Boyle Abbey, County Roscommon

Conservation, Architecture and Archaeological Excavations 1982–2018

Boyle Abbey, County Roscommon
Conservation, Architecture and Archaeological Excavations 1982–2018

EDITED BY
Fionnbarr Moore and Geraldine Stout

Archaeological Monograph Series: No.13
Boyle Abbey, County Roscommon

WITH EXCAVATION SECTIONS
Dr Ann Lynch, Fiona Rooney, Annette Quinn and Anne Carey

SPECIALIST CONTRIBUTIONS BY
Catriona Devane, Roger Stalley, Rosanne Meenan, Margaret McCarthy, Clare McCutcheon, Órla Scully, Siobhan Scully,Elizabeth Wincott Heckett, Laureen Buckley, Joanna Wren, Linda Lynch, Miriam Carroll, Raghnall Ó Floinn, Jo Moran, Mary-Liz McCarthy, Denis Walsh, Kevin Clancy, Susan Lyons, Fionnbarr Moore and David Swift.

National Monuments Service
Archaeological Monograph Series
General Editors, Anne Lynch and Conleth Manning

1. *Excavations at Roscrea Castle*, ed. Conleth Manning (2003).
2. *St. Audeon's Church, Cornmarket, Dublin: Archaeology and Architecture*, Mary McMahon (2007).
3. *Kells Priory, Co. Kilkenny: Archaeological Excavations*, T. Fanning and M. Clyne (2006).
4. *The history and archaeology of Glanworth Castle, Co. Cork: Excavations 1982–4*, Conleth Manning (2009).
5. *Tintern Abbey, Co. Wexford: Cistercians and Colcloughs*, Ann Lynch (2010).
6. *Trim Castle, Co. Meath. Excavations 1995–1998*, Alan R. Hayden (2011).
7. *Parke's Castle, Co. Leitrim: Archaeology, History and Architecture*, Claire Foley and Colm Donnelly (2012).
8. *Clogh Oughter Castle, Co. Cavan: Archaeology, History and Architecture*, Conleth Manning (2013).
9. *Poulnabrone: An Early Neolithic Portal Tomb in Ireland*, Ann Lynch (2014).
10. *High Island (Ardoileán), Co. Galway: Excavation of an Early Medieval Monastery*, Georgina Scally (2014).
11. *Barryscourt Castle, Co. Cork: Archaeology, History and Architecture*, Dave Pollock (2017).
12. *Magheracar, Co. Donegal: Excavation of passage tomb on Ireland's north-west coast*, Eamon Cody (2019).

These monographs are subject to international peer review.

BAILE ÁTHA CLIATH
Arna Fhoilsiú Ag Oifig An Tsolatháir

Le ceannach díreach ó
Foilseacháin Rialtais,
52 Faiche Stiabhna, Baile Átha Cliath 2
(T. 076 1106 834 *nó* R. publications@opw.ie)
nó trí aon díoltóir leabhar.

DUBLIN
Published by The Stationery Office

To be purchased from
Government Publications,
52 St. Stephen's Green, Dublin 2.
(T. 076 1106 834 *or* E. publications@opw.ie)
or through any bookseller.

ISBN: 978-1-4468-8070-8

Designed and typeset by Atelier David Smith
Cover design by Atelier David Smith
Copy-edited by Sheelagh Hughes, Editorial Solutions
Printed by W&G Baird

Contents

Acknowledgements

The regular meetings and on-site discussion by the project team on every aspect of the conservation project for the north aisle, under the chairmanship of Paul McMahon, Senior Architect OPW, was essential to the success of what was an extremely complex and challenging undertaking. The team comprised John O'Brien, Architectural Assistant, OPW, John Corcoran and John Warren, successive OPW Districts Works Managers, Dromahair District, Peter Cox, Mary-Liz McCarthy and Andrzej Czaplicki, Carrig Conservation, Kevin Clancy of Michael Punch and Partners (PUNCH Conservation), John Goldrick, OPW, Health and Safety, Niall O'Donovan, Assure Health and Safety Consultants, Fionnbarr Moore, National Monuments Service, project archaeologist.

Also crucial to the conservation project were the OPW Dromahair District works team, in particular Lorcan Higgins, Pat Egan, Alan Graham and John Nicholson who worked tirelessly in all weathers to see the project through to completion. Also Robert Howard and David Little, OPW, Athenry District, who prepared the mortar recipes, which were essential for the authentic rebuilding of the north aisle wall and arcade and Pat Heraghty, District Works Manager, for his support on this aspect of the project. Annette Quinn and Miriam Carroll of Tobar Archaeology made a major contribution to facilitating and informing the project as a result of their meticulous excavation of the north aisle area

Lisa Edden of CORA Consulting Engineers provided specialist advice on structural matters. Mark Cullen of FDK Engineering provided the steel fabric for the new north aisle glass roof and exterior wall. Karl Kavanagh of Hodgkins Architectural Facades provided the glass. All deserve special mention for what was an innovative, difficult and delicate operation.

Con Brogan, former Senior Photographer, National Monuments Service, made a detailed photographic record of every phase of the project (archived by Tony Roche, National Monuments Service), and Crossing the Lines Films also recorded every phase of the project. Murphy Surveys undertook a photogrammetric survey of the building prior to the works commencing. Pixelbrick, Architectural Models and Architectural Presentations provided excellent information panels to inform the general public on what was taking place in the Abbey.

Senior OPW management, in particular Dermot Bourke and Frank Shalvey were very supportive of the project as were former NMS Director, Finian Mathews, Chief Archaeologist, Brian Duffy, former Acting Chief Archaeologist, Dr Ann Lynch and Con Manning, Senior Archaeologist.

Fionnbarr Moore and Geraldine Stout would like to thank all the contributors to this volume. They would like to thank the many individuals in the National Monuments Service who assisted in the preparation of this publication including Dr Ann Lynch and Con Manning for reading an early draft of this monograph; their comments and changes were invaluable, to Michael MacDonagh and Pauline Gleeson for their managerial assistance, to Máire Ní Chonghaile for her administration of contracts and to the NMS Photographic Archive Unit, John Lalor, Tony Roche and Lynn McDonnell for providing illustrations. They are indebted to Dr David Robinson for peer reviewing an early draft of this report and sharing his invaluable expertise. They would also like to thank the National Library of Ireland, the Royal Irish Academy and National Gallery of Ireland for permission to reproduce their images. Sincerest thanks to Matthew Stout for assistance with drawings and text. Special thanks to Sheelagh Hughes for her excellent editing of this volume, Atelier David Smith for design and typesetting and W&G Baird for printing.

Dr Ann Lynch would like to thank the following: those who worked on the excavations; supervisors Anne-Marie Lennon and Paula Harvey and workmen Gary Beirne, Thomas Beirne, Patrick Cregg, John McDermott, Sean McLoughlin, Gerry Quinn, Martin Roche and Michael White. Paul McMahon (National Monuments Service) was the project conservation architect and special thanks are due to Clerk of Works John Corcoran and the workmen from the OPW Depot in Dromahair who serviced the excavations. The assistance of those who provided specialist reports is greatly appreciated, in particular Dr McBride of Forensic Science Ireland (Garda HQ) who analysed the human hair. The site drawings were prepared for publication by Conor McHale and Patricia Johnson is responsible for the artefact drawings.

Annette Quinn would like to thank the following for their assistance in the Boyle Abbey North Wall Conservation Project: Miriam Carroll for her assistance with the excavation and post-excavation, the excavators without whom the project would not have been possible, Maureen Murphy for her painstaking work on the post-excavation, Laura O'Connor for her assistance in cataloguing artefacts, the OPW site staff who provided assistance with logistics, the National Monuments Service staff, including Con Manning, Fionnbarr Moore and Geraldine Stout, all of whom were involved in overseeing the work. The author would also like to thank the archaeologists who provided specialist work for the final report and publication, Hugh Kavanagh who was responsible for site survey, digitising of site plans and preparation of images for this monograph, Margaret McCarthy (faunal remains), Linda Lynch (for an outstanding and detailed report on the osteological remains), Miriam Carroll (ferrous and non-ferrous, stone and artefacts of skeletal material), David Swift (the Boyle Abbey sword), Jo Moran (window glass), Clare McCutcheon (pottery and bottle glass), Joanne O'Sullivan (bead report), Joanna Wren (roof tiles) and Susan Lyons (archaeobotanical material). Also, thanks to the locals in Boyle and those who visited the site over the years (including my parents!) who showed great interest in the site and the findings. All artefact illustrations in this report were undertaken by Sara Nylund (unless otherwise stated). All photographs (site and artefacts) were undertaken by the author (unless otherwise stated).

List of Illustrations and Tables

LIST OF FIGURES

LIST OF PLATES

Pl. 6.3	Pier 3 base F376.
Pl. 6.4	Pier 3 moulding (F298) looking west.
Pl. 6.5	Pier 5 foundation pit (F386) looking south.
Pl. 6.6	Pier 5 fill of foundation cut F386 looking west.
Pl. 6.7	Pier 5 base (F375).
Pl. 6.8	Pier 5 moulding (F297).
Pl. 6.9	Pier 7 foundation pit (F385) with blue clay F369 surrounding pit.
Pl. 6.10	Pier 7 fill of foundation pit F385.
Pl. 6.11	Pier 7 base (F374) looking north.
Pl. 6.12	Pier 7 moulding (F296) looking north.
Pl. 6.13	Pier 9 foundation pit (F544).
Pl. 6.14	Pier 9 base (F522) looking north.
Pl. 6.15	Pier 9 moulding from above.
Pl. 6.16	Pier 9 moulding looking north.
Pl. 6.17	Pier 11 foundation pit (F545).
Pl. 6.18	Pier 11 base (F509) looking north.

Pl. 6.19	Pier 11 base moulding.
Pl. 6.20	Pier 13 foundation pit (F546) looking north.
Pl. 6.21	Pier 13 base (F510) looking north.
Pl. 6.22	Pier 13 moulding.
Pl. 6.23	Posthole (F277) adjacent to north wall looking east.
Pl. 6.24	Posthole F347 (right) and F349 (left).
Pl. 6.25	Postholes F342 (foreground) and F340 (background) looking west.
Pl. 6.26	Post-medieval wall (F4) overlying remains of F42 (west wall, arrow).
Pl. 6.27	West wall (F42) looking south-west.
Pl. 6.28	Flagstone foundation (F148) under west wall (F42) and forming base of annex (F25) looking south.
Pl. 6.29	Flagstone foundation (F148) indicated by arrow (west side of north aisle).
Pl. 6.30	North wall (F19/F211) looking east towards north transept.

Pl. 6.53	Robbing out trench (F219, post-excavation) along central and eastern end of north aisle.
Pl. 6.54	Section of robbing out trench (F41/F219) in western side of north aisle.
Pl. 6.55	Ditch (F222) with cobbles (F207) subsided into cut.
Pl. 6.56	West-facing section of ditch at east end of north aisle.
Pl. 6.57	Linear ditch (F222) post-excavation looking east.
Pl. 6.58	Ditch (F604) to right looking south.
Pl. 6.59	Post-medieval drain (F407) looking north.
Pl. 6.60	Pier 7 base moulding and wall (F259) to south and wall (F236) to the north.
Pl. 6.61	Wall (F409) in between piers 11 and 13.
Pl. 6.62	Wall (F703) constructed between piers at west end of aisle/nave F703.
Pl. 6.63	Wall (F703) looking east.
Pl. 6.64	Cobbles (F13).
Pl. 6.65	Cobbles (F8/F10) and walls (F4 and F5) at western end of north aisle looking east.
Pl. 6.66	Cobbles (F902) in south-east corner of aisle against transept wall.
Pl. 6.67	Wall (F397) looking north (note test trench excavated by Fiona Rooney to right of wall).
Pl. 6.68	Buttress foundation (F393, Pier 9).
Pl. 6.69	Buttress foundation (F393, Pier 9), north wall to right and cobbles F207 either side of buttress.
Pl. 6.70	Buttress (F203, Pier 3) at east end of north aisle.
Pl. 6.71	Buttress (F201, Pier 7) looking south
Pl. 6.72	Buckle E2399:205:114.
Pl. 6.73	Buckle E2399:401:137.
Pl. 6.74	Stick pin E2399.91.63.
Pl. 6.75	Stick pin E2399:146:90.
Pl. 6.76	Stick pin E2399:439:186.
Pl. 6.77	Dress hook/clasp E2399.87.59.
Pl. 6.78	Button E2399:2:113.

Pl. 6.113	Glass fragment E2399:221:2024.
Pl. 6.114	Glass fragment E2399:218:193-4.
Pl. 6.115	Bone handle E2399: 910:50.
Pl. 6.116	Bone handle E2399: 58:3070.
Pl. 6.117	Bone handle E2399:204:349.
Pl. 6.118	Bone handle E2399:205:1052.
Pl. 6.119	Pin E2399:480:190.
Pl. 6.120	Pin E2399:542:221.
Pl. 6.121	Disc E2399:221:2005.
Pl. 6.122	Comb E2399:33:11.
Pl. 6.123	Comb fragment E2399:0:02.
Pl. 6.124	Domino piece E2399:2:313.
Pl. 6.125	Clay pipe E2399:212:1708.
Pl. 6.126	Clay pipe E2399:27:536.
Pl. 6.127	Clay pipe E2399:221:2000.
Pl. 6.128	Clay pipe E2399:2:196.
Pl. 6.129	Clay pipe bowl E2399:2:197.

Pl. 6.130	Bead E2399:142:89.
Pl. 6.131	French medieval pot sherd E2399:77:60.
Pl. 6.132	Martincamp-type pot sherd E2399:205:560.
Pl. 6.133	Transition-type pottery (E2399:139:92, 98,101,111).
Pl. 6.134	Eighteenth-century bottles.
Pl. 6.135	Late eighteenth-century Mallet-type bottle base (E2399:901:314).
Pl. 6.136	Eighteenth-century bottle.
Pl. 6.137	Possible eighteenth-century medicinal bottle.
Pl. 6.138	Quern stone E2399:231:18.
Pl. 6.139	Quern stone E2399:439:183.
Pl. 6.140	Architectural fragment E2399:13:18.
Pl. 6.141	Peg tile E2399:395:2681.
Pl. 6.142	Peg tile E2399:207:1636.
Pl. 6.143	Uncrested ridge tile E2399:393:2658.

LIST OF TABLES

Preface

Boyle Abbey is a National Monument in State Care in the town of Boyle, Co. Roscommon. It was the principal Cistercian house in the kingdom of Connacht in the medieval period and its ruins today are among the best preserved of the order to be found in the country. Since 1892 it has been in the guardianship of the Commissioners of Public Works who have maintained the site. In the 1980s the Office of Public Works (OPW) undertook conservation works which involved archaeological excavation. Subsequently, in 2006 the OPW commenced a major programme of conservation works on the abbey, which involved dismantling and restoring the north aisle wall of the church, which had bowed. This was one of the largest stone conservation projects undertaken by the state and involved a multi-disciplinary team of experts, including engineers, architects and archaeologists who worked closely together to oversee the entire project through to completion. These works have produced a vast body of new information on the history, architecture and archaeology of Boyle Abbey, which is presented in this volume.

Interior view of newly conserved North aisle.

Chapter 1

Introduction

Geraldine Stout

Physical setting

Boyle Abbey is a National Monument in State Care in the town of Boyle, in north Co. Roscommon. It lies in the barony of Boyle and townland of Knocknashee (National grid: 580833 802767) (Pl. 1.1, Fig. 1.1). The abbey is situated on a fording point in the River Boyle and lies on the margins of Lough Key. A settlement known as Abbeytown built up around the abbey and this bridging point.

Boyle stands at the foot of the Curlew Mountains where the Dublin to Sligo road follows the Curlew Pass. It is on a junction of an elaborate system of early roadways which linked directly with the Slighe Assail, the main route from the east to Connacht and Slighe Mhor a primary route across Ireland (Doran 2004, 64). (Fig 1.2) This allowed the monastery to become a prominent medieval centre of pilgrimage.

The Boyle area is part of the Central Lowlands of Ireland. Soils around the abbey area are fine loamy drift. The Irish Soil Information System (Teagasc and the EPA n.d.) classifies them as the Kilrush association composite with siliceous stones (Fig.1.3). It is surrounded by rich agricultural land, the limestone pasturages on the plains of Boyle being amongst the best in Ireland. Today the land is devoted to grazing with cattle dominating, especially in north Roscommon. The abbey lands were served by a water system of navigable rivers, and the north Sligo coastline; the River Boyle, a tributary of the River Shannon, flows out of Lough Gara and through Lough Key.

The Geological Survey map for the area shows Boyle Abbey situated on a junction of the Palaeozoic Carboniferous and the Lower Avonian shales and sandstones (Fig. 1.4). This has been supported by bore tests carried out by IGSL Ltd in the grounds of the abbey which retrieved limestone or sandstone fragments in the lower level of the boreholes (Carrig 2005, Appendix1). Both the ashlar and rubble stone used to construct the church at Boyle are reputed to have been sourced from a local quarry, known as John's hole, upstream from

Fig. 1.1. Location maps of Boyle Abbey and immediate environs.

Boyle (Fig. 1.4). This is probably where the monks obtained good sandstone for the construction of the abbey. The stone was transported along the river which runs alongside the abbey site.

Historical outline

Boyle Abbey, Co. Roscommon (variously referred to as *St Maria Virginis*, *Buellium*, *Ath da Laarc*, *Mainstir-na-Buill*) was established by Cistercian monks from Mellifont, Co. Louth, in 1161 (Gwynn and Hadcock 1970, 128; Moore 2015). It was one of nine daughter houses affiliated to it (Fig.1.5). In 1148 a group of 12 monks and their abbot set out from Mellifont with the aim of establishing the first Cistercian house in Connacht. Initial efforts were made to establish a daughter house on three sites including the west side of Ballysadare Bay, Co. Sligo, where there are upstanding remains of a grange at Ballinlig, but the foundation finally settled in Boyle on the early ecclesiastical site of Ath da Lairg on lands belonging to the McDermots, Lords of Moylurg representing the northern part of modern County Roscommon in Connacht. The abbey was not consecrated until 1220, by which time it had two daughter houses of its own, Assaroe, Co. Donegal (1178) and Knockmoy, Co. Galway (1190).

Their monastic estate mainly included the present town of Boyle and lands extending to the south and west, but their holdings were scattered throughout counties Roscommon, south of Lough Gara, Sligo as far as the Leitrim border and even into Galway. Stout (2015, 39–45) has mapped and described this estate which encompassed an estimated *c.* 5,336ha (Fig. 1.6) Table 1.1). They exploited their lands through a series of 'model farms' known as granges, a generic term for buildings, especially store houses devoted to agricultural production and worked directly by monks. The order had created the institution of the lay brother or *conversi* for the provision of agricultural labour and they were involved in all trades and crafts needed for the efficient running of a grange including sheep herding. They were thus able to establish a self-sufficient economy where the farms supplied their mother house with agricultural products.

There was a hierarchy of granges ranging from sheep runs to larger farms with precinct walls,

Pl. 1.1. Aerial view of Boyle Abbey from the south-west.
© Photographic Archive, National Monuments Service. Government of Ireland.

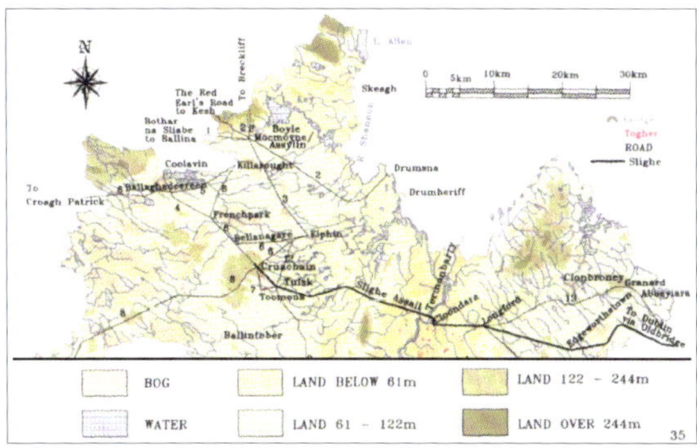

Fig. 1.2. The early road network at Boyle (after Doran 2004, 64).

barns and mills. The granges on the Boyle Abbey estate range in size from that at Tulsk with 14ha to that on Grange of O'Fallon with 836ha. Boyle Abbey had both upland and lowland granges. Most of these lands can be identified and some remains of settlement survive. By the sixteenth century these granges had developed into nucleated settlements sometimes associated with a castle. For example, there was a small stone castle and a church attached to Grange Beg in the parish of Templeboy not far from Aughris Head. The grange in north Sligo was in the possession of Hugh O Harte who by 1577 built a new castle there. The grange known as Grange of O'Fallon was located in south Roscommon and by the sixteenth century had developed into a nucleated settlement of cottages around a castle.

The McDermots had been amongst the abbey's earliest benefactors and were inextricably linked with the community through the centuries and second only in importance to the O'Connors in Connacht. Various members of the family were buried within the abbey precinct. The vision today of peaceful monastic ruins belies a turbulent past. Boyle Abbey provided a stronghold for the McDermots

Table 1.1 Lands of Boyle Abbey

Name	Date	Townland name (OS)	County	Area ('acres')	Ha (OS)	Structures
Maghermoney (Gr. of)	1569	Monivea Demesne	Galway	160	374	Chapel
Aghnagrange	1606	Aghnagrange	Roscommon	1.25	40	
Ardkeran	1606	Ardcorcoran	Roscommon	1.25	22	
Ardmore	1606	Ardmore	Roscommon	1.25	106	
Ardsillagh	1606	Ardsallagh	Roscommon	150	78	
Boyle Town	1569	Knocknashee	Roscommon	360	47	Abbey
Carreronenalta	1569	Carrownanalt	Roscommon		87	
Cornebole	1569	Curraghnaboley	Roscommon	70	29	
Coulhurey grange	1577	Ballytrasna	Roscommon	1.25	102	
Creavollan	1585	Reevolan	Roscommon	1.25	70	
Derrymaguirk	1606	Derrymaquirk	Roscommon	1.25	114	
Fallon (Gr. of) / Folan (Gr. O)	1569 / 1577	Grange / Milltown	Roscommon	80	836	Castle
Fynisklyne	1577	Finisclin	Roscommon			Rectory
Grange	1569	Grange	Roscommon		639	
Grange	1569	Grangemore	Roscommon		206	
Grange-Beagh	1606	Grangebeg	Roscommon	1.25	221	
Grange-Mulconry	1569	Grange	Roscommon	190	100	Mill
Graunge	1577	Carrownageeragh	Roscommon	1.25	121	
Graunge Mownwy	1569	Mocmoyne	Roscommon	180	82	
Killummod	1604	Killumod	Roscommon		141	Church
Knock doe Mannaghe	1606	Knockadoo	Roscommon	1.25	43	
Knockabroe	1606	Knockvaroe	Roscommon	1.25	94	
Knocknecloygh	1606	Knocknacloy	Roscommon	1.25	36	
Lecarrow	1606	Lecarrow	Roscommon	1.25	54	
Lisogevoge	1606	Lismageevoge	Roscommon	0.5	44	
Loughurt alias Longfort	1606	Longford Hill	Roscommon		109	
Moynterolys (Gr. of)	1569	Grange	Roscommon	210	110	
Tinacarra	1606	Tinacarra	Roscommon	1.25	55	

Table 1.1 Lands of Boyle Abbey *continued*

Name	Date	Townland name (OS)	County	Area ('acres')	Ha (OS)	Structures
Tullaghboy	1606	Tullyboy	Roscommon	1.25	67	
Tullestermy	1570	Esternow	Roscommon	79	87	
Tulskirrie (Gr. of)	1578	Grange	Roscommon	70	41	
	c. 1840	Coolnagranshy	Roscommon	1.25	28	Nunnery
Altferannan	1611	Alternan Park	Sligo		14	
Cowlhenrie (Gr. of)	1569	Grange East / North / West / Primrosegrange	Sligo	37	279	Castle
Gr. in O'Conor Sligaghe's country	1569	Grange	Sligo		223	Castle
Graungenemangh	1569	Grangiaroe	Sligo		33	
Graungenemangh	1569	Graniamore	Sligo	150	34	
Graungenemanagh	1569	Drumnagranshy	Sligo		155	
Templenemanagh	1569	Templevanny	Sligo		72	Church
Tireherage (Great Gr. of)	1569	Grangemore	Sligo	150	148	
Tireherage (Small Gr. of)	1569	Grangebeg	Sligo	60	197	
Total				1,965	5,338	

who played an active role in defending Connacht against the Anglo-Normans in the twelfth and thirteenth centuries. The abbey was strategically placed to protect the 'great pass' over the Curlew Mountains and found itself in the centre of a power play and internecine wars in Connacht through the centuries. It had to contend with physical attacks on its monastery and property and was badly damaged by the Anglo-Norman wars against the Irish in 1202, 1235 and 1284. It continued to be a centre of conflict into the post-medieval period.

In 1569 Lord Deputy Henry Sydney took the abbey from the McDermots and there followed a succession of tenants. In the late sixteenth century, it was fortified and being used as a military barracks by Richard Bingham, governor of Connacht. Then known as 'Boyle Castle', the abbey was modified to meet its military needs. Boyle Abbey was granted to John King and John Bingley on 20 November 1617 and John King's grant of the manor of Boyle Abbey was confirmed in 1619 (D'Alton 1845 i, 228–32; Weld 1832, 225). The abbey was besieged in 1645 during the Cromwellian wars and it is likely that the outer wall of the north aisle was demolished at this time. Military occupation ended in the eighteenth century (Stalley 1987; Kalkreuter 2001, 23–4; Fig. 1.7). The precise timing of the withdrawal of troops from the abbey is unclear but is likely to have occurred between 1714 and 1727 (Kerrigan 1985). The abbey was vested in the guardianship of the Commissioners of Public Works by the King Harmon family of Rockingham in November 1892.

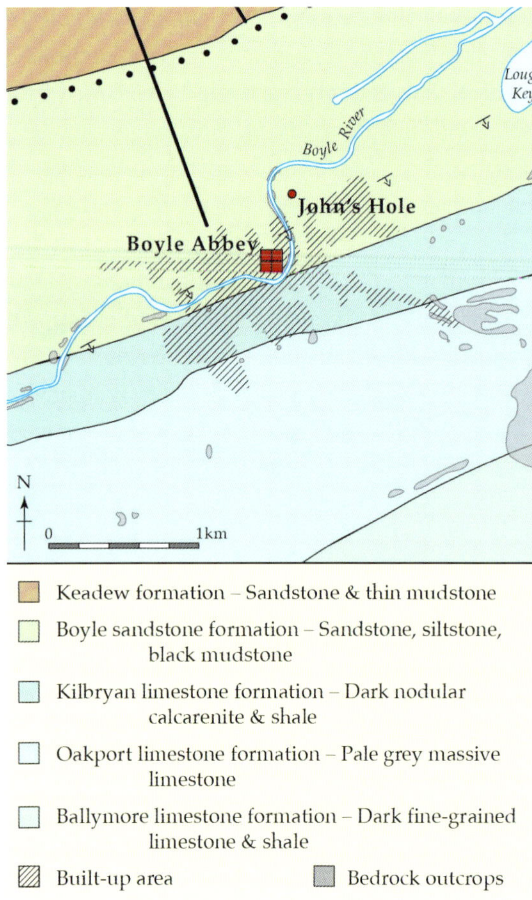

Fig. 1.3. The soils at Boyle Abbey based on the Soil Survey of Ireland.

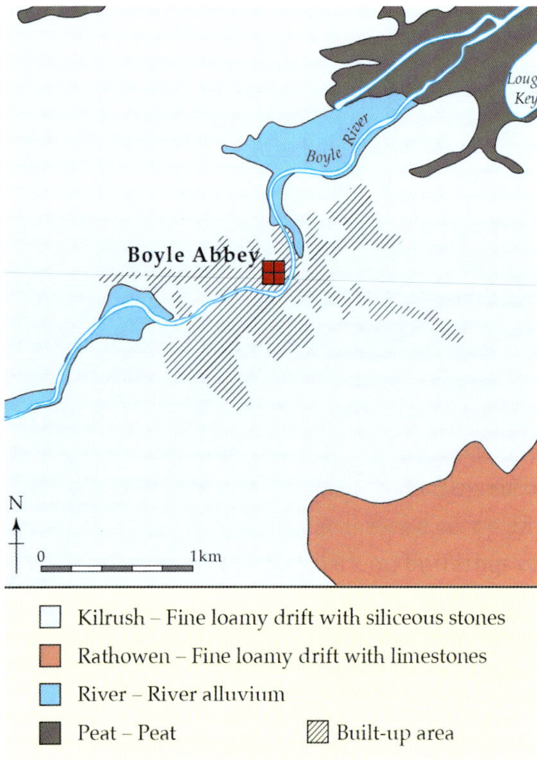

Fig. 1.4. The geology of Boyle Abbey based on the Geological Survey of Ireland.

Art and architecture

The medieval fabric of the church is largely intact but most of the conventual buildings have been altered during military usage of the site in the post-medieval period, so that substantial remains of the medieval fabric only survive in the eastern range. Amongst the earliest descriptions of the surviving buildings at Boyle are found in Colonel William Burton Conyngham's *Journal of two tours made from Connaught in 1779* and in Archdall's *Monasticon Hibernicum* (Archdall 1786). The earliest known drawing is by Gabriel Beranger in 1779 (Fig. 1.8). Burton Conyngham commissioned a number of artists including Bigari, who was an Italian stage-scene painter working in Ireland, to record ancient churches and castles. Bigari's view of Boyle Abbey (Fig. 1.9) on a sketching tour of Connacht in the summer of 1779 (Harbison 2001, 64) monumentalises the building and makes it appear much longer and deeper than it is in Francis Grose's *Antiquities of Ireland* (1791–5) engraving of Boyle (Fig. 1.10). Austin Cooper's *Tracings of drawings and plans of various ecclesiastical antiquities* (1783) provide important information about its architectural details before conservation works were undertaken in the nineteenth century (Fig. 1.11). There are also sketches of the abbey in Brewer's *Beauties of Ireland* (1825–6) and George Du Noyer's *Antiquarian Sketches* (1840).

Arthur Champney in his *Irish ecclesiastical architecture* (1910) identified in Boyle Abbey and some other churches in the west of Ireland a Transitional style of carving which was distinctively Irish and this became known as the School of the West (Kalkreuter 2001). Harold Leask (1960, ii, 53) branded the School of the West the 'royal style' of Connacht which he thought to have developed as an anathema to Anglo-Norman influence. In a wider European context, it may also have represented non-compliance with the building norms of the Cistercian order giving way to an Irish vernacular style and continued use of the Hiberno-Romanesque tradition (Kalkreuter 2001).

Boyle Abbey is particularly prestigious for having a *scriptoria* and professional scribes Donnachadh Mór O'Daligh, who was buried at Boyle in 1244, and Diarmaid O'Culechain, who wrote a missal for its daughter house at Knockmoy. The

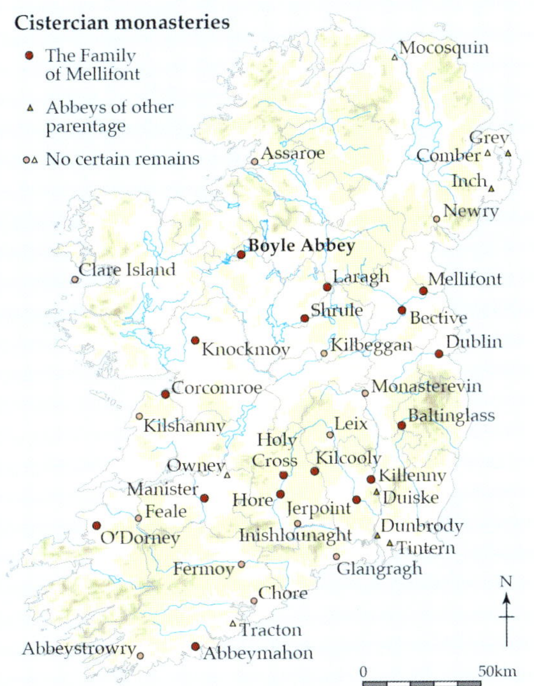

Fig. 1.5. The Cistercian abbeys of Ireland (after Leask 1960).

Fig. 1.6. The monastic estate of Boyle Abbey (after Stout 2015).

Fig. 1.7. Detail from the parish map of the Down Survey showing Boyle and its environs. (National Library of Ireland).

thirteenth-century Annals of Cotton MS Titus A XXV, also known as the Annals of Boyle, are thought to be based on an earlier chronicle written at Boyle Abbey. These developed into the Annals of Loch Cé associated with the Premonstratensian house of the Holy Trinity. The life of Athracht, patron saint of Cill Athrachta (Killaraght) in the barony of Coolavin, Co. Sligo, not far from Boyle, published by John Colgan (ASH 277–82) was probably written by a Cistercian monk at Boyle at the end of the twelfth century or in the early thirteenth century. Illuminated manuscripts from Irish Cistercian houses are rare. Stalley (1987, 187, 217–19) has postulated that Cormac's Psalter now in the British Library may have come from Boyle Abbey because of comparison with carvings and faces which are similar to initials in the manuscript.

References to Boyle Abbey in international Cistercian literature are rare. James France (1998)

Fig. 1.8. An eighteenth-century drawing of Boyle Abbey by Gabriel Beranger. (By permission of the Royal Irish Academy).

in his book on *The Cistercians in medieval art* draws attention to a grave slab from Boyle with an unusual depiction of a staff grasped by a robed arm expressing the authority of the abbot, which is similar to an example from Flawley in Gloucestershire (111–12; Stalley 1987, 205, Pl. 240). In D.H. Williams *The Cistercians in the early Middle Ages* (1998) there are numerous allusions to Boyle Abbey including its thirteenth-century great stone guest house and the unusual presence of a crypt containing its treasures. In David M. Robinson's *The Cistercians in Wales* (2006, 64, 74), the author draws attention to the French influence in the ground plan of Boyle Abbey which reflects the 'Bernardine plan', a proportional system used in the setting out of the early Cistercian churches and the organisation of its presbytery and transepts which follows a pattern seen at the mother house in Clairvaux, France. Robinson (*ibid.*) also draws attention to the refectory at Boyle, which is arranged on an east-west axis, parallel to the church and adjacent to the south walk of the cloister like the earliest stone refectories and at Dunbrody, Co. Wexford, Hore, Co. Tipperary and Monasteranenagh, Co. Limerick, in Ireland. This is, he states, precisely what occurred in the primary stone layouts in Britain; for example, Waverly, Surrey, as early as the 1130s, Byland, York, from the 1140s–1150s, Fountains, Yorkshire, Furness, Cumbria, Kirkstall, Leeds and Rievaulx in the north of England (*ibid.*). The eventual Cistercian preference for a north-south refectory arrangement did not take place until the mid to late twelfth century.

Conservation

Boyle Abbey was the principal Cistercian house in the kingdom of Connacht and its ruins today are among the best preserved of the order to be found in the entire country. The abbey is considered to be one of the most attractive and stylistically intriguing of the Irish Cistercian monasteries (Stalley 1987). Since 1892, the ruins have been in the guardianship of the Commissioners of Public Works who have maintained the site. Their annual report 1894–1895 records that they had partially removed ivy which had completely covered the abbey and was endangering the fabric (Commissioners of Public Works 1896, 80).

The annual report of 1903–4 also refers to these early works and observed that five buttresses built against the northern wall of the nave, about 70 to 80 years previously, were considered useless (Commissioners of Public Works 1905, 14–16). During the 1903–4 phases of work, the tops of the walls throughout the abbey were cleaned down. The loose masonry of the four buttresses at the northern wall of the nave was taken down and rebuilt. Timber lintels over the opes in the dormitory wall and refectory were removed and replaced with lintels. The north arcade was recorded at this time as being 'two feet six inches out of plumb'. This report includes a series of detailed plans and drawings of the abbey (Fig. 1.12). The Commissioners reports from 1940 and 1941 document further works on the abbey which involved further removal of ivy and extensive pointing and weathering carried out to stabilise the fabric of the buildings. In 1975 a report by the Office of Public Works (OPW) stated that cracks on the buttresses were being monitored.

In the early 1980s, archaeological investigations were undertaken by the National Monuments Service (NMS) at Boyle Abbey in advance of the restoration of its gatehouse and further excavation in 1984 was required to expose the north cloister walkway. Subsequently, in 2004 pre-conservation archaeological testing under contract on behalf of the OPW took place in two areas of the abbey: along the north wall of the nave and inside the refectory. Given the structural instability of the north aisle arcade, engineering test trenches were required to establish the depth of natural ground prior to

Fig. 1.9. Bigari's view of Boyle Abbey in 1779. (By permission of the National Gallery of Ireland).

Fig. 1.10. Francis Grose's engraving of Boyle Abbey (1791–5). (By permission of the National Library of Ireland).

Fig.1.11. Austin Cooper's engraving of Boyle Abbey (1783) (after Harbison, 2000).

proposed insertion of cores and supports for the outward leaning north wall. In the refectory, where there were also proposals to construct a lean-to roof to provide shelter for the collection of architectural stone fragments from the abbey, extensive pre-conservation archaeological excavations took place. Between 2006 and 2012 the OPW undertook major conservation works alongside archaeological excavation carried out under contract to the OPW to clarify the original line of the north aisle wall, which had been largely robbed out in the past. As the buttresses were no longer providing adequate support to the surviving north aisle wall, a radical intervention was needed to stabilise the structure. This included the dismantling of the buttresses and blocking walls, as well as the dismantling, underpinning and reconstruction of the arcade between the centre bays.

This was one of the largest stone conservation projects ever undertaken by the state and involved a multi-disciplinary team of experts, including engineers, architects and archaeologists who worked closely together to oversee the entire project through to completion. This conservation project is described in detail by the engineers involved in Chapter 7 of this monograph. The controlled dismantling of the north arcading and subsequent excavation of the pier bases provided a unique opportunity to examine the make-up of the foundations especially given the poor structural condition of the north arcade which gave rise to the 'North Wall Project'. The easternmost foundations showed more signs of subsidence than their western counterparts, with the underlying foundation stones being completely shattered and crumbled; this may have had an impact on the form of pier used for the remainder of the wall. It was concluded that the leaning arcade at Boyle was undoubtedly a result of the poor foundations that lay beneath the piers, a consequence of the constant change in water levels. The most dramatic movement of the wall is likely to have occurred following the removal of the north aisle in the post-dissolution period when the abbey was transformed into a barracks.

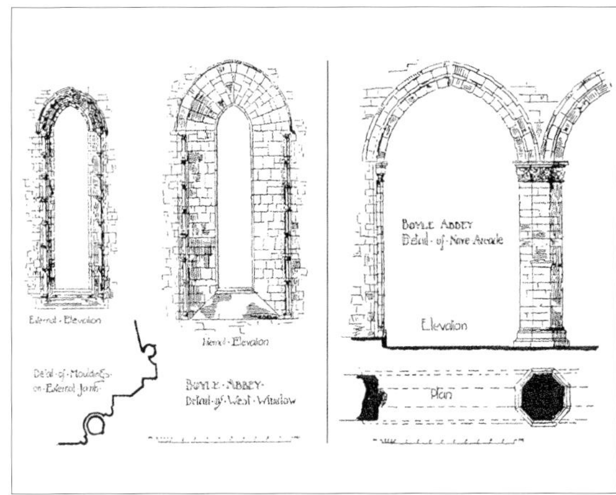

Fig. 1.12. Plans and detail drawings of Boyle Abbey. (Office of Public Works 1904).

These phases of conservation have ensured the better presentation of the ruins and their safety for the foreseeable future. Opportunities afforded for excavation by the conservation programmes have produced a considerable body of new material on the full history of the site. Three separate excavations were undertaken as part of these conservation works. These are presented here as standalone reports with discussion, and a final summary provides a general overview of all results. A comprehensive history of the site and architectural review of the buildings provide a broader canvas on which to place this new information.

View of church interior at Boyle Abbey.

Chapter 2

Historical Background

Catriona Devane

The journey to Boyle

On 16 August 1148 Abbot Peadar Ua Mórdha and a group of 12 monks, accompanied by lay brothers (Gwynn and Hadcock 1970, 128–9) set out from Mellifont, in County Louth, to establish the first Cistercian house in Connacht (Fig. 2.1). They passed along Slige Assail, one of the three primary route ways of Ireland (Ó Lochlainn 1940, 472, 594; Meyer 1906, 6, 7). Slige Assail was the road from Mide (Meath) to Cruachu (Rathcroghan) in Mag nAí which was the heartland of the Uí Briúin Aí kingship of Connacht. The Cistercian monks would have crossed the Shannon into Mag nAí, where Tarmonbarry is today. From there they turned northwards, off Slige Assail into Mag Luirg at Tulsk, before reaching the River Boyle. Their path continued across the Curlew Mountains as far as Ballisadare Bay in County Sligo. A circuitous route brought the monks from Mellifont to three different locations in Connacht before they finally put down permanent roots at Áth Dá Laarg (Boyle) on the River Boyle in 1161 (AB). According to folklore, the *áth* (ford) is named after Fer dá Laarc who was killed on the banks of the Boyle (Met. Dinn. iv, 282).

Their journey from Mellifont into Connacht coincided with a campaign by Tairrdelbach Ua Conchobair, and subsequently by his son and successor Ruaidrí, to secure the Uí Conchobair sovereignty of Connacht and the high kingship of Ireland. When Ruaidrí was inaugurated as king of Connacht in 1156 he was supported by the Uí Máel Ruanaid dynasty, with whom he shared a common ancestry. Both Uí Conchobair and Uí Máel Ruanaid belonged to Síl Muiredaig, the dominant branch of Uí Briúin Aí whose forefather Brión was a son of Conn Cét Chathath (Conn of the hundred battles), the eponymous ancestor of the Connachta. Brión had two brothers, Ailell and Fiachrach, whose descendants were called Uí Ailella and Uí Fiachrach. They gave their names to two modern baronies, Tireragh (Tír Fiachrach – the land of Uí Fiachrach) on the southern shore of Ballisadare Bay, and Tirerril (Tír Ailella

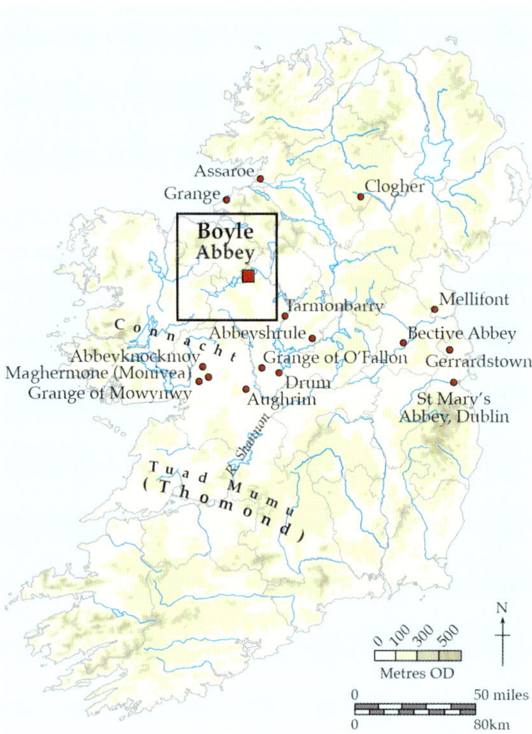

Fig. 2.1. Location map showing places mentioned in the text.

– the land of Uí Ailella) on the northern shore. The barony of Leyny, an anglicisation of the population group, Luigne, divides Tireragh from Tirerril. Áth Dá Laarg (Boyle), where the monks finally settled, was located in Mag Luirg, also known as Mag Luirg an Dagda – the plain of the tracks of the Dagda – in central Roscommon. The Dagda was a godly and powerful figure who was king of the otherworld Tuatha de Danann (SG 279; ALC 1497; AFM 1597; Walsh 1948, 80, 124, 168).

Boyle: an early ecclesiastical backdrop

Boyle Abbey lies in the townland of Cnoc na Sidhe (Knocknashee – the hill of the otherworld people), while the nearby parish church of Boyle is in the neighbouring parish of Drum, to the east. Both are in the diocese of Elphin. Mag Luirg, through which the River Boyle runs, is more or less co-extensive with the modern barony of Boyle (Pl. 2.1). In the fifth century, according to tradition, St Patrick appointed Comgell/Conall as bishop of Áth Dá Laarg (TT 136, 173, 177; ASH 281, §11; Sharkey 1927, 62–4). This suggests that Áth Dá Laarg was affiliated with the *paruchia* of Armagh many centuries before the abbey was built (TT 136, 173, 177; ASH 281, §11; Sharkey 1927, 62–4; Ó Riain 2011, 222). The memory of Conall survived at Áth Dá Laarg alongside the Cistercian foundation, and in 1487 – when the parish church at Boyle was burnt – it was called Druim Conaille (AU; AFM).

An incident outlined in the mid ninth century *Vita Tripartita* describes how St Patrick fell into the River Boyle at Áth Carbaid (the ford of the chariot) near Eas Mac nEirc (the waterfall of the son of Eirc), about 1km west of Boyle. He cursed the water to the east of the ford but not to the west and prophesied that when St Colmcille came to the spot, he would appreciate fruitful water. The story is reiterated in Maghnus Ó Domnaill's *Bethu Colaim Chille* and suggests that a rival church to the Patrician church of Conall was established at Eas Mac nEirc in the sixth century under the patronage of the *paruchia* of Derry and St Colm Cille (Stokes 1887, i, 142–5; BCC 14–17, 156–7; Herbert 1988, 236; Ó Riain 2011, 269–70; O'Hanlon 1875, iii, 266). The church at Eas Mac nEirc was dedicated to St Dochonna (*ibid.*). When the obit to St Fursa, who died at Eas Mac nEirc in 748, was recorded in the annals, it was stated that it was now known as Eas Uí Fhloinn (AFM). This has been anglicised as Assylin and comes from the family name O'Flynn, who were hereditary *comharba* (coarbs) of St Dochonna of Eas Mac nEirc. This office holder had the honour of being present at the Uí Briúin Aí inaugurations at Carnfree in Rathcroghan (Dillon 1961, 188).

Little is known about the church of Druim Conaille at Áth Dá Laarg, other than that St Maccán was associated with it (Archdall 1786, 599). In *Corpus Genealogiarum Sanctorum Hiberniae*, a Maccán is listed among deacons (Ó Riain 1985, 139). There is no surviving archaeological evidence of an earlier ecclesiastical foundation on the site of the Cistercian abbey of Boyle.

The circuitous route to Boyle

The community of monks that left Mellifont for Connacht in 1148 first settled at Grellach Dínach under Abbot Peadar Ua Mórdha (AB; AU). It has been suggested that Grellach Dínach is Kinnagrelly in the parish of Ballisadare in the kingdom of Luigne in the modern County Sligo (O'Rorke 1900, ii, 398). It is plausible that Tairrdelbach Ua Conchobair, having plundered Luigne in 1148 (AT), granted swordland to the Cistercians in order to neutralize attempts by the defeated rulers of Luigne, Uí hEadhra/Uí Gadhra (O'Hara/O'Gara), to regain control of their kingdom. It should be borne in mind, however, that there are townlands named Grallagh[more] and Grallagh[beg] in the parish of Boyle where the monks could have settled.

Peadar Ua Mórdha became Bishop of Clonfert *c.* 1151–2, and the community at Grellach Dínach moved to Druim Connaid where they remained for two years under the abbacy of Aédh Ua Maccáin. Druim Connaid may be Drumcunny in the parish of Ardcarn, a short distance from Boyle (D'Alton 1845 i, 178). Ua Maccáin was succeeded as abbot of Druim Connaid by Muirgius Ua Dubthaig who, after six years, *c.* 1158–9, moved his community to Bun Finne (Buninny) in the parish of Dromard in County Sligo, where he spent two and a half years (AB).

Bun Finne lies in the ancient kingdom of Tír Fiachrach where the River Finn enters the southern shore of Ballisadare Bay. Tír Fiachrach was the land of Uí Fiachrach who had contested the kingship of Connacht with Uí Briúin. Uí Fiachrach were rivals of Uí Briúin for the kingship of Connacht from the late fifth century until the end of the eighth century when Síl Muiredaig, the branch of Uí Briúin Aí from which Uí Conchobair and Mic Diarmata descended, took power. From 773 on, all the regional kings of the Connachta belonged to Uí Briúin. By the mid twelfth century, the northern side of the bay, Tír Ailella – the land of Uí Ailella – was under the control of Uí Conchobair. So, too, was Luigne, which separated Tír Fiachrach from Tír Ailella. According to Uí Fiachrach tradition, Bun Finne, where the Cistercians now settled, was one of ten principal seats of Uí Fiachrach where Sliocht Lochlainn had an inheritance of eight quarters of land (O'Donovan 1844, 118–21, 172–5). It seems that Uí Conchobair controlled Ballisadare Bay since Uí Dubda, the ruling sept of Uí Fiachrach, supported them in 1153 when Brian Ua Dubda died in combat; in 1155 the fleet of Tír Fiachrach accompanied Uí Conchobair in an attack on Inis Eógain (AFM).

It has been argued that the site 'Abbey Field', in the townland of Ballinley/Ballinlig adjacent to Bun Finne, was the location of the first Cistercian foundation (Stout 2015, 40, 52–3; O'Rorke 1900, ii, 398; Recorded Monument SL019-043002). It is a large, raised, rectangular enclosure, measuring 62.5m by 82m (enclosing 0.5ha) and defined by remnants of a bank, ditch and outer bank (Fig. 2.2). In the interior is a long rectangular building, possibly a barn, defined by a low, grass-covered bank of earth and stone. Also found near the site in a farmyard wall is a small fragment of cut stone, which may be a water stoup (Stout 2015, 52–3).

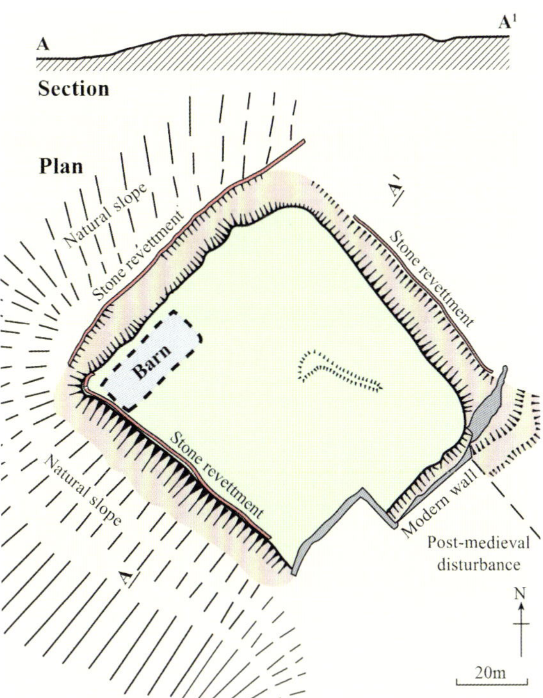

Fig. 2.2 The grange at Ballinlig, Co. Sligo (after Stout 2015).

Abbot Muirgius Ua Dubthaig left Bun Finne in 1161 and put down permanent roots at Áth Dá Laarg (Boyle) where work began on the monks' first stone building (AB; HD; Weld 1832, 227; D'Alton 1845 i, 178; Gwynn and Hadcock 1970, 128–9; Mac Niocaill 1959, 9, 127). Ua Dubthaig spent 13 and a half years as abbot in Boyle and was buried there when he died in 1174 (AB; AT; AFM; ALC). The name Áth Dá Laarg was subsequently used in relation to a burial in Boyle Abbey in 1197 (AU). By 1161, Mic Diarmata were established as the local rulers of Mag Luirg. There is no evidence, however, to confirm that Mic Diarmata endowed the Cistercian monks with the site on which Boyle Abbey was built. Likewise, there is no proof that Uí Conchobair were the benefactors. It may be that the abbey lands were granted from land taken from one of the older Mag Luirg chiefs by either Mic Diarmata or Uí Conchobair.

The seantaoisigh (ancient chiefs) of Mag Luirg

Cenél Mic Erca, in whose territory Boyle Abbey was built, were a sept of Uí Ailella who had lost control of their lands by the mid-ninth century (ASH, 277–82, 281 n.11; Bieler 1979, 148–9; Stokes 1887 i, 108–09, 142–5; Ó Riain 2011, 82, 222, 269–70; BCC 14–17, 156–7; Herbert 1988, 236; O'Hanlon 1875 iii, 266). They are one and the same as Corca Achlainn who rebranded themselves as Uí Briúin Sinna, adopting a spurious genealogy that tied them to the more successful Uí Briúin Aí (Byrne 1973, 232). They were described as 'the mightiest and strongest among the Connachta' but that 'they do not rule like over-kings' (Stokes 1887, i. 94–5).

Mic Riabhaigh (the McGreevys), another important family, belonged to a number of dynasties known as 'Fir Sceindi' (Ó Raithbheartaigh 1932, 180) who were significant in the vicinity of Boyle (Carney 1943, 26). Although they lost status with the rise of Uí Briúin, Mic Riabhaigh had prominence in Mag Luirg until at least 1238 when there is an obit to Cathal Mac Riabhaigh *taoiseach* Fir Sceindi. (AFM). It is unlikely that they were in a position to endow the Cistercians with monastic land in the twelfth century.

Uí Conchobair and Mic Diarmata

At the end of the eleventh century, the leading family of Síl Muiredaig of Mag nAí, Uí Conchobair (the descendents of Conchobar), adopted the name of their ancestor Conchobor († 971) as their surname.

It was not until after Diarmait mac Taidg mac Máel Ruanaid, *tigherna* (lord) of Uí Máel Ruanaid, died in 1159 (AFM) that his kinsmen, Uí Máel Ruanaid adopted Mac Diarmata (singular name – son of Diarmait) and Mic Diarmata (plural family name,) as their family name. Diarmait was called King of Mag Luirg in his obit in 1187 (ALC; AFM; AB; AU). Diarmait's son, Conchobar, was the first to use Mac Diarmata as a surname. Conchobar Mac Diarmata established the Mic Diarmata *caput* on 'MacDermot's Island', i.e., the rock on Loch Cé near Boyle (AT) and died in a monk's habit in Boyle Abbey in 1196 (ALC; AU; AFM; = AB 1197). He was succeeded as king of Mag Luirg by his son Tomaltach na Carraige – Tomaltach of the Rock.

According to tradition, in the tenth century Diarmait's forefather Máel Ruanaid came to an agreement with his brother Conchobar, as a result of which Máel Ruanaid's descendants took possession of Mag Luirg in return for surrendering any claim to the regional kingship of Connacht to Conchobar's heirs (McKenna 1939, 124–8; 1940, 74–7).

The kingship of Connacht in the twelfth century

Unrest during the reign of Tairrdelbach Ua Conchobair (1106–56) was compounded by discord within Uí Conchobair which led to Tairrdelbach imprisoning his son Ruaidrí. Ruaidrí was released in 1144. He gradually gained his father's confidence and became king of Connacht on his father's death in 1156 and high king of Ireland in 1166. Ruaidrí abdicated in 1183 in favour of his son, Conchobar Máenmaige (AFM) but resumed the kingship in 1185 with support from the forces of Munster and the Normans. Conchobar Máenmaige's son, Cathal Carrach Ua Conochobair, retaliated and Conchobar Maenmaige regained the sovereignty of Connacht before the year was out and expelled his father. When Conchobar Máenmaige was assassinated in 1189, his kinsman, Muirchertach mac Cathail Mac Diarmata of Mag Luirg, was among his assassins. Ruaidrí Ua Conchobair died as a monk in the Augustinian monastery of Cong in 1198.

When Ruaidrí's brother, Cathal Crobhdearg Ua Conchobair, became king of Connacht in 1189 he was challenged by his grand-nephew Cathal Carrach. In 1199 they made peace and the latter was granted land in Connacht. The peace was short lived, however, and in 1200 Cathal Crobhdearg went to Tír Fiachrach hoping to capture Cathal Carrach, but the latter got the upper hand. We know that Mac Diarmata supported Cathal Crobhdearg because the hostages of Tomaltach na Carraige were taken by Cathal Carrach. Cathal Carrach devastated all of Connacht and burnt nearly all the churches. Because the churches are not named, we cannot be certain that Boyle suffered. In 1201 Cathal Crobhdearg went to war with Mac Diarmata and plundered their territory in Mag Luirg and in Tír Ailella where they now also had land (ALC; AFM).

Pl. 2.1. View of Boyle Abbey looking west onto the Boyle River. © Photographic Archive, National Monuments Service. Government of Ireland.

In 1202 Cathal Crobhdearg and William de Burgo (d. 1205/06?), with forces from Munster, marched through Connacht to Boyle Abbey which they used as military quarters. They spent three days defiling the abbey and the buildings were broken and burnt. De Burgo spent two days erecting a stone wall 'round the great stone house of the guests' (ALC; = AFM 1201). The next day Cathal Carrach was killed by the Normans in a skirmish elsewhere (ALC; AFM; AU; AClon). When they got word of his death, Cathal Crobhdearg and William de Burgo left Boyle Abbey. Muirchertach and Conchobar Ua Briain who had accompanied them to Connacht were brothers-in-law of both Cathal Crobhdearg and de Burgo. They decided to send their mercenaries throughout Connacht to levy their wages. A rumour spread throughout the province that de Burgo had died. The Irish chiefs resolved to take advantage of this by killing de Burgo's men as soon as they arrived on their doorsteps. De Burgo returned to Tuad Mumu (Thomond), blaming Cathal Crobhdearg for the massacre of his men. In 1203 de Burgo built a castle at Meelick and attacked Connacht soon afterwards (ALC). According to the Annals of Clonmacnoise, he took the spoils of all the churches of Connacht including 'the abby of Ath-da-laragh' (AClon 1204). In the winter of 1205/1206, however, 'God and the saints took vengeance on De Burgo for plundering the churches of Connacht for he died of a singular disease, too shameful to be described' (AFM).

The development of the ecclesiastical foundation at Áth Dá Laarg did not happen overnight, and it is interesting that in 1230 Donnsléibhe Ó hIonmhainéin, a holy monk and chief master-mason of the monastery of Boyle, died. He may have overseen the building of the abbey church, 'the decorative carvings being more ornate than the official Cistercian ideal required' (AConn; ALC; AU). The completion of Boyle Abbey, as reflected in the various architectural styles, was undoubtedly held up by the numerous attacks listed above. It was not consecrated until 1220.

Daughter Houses of Boyle

Boyle Abbey at Áth Dá Laarg was in origin a daughter house of Mellifont and, in time, Boyle gained its own daughter houses, Eas Ruadh (Assaroe, Co. Donegal), founded in 1178, and the abbey of Collis Victoria, founded by Cathal Crobhdearg at Cnoc Muaidhe (Knockmoy, Co. Galway) in 1190 (ALC; Lanigan 1822, 338; Gwynn and Hadcock 1970, 124). The introduction of the Cistercian order coincided with the adoption of the European Latin charter by Irish kings. The charter provided a means for Irish kings to promote themselves at the expense of their rivals. The earliest surviving charter is dated 1156. There is no direct evidence that Tairrdelbach Ua Conchobair or his son Ruaidrí directly patronised the foundation of the abbey at Boyle or that they or Uí Máel Ruanaid offered a charter outlining their rights to the monks. Áed Uí Máel Ruanaid became king of Connacht in 1224, before his father, Cathal Crobhdearg, died as a monk at Knockmoy. One of Áed's first acts was to sign a charter for the abbey of Knockmoy. The abbot Áed Uí Máel Ruanaid died as a result of bloodletting in 1225 (Flanagan 2005, 353; AC; ALC; AFM). It has been suggested that the charter given to Knockmoy by Áed was issued to mark Cathal Crobhdearg's funeral (Flanagan 1998a, 113–14; 1998b, 115, 117; 2005a, 120, 227). Boyle Abbey, meanwhile, was not consecrated until 1220 (ALC; = AFM 1218; = AU 1219).

Boyle Abbey had privileges granted by Ruaidrí Ua Conchobair, who had abdicated in 1183. One such concession was a rent of 25 bushels of barley due annually from three cantreds in Connacht as a gift from Ua Conochobair. The justiciary Maurice FitzGerald was mandated in 1233 to find out if his predecessor, Richard de Burgo (d. 1243), had divested the monks of their rights; if this was the case, the monks should be paid the rent owed to them. The property was in the cantreds of Tyrmany, Trichata and Magne (CDI i, 299). The inferred inquiry into the theft of the monks' barley did not deter Richard from plundering Boyle Abbey in 1235. His army crossed through Connacht from Athlone to the churches of Roscommon and Elphin which they burnt and plundered. They continued to Boyle Abbey and 'overran the monastery and broke open the *scribhta*; and all its valuable things, and its mass-chalices and vestments, were taken out of it' (AConn). A corresponding entry has *cripta* (cript) instead of *scriphta* (AB). Crown officials were appalled at the violation and all that could be recovered was returned and everything else was paid for (AB; ALC; AU; AFM; AClon).

Monastic discord

The expansion of reforming monastic orders from the Continent in the twelfth century and throughout the early thirteenth century led to two main groups of Cistercian houses in Ireland – those founded from Mellifont Abbey and its daughter houses and those founded from St Mary's Abbey, Dublin, which were under the influence of the Normans (Conway 1958, 30–70; Gwynn 1949, 110–25). Norman officials such as Gerald of Wales complained that some Irish monasteries had departed from the general rule of the Cistercian order (GC iv, 178–81, 183). Although Mellifont was a daughter house of Clairvaux (Aube), the Mellifont filiation to which Boyle Abbey belonged was Irish in character. Monks did not embrace communal living and slept in individual cells. The reluctance of Irish monks to travel to the Cistercians' General Chapter at Cîteaux (Côte-d'Or) was seen as a lack of discipline among the Irish. It was discussed at the annual meeting at Cîteaux in 1216 and the abbey at Clairvaux was nominated to solve the problems that had developed in Mellifont. Visitors sent to Mellifont by the abbot of Clairvaux in 1217 were refused admission as a result of which Abbot Thomas of Mellifont was deposed at the General Chapter (Conway 1958, 54–6; Smith 1991, 33–4; O'Dwyer 1979, 54; Mac Niocaill 1959, 84–5). A decade later (1227) a visitation was carried out by the abbots of Trois-Fontaines (Marne) and Froidmont (Oise) on behalf of the abbot of Clairvaux (CDI i, 225). Their mission was to address and solve the problems in the Cistercian houses in Ireland. Efforts were made to exclude Irishmen from ecclesiastical office and to introduce Norman practice (Conway 1958, 58–9). The efforts at reform were resisted by Mellifont and its daughter houses, which included Boyle, and the abbots of Boyle and Assaroe were among those deposed (Mac Niocaill 1959, 85–6, 89). The standoff between the Cistercian central authorities in France and the monastic filiation of Mellifont became known as 'the Conspiracy of Mellifont'.

As a consequence, the daughter houses of Mellifont were transferred to new mother houses at the council of abbots convened in Dublin in 1228 by the appointed visitor, Stephen of Lexington (d. 1258). The prior and community of Boyle were not represented at the council because the abbot had been deposed. Boyle and Knockmoy were transferred to the jurisdiction of Clairvaux. Stephen also tactically placed Bective under Clairvaux while the monastery at Abbeyshrule, Co. Longford, a daughter house of Mellifont, became affiliated with Bective. The plan had ramifications for Boyle because Stephen of Lexington saw the strategically placed and strongly fortified abbey at Bective as a base from which Boyle could be disciplined and reformed. Stephen nominated the abbot of Shrule as a visitor to Boyle representing the abbot of Clairvaux. The fact that Shrule was answerable to Bective made Boyle Abbey answerable to the French abbot of Bective. In August 1228 Stephen ordered the abbot of Shrule to visit Boyle to oversee the election of a new abbot. Two out of four candidates were Irish, one of whom was Nehemias Ó Brógáin, titled 'prior of Mellifont'. This occurred despite Stephen attempting to eradicate the Irish language from the practices of Cistercian houses. It is possible that Prior Nehemias, who was bishop elect of Clogher, was an asset in Stephen of Lexington's dealings with Mellifont. Stephen anticipated a backlash from the monks in Boyle and directed the abbot of Shrule in how to handle the situation: he gave him the power of excommunication. Nehemias did not become abbot of Boyle and was appointed to the see of Clogher, where he remained bishop until his death in 1240 (Mac Niocaill 1959, 89–90, 94; O'Dwyer 1972, 87–8, n.21).

The changes imposed by Stephen of Lexington in 1228 may have encouraged members of the Cistercian community at Boyle to join the Premonstratensian Abbey on Trinity Island, Loch Cé (Flower 1927, 340, 344; Clyne 2005, 24; O'Dwyer 1972, 83–5). The possibility may be reflected in a dispute that took place at Boyle between the Cistercians and the Premonstratensians following the death of Diarmait Mac Gilla Cárthaig, *airchinnech* (chief steward) of Tibohin, in 1229. Diarmait's body lay unburied for two nights because the monks on Trinity Island demanded to keep it. The body did not repose in Boyle Abbey, however, but in the church of Drum. Arbitration took place after which the deceased was removed at the end of the third day for burial on Trinity Island (AB; AConn).

The General Chapter in Cîteaux

Although Cistercian houses were exempt from paying tithes because their lands were privileged by the pope, they were liable for payments to their own General Chapter. The General Chapter required financial aid from its abbeys to help with running costs. Payments were first introduced *c.* 1235 as voluntary contributions but soon became a form of taxation to defray the expense of administration (Burton and Kerr 2011, 900). The General Chapter met annually in Cîteaux to the south of Dijon in France. Due to distance and the hardship of travel it was agreed in 1190 that the abbots of Irish Cistercian houses were only obliged to attend every fourth year (Fr. Colmcille 1958, 43). The abbot of

Mellifont was responsible for fixing the annual rota of alternate attendees. The dangers of travel were expressed in the annals of 1217 when it was recorded that many were killed on the way.

Attendance in Cîteaux was somewhat erratic and in 1195 the abbot of Mellifont was reminded that he should implement the rota directive. The first record of the attendance of the abbot of Boyle at the General Chapter was in 1197 (Mac Niocaill 1959, 77–8). He was reported absent in 1237 and in 1276 when he and four other absent Irish abbots were suspended due to 12 years' non-attendance at the General Chapter without good reason (*ibid.*, 78, 79). In 1278 the abbot of Boyle was officially excused from attending the Chapter at Cîteaux (*ibid.*, 81–2). An instance of complaint by Boyle Abbey was recorded by the General Chapter in 1239 against the abbey's then former daughter house, Knockmoy (*ibid.*, 82–3). In 1352, the General Chapter dealt with Donnchad (Donatus), abbot of Boyle who, although he had been deposed by the abbot of Mellifont, acting on behalf of Clairvaux, for being unworthy, and a new abbot installed, was still acting as abbot (Mac Niocaill 1959, 103, 109; Conway 1958, 109).

The scriptoria at Boyle and Trinity Island, Loch Ce

The Premonstratensian order was introduced to Mag Luirg by Clarus Mac Mailín, archdeacon of Elphin, between 1215 and 1224, as part of the Church reform movement. As suggested above, attempts by Stephen of Lexington to reform Boyle Abbey in 1227/1228 may have influenced disaffected monks to join the new community on Trinity Island (AFM 1237; Clyne 2005, 23).

The Annals of Boyle, also known as the Annals of Cotton MS Titus A XXV, are reputed to be the original chronicle of the Premonstratensian house of the Holy Trinity at Loch Cé. The thirteenth-century manuscript is in the British Library in London. It has been suggested that the manuscript is based on an earlier chronicle written at Boyle Abbey and that the scholar James Usher, Archbishop of Armagh and Primate of All Ireland (1625–56), gave it the name Annals of Boyle (Flower 1927, 340, 344). The annals contain an abbreviated version of the pre-Palladian Irish World Chronicle, the Chronicle of Ireland, and annals up to 1228 that are believed to have been written at Boyle. The annals were continued up to 1257, perhaps at Premonstratensian Holy Trinity (O'Dwyer 1972, 83–5; Clyne 2005, 24–5; Conway 1958, 116, n.16). These annals developed into the Annals of Loch Cé, which were copied for Brian MacDiarmata. In 1577 he was described as the superior of the monastery of Holy Trinity and was also head of the MacDiarmata clan. Some entries in the Annals of Loch Cé point to the use of a Cistercian chronicle in their compilation, such as that of 1217 which equates 'all the abbots of Ireland' with Cistercian abbots (ALC).

The life of Athracht, published by John Colgan (ASH 277–82) was probably written by a Cistercian monk at Boyle at the end of the twelfth century or in the early thirteenth century. Athracht, whose name has been anglicised as Attracta, is the patron saint of Cill Athrachta (Killaraght) in the barony of Coolavin (County Sligo) not far from Boyle. Athracht was persuaded by her brother, Conall of Drum, not to erect a church too close to his own (Mooney 2000, 28; Ó Riain 2011, 81–2).

Pilgrimage, interment and refuge

The office of abbot of Boyle was a political position within the remit of a select group of families such as Uí Mocháin, Mic Dáibhí and ultimately Mic Diarmata (Mac Niocaill 1959, 172–3). Patronage worked in two ways: the monks provided services and were materially rewarded, often with land, some of which was swordland. Pilgrimage, interment and refuge formed part of the economy of Boyle. Pilgrimage was hazardous throughout the Middle Ages and in 1242 Brian Ua Dubda, chief of Tír Fiachrach, Tír Ailella and Iorras was killed on his way to the abbey of Boyle (AConn). The circumstances are unknown. The abbots, such as Ua Máel Brénainn who acted as a signatory for Áed Ua Conchobair to the charter of Knockmoy, were presumably buried in the abbey. The former died as a result of a bloodletting in 1225 (AC; ALC; AFM), a regular feature of monastic life as a means of encouraging good physical and mental health (Williams 1988, 252–3). In 1230 Donn Sleibhe O hIonmainen, a reverend and holy monk and principal master of the carpenters in Boyle Abbey, was buried there (AFM). That there was status to burial in Boyle Abbey was illustrated in 1244 when Donnchad Mór Ua Dálaig, a master of poetry, was buried in the monastery of Boyle (AClon; AC; AFM). The Uí Dálaig were advisors to the Uí Conchobair kings. Women were also buried at Boyle Abbey in the medieval period: in 1253 the daughter of the earl of Ulster, the wife of Milo Costello, was interred at Boyle (AConn; ALC). In 1264, the abbey was also the last resting place of Oengus Ua Clúnáin, a retired bishop of Achonry who had taken up the monastic habit. The Annals of Connacht call him Bishop of Luigne. In the mid nineteenth century a tree in the cemetery at the abbey was known to mark his grave (O'Donovan 1852, 8). Áed na nGall Ua Conchobair, who was credited with stemming Norman expansion into Connacht and ruled Connacht between 1265 and 1274, was buried with the monks in the abbey of Boyle (AU; AFM; CS). Meanwhile, the abbey regularly served as a place of refuge. In 1256 the annals record the death of Sitric Mac Senlaich following an escape to the monastery of Boyle to seek the protection of the order (ALC; AConn; AFM). When Domnall Ua Conchobair, tanist of all Connacht, was killed in a skirmish by Áed Brefnech Ua Conchobair in 1307, his funeral procession was accompanied by many droves and flocks and cattle and companies of horse and foot and mercenaries to his burial; and he was then interred in the monastery of Boyle with reverence and honour. There is a reference to a Holy Cross being erected in the abbey in 1312 (ALC).

Despite its strong economy from royal grants, revenue generated from agricultural activity, and payment for the above-mentioned services, Boyle Abbey was under scrutiny during the General Chapter of 1277 when it was decreed that its abbot be deposed. He was found guilty of not making payments that were due to the General Chapter (D'Alton 1845 i, 190).

Boyle in the thirteenth and fourteenth centuries

Warfare broke out in Connacht between the Irish and the Normans in 1284. There was plundering in Mag Luirg and the Curlew Mountains and the Crown repaid the losses suffered by the communities of Boyle and Trinity Island (AFM; ALC; AConn). In 1296 Boyle was targeted by Áed Mac Eógain Ua Conchobair, king of Connacht (1293–1309). Civil war meanwhile occurred among Uí Conchobair and Áed was deposed. In retaliation, he enlisted a large army under the leadership of William and Theobald de Burgo. They proceeded to the abbey where they spent four nights. They destroyed all the corn and property throughout the district and the local chieftains made submissions to them (AFM; ALC). They seem to have used the abbey as their military headquarters. In 1297 Conchobar, king of Mag Luirg and Airtech, was buried in Boyle 'in the grave of his ancestors and elders' (ALC).

Pl. 2.2. View of church interior at Boyle Abbey.

The Bruce War

A relatively peaceful time following the inauguration of Feidlimid Ua Conchobair as king of Connacht in 1310 was interrupted by the invasion by Edward (d. 1318), the younger brother of the Scottish king, Robert Bruce, in May 1315. Although Bruce did not cross into Connacht, Feidlimid, who was subservient to Richard Ruadh de Burgo, earl of Ulster and lord of Connacht, saw Bruce's presence as an opportunity to consolidate his kingship of Connacht. Bruce sent emissaries to Feidlimid offering him the province of Connacht in exchange for abandoning Richard de Burgo. Feidlimid acceded. His cousin Ruaidrí, son of Cathal Ruadh Ua Conchobair, meanwhile contacted Edward Bruce and promised to banish the Normans from Connacht. Edward agreed, provided that Ruaidrí did not encroach on Feidlimid's territory. Ruaidrí ravaged Connacht instead. The only Síl Muiredaig chief that did not submit to him was Feidlimid's foster father, Máel Ruanaid Mac Diarmata, king of Mag Luirg. Ruaidrí was inaugurated on Carnfree in his cousin's absence. On hearing this, Feidlimid, who was supporting in the north, returned to Connacht. His troops were, however, decimated on the return journey and as a result of this Feidlimid encouraged his followers to submit to Ruaidrí. De Burgo, meanwhile, was defeated in Ulster and returned to Connacht where the Norman settlements had been attacked by Ruaidrí. Máel Ruanaid Mac Diarmata made peace with Ruaidrí in order to recover his confiscated lands. Soon afterwards he contravened his agreement with Ruaidrí and brought a great prey to Feidlimid (ALC; AConn).

When Ruaidrí got word that Mac Diarmata had joined Feidlimid, he attacked Mag Luirg and destroyed the sanctity of Eas Dachonna, and that of the monks of Boyle Abbey and other churches by stealing their cattle and corn. Máel Ruanaid Mac Diarmata meanwhile heard that his kinsman Diarmait Gall had grabbed the kingship of Mag Luirg, taken the rock at Loch Cé and was inaugurated at Cruachu (ALC; AConn). He plundered a wide area in retribution. When Feidlimid Ua Conchobair and his foster father got word that there were still some cows in Mag Luirg they went in search of them and plundered all the cows and horses they could find. The effect that this had on Boyle Abbey is undocumented.

In 1316, Feidlimid Ua Conchobair and Máel Ruanaid Mac Diarmata gathered forces. They encountered and outfought Ruaidrí who was killed alongside Diarmait Gall Mac Diarmata. Máel Ruainaid Mac Diarmata was wounded. Feidlimid had thus briefly secured the kingship of Connacht but was killed at the battle of Athenry the same year. Edward Bruce continued his campaign until 1318 when he was defeated and killed at Faughart, Co. Louth (ALC; AConn).

Máel Ruanaid Mac Diarmata took the habit of a Cistercian monk at Boyle in 1331 and his son Tomaltach na Carraige became king of Mag Luirg (ALC; AFM; AClon). Walter de Burgo went into Mag Luirg and burnt, preyed upon and destroyed all before him except for churches and church lands for which he had great respect. Tomaltach opposed him, an act that was apparently not unavenged. Tomaltach died in 1336 in his house at Caladh na Carraige, on the shore of Loch Cé, and was succeeded by his son Conchobar. Tomaltach was buried in Boyle Abbey and not on Trinity Island (AClon; ALC; AConn). In 1349 the plague known as the Black Death was rampant and Mag Luirg, where 'great numbers were carried off', was especially mentioned in the annals (AFM; AC; = AClon 1348). Between 1367 and 1393 there were numerous raids on Mag Luirg when corn and buildings were burn t and people killed (AC; ALC). Although Boyle Abbey inevitably suffered throughout this period, no specific detail is given.

In 1393 Tomaltach na Carraige's grandson, Máel Ruanaid Mac Diarmata succeeded his cousin Áed (1368–93) as king of Mag Luirg. In 1398 he went to the monastery of Boyle and transferred all their food to the Rock of Loch Cé. Conchobar, the son of Áed, tracked him as far as Echdruim (Aughrim in the barony of Ballintubber North) and burned the church. Máel Ruanaid Mac Diarmata was captured and many of his followers killed, and their horses and armour were taken from them. Conchobar now became king (ALC; AConn). In 1462–3, a monk named Cornelius in the monastery of Boyle informed the pope that Malachy, abbot of Boyle had 'dilapidated' the belongings of the abbey, 'committed simony and perjury', and openly kept a concubine in his own house. It was decided that Cornelius, despite being the son of unmarried parents, would now become abbot (Cal. Pap. Reg. vol. 11, 1455–1464, 481). Such accusations were frequently made to the Vatican, often for ambitious and mercenary reasons.

In 1471 Boyle was flooded at Beltaine (May Day). There were showers of hail, and thunder and lightning that destroyed the fruit of the land, and 'a boat could have floated over the floor of the great church of the monks' (AC) (Pl. 2.2). Mic Diarmata fought against each other in 1478 and destroyed each other's territories. After wasting and plundering the churches and the work of the artisans of Conchobar Mac Diarmata, Ruaidrí Mac Diarmata placed creaghts in Ardcarn and around Boyle. The word creaght, a derivative of *caoraíocht*, refers to nomadic herdsmen (Byrne 2004, 89). He was then inaugurated as king of Mag Luirg at Cruachu (ALC) and remained king until his death in 1486.

Tension between Ulster and Connacht continued and in 1526 a 'great war' broke out. Áed Dubh Ua Domnaill, king of Tír Conaill (1505–37), entered Mag Luirg, which he destroyed and burned. He came again in 1527, and in 1528 with gallowglasses. Mag Luirg was again destroyed in 1530, on which occasion Ua Domnaill passed Boyle Abbey southwards through the Mac Diarmata *tánaiste*'s land and into Mag Luirg, which he destroyed. He came again in 1532 after which he made peace with Mac Diarmata (AC; ALC). This hostile activity inevitably affected the economy of the Cistercian monks at Boyle. Diarmait an Einigh (Diarmait the hospitable), a son of Ruaidrí Óg who died in 1486, succeeded his brother Cormac as king of Mag Luirg in 1528 and ruled until 1533 when he was beheaded by his grand-nephew Cormac Carrach mac Eógain (AC; ALC). Diarmait was succeeded for a year by his nephew Eógan Mac Diarmata (1533–34), a grandson of Ruaidrí Óg and father of Diarmait's assassin. Following Eógan's death on the Rock in Loch Cé in 1534 (AC; ALC), his descendants, Sliocht Eógain, became key players in Mag Luirg and used Boyle Abbey as their headquarters.

Eógan Mac Diarmata was succeeded as king of Mag Luirg (1534–49) by his first cousin, Áed mac Cormaic, the abbot of Boyle. In 1538 Áed's kingship was opposed by a first cousin, Ruaidrí mac Taidg, and war broke out. An agreement was reached by which each was deemed half-king. Abbot Áed now concentrated on administering Boyle Abbey and its estates. When Ruaidrí and his wife Sadhb convened a school for *filí* and *ollaimh* (poets and professors) in 1540, Áed was first on the list of invitees. Following Áed's death in 1549 Ruaidrí was the undisputed king of Mag Luirg until his death in 1568 (ALC). The next known abbot of Boyle is Tomaltach mac Eógain of Sliocht Eógain.

A war broke out in 1555 between Ruaidrí Mac Diarmata and Sliocht Eógain in the course of which Boyle Abbey was captured by Ruaidrí's son, Brian. Tomaltach Mac Eógain Mac Diarmata, abbot of Boyle and leader of Sliocht Eógain, was captured. Sliocht Eógain retaliated and burnt the abbey and carried away seven horses (ALC). Afterwards, they regained possession of the abbey. In 1562 Ruaidrí Mac Diarmata discovered that Sliocht Eógain retained an army of 300 gallowglasses which they used to burn and plunder the property and strongholds of Ruaidrí's allies in Mag Luirg. When Ruaidrí, who remained on the Rock in Loch Cé, realised the extent of the destruction, he waylaid Sliocht Eógain as they crossed the River Boyle on their way to Boyle Abbey. Sliocht Eógain was routed by Tadhg Mac Diarmata and Ruaidrí's son Brian and Ruaidrí captured Boyle Abbey the same day (ALC).

Dissolution of the monastery

When Pope Clement VII refused Henry VIII's petition to annul his marriage to Catherine of Aragon, the Tudor king put his authority over the Catholic Church into a legal framework. The Act of Supremacy was passed in 1534 and by 1541 the Irish Parliament had voted to change the status of Ireland from that of a lordship to that of the Kingdom of Ireland. From the late 1530s the king's administration set about influencing Irish kings in adopting the policy of 'surrender and regrant' and accepting the Protestant religion. Henry set about suppressing dynasties that were beyond the control of his administration in Dublin. He also set about suppressing the monasteries and confiscating their property. The dissolution of the religious houses in Ireland under Henry VIII did not de facto extend beyond the Pale, the territories of the earl of Ormond and certain other territories in south Munster. In Gaelic areas the suppression of monasteries usually happened some decades later than in the east of Ireland as the Crown did not have the authority to put its policy into effect, especially when a monastery was protected by a powerful local family. Men who benefited from the grants of monastic lands did not necessarily show enthusiasm for expelling the monks. After the decree of suppression in 1541, Boyle Abbey came under the protection of Ruaidrí mac Taidg mac Diarmata, the half-king of Mag Luirg whose cousin Áed was abbot until 1549. There is no evidence that Ruaidrí banished the Cistercian monks from Boyle. Áed was succeeded as abbot by Tomaltach mac Eógain. Henry Sidney took the abbey of Boyle on his return from a campaign to Ulster in 1566 and put a tenant in it (Brady 2002, 47). Describing his earlier tour of Connacht, Sydney wrote in 1569 that 'I took the great abbey of Boyle in Connaught. Mac Dermode submitted' (Cal. Car. MSS 1578–88, 334–5). The 'Mac Dermode' quoted was Tairrdelbach Mac Eógain Mac Diarmata who had become king of Mag Luirg in 1568 and ruled until 1576. His brother Tomaltach was abbot of Boyle. After Ruaidrí's death in 1568, Elizabeth I granted Boyle Abbey and its possessions to the sheriff of Meath, Patrick Cusack of Gerrardstown on 30 November 1569 (Griffith 1991, 232). Cusack paid no rent so his patent was therefore declared void by 1577. The document relating to the forfeiture of this patent by Patrick Cusack on 9 June 1577 provides a detailed account of the survey of Boyle Abbey property by Michael FitzWilliam, the Surveyor General of Ireland:

> On 30 Nov 1569 the Queen granted to Patrick Cusack of Gerrardeston, Co. Meath, esq., the site & precincts of the abbey of Boyle in McDermyt's country, containing 1a, in which are the stone walls of a church, a belfry, a cloister, a hall, a dormitory, a cemetery, 6 gardens or orchards and other ruined buildings, 3 ruined mes. & 360a in Boyle, 9 cottages & 280a. in Grange of Monwye in Clanrichardes county, 10 cottages & an enclosure & 120a. in Grange Offallon in Offallon's county, 180a in Cortenebole in O Connor Reaghe's country, 70a. in Tulskie, 180a. in the grange of Moyneterrolis, now laid waste, in Mc Granilles country, 6 cottages, 270a. & a piece of land called Carrevenalta in Graunge Mannaughe & Tamplemannaughe in Mc Donnoughe Corren's country, 6 cottages & 220a. in Great and Little Graunge in Tiroheraghe in O Doudes country, a castle, 6 cottages, 7 260a. in Cowlkenrie in O Connor Sligaghes country, a new castle beside Oharte & 7 cottage & 70a. in the Graunge in O Connor Sligaghes country, & a head rent from 100a. in Mc Dermottes county, all formerly the property of Boyle abbey , the rectory & tithes of Killenemannaughe in Mc Dermotts county, which extends into Killenemannauhe , Balleneckhall, Finiskline and other ruined vills, the chapels & tithes of Grange Monwye, Cornabole, the Graunge, Monterrolis, Tamplenemannaughe, Graungenemannaughe beside Ballenmote, Graunge, Moore, Grange Bege & Cowltre, extending into the vills of Mowvye, Cornabole, Graunge of Monterolis, Templenemannaughe, Graunge na Mannaughe, Grange Moore, Grange Begge, & Cowlekirry & other vills, the rectory & tithes of Tomna in Mc Dermit's country which extends into Tomna' and other ruined vills & hamlets, the rectory & tithes of Killunte in Mc Dermites country which extends into the vill of Killunte, the Graunge & other ruined vills, the tithes of the Graunge & Tulskie, all formerly the property of Boyle Abbey, for 21 years from the previous Michaelmas at 18-16-4 p.a.. The rent was never paid up to Michaelmas 1576 & the patent is therefore void.

Boyle Abbey was described as a one-acre site with the walls of a church and belfry, a cloister, a hall, a dormitory and some ruined buildings (Pl. 2.3). The possessions of Boyle Abbey included *c.* 1,700 acres (688ha), three castles, several granges, many cottages, six gardens and orchards; six other gardens and orchards, and three messuages in the town of Boyle; 200 acres (81ha) of arable, and 160 of mountain pasture in the townland of Boyle; besides three castles, 44 cottages, 540 acres (218.5ha) of arable land, and 729 acres (295ha) of mountain and rough pasture, dispersed in small parcels, under various denominations, chiefly given from the names of the chiefs of the several districts. By the description, the church and belfry were already stripped (Griffith 1991, 232–3).

It is clear that not all of Boyle Abbey's monastic possessions were acknowledged in FitzWilliam's survey because lands that became rectories and vicarages attached to Boyle appear in later inquisitions. Stout (2015) has argued that the sixteenth-century estimate is a misrepresentation of the size of their estate which is thought to have exceeded 5,336ha (Fig. 1.6; Table 1.1). The survey of its monastic possessions gives a detailed breakdown for only a portion of the estate with 1,956 Irish acres and 15.5 quarters listed. Land described as 'arable' comprised about one-third of the estate and the remaining holdings were described under a mixed heading of mountain, pasture, underwood, moor and bog. The emphasis was on pastoral farming rather than tillage. The grange farms ranged in size from that at Tulsk with 14ha to that on Grange of O'Fallon with 836ha.

The conquest of Connacht

When Ruaidrí Mac Diarmata died in 1568, he was succeeded as king of Mag Luirg by Tairrdelbach Mac Eógain Mac Diarmata of Sliocht Eógain who now took over the Rock of Loch Cé. War broke out in 1570 between Tairrdelbach and his brothers on one side, and Brian Mac Ruaidrí and his brother on the other. When Brian was besieged near Castlerea, Co. Roscommon, in 1571, Fytton, the president of Connacht, came to his assistance. Brian then attacked Boyle Abbey and plundered it (ALC). On 6 June 1571 Brian was made seneschal of the barony of 'Moylurge' by Queen Elizabeth, with 'licence to attack and punish by all ways malefactors and their adherents, rebels, vagabonds, rhymers, Irish harpers, and idle men and women; and to hold a court baron' (*Fiant* 1817) The conquest of Connacht was well and truly underway. Abbot Tomaltach Mac Eógain Mac Diarmata was still 'in tenure' of the abbey in 1577. The seneschal, Brian Mac Diarmata, meanwhile, remained in office until at least 1578, receiving 'great honour from the Council of Éirinn' when he attended a 'great council' in Dublin (ALC).

Although in possession of abbey lands into the seventeenth century, Tomaltach Mac Diarmata did not remain abbot of Boyle. On 21 November 1580, Abbot Glaisne (Gelasius) Ua Cuillenáín, a strong advocate of the counter-reformation, was martyred (Mac Earlean J. 1922, 77–121). According to the *Catholic Encyclopaedia* (1913, viii, 163), when Glaisne returned to Ireland, he had Boyle Abbey restored to him. Patrick Cusack appears to have supported his attempts to re-establish monastic life at Boyle. On a visit to Dublin, Glaisne and the abbot of Holy Trinity, Loch Cé, Eógain Ua Máel Ciaráín, were imprisoned after refusing to renounce their allegiance to Rome. They were tortured and subsequently hanged outside Dublin. It is said that Glaisne's body was not mutilated due to the intercession of his friends. His clothes were divided as relics (*ibid*.; Mac Niocaill 1959, 122). One of these relics, a rosary beads comprising large amber beads on silver wire, with a silver medallion, is now in the Dominican abbey in Kilkenny. The medallion, which portrays the statue of Our Lady of Atocha in Madrid, indicates that the relic came from the Dominican monastery of Atocha (Hogan 1992; Gaffney 1961). A letter written in Italian by Glaisne's brother, Bernard, to the 'Cardinals of Propaganda' in Rome, between September 1637 and November 1639, that refers to Bernard as 'abbot of Boyle', survives. Bernard died in 1639 (Jennings, B 1949, 1–49).

Richard Bingham and Boyle

Henry Sidney, Lord Deputy of Ireland, 1565–71 and 1575–78, played a key role in establishing the presidency of Connacht and in 1569 Edward Fytton was appointed the first Lord President. This office was to be financed from within the province leading to a system being put in place in 1577 that became known as the first Composition of Connacht. Fytton outlawed Gaelic customs and suppressed Catholic shrines and practices. The customs and practices of Irish kings and cess, such as coign and livery, demanded by English garrisons, would be replaced by annual rent on specific tracts of land. The administration set out to undermine the authority of Irish rulers by taking responsibility for the defence of the province. Some landowners welcomed this as it exonorated them from onerous military obligations to their Irish overlords. In 1583, William Usher of Dublin was granted the abbey of Boyle for 21 years after which the lease would transfer to John St. Barbe. The following year Richard Bingham became governor of the presidency of Connacht and set about imposing martial law on the province.

On 8 February 1585 Bingham petitioned for the 'charge' of the abbey of Boyle, the heir of which had run away from school in Oxford (CSPI 1574–85, ii, 552). On 15 March, Bingham petitioned the Privy Council for a 60-year lease of Boyle Abbey, adding that the 'M'Dermots' and others were very bad neighbours (*ibid*., 555). Although Boyle Abbey was a garrison, the chancellor wrote to Richard Bingham on 24 June 1585 ordering that an injunction be given to William Usher of Dublin to give up

Pl. 2.3. General view of Boyle Abbey from the north. © Photographic Archive, National Monuments Service. Government of Ireland.

the abbey of Boyle (CSPI 1686, 92). John King was, by now, acting as secretary to Richard Bingham (CSPI 1574–85, 571). His services were rewarded by Queen Elizabeth with lease of the abbey of Boyle.

In 1585 John Perrot, Lord Deputy of Ireland, put in place the *Compossicion Booke of Conought* (Freeman 1936). The Composition of Connacht was a 1585 agreement between the Gaelic chiefs of Connacht and the English Dublin Castle administration of the Kingdom of Ireland, which replaced the multiple existing levies with a single tax on land holdings. The Composition was a form of surrender and regrant, a part of the Tudor reconquest of Ireland. It took place under the government of the Lord Deputy, Henry Sydney, and Sir Richard Bingham as Governor of the Presidency of Connacht. The boundaries of Roscommon were established subject to the president of Connacht, Edward Fytton. Landholders were indentured by having to pay a composition rent to the Crown. The extents of the barony of Boyle were based on those of the Mac Diarmata kingship of Mag Luirg when shiring Roscommon in 1570. The Composition of Connacht mentions Boyle Abbey and its 27 quarters of land (*ibid.*, 154). It also refers to lands in Roscommon, Sligo and Leitrim being held from the queen including the house or manor of Boyle and the court baron and court leet of the manor (*ibid.*, 120, 123, 126, 141, 144, 153–4, 157, 161–4, 168). In October 1586 Bingham wrote that Boyle Abbey would soon be 'worth to him above' the yearly rent of £66l. 13s. 4d. (CSPI 1586–8, 189). The abbey comprised 27 quarters of land, which Bingham let to farm for 20s. a quarter. The tithe was not worth more than £3 per annum. He had two granges in Sligo, worth about £8 per annum, and a grange or two in O'Rourk's country which were worth nothing. Bingham was receiving £34 in rent, almost half of which came from his servants and soldiers who were tenants and wanted it for free (*ibid.*). Bingham paid £12 annual rent to the Exchequer and a composition rent of £11. He had also paid William Usher over and above the 'said rent' for the previous two years, £20. He claimed to have paid £33 yearly and that Boyle Abbey was not yet worth anything to him nor would it be for the following five years (*ibid.*). In 1587 Bingham's lease of Boyle Abbey was described 'as a consideration for the withdrawing of Athlone from him' (CSPI 1586–8, 297).

In September 1589, Bingham wrote that 'the Boile' lay waste and would be given to Richard Dyre (CPSI 1588–92, 236). In September 1590 Bingham suggested that bringing Englishmen to Boyle would curtail the Irish. The abbey lands were described as wasted and Bingham was of the opinion that no Englishman would be willing to settle in Boyle without a long lease (*ibid*., 363). On 31 December he wrote that 'there is never a house on the whole demesne of the abbey, but only a desolate place, and the lands are wasted' (*ibid*.). In May 1592 the governor complained that most of his own tenants in 'the Boile' had gone away in May and left the land waste (*ibid*., 482). In 1592 Bingham was paying an annual fee of £16 for Boyle Abbey (CSPI 1592–6, 438). On 2 July 1593, Captain Robert Fowle wrote to Burghley offering to repair 'the Boyle' in return for a long lease of Athlone (CSPI 1592–6, 121). Bingham corresponded with Burghley on 19 July saying that 'if the Boyle had been inhabited and a town planted', that 'Maguire' would not have recently raided Connacht. He dared Fowle to contradict his account (*ibid*., 128). Bingham had written a similar letter to Robert Cecil the previous day saying that the Curlew 'Mountes' were 'still haunted with a most rebellious sept called Clandermonds, and by reason that the Boile is waste the said rebels hath free passage to and fro in all those parts and keepeth wast whole countries on both sides of the mountain...and there is no question of it...but the inhabiting of the Boile will be the only stay of three counties, Roscommon, Sligo and Leitrim' (Cal. Car. MSS, XXX).

Boyle and the Nine Years war

The Nine Years war was fought between the Irish chiefs, Aodh Ó Neill (Hugh O'Neill) and Aodh Ruadh Ó Domnaill (Red Hugh O'Donnell) and their allies, and the proponents of English rule in Ireland. It lasted from 1593 to 1603. Bingham had already identified the strategic importance of Boyle and used the abbey as a barracks in 1592. Bingham's comments after MacGuidhir raided Connacht in 1593 were reiterated by Lughaidh O Clerigh in his biography of Aodh Ruadh Ó Domnaill. After MacGuidhir crossed the bridge at Boyle to access Mag nAí, Bingham's cavalry encountered them in the vicinity of Tulsk. Bingham counter-attacked MacGuidhir but had to retreat. Later in the year Bingham attacked the MacGuidhir lands of south Ulster, after which his army returned to Boyle Abbey (Walsh 1948, 62–7; AFM). On 18 July 1593 Richard Bingham explained to Robert Cecil that he had previously petitioned Cecil's father 'for some estate to myself in the Abbey of Boile, a waste thing'. He went on to explain its strategic value (CCPH iv, 338–9).

Early in 1594 Bingham got word that Aodh Ruadh Ó (= Ua) Domnaill was plundering the countryside. He came to meet him. Anticipating that Ó Domnaill would be easily beaten, Bingham assembled an army to meet him at the 'Segais called the Boyle', a place he believed Ó Domnaill would pass on his return journey to Donegal. The placename 'Segais' was on occasion used as the name of the River Boyle and Boyle Abbey. Corrsliab na Segsa was an alternative of Corrsliab, the Curlew Mountains (Hogan 1910, 594). Ó Domnaill outwitted Bingham and no more than a skirmish took place. Ó Domnaill revisited his neighbours early in the summer to persuade them to fight for their hereditary lands. Troops assembled on 18 April and agreed to attack the English who were in 'the monastery of the Segais'. Two hundred soldiers who 'wasted the neighbouring lands so that they were wildernesses without residence or dwelling' were garrisoned in the abbey church. Ó Domnaill sent cavalry across the River Boyle to the monastery both as reconnaissance and with a view to driving away the cattle that belonged to the English. Ó Domnaill hoped that the soldiers would be drawn out of the abbey. English garrisons in Newport, between Loch Cé and Loch Arrow, were aware of Ó Domnaill's presence and 'started shooting leaden balls and exploding powder' to warn the soldiers in the abbey. As a result, the garrison remained within the abbey (Walsh 1948, 82–9). Ó Domnaill's people took their cattle from the English of the monastery of Boyle and plundered the plain of Connacht (*ibid*., 93–4).

Aodh Ruadh Ó Domnaill visited Boyle once more. His biographer, Lughaidh Ó Clérigh (Walsh 1948) explained that the necessity for so much cattle raiding was 'the remoteness and distance of their own territory and the weakness and feebleness of all kinds of cattle then'.

In May 1595 Thomas Reynolds was Constable of Boyle Abbey. Efforts by commissioners appointed in Connacht to bring the Irish to heel were failing. In July 1596 Boyle Abbey was besieged by allegedly a thousand Irish. On 13 August Reynolds wrote that, because of a shortage of food, the garrison was in 'very great danger' of losing the abbey (CSPI 1592–6, 525, 531). In December 1596 an inventory of 'her majesty's forces in Ireland' noted that Richard Bingham's horsemen in Ballymore, Boyle and Athlegue amounted to 100. The figure was amended, in Lord Burghley's handwriting, to 150 (CCPH vi, 544).

A new Lord Deputy named Thomas Burgh was appointed in 1597. He immediately ordered Bingham to attack Aodh Ruadh Ó Domnaill. Bingham mustered the English forces of Connacht and many Irish and arranged to meet them at the monastery of Segais (Boyle) on 3 August. Bingham and his army marched to Cenél Conaill (Donegal) where they were routed (Walsh 1948, 146–61). Notwithstanding this defeat, the war continued with varied outcomes and on 18 February 1598 Brian Ua Ruairc 'submitted to the Queen' at Boyle Abbey. The following day Seán Mac Maghnuis Óig Ó Domnaill of Tír Conaill did likewise for himself and others (CCPH viii, 55–6).

On 5 August 1599, an army under the command of Conyers Clifford was attacked with resulting casualties (CSPI 1599–1600, 113). On 10 August 1599 instructions were given by the earl of Essex to Lord Dunkellin and Arthur Savage, commissioning them to command the Crown forces in Connacht. They were directed to make sure that Boyle and Tulsk had sufficient wards to garrison them and enough provision for two or three months (*ibid.*, 119). On 14 August, Essex wrote that in Connacht, Queen Elizabeth held the town of Galway, the castle of Athlone, and the wards of Roscommon, Tulsk and the Boyle (*ibid.*, 123). Essex's unease is apparent in a letter written five days later in which he outlines the travails of Connacht. He says that 'the Abbey of the Boyle' had surrendered and that most of the province was revolting (*ibid.*, 125). By 8 October the garrison at Boyle Abbey was short of provision. It was believed that Aodh Ruadh Ó Domnaill was meeting 1,000 rebels in Clanrickard, making it impossible to relieve the ward in Boyle (*ibid.*, 179). Plans were afoot by the end of the month to provide for the garrison, despite 1,000 men waiting to intercept the food destined for the soldiers at Boyle. The food was eventually stored for safekeeping in Ballinasloe and the soldiers who came to collect it were sent home. Mac Diarmata and Ua Conchobair Ruadh had a similar plan and waited near Elphin with their forces. Boyle could not be relieved (*ibid.*, 207). De Burgo, earl of Clanrickard, complained that Ó Domnaill had drawn his forces upon them. They heard that Boyle was 'lost' and Roscommon in great danger (*ibid.*, 259). On 27 November 1599 Arthur Savage addressed concerns for the men and provisions in Boyle, mainly lack of clothing for his men (*ibid.*, 272).

Oliver Lambert wrote to the Lord Deputy on 18 June 1602, indicating his intention to find a way to pass. If the plan succeeded and Boyle Abbey was guarded, the passage would be free and the so-called Irish rebels confined to Breifne. The English hoped to hunt the Irish down before the winter ended (CSPI 1601–3, 419–20). By 26 June, Lambert reported that the Irish were still around Boyle Abbey (*ibid.*, 422). But by the beginning of August the English undertook a 12-mile march towards Boyle Abbey to confront the Irish, who subsequently fled (*ibid.*, 465–6).

Inquisitions

On 4 December 1603 the Lord Deputy, George Carew, was directed by King James I to make John King and John Bingley tenants of four abbeys, one of which was Boyle. It was 'a lease in reversion for fifty years' (CSPI 1603–6, 113). The grant was confirmed in 1619, with the additional privilege of holding courts, both leet and baron. The vicarages of Drum and Dryne were included in the grant (D'Alton 1845 i, 244). A leet court is a manorial court that tried petty offences; a baron court must be granted by royal prerogative as it recorded the surrender of and admission to land, disputes and so on (Byrne 2004, 87; CSPI 1633–47, 65).

Inquisitions were held in 1603, 1606 and 1611 to determine the extents of the lands and possessions of Tomaltach Mac Eógain Mac Diarmata, the former abbot of Boyle. His estate amounted to 23 quarters, nine half quarters, and one cartron of land, some of which was in the vicinity of the abbey. The rest was scattered around counties Galway, Sligo and Roscommon. The monastic estate included '24 eel weirs on the Boyle river; all the tithes, great and small, of the said lands and eel wiers; besides a moiety of the tithes, being the rector's part, of 13 townlands, and the fourth part or vicarage tithes of Isselyn' (Weld 1832, 230). The abbey was granted exclusively to John King on 20 November 1617.

Boyle Castle and the borough of Boyle

It was recorded on 29 September 1606 that John King, Constable of Boyle, had 15 wardens. The reason for this being recorded was that the number of wardens was about to be reduced to 10 (CSPI 1874, 581). Boyle was about to be fortified and by 26 May 1607 John King and John Bingley were 'erecting a strong castle' (CSPI 1606–8, 150). This is the bastioned fort (RMP RO006-068001-) situated on a commanding height overlooking the town of Boyle in the townland of Bellspark and Mocmoyne. It had a garrison of 94 in 1659 (Pender 1939). It is a regular pentagonal fort with five triangular bastions (O'Conor 2002, 189–203)). King was knighted on 7 July 1609 (Metcalfe 1885, 161). In 1610 the ward at the abbey comprised 10 wardens (CSPI 1608–10, 508). King expected to be elected as an MP for Boyle in 1611 (CSPI (1611–1614), 1877; Cal. Car. MSS 1611, 50) but did not succeed. In 1613, however, he was returned as an MP for County Roscommon with the help of the soldiery of Vice-President Oliver St John (CSPI 1611–14, 138, 362, 496). Constables and wardens remained at Boyle Abbey during 1611 and the surrounding district was growing as a town. On 9 December 1612, an order was given to draw forth a fiant of incorporation to 13 individuals 'by the name of Borough-master and burgesses of the Town of Boyle and Tulsk' enabling them to send burgesses to Parliament (CSPI 1611–1614, 1877, 9, 307–8). On 1 April 1613, the names of towns and boroughs within each county that are enabled by charter to send burgesses to Parliament are listed. There is a distinction of the old borough from the new. Roscommon and Boyle are listed as new with no reference to Tulsk (CSPI 1611–1614, 1877, 333–4).

The district adjacent to Boyle Abbey was growing as a town and on 9 December 1612, an order was given to draw forth a fiant of incorporation to 13 individuals 'by the name of Borough-master and burgesses of the Town of Boyle and Tulsk' enabling them to send burgesses to Parliament (CSPI 1611–1614, 1877, 9, 307–8). There is a distinction between an old borough and the new. Roscommon and Boyle are listed as new with no reference to Tulsk (CSPI 1611–1614, 1877, 333–4).

The borough of Boyle

On 25 March 1614, King James gave a governing charter to the borough of Boyle following 'the humble petition of the inhabitants of the town of Boyle, in our County of Roscommon, as for cultivating and planting those western parts in our said kingdom, which have been depopulated and made waste'; Boyle became 'one entire free borough of itself by the name of the Borough of Boyle' (D'Alton 1845 i, 240–1). As a corporate town, it could return two members to the Irish Parliament under the patronage of the King family, i.e., the earl of Kingston. Parliamentary representatives included Robert King, who was elected in 1639, Captain John King – 1688, John King – 1695 and both Robert King and John King who were elected in 1703 (*ibid.*, 35). Boyle Abbey was granted to John King and John Bingley on 20 November 1617 (D'Alton 1845 i, 228–32; Weld 1832, 225).

John King's grant of the manor of Boyle Abbey was confirmed in 1619. It included the possessions of the dissolved monastery of Boyle, and the tithes of many churches including those of the vicarage of Assylyn. The vicarages of Drum and Dryne were in the portfolio, and a number of vicarages in the barony of Tyrerill and elsewhere (D'Alton 1845 i, 244). The successful suppression of the monasteries is summed up in a report presented in Rome by James Fallon (Vicar General) on behalf of Bishop Boetius Egan, the Bishop of Elphin, in January 1631, which describes the ruinous state of the Cistercian monastery.

Formerly there were 65 churches in the diocese: only five of these remained and were used by the Protestants. In many cases not even a trace of them was to be found. Forty priests ministered to the faithful. The monastery was in ruins with the exception of one chapel, which the Protestants used as a parish church. The cloister was adapted for use as a barracks (Beirne 2000, 84–5). Although Thomas Kiernan, who lived until at least 1650, was the last 'Abbot of Boyle', he did not live in the abbey (CR iv, 425).

On 9 May 1635 Lord Strafford opened a commission by which he sought to establish the title of the English Crown to all the lands of Connacht. The commission was based in Boyle Abbey from where Strafford set about surveying the province of Connacht (Simington 1949, xxxiv). The Strafford Survey for Roscommon does not survive except in so far as it was used in the Books of Survey and Distribution. Knocknashee does not appear as a placename in the survey. Instead, Boyle Abbey is placed within a parcel of land called Tullogh which comprised 'one quarter of arable and pasture'. The latter was made up of 83 acres (33.5ha), 45 acres (18.2ha) of shrubby wood pasture and 'the "situation" of ye Abbey and Towne of Boyle'. It comprised 13 acres (5.3ha). Robert King was the proprietor (*ibid.*, 143). Neighbouring Irish landholders such as Bryan Mc Dermot and Owen McConnor McDermot forfeited their remaining ancestral lands to Robert King (*ibid.*, 143–4).

John King died in England on 4 January 1637 and his body was shipped to Ireland and buried at the church in Boyle.

The 1641 Rebellion and the Confederate War

The Confederate War began when Catholics of both Irish and Norman (Old English) descent opposed English and Scottish Protestant settlers and English rule. The war coincided with civil war in Britain and resulted in Irish Catholics and Presbyterians in Scotland supporting the Royalist cause against Oliver Cromwell and the English Parliament. The war, which began with a revolt in 1641, ended with the defeat of the Irish by Cromwellian forces between 1649 and 1653.

In 1641 Robert King was appointed constable of the 'Castle of Abbey Boyle' and given wardens to protect it. In 1642 the abbey, described as an 'active defence', surrendered to the Irish after a long siege 'for lack of water' (D'Alton 1845, 249). An artillery fort just north of the town of Boyle possibly dates between 1641 and 1660 (Kerrigan 1995, 102–3). The Irish were ultimately defeated, and a policy of confiscation and transplantation was imposed by which the counties west of the Shannon were reserved as an enclave for transplanted Irish landholders. Conditions for the local population in the vicinity of Boyle at the time the transplantees arrived were also wretched and on 11 July 1655 a levy of £200 was authorised to establish a workhouse at Boyle Abbey. The English Government agreed to provide an additional £100 (Barnard 2000, 75).

Transplantation

In 1642 John King made his son John commander of 'Boyle Castle' and in 1650 he was fighting on the side of the Parliamentarians against the Irish. On 7 June 1658 he was knighted by Henry Cromwell, the son of Oliver Cromwell. Henry was Lord Deputy-General of Ireland. Meanwhile, in 1656 Robert King sat on a committee in Dublin which allocated certain regions to particular groups, with criteria based on matching like with like. The barony of Boyle 'comprising the famous plains of Boyle that fatten a bullock and a sheep to the acre' was reserved for transplantees from Kildare, Meath, Laois and Dublin 'coming from the finest feeding and fattening lands in Ireland'. Artagh, in the barony of Boyle, was not included and was allocated to inhabitants of County Kerry. The baronies of Roscommon, Ballintubber and Bellamo were likewise granted (Prendergast 1875, 160–2).

The Census of Ireland 1659 indicates a garrison at Boyle with Captain Francis King's Foot Company and their wives totalling 94 people including Lt. Robert Folliott and Ensign Mathew Curtis (Pender 1939, 585). King was elevated to peerage on 27 August 1660 when a 'draft of warrant in favour of John King of the Abbey of Boyle' ordered that a bill be prepared to make him a baron with the title of Baron Kingston (CSPI 1660–1662, 28). On 21 August 1682 Robert King of 'Abbey Boyle' was given a baronetcy that would be inherited by his male heirs (CSP Domestic 1682, 321–62).

A new charter was given to Boyle by James II on 21 March 1687 in which King James appointed 'Bryan, son of Henry Mac Dermot, Burgomaster; and the following 19 Burgesses, viz.: Robert King, Baronet; John King, Theobald Dillon, Roger Oge Mac Dermot, Oliver O'Gara, Edward Mulloy, Hugh Mac Dermot, Cornelius Mac Dermot, Thady O'Byrne, Thomas Mac Dermot, senior, Thomas Mac Dermot, junior, Esquires; Edmond Frency, Laurence Dowdal and Martin Lynch, merchants; John Conry and Daniel Kelly, gentlemen; Bryan Mac Dermott Roe; Edward Connor, shoemaker; and Henry Mac Dermot'. The charter was never acted on due to warfare (D'Alton 1845 i, 255).

The war of the two kings

The 'war of the two kings' (1688–91) was a conflict between the supporters of the Catholic King James II of England and those of the Dutch Protestant Prince William of Orange who had deposed James as king of England, Scotland and Ireland in November 1688. James fled to France and got military support from Louis XVI, at the same time looking to Ireland for help. The Lord Deputy, Richard Talbot, was loyal to James and set about placing garrisons at key points in Ireland. Derry, which had a Protestant garrison, was besieged.

In December 1688 Colonel Mac Donnel, who was garrisoned at Boyle Abbey, would not allow Protestants to pass towards Sligo with goods and provisions. He seized the items instead. Robert King wrote to him asking that he allow the Protestants free passage since the garrison in Sligo did not interfere with Catholics visiting friends in such places as Boyle. Mac Donnel resisted, and the matter was dealt with at a council held in Sligo. It was decided that Robert King and Chidley Coote should, 'with a party of horse and foot march to Abbey Boyle'. When King arrived at the abbey, Mac Donnel brought his own horse, foot soldiers and dragoons inside Boyle Abbey and its gardens. His troops exceeded King's retinue by five to one. On the face of it, Mac Donnel agreed to King's request but did not deliver on his promise (D'Alton 1845 i, 257–8).

A letter written by Fr John Delap of Ballyshannon in 1688 reported that 'many hundreds of men, foot and dragoons, were arming themselves in the Counties of Roscommon and Mayo, with an intent to fall on our friends in Boyle and this county'

(D'Alton 1845 i, 256–7; Trimble 1919–21, 699). The rebels were commanded to meet 'at the Boyle' and surrender their arms and horses. They were also commanded to give hostages as a security 'for their future peaceable deportment' (Trimble 1919–21, 430).

The Jacobite–Williamite War

Patrick Sarsfield, an Irish soldier in the Jacobite army, is credited with securing Connacht for the Jacobites in the earlier part of the war. Enniskillen, Derry and Sligo were captured by King William's forces in 1689 (Trimble 1919–21, 615). Following a heavy defeat in Newtownbutler, Sarsfield withdrew to Sligo and then to Boyle. Colonel Thomas Lloyd was, meanwhile, sent by the Williamites to Sligo. When he heard that Sarsfield would come from Boyle to retake Sligo Castle, he left Sligo and crossed the Curlew Mountains. He sent an advance guard of 20 men, supported by Enniskillen dragoons, to Boyle. When Lloyd's advance party reached the outposts of Boyle Abbey in the Curlew Mountains, the soldiers killed a sentry and captured three others. Lloyd's troops were spotted at sunrise and allegedly 500 foot soldiers, under Colonel Kelly, advanced from Boyle Abbey to attack Lloyd. Sarsfield was not in Boyle Abbey at the time as he had left for Dundalk. Although Lloyd had fewer men than Colonel Kelly, his strategy was successful and the Irish foot soldiers and cavalry fled. Lloyd left a small garrison in Boyle under the command of Captain Weir (*ibid.*, 619–21). To commemorate the victory, chalice-shaped drinking glasses with long shanks were made. The glasses had an inscription around the rim that said, 'The Battle of the Boyle, September the 20th, 1689' (D'Alton 1845, 266).

Lloyd was aware that Sarsfield had strong foraging parties in County Roscommon while his own force was small and in danger of becoming insignificant. He appealed to Enniskillen for reinforcements. There was no outcome to his plea because General Schomberg's camp 'was wasted with fever and prostrated with malaria'. Troops were eventually sent to support him in Boyle (Trimble 1919–21, 623; Childs 2007, 160–8). When James II heard that troops had been sent to Boyle to support Lloyd, he sent instructions to Patrick Sarsfield 'to clear the English out of Connacht'. Sarsfield headed to Connacht, allegedly gathering 2,000 troops on the way. In mid November, when Sarsfield was within four miles of Boyle Abbey, Captain Weir slipped out in the darkness.

In August 1691 Robert King wrote from Boyle Abbey to Colonel Caulfield, the commander-in-chief in Athlone, that 'we are here making up our several troops of militia, pursuant to the Government's commands, and for the preservation of this side of the county, but we are in the greatest want of ammunition, having some firearms, but neither powder nor ball to use them, which makes me desire the favour of you to order out of the stores there, only half a barrel of powder, and the like proportion of musket-balls, in which you will oblige many, and Sir, your most humble servant, Robert King' (D'Alton 1845, 273–4).

After the defeat of King James at the Battle of the Boyne in 1690, followed by the siege of Limerick in 1691, Sarsfield and thousands of Irish soldiers with their followers went into exile in France, where they continued to serve James II. Sarsfield was mortally wounded fighting the troops of William of Orange in July 1693 in the Battle of Landen in Flanders.

On 4 September 1691 Robert King wrote to Colonel Thomas Lloyd, now Governor of Athlone, from Boyle Abbey, about proposed engineering works. An engineer could judge the usefulness of 'some place of strength, of which it has yet none', and the trouble it would cause 'for their enemie'. He wrote that Boyle Abbey was always thought of as a place that was useful for protecting the 'great pass' over the Curlew Mountains and that the pass never needed part of the army to guard it. It appears that the earl of Ormond, as Lord Lieutenant, issued an 'order of council' for building a fort near the strategic pass. King explained that he was in Boyle Abbey by Government command with 20 men. He considered this to be a small number 'for so great a post' because of several groups of enemies nearby. One particular group comprised *c.* 100 men within four miles of Boyle Abbey. King requested foot soldiers to be sent to Boyle Abbey, and an engineer, to defend it (D'Alton 1845 i, 273–6). By 10 September Boyle had been relieved by 1,500 men of the Northern and Dublin Militia (*ibid.*, 277).

Eighteenth century

A list of barracks in the midlands in 1704 includes Boyle which had 36 troopers (Kerrigan 1985, 101). The garrison at Boyle Abbey appears to have been abandoned sometime between 1714 and 1727 (*ibid.*). Beranger in 1729 states that Lord Kingston 'keeps it locked up'; 'is a complete forrest, covered with large trees, underwood and thorns, beside weeds'; cloisters 'having been a horse barrack yard with stables about it' (Harbison and Shields 2002, 80–1). A view of Boyle Abbey in 1792 by Cooper (Harbison 2000, 218) shows a roofed building running south from the gatehouse (Fig. 1.11). There may have been no garrison in Boyle between *c.* 1720 and 1795 when the King family sold their town. *The Irish Penny Magazine* (1833, 201–4) includes two prints of Boyle Abbey; the interior one shows railings around a burial plot in the nave and some headstones. It also records that a Captain Robertson, in whose garden the abbey was, did clearance works around the monument some 15 years earlier.

The possibility of a French invasion following a landing on the west coast resulted in the defence of the Shannon crossing in the late eighteenth to early nineteenth century (Kerrigan 1995, 214ff). Boyle was also included in a list of barracks in 1811 when it had an infantry of 9 and 280 privates (Kerrigan 1985, 106). Barracks to the west of the River Shannon at Roscommon, Tulsk, Elphin and Boyle provided accommodation for over 800 troops in 1811, available to defend the Shannon crossing points between Lanesborough and Jamestown (Kerrigan 1995, 233).

Boyle in state care

The King family owned Boyle Abbey when it was taken into state care. Harold Leask's list of National and Ancient Monuments names the Irish monuments that were brought into state care in the nineteenth century. Boyle Abbey was listed as a Class D 'ancient monument' 'of which the Commissioners of Public Works had consented to become Guardians under Section 1 Ancient Monuments Protection Act 1892' (NMS File no. NM03242). The Commissioners of Public Works subsequently undertook works at the site; the first documented works date to their annual report in 1904. It refers to five buttresses being built against the northern wall of the nave, about 70 years previously. They were described as almost useless (Commissioners of Public Works 1905, 15). This report also refers to works carried out in 1894 including the removal of ivy and repair of walls where masonry was dislodged (*ibid.*). During the 1903–4 phases of works, the tops of the walls throughout were cleaned down and concreted. The loose masonry of the four buttresses at the northern wall of the nave were taken down and rebuilt with concrete. The north arcade was recorded at this time as being 'two feet six inches' out of plumb. The Commissioners' reports from year end 1940 and 1941 document further work on the abbey including removal of ivy and extensive pointing and weathering to stabilise the condition of the fabric (Commissioners of Public Works 1939–40). In 1975 cracks on the buttresses were monitored to check for further movement and the serious state of the north aisle wall resulted in major conservation works undertaken by the OPW in 2006.

Pl. 3.1. Interior view of the abbey church looking east.

Chapter 3

An Architectural History of Boyle Abbey and its Cloistral Buildings

Roger Stalley

Introduction

The church at Boyle is one of the most distinguished pieces of medieval architecture in Ireland, with outstanding features in both the Romanesque and early Gothic styles (Pl. 3.1). The quality of the stonework throughout the church is impressive, so too the range of carving that decorates the fabric. Equally significant is the way in which the church was built in stages, providing a visible demonstration of the incremental manner in which medieval buildings were constructed. Moreover, the architecture itself has an international dimension, key elements of the design being derived from Cistercian practice in France and Britain. At the same time, the work was important in a local context, for it was the masons at Boyle who provided a stimulus for what has come to be known as the 'School of the West' (Leask 1960, 53–76; Kalkreuter 2001). Boyle, in fact, offers an outstanding demonstration of the way in which the Cistercians, as an international order, brought new methods of design to some of the more remote outposts of Europe.

The monastery at Boyle was founded at a key moment in the history of Irish architecture, as pan-European modes of building began to exert an impact. Until the 1140s, Irish monastic churches were modest in design, most comprising single cell buildings with a chancel attached at the east. The arrival of the Cistercians in 1142 brought a new approach and within a few years stone churches on a scale never seen before were being erected in various parts of the country. The impact is particularly obvious at Mellifont (Louth), where a church designed on Continental lines, complete with a presbytery, transepts and an aisled nave, was dedicated in 1157 (Stalley 1980; Stalley 1987, 56–7, 248). The monks who founded Mellifont had been trained at Clairvaux under the watchful eye of St Bernard (d. 1153), and it is no surprise that the early buildings there reflected architectural practice as found in the early French monasteries. Indeed, St Bernard had sent a monk, Robert by name, to advise on the organisation of the abbey (James 1953, 454–5; Stalley 1980, 268). Cistercian architecture is well known for its austerity and lack of adornment, as befitted the ideals of the order, and for the most part this is reflected in the Irish buildings.

The community that eventually settled at Boyle had departed from Mellifont in 1148, long before the great stone church there had been completed (Gwynn and Hadcock 1970, 128–9). This was one of several groups that set out in the late 1140s to establish new houses in different parts of the country. The rapid expansion reflects the appeal of the Cistercians, who managed to attract recruits in extraordinary numbers (Stalley 1987, 11–16). The Boyle community was the first to travel to Connacht, where presumably they had the blessing of the king, Tairrdelbach Ua Conchobair. Their early experiences, however, were far from auspicious, as they abandoned three potential sites in the space of 13 years. False starts were not unknown within the order, but this was an extreme case (Kinder 2002, 81–5, 105). Other communities that moved to a new site after a few years included Abington (Co. Limerick) and Graiguenamanagh (Co. Kerry) (Gwynn and Hadcock 1970). Several English communities began life at previous sites, notably Louth Park, Lincolnshire, Kirkstall, Leeds, Thame, Oxfordshire Byland, York, Stanley, Wiltshire and Vaudey, Lincolnshire (Donkin 1978, 31–6, 179–80; Fergusson 1984, 24). Quite why the initial sites proved unsuitable is unclear: various factors could be at work, not least the quality of the land or the reliability of the water supply, plus the degree of solitude and the extent of interference from outside sources. In England sites are known to have been abandoned because the land proved to be marshy or prone to flooding, or not sufficiently fertile. It is not known whether the Boyle community erected permanent structures at any of their abandoned sites. Seven years was spent at Grellach Dínach the first location to be occupied, time enough perhaps to embark on buildings of substance (Gwynn and Hadcock 1970, 128). After Grellach Dínach (the site of which is unknown) the monks stayed at Drumconaid for three years and at Bun Finne for two and a half years.

The monks would not have made their final move from Bun Finne in 1161 unless the site at Boyle was well prepared in advance. The statutes of the order decreed that no abbot was to be sent to a new place without the prior construction of an oratory, refectory, dormitory, guest quarters and gatehouse, 'so that they may straightaway serve God there and live in keeping with the Rule' (Robinson 2006, 50; Waddell 1999, 408, 461). Secular patrons normally provided this initial accommodation, which might take the form of temporary wooden buildings or involve the re-use of existing structures (Robinson 2006, 50–2). There is a detailed account of the way in which a site might be prepared in the chronicle of the Cistercian abbey at Meaux (Yorkshire), (Fergusson 1984, 133). Given their previous experience, it is unlikely that the monks at Boyle were in a hurry to embark on major works until they had absolute confidence in the site. There is some evidence that Boyle or Áth Dá Laarg was already an ecclesiastical site (Gwynn and Hadcock 1970, 128). Five or ten years may thus have elapsed before they were ready to invest their energies in major construction. While the new location beside the River Boyle provided an excellent supply of fresh water, the land was low-lying and, as future generations were to discover, prone to flooding. Following a thunderstorm in 1471, the annals report that 'a boat could have floated over the floor of the great church of the monks' (AC). In later centuries the damp conditions may well have contributed to the instability of the church; as the recent excavations revealed, the foundations of the piers in the nave were not particularly deep (see Chapter 6). In such circumstances it would have been advisable to set the piers on a continuous sub wall, rather than rely on a set of individual foundations, as was the case. Sleeper walls were used, for example, in the church of the Cistercian abbey at Buckfast, Devon (Robinson 2017, 40). One particular advantage of the site, however, was the presence nearby of excellent local sandstone.

Constructing the church: the first campaign

When it came to the erection of permanent buildings, the Cistercians usually gave priority to the church, the prime focus of their life. Churches were not, however, laid out in isolation, for they formed part of an overall scheme based around the

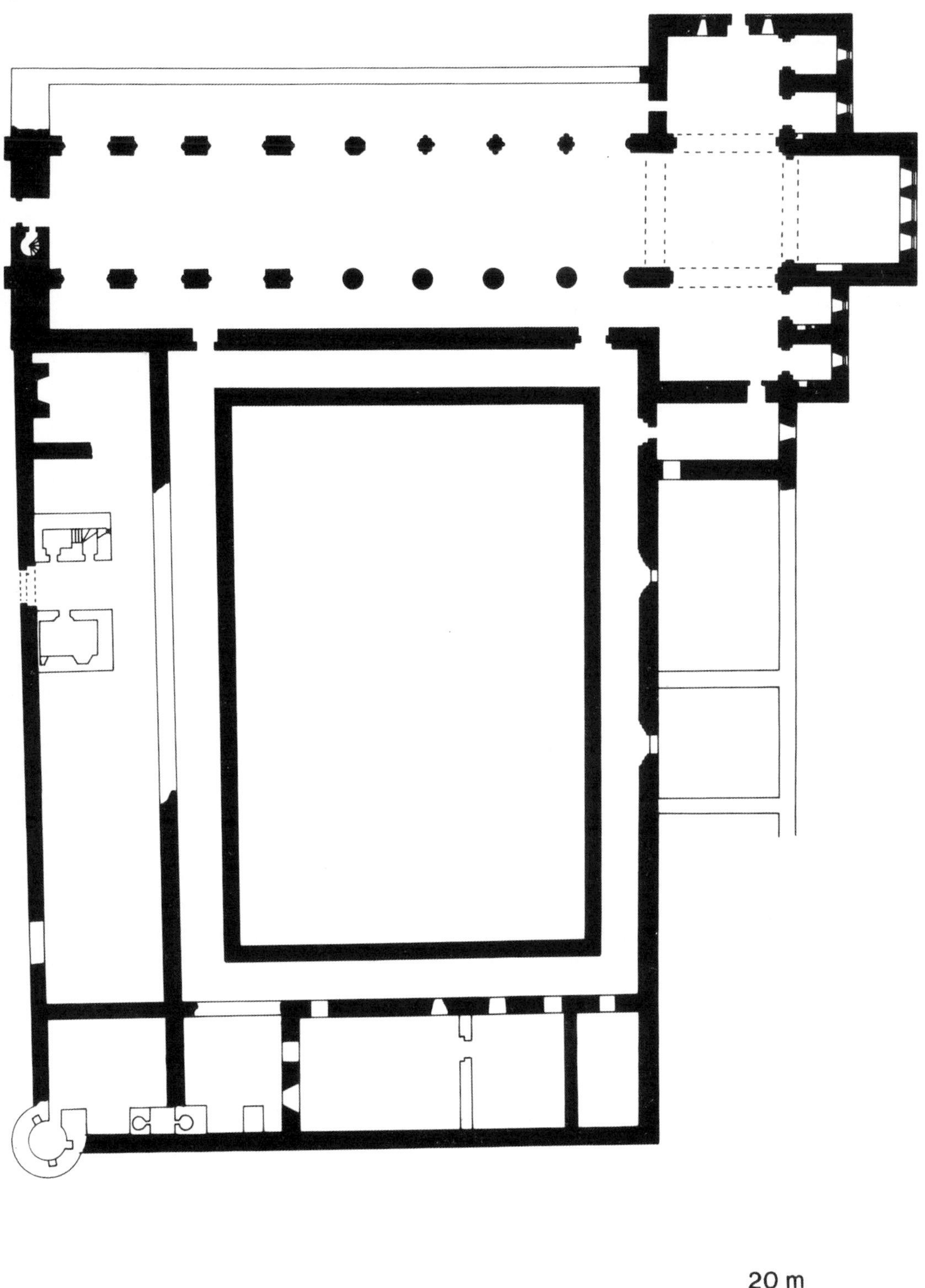

Fig. 3.1. Plan of the abbey and cloistral buildings.

Pl. 3.2. North transept chapel entrances.

cloister. In many cases, proportional ratios derived from the cloister were used to generate the layout of the surrounding buildings (Hahn 1957, 66–82; Stalley 1987, 68–75; Stalley 2012, 208–9). At Boyle the first phase of building included the presbytery, the transepts and probably the first four piers on the south side of the nave (Fig. 3.1). With the presbytery and transepts complete, a temporary barrier may have been placed across the opening to the nave, allowing the church to be put to use, though the cramped conditions in a half-finished building must have been far from ideal.

It is likely that work began on the church within a decade or so of the community's arrival, perhaps about 1170–5. A piece of sculpture on the sedilia in the presbytery provides some general support for this: it takes the form of a monstrous bird with a predatory beak and sleek sinister eyes, the carving still remarkably crisp. The style and design have similarities with a capital on the rebuilt doorway at Kilmore (Cavan), where a monster with open jaws appears to devour a shaft (CRSBI 2020). A related carving can be found on the doorway of the Nuns Church at Clonmacnoise (Offaly), constructed in 1167 (AFM); there is, however, some doubt as to whether the relevant carving at Clonmacnoise actually formed part of the Nuns Church (Ní Ghradaigh 2003, 183–7).

The church follows a formula that was widespread in the Cistercian order, especially in the affiliation of Clairvaux. The square presbytery is flanked by a pair of chapels entered from the transepts (Fig. 3.1). There is a rectilinear flavour to the layout, though in geometrical terms it is not entirely consistent as the chapels vary in width, a curiosity also found at Jerpoint (Kilkenny) (Stalley

1987, 81). The south chapel at Boyle is considerably narrower than the others. Pointed barrel vaults, built of rubble masonry, cover the presbytery and chapels, the only parts of the church to be vaulted. This was common practice in both England and Ireland, reflecting a long-standing tradition in Christian architecture: acting as a solid *baldachino*, a stone vault accentuated the most sacred spaces within the church.

Six round-headed windows in the east wall, arranged in two rows of three, originally illuminated the presbytery. These were replaced in the thirteenth century by Gothic lancets, but their position is marked on the outside by the original string courses. The whole of the east end is articulated by such string courses, some of them lining up with the hood mouldings of the windows. This was the cause of some irregularity on the exterior of the north transept, the windows here being slightly shorter; one of the string courses coming round the building from the east was too high and made an awkward junction with the hood mould, a problem evidently not anticipated by the mason in charge. The main source of the problem lay in the inconsistencies of the window dimensions. In the north transept the two lower windows differ in size, which means that the string course between them is set at a disturbing angle. The string courses, together with moulded eaves at the base of the roofs, served to enliven the exterior walls of the church in a Romanesque manner.

Some of the finest masonry at Boyle is associated with the arches leading into the presbytery and transept chapels. The presbytery arch is composed of three orders, with corresponding shafts on the jambs below, the largest being on the inner face. The entrances to the chapels were treated in contrasting ways – the outer chapels with a single engaged shaft, the inner ones with a group of three shafts (Pl. 3.2). The capitals are decorated with a variety of scallops and simple foliage; between the northern chapels the carving was extended as a frieze along the surface of the wall, an arrangement also found at Jerpoint (Stalley 1987, 80–1, 180–1). The most northern chapel at Boyle is especially interesting: the arch includes a hollow moulding not found elsewhere, and one of the capitals is quite unique (Fig. 3.2). Between two broad spreading leaves a grotesque face can

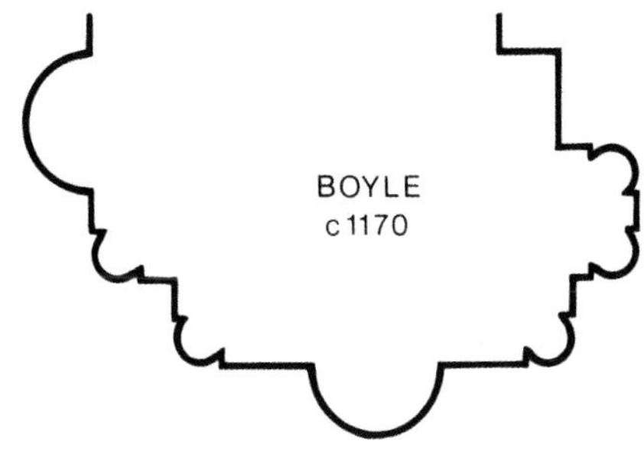

Fig. 3.2. Plan of south-east crossing pier.

be seen emerging from the foliage scrolls. This is not the sort of decoration expected in a Cistercian house, more a reflection of the type of sculpture found on churches outside the order; the face has echoes of those carved on the chancel arch at Tuam Cathedral (Galway) in 1184 (Henry 1970, 168, pls 86–7; Stalley 1981, 180–2).

In fact, the carved details in this early phase of building are clearly embedded in Hiberno-Romanesque practice and this is likewise true of the bases associated with the various shafts and responds. Some of these are emphatically bulbous in form and most are furnished with decorated spurs on the angle (Pl. 3.3). There are many parallels for such features in Irish Romanesque, as at Killeshin (Laois) and Baltinglass (Wicklow) (Stalley 1999, 97–9, 118, fn 39). In some cases the spurs are carved like simple claws, in other instances they take the form of a flat leaf. The most intricate examples appear to be modelled on a buckle or some form of ornamental metalwork. Several bases have an unusual form in which a plain 'leaf' emerges from the top of a large roll (north transept, south chapel, north respond). This anticipates a type found in the claustral buildings at Boyle, where similar tricks were employed in more exaggerated form.

On the south side of the south transept, a door led into the sacristy, and at a high level there was an entry to the dormitory, as routinely found in monastic architecture. No trace survives of the staircase that allowed the monks to descend directly into the church for services at night. In the north transept a doorway led out of the church towards the monastic cemetery, an exit known as the *porta mortuorum or porte des mortes* (Aubert 1947, i, 355). The portal at Boyle is surprisingly

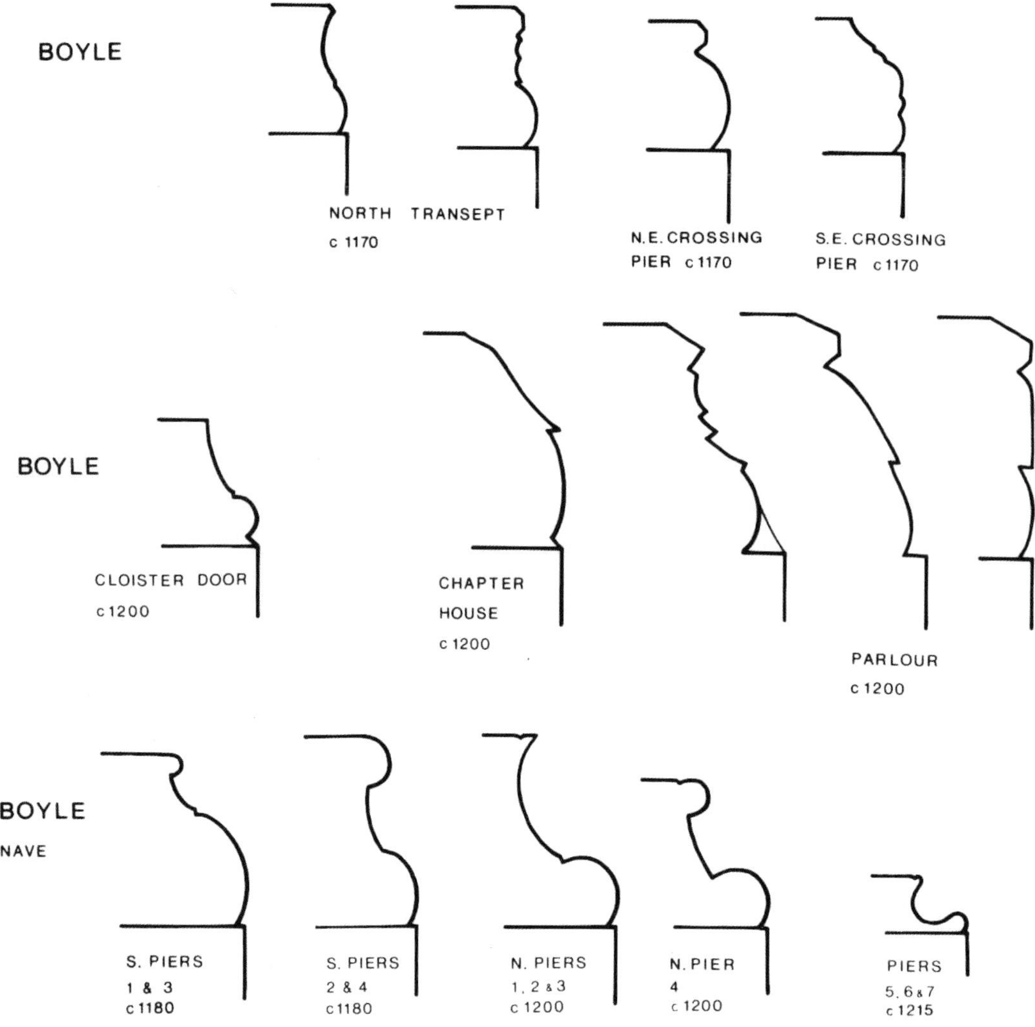

Fig. 3.3. Profiles of base mouldings in Boyle Abbey.

wide; although the exterior was remade in the early twentieth century, the interior jambs are authentic. A doorway (blocked) in the west wall provided access to the north aisle of the nave and must have been made before the north aisle itself was erected. The most curious feature of the north transept is that a doorway high in the east wall can only be reached by means of a ladder (Pl. 3.4). This allowed workmen to get into the roof space over the north transept chapels; similar arrangements can be found in France and Germany, notably in a group of churches associated with Clairvaux, a group often described as 'Bernardine', a term derived from the controversial assumption that St Bernard himself may have had a role in the formulation of their design (Esser 1953, 204–11; Hahn 1957, 84–128; Stalley 1987, 77–83; Stalley 1994; for a recent judicious assessment see Robinson 2006, 62–4). Such doorways can be seen at Fontenay (Côte-d'Or), Noirlac (Cher), and Eberbach (Hesse); there is a similar example at Abbeyknockmoy (Galway), one of the daughter houses of Boyle (Hahn 1957, 106). At Eberbach the doorway was in the south transept as the cloister here was situated to the north.

Substantial piers, rectangular in form, marked the junction of transepts and nave (Fig. 3.3). They were treated like continuous sections of wall, the narrow face towards the nave being furnished with a large, engaged shaft, serving as a respond for the nave arcade.

The masons responsible for the east end of the church evidently made a start on the nave, erecting the four cylindrical piers on the south side. The masonry here is outstanding, the various blocks precisely cut in the local sandstone (Pl. 3.5). The choice of cylindrical piers is interesting. The form, which is associated with English Romanesque, was adopted by the Cistercians in several of their English monasteries, as at Buildwas, Shropshire, Dore, Herefordshire, Cleeve, Somerset, and Fountains, North Yorkshire (Fergusson 1984, 39–48, 91–100, 119). In Ireland similar piers were employed (in alternating sequences) at Baltinglass in the 1150s and a decade or so later at Jerpoint (Stalley 1987, 84–7). Cylindrical piers were also used at Inislounaght (Tipperary); in the seventeenth century the stones were re-used in the Main Guard at Clonmel (Stalley 2012, 209–11). In these latter examples the piers were surmounted by square capitals, resulting in a clumsy overhang at the corner, but at Boyle the design was much improved with the introduction of an octagonal capital. A similar refinement can be seen in England at Dore, where the capital was circular in form. The plinths on which the piers rest, however, were still square in plan, the angles being embellished with extravagant foliage spurs, those on the first pier conceived on a giant scale. In contrast to Baltinglass and Jerpoint, the cylindrical piers at Boyle were not combined with other forms, nor were they disturbed by the presence of perpyn walls; as a result, they are far more striking and majestic in effect. Two different mouldings were employed at the foot of each cylinder, a subtlety easily missed. At the same time the aisle wall must have been constructed, probably along its full length, for this served as the north wall of the cloister. This wall appears to have been constructed in one piece, as noted by Lynch (see Chapter 4). The processional doorway that led directly from the cloister to the monks' choir, however, belongs to a later period, its jambs containing large, keeled mouldings of a type associated with a period several decades later (Fig. 3.4) (Stalley 1980, 319). These very precise keels are found at Mellifont, notably on the lavabo of *c.* 1210. Once the piers and arches were complete, the wall immediately above could have been constructed, though this may not have happened until the rest of the arches had been erected.

Pl. 3.3. Base with ornamental spur at entrance to the presbytery.

Pl. 3.4. North transept seen from the south arcade of the nave.

The work of the first campaign at Boyle incorporated elements derived from Burgundy, England and Ireland, producing a synthesis that was both distinctively Irish and distinctively Cistercian. Someone at Boyle knew a fair amount about Cistercian architecture in Burgundy and neighbouring Champagne, though whether this knowledge came directly from France or from earlier experience in Ireland is difficult to judge. The elements are all associated with the so-called 'Bernardine' churches. First there is the plan type, with one or more chapels opening off each arm of the transept. Then there is the short presbytery covered with a pointed barrel vault, a form adopted from Burgundian architecture. Equally specific is the height of the presbytery, considerably lower than the nave, the latter forming the dominant space within the church. The high-level access to the roof spaces over

Pl. 3.5. Cylindrical piers forming the south.

the north transept chapels has obvious links with French building, as we have seen. Another detail found in many Cistercian churches is the ovoid window high in the gable of the south transept. More significant are the pointed arches in structural positions, another feature with obvious precedents in Burgundy. Many of these features, though not the plan, may have been derived from Mellifont, the mother house of Boyle. Perhaps a monk or lay brother, familiar with construction of Mellifont or another early house, lent his services to Boyle in a supervisory role. Although the cylindrical piers in the nave were ultimately derived from England, the form was already in use in Ireland. The same could be said of the scalloped capital. In fact, the many parallels with Hiberno-Romanesque sculpture leave little doubt that the stone was carved and dressed by locally recruited masons.

The conventual buildings

Members of the same team evidently constructed the east range of the cloister. With a part of the church in use, it made sense for the monks to turn their attention to the conventual buildings. The sacristy formed a natural extension of the transept and beyond came the chapter house and the so-called parlour. Unfortunately, this part of the abbey was badly mutilated when the abbey was transformed into a barracks. Remains of two elaborate doorways survive, but it is hard to make much sense of the architecture. The inner wall of the east range was substantially rebuilt after the dissolution of the monastery when it became the outer boundary of a two-storey building that extended into the cloister garth. It is the inner face of what was once the east wall of this later structure that we now see, a line of joist holes clearly marking the position of the floors. This building was still intact at the end of the eighteenth century, when it was illustrated in Grose's Antiquities of Ireland (Fig. 1.10). The main priority in military terms was evidently the construction of a high defensive wall to protect the cloister garth. It is curious that more of the monastic east range was not retained by the military: the dormitory on the upper floor would surely have been ideal for housing soldiers. It rather suggests that the east range was damaged or destroyed before the soldiers took over. There is a certain irony in the re-use of the abbey as a barracks since the early Cistercians were accustomed to referring to themselves as *milites Christi*, or soldiers of Christ (Waddell 1999, 400; Smith 2010).

The first chamber south of the church was the vaulted sacristy, a utilitarian space entered through simple doorways from the cloister and the church. In many Cistercian monasteries the west end of the chamber was separate from the sacristy itself and used as the book room or *armarium* (Robinson 2006, 150–1). It is not clear whether this was the case at Boyle; if it was, the door from the cloister would have led only into the book room and not the sacristy. The sacristy housed the liturgical items required for services in the church. Even in a Cistercian house, some of these were potentially valuable, which explains a raid that took place at Boyle in 1235. The Annals of Loch Cé describe how an army led by Richard, son of William, and other Norman lords arrived at Boyle on Trinity Sunday: the troops appear to have been out of control, judging by what happened: '... and their soldiers attacked the monastery, and broke open the sacristy; and all its valuable things, and its mass-chalices and altar-cloths, were taken out of it' (ALC 1235). In this case the monastery suffered no long-term damage, as the annalist goes on to explain: 'And this was very hateful to the chieftains of the Foreigners, who returned every article of them that was to be found; and they paid for the things that were not found' (*ibid.*).

After the sacristy came the chapter house, the plan of which remains uncertain. The chapter house might have been rectangular in form and contained within the line of the east range, though in many cases monastic chapter houses were extended further east. They were usually vaulted: assuming a rectangular plan, it could have been divided into six bays, arranged 3 × 2 (Stalley 1987, 162–6). What survives are the lower sections of the doorway that clearly formed part of an ambitious design (Fig. 3.4). It contained no less than five orders, four of them defined by shallow sub-quarter shafts. Although the actual entrance was quite narrow (0.83m), the overall width of the portal (3.63m), with its sequence of separate orders, was over four times as great. In normal circumstances the wall would have been too thin to incorporate a portal of five orders, a problem that the masons solved in an ingenious way. Although the engaged shafts were broad, their curvature was shallow, which meant that each order was recessed far less than might be expected with shafts of this size. The monks thus acquired a portal that gave an impression of exceptional grandeur; unlike most Romanesque or early Gothic doorways, where each order is firmly recessed, the rolls at Boyle are formed of what is in effect just a segment of a curve. The design of the bases is equally remarkable: on the four outer orders there is a thick, slightly bulbous moulding that is surmounted by a concave flange-like feature; the inner order has a variant of this scheme, with a robust upper roll along with an elaborate foliate spur. These unconventional forms had been foreshadowed at the east end of the church; they were further developed at Cong and other sites in Connacht.

The character of the doorway underlines the importance of the chapter house in the life of the monastery. This is where the monks assembled each day after Mass to hear passages read from the rule of St Benedict, to listen to a homily from the abbot and to make confession (Kinder 2002, 245–68). It was the place where abbots were buried and as such embodied the very history of the monastery. If the interior matched the splendour of the doorway, it must have been one of the most remarkable chapter houses in the country. In most monastic houses, windows flanked the chapter house doorway but there is no trace of them in the surrounding wall, which was almost totally rebuilt in the military period. A long section of stone to the right of the doorway might possibly have served as some form of lintel or string course at the base of the windows. Part of the inner order and hood mould of the chapter house door is visible from the private garden on the opposite side of the wall. The parlour, as its name suggests, was a chamber where speaking was allowed, serving as a place where the prior might issue instructions on particular issues (Robinson 2006, 152). At Boyle its doorway was impressive and, judging from what survives, the design was as extravagant as the chapter house. In this case the engaged shafts are more orthodox. As three orders were involved, the recession of the three orders was more consistent with the width of the surrounding wall. The interior face of the doorway was embellished with further orders. Parts of the north jamb are visible from the private gardens to the east of the abbey. In this case there are three orders, each with bases

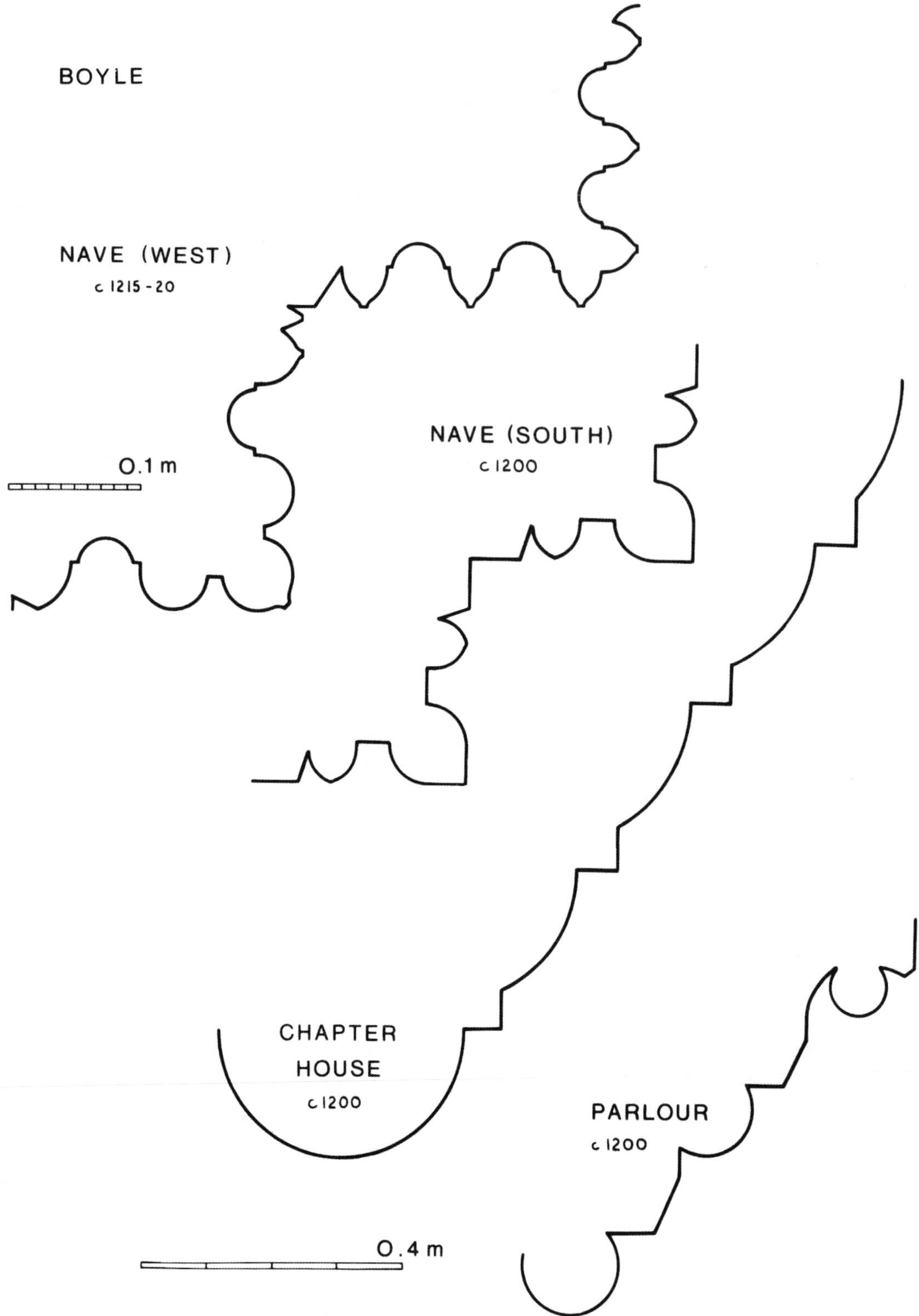

Fig. 3.4. Moulding profiles of door jambs employed in Boyle Abbey.

of different design (Fig. 3.4, Pl. 3.6). That on the inner order is especially fine, with broad leaves emerging from the lower moulding, spreading out across the angle of the plinth. The mason, or masons, responsible for both this and the chapter house doorway obviously had no interest in, and perhaps no familiarity with the more orthodox, classically derived forms encountered more generally in Romanesque. In their eyes, base mouldings provided an opportunity to display their inventive powers. While their choices may have been unorthodox, they were talented craftsmen, who handled the local stone with impeccable precision.

Beyond the chapter house and parlour once lay a chamber often described as the dormitory undercroft. In practice it served as a dayroom for a variety of monastic activities, especially in inclement weather. Above, running along the entire upper floor of the east range was the monastic dormitory. At its south end lay the latrines, at Boyle conveniently situated so that the contents of the sewer could be flushed into the river close by. It is disappointing that virtually no trace of any of these rooms survives.

Equally disappointing is the complete destruction of the cloister arcades. Excavations in recent years have established the line of the walkways on the west, north and east sides of the garth, but all evidence of the arcades themselves has vanished (see Chapter 4). Following standard practice, the arcades would have supported the roofs over the cloister walks while at the same time defining the open space at the heart of the monastery. In view of the elaborate masonry found in the chapter house and parlour, it would be remarkable if the monks of Boyle had not erected a set of impressive arcades, perhaps along the lines of those reconstructed at Mellifont (Stalley 1980, 312; Stalley 1987, 153–4). The fact that no fragments were discovered when the cloister walks were excavated suggests that the arcades were cleared away in a systematic fashion following the dissolution of the monastery. Cloister arcades were especially vulnerable when monastic buildings were put to new uses, since a line of arches resting on a low wall obstructed easy access to the buildings around the cloisters, especially for horses and carts. During the excavation of the cloister walks at Tintern (Wexford) in 1985, many pieces of column and arch stones were found embedded in the ground, suggesting that here too the arcades had been systematically demolished (Lynch 2010, 61–75). At Boyle there appears to have been a wholesale clearance. One can only hope that at some stage in the future pieces may be found, either close to the abbey or re-used in local buildings.

Most Cistercian cloisters are approximately square in plan and, in this respect, Boyle differs somewhat from the norm (Fig. 3.1). It is likely that a square arrangement, with sides of approximately 100 feet (30.5m), was envisaged when the church was first laid out. At Mellifont there are signs that the cloister was extended to the south and something similar may have happened at Boyle (Stalley 1980, 309–10). The east–west dimension at Boyle is 30.56m (100ft 5 inches) and, given the popularity of the 100 feet width for cloisters, this is unlikely to be a coincidence. The north–south dimension is 40.61m (133ft 3 inches). Even as a rectangle, however, the layout at Boyle is far from regular: the existing walls of the west range, for example, are not aligned at right angles to the church, as is normally the case.

The monastic refectory has fared no better than the chapter house and cloister walks. It occupied much of the south range, lying parallel to the cloister walk, as found in several of the Irish houses (Stalley 1987, 169–70). The position of the refectory at Boyle followed the traditional monastic model, in contrast to many Cistercian houses, including some in Ireland that, set the building at right angles to the cloister as a means of gaining additional space. Although the walls stand to a considerable height, the absence of dressed masonry makes it difficult to date, and there is serious doubt as to whether any of the masonry above 1.5m belongs to the monastic era. A gabled section of wall, aligned to the east cloister walk, was clearly built after the dissolution since it contains moulded stone recycled from the medieval buildings.

Cistercian refectories were normally equipped with a pulpit, from which one of the community read aloud as the monks consumed their food in silence. Excavations conducted in the floor of the refectory failed to uncover compelling evidence from the monastic era, (Archaeological Consultancy Ltd 2004, 9–15; see Chapter 5). A cobbled floor found at a depth of 1.40m below the present ground level is described as the 'original cobbled surface of the refectory'. This would be an unusual floor for a monastic refectory, though it might have been suitable for an undercroft below a refectory on an upper floor. At Boyle the pulpit must have been incorporated in the south wall towards the east end. A lavabo or washbasin in the form of a stone basin was usually incorporated into the outer wall, close to the doorway. In a few cases, as at Mellifont, it was housed inside a separate pavilion that projected into the cloister garth (Aubert 1947, ii, 24–8; Kinder 2002, 137–9; Stalley 1987, 170–2; Stalley 1996). Every lavabo needed a supply of fresh water and at Boyle this was presumably piped from a spot upstream from the abbey. The washing of hands was more than a hygienic exercise, for in a monastic environment the act of washing had spiritual overtones as well (Stalley 1996, 263). Unfortunately, the lavabo, wherever it was situated, was obliterated in the aftermath of the dissolution.

The monastic kitchen was normally situated at the west end of the south range, and at Boyle there is a substantial fireplace, with an impressive seventeenth-century chimney above, suggesting that the military re-used the site for their own kitchen. A circular tower was added at the south-west angle, providing defensive cover along the south and west walls. Although occasionally misinterpreted as an ancient round tower, its form is consistent with other defensive turrets of the seventeenth century. The much rebuilt outer wall of the west range formed part of the defences of the barracks. The basic layout of the range is clear enough, but the absence of dressed masonry makes it difficult to establish when the range was built, how it was used and how much of it is medieval. In the typical Cistercian monastery, the ground floor contained the lay brothers' refectory, with their dormitory located above. While lay brothers often outnumbered choir monks in the early years, they had largely died out by the fourteenth century, as monastic land was rented rather than farmed directly. A passage through the west range normally served as the main access to the cloister; it is likely that the current two-storey entrance occupies the original site.

1201 and the desecration of the monastery

In 1201 the monastery at Boyle was occupied for three days by a combined force of Norman and Irish soldiers, led by William de Burgo. The author of the Annals of Loch Cé was scandalised by the desecration, giving a lurid description of what happened, as if the whole place had been turned into a brothel:

> ...they were three days in it, so that they polluted and defiled the entire monastery; and such was the extent of the defilement that the mercenaries of the army had the women in the hospital of the monks, and in the houses of the cloister, and in every place in the entire monastery besides. No structure in the monastery was left without breaking and burning, except the roofs of the houses alone; and even of these a great portion was broken and burned. No part of the buildings of the entire monastery was allowed to the monks and brothers, excepting only the dormitory of the monks, and the house of the novices. A stone wall was commenced by William Burk, on this occasion, round the great stone house of the guests, and two days' work was devoted to its erection (ALC 1202, recte 1201).

The description is extremely valuable in giving an impression of the extent of the buildings that existed at this time, exactly 40 years after the monastery's foundation. It is clear that most of the buildings around the cloister were complete, but more interesting are the references to a guest house, the monks' infirmary, and a house for the novices. The guest house sounds imposing, the annalists describing it as the 'great stone house of the guests' as if it was something out of the ordinary. The construction of a stone wall around the house gives the impression of an isolated structure, one that could easily be converted into a fortified residence. The infirmary and house of the novices might also have been made of stone, though the annalist does not specifically say so. The dormitory of the monks gets a specific mention, suggesting that the east range was finished. In fact, one gets the impression that the architecture of the whole monastery was substantially complete. There is, however, no mention of the church and the silence of the annalist suggests this suffered no harm; if damaged, it surely would have been mentioned. The critical question is just how much of the church had been finished at this time. The architectural evidence suggests that much of the nave that we see today had yet to be built.

Pl. 3.6. Parlour doorway, south jamb.

The annalist is keen to outline the physical damage. He talks about buildings being 'broken and burned' and roofs being seriously damaged. The reference to burning is curious, as if the troops were scavenging for firewood. Ecclesiastical chroniclers are noted for their capacity to exaggerate damage, especially to religious buildings, and one must be slightly wary in such cases. Most of the damage related to timber and presumably stone slates, the sort of damage that might be repaired in months rather than years. While the 1201 episode may have disrupted the life of the monastery, it is unlikely that it had any long-term impact on the progress of building.

Constructing the church: the second campaign

Once the monks had completed the more urgent domestic buildings, especially in the east range, it is likely that work resumed on the church, perhaps in the years after 1201. Four bays of the south arcade had already been constructed, and the next task was to erect the corresponding bays to the north. In the interests of symmetry, one might have expected the cylindrical piers of the south side to be repeated, but this is not what happened. Instead, there was a fundamental change in design, suggesting the arrival of a new master mason. Instead of cylindrical piers, a more complex clustered form was introduced, at variance with what had gone before (Fig. 3.5). The term 'clustered pier' is generally used for this form, though they are sometimes described as 'fasciculated piers', as by Fergusson (1994). The new piers consisted of eight shafts grouped around a central core, a type that involved far more labour on the part of the masons. The shafts alternate in size, those on the diagonals having a larger diameter. This type of pier had become fashionable in England during the second half of the twelfth century, especially in the north, as at Roche, South Yorkshire and Byland, York; broadly speaking there were two types, one in which the shafts were made from separate sections of stone, the other in which the shafts were 'engaged' or bonded into the core. The Boyle piers belong to the latter category, though they were not constructed in the English manner. Rather than

Fig. 3.5. Plan of one of the clustered piers employed in the north arcade of the nave.

tightly clustered together, the shafts are widely spaced, leaving a gap between each shaft. Moreover, all the shafts are round, whereas in England by 1180, if not before, circular shafts were generally combined with keeled forms. The latter approach was introduced to Ireland at Inch (Down), a monastery founded in 1180 by John de Courcy after his conquest of Ulster (Stalley 1987, 95). In typological terms the piers at Boyle pre-date those at Inch and appear to be unique in Ireland, created perhaps by a mason with limited experience of this type of design.

When the three clustered piers were dismantled during the conservation works of 2006–12, the ingenuity of their construction was revealed. The eight shafts were locked together through an elaborate system of joints: behind some of the shafts was a long angular tongue that tied the stones together (see Chapter 6). Many of these tongues had cracked or broken, threatening the stability of the whole pier; over time the piers had been heavily patched and repaired.

The introduction of the clustered piers is hard to understand. The choice would have been more understandable if they were replacements for orthodox piers that had failed or been damaged in some way. However, the excavations demonstrated that they were not replacements, the pit and sub foundations of each pier being specifically intended for the new design (see Chapter 6). The radical change in style includes the carved details, confirming that a new team of masons had arrived at the monastery.

An important feature of the new piers is that they were specifically designed with choir stalls in mind. A well-known feature of Cistercian life was the manner in which the monks and the lay brothers were firmly separated from each other, occupying different parts of the church: the stalls of the choir monks were located in the area of the crossing stretching west for a short distance into the nave. Then came a transverse screen, behind which lay a small retro choir for the use of the elderly and infirm. This was separated by a further screen from the choir of the lay brothers, which took up much of the remainder of the nave. In most Cistercian abbeys the medieval stalls have long since been destroyed, leaving little sign of the medieval arrangements.

At Boyle some of the shafts of the clustered piers have flange-like projections, designed to provide a flat surface so that the back of the stalls would fit snugly against them. Such expedients were well known in Cistercian churches, their purpose being to maximize the width of the choir, while guaranteeing a tight a fit between stalls and pier (Stalley 1987, 86). The 'perpyn walls' at Baltinglass and Jerpoint were designed for the same purpose, but the arrangements at Boyle are far more sophisticated. The scheme was obviously well thought out by someone familiar with Cistercian requirements. The arrangement could not be duplicated on the south side, for here the stalls were backed against the cylindrical piers. The 'flanges' would have allowed for stalls in the first three or four bays of the nave, though this would have been too far west for the monks choir and too far east for the lay brothers choir. They must have butted up against the plinths, leaving an awkward gap. A second modification, again with wooden stalls in mind, explains the treatment of the central shaft on the main face. If this shaft had continued to the ground it would have disrupted the back of the stalls; it was thus terminated at a point just above the stalls themselves. This shaft continued its upward trajectory by squeezing its way between the hood moulds of the adjacent arches. It was later fitted with a tripartite capital in the main spandrels.

As if the contrast in pier design was not enough,

a further inconsistency in this campaign of building came with the construction of the arches. These were given a pointed profile, in defiance of the semi-circular forms on the opposite side.

The asymmetries at Boyle seem strange to the modern viewer, though they were far from unique at the time, especially in English architecture. Striking examples can be found at Selby Abbey (North Yorkshire) and the parish church at New Shoreham (West Sussex), in both cases arcades north and south being constructed with different designs (Stalley 1995). The arcades in the thirteenth-century nave at Gowran (Kilkenny) likewise differed north and south. Such architectural schizophrenia, in which variety triumphed over consistency and symmetry, is not easy to explain. Perhaps the monks at Boyle found it hard to resist the ideas of a recently arrived master mason with firm ideas of his own; in England there are examples of a newly appointed abbots promoting radical architectural change, a way of demonstrating that they could do better than their predecessors. An extreme example of this occurred at the Cistercian abbey of Meaux in Yorkshire, where successive abbots destroyed the work of their predecessors (Fergusson 1984, 133–4; Robinson 1998, 141–3). When embarking on ambitious architectural projects, the role of personal ambition cannot be ignored, as noted by Robinson (2017, 49, 51). The changes at Boyle surely engendered debate within the community, perhaps even heated argument. Had the monks so desired, the cylindrical piers could easily have been repeated on the north side. There is a certain irony in the fact that, once the choir stalls were in place, the clustered piers would have been largely invisible anyway, their subtleties fully visible only from within the aisle. It is also interesting to note that the Cistercian church at Furness (Lancashire) employed both clustered and cylindrical piers, in this case carried out in a systematic alternating sequence along each arcade (Fergusson 1984, 58). Such alternation was common in Romanesque architecture; it had obvious aesthetic appeal, something not so apparent when the two types were simply opposed to each other, north and south.

Only three piers of the clustered type were constructed, the next in line taking a simple octagonal shape. Again, it is not easy to explain the reasoning behind this decision, unless there was a desire to provide something cheaper and faster. It might have marked the location of the screen separating the retro choir from the lay brothers, though it seems too far west for this. Halfway up the pier is a projecting stone, its upper surface 1.97m above the floor; it was presumably related in some way to the lay brothers' stalls. The details of the pier itself are quite a puzzle. The substantial plinth has no obvious parallels in the abbey and the base moulding does not accord with what had gone before. However, the foliage ornament that wraps around the huge frieze-like capital echoes that on the last of the clustered piers. Adding to the confusion, the same style of carving is found throughout the third and final campaign of construction; in particular it includes a tiny, upturned semicircle of berries, one of the leitmotifs of the later sculpture. Is this the work of a mason who worked at Boyle over a long period, perhaps under the authority of different master masons?

With the fourth pier erected, the first four bays of the nave were close to completion. At this point a section of the upper walls, along with the clerestory windows, could have been constructed. There is some evidence in the coursing to suggest that the first three or four bays of the nave were built before those, further west, though it is hard to be certain, given the rough coursing of the masonry. If the upper walls were finished at this time, then a temporary wall could have been erected across the nave to separate the completed work from construction activities further west, a frequent strategy in medieval building programmes. In this way a sizeable part of the church could have been brought into use. Whether or not this happened remains an open question.

Constructing the church: the third campaign

The final campaign of building involved the last four bays of the church (Pl. 3.7). Compared with what had gone before, this was a remarkably consistent piece of design, with both north and south sides being erected at much the same time. It is also the one part of the church that can be assigned a date with some degree of confidence. A formal consecration of the church took place in 1220 and

Pl. 3.7. Nave, south arcade showing western extension of the church.

the whole church was presumably completed and roofed at this time (ALC 1220). A small detail on the corbel on the north side of Pier 7 south confirms this date. A continuous line of small lobes at the base of the capital can be paralleled on the lavabo at Mellifont generally attributed to the period *c.* 1210 (Stalley 1980, Pl. vii, c). The date is confirmed by parallels with the early work at Ballintubber Abbey, Co. Mayo, where the chancel was erected between 1216 and 1225 (Dugdale 1693, ii, 259, no. 1037). According to the Annals of Connacht 1215: 'Moelbrigte O Maicin, abbot of Ballintober, a virgin and sage, rested in Christ. By him the church of Ballintober was begun, and its sanctuary and crosses finished with great labour, in honour of Patrick, Mary our Lady, John and the Apostles'. The same workforce was employed at both abbeys and this included a sculptor popularly known as the 'Ballintober Master'.

With these final bays, the monks were faced with a dilemma. Three different types of pier had already been employed; should any of these be copied or was it time to adopt a fourth, and if so in what form? There was also the problem of the arches, round and pointed forms having been employed on opposite sides of the church. As it turned out, they took a rational and practical approach, presumably on the advice of their current master mason. Previous pier designs were ignored and a robust rectangular form adopted instead. Admittedly, the new supports were more like sections of wall, rather than free-standing supports. The angles were given a chamfered edge, relieving the harshness of the outline. A cluster of three shafts supported the inner order; further clusters towards the nave and aisles terminated in a graceful point well above floor level (Pl. 3.7). Like the central shaft on the clustered pier further east, these tapering shafts were designed to avoid interference with the stalls, in this case the stalls of the lay brothers (Pl. 3.8). They were in effect elongated corbels, a characteristic of Cistercian architecture throughout Europe.

When it came to the arcades, the monks made the only sensible choice available: round arches were continued on the south side, pointed arches to the north, a solution that maintained a modicum of consistency. The outer order is provided with a narrow-keeled roll, supported by a small, moulded corbel at the springing point, thus distinguishing the arches from those erected earlier: on the north side the two types meet over the octagonal pier, where a slight difference of alignment is visible.

What is less obvious is that the final two bays are narrower than the others by almost half a metre (0.44/0.46m). There was a danger, therefore, that the arches in this bay would not rise to the same height as the others. To compensate, the masons sprung the arch at a higher level, which in turn meant raising the level of the supporting capitals (Pl. 3.9, Fig. 3.4). This applies to the round-headed arches in the south arcade only. Quite how the builders got themselves into this mess is not clear, but it must indicate that the position of the west façade was already fixed: too little space had been left for the final bays.

One of the unusual features of Boyle is the substantial drain that crossed the church from north to south just below floor level. This was excavated by Ann Lynch in the 1980s, when its route was traced into the cloister walks (see Chapter 4). Its position is clearly identified by the relieving arch, low down in the wall of the south aisle (Pl. 3.9). The drain gives an indication of the height of the water table, showing how vulnerable the site was to flooding. It may also explain the design of the piers at the west end of the church, which were far more substantial than those erected earlier. Had the builders become wary of the moist nature of the ground? Whether or not the design was chosen for structural reasons, it was a wise choice, for over time they proved to be more stable than the clustered piers erected earlier. Nonetheless, it is curious that the monks chose to run the drain straight across the nave, rather than diverting the flow around the west end of the building. If the drain pre-dated the nave, perhaps the monks felt its route was best left undisturbed?

The final campaign also involved the construction of the west façade, which houses an elaborate portal, furnished on the exterior with two orders of Gothic mouldings carried continuously around the arch (Pl. 3.10). The façade was deep enough to allow for a spiral staircase in the thickness of the wall, its position clearly marked on the exterior by square-headed windows. The centre of the façade is articulated by projecting buttresses, the angles of which are enhanced by narrow mouldings. The moulding itself consists of a small roll with a very narrow fillet; from a distance it can be mistaken for a nibbed roll or pointed bowtell. The sheer depth of the façade meant there was room for a short porch,

Pl. 3.8. Corbels inserted into nave arcade.

the entry to the staircase being located on its south side. Above the doorway is an impressive window, strikingly Gothic in proportion, its cavernous 'reveals' reflecting the thickness of the whole wall (Pl. 3.11). The head of the window is decorated with a late form of chevron ornament, identical to a type found at Ballintubber, but the most remarkable feature of the design is the way in which the window is framed by detached shafts, set into deeply moulded jambs. The shafts were made in short sections and held in place by rings bonded into the adjoining fabric. Similar shafts were employed on the interior of the window, some of them cut in a grey sandstone forming an attractive contrast with the surrounding masonry. Detached shafts of this type were employed universally in English Gothic architecture, but this is one of the first occasions they were employed in the west of Ireland. The internal head of the window is surprisingly plain, an anti-climax after the ornate jambs. The face of the doorway below is likewise undecorated.

One peculiarity of the façade is that it does not terminate in a gable, as might be expected: rather, there is a turret-like projection in the centre, the interior of which is hollow. As Britta Kalkreuter (2001, 61) has pointed out, the façade must have been considerably higher, given the height of the roof outlined on the wall of the crossing tower. What initially appears to be a bell turret was in fact a defensive turret, erected when the abbey functioned as a barracks (Pl. 3.10). Parts of the abbey were already in ruin at this stage, since medieval dressed stone was recycled in the fabric, including three pieces with foliage carving. Nonetheless the staircase is original and for over half its height it was constructed with a well-formed newel. Boyle appears to be the only house in Britain and Ireland with a stair in this position. In Britain newel stairs are occasionally found at the south-west corner of the façade, as at Kirkstall (Leeds), Fountains (York), Rievaulx (North Yorkshire) and Strata Florida (Wales), but these are linked to the lay brothers' quarters. Apart from providing access to the nave roof, its function is not immediately obvious.

The final campaign also involved the completion of both the clerestory and the roof of the nave. Unfortunately, none of the windows over the western bays survive, so we do not know whether they followed the design established in earlier campaigns. The surviving examples are round headed, each being provided with a thick hood mould, following the pattern seen in the transepts. From the outside the windows appear remarkably small, though they were given wide internal splays to spread the light as far as possible. There is nothing to suggest that any of the nave windows were enlarged with tracery in the later Middle Ages. The collections of loose stone at Boyle include one group from a traceried window. The style belongs to the fifteenth century. As there is no obvious place for such a window in the church, it presumably came from one of the conventual buildings.

Judging from the lines visible on the wall of the crossing tower, the roof was formed of coupled rafters, presumably tied together by a collar (Pl. 3.12). A low-level tie beam or truss would have provided greater strength, but this would have cut across the face of the tower arch in an intrusive and unsightly way. The absence of a strong tie beam exposed the roof to tensile stress, making it vulnerable to lateral spread. This is exactly what happened, the north wall eventually being pushed out of vertical alignment. It is not clear whether the north wall began to rotate outwards before the dissolution of the monastery and the subsequent destruction of the roof. Roofs made of coupled rafters were standard in thirteenth-century Ireland and Boyle is not the only place where they gave trouble. The same type of roof covered the chancel of Ardfert Cathedral (Kerry), in this case forcing the south wall out of alignment. The addition of a large buttress at Ardfert in the nineteenth century prevented the wall from collapse. This was removed during conservation work undertaken between 1989 and 1998, the wall being stabilised (Moore 2007, 111). (For the original roof form see Leask 1960, 111–13; Stalley 2012, 46–9, figs 28, 31.) Here the problem may have been exacerbated by the addition of battlemented parapets, a modification widely adopted in later medieval Ireland, though not at Boyle.

Pl. 3.9. Nave, western bays showing differences in length.

A unique feature of Boyle was the presence of wall posts corresponding to each of the main rafters. These rested on sculptured corbels fitted into the spandrels of the arches (Pls 3.7, 3.8). In the west bays the corbels were included from the start, elsewhere they had to be inserted into older masonry, a point very obvious above the clustered piers. The corbels are composed of three short shafts, implying that the wall posts themselves consisted of three elements. Had these posts survived, our impression of the interior of the church would have been very different, the bare walls being divided into a series of well-defined bays, thereby giving the interior a decidedly Gothic flavour. Similar corbels were provided in the aisles, where wall posts were presumably also employed.

The architecture of the final campaign is closely related to practice in the west of England in the years around 1200, the so-called west country 'school' of masons that operated in the area around the Bristol Channel (Brakspear 1931, 1–18). Common features comprise a series of specific details,

Pl. 3.10. West façade.

Pl. 3.11. Head of window in the west façade.

rather than any overall approach to planning or design. Of the 16 characteristics listed by Brakspear, who sought to define the 'school' in 1931, approximately half can be found at Boyle. They include:

- mouldings that flow continuously around an arch without interruption by capitals
- triple shafts supporting the inner order of arcades
- semi-octagonal capitals
- the use of pointed nibs on shafts
- nibbed mouldings down the angles of buttresses
- capitals without a 'neck' moulding at the base.

To this list can be added the use of tall concave scalloped capitals, along with the survival of late forms of chevron ornament. The works of the third campaign at Boyle were evidently the charge of a master mason with direct knowledge of English methods, the English forms being well understood and executed with precision. It would be interesting to know the identity of this individual: perhaps he was recommended to the monks by one of the Cistercian abbeys in England or Wales. In the years around 1215, however, Boyle would have been an uncomfortable place for such a craftsman. Quite apart from language difficulties, ethnic tensions within the Cistercian order in Ireland were already becoming apparent, the older Irish monasteries viewing the French-speaking communities in the newly founded Anglo-Norman houses with suspicion (see Chapter 2) (O'Dwyer 1970; Stalley 1987, 17–20). There is no doubt about where the loyalties of the Boyle community lay. The local kings of Mag Luirg were closely identified with the monastery and the abbot was to play a role in the so-called 'conspiracy' of Mellifont, a movement that resisted Anglo-Norman influence within the order. In these circumstances the presence of an English master mason would be a surprise.

While connections with the Bristol area are not in doubt, there are equally obvious links with Dublin, in particular with the reconstruction of

Christ Church cathedral. The work carried out at the cathedral in the years around 1190 was in part inspired by Brakspear's west country school: this included the use of triple shafts, trumpet scalloped capitals, the absence of a neck moulding on some capitals, the retention of chevron ornament and the use of nibbed shafts and colonettes (Stalley 1979, 109–16). Especially telling is the presence of a tiny corbel that finishes off the narrow outer order of an arch, as found in the western bays at Boyle. Moreover, the west window at Boyle, in particular the way it is framed by shafts with multiple rings, can be compared with the original windows in the nave aisles at Christ Church. This is surprising, for the windows in question are thought to belong to the early Gothic campaign at the cathedral, a campaign usually placed in the 1230s (Stalley 2000, 68–74). This is an intriguing stylistic connection, with implications for the chronology of both buildings. A further link with the Christ Church nave comes in the form of the wall shafts situated against the interior face of the Boyle façade. These are triple filleted shafts, in other words shafts with three narrow vertical ridges, an early Gothic variation and one that was employed on the main piers in the nave of Christ Church. In the years around 1220 the Boyle masons were evidently in close touch with the latest fashions and techniques. Triple filleted shafts can be found at a number of Irish buildings in the early decades of the thirteenth century, as at Graiguenamanagh, Lismore, Co. Waterford, and Abbeyknockmoy.

Christ Church was of course not the only centre of activity in Dublin and it is possible that workshops in other monastic houses exerted just as much influence, those operating at the Cistercian abbey of St Mary's, for example, or the Augustinian houses of St Thomas and All Hallows. Given the uncertainties, the background of the masons who worked at Boyle in the years before 1220 thus remains an open question. As well as architectural connections, there are also sculptural links with Christ Church, in particular the way in which animals or figures were portrayed on capitals in a manner not seen in Ireland before.

The architecture of the third campaign at Boyle had repercussions throughout Connacht, an impact that has been explored at length by Britta Kalkreuter

Pl. 3.12. Tower, west wall showing marks of the nave roof.

(2001, 67–167). The abbey in fact occupies a crucial position in Ireland's own version of the west country school, one that Harold Leask (1960, 53–4) termed the 'School of the West'. The word 'school' is perhaps a misnomer, for we are looking at a loose band of masons using similar techniques, rather than a specific group of individuals that had been trained together. Experience gathered at Boyle had an impact at Assaroe, Co. Donegal. and Abbeyknockmoy, the two daughter houses of Boyle, but the most explicit link is with the Augustinian abbey of Ballintubber, founded by the king of Connacht, Cathal Crobhdearg O Conor in 1216 (Dugdale 1693, ii, 259, no. 1037). There is no doubt the same sculptor (or sculptors) was employed at both places. Amongst many common features is the type of chevron found in the west window at Boyle, a type repeated on one of the chancel windows at Ballintubber (Pl. 3.11) (Stalley 1971, 108–17).

The windows of the presbytery

Although the fabric of the church was complete by 1220, two substantial changes were introduced shortly afterwards. One was the remodelling of the windows in the presbytery, the other was the construction of a substantial tower.

At some point in the thirteenth century, the six Romanesque windows in the presbytery were replaced by Gothic lancets, a modification that transformed the visual appearance of the east end of the church. The presbytery, the focal point of the monastic liturgy, must have been a gloomy space until this time. The lancets effectively doubled the size of the openings providing a vertical élan not present before. The combination of three (and sometimes five) lancets, filling the east gable of a church became one of the most striking features of early Gothic architecture in Ireland and there are several examples in those Cistercian monasteries founded by Anglo-Norman patrons. Notable examples include Graiguenamanagh, Inch, Abington and Dunbrody (Wexford) (Stalley 1987, 92–103; Stalley 2012, 44–52). The monks of Boyle must have been impressed by what they saw elsewhere, the changes immediately giving their church a more fashionable appearance. Following Cistercian conventions, the windows were no doubt filled with panels of grisaille glass.

The details of the work are informative. The reveals of the outer lancets were supported on cone-shaped corbels, finished off with attractive foliage terminals (Pl. 3.13). Similar tricks can be found elsewhere, as in the early Gothic work at Newtown Trim (Meath) and Dunbrody. Foliage terminals can also be found at Abbeyknockmoy and they became widespread in Irish late Gothic buildings. The central lancet at Boyle was given grander treatment. Here the window moulding was linked to a detached shaft (now missing), which in turn rested on a corbel ornamented with scallops. The rounded form of the capital differs from anything seen before at Boyle and can be compared with early Gothic work *c.* 1220–40 in the cathedrals of Dublin. The remodelling of the windows presumably took place at much the same time.

The construction of the tower

The second modification concerned the crossing tower, another response to Anglo-Norman architecture (Pl. 3.14). By the 1160s, Cistercian communities in England were building low towers over the crossing, a practice derived from contemporary English architecture. The various sections of the church – presbytery, transepts and nave – were constructed to the same height, each with a separate roof abutting the walls of the tower, as at Buildwas and Kirkstall. This practice was subsequently followed by the Anglo-Normans in Ireland, one of the first being Grey Abbey (Down), where the Cistercian house was founded by John de Courcy in 1193 (Stalley 1987, 92–5).

Against this background, Boyle emerges as something of a hybrid. It contains elements of the so-called 'Bernardine' scheme, most noticeably the relatively low pointed arch leading into the presbytery. The other arches around the crossing, however, are set at a much higher level. In fact they are surprisingly tall, rising well above the wall heads of the adjoining clerestories, giving the impression of a tower perched high above its surroundings. The distinctiveness is brought out by a comparison with Buildwas, where the four crossing arches rise to the height of the adjoining walls but no further (Fergusson 1984, pls 106–7; Robinson 2006, Fig. 58). At Roche and Kirkstall, the crossing arches are likewise the same height as the adjoining wall heads. The original round-headed crossing arches at Dunbrody were also set within the walls, though later remodelled with the addition of steep pointed arches. At Boyle they rise well into the roof space, an arrangement that precluded the use of a transom or tie bar at the base of the roof. This manner of construction became common in the early Gothic era, the cathedral of Ardfert providing a good example (Stalley 2012, 46–9, figs 28, 31).

This is the first hint that the tower of Boyle was not part of the original design. Further evidence shows that it was in fact an afterthought, constructed after the church was finished: one crucial feature furnishes the proof. The western arch of the crossing is supported on corbels, the style of which belongs to the period 1220–60. Disturbed masonry either side confirms that the corbels are later insertions (Pl. 3.15). They support the western arch of the crossing arch, which in turn supports the tower. The tower itself, therefore, must belong to the mid thirteenth century, long after the fabric below had been completed.

There is, however, one difficulty with this explanation. The western arch of the crossing is identical in form to the arches that lead into the transepts, even down to tiny details like the small centring slots at the springing of the arch. Immediately above the dressed stone of the arch itself are two lines of relieving arches, made of narrow stones set radially, again a feature encountered on all three arches. There can be no doubt, therefore, that these arches were constructed at the same time. But the arches opening into the transepts are not supported on inserted corbels. Rather they rest on engaged shafts

Pl. 3.13. Presbytery window, detail of north lancet.

Pl. 3.14. Tower viewed from the south-west.

that form part of the fabric of the twelfth-century building. Even the capitals are consistent with this date. So, it would appear that the high arches into the transepts were at least planned in the years around 1180, even if the existing arch was not built at this time. This opens a further issue. If transept arches were planned in the first campaign of building, why was an equivalent arch not planned on the west side? There appears to be no easy explanation.

The insertion of the tower must have involved some rebuilding of the roof over the nave and the tower walls contain the marks of two separate roofs, each with a different pitch (Pl. 3.12). The lower marks appear to be earlier, and the remains of stone slates can be seen embedded in the fabric. The masonry details (notably on the west face) suggest that the walls of the tower were built on top of this roof; the first roof rested on a gable that was later extended upwards to form the square tower. The point to remember, however, is that this roof was built above an arch that belonged to the middle years of the thirteenth century. There must therefore have been an earlier roof that covered the church before the building of the tower.

If the western arch was a late addition, the original nave roof could have continued without interruption to the presbytery arch, as found in examples of 'Bernardine' churches. If arches had been constructed at a high level in the transept, the nave roof would have had to rise up over them in some way. The apex of the arches was too high to allow for a continuous roof, running from the west façade to the presbytery. It is thus hard to avoid the conclusion that the transept arches were lifted when the tower was constructed. How such roofs might have related to roofs over the transept is hard to imagine. At this time the existing high arches could not have existed; indeed, their very height would have prevented the construction of a continuous gabled roof running the length of the building.

The history of the tower itself is equally difficult to unravel. Judging by the amount of concrete in the fabric, substantial sections have been repaired and rebuilt, probably in the early years of the twentieth century. There are several peculiarities, two of which deserve attention. First, the upper edging of the roof, which is made of dressed stone and bonded deep into the wall, stops abruptly about halfway up (Pls 3.12, 3.14). Either the levels above have been rebuilt or preparations for this more steeply pitched roof were abandoned. Second, if the roof-edges had been continued, they would have blocked the windows above. The most plausible explanation of these anomalies is that this second roofline was abandoned when construction had reached a point just below the windows. This is confirmed by the way in which the masonry courses straight across the top of the incomplete roof-edge. There must have been a radical change of mind, the community deciding to keep the existing roofline, perhaps because it allowed room for large windows above. Such a decision might make sense if the tower was intended to house bells.

Access to the floor of the tower was another problem facing the thirteenth-century builders. The solution was quite complex. Starting in the dormitory, in the upper level of the east range, it was possible to walk into the roof space over the south transept chapels; from here there were steps up into the space over the presbytery vault. At this point a spiral staircase was built into the thickness of the east wall of the tower, its location clearly visible from inside the church below. As for the roof of the tower, antiquarian drawings show that it had a gabled roof running east to west. This would have been an unorthodox form for a medieval monastery; it presumably represents a modification that took place after the dissolution of the abbey.

Pl. 3.15. North-west pier of the nave, corbel inserted to support the western arch of the crossing.

The addition of crossing towers has particular relevance in the light of a decision taken by the General Chapter of the Cistercian order in 1157. Simply stated, this said: 'Let stone towers with bells not be built' (Norton 1986, 328). The wording is somewhat ambiguous, and it is unclear how it was interpreted: by 1200 many abbeys had ignored the instruction. It appears the statute was aimed at bell towers, rather than towers in general, with a desire to eliminate the more ostentatious designs (Fergusson 1984, 46–8; Stalley 1987, 141–3; Kinder 2002, 57). In 1217 the abbey of Bohéries (Picardie) in France was forced to demolish a tower because it was deemed 'contrary to the form of the order' (SCGOC 217, 27). Low towers over the crossing were evidently regarded as acceptable, perhaps because they had a practical value, allowing the various sections of the church to be roofed independently. What began as an Anglo-Norman fashion eventually became accepted throughout the order in Ireland; in the later Middle Ages towers were added to a number of Cistercian churches, including Mellifont, Jerpoint and in County Tipperary, Holycross, Hore and

Kilcooly (Stalley 1987, 144–52). Despite the wording of the 1157 injunction, comments at the time of the dissolution describe such towers as 'belfries'.

The construction of the tower at Boyle had implications for the roof of the church, sections of which had to be rebuilt at the same time. It is clear that the thirteenth-century builders erected a roof of coupled rafters, held together by a collar and perhaps a tie beam below. But what form of roof existed before the tower was erected and before the three arches opening into the transepts and nave had been constructed? The evidence is inconclusive, one of the many architectural uncertainties of Boyle. If arches had been constructed at a high level in the transept, the nave roof would have had to rise up over them in some way. The apex of the arches was too high to allow for a continuous roof, running from the west façade to the presbytery. It is thus hard to avoid the conclusion that the transept arches were lifted when the tower was constructed.

With an impressive tower and three dramatic lancets in the east wall, the architecture at Boyle was now on a par with more recent Anglo-Norman designs. Was this a deliberate response to the tensions within the order? At the very least it suggests a degree of ambition on the part of the community, one that must have considered itself the principal Cistercian house in the kingdom of Connacht.

The labour force

Although the Norman chronicler, Orderic Vitalis, stated that the Cistercians were accustomed to build their 'monasteries with their own hands in lonely, wooded places' (Chibnall 1973, iv, 326–7), the notion of monks toiling away on heavy building tasks gives a false impression of what actually took place. The choir monks may have lent a hand in the early days, when temporary structures of wood were required, but masonry construction was a job for professionals, as was self-evidently the case at Boyle. The quality of the stone cutting and the complexity of much of the design leave little doubt about this. The lay brothers, who attended church only twice a day, might well have assisted, especially any who had been trained as masons or carpenters, this was probably the exception. The many changes of style at Boyle demonstrate that paid professionals were recruited as the need arose. Had the monastery possessed its own team of masons, the style of building would surely have been more consistent throughout the church.

The local sandstone lent itself to fine carving and in a few places high quality ashlar was used for sections of wall. There are good examples in the transepts, between the chapels (Pl. 3.16), and on the interior walls of the western porch. The north side of the porch is especially interesting, since many of the blocks are interlocked creating a veritable geometrical puzzle. At one point the mason strayed from the horizontal, making up for his error by cutting a trapezoidal stone to get back on track. With these few exceptions, the fine sandstone was limited to the architectural details, rather than general walling. During the dismantling of the nave piers, setting out marks were revealed on the inner surfaces of the stones. At various places in the church there are occasional mason's marks, especially in the western bays and around the Gothic windows in the presbytery (P. Egan pers. comm.; see also Dornan 2009, 7). The local sandstone varies in colour and in the final campaign the masons used both grey and yellow blocks together, in one case (the responds of the west bay) in a roughly alternating sequence. Similar experiments along these lines were later tried at Dunbrody and St Canice's in Kilkenny, though such schemes were rarely maintained with any consistency. At Boyle it seems unlikely the mixed material was done for visual effect, since the walls of Cistercian churches were usually lime washed and then embellished in paint with false masonry joints. Although no trace of this has survived at Boyle, there is evidence of such treatment in other Irish Cistercian churches (Stalley 1987, 214).

During the first campaign one gets the impression that the masons were learning from experience and in one instance a significant change has, in effect, been fossilized in stone. The first cylindrical pier in the nave has a capital formed from a number of blocks, arranged in a circle. One of these blocks contains two alternative designs, disrupting the continuity of the pattern; it is surprising the stone was put to use and not discarded. Furnished with one large overhanging scallop, it is easy to understand why the initial scheme was

Pl. 3.16. Masonry pier dividing the chapels of the north transept.

abandoned. Even more curious is a piece of carved stone set within rubble masonry in the north-east corner of the presbytery. This must pre-date the church, though where the fragment came from remains a mystery.

Although professional master masons controlled operations on a day-to-day basis, Cistercian monks had a clear idea about what they wanted, especially on matters of planning and proportional layout. Advice might come from the mother house, as happened at Mellifont in 1142 when St Bernard sent the monk, Robert, from Clairvaux to assist with 'the buildings and other things necessary for the wellbeing' of the house (James 1953, 454–5). Robert was evidently an advisor, rather than a builder himself. In this manner guidelines and instructions could be passed from one monastery to the next. At Boyle in the 1160s someone had a good grasp of Cistercian design in France, even to the extent of including an access door high up in the wall of the north transept. Was this a member of the community or a monk sent out from Mellifont to advise? In some cases, the mason in charge might have been recruited via other Cistercian houses in Ireland; at the very least such men could have prepared themselves by inspecting Cistercian work elsewhere. In a monastic community it was the cellarer who was usually charged with overall supervision of building projects, acting as a *custos operis*, or keeper of the works. At Boyle, Donnsleibhe O'hInmhainén was described as 'a holy monk and chief master of the carpenters' when he died in 1230, bearing out the supervisory role that monks might undertake (ALC 1230).

Pl. 3.17. Capital in the nave with foliage and berries.

The sculptural programme

During the final campaign a considerable amount of time was devoted to the carving of capitals. As well as the 16 examples on the piers, another 30 were required for the various corbels, an output sufficient to occupy a mason for at least a year, though it is unlikely that the work was restricted to one individual. The designs are quite diverse, and none appear to be an exact repeat. The designs have been analysed at length by Kalkreuter (2001, 52–9). The most frequently used motifs are varieties of palmette ornament, with leaves that consist of three lobes of diminishing size. The lobes themselves are concave except for one curious example in which the design was turned inside out, the lobes being convex and strikingly bulbous. This is found on the east side of Pier 7 in the south arcade. The foliage is usually arranged in one or more rows around the surface of the capital, with the 'leaves' themselves being framed by an encircling stem; in a few cases the foliage is turned over at the top, a technique reminiscent of that found on two of the clustered piers. In several cases a line or double line of berries hangs from the lower edge of the leaves, a highly distinctive feature (Pl. 3.17). Occasionally pieces of a rope-like moulding were introduced. Several capitals are formed of trumpet scallops, in some cases the head of the 'trumpet' being hollowed out. In other instances, more conventional scallop designs were combined with foliage. One curiosity is the occasional omission of the necking ring, for which there appears to be no pattern or specific rationale.

Seven capitals fall outside this general scheme, being decorated with figures or animals in a typically Romanesque manner. Given Cistercian disapproval of this type of carving, the capitals are quite a surprise. Especially notable is the skilful adaptation of the designs to the awkward shape of the tripartite capitals; it is worthwhile considering each of them in turn.

1. (South arcade) A composition depicting a cock and a lion tussling over ambiguous looking prey (a small creature of some sort) (Pl. 3.18). The design is doubled but reversed so that the two lions are placed back-to-back, their tails entwined and ending in leaves. The cock's feathers terminate with a fine spiral swirl. The animals are deeply cut and stand out from the background in bold and well-rounded relief. The action takes place above a leaf-like frame. This is rightly regarded as one of the finest pieces of Romanesque sculpture in the country.
2. (South arcade) The sculptured field is divided into two horizontal sections. The upper part contains three dogs, carved in a line, two of them fighting over prey, the third biting the tail of the animal ahead. The composition lacks the vitality shown in the previous capital and the carving is lacking in depth. For this reason, it has usually been attributed to a less gifted craftsperson. The lower part of the capital has a sequence of simple upright leaves. There is no necking.
3. (South arcade) Four figures in line, separated by trees from which each of them grasps the leaves or fruit (Pl. 3.19). The two central figures hold up their arms in a traditional orans pose. Those at the sides have more difficulty reaching the tree, one arm being stretched across their stomachs. The figures are emphatically frontal, and each is clothed in a short knee-length tunic, those in the centre with well-defined belts. Below the action there is a cup-like design, forming a base over the outer shafts. The style of the figures can be compared with carvings elsewhere in the School of the West, not least on a capital at Killaloe cathedral.
4. (Corbel nave south) This is the most ambitious but also the most damaged of the figural capitals. It depicts two naked figures back-to-back, their ribs clearly articulated. Both are involved in a struggle against rampant lions, the latter furnished with foliate tails: the right figure wields a sword in his right hand and grasps the jaw of the lion with his left. The other figure is forcing open the jaws of the second lion. The action is laid out above simple leaves that have a jagged upper edge. The long ovoid faces, seen in profile, are typical of facial types encountered in the School of the West.
5. (Corbel nave south) An impressive zoomorphic composition, with a series of dragons with their necks entwined and their claws locked together; the lengthy tails include various twists before eventually terminating in what appear to be small leaves. Palmette-type foliage lines at the base of the capital. The sequence of affronted beasts combined with the insistent symmetries are characteristic of Romanesque art: a similar approach can be seen in the well-known griffin capital in the north transept at Christ Church cathedral Dublin *c.* 1190–1200 (Stalley 1979, 110–11).
6. (South arcade) A capital combining a series of narrow scallop-like forms below with a double row of leaves above. A series of tiny heads are fitted into the gaps between the leaves (Pl. 3.20). Although there is no sign of bodies, tiny hands grasp the stems of the adjacent leaves. The heads were all modelled individually, and none are exactly the same. Small, isolated heads of this type are not unique to stone carving and similar heads can be found amidst the foliate scrolls of Cormac's Psalter (British Library Add. MS 36929), a manuscript with Cistercian associations. There is a possibility that it was made at Boyle (Stalley 1987, 128–9).
7. (Corbel nave south) A single capital, the entire block occupied by a human head, seen frontally. The closely spaced eyes have prominent eyelids. There may have been a beard, though this is hard to identify as the lower sections of the capital are badly damaged.

Although the seven capitals discussed above are varied in quality, they have features in common,

Pl. 3.18. Capital in the nave depicting a cock and lions.

and one cannot automatically assume that they were carved by different craftsmen. Much may have depended on the models available and perhaps too the amount of time a mason was given to carry out the work. The compositions fall within the common repertoire of Romanesque art and there is no reason to believe that they had any intentional Christian meaning. That is not to say that a pious monk might not have read them in Christian terms: confrontations of man and beast, for example, are frequently encountered in the words of the Old Testament, particularly in the psalms.

The choice of subjects is especially interesting, given Cistercian criticism of meaningless works of art. St Bernard's diatribe against superfluous and distracting sculpture, written in the 1120s, specifically identified the type of subjects found at Boyle, as he demanded to know 'in the cloister ... what profit is there in those ridiculous monsters ... To what purpose are those unclean apes, those fierce lions, those monstrous centaurs, those half men, those striped tigers, those fighting knights, those hunting their horns' (Davis-Weyer 1971, 169–70). Bernard's views informed the subsequent statute of *c.* 1122–35 that forbade sculpture and pictures in Cistercian buildings 'because while attention is paid to such things the positive value of meditation or the discipline of religious gravity is often neglected'. Some phrases in the Latin are not easy to convey in English: '*Sculpture vel picture in ecclesiis nostris seu in officinis aliquibus monasterii ne fiant interdicimus, quia dum talibus intenditur, utilitas bone meditationis vel disciplina religiose gravitatis sepe negligitur*' (Norton 1986, 324; Waddell 1999, 446). Admittedly, the carvings at Boyle count as relatively modest contraventions of the rule and they are all to be found in the area of the church occupied by the lay brothers, rather than the choir monks. Even so, during his visitation of 1228, Stephen of Lexington felt the need to remind the Irish monasteries of the need for simplicity in such matters (Griesser 1946, 104, no. 70). The Latin in this passage is ambiguous, especially the phrase '*aliqua varietas picturarum marmorea vel alia*' which was translated as 'any different styles of painting, to look like marble or anything else' (O'Dwyer 1982, 166). This may not capture the full meaning of the text. Stephen of Lexington's remarks were not specifically directed at Boyle. The introduction of 'profane' subjects lends further support to the belief that the mason or masons responsible were recruited from outside the order.

Pl. 3.19. Capital in the nave with figures.

Sculpture was usually painted at this time and, if this was the case at Boyle, the array of capitals and corbels would have been far more prominent than they are today, with spots of colour enlivening the limewashed walls. In Cistercian houses one suspects the paint would have been relatively subdued, the foliage capitals predominantly green; it would be interesting, nonetheless, to know how the animals and figures were treated.

The type of sculpture found at Boyle was reflected in a range of buildings elsewhere in Connacht. Similar foliage patterns, for example, are encountered at Abbeyknockmoy, Boyle's daughter house. The closest connections, however, are with Ballintubber Abbey, where the tripartite capitals in the chancel include similar confrontations of animals and beasts. The same stylistic features can be found in both places, though none of the compositions were repeated. At Ballintubber the leaf formations around the base of the capitals occupy rather more space and they take a slightly different form. It is not easy to decide where the

Pl. 3.20. Foliate capital embellished with human heads.

mason (or masons) worked first: on balance it is perhaps more likely that the carvings at Boyle preceded those at Ballintubber.

The later Middle Ages

Once the tower and eastern lancets had been added to the church, there is no evidence of major alterations to the fabric. The fashion for bar tracery appears to have had little effect and none of the windows in the church was subsequently enlarged. There are, however, several loose stones from a traceried window that presumably came from one of the conventual buildings. There is also a fragment of ballflower decoration, an ornament favoured in the first half of the fourteenth century (Dornan 2009, 11). It is rarely found in Ireland though the ornament was employed around the east window of the church at Jerpoint. The collection of loose stone includes a number of slabs decorated with pointed trefoil arches, cut as blind decoration against a series of solid blocks. They include an angle piece, suggesting the stones belonged to a rectangular feature of some sort: this could have been an altar, a tomb or perhaps part of the screen separating the monks' and lay brothers' choirs. This is accomplished work, probably from the late thirteenth century. An obvious lacuna at Boyle is the absence of floor tiles. Although widely used in Cistercian churches abroad, the fashion in Ireland was limited to areas of Anglo-Norman settlement.

In general, the architecture and sculpture of the abbey suggests that the relative prosperity enjoyed by the community in the early years did not survive into the later Middle Ages, a time when the monastery was firmly under the control of the MacDermots, the local lords of Moylurg (see Chapter 2). In 1402 the abbey was granted an indulgence for the conservation of the church, which suggests the community was struggling to maintain its buildings. In 1569, when the abbey was granted to Patrick Cusack, the site contained 'the walls of church and belfry, cloister, hall dormitory and some ruined buildings', the latter phrase suggesting parts of the monastery were in poor repair (Gwynn and Hadcock 1970, 129). The MacDermots had been amongst the abbey's early benefactors and various members of the family were buried within the walls. It is likely that there was once a significant tomb on the north side of the presbytery, the standard location for a benefactor's tomb, the rough masonry in this area suggesting that something has been removed. Conspicuously absent, however, are grand sculptured memorials, like those in the Cistercian monasteries at Jerpoint (Kilkenny) and Kilcooly (Tipperary) (Dornan 2009, 12–13).

View of the exterior of the west gatehouse.

Chapter 4

Excavation of the Gatehouse and Cloister Walks

Dr Ann Lynch

SPECIALIST CONTRIBUTIONS BY

A. Carey, R. Meenan, M. McCarthy, C. McCutcheon, S. Scully, E. Wincott-Heckett

Introduction

Trial excavations and archaeological monitoring were undertaken at the Cistercian abbey at Boyle in October 1982 and May 1983 in advance of the restoration of the gatehouse by the National Monuments Service. More extensive excavation was undertaken in April/May 1984 to expose the north cloister walkway. Before excavation, the cloister area comprised a grassed surface with the east walkway, at a lower level, the only visible monastic feature (Fig. 4.1). It was evident that considerable build-up of material had occurred, particularly around the perimeter of the cloister garth where the walkways had become obscured. It was decided that in order to improve the presentation of the site and to aid with the interpretation of the cloister area, the original monastic surface of the north walkway should be exposed thereby enabling visitors to walk along two sides of the cloister garth. The results of all phases of work directed by the writer are presented here.

The gatehouse

The abbey is entered through a passage in the gatehouse (external dimensions 9.85m east–west by *c.* 5.2m north–south) along the west range (Fig. 4.1). It is a two-storey structure with an attic and a fireplace on the upper floor. There are two chambers at ground level, one on either side of an entrance passage (W. 2.6m). A stairs leads from the ground floor of the northern chamber to a first-floor room with square hood mouldings defining two rectangular windows. It has a wooden floor. The ground-floor chamber on the south side of the passage measures 3.80m by 2.m The present, red tiled roof is a reproduction of the original, evidence of which was recovered in this excavation.

Limited archaeological works were carried out within the gatehouse during its renovations in 1982/1983. Two cuttings were opened within the passage (Fig. 4.2, Cuttings 1, 2) from

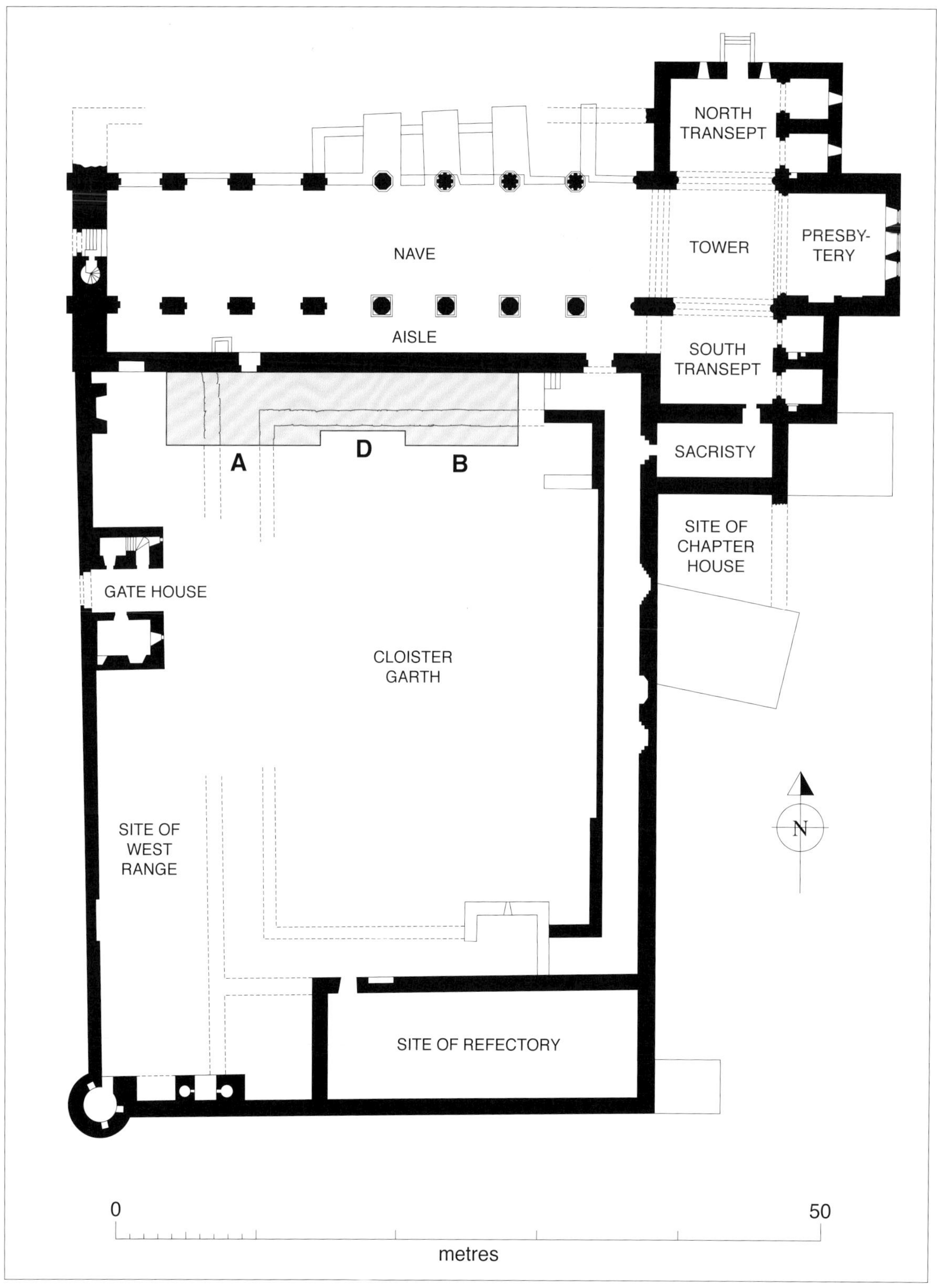

Fig. 4.1. Plan of the abbey showing area excavated in 1984. (Plan dated 1903, courtesy of OPW)

which the topsoil, comprising loose dark brown/black soil (*c*. 120mm deep) containing fragments of red brick, animal bone and a 1921 penny, was removed. Beneath the topsoil, there was a well-preserved cobbled surface which was later exposed throughout the passage and left *in situ*. The cobbles average 120mm × 100mm and incorporate a shallow drainage gully running east–west through the passage. Modern disturbance was evident adjacent to the entrance to the small chamber at ground level on the north side of the passage. The re-used stone forming the sill of the chamber was exposed at a slightly lower level than the cobbles and evidence of fixings on each jambstone suggests the entrance was once secured by a metal grille.

The ground-floor chamber on the south side of the passage measures 3.80m × 2.50m and a cutting 1m wide was opened running the full length of the room (Fig. 4.2, Cutting 3). Here, the topsoil varied in depth from 120mm at the west end to 250mm at the east, following the sloping cobbled floor underneath. The topsoil contained large quantities of red/orange ceramic roof tiles. A narrow trench (600mm wide) had been cut through the cobbles against the west wall and this extended below the foundations of the wall to the boulder clay (at a depth of 700mm). This trench had been backfilled with moist black soil containing further fragments of ceramic roof tiles, mortar and animal bone of recent appearance. This disturbance must have occurred during repair works undertaken by the OPW in the late nineteenth/early twentieth century. A small cutting was also opened immediately inside the entrance to the chamber to facilitate ESB cabling (Fig. 4.2, Cutting 4). Underneath the cobbling that was at threshold level there was black soil with small amounts of animal bone and mortar fragments. At 380mm depth, the wall footing was exposed, and the soil changed to a sandy consistency with charcoal flecking.

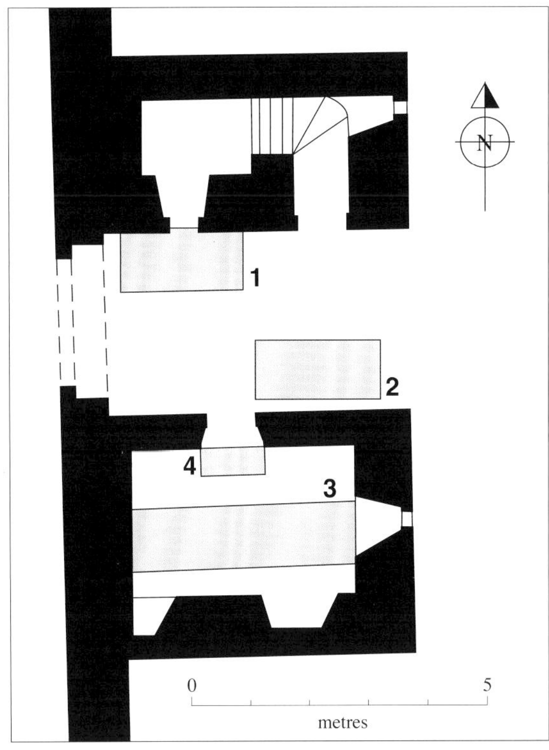

Fig. 4.2. Plan of the gatehouse showing areas excavated in 1982–3.

The nave

Initially two cuttings (A: 5m × 11m; B: 5m × 8m) were opened against the south nave wall in 1984 and the area between them (Cutting D: 3m wide) was subsequently investigated. This resulted in a total excavation area of 24.8m east–west × 5m (maximum) north–south (Fig. 4.1). Cutting C was a narrow 2m-wide strip opened against the wall of the refectory to check for the remains of a cobbled surface and is not described here.

The south face of the nave wall (F14) was exposed to foundation level within Cuttings A, B and D. The original masonry survives to an average height of *c*. 1.10m with an additional *c*. 250mm of modern (OPW) masonry on top (Fig. 4.3). The facing of the Cistercian wall comprised large, mostly rectangular limestone blocks laid horizontally in courses with smaller stones filling the interstices. The only visible evidence of mortar bonding was at the threshold of the doorway and in the relieving arch of the drain (see below). The nave wall sits on a footing that projects *c*. 250mm from the base of the wall and averages 150–200mm in height (Figs 4.3, 4.4) and the footing in turn rests on a compact light brown/orange clay (F44). The masonry of the south nave wall as revealed during the excavation appears to be of single-phase construction suggesting that it was built during the first building campaign in the late twelfth century (see Chapter 3).

Before excavation, a gap in the nave wall *c*. 10m from the west end of the church provided access from the cloister down into the nave (Figs 1.1, 4.3). Excavation revealed that this gap in fact

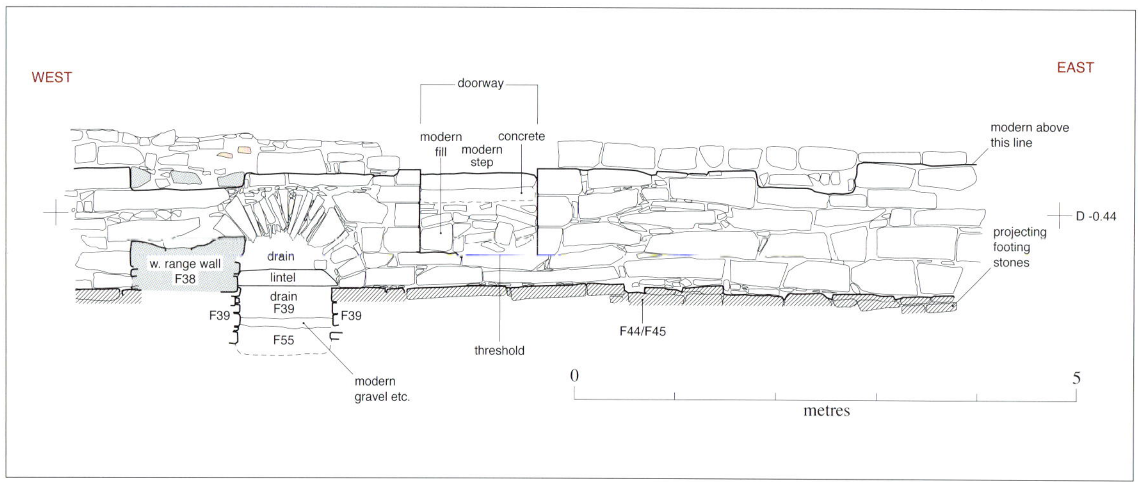

Fig. 4.3. Elevation of south wall of nave, Cutting A.

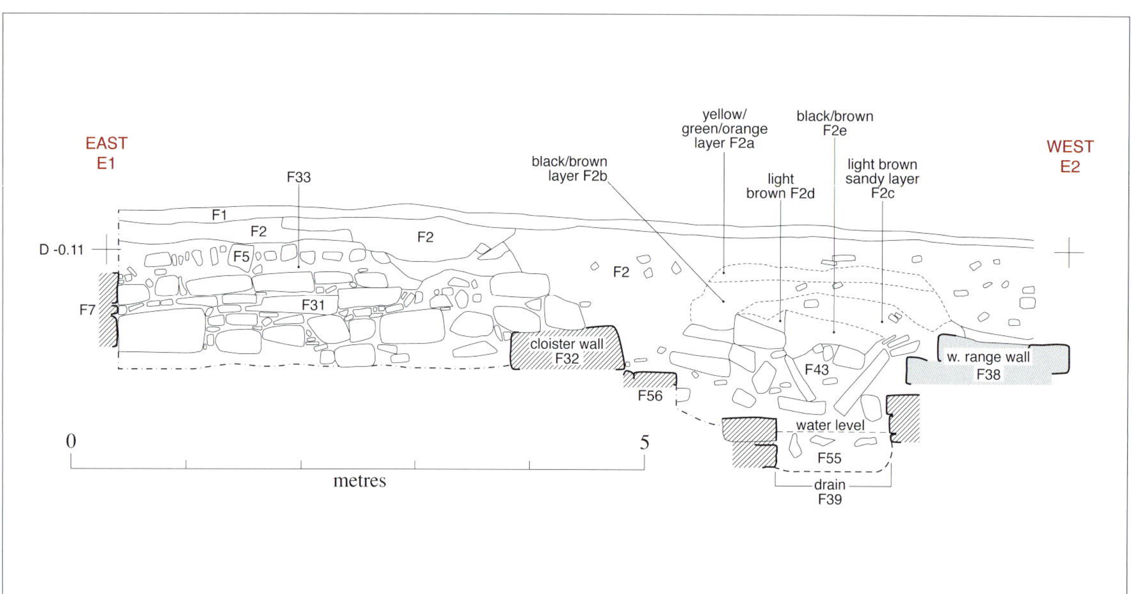

Fig. 4.4. South section face, Cutting A. (See Fig. 4.5 for locations.)

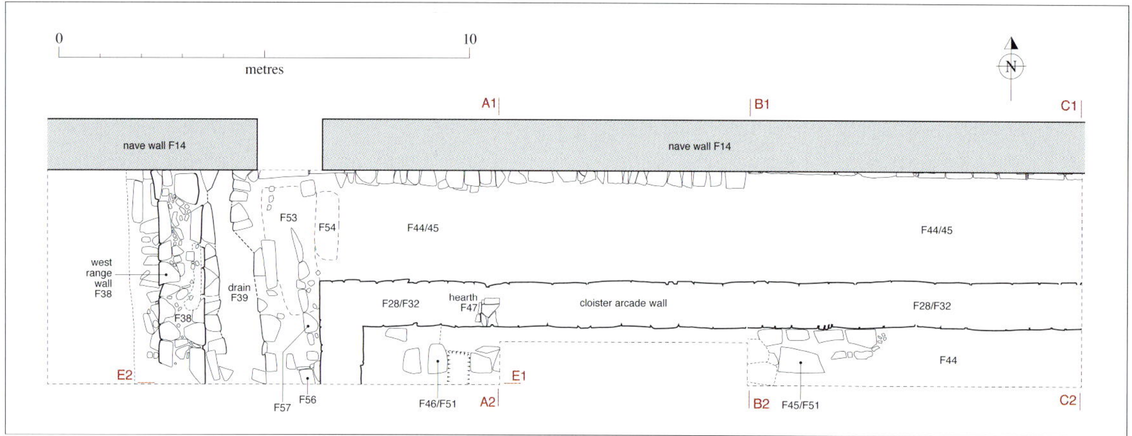

Fig. 4.5. Plan of monastic features, north cloister walk.

marked the position of an original doorway, the threshold of which was uncovered *c.* 800mm below the modern steps (Fig. 4.3, Pl. 4.1). The doorway is 1.90m wide and the surviving jambstones (four on the west side, three on the east) are finely cut with chamfered angles. The threshold consists of two rectangular slabs on top of which a fill of stones and clay covered by concrete provided a base for the modern steps.

Immediately west of the doorway, a relieving arch partly visible before excavation was shown to span a drain (F39) that extends southwards from under the nave and which continues beneath the west cloister walk (Figs 4.3–5). The drain, originally *c.* 700mm in depth, averages 850mm–950mm in width and its side walls were constructed of roughly coursed limestone slabs with the relieving arch springing from the footing of the nave wall (Fig. 4.5, Pl. 4.2). Extensive disturbance had taken place along the eastern side of the drain, in particular, resulting in the removal of much of the eastern side wall and all but one of the covering lintels. A number of displaced lintels were recovered from backfill material (F43) above and to the east of the drain and the extent of the disturbance was clear from the recovery of seventeenth-/eighteenth-century ceramics and a clay pipe stem (106) of late seventeenth-/early eighteenth-century date from this backfill deep within the drain. Undisturbed waterlogged deposits (F55) survived in places within the drain, especially close to and underneath the nave wall. These consisted of dark brown/black silty clays with lenses of grey clay and sand, and they contained about 130 animal bones in addition to some organic material including twigs, hazel nuts, oyster shells and scraps of leather (105, 110) (see below). A small number of human bones were found intermingled with the animal bones. Two pieces of architectural cut stone were recovered from the top of the drain sediments; a fragment of an ogee-headed window (including a spandrel and part of a cusp) and a piece of limestone column, 100mm in diameter. This drain was constructed as an integral part of the west end of the church probably in the early thirteenth century and would have been a vital element of water management on a site that must have been prone to flooding, given that the River Boyle bounds the site to the south and east. Traces of a second drain (F56) were uncovered in the west cloister walkway, running under the cloister arcade wall (Fig. 4.5, Pl. 4.3). This was a small box drain (200mm wide × 200mm high) with a stone-lined floor and was filled with mottled yellow/grey sandy clay with charcoal flecks.

Pl. 4.1. Remains of original doorway in south wall of nave. (Photo: A. Lynch)

Pl. 4.2. Drain extending southwards from underneath the nave. (Photo: A. Lynch)

The east wall (F38) of the west range was exposed abutting the nave wall (Figs 4.3, 4.5, Pl. 4.2). The range wall averages 1.15m in width and survives two to three courses in height. It consists

Pl. 4.3. Box drain (F56) in west cloister walk. (Photo: A. Lynch)

Pl. 4.4. The north cloister walk after excavation, looking east. (Photo: Con Brogan, NMS)

of a mortar-bonded rubble core with large limestone facing stones. The east face of this wall was built on the west wall of the drain (F39) while the west face rests on a footing of flat slabs that project 200mm–400mm from beneath the wall.

The remains of the north cloister arcade wall and its return on the west side were revealed, indicating a width of 2.55m for the north walk and 2.75m for the west walk (Fig. 4.5, Pl. 4.4). The arcade wall survives to heights ranging from 300mm to 750mm and averages 1.0m in width (Figs 4.5–7). It appeared to be clay bonded with a rubble core and a vertical, roughly coursed limestone face on the side facing the walk while the inner (garth side) face displayed a slight batter. The facing stones varied considerably in size and shape, ranging from large rectangular slabs similar to those in the nave wall to smaller rectangular and blocky stones (Fig. 4.6). No trace of the sill stones on which the arcading would have sat or of the arcading itself, were recovered.

Both the nave wall and cloister arcade wall were built on a compact, light brown/orange clay (F44/F55) that formed the floor of the cloister walk. Along the north walk it had the appearance of a well-trodden surface with frequent pebble inclusions, charcoal flecking and occasional small patches of mortar. At the north-west corner, in front of the doorway leading into the nave, remnants of rough cobbling (F53) were exposed extending north–south for *c.* 3m. This comprised pebble-sized stones interspersed with small/medium sized angular stones set into a thin layer of mortar. A spread of similar mortar (F54) was uncovered just to the east that may also have originally been bedding for a cobbled surface (Fig.4.5).

A line of eight stones (F57) running north–south for a distance of 3.40m in the west walk appears to pre-date the cloister arcade wall (Fig. 4.5). The stones are set within F44/F45, at a depth of 250mm where the southernmost slab runs under the arcade wall. Their function is unclear but the occurrence of angular stones averaging 120mm × 100mm between these slabs and the cloister arcade wall suggests they may be the facing stones of an earlier wall.

The excavations extended south of the cloister arcade wall, thereby exposing a narrow strip (*c.* 1.30m wide) of the cloister garth. A number of large flagstones (F46/F51) were uncovered resting on the boulder clay (F44/F45) and abutting the base of the arcade wall (Fig. 4.5, Pl. 4.5). Originally it was thought these could be the lintels of a drain, perhaps an extension of F56, but when one flagstone was lifted, this did not prove to be the case. It is likely therefore that this northern part of the garth was paved with flagstones at least during the later monastic period. A fragment of cut silk cloth was recovered from between two of these flagstones (see Wincott Heckett below).

The limited excavations undertaken at the north side of the cloister revealed details of late twelfth-/early thirteenth-century monastic structures. The south nave wall was exposed to foundation level and an original doorway leading from the nave onto the west cloister walk was revealed. A substantial drain extending north–south underneath the full width of the nave was built as an integral part of the church structure and even though in the area excavated, this feature had been extensively disturbed in post-medieval times, a little of the primary waterlogged sediment had survived. Drainage was obviously of some concern at the time of construction as a second small box drain was constructed in the west walk and was traced to the south-east extending under the cloister arcade wall. It is possible that this latter drain was associated with a lavabo sited within the cloister garth, similar to that revealed during excavations at the Cistercian abbey at Dunbrody, Co. Wexford (Moloney 2009, 32). The east wall of the west range was built against the nave wall and on top of the north–south drain indicating that what is traditionally the lay brothers' accommodation was constructed late in the building campaign, possibly in the second quarter of the thirteenth century or even later.

The full extent of the north cloister arcade wall and walk was uncovered. The floor of the walk appeared to have been trampled gritty clay although at its western end traces of rough cobbling set in mortar were uncovered in an area of probable heavy usage in front of the doorway into the nave. Recent excavations suggest that Cistercian cloister walks were floored in a variety of ways – those at Tintern, Co. Wexford, were of clay with a gravel-type surface (Lynch 2010) while at nearby Dunbrody, they appear to have been paved with shale flagstones (Moloney 2009, 39). Interestingly, there are indications that part of the cloister garth at Boyle may have been paved with flagstones. Unfortunately, apart from a fragment of silk cloth, no artefacts were found associated with the medieval structures.

The cloister

In 1983, two trial trenches were opened within the cloister (Figs 4.5, 4.6). Trial Trench 1 (4m × 2m) was opened to check for the remains of the cloister arcade wall. Underlying rubble and modern fill, a layer of paving was uncovered at a depth of *c.* 720mm. This paving had been disturbed (probably during OPW works) to expose remains of the cloister arcade wall which lay *c.* 300mm–350mm below the paving. Trial Trench 2 (4m × 1m) was opened across the conjectural line of a north–south wall shown on the OPW plan dated 1903 and that was thought may have represented the west range wall. Remains of this wall were revealed immediately under the sod but it clearly belonged to a late phase of use of the site as it had been built at a higher level than traces of two further structures exposed at both the western and eastern ends of the cutting. The results of excavation of these two trial trenches are integrated below with those of the more extensive excavations undertaken in 1984.

Pl. 4.5. Flagstones in cloister garth with cloister arcade wall. (Photo: A. Lynch)

The post-dissolution features

It is difficult to determine when exactly the monks departed from Boyle Abbey and when the conventual buildings and structures within the cloister were demolished. It is possible that immediately after its dissolution in the mid sixteenth century, the monastic buildings were stripped of everything of value, but the wide-scale demolition and modification of the cloister area is more probably the result of the military occupation that commenced at the end of the sixteenth century (see Chapter 2). As described above, the north cloister arcade wall had been reduced to varying heights and the excavation also revealed that the area between it and the nave wall had been backfilled with a range of different deposits. At its eastern end (Area B) a deposit of mid-/dark brown sandy clay (F29) had been dumped on top of the clay floor (F44) to depths ranging from 600mm–700mm which coincided with the surviving top of the arcade wall (Fig. 4.7). This backfill material, which had also been deposited on the garth side of the arcade wall, contained a moderate amount of small stones, occasional large stones, disarticulated human and animal bone, patches of mortar, charcoal and small brick fragments. A dump of disarticulated human bone intermixed with animal bone rested against the nave wall (Fig. 4.8, Pl. 4.6). Two sherds

Pl. 4.6. Kiln overlying remains of cloister arcade wall with dump of disarticulated bone visible against nave wall. (Photo: A. Lynch)

Pl. 4.7. Hearth (F47) built on top of remains of cloister arcade wall. (Photo: A. Lynch)

Pl. 4.8. Remains of kiln during excavation, with rubble platform (F23) visible in foreground. (Photo: A. Lynch)

of eighteenth-century pottery (50, 69), one sherd of possible medieval pottery (75) and a possible hammerstone (68) were recovered from this backfill material. Large stones (F3) had been loosely placed on top of the arcade wall itself. Midway along Area B, the nature of the backfill material changed to a loose rubble (F23) intermixed with brown sticky clay, which partially overlay F29 but which rested directly on the clay floor (F44) at the western end of the cutting (Figs 4.7, 4.8). This rubble included very large boulders (up to 600mm × 700mm) but no cut or dressed stone. It overlay the arcade wall, which had been reduced to one course in height here, and its west and south-east edges were faced with roughly coursed blocks of limestone (Fig. 4.8, F13). This rubble deposit provided a platform for the kiln (F12) described in detail below. To the west of the rubble, the fill overlying the floor of the cloister walk was a brown/black clay (F36/F50) similar to F29 and containing some large stones (including cut stone), disarticulated bone (human and animal) and a sherd of eighteenth-century glazed red earthenware (93). In places this clay extended over the remains of the arcade wall.

A small, stone-built hearth (F47) had been constructed on top of the remains of the arcade wall, *c.* 4.1m from its north-west corner, and was probably used during the reconfiguration of the cloister area (Figs 4.5, 4.7, Pl. 4.7). The floor of the hearth, paved with three flat slabs, measured 480mm × 500mm and was defined on its north and west sides by stones set on edge. The stone on its north side was a re-used cut stone. The floor of the hearth was covered with brown sandy soil (F48) containing burnt clay and charcoal from which oyster shells, animal bone and an iron object (96) were recovered.

The kiln

Following the partial demolition of the cloister arcade wall and the backfilling of the north cloister walk, a drying kiln (F12) was constructed on top of a rubble platform (F23) described above (Fig. 4.8, Pl. 4.8). The bowl of the kiln which was of classic keyhole shape abutted the nave wall and measured *c.* 1.35m in diameter. Only its basal course (up to 500mm wide) survived, and it was comprised of large, mortared stones. The floor of the bowl (F35), sloping downwards from west to east, was paved with flags of varying sizes, some of which were set in mortar. Evidence of heat damage was particularly evident along the eastern side of the bowl where the structural stones and paving stones were pink/red in colour and crumbly to the touch. There was no well-defined flue but a large flagstone, projecting *c.* 70mm above the level of the floor, had been set in the narrow (520mm wide) entrance to

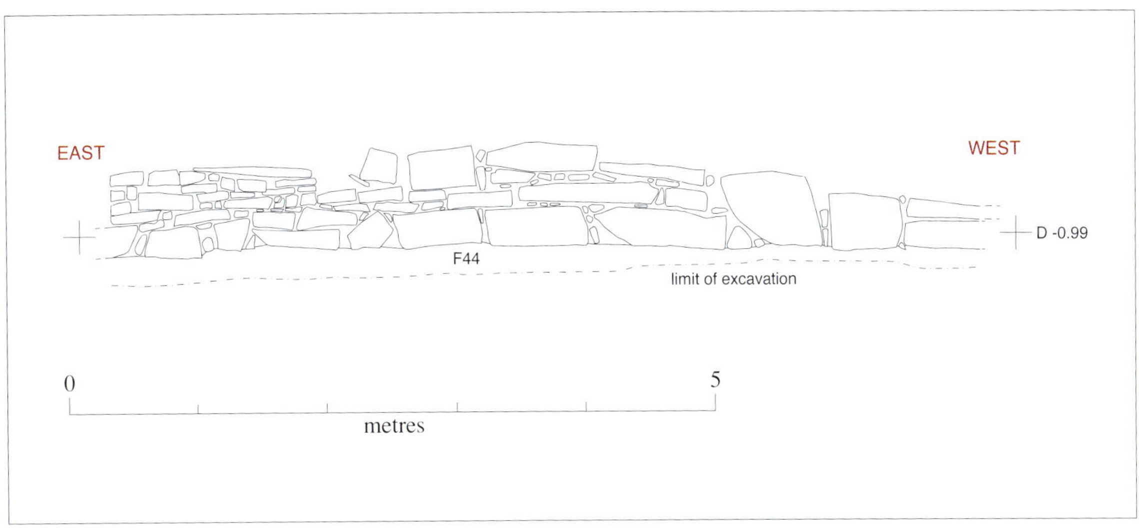

Fig. 4.6. Elevation of north face of cloister arcade wall, Cutting B.

the bowl (Fig. 4.8). This may have functioned as a type of baffle stone to direct the hot air from the fire pit upwards into the drying chamber (Monk and Kelleher 2005, 102). The fire pit (F24) lay directly outside the entrance to the bowl and comprised a rectangular area (1.20m × 900mm) defined by mortared facing stones on the east and south sides and floored with rough paving and mortar. A deposit (F34) of burnt clay, mortar fragments and lenses of charcoal and ash covered the floor of the fire pit to a depth of 80mm–100mm, with concentrations of mortar evident along the eastern and southern sides. Small pieces of oyster shell, animal bone fragments, an iron blade (76) and nine fragments of lead window cames (77) were recovered from this deposit.

This structure most likely functioned as a corn-drying kiln. In areas prone to damp harvests, it was necessary to use some indirect source of heat from an open fire to reduce the moisture content of harvested grain before storage and also to facilitate its threshing and milling. It is possible that non-cereal crops such as flax, hemp and pulses (peas and beans) also had to be dried after particularly wet harvests. Corn-drying kilns have been recorded in Ireland from as early as the early medieval period and were still used into the late nineteenth century along the Atlantic fringes. Since the 1980s, such kilns have been recorded in increasing numbers on Irish archaeological sites (Monk and Kelleher 2005, 77–9). The shape of the Boyle Abbey kiln is the classic keyhole type that generally tends to date to the late medieval or post-medieval period (*ibid.*, 105) although the lack of a well-defined flue is unusual. The stone platform surrounding the thirteenth-/fourteenth-century keyhole kiln at Kilferagh, Co. Kilkenny, is reminiscent of that at Boyle and archaeobotanical analysis of samples from the entrance of its flue produced mostly wheat (*ibid.*, 89; Hurley 1987, 90). Other kilns sampled have produced evidence for the presence of oats and barley as well as wheat. Unfortunately, no samples were taken from the bowl or fire pit at Boyle that might have indicated the crop(s) being dried.

No dating evidence was retrieved from the kiln but its construction over the partially demolished cloister arcade wall indicates a late sixteenth-century date at the very earliest, but it is more likely to belong to the eighteenth century as indicated by the pottery retrieved from the fill of the cloister walk, which is coeval with the rubble platform for the kiln. Corn-drying kilns have been recorded within castles in Britain and Ireland including Glanworth Castle, Co. Cork, where the remains of a kiln were located close to a bread oven, both dating to the seventeenth century (Manning 2009, 146). A keyhole type kiln dating to the fourteenth/fifteenth century has also been recorded within the precinct of Adare Castle, Co. Limerick (Dunne and Kiely 2013, 89). The location of a kiln within the walls of 'Boyle Castle' would likewise have ensured a secure source of grain suitable for grinding, for the military garrison. In the absence of a flue, however, which in keyhole kilns normally ranged from 1.2m–5m in length, it is difficult to know how effective the kiln would have been. The presence of fire-reddened stones within the bowl suggests a conflagration

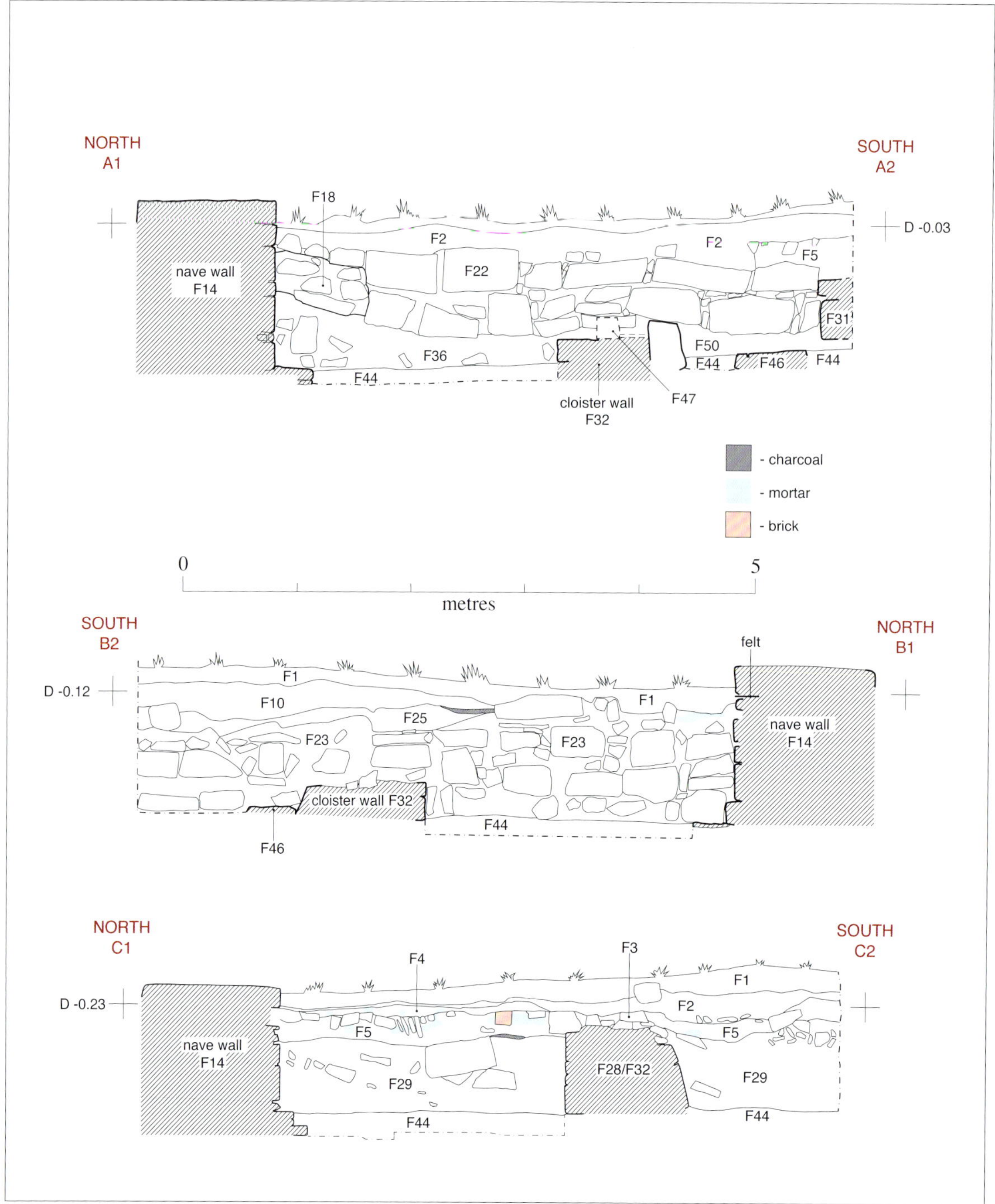

Fig. 4.7. Sections across cloister walk. (See Fig. 4.5 for locations.)

and it is possible that the kiln never functioned properly, with sparks migrating from the fire pit to the drying floor with disastrous consequences.

The floor of the bowl of the kiln was covered by a layer of soft pink/brown soil (F17) with lenses of silt and sand and stones ranging from small pebbles to examples 100mm–150mm long. Small fragments of brick, mortar and pockets of fine powdery charcoal were also recorded within this deposit. The deposits within the fire pit were partly covered by clay with a very high mortar content and occasional brick fragments (F25) and this also extended westward over the rubble platform (F23). A single iron nail (67) was recovered from this layer. A concentration of compact mortar and stones (F26) lay to the south (Fig. 4.8). The prevalence of mortar within, over and around the kiln is of interest and during excavation, the possibility of the kiln having been used for the production of lime was considered. It is more likely, however, that following the kiln's abandonment, the

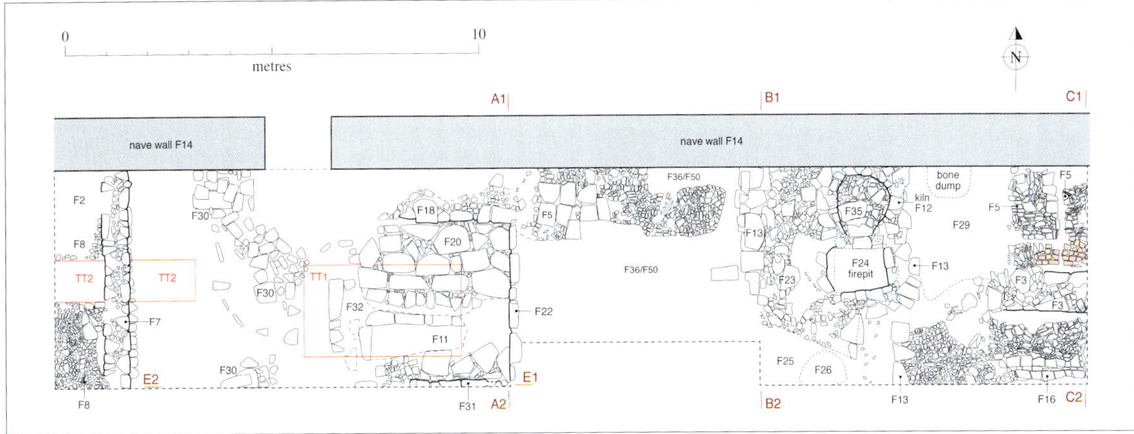

Fig. 4.8. Post-dissolution features revealed in the north cloister walk.

area around it was used for the mixing of mortar during a period of military activity.

The paved structure

The remains of a paved structure were uncovered *c*. 8m to the west of the kiln and at the same stratigraphic level. The paved floor (F20) measuring *c*. 3.4m east–west × 3.4m north–south was bounded by coursed masonry on the north (F18), east (F22) and south (F31) sides (Fig. 4.8, Pl. 4.9). This masonry, surviving on average two to three courses in height was in fact facing built against rubble deposits behind (Figs 4.7, 4.8). The stone facing on the east side (F22) extended over the remains of the cloister arcade wall (F32). Little mortar appears to have been used in the masonry of these three structures that abut one another. Although some disturbance had been caused by the modern trench (F11), there is no evidence that the paved area was enclosed by masonry on the west side, suggesting an open-ended structure. The paved floor was well laid and comprised mostly square or rectangular slabs, some over 1m in length (Fig. 4.8, Pl. 4. 9). These paving stones were set into light brown coarse sandy soil (F37, F40) from which oyster shells, small fragments of wine bottles and a small sherd of Chinese porcelain (99) dating to the eighteenth century were recovered. The precise nature and function of this structure are not clear. It may have been used as a storage area in connection with the nearby kiln in the eighteenth century before the final withdrawal of the military troops.

Another feature that appears to belong to the later phase of military occupation is the wall (F7) that runs southwards from the nave just 0.80m west of the west range wall (F38) (Fig. 4.8). This wall was first recorded in Trial Trench 2 and was subsequently examined in more detail in Trench A. It lay immediately beneath the cobbling (F8) and where this had been disturbed, it appeared just below the sod layer. The wall, which averages 600mm in width, survives two to three courses in height with no visible mortar bonding but incorporates re-used stones with old mortar adhering. It rests on a footing, one course deep, that in turn overlies lenses of clay, charcoal and sand from which sherds of late seventeenth-/early eighteenth-century Staffordshire ware were recovered. Eight sherds (3A–H) of Bristol/Staffordshire drinking vessels of similar date were found resting on top of the remains of this wall at its northern end.

The entire cloister area appears to have been surfaced with either cobbles (F5/F8) or flagstones (F13) that had been set into a layer of grey/brown clay (F6). Items recovered from this clay include iron nails (14), eighteenth-century pottery (15, 16, 19) and a possible iron chisel (17) suggesting that the surfacing was carried out in the later eighteenth or perhaps the nineteenth century. This in turn was covered by a layer of topsoil (F2) before the area was finally grassed over. A large number of artefacts were recovered from the topsoil ranging from glass, pottery and clay pipes to coins and a bronze needle.

The Finds

Approximately 110 artefacts were recorded from the excavation and all have been numbered with the registration prefix E283.

Pl. 4.9. Paved structure, looking east. (Photo: A. Lynch)

POST-MEDIEVAL POTTERY
Rosanne Meenan

INTRODUCTION
An assemblage of 103 sherds of post-medieval pottery was examined, the majority of which were recovered from the redeposited topsoil (F2) (Table 4.1).

The total of 11 vessels was computed using the number of rims present unless otherwise stated. The individual wares that were found are not described in detail here; the reader is referred to the post-medieval pottery report in the Galway City excavation publication (Hurley and Scally 1997) and to the Norwich pottery report (Jennings 1981) for this background information.

BRISTOL/STAFFORDSHIRE SLIPWARE
At least two drinking vessels were present in this group. A rim (43) formed part of a wide mouthed mug or cup and was decorated with marbled brown slip; another cup rim (55) was decorated with trailed brown slip. A base (3c) came from a smaller drinking vessel with a base diameter of 50mm. Its body was decorated with swirls, loops and lines of trailed brown and pale yellow slip.

WESTERWALD STONEWARE
Six sherds (12, 13, 27, 36, 39, 87) came from the same small jug or mug. This would have been a globular vessel with a cylindrical neck. The neck sherd (36) had concentric rilling. The body sherds were decorated with stamped foliage motifs and one (87) had an incised strapwork motif. The neck sherd was glazed in purple (manganese), a colour used in decoration from the 1660s onwards (Hurst *et al.* 1986, 223). The seventh sherd, a handle (72), may have come from a different vessel as it may have been too heavy to have formed part of the mug.

FRECHEN STONEWARE
All the sherds came from bottles. There was one base sherd (46), the bottom of which shows the wiremarks typical of Frechen manufacture. Another sherd (56) featured the edge of a stamped medallion but not enough survived to be able to distinguish the motif.

YELLOW WARE OINTMENT JARS
These ointment jars were made with buff coloured clay with a clear lead glaze which fired yellow. They probably formed part of the same production tradition as the Bristol and Staffordshire slipwares with approximately the same date range. The largest example (104) had a rim diameter of 90mm.

PORCELAIN (CHINESE)
Eighteen sherds from a minimum of two vessels were recovered. The plate (1B/100) had diaper pattern in blue on the rim and a blue floral pattern on its base augmented with overglaze red paint. The tea bowl base (102) had a diameter of 30mm. The remaining sherds may have come from the tea bowl or other bowls.

TIN-GLAZED EARTHENWARE
There were eight sherds of tin-glazed earthenware. At least two washbowls were represented, one of them (101) with a plain white glaze and the other (83B) with a light blue glaze decorated with broad blue brush strokes. Plate body sherds were present along with a body sherd from a drug jar.

STAFFORDSHIRE EARTHENWARE
There was one base sherd (61) of an unidentified vessel form. The fabric is earthenware with an even buff colour and there is an all-over brown glaze similar to that used on Nottingham-Derbyshire stonewares. This is an eighteenth-century ware. It does not resemble locally made earthenware and is more likely to have been imported from Britain, possibly from Staffordshire.

BLACK GLAZED WARES (COAL MEASURE CLAY)
One body sherd (59) may have originated from a

drinking vessel as the walls are very thin.

Two rim sherds (69A, 69C) came from the same milk pan although non-joining. Based on the style of the patchy glaze, they probably date from the first decades of the eighteenth century. A body sherd (69B) came from an upright storage vessel which dated to the second half of the eighteenth century as indicated by the prominent throwing rings and the evenly applied glaze.

POSSIBLE MEDIEVAL WARE

One sherd (75) of possible medieval pottery ware was present in the assemblage. It had a red sandy fabric with many inclusions including stone and white quartz, and a clear shiny brown exterior glaze.

WHITE SALT GLAZED STONEWARE

This was half (107) of a lid from a small jar with a diameter of 40mm. Undecorated.

NORTH DEVON SGRAFFITO

There was one base sherd (73) from a dish.

SLIPWARE

Two sherds (50, 94) came from different vessels; both were made in a fine oxidised red fabric and their internal surfaces were covered in white slip before being glazed. The dish rim (94) had a much lighter yellow glaze.

GLAZED RED EARTHENWARES

There was a group of four sherds, three (22, 26, 93) possibly from the same vessel, made in a highly fire-reduced fabric with an olive green interior glaze. The bottom surface of the base sherd (22) shows parallel streaks created when the vessel was being removed from the wheel. The fourth sherd (58) of the group, also with a reduced fabric and olive green glaze, may have formed part of a small jug or cup as it was waisted with a raised ridge.

There were two rim sherds (16, 60) from different bowls with plain upright rims, made in fine red earthenware with a glossy all-over brown glaze; the glaze on 16 was slightly darker.

There was one jug base (53) which featured small fragments of grog on top of the glaze on the interior base; there is also the impression of a piece of grass, straw or rush. This suggests that the sherd may have been a waster and that it was manufactured close to the find spot. An area within the south range of Boyle Abbey was excavated by Fiona Rooney in 2004 (see Chapter 5). The remains of a kiln were found which was dated, by associated glass, to the early eighteenth century. It is possible therefore that some, or all, of the glazed red earthenware found on this excavation may have been manufactured on the site.

DATING

The pottery was recovered from backfill layers and from above and below the post-medieval cobbling. The majority of sherds were recovered from F2, the redeposited topsoil.

The assemblage can be dated in general from the middle of the seventeenth century to the middle of the eighteenth century. The Rhenish stonewares fit into the earlier half of this time bracket as they are more likely to date to the second half of the seventeenth century. Their presence here at Boyle is further clear evidence that they were transported into the north-west of the country; they were also found at Clogh Oughter Castle in Cavan where there was military activity in the 1640s (Manning 2013, 21–33).

The Bristol/Staffordshire slipware, the yellow ware, the tin-glazed earthenware and the North Devon ware all fit comfortably with a date in the decades on either side of 1700, as does the black glazed ware which belongs to the first half of the eighteenth century. The white salt glazed stoneware dates to the middle years of the eighteenth century; the black glazed ware with the even glaze dates to the second half of the eighteenth century. The porcelain can also be dated to the eighteenth century. As individual sherds of glazed red earthenware are very difficult to date, they offer no assistance in the overall dating though, if produced nearby (see above), they may have dated to the early eighteenth century.

The bulk of the vessels represented here were table wares of middling status. The milk pans may represent some kind of food processing nearby, but the rest of the assemblage comprised vessels that were used at the table. There was no evidence for ceramic cooking vessels, but no metal cooking vessels were found either suggesting that the remains of these vessels, if they were used and survived, were dumped elsewhere. The pottery was presumably associated with the military occupation of the site.

CLAY PIPES

Clare McCutcheon

INTRODUCTION

Eight bowls and nine stem fragments were recovered ranging from the seventeenth to the twentieth century in date.

SEVENTEENTH/EARLY EIGHTEENTH CENTURY

The earliest of the bowls (65), dating to the early seventeenth century, is very small with a bowl diameter of *c.* 8mm and a flat undecorated heel.

A further three bowls (32, 52A and 52B) also have flat undecorated heels with rouletting on the two latter, all three dating to pre-1640. A single bowl without heel or spur (98) has a very similar shape to these earlier bowls.

Two bowls (72 and 80A) have later seventeenth- to early eighteenth-century spurs rather than the earlier flat heel and have milling around the rim. One of these (80A) is marked incuse with the letters I.E. on the back of the bowl, possibly a member of the Edwards family of Bristol (Lane 1997, 228).

The diameter of the other six bowls of the period is approximately 11mm.

NINETEENTH CENTURY

A complete bowl (diameter 16mm), spur and partial stem dates to the nineteenth century. It is very possible that it was made in one of the famous Knockcroghery production houses. The bowl is marked on the rear with the number 43, stamped incuse. On the stem are the number 12 and the start of lettering possibly DE but all of the lettering is somewhat smudged. It has been suggested that the number 43 relates to an address (Norton 2004, 434):

> The '43' element of Samuel's address was used to denote a pipe type in the second half of the nineteenth century. Patrick Devlin, the last Dublin pipe-maker, stated in an interview (Irish Press, 16 January 1937) that the '43' was the trademark of an 'Old Galway House.

In addition to Samuel Gorman of Galway, other manufacturers – notably Patrick Devlin of Dublin – made '43s' up until the 1930s (*ibid.*, 445). However, given that the number '43' appears on several pipes identifiable to different makers with varying addresses, another explanation may also be offered. The date 1843 in association with the name 'Conciliation Hall' and 'Repeal' was noted on a pipe recovered at Kilmainham (Sweetman 1982, 73). It is more likely that, rather than an address for a single pipe-maker in Galway, the '43' relates to 1843, the year that Daniel O'Connell had proclaimed to be the great Repeal Year when a large meeting hall, Conciliation Hall, was built on Burgh Quay, Dublin. The numbered pipe found at Boyle may have been a Repeal type in the Galway/Roscommon area and no pipe of this type has been found in extensive excavations in either Cork or Waterford. A web search (https://www.flickr.com/photos/23885771@N03/sets/72157641456389435/with/12502171803) located photographs of two pipes, one showing DAN O'CONNELL encircling the number 43 and the second stamped with HOME RULE JOHN LYONS in a double oval with the number 43 in the centre.

STEMS

Of the nine stems recovered, just one (79A) is undecorated.

One stem (106) is marked with rouletting and the letters NGOUDA. Three stems (10, 66, 80B) are stamped incuse with L and LE between lozenges with rouletting above and below. This is understood to be the mark of Lluellin Evans of Bristol, dating to 1661–88 and a similar stem was recovered at Skiddy's Castle, Cork (Lane 1997, 235). Two other stems (33A and 33B) have rouletting and could also be Evans pipes but without the initials they cannot be identified as such and rouletting is a typical pattern on stems.

Two further stems (33C and 79B) have both rouletting and triangular stamping around the stem.

CERAMIC ROOF TILES

A large number of fragments of curved ceramic roof tiles were recovered from the topsoil in Cutting 3 within the ground-floor chamber of the gatehouse and to a lesser extent from the topsoil generally within the cloister. These single-curve pantiles have a smooth concave surface while the convex underside is quite rough and unfinished. The nib, where it survives, appears to be roughly rectangular in shape and was located at the end

Table 4.1 Seventeenth- and eighteenth-century wares

Ware	Number of sherds	MVN	Vessel form
Bristol/Staffordshire slipware	13	2	2 drinking vessels
Westerwald stoneware	7	–	
Frechen stoneware	9	–	
Yellow ointment jars	7	–	
Porcelain (Chinese)	18	2	1 plate (recognisable by base), 1 tea bowl (recognisable by base)
Tin-glazed earthenware	8	2	2 washbowls
Staffordshire earthenware	1	–	
Black glazed earthenware (coal measure clay)	4	1	1 milk pan
Possible medieval	1	–	
White salt glazed stoneware	1	1	1 lid from small jar
North Devon sgraffito	1	–	
Slipware	2	1	1 dish
Glazed red earthenware	31	2	2 bowls
Total	103	11	

of the tile. The fragments recovered suggest at least two distinct fabrics – a bright orange/red and a lighter salmon pink. Both types were intermingled and do not appear to represent different roofing phases.

Pantiles were imported in great quantities from Europe into Irish ports in the seventeenth century and continued in use into the first half of the eighteenth century. Clay tile as a roofing material became less common in the later eighteenth century when slate became the preferred material for cladding roofs (Department of Environment, Heritage and Local Government 2010, 35). Given that many of the tile fragments were recovered from within the gatehouse, it is likely that this building at least, had a red tiled roof during the period of military occupation during the seventeenth and eighteenth centuries.

BOTTLE AND VESSEL GLASS

Siobhan Scully

INTRODUCTION

Eight glass fragments were recovered from the excavations at Boyle Abbey. Five are from wine bottles, two are from drinking glasses and one is possibly a handle fragment from a glass flask. All the fragments date between the late seventeenth century and the eighteenth century.

WINE BOTTLES

There are five fragments of wine bottles. There are two lip and neck shards, both from 'onion' bottles. This type of bottle tended to have a squat bulbous body with a short neck. Both lip and neck shards have sheared lips and applied string rims around which a cord would have been wound to keep the cork in place. One (21) dates to between the 1680s and the 1710s and the other (2) dates to around the 1680s to the 1720s. The base shard (6) is a fragment of a wide base, probably also from an 'onion' bottle. It dates to between *c.* 1700 and the 1730s. One body shard (20) has a fragment of an applied glass seal. The seal possibly has the letter 'E' on it. This and the other body shard (91) date to the seventeenth or eighteenth century.

CATALOGUE

Wine bottle. E283:2. Lip and neck shard. Sheared lip with applied string rim. Dark green glass. Heavy patina, crizzled. Neck widens towards shoulder. 'Onion' bottled. *c.* 1680s–1720s. From topsoil F2.

Wine bottle. E283:6. Base shard. Fragment of wide base from 'onion' bottle with kick. Dark green glass. Very heavy patina. *c.* 1700–1730s. From topsoil F2.

Wine bottle. E283:20. Body shard with fragment of seal. Olive green glass. Heavy patina on interior, crizzled. Fragment of seal possibly has letter 'E'. Seventeenth–eighteenth century. From F4, overlying cobbles.

Wine bottle. E283:21. Lip and neck shard. Short neck with applied string rim and sheared lip. Dark green glass. Sloping shoulders. 'Onion' bottle, *c.* 1680s–1710s. From topsoil F2.

Wine bottle. E283:91. Body shard. Dark green glass. Heavy patina. Seventeenth–eighteenth century. From topsoil F2.

VESSEL GLASS

There is one fragment of a foot (85B) from a drinking glass. It is of clear glass and the foot is folded. It dates to the late seventeenth century. There is one small clear glass body shard (85A) which is probably from the bowl of a drinking glass. The fineness of the glass would suggest a late seventeenth-century date. One glass fragment (86) is possibly a handle fragment from a flask. The clear glass appears to have been coloured with a white circular diaper pattern and may also be seventeenth century in date.

CATALOGUE

Drinking glass. E283:85. Possible fragment of bowl of drinking glass. Clear glass with patina. Seventeenth century. From topsoil F2.

Drinking glass. E283:85B. Fragment of circular foot, folded at the edge. Clear glass with patina. Seventeenth century. From topsoil F2.

Possible handle of flask. E283:86. Clear glass which appears to have white colouring in a circular diaper pattern. From topsoil F2.

FLAT GLASS

A sample of six pieces of flat glass (51) was kept from the topsoil F2, all of which are probably window glass. Four pieces are light green in colour and the remaining two are clear with some patination. One of the green pieces is a dagger shape (L. 45mm) and appears to be a quarry with marks from a frame visible along one edge. The two clear pieces also appear to be quarries. One is rectangular (49mm × 15mm) and the other triangular (L. 51mm). All six pieces are likely to be post-medieval in date.

LEAD WINDOW CAMES

Ten fragments of lead window cames were recovered. These may have originated in the monastic buildings and subsequently escaped the salvaging/stripping of building materials following the dissolution of the monastery.

CATALOGUE

E283:92. A single piece (L. 47mm) of flattened and slightly twisted lead window came. Found in the topsoil (F2), Area A.

E283:77. A collection of nine flattened and twisted lead window cames (maximum L.

120mm) with white patination as a result of exposure to heat. Found in the deposit (F34) resting on the floor of the fire pit belonging to the corn-drying kiln.

IRON OBJECTS

CATALOGUE

Iron bar. E283:17. A fragment of a tapering, wedge-shaped iron bar; L. 62mm; W. 9mm maximum; T. 6mm maximum (Fig. 9). Could be part of a chisel or small wedge. Found in the underlay (F6) for cobbling, Area A.

Iron rod. E283:96. Tapering iron rod, broken at narrow end and with indeterminate organics adhering to the wider end (Fig. 4.9). Sub-rectangular in cross section; L. 93mm; W. 12mm maximum; T. 4mm maximum. May be the handle of a spoon or other cooking/eating implement. Found on the floor of the hearth (F47) built on top of the cloister wall, Area A.

Iron blade. E283:76. Narrow iron blade found in three pieces (Fig. 4.9). Both sides taper towards point, broken at opposite end. Highly corroded with some charcoal adhering; L. 95mm; W. 12mm maximum. Found in the deposit (F34) resting on the floor of the fire pit of the corn-drying kiln.

NAILS

Iron nails in various stages of corrosion were found in mostly redeposited contexts. Those described below are a sample of the best preserved.

CATALOGUE

E283:67. A nail with roughly rectangular head and shaft; L. 52mm; W. and T. of shaft near head: 5mm × 3mm. Found in mortar layer F25 in the vicinity of the corn-drying kiln.

E283:14. A collection of six small nails found in the clay underlay (F6) for the cobbles in Area A. They range in length from 41mm to 22mm. All appear to have been rectangular in section; two have slightly domed heads, the remaining have what appear to have been rectangular heads.

COPPER ALLOY OBJECTS

Copper alloy needle. E283:18. A well-preserved copper alloy needle, L. 99mm (Fig. 4.9). The shank has been formed by folding over the bronze strip to give a roughly oval section (W. *c.* 4mm close to the head). The flattened head of the needle has a punched rectangular eyelet measuring 5mm × 3mm. The shank is highly polished suggesting extensive usage. Copper alloy needles have been recorded from at least the Viking period and are well documented in the medieval and post-medieval periods. Numerous examples were recovered from the Viking and medieval levels in Waterford City (Scully 1997, 451–6). The Boyle Abbey needle is longer than the average Waterford example (60mm) and may well have been used for a specialised purpose such as sack making. It was found in the redeposited topsoil (F2) in Area A.

COINS

CATALOGUE

Groat, silver. E283:48. Henry VIII, harp coinage. Reverse, crowned harp dividing crowned h a (Henry and Anne Boleyn). 1534–5. Found in redeposited topsoil (F2) close to late wall (F7), Area A.

Halfpenny. E283:97. Charles II. Reverse, crowned harp, large lettering. 1680. Found just under sod in redeposited topsoil (F2) in Area D.

Shilling. E283:28. William III. Extremely worn. 1695–98. Found in redeposited topsoil (F2), Area A.

Two pennies. E283:49. Victoria. 1862, 1860.

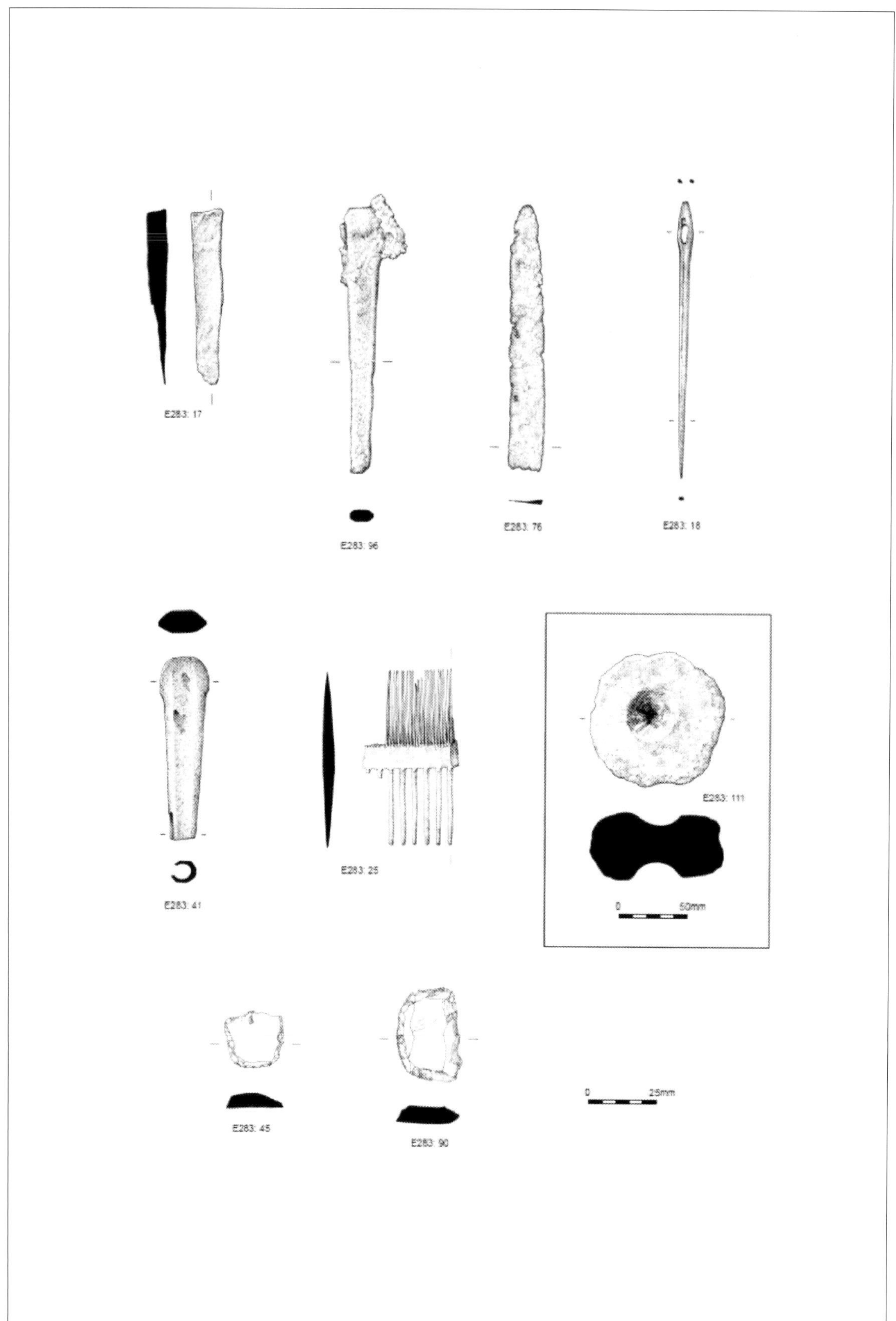

Fig 4.9. Metal, bone and stone artefacts recovered during excavation.

Found in redeposited topsoil (F2) over paved floor (F20).

Seven pennies. E283:7. Five English and two Irish ranging in date from 1842 to 1917. Found in redeposited topsoil, Area A.

BONE OBJECTS

CATALOGUE

Handle. E283:41. Handle for tanged implement, possibly a knife. Broken at socket end. Slightly polished with facets of carving visible (Fig. 4.9). Surviving L. 65mm; W. 9mm at broken end, 18mm maximum at opposite end, Diameter of socket *c.* 5mm. Found in redeposited topsoil (F2), Area A.

Comb. E283:25. Double-edged, single piece comb, with a row of fine and a row of coarse teeth, belonging to Dunlevy's Class J (Dunlevy 1988a, 350) (Fig. 4.9). Fragmentary, surviving L. 33mm, Depth 63mm, T. 5mm. This type of comb continued to be made into the post-medieval period. Found in redeposited topsoil (F2), Trial Trench 2.

STONE OBJECTS

CATALOGUE

Quartzite pivot-stone (Fig. 4.9). E283:111. The quartzite stone has been roughly fashioned into a circular disc shape, Diam. 95mm, T. 40mm. A pivot-hole has been worn roughly in the centre of both flat surfaces and they measure 40mm diam. × 13mm depth and 35mm diam. × 9mm depth. Both holes have rills, display a high degree of polish and have been worn at a slight angle. Found below the level of the base of wall F7 in Trial Trench 2, exact context uncertain. It is difficult to ascertain the precise function of such a pivot-stone but one found at Glanworth Castle has been interpreted as belonging to a horizontal mill with the positioning of pivot-holes changing as they became too large from the spigot turning in them (Manning 2009, 86).

Cobble-like stone. E283:68. Rounded cobble-like stone with large flake removed from one end suggesting possible use as hammerstone. Black staining on one side suggests exposure to fire. L. 75mm, W. 68mm, T. 25mm. Found in backfill material (F29) overlying cloister walk in Area B.

Cobble-like stone. E283:95. Rounded cobble-like stone (similar to 68) with large flake removed from one end suggesting possible use as hammerstone. Extensive black staining suggesting exposure to fire. L. 80mm, W. 70mm, T. 29mm. Found in redeposited topsoil (F2), Area A.

GUNFLINTS

The flintlock musket and pistol were developed in France in the early seventeenth century and continued in use until the nineteenth century. A piece of flint had to be placed in the flintlock's hammer to strike the spark that ignited the charge. Two of these gunflints were recovered at Boyle Abbey and must belong to the period of military occupation (Fig. 4.9).

CATALOGUE

Gunflint. E283:45. Rectangular honey-coloured gunflint, heavily retouched on one long side resulting in rounded corners. L. 32mm, W. 22mm, T. 6mm. Found in redeposited topsoil (F2), Area A.

Gunflint. E283:90. Thumbnail-shaped grey/beige gunflint with retouch along its curved edge. L. 19mm, W. 21mm, T. 5mm maximum. Found in redeposited topsoil (F2) overlying the west range wall (F38), Area A.

LEATHER

Several small scraps of leather were recovered from the silty deposits (F55) in the bottom of the drain that runs north–south under the nave of the church and consequently probably date to the monastic period. One short narrow strip (105) has three stitching holes; other small fragments (110) may have been parts of shoes but these were not located.

TEXTILE

Elizabeth Wincott Heckett

E238:108. A narrow strip of cut silk cloth, 460mm long, and ranging in width from *c.* 4mm to 45mm was recovered from the dark brown/black clay (F50) between the slabs (F46) interpreted as paving within the cloister garth in Area A.

The cloth is woven in 3/1 twill which is not often used. It could be a cutting from a choice piece, such as an orphrey (see glossary below), which was subsequently used perhaps as a bandage or decoration. Since it seems to have been circularly and loosely folded, it may have covered or enhanced some small part of a body. The strip of cloth may originally have been part of a Boyle Abbey vestment, such as a chasuble that was no longer in use because fashions had changed. Since one edge of the silk cloth was folded and stitched, it could also have been a remnant of another item of dress, perhaps of religious or priestly origin. In the sixteenth century and before, vestments were judged to be extremely significant religious items and so were cherished. Perhaps the remnant of silk 3/1 twill was seen as a holy relic and a significant safeguard against evil.

Nine hairs or hair fragments were found attached to the cloth fragment and these have been analysed courtesy of Dr B.M. McBride of Forensic Science Ireland (Garda HQ). One intact human head hair was identified; it was 130mm long, had a natural taper at one end indicating that it had not been cut for some time and, while it was dark near the root, it gradually became blonder along its length due to bleaching by the sun. This hair had been pulled or brushed from the head and had not been shed naturally. Seven other fragments of human hair were identified ranging in length from 5mm–15mm and most had been cut or broken at both ends. These hairs were dark brown/brown in colour. One hair, 40mm in length was grey coloured and was not of human origin.

The textile was found while cleaning between the slabs (F46) within the garth, just south of the cloister arcade wall. These slabs may be the remains of monastic paving within the garth and the textile could have been discarded/lost around the time of the dissolution and before the area was built up when first occupied by the military in the late sixteenth century.

In the late fifteenth/sixteenth centuries a similar 3/1 silk cloth (616:51B) was thrown out with a bundle of 17 other cloth pieces, probably from a tailor's shop, onto a rubbish heap in Bridge Street Upper, close to Dublin Castle. Coins of 1534 and 1586 were associated with the 3/1 cloth suggesting that the Boyle Abbey cloth may be of a similar date (Wincott Heckett 2005).

The excavations at South Main Street, Cork (2003–2005) retrieved 24 textiles from a seventeenth-century cess pit. Among the 14 silk textiles were four twill pieces with similarities to the Boyle Abbey example. Three of the Cork silk twill pieces were badly worn suggesting use over a long period and the possibility of a sixteenth-century date. This date is reinforced by the fact that two of the four pieces were seemingly decorated with ribbons or laces, a very popular way of dressing in the sixteenth and earliest seventeenth centuries (Wincott Heckett 2014, 221).

Fragments of cloth have also been recorded from infant burials. Twenty-one small textile fragments, mostly attached to small, thin, copper alloy pins, were found with burials in the *cillín* site in Mackney Ringfort, Co. Galway. Almost all are linen, while one other cloth was possibly made of wool. Probable human hairs were also found on two sets of pinned cloths (Wincott Heckett 2009, 480).

At the site of a medieval church at Killalee, Killarney, Co. Kerry, the retrieval of copper pins from the graves of two infants in the *cillín* indicates that they were wrapped in shrouds prior to burial. Cream silk fibres were found attached to the pins from one burial that had also been placed in a stone-lined grave indicating special care and attention (Dennehy and Lynch 2001).

GLOSSARY

CHASUBLE	A loose sleeveless vestment worn by the celebrant priest at the Christian service of Mass. From casula (little house), the name indicating a protecting and covering purpose.
END	An individual warp end.
LACES	Narrow woven trimmings, often incorrectly called 'braids'.
ORPHREY	Decorative band on chasubles and other clerical vestments .
PICK	A single pass of the tool (shuttle) carrying weft threads through the shed (an opening in warp).
RIB	A ridge on a cloth formed by the interplay of picks and ends.
TWILL	A weave created by the weft system crossing over two or more warp ends, and continuing under one, over one. In the next row the sequence begins one warp end over thus creating a diagonal pattern in the cloth and under one as above. In 2/2 twill the weft picks pass over two warp and then under two.
VESTMENT	Clothes worn by monks or priests.
3/1 SILK, 7-END SATIN, 5/2 RIBBED, 2/3 LOOSELY WOVEN TWILL	Weaves with warp effects.
WARP	The system of threads that runs from top to bottom or from front to back on the loom. The warp ends are the individual warp threads.

THE ANIMAL BONES

Margaret McCarthy

INTRODUCTION

The animal bones under discussion came from a sediment deposit (F55) in the bottom of a drain (F39) which extended under the western end of the nave of the church. This deposit also contained scraps of leather, twigs and pieces of wood, items which are interpreted as belonging to the medieval monastic period of occupation. The animal bones are extremely well preserved which allowed for many positive identifications, and from their overall composition can be regarded as the discarded meat waste of the Cistercian monks. In 1335 Pope Benedict XIII allowed that carnis could be served to healthy Cistercian monks on Sundays, Mondays, Tuesdays and Thursdays except during feasts such as Lent and Advent. This could not be eaten in the refectory where only 'regular' or approved foods could be served and so a 'misericord' or additional dining room was constructed or sectioned off and the food for this area was prepared in the infirmary kitchen (Beglane 2016, 158). A few small indeterminate fragments are burnt to a white chalky condition from being in contact with intense heat related presumably to cooking activities.

All of the recovered faunal material was assessed for this report and the bones were identified using the writer's reference collections. Data were recorded onto an Excel database, which includes categories for butchery, ageing and sexing as well as species and element identification. Bones not identified to species were categorised according to the relative size of the animal represented, namely large mammal, medium mammal and indeterminate. The material recorded as 'large mammal' in Table 2, for instance, is likely to belong to cattle but was too small to eliminate the possibility of horse and red deer, although the remains of these animals are not present in the assemblage. Similarly, specimens that in all probability were sheep but which may have also originated from goat, pig or large dog were recorded as 'medium mammal'. Due to the anatomical similarities between sheep and goat, bones of this type were assigned to the category 'sheep/goat' unless a definite identification using guidelines from Boessneck (1969) and Prummel and Frisch (1986) was achieved. Ageing data were determined using procedures outlined by Silver (1971) for long bones and Grant (1975) for mandibles. The relative proportion of the different species was assessed using the fragments total (NISP) and the minimum number of individuals (MNI) represented.

ANALYSIS

In total, the excavation yielded 131 animal bones, all of which, with the exception of single piece of antler tine, were found in the sediment of the medieval drain in Area A. The overall composition of the assemblage is given in Table 2, which shows that, with the exception of the single piece of red deer antler, the sample is made up solely of the remains of the three main livestock species.

Cattle constitute the greater part of the identifiable assemblage with 41 specimens representing at least three individuals. Most parts of the skeleton including the main meat-bearing upper elements and the lower extremities such as phalanges and metapodial bones are present indicating that primary butchery was undertaken within the precincts of the abbey. Limited ageing evidence indicates that these were killed at a prime age for meat provisioning, that is between two and a half to four years of age. The bones display frequent cut marks including heavy chops on the upper limb bones, axially chopped vertebrae, fractured skulls and skinning traces with a finer implement on scapulae and pelves. A single horn core indicates a small, short-horned breed of cattle and polishing on the proximal articular surface of a metacarpus is suggestive of this animal being used for traction.

Sheep are second in importance numerically with the 21 identified bones indicating that at least two adult individuals are present based on distal femora. Butchery marks are less common than on cattle remains but there is evidence for heavy chopping of upper limb bones, and skull fragments have been broken and smashed to gain access perhaps to the brains. Pigs were also kept and eaten and at least two adult sows are estimated based on lower canines. The only category of other fauna present is red deer, *Cervus elaphus*, represented by a fractured tip of an antler tine.

POST-MEDIEVAL ANTLER

A layer of rubble (F10) in Area B contained a fragment of a red deer antler tine. The tip was sawn from the main beam and represents waste from craft-working.

DISCUSSION

This small collection of animal bones was recovered from a medieval drain that runs north–south under the western end of the nave (Table 4.2). Excavations in the north aisle of the church uncovered a continuation of this drain (F63) which extended under the north wall. A total of 88 animal bones were recovered from various fills of the northern section of the drain and the faunal composition is similar to the sample recovered in 1984, being dominated by cattle bones with lesser quantities of sheep and pig. Goat, horse, cat and rabbit were also represented. A female goat is represented by a finely sawn horn core indicating that the sheet had been carefully removed for craft-working. Horse, cat and rabbit are all represented by just a single bone but their recovery does point to the presence of these animals in and around the abbey during the medieval period. Both faunal samples are characteristic of domestic refuse and the analysis indicates that the monks' meat diet consisted almost entirely of beef, mutton and pork. For both samples, there is a noteworthy high frequency of cattle bones and beef seems to have played a significant dietary role. The pattern of cut marks on the bones is consistent with food waste and from the skeletal elements present it is clear that live animals were slaughtered and butchered in the immediate environs of the abbey whenever meat was required. While the samples are too small to read much significance into ageing data it would seem that animals were killed mostly when they had reached their optimum age for meat provision, that is, two and a half to four years. This analysis has established the expected occurrence of the three main livestock species in the diet but data obtained from a larger assemblage recovered during excavations within and around the church have shown that fish and both wild and domestic bird species were also exploited to augment the meat supply from domestic husbandry (see McCarthy below). As it stands, the faunal sample recovered during the excavations in 1984 is too small for valid comparisons to be made with other contemporary sites but the results will ultimately be integrated with those from the larger assemblage to

Table 4.2 Representation of species and element

	Cattle	S/G*	Pig	Red deer	LM*	MM*	Total
Antler	–	–	–	1	–	–	1
Skull	4	3	–	–	–	–	7
Mandible	2	2	2	–	–	–	6
Maxilla	–	1	1	–	–	–	2
Tooth	5	1	5	–	–	–	11
Horn core	1	–	–	–	–	–	1
Atlas	1	–	–	–	–	–	1
Axis	1	–	–	–	–	–	1
Vertebrae	4	4	1	–	–	–	9
Sternum	1	–	–	–	–	–	1
Scapula	1	–	1	–	–	–	2
Humerus	1	–	–	–	–	–	1
Radius	2	–	–	–	–	–	2
Ula	–	1	–	–	–	–	1
Metacarpus	2	–	–	–	–	–	2
Sacrum	–	1	–	–	–	–	1
Pelvis	6	2	1	–	–	–	9
Femur	2	2	–	–	–	–	4
Tibia	5	2	1	–	–	–	8
Metatarsus	2	2	–	–	–	–	4
Astragalus	1	–	–	–	–	–	1
Calcaneum	1	–	–	–	–	–	1
Phalanges	1	–	–	–	–	–	1
Sesamoid	1	–	–	–	–	–	1
Rib	–	–	–	–	22	–	22
LBF*	–	–	–	–	18	13	31
Total	44	21	12	1	40	13	131

S/G* (Sheep/goat); LM* (Large mammal); MM* (Medium mammal); LBF* (Long bone fragment) provide a more complete picture of Cistercian diet and animal husbandry practices in Boyle.

SUMMARY AND CONCLUSIONS

Although limited in scope, these excavations have thrown some light on the form and layout of the medieval cloister and on the post-dissolution use of the abbey buildings. The south wall of the nave was shown to be of single-phase construction with a doorway leading into the north-west corner of the cloister. This is in contrast to the three separate phases of construction evident in the design of the aisle arcades (Stalley 1987, 87; see Chapter 3). A substantial drain runs north–south under the western end of the nave and appears to have been constructed as an integral part of the nave indicating that drainage was of some concern at the time of construction, most likely prompted by the risk of flooding from the fast-flowing River Boyle that bounds the site to the south and east. Traces of a smaller drain were also revealed in the north-west corner of the cloister, extending under the cloister arcade wall, suggesting that a lavabo may perhaps have been located within the cloister garth. The width of the north and west cloister walks was established as 2.55m and 2.75m respectively and no evidence of a collation bay or collation bench was recovered in the north walk as revealed during excavation at the Cistercian abbey at Tintern, Co. Wexford (Lynch 2010, 66). The surface of the north and west walks appears to have been a compact clay with some evidence of rough cobbling set in mortar, in front of the doorway into the nave. The cloister arcade wall had a slight batter on the inner (garth) side but no trace of the sill stones on which the arcading would have sat, or of the arcading itself had survived. It is possible that the cloister garth was at least partially paved at the time of the dissolution as evidenced by the stone paving exposed in the narrow strip excavated immediately adjacent to the arcade wall.

Animal bone retrieved from the sediment within the drain that runs under the nave of the church provides the only insight into the monks' way of life. Taken together with additional bone recovered from a continuation of this drain on the north side of the church during more recent excavations, this domestic waste suggests a meat diet dominated by beef, with mutton and pork also represented. The skeletal elements present also indicate that live animals were slaughtered in the immediate environs of the abbey, presumably as meat was required.

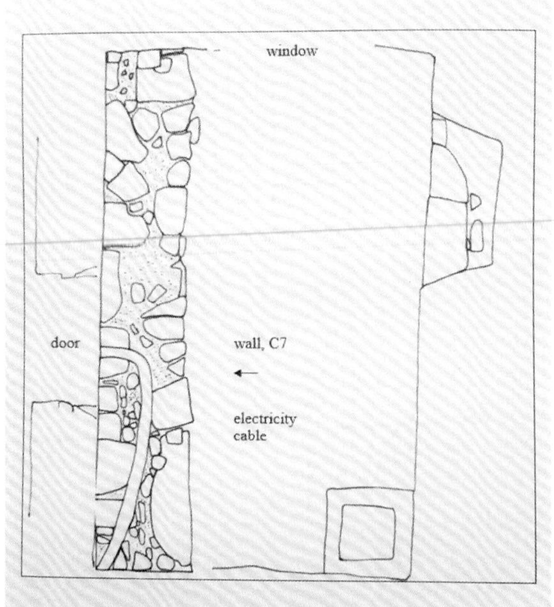

Fig. 4.10. Plan of excavations in the south chamber of the gatehouse in 2018.

The cut strip of silk cloth with associated fragments of human hair is intriguing. The comparanda for this type of 3/1 silk cloth suggest a sixteenth-century date and this fits with the context in which it was found – wedged between two flagstones in the cloister garth, covered by the post-dissolution fill. It is likely that this item was lost/discarded in the mid sixteenth century, possibly at the time of the dissolution and just before the cloister was modified for military purposes. The cloth, which probably originated from a religious vestment, could in itself have been cherished as a holy object but the presence of adult human hair wrapped within the cloth raises the possibility of a relic of a venerated person – perhaps relating to one of the abbots or another senior member of the Cistercian community.

The cloister was extensively modified between the late sixteenth century and the end of the eighteenth century when the abbey was occupied by the English garrison. The arcade wall was reduced in height and large quantities of clay, stones and mortar were dumped in the cloister walks and within the garth area in order to raise the ground level. Traces of cobbled and paved surfaces have

Pl. 4.10. Excavations in the south chamber of the gatehouse in 2018.

survived, and the remains of a corn-drying kiln were revealed overlying the arcade wall and the backfilled cloister walk. The construction and use of the kiln could have taken place as late as the eighteenth century as suggested by the few sherds of eighteenth-century pottery found in the backfill of the cloister walk. The discovery of a tile kiln in the refectory within the south range during more recent excavations by Fiona Rooney (see Chapter 5) is of particular interest as it suggests considerable industrial usage of the abbey buildings during the military occupation. The two-storey gatehouse with its red tiled roof appears to have been largely rebuilt during Elizabethan times but it most likely incorporates the remains of the main Cistercian gateway that would have led into the west cloister walk.

The artefactual evidence relates mostly to the post-dissolution period and all objects were found in redeposited contexts. The pottery comprises table wares dating to between the middle of the seventeenth century and the middle of the eighteenth century and must have been used by the military. The fragments of wine bottles and vessel glass are of similar date. The only objects of definite military usage are the two gunflints. The lack of artefacts relating to the monastic period is disappointing but not surprising given the limited area excavated and the extent of post-dissolution destruction of the cloister area.

ARCHAEOLOGICAL EXCAVATIONS AT THE GATEHOUSE (2018)

Anne Carey

In October 2018 further archaeological excavations were undertaken within the interior of the gatehouse in the south chamber under Ministerial Consent C000878. The entire floor area of the south chamber as excavated. Directly underlying the flooring was a small area of cobbles thought to be post-medieval in date. A broad mortared stone wall was discovered adjacent to the northern wall of the chamber at a depth of 350mm below current ground level. Its northern limits underlie the north wall of the chamber. It was orientated east–west and had a partially exposed width of 7000mm. It stands to a maximum height of 600mm (Fig. 4.10, Pl. 4.10). This wall appears to be part of the medieval west range of the abbey and pre-dated the remodelling of the gatehouse in the late sixteenth century. Excavation of the area adjacent to the east wall of the gatehouse revealed a number of phases of wall construction.

View of the Abbey Church from the cloister.

Chapter 5

Excavations Within the South Range and Abbey Church

Fiona Rooney

SPECIALIST CONTRIBUTIONS BY
L. Buckley, C. McCutcheon, R. Meenan, O. Scully and J. Wren

Introduction

This chapter is concerned with archaeological pre-development and archaeological investigations in the south range and along the north arcade wall of the north aisle at Boyle Abbey. As part of the conservation works at Boyle, archaeological testing was required in the refectory and along the north arcade wall of the nave of the abbey church. In the refectory, a lean-to roof against the south wall was to be constructed in order to provide shelter for the collection of architectural stone fragments from the abbey. Along the north arcade wall of the north aisle engineering test trenches were required to establish the depth of natural ground prior to the proposed insertion of cores and supports for the outward leaning north arcade wall as part of conservation works. The testing was carried out over a period of 13 weeks from June to November 2004.

Refectory

Initially two trenches were excavated in the centre of the refectory, both orientated east–west and measuring 5m in length and 1.5m in width. These two trenches were subsequently joined and extended to the full length of the refectory. The trench, orientated east–west, measured 22m in length and 1.5m in width (Fig. 5.1, Pls 5.1, 5.2). Towards the west, the trench was extended to the north and south in order to facilitate the full excavation of a post-medieval kiln base. This area measured 7.40m × 4.20m.

The earliest phase of activity recorded in the refectory was a cobbled surface found 1.45m below the present ground level (Figs 5.1, 5.2, Pl. 5.3). This was covered by successive layers of burning (C27 and C28) measuring 0.44m in depth; a deposit of mortar, slates, nails and burnt wood (C26) measured 0.20m in depth. This was overlaid by sand (C25) and boulders (C24). These layers are interpreted as building collapse. The burnt

Pl. 5.1. View of eastern part of trench in refectory, taken from t he west.

Pl. 5.3. View of leaning arcade wall

Pl. 5.2. View of western part of trench in refectory, taken from the north.

deposits produced an assemblage of nails with L-shaped heads and these 'are either floor or joiners' brads' (see Scully below). A row of five stone pads (C23a–e) was found on a deposit of large boulders (C24) above this cobbling (Fig. 5.1, Pls 5.1, 5.2). The square pads were made up of uncut limestone and had extensive mortar throughout. These measured on average 1.10m × 1.20m and 0.40m–0.60m in depth. They may have been used to support a column which in turn supported a roof over the refectory during the later phase of occupation of the abbey. A central channel measuring 0.16m in depth was located in four of the bases (C23b–e). A north–south wall was partly revealed which came down onto the cobbling. It was constructed of uncut limestone blocks with mortar throughout (Pl. 5.2).

Kiln

The remains of a dismantled kiln base were revealed in the west end of the refectory, directly inside the doorway from the cloister and on top of one of the stone pads (C23b; Figs 5.1, 5.3, 5.4). It was initially apparent as a layer of sticky red clay with a high concentration of broken ceramic tiles, red brick, kiln furniture and red-bricked flues in the south-west (Pl. 5.4). The kiln comprised the base of a west section of wall and a spread of burnt clay (measuring 2m in diameter and 0.22m in depth) with rows of vertically placed brick along the east side enclosing an area measuring 8.40m north–south. The row in the west measured 6.70m in length and the tiles measured 0.30m × 0.20m × 400mm (Fig. 5.4, Pl. 5.5). A circular clay spread and curved walling

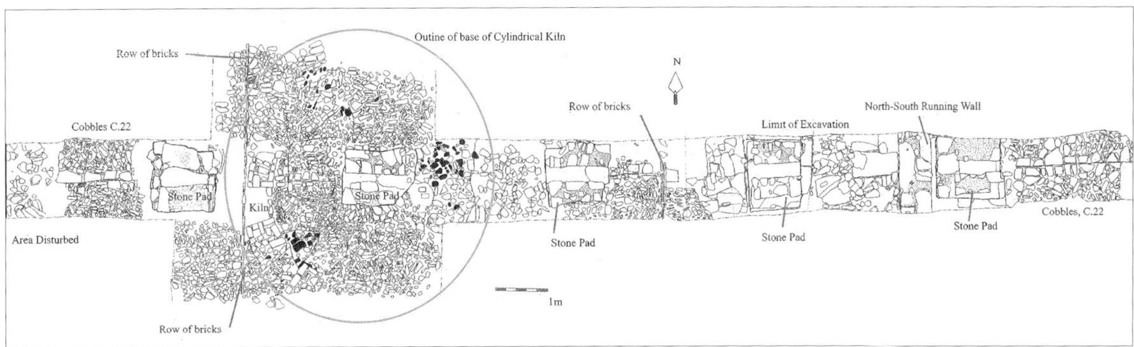

Fig. 5.1. Plan of excavations in the refectory.

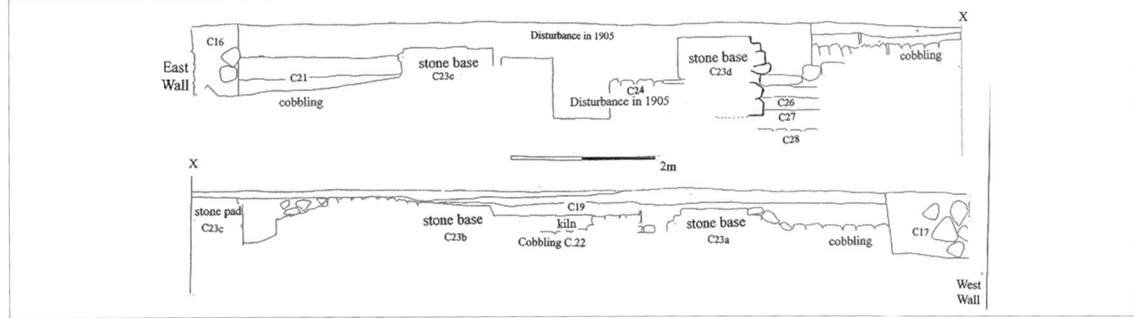

Fig. 5.2. Section drawing of stratigraphy in the refectory.

Fig. 5.3. Plan of kiln after excavation.

indicated that the kiln was cylindrical (Pls 5.5–7). Excavation of the combustion chamber revealed burnt clay (C20) containing fragments of pottery, kiln furniture and tile (Pl. 5.7). Two openings were revealed in the west and south-west. The opening in the west, measuring 0.60m in length and 0.60m in width, was edged with red brick and burnt sand on the base. The opening in the south-west measured 0.70m in length and splayed out from the internal edge (0.30m in width) to the external edge (0.54m in width). These openings are the remains of flues through which the hot air from the firebox entered the kiln. Examination of the kiln waste recorded a collection of small discs resembling biscuits, together with a collection of rods and strips of clay, which may have been used as spacers or supports

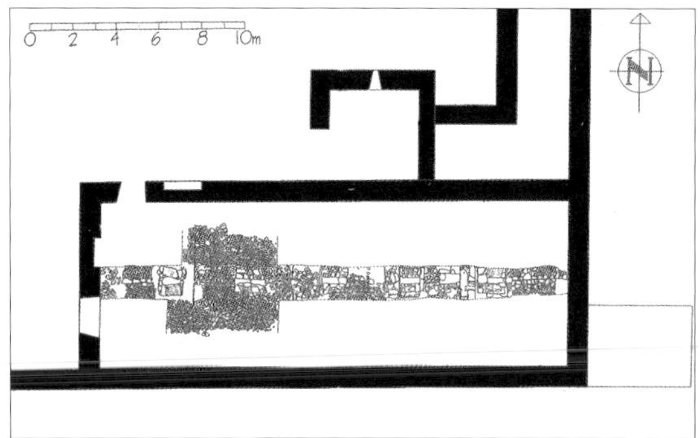

Fig. 5.4. Plan of area excavated in the interior of the refectory.

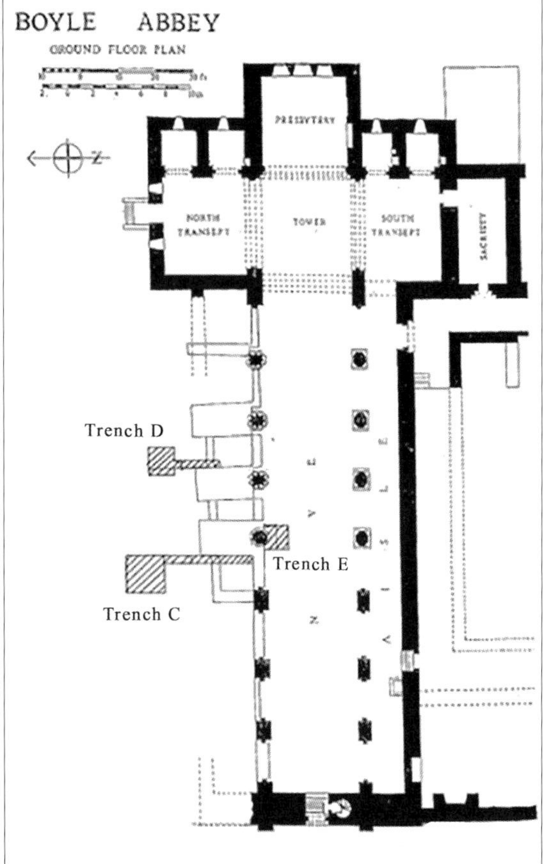

Fig. 5.5. Location of trenches C, D and E along the north wall.

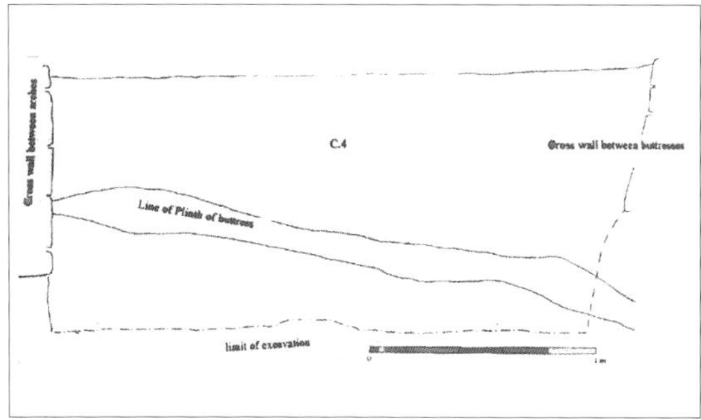

Fig. 5.6. Profile drawing of layers in Trench C, between the buttresses.

during the firing process. It is usual for the kiln ware chambers to be supported by a form of cross walling, and the stone pad appears to have been used in some way to form part of the structure.

Pottery from the kiln consisted of Sandy ware (saggers) which according to Meenan (see below) were 'used in the manufacture of pottery to protect smaller, finer vessels during firing'. A deposit of red brick, red clay and glass (C21) (Fig. 5.2) overlay the kiln and would appear to be contemporary with it. It contained a large quantity of early eighteenth-century glass bottles and large tiles. Some of these tiles were rounded in shape and had mortar on both sides. They may have been used in the kiln and dumped here after the kiln was dismantled.

A dark brown clay (C19) overlay the base of the kiln (C20) in the west of the refectory, the stone pads (C23) and the cobbling (C22). In the east of the trench, near the wall, it overlay a deposit of red brick, red clay and glass (C21). Excavation of C19 in the area of the kiln produced a number of clay pipe fragments. One clay pipe fragment (281), identified by Clare McCutcheon, had a bulbous bowl dating from the late seventeenth century (see below). Excavation of C21 to a depth of 0.20m revealed later cobbling (C22). This cobbling was found at different levels throughout the trench excavated in the refectory. It sloped down from the side walls forming a drain along the centre of the refectory, rising up to overlie four of the stone bases. This layer was covered by a dark brown stony fill (C18) in the eastern half of the refectory. It measured 6.30m in length, had a maximum depth of 0.80m, and contained inclusions of glass, metal, clay pipe, roof tile, red brick and modern material. This layer would appear to be associated with works carried out by the OPW in 1905.

North arcade wall

Along the north arcade wall of the north aisle, three engineering test trenches were required to establish the depth of subsoil prior to the proposed conservation of the outward leaning north arcade wall (Fig. 5.5, C, D and E, Pl. 5.3). Trenches C and D were excavated on its north side beside the supporting buttresses and Trench E was excavated within the nave beside a column.

In Trench C burials were found on the grey marl subsoil (C13). Five were aligned east–west, and preliminary examination by the osteo-archaeologist identified four adults and one child (Figs 5.6–9, Pls 5.8–11). Removal of Burial IV revealed further disarticulated remains (Fig. 5.10, Pl. 5.12) representing three more burials (Burials VI–VIII) (Fig. 5.11, Pls 5.13, 5.14). The findings of the skeletal report identified one male middle-aged adult, two older male adults, one female middle adult and one juvenile. The burials were overlain by a black/brown layer (C9) (Fig. 5.11). This contained inclusions of animal bone, metal objects, pottery and glass. Examination of the pottery from this layer has revealed that it dates from the seventeenth to the nineteenth century, including unglazed roof tiles dating from the late seventeenth century and fragments of nineteenth-century pottery. Some glass fragments (616–18, 631–4) were identified as dating from the seventeenth to the eighteenth century, and a clay pipe bowl (419) dated to the nineteenth century.

Excavation of Trench C also revealed the base of a wall below the plinth of a buttress (C5) (Fig. 5.12). Overlying this was a stony fill (C6) with stones ranging in size from 0.10m × 0.08m × 0.05m to 0.32m × 0.22m × 0.15m and loose brown clay. Architectural stone fragments were contained within this layer and have been retained on site (Pl. 5.15). Other inclusions in this layer were red brick, slate, nineteenth-century pottery, animal bone and metal objects (Fig. 5.12) and a fill of dark brown gritty clay (C4) measuring 1.05m in depth. C4 contained fragments of pottery, glass, animal bone and metal objects. These included one clay pipe bowl (420) of early eighteenth-century date, glass (628) of a similar date, and pottery (387) dating from the seventeenth to the twentieth century. To the north of the buttress, excavation uncovered a layer of stone chippings that may have been laid down during the 1970s when work was carried out on the buttresses. The topsoil contained fragments of clay pipe, animal bone, modern pottery, metal objects and glass.

Excavation of Trench D revealed three more burials, aligned east–west (Figs 5.13, 5.14, Pls 5.16–18). Only the skull and shoulder of Burial I was revealed as it extended into the east baulk. Excavations of Burials II and III found that Burial

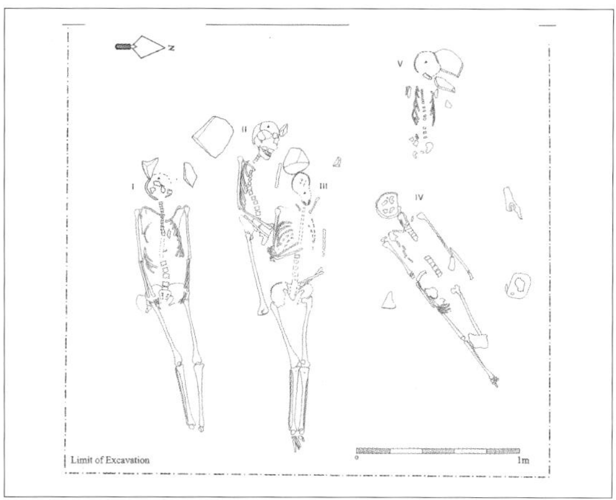

Fig. 5.7. Plan of burials I to V in Trench C.

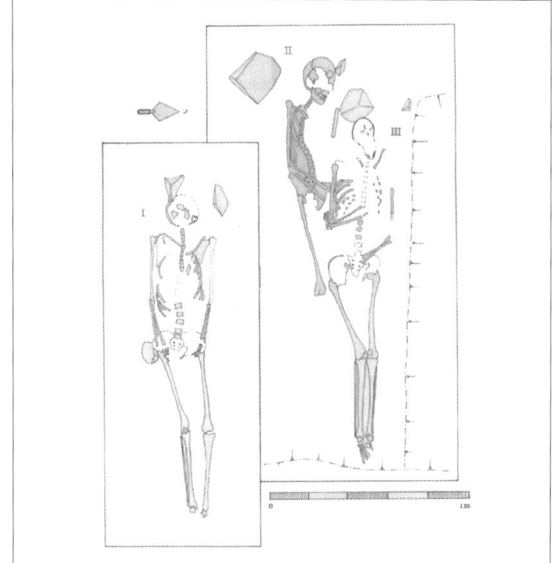

Fig. 5.8. Plan of burials I to III in Trench C.

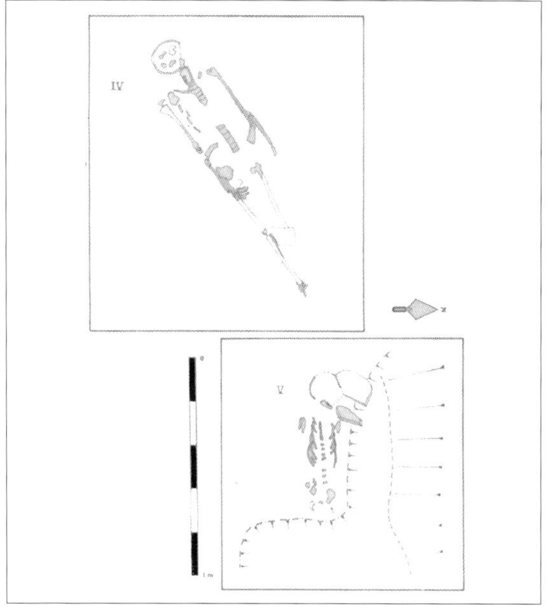

Fig. 5.9. Plan of burials IV to V in Trench C.

Pl. 5.4. Detail of context 19, over the kiln, after the removal of sod, taken from the east.

Pl. 5.5. View of kiln during excavation, taken from the north-east.

Pl. 5.6. View of black layer below kiln.

Pl. 5.7. View of kiln (post-excavation) and cobbling, taken from the west.

Pl. 5.8. View of Burial I in Trench C, taken from the east.

Pl. 5.9. View of burials I and II in Trench C, taken from the east.

Pl. 5.10. Detail of Burial V in Trench C, taken from the north.

Pl. 5.11. Detail of Burial IV in Trench C, taken from the east.

Pl. 5.12. View of disarticulated bone after removal of Burial IV in Trench C, taken from the south.

Pl. 5.13. View of Burials VI and VII in Trench C, taken from the north.

Pl. 5.14. Detail of Burial VIII in Trench C, taken from the north.

Pl. 5.15. Detail of stones below buttress in Trench C, taken from the west.

Pl. 5.16. Detail of Burials I and II in Trench D, taken from the east.

Pl. 5.17. View of west-facing section of Trench D, taken from the east.

Pl. 5.18. View of C10 (layer with burials) in Trench D, after removal of C9 – the black layer, taken from the west.

Pl. 5.19. General view of stony layer in Trench D, taken from the west.

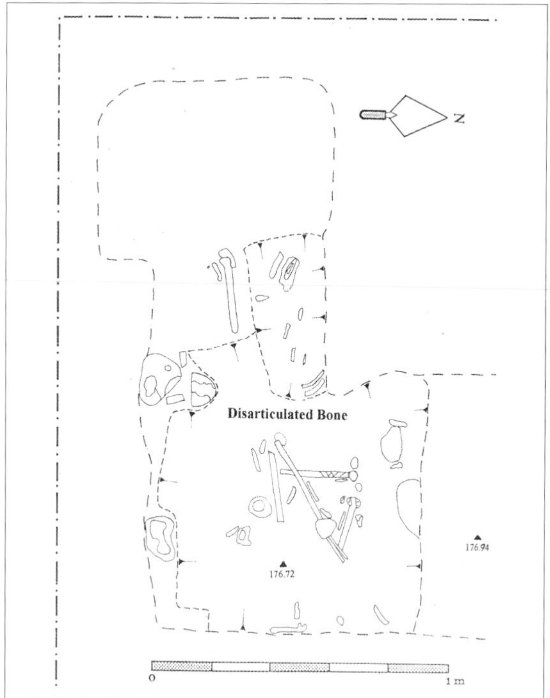

Fig. 5.10. Plan of disarticulated bone after removal of Burial IV in Trench C.

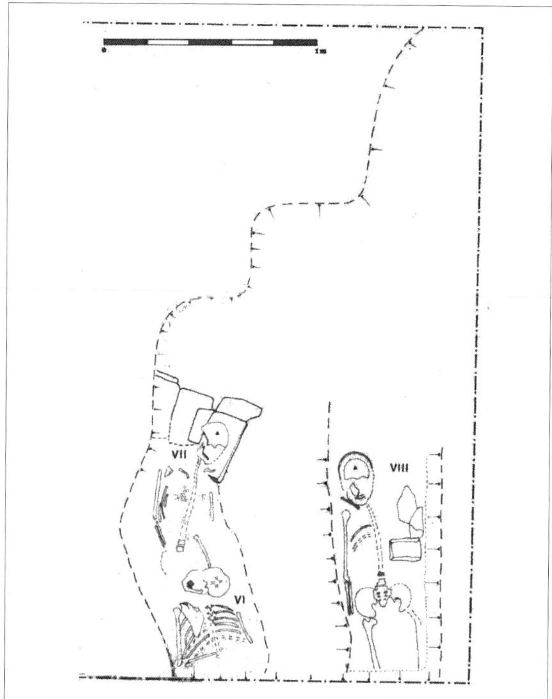

Fig. 5.11. Plan of Burials VI to VIII in Trench C.

II cut into Burial III. The findings of the skeletal report indicate two male middle adults and one female middle adult. The burials overlay the natural grey marl (C13). Examination of the disarticulated bone by Laureen Buckley identified four adults, one juvenile and two infants present in C9. The findings of the skeletal report indicate three adults, one adolescent, one juvenile and one infant present. Seven nails and one wedge were recorded from C10. The wedge is similar to an iron wedge found in excavations by Ann Lynch (E283:17; see Chapter 4). These implements were used to slice wood, with similar examples recorded in Anglo-Scandinavian levels in York, as well as from the medieval Augustinian Priory of Kells in County Kilkenny.

Overlying the burials was a stony layer with rough cobbling (C3) in the centre of the trench (Fig. 5.15, Pl. 5.19). The cobbled area appeared to form a drain as it sloped down from the north of the trench. The average size of the stones was 0.1m × 0.12m × 0.8m. Finds from this layer included tile identified as BA1 and BA2 and ceramics dating from the seventeenth century. The cobbling in the extension to the trench overlay a layer of redeposited natural ground (C7) which measured 0.5m in length, 0.12m in depth and extended into the eastern baulk. A number of fragments of willow ware were recovered from this context dating from the late eighteenth to the twentieth century. The cobbling in the rest of the trench came down onto a stony fill with light brown clay (C6) and a layer of mortar (C8). Stone foundations of the buttresses (C5) were revealed immediately below the sod (Fig. 5.14, Pl. 5.19).

Excavation at the base of Trench E beside a column inside the nave uncovered a grey-brown gritty clay (C15) (500mm in depth) and a light, brown gritty clay (C14) which contained human remains (Fig. 5.16, Pls 5.20, 5.21). The findings of the skeletal report of the disarticulated bone identified a minimum of three adults and one juvenile. A plinth and stone foundations were revealed (Fig. 5.17).

The Finds

CLAY BUILDING MATERIALS

Joanna Wren

INTRODUCTION

This assemblage consisted of 1,806 sherds of post-medieval clay building material, including

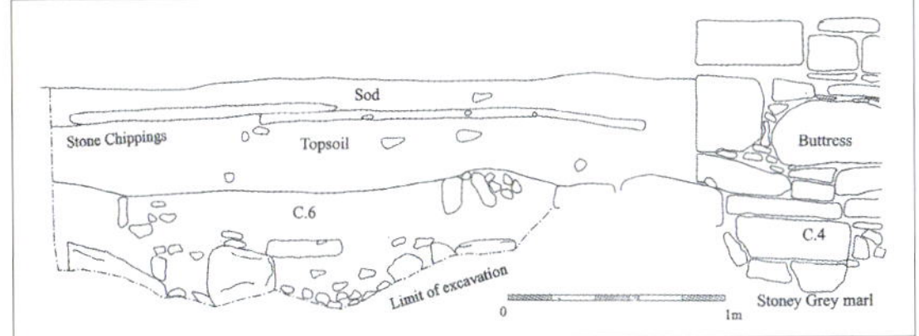

Fig. 5.12. West-facing section drawing of Trench C.

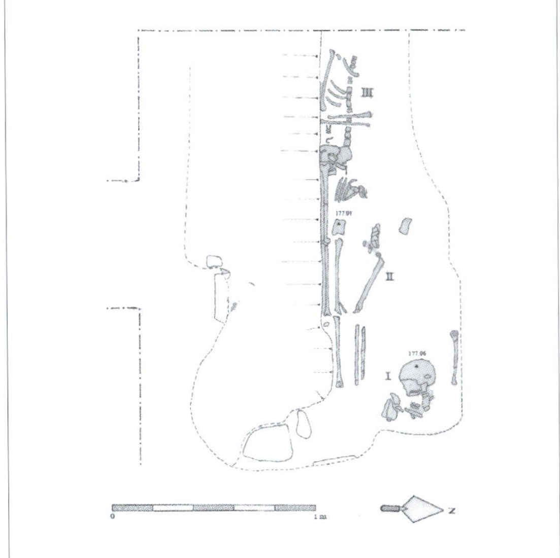

Fig. 5.13. Plan of burials I to III in Trench D.

Pl. 5.20. View of Trench E, post-excavation, taken from the south-east.

Pl. 5.21. View of Trench E, post-excavation, taken from the south.

peg tiles, pantiles, floor tiles, roof tiles and bricks. The bricks included structural material from a kiln. The largest single category in the assemblage was the pantiles representing 61%.

METHODOLOGY

Three different fabrics were identified. Two of these were used in the manufacture of a number of different forms of tile and were probably made locally. They were numbered Boyle Abbey Tile one and two (BAT1, BAT2). The first fabric (BAT1) was used in the manufacture of peg tiles, ridge tiles and pantiles and the vast majority of the assemblage (93%) was comprised of roof tiles in this fabric. The second fabric (BAT2) was used to make peg tiles and bricks (6%). Lastly there was a single sherd or ridge tile made in gravel tempered fabric imported from North Devon.

The tiles were grouped according to these fabrics and then subdivided on the basis of form. They were weighed as the most accurate way of assessing quantity. The total numbers and weights of each form of tile were recorded according to context. The report is divided for discussion on the basis of the fabric groupings and ordered chronologically. Dating is based on a combination of typology, contextual information and comparative material from other sites.

BOYLE ABBEY TILE ONE FABRIC
(PEG TILES, PANTIL AND RIDGE TILES)

Almost all the sherds, some 1,720 fragments, came from tiles made in this hard, coarse fabric, which fired to buff or brick orange, with swirls of both colours visible in cross section. It contained sparse angular inclusions of red or buff matter, and voids where material had burnt out during firing. Sherds made in BAT1 fabric included examples of at least three different forms of tiling and some structural bricks from a kiln. Only 80% of the sherds were complete enough to classify and the majority of these (59%) were identified as pantiles, with smaller amounts coming from peg tiles (10%), ridge tiles (3%) and kiln brick (8%).

A significant number of sherds in BAT1 fabric were found in deposits associated with the post-medieval kiln. Small amounts also occurred in contexts

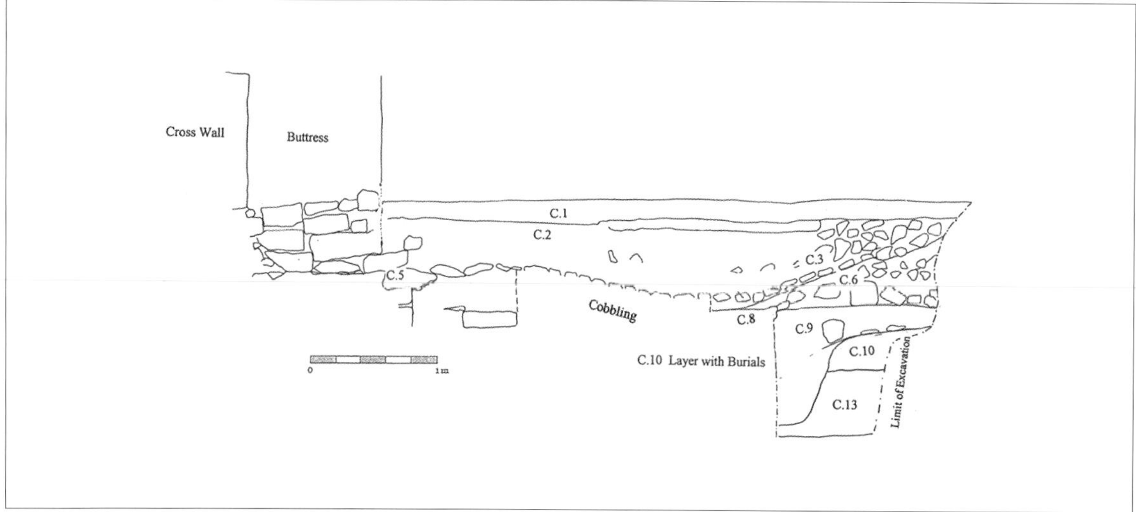

Fig. 5.14. East-facing section drawing of extension to Trench C.

along the north aisle wall and the rest came from unstratified deposits scattered across the site.

- Pantiles
  The vast majority of the sherds made in BAT1 fabric, 1,110 fragments, came from pantiles. These are a post-medieval development of earlier curved roof tiles and they were used on the body of the roof with other tiles along the ridge. Complete pantiles are sub-rectangular in shape with an S-shaped profile and nibs attached inside their upper edges. The nibs were used to attach the tiles, by hooking them over the timber roof laths and they were then further secured by back pointing with mortar from inside the building (Moorhouse 1988, 36).

- Peg tiles
  There were also 150 fragments of peg tiles. These were clay imitations of the flatter forms of roofing, like slates or wooden shingles, which functioned better on the steep roofs used in the wet Irish climate. They consisted of flat rectangular slabs of clay with peg holes and/or clay nibs along their upper edges. They were attached to the roof in horizontal rows, using pegs or clay nibs and each row overlapped the one below it. The exposed lower sections were usually protected with a glaze.

  No nibs survived on the Boyle Abbey tiles and they would have been attached using pegs or nails. The remains of holes were found on 43 of them including 39 sherds with round holes and four sherds with square holes. The tiles with round holes were found in the same contexts as the square ones and their use was probably arbitrary, determined by an individual tilemaker's preference. None of the sherds showed evidence for glaze.

- Ridge tile
  There were 20 fragments of ridge tile made in BAT1 fabric, The remains of low cockscomb cresting survived on one sherd (04E0945:2422) and another two were definitely uncrested (04E0945:0881;04E0945:1075).

BOYLE ABBEY TILE TWO FABRIC
(PEG TILES AND BRICK)

Eighty-four sherds were made in this coarse dark red fabric, which contained frequent inclusions of quartzite and unidentified cream matter all *c.* 1mm in size. The vast majority of them (87%) were from brick, but there were also 11 sherds of roof tile.

- Peg tiles
  The roof tile sherds probably came from peg tiles. Substantial quantities of peg tile made in this fabric were recovered during excavations in the north aisle. None of them had nibs but the remains of round peg holes survived on 11 sherds and they would probably have been attached to the laths on the roof with wooden pegs. None of the sherds showed evidence for glaze.

- Bricks
  The bricks in this fabric were thick and were probably handmade, factors which combine to suggest a date in the eighteenth century for their manufacture (Lynch and Roundtree 2009, 15). Three small fragments of brick were found along the north aisle wall, some more (30%) came from the area of the refectory and the rest (69%) were scattered across the site in unstratified material.

NORTH DEVON GRAVEL TEMPERED WARE (FLOOR TILES)

There was a single sherd (04E0945:2567) from a ridge tile made in a gravel tempered fabric imported from North Devon. No cresting or decoration survived on this piece but gravel tempered tiles usually have low cockscomb crests and are occasionally decorated with either straight or curving lines, incised or thumbed. This form of tile is found throughout Ireland, normally in contexts dating to the seventeenth and eighteenth centuries. The Boyle Abbey sherd came from a deposit within the refectory.

DISCUSSION

The most significant aspect of this assemblage is the fact that it consists almost exclusively (95%) of tiles in one fabric (BAT1) which were fired in the on-site kiln. Comparative evidence indicates a date range from the early seventeenth to the early eighteenth century, for the various forms of tiling in this fabric (Wren 2006, 492; Wren 2010, 141; Wren 2013, 374). The kiln, therefore, must have been in operation during the period when the abbey was in use as a military barracks. At the time, the refectory was one of the few standing buildings on the site and the kiln was probably built inside it to capitalise on the shelter provided by its walls. Tilemakers often manufactured on site (Eames and Fanning 1988, 12).

The kiln (C20) was severely truncated and all that survived was part of the basal levels of its western wall and a spread of burnt clay, measuring 2m in diameter. It was flanked to the east and west by rows of vertically placed brick, enclosing area 8.40m north-south. The clay spread was circular, and the walling was curved, indicating that they represented the foundations of some form of cylindrical kiln (Dawson and Kent 2008, 213).

The area enclosed by the stone walling was the combustion chamber where the tiles were fired (White *et al.* 2015, 37). The two openings in the chamber wall were the remains of flues through which the hot air from the firebox entered the kiln. The air circulated below an elevated platform, a ware chamber, where the tiles were laid to be fired. The burnt clay and kiln waste covering these foundations may be the remains of a clay superstructure for the kiln but is more likely to be part of a temporary roof, replaced with each firing.

Kiln ware chambers were normally supported

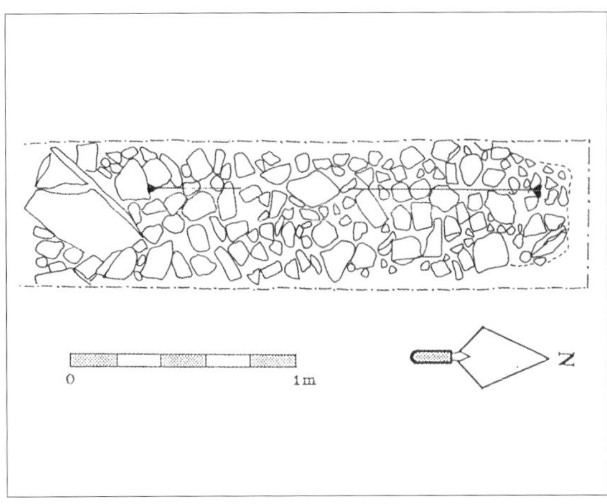

Fig. 5.15. Plan of cobbles in Trench D.

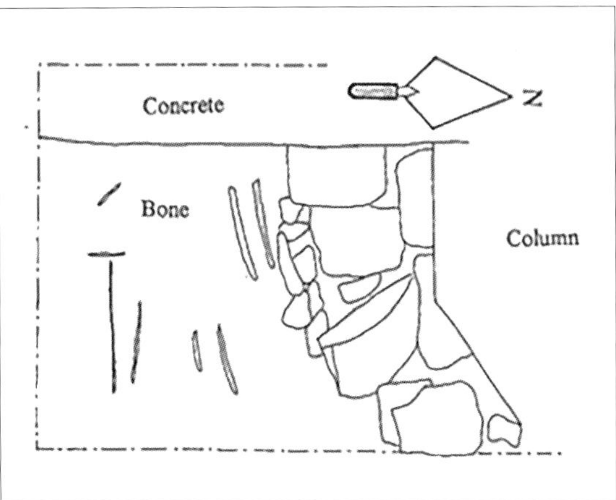

Fig. 5.16. Plan of Trench E after excavation.

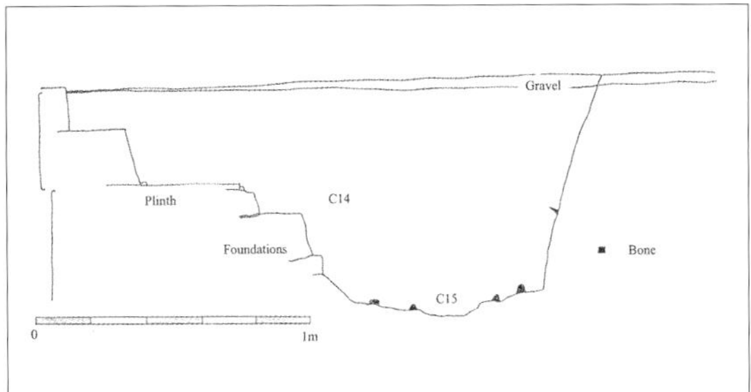

Fig. 5.17. West-facing section drawing of Trench E.

by some kind of cross walling. The fact that the Boyle Abbey kiln is built on top of one of a row of stone pads (C23) is interesting in this regard, especially in view of the fact that these were partially bonded with re-used tiles. These pads extend east and west beyond the kiln and do not form an integral part of its structure. It is possible, nonetheless, that the tilemakers made use of an earlier wall as a foundation for their ware chamber.

The rows of vertically placed brick on either side of the kiln indicate the presence of some kind of shelter or windbreak. This would have been important to regulate the flow of air to the kiln and ensure an even firing. The rows of bricks would have to be the remains of a temporary shelter as they are too flimsy to have supported anything permanent. When taken in conjunction with the stone refectory walls, they could have been highly effective. Evidence for even simpler post and wattle windbreaks was uncovered at a medieval kiln in Nuneaton in Warwickshire (Mayes and Scott 1984, 37).

Cylindrical pottery kilns have a long history. In Britain they were in use from the Roman period right up to the nineteenth century (White *et al.* 2015, 35). The later eighteenth- to nineteenth-century kilns were large with walls supported by steel bands, multiple flues and elaborate surrounding chimneys or hovels. The dimensions and structure of the Boyle Abbey kiln are suggestive of a simpler earlier kiln, like those used in the seventeenth century at Barnstaple in Devon (Dawson and Kent 2008, 215).

The Barnstaple kiln was slightly smaller than the one at Boyle Abbey, with an internal diameter of 1.55m, but it resembled it in other respects. As suggested for Boyle, it was an open cylinder kiln, topped with a temporary roof of clay and wasters for each firing. It was also fired by a pair of twin flues. The same may have been the case at Boyle, as – despite the fact that the kiln was very fragmentary – the two surviving flues were quite deliberately orientated to the prevailing winds. The combustion chamber of the Barnstaple kiln also had central piers to support its ware chamber, in this case made of brick. The brick wasters from Boyle may have been used in walling some kind of superstructure, or more likely in lining the upper levels of the flues.

A date sometime in the seventeenth century for the Boyle Abbey kiln is consistent with the forms of tile it produced. Tiles in BAT1 fabric were found during all phases of excavation at the site, and when talking about the kiln it seems logical to discuss them as a whole. Amongst the sherds that were complete enough to classify, the vast majority came from pantiles, with smaller amounts of peg tile ridge tile and kiln brick.

Pantiles occur widely on sites in Ireland, normally in contexts with a broad seventeenth- to eighteenth-century date and the same is true of the form of low cockscomb ridge tile found at Boyle (04E0945:2422). Uncrested ridge tiles are normally dated even later. It is the presence of peg tiles in this assemblage, however, which may provide a tighter date for the kiln.

Comparative evidence indicates a fashion for peg tiled roofing in the west and north-west during the seventeenth century. For the most part these tiles have been found at fortified structures in lakeland regions. At Clogh Oughter Castle, in particular, the remains of a collapsed roof of peg tiles were uncovered in secure contexts, which dated them to the first half of the seventeenth century (Wren 2013, 374).

Similar tiles were found in an early seventeenth-century context at Portumna Castle, Co. Galway (C. Manning pers. comm.), and amongst seventeenth-century material at Limerick Castle (Wren 2015, 472). There is also evidence that some forms of low cockscomb cresting can be dated to the same period, and on balance it seems likely that this kiln was in operation sometime in the seventeenth century.

Excavations outside the north aisle wall, between 2006 and 2012, uncovered significant amounts of peg tile and it was suggested that they were used in roofing one of the outbuildings there. A depiction of the abbey by Beranger in 1779 shows a building roofed with red tiles, which could be one of these, although it appears to be located closer to the presbytery window. In the area of the refectory there was a preponderance of pantiles, possibly the remains of the last firing from the dismantled kiln. Pantiles also occurred in large numbers in the abbey gatehouse where they probably represent the remains of a dismantled roof.

As discussed above, an eighteenth-century date is likely for the second fabric (BAT2), based on the kind of bricks it was used to make. The fact that both bricks and roof tiles were made in this fabric could suggest that it too was locally made, if not at the abbey somewhere in the wider vicinity of Boyle.

THE CLAY PIPES

Clare McCutcheon

INTRODUCTION

A total of 78 pieces of clay pipe were recovered during the 2004 season of excavation of which 61 are undecorated stem fragments. The pipes have been divided into roughly seventeenth, eighteenth and nineteenth century in date, with a closer date listed where a positive identification can be made.

LATE SEVENTEENTH CENTURY

265: bulbous bowl, milling around rim, oval spur.
266: bulbous bowl, trace of milling around rim, oval spur.
281: bulbous bowl, broken spur.
301: bulbous bowl, fragment, milling on rim.
420: bulbous bowl, milling on rim, spur

EIGHTEENTH CENTURY

315; 342; 384: three stems, no bowl remaining, similar shaped small sub-rectangular spurs.

NINETEENTH CENTURY

300: large plain bowl, knife trimmed, no spur or heel.
316: stem fragment, incised spiral marking.
419: large complete bowl, (external diameter 29.6mm–30.54mm × internal diameter 14.05mm–14.85mm), rouletted and stamped with the number 43 within a circle, three lightly incised combed lines on back and front of pipe along mould marks, through number 43. Spurred, stem stamped with indistinct numeral (322?) and lettering on one side and the final letters of a name (LLY) on the other. This was possibly made at Knockcroghery although no maker with that name is listed as working there (Norton and Lane 2013, 36) and the closest probable maker could be in Limerick where Daniel or Michael Kennelly are listed (*ibid.*, 33). Two other bowls stamped 43 have been recovered at Boyle Abbey (E283; E2399:2:197). It is most likely that the number refers to the Repeal Year, 1843, rather than a series of addresses and may have been a Repeal type local to the Galway/Roscommon area (see McCutcheon below).

STEMS

267: stem fragment, faint overlapping lines.
272: stem fragment, distorted to oval at one end.
273: stem fragment, spiral hachuring with incised dot-in-circle above and below.
275: stem fragment relief marked .95
293: stem fragment, incised spiral marking, circles at top.
295: stem fragment, undecorated, L. 115mm.
316: stem fragment, incised spiral marking.
418: stem fragment, relief marked 290?

GLASS

Clare McCutcheon

INTRODUCTION

A total of 95 pieces of bottle glass and a fragment of window glass were presented for study, recovered from the site of the refectory and along the north aisle buttresses. The bottle glass consisted of the rims and bases from the original assemblage and, following identification and some reassembly, this total was reduced to 89 shards of diagnostic items.

EIGHTEENTH CENTURY

The majority of the bottles represent two types of wine bottle. The first is the typical early eighteenth-century short-necked onion bottle with string ring at the top of the neck and a low kick up underneath. There are eight complete rims with some few further partial rims surviving. The slightly later mallet-type bottles can be seen in the engraving of William Hogarth's picture 'Charity in the Cellar', dated 1740 (Pl. 5.22).

The second group of early to mid eighteenth-century bottles, however, are far more unusual and more interesting. These are French wine bottles, with long necks and no string ring, described as 'wrythen' as the glass has a distinct twist visible on the finish (Hanrahan 1978, 56). These were also found in colonial Virginia (Noël Hume 1961, 105). These bottles can also be seen in the Hogarth engraving, both on their sides at the feet of the drinkers and hanging on pegs at the back of the room. While covered in wicker in the manner of some modern Chianti bottles, they did not have the wicker foot that would allow them to be stood up, and the modern shape would be similar to that of the Mateus Rosé brand, although in a much thinner body. Because they were so identified with France, it appears that even those made in England were known as 'long-necked French quart bottles' (Hanrahan 1978, 56).

Only one rim/shoulder (519) in this assemblage hints at the oval shape and a second rim/neck (520) from the same context (east end of the refectory) has the blackening and sugar-like consistency described above. Two other wanded bottles were recovered from subsequent excavations at Boyle Abbey (see McCutcheon below).

There are also some base fragments from later eighteenth-century wine bottles but no complete ones or diagnostic rims.

NINETEENTH CENTURY

In the early nineteenth century, blown glass bottles were replaced by moulded bottles, primarily produced in Bristol. Three moulded rims and a complete base with a central nipple are typical of these bottles. An amber coloured bottle (452) has a short neck but unfortunately the base does not survive. This would have been marked with a registration diamond indicating a later nineteenth-century date.

TWENTIETH CENTURY

Two clear base shards from a MiWadi squash bottle which was most likely made at the Irish Glass Bottling Company in Dublin. The company was founded in 1927 and used glass bottles until the late 1980s when they switched to plastic (Miwadi 2021).

METAL ARTEFACTS

Órla Scully

INTRODUCTION

There were 82 artefacts in the assemblage from Boyle Abbey, most of which were in poor condition, indicating exposure to a combination of moisture and oxygen, usually indicative of a well-drained subsoil. Many of the finds were structural, mostly nails, with all but one of the artefacts made of iron. The majority of the artefacts in the metal assemblage are post-medieval.

METHODOLOGY

The following discussion is sub-divided into groups according to the function of the artefact, which in this assemblage consists of dress; horse equipment; locks and keys; miscellaneous; structural and tools.

ARTEFACT GROUPS

- Dress
  The best-preserved artefact in the metal assemblage from Boyle Abbey is the only non-ferrous object: a copper-alloy dress pin with a spiral-wound head. It is unusual, and not a type of stick pin per se, but a dress or hair pin, fashioned in much the same manner as a sewing pin, though larger and longer. Smaller sewing pins of this type of manufacture are known from thirteenth-century contexts in Dublin Castle and medieval deposits in Winchester (Biddle and Barclay 1990, 561). This is not a domestic sewing pin, but a larger 'dress' pin. A wire-wound headed pin with an exceptionally long shank was recovered from fourteenth-century deposits in London (Pritchard 1991, 303). The object is most closely paralleled by a find from a late sixteenth- to early seventeenth-century context in Winchester (Biddle 1990, 559).

- Horse equipment
  There were five horseshoe nails in the assemblage, all from the same context (C19). These had quite short rectangular shafts, with the rectangular heads a simple extension of the shaft. They did not have any early characteristics, such as fiddle key heads or expanded head with 'ears', and indeed differed little from modern day horseshoe nails. 'Nails [with] a square or rectangular head seem generally to have stood proud of the shoe, though often worn level...the shank rectangular in section, often quite broad to suit a rectangular hole are found with Type 4 shoes from London dated by ceramics to the late fourteenth and early fifteenth century (Clark 1995, 88). The examples from Boyle Abbey are likely to date from the English army's occupation of the site in the sixteenth to eighteenth centuries.

- Locks and keys
  A tentative identification of an unusually shaped iron bar is that it may have functioned as a latch rest. It has an outline like that of a knife, but with

a flat terminal rather than a point, and the bar is an even thickness throughout. The rectangular-sectioned bar is straight on one side, while the opposite side drops halfway to a tapered end. As such it is somewhat similar to two objects identified as latch rests from medieval levels in York. The York examples are described as having 'a tapering tang which is widened out into a triangular catch at the thicker end' (Ottaway and Rogers 2002, 28–36). Egan has cast doubt on the identification of these objects and suggests that they are simply a form of hook as no suitable latches are known from medieval context. The Boyle Abbey example is from a post-medieval context within the refectory area (C19).

- Miscellaneous
  There are seven iron bars in the assemblage, ranging from 46mm to 232mm in length. None exceeds 11mm in width. Two come from the post medieval kiln built in the area of the refectory. It is possible they originated as part of a grille within the kiln. The other four come from a post-medieval context also within the refectory (C19) and could also have been associated with the kiln. The remaining two (690 and 692) are relatively small, but both have an angled terminal at one end, with the opposite terminal broken. Though incomplete, and thus shorter, they are similar to the angled terminal of a 'sear' from a matchlock musket, such as was found in Clogh Oughter, dating from the siege there in the seventeenth century (Shiels 2013, 148). An iron disc with an inner rim around the edge is most probably the covering of a button. It would have had an inner plate with a central loop, or eye, to attach to the cloth.

- Structural
  The majority of the structural items were nails. There were 62 nails, 50 of which were hand-wrought rectangular-shafted examples, usually with an originally round head, though much damage had been caused to most through use and subsequent corrosion. These are ubiquitous from the Iron Age to the later medieval period, until mechanisation became widespread from the late eighteenth century. Several of these simple nails had adhesions of charcoal in the corrosion products. Interestingly, the remaining 12 nails had L-shaped heads. These are either floor or joiners' brads. These 'tapering nails of parallel thickness with heads projecting only on one side, are used to connect parts together where nail hole is required to be of the minimum size (Mitchell 1944, 205). All of them are from the same context: a layer below the stone layer in the refectory. It is possible they indicate the former presence of a wooden floor. Also from this context came two iron brackets, with rivets still *in situ*.

Pl. 5.22. William Hogarth 1740 'Charity in the Cellar' engraving.

- Tools
  Only one artefact can be classified as a tool, and this is the small iron wedge from Trench D (C10). It is comparable to a similar iron wedge found in an earlier phase of the excavations at Boyle Abbey conducted by A. Lynch (E283:17). The tapered bar has a flat end, as the wedge was needed to slice into wood, not become embedded in it. These tools have a long history, found for example in Anglo-Scandinavian levels in York. Three similar objects were recovered in excavations in the medieval Augustinian priory of Kells, Co. Kilkenny (Ottaway 1992, 530).

POTTERY

Rosanne Meenan

INTRODUCTION

The assemblage of pottery retrieved during archaeological excavations at Boyle Abbey in 2004 comprised material probably manufactured in the kiln that was exposed during the excavation and other wares commonly found on excavation sites dating from the second half of the seventeenth century until the nineteenth century.

The assemblage, comprising 306 sherds, was examined and recorded according to the context in which it was found; each sherd has its individual find number recorded on it. Table 5.1 shows the number of sherds in the assemblage and the minimum number of vessels represented (MVR) which is based on the presence of differently shaped and decorated rims and handles. The kiln waste was weighed.

The assemblage was recovered from mixed contexts and was in the main unstratified. Some pieces were found in the vicinity of the kiln, in layers overlying the remains of the kiln and the burnt red clay layer. Two groups could be distinguished in the assemblage. The first group consisted of the domestic pottery which was used when the site was a barracks; the second group comprises a corpus of saggars that was probably manufactured in the kiln on the site.

SEVENTEENTH- TO MID EIGHTEENTH-CENTURY WARES

- Black glazed ware
  There were eight sherds made from clay found in the coal measure clays of western England and north-east Wales, including the production centre of Buckley. Two storage vessels were represented. The Boyle sherds can probably be dated to the late seventeenth century and to the early years of the eighteenth century, as they featured the brown-purple glaze typical of production at that time.

  There were two sherds of black glazed ware from a different source of production and which could have been produced more locally to Boyle. One milk pan was represented.

- Frechen and Fulham stonewares
  Jugs were made in these stonewares, the former from the Rhineland dating from the seventeenth century, the latter made in London in imitation of the German wares and dating from the end of the seventeenth century.

- North Devon wares
  There was a small amount of material from the North Devon production sites, which dates predominately in Ireland to the last third of the seventeenth century and into the eighteenth century. One vessel was represented by the base of an unusual form (368) on which a handle or foot springs out horizontally from the angle of the base and the wall; the remainder comprised fragments of roof tiles.

- Portuguese faience
  This was a sherd (246) of Portuguese faience comprising the rim of a plate. There were two shades of blue paint on both surfaces; a spiral was the only pattern to be identified. The quality of glaze and paint suggests that the sherd was Portuguese, and thereby dating from the middle years of the seventeenth century.

- Tin-glazed earthenware
  Four vessels were represented here comprising a bowl, a charger, a chamber pot and a drug jar identified by its base. The charger (256/257) was decorated with a floral pattern along the rim and dates to the middle years of the eighteenth century. Apart from one other sherd that was decorated with a floral pattern the remainder of the sherds featured plain white glaze.

- White salt glazed earthenware
  There was one sherd of this fine stoneware dating from the first half of the eighteenth century.

- Yellow ware
  There was one sherd of this yellow-glazed earthenware.

- Westerwald
  There was one sherd from a stoneware jug, dating from the eighteenth century.

MID EIGHTEENTH- TO NINETEENTH-CENTURY WARES

- Nineteenth-century stoneware
  Of the eight sherds in this group, there was one ink bottle present.

Table 5.1 Seventeenth-, eighteenth- and nineteenth-century wares

Ware	Number of sherds	MVR	Forms
Nineteenth-century stoneware	8	1	1 ink bottle
Banded ware	1	1	1 bowl
Black glazed ware (coal measure)	8	2	2 storage vessels
Black glazed ware (local?)	2	1	1 milk pan
Brown glazed white earthenware	1	–	
Brown Staffordshire	1	1	1 teapot (lid)
Creamware	4	–	
Frechen stoneware	4	1	1 jug (by handle)
Fulham stoneware	1	–	
Glazed red earthenware	33	8	4 jars, 1 dish, 1 milk pan, 1 chamber pot, 1 mug (possible identification by base)
Ironstone	1	–	
Sandy ware (saggar)	134	8	3 bowls, 4 saggars, 1 milk pan
North Devon gravel-free	1	–	
North Devon gravel-tempered	10	2	1 footed vessel (identified by foot), 1 roof tile
Portuguese faience?	1	1	1 plate
Shell edged	1	1	1 plate
Slipware	2	–	
Tin-glazed earthenware	19	4	1 charger, 1 chamber pot, 1 bowl, 1 drug jar (identified by base)
Transfer-printed ware	29	7	1 saucer, 6 plates
Unglazed	39	4	4 flowerpots
White earthenware	3	–	
White salt glazed stoneware	1	–	
Yellow ware (Staffordshire?)	1	–	
Westerwald	1	–	
Total	306	42	
Kiln waste	14,110g		

- Nineteenth-century white earthenware
  Three sherds of this undecorated ware were found.

- Banded ware
  This ware dates to the early nineteenth century. One bowl was represented.

- Brown glazed ware and brown Staffordshire ware
  These wares may have been produced in Staffordshire, dating from the late eighteenth century or into the nineteenth century. A tea pot was represented by a lid.

- Creamware
  There were four body sherds of this fine table ware of the mid to late eighteenth century.

- Glazed red earthenware and slipware
  Glazed red earthenwares were made locally around the country although little is known of the industry. There was production from the seventeenth century up until the twentieth century, but as forms and styles changed little over those decades and centuries, it is very difficult to suggest close dating for different forms. The assemblage here was not unusual, comprising jars, a dish, a chamber pot and a possible mug identified by the straight profile rising from the base. A number of the glazed red earthenware sherds may have been made in the Boyle kiln, as the fabrics resemble that of the saggars. Others, however, were clearly not of the same fabric and were probably made in kilns elsewhere. These were domestic wares, probably used by the garrison stationed in the barracks. There were also sherds decorated with trailed slip.

- Ironstone
  One sherd (192) was present. It came from an upright bowl with plain white glaze and a moulded thistle pattern on the exterior.

- Shell-edged ware
  One sherd was present.

- Transfer-printed ware
  There were 29 sherds of transfer-printed ware comprising one saucer and six plates. The individual plates were identified by the patterns on them. The willow pattern was present along with other Chinese patterns and there was also a pattern of intertwined ropes.

- Unglazed earthenware
  This was a group of sherds which overwhelmingly comprised flowerpots identified by the base perforations and by their rims. The fabric was very fine and dense, with very few visible inclusions but with some voids where inclusions have fallen out, and buff in colour. They were highly fired, very well made with throwing rings on the interior. The rims were very slightly squared, beaded or undifferentiated. Bases were perforated. There was no evidence for glaze. Rim diameters ranged from 120mm–200mm. There was one other sherd of unglazed earthenware, probably also from a flowerpot in a different fabric.

- Sandy ware (saggars)
  This was a distinct group of vessels recovered from the excavation. It was distinctive by its fabric and by the characteristics of the vessels which were made in the fabric; they were primarily saggars, used in the manufacture of pottery to protect smaller, finer vessels during firing. The fabric was sandy with grains of quartz and very sparse mica. The texture was fine and dense. There were voids in the fabric, as if the clay had not been blended thoroughly or as a result of inclusions falling out. The colour ranged from pale grey to very light brown-cream. The surface on some sherds had a rough feel. The vessels were wheel-thrown, in one piece, with very prominent throwing rings on the interior walls of the vessels. In general, the walls of the vessels were very thick.

  The bulk of the vessels in this fabric were saggars. They were identified by their rims which ranged in diameter from 120mm–200mm. The rims were heavy, squared and everted. No profile survived so it was not possible to determine original heights. The walls of the jars were not straight sided; rather they were constricted below the rims and occasionally the bases were splayed.

There was no evidence on any of the rim sherds for handles. Some bases had been wiped with a blade leaving parallel scoring but otherwise they did not appear to have been treated in any way.

Five sherds were perforated. One of them showed the perforation 110mm below the rim; otherwise it was not possible to determine where the perforations were located on the vessels. None of sherds showed evidence for glazing. The reason for the absence of glaze on the sherds is not clear. Saggars themselves would not be glazed but they would show drips and blobs of glaze from the other vessels that were being fired in the kiln at the same time. Interestingly, none of the roof tiles, also produced in the kiln, was glazed.

None of the sherds feature sooting or other evidence for use; there was no visual evidence that smaller vessels had been inserted inside them. There are some badly formed sherds that could be counted as wasters and therefore useless. There are other sherds that were faulty, but which nevertheless would have been functional. It is highly likely that these saggars were manufactured in the kiln. However, no direct link could be observed between the saggars and the items of glazed red earthenware that were found on the excavation. Small vessels which would have been fired inside the saggars were not observed in the assemblage.

- Other vessels in sandy fabric

  There were a small number of vessels made in the same fabric as the saggars. They included a flowerpot (92), recognisable by the perforation through the base and distinct from the other flowerpots that were found on the excavation. There were remains of a milk pan (81) with a rim diameter of 300mm and with a flat everted rim; this vessel showed no sign of glaze. The profiles of three shallow bowls (95, 164, 224) were present, all of them straight sided with flat everted rims. The base diameters ranged from 120mm–26mm, the rim diameters from 130mm–180mm and the height from 42mm–50mm. The flat rim of 164 featured two stamped circles. They were all wheel-thrown in one piece and none showed any evidence for glaze. Similar vessels were classified as pans when excavated at the Donyatt potteries although they tended to be glazed on the interiors (Coleman-Smith and Pearson 1988, 239, no.12/59). It is also possible that the Boyle vessels were small saggars although they were very finely made.

PARALLELS

Three saggars with splayed bases were found during investigation of a dump of wasters from a kiln at Castle Hill, Great Torrington, North Devon (Allan *et al.* 2007, 140–2); the excavators were of the opinion that production at this kiln ceased before 1735. The Castle Hill saggars would have held small vessels only and the excavators observed that very few small vessels were found in the waste material suggesting that the saggars had served their purpose in protecting their contents during firing (*ibid.*168). Saggars were also found during examination of another deposit of kiln waste in Bideford, North Devon. The illustrated rims showed the same heavy profiles with approximately the same diameters as the Boyle examples; splayed saggar bases were also found here (Allan *et al.* 2005, 188). There was little dating evidence for the deposit, but the excavators suggested a date in the later seventeenth century due to the absence of certain forms (*ibid.*, 174).

THE KILN WASTE

An estimated 14,110kg of kiln waste were recovered from the excavation. All of this waste was fired. There was a collection of small discs which resembled biscuits, flattened on one surface but rougher on the other surface; they had diameters of approximately 50mm. There was a collection of crudely formed rods and strips of clay of differing diameters and thicknesses; many of them featured notches or regular depressions as if either they had been pressed down on an object or objects had been pressed down on them before firing. They may have been used as spacers or supports during the firing process, but again there was no evidence for glaze on them. There was little or no evidence for pieces of pots stuck to each other as a result of misfiring. The evidence indicates that this was just a tile kiln.

DATING OF ASSEMBLAGE

The range of wares from all the contexts in which they were found was mixed in date. The assemblage

Table 5.2 Minimum number of adult individuals in Trench C

Bone	Location	Left	Right
Humerus	Burials	3	3
	Disarticulated	3	4
	Total	6	7
Radius	Burials	2	3
	Disarticulated	2	3
	Total	4	6
Femur	Burials	3	4
	Disarticulated	2	2
	Total	5	6
Frontal Bone	Burial	4	3
	Disarticulated	2	2
	Total	6	5
Parietal	Burial	3	3
	Disarticulated	2	3
	Total	5	6

of domestic vessels dating from the late seventeenth century/early eighteenth century was not large. The range of vessel types, on the whole, was standard for its time and was more than likely used by the occupants of the barracks who were in residence at this period. The pottery that can be dated to the later eighteenth century may also have been deposited by the troops if they were still in occupation at that time; alternatively, they could have been deposited by other occupants of the abbey if such existed or by the townspeople of Boyle.

A seventeenth- or early eighteenth-century date for the use of the kiln is suggested by Wren in her discussion of the roof tiles found on the excavation. This is based on the typology of the numerous peg tiles found in association with the kiln. If the tiles date to that period and if the saggars and tiles were in production at the same time, then it is clear that the manufacture of the saggars must date to the seventeenth or early eighteenth century.

POTTERY PRODUCTION IN CONNACHT

Lewis (1837) cited clay sources in Roscommmon south of Boyle at Kilmean (176) and near Roscommon town (526); coarse pottery was made near Dromahair and Leitrim (255) but Lewis did not refer to the clay source in the latter cases. The clay sources in Roscommon were at least 30km distant from Boyle and other closer clay sources are not known to the writer.

A destroyed kiln was excavated by Anne Carey in the centre of Tuam, Co. Galway in 1992 (Carey and Meenan 2004, 37–45). It was a brick structure, comprising a circular oven with a single flue. The oven was 1.74m in diameter and the flue was *c.* 1.96m long with a mortared limestone entrance. It appeared that the kiln had been deliberately destroyed, with many pottery finds inside the oven. Carey suggested that this kiln operated in the mid eighteenth century and was probably destroyed in the 1770s (*ibid.*, 44–5). Small straight-sided bowls were also found here (*ibid.*, 42).

Table 5.3 Minimum number of adult individuals in Trench D

Bone	Location	Left	Right
Radius	Burials	1	2
	Disarticulated	4	4
	Total	5	6
Femur	Burials	1	2
	Disarticulated	5	4
	Total	6	6
Frontal Bone	Burial	1	2
	Disarticulated	2	3
	Total	3	5
Parietal	Burial	0	1
	Disarticulated	5	2
	Total	5	3

SKELETAL REPORT

Laureen Buckley

INTRODUCTION

Trench C contained five burials and Trench D contained three burials. Some disarticulated human remains were found in Trench E.

POPULATION CHARACTERISTICS

In total there were eight burials excavated, five from Trench C and three from Trench D. The amount of disarticulated bone from Trench C indicates that there were at least four adults, three juveniles and one infant represented in it. In Trench D, context 9 had four adults, one juvenile and two infants present. Context 10 in Trench D had three adults, one adolescent, one juvenile and one infant present. The disarticulated bones with no context in Trench D, do not increase the minimum number of individuals from either context 9 or context 10. In order to assess whether any of the disarticulated adult remains could have come from the burials, the most common skeletal elements from the burials and disarticulated remains from each trench are summarised in Tables 5.2 and 5.3.

Thus, it can be seen that, when the bones missing from the burials are taken into account, the absolute minimum number of adult individuals from Trench C is seven, based on the number of right humeri.

As there were three juvenile skulls present among the disarticulated remains from Trench C, and Skeleton 5, the juvenile in Trench C, also had skull present, then the minimum number of juveniles in Trench C is four. There was also one infant represented.

TRENCH D

There were three adult burials in Trench D. The disarticulated remains indicated a minimum of four adults from context 9, three adults from context 10, one adolescent from context 10, one juvenile from context 9, one juvenile from context 10, two infants from context 9 and one infant from context 10. Bones from other contexts in Trench D did not influence the number of individuals.

Again, as there was a possibility that some of the disarticulated bone could have come from the burials in Trench D. The most common bones from the burials and all disarticulated contexts were

Table 5.4 Minimum number of individuals in Trenches C, D and E

	Adults	Adolescents	Juveniles	Infants	Total
Trench C	7	0	4	1	12
Trench D	7	1	2	2	12
Trench E	3	0	1	0	4
Total	17	1	7	3	28

summarised to ascertain the minimum number of individuals.

It can be seen from Table 5.3 that the most common bone in Trench D is the right humerus. Therefore, the minimum number of adults in Trench D is seven, based on the numbers of right humeri.

There was also a minimum of two infant, two juvenile and one adolescent skeletons present in Trench D.

Trench E also contained disarticulated bone representing a minimum of three adults and one juvenile.

This information is summarised in Table 5.4. The total number of individuals recovered from Boyle Abbey excavations in 2004 is therefore 28, with 17 (60%) being adults and the remaining 40% being under 15 years, adolescents and juveniles. Only 11% of the population were infants. Infant bones are usually under-represented in disarticulated remains as they decay quickly when they are disturbed.

AGE AND SEX

Five of the *in situ* burials were male and two were female. A further four males and two females were identified in the disarticulated remains. Most of the *in situ* burials were late middle adult or older adults with two being classed as middle adult. Among the disarticulated remains one female was an early middle adult, one was a middle adult, there was one young adult male, two early middle adult males and one late middle adult.

The numbers are too small for a full statistical analysis of the results. All that can be said is that there were more males than females and more of the males were older adults. The one *in situ* juvenile burial was aged 9–10 years.

LIVING STATURE

It was possible to estimate the living stature of four of the males and one female. The female stature was 153cm and the males ranged from 164cm–173cm with an average of 170cm.

DENTITION

With only three individuals among the *in situ* burials having dentition remaining it was not possible to statistically analyse the dentition. There were a few partial maxilla and mandibles among the disarticulated remains but very few teeth remained in place. All that can be said is that attrition seemed to be moderate to heavy particularly on the molar teeth and that calculus deposits were moderate to heavy with some associated alveolar recession indicating periodontal disease. There were no cavities on the adult teeth but one male had an abscess. The juvenile had very small cavities on two molars.

CONGENITAL ABNORMALITIES

- Cleft neural arch/spina bifida occulta
  Small gaps in the neural arches of the vertebrae are the most commonly known developmental defects of the vertebral column (Barnes 1994, 119). Barnes (*ibid.*) prefers the use of the term 'cleft neural arch' although this condition is more commonly referred to as spina bifida occulta. Barnes has highlighted that a cleft neural arch without neural tube defect is in fact much more common than cleft vertebrae with neural tube defect (spina bifida), as high as 25% in some populations (*ibid.*, 49, 119). A cleft neural arch is caused by slight delay in the development of the neural arches and is asymptomatic as the cleft is covered with fibrous tissues

that protect the spinal cord. It can be difficult to differentiate between the two conditions in ancient bone. They both commonly occur in the sacrum and both can result in the dorsal surface being open for some or all of its length.

In the Boyle population there was one individual, Burial 4 in Trench D, with the dorsal surface of the sacrum open for all its length.

- Cribra orbitalia and porotic hyperostosis

These conditions are characterised by expansion of the diploë or 'hematopoietic marrow hypoplasia' (Ortner 2003, 102), and a thinning of the cortical bone of the outer table. This results in visible areas of porosity on the cranial vaults (porotic hyperostosis) and in the orbits (cribra orbitalia). In the vault the parietal bones are frequently affected, around the temporal line, although the porosity may also be visible on the occipital.

Both of these conditions are more frequently found in juvenile skeletal remains (Stuart- Macadam 1985). It is suggested that cribra orbitalia is an early expression of porotic hyperostosis (Blom *et al.* 2005). These two stress indicators are believed to be related, often viewed as being manifestations of anaemia, predominantly iron deficiency anaemia (Grauer 1993; Carlson *et al.* 1974). It is argued that these lesions are indicative of a deficiency of iron in a young child; however, blood loss, parasites and poor hygiene may also contribute to this condition (Hengen 1971). Children under five and nursing mothers are more likely to be affected by iron deficiency anaemia.

There were four individuals, three males and one female, with cribra orbitalia. Burial 1 in Trench C had mild cribra orbitalia in the right orbit, Burial 2 had moderate cribra orbitalia in the left orbit. Burial 4 in Trench C, a female, had severe cribra in the right orbit. Burial 3 in Trench D had mild cribra in the right orbit.

- Enamel hypoplasia

Enamel hypoplasia is a defect in enamel formation, where there is a temporary cessation or disruption in ameleoblast activity during their formation of enamel matrix. It can take the form of horizontal lines or grooves or pits in the surface of the enamel (Hillson 1986, 129). As enamel is produced in incremental bands, the age of disruption can be assessed with accuracy. The most common teeth affected are the canines and the molars, usually the first molar.

Dental enamel hypoplastic defects are commonly regarded as representing episodes of nutritional stress in infancy or childhood that result in the malformation or imperfect formation of dental enamel. However, they can also be caused by acute fever. Clearly defined hypoplastic lines or bands can therefore be attributed to a specific period of stress that stunted enamel growth.

Its presence was noted in two of the individuals with teeth.

- Non-specific infection

Non-specific infection is commonly seen in archaeological human remains. As bone has a limited number of responses to infection it is not always possible to attribute a cause to changes seen on the skeleton. Periostitis is an inflammation of the periosteum (the outer surface of the bone) and can be the result of an infection, trauma, or may be part of another disease process. Where the disease process is not identified, it is known as a non-specific infection. Active periostitis is easily identified in skeletal material as the inflammation stimulates the bone-forming process so that a new layer of porous, fibre bone is laid down over the original bone surface. As the condition becomes chronic the new bone becomes thicker and more organised so that it becomes sclerotic and normal bone colour. As it heals the new bone becomes incorporated into the original bone surface so that only striations with some porosity are visible on the surface.

Periostitis was found on Burial 1 in Trench C, a late middle adult male. It was located on the left femur and fibula and was active at the time of death.

There were some isolated bones in the disarticulated remains also with active periostitis. In all cases it was the leg bones that were affected, and this included a femur from a young juvenile.

- Degenerative joint disease

Degenerative joint disease is a term used to describe the deterioration of joint surfaces with age. It is caused mainly by the accumulative effect of everyday stresses and strains on the joints but there are many factors involved including age and the genetic predisposition of the individual (Rogers and Waldron 1995). Sometimes it can arise as a result of trauma to the joint or to a bone near the joint.

The changes that occur in the joint are an attempt by the bone to relieve mechanical stress. Initial changes are osteophytes or lipping at the joint margins, which are an attempt to increase surface area and so reduce stress. New bone can develop on the joint surfaces, which is also an attempt to strengthen the joint and these are described as surface osteophytes. The surface of the joint can also appear pitted and porotic. Eburnation of the joint surface caused by bone rubbing on bone when the cartilage is destroyed is considered the final stage of the disease. Eburnation of the joint surface is considered the only definitive feature of osteoarthritis. However, the presence of marginal osteophytes or surface osteophytes coupled with pitting of the surface or alteration of the contour of the joint can also be considered to be osteoarthritis. Marginal lipping on its own cannot be used as a diagnosis for osteoarthritis as it could be simply a sign of ageing (Rogers and Waldron 1995, 44).

Among the *in situ* burials, degenerative joint disease was seen mainly in the spine with five individuals affected. Severe eburnation of the joint surfaces was seen in the older male. Most of the vertebral columns were too fragmented to analyse fully.

One individual also had osteoarthritis of the shoulder and degenerative joint disease of both hips. Degenerative joint disease was present in the right hip of another individual. Both these individuals were male.

- Schmorl's nodes

Schmorl's nodes are depressions in the middle of the end plates of the vertebral column often associated with vertebral osteophytosis. They are caused by herniations of the disc material often caused by sudden traumatic incidents and chronic heavy stress. Therefore, they occur more often in individuals engaged in heavy labour and accumulate with age. They were seen in three individuals, all males, late middle adult or older.

- Spondylolysis
  In this type of fracture the neural arch becomes detached from the vertebral body. The fracture site is usually just below the superior articular surfaces. Sometimes only one side is fractured but more often the fracture is complete, occurring at both sides. Spondylolysis is thought to be caused by stress in the lower back area, acting on a congenital weakness. In the population from Abbey Street, Kilkenny, three individuals had complete spondylolysis of the fifth lumbar vertebrae. They were all females, one was a young adult, one was a late middle-aged adult and one was an older adult. The condition tends to become more frequent with age.

  The detached neural arch never fuses again to the rest of the body and a pseudo-arthrosis is set up at the area of detachment. Apart from a low ache in the back they do not usually cause serious problems unless the body becomes unstable and slips forward, a condition known as spondylolysis.

  Burial 3 in Trench C had bilateral spondylolysis on the fifth lumbar vertebra.

- Enthesophytes
  Three individuals had evidence of enthesophytes. Burial 2 in Trench C had bowing of the femurs and strong muscle insertions on the right patella. Burial 3 in Trench C had enthesophytes gluteal tuberosities of both femurs and on the back of the calcaneum. Enthesophytes were also present on the femurs of Burial 2 in Trench D, a female.

SUMMARY AND CONCLUSIONS

A total of 28 individuals were recovered from this site, most of them from the disarticulated remains. It was possible to identify nine males and four females, with one adolescent, seven juveniles and three infants also present. Some of the burials showed evidence of nutritional stress with cribra orbitalia and linear enamel hypoplasia present on the teeth. It is not possible to do a statistical analysis of the results due to the low number of individuals. Evidence of joint disease, particularly in the spine, was evident on the late middle adult and older individuals. There was also evidence for stress on the spine in the form of Schmorl's nodes and in one case spondylolysis, a fracture of the vertebrae. There was also evidence for non-specific infection suggesting that the population was under stress. Despite the small number and fragmentary nature of the assemblage it was interesting to obtain a snapshot of the biological stress of this population.

Chapter summary and conclusions

In the refectory, multiple phases of activity were revealed during the course of the pre-development testing. The earliest phase of activity recorded was a cobbled surface found 1.45m below the present ground level. Overlying this were two layers of burnt material and collapse which may date from the thirteenth century when the abbey was laid siege (Chapter 2 and Chapter 3). This would indicate that the original floor of the refectory was at the lower level, tying in with the level of the cloister. Examination of the nails recorded from the layer of collapsed material identified some of them as having L-shaped heads and describes them as either floor or joiners' brads. These may have been used in the roofing and this layer may represent roof collapse. A dress pin was also recorded from this layer and Scully considers that it can be most closely paralleled by a find from a late sixteenth- to early seventeenth-century context in Winchester.

Above the layers of burning was a layer of boulders, which may be associated with collapse, or may have been deliberately laid down. Stone pads were built on top of these stone boulders which partly cut into the burning layers. These stone pads may have been constructed to support a roof over the refectory during the later phases of occupation of the abbey, or they could have carried a timber floor. In the annual report of 1904, the Commissioners of Public Works recorded that there were a number of benches of solid masonry, and it was thought that they were associated with cellars below the kitchen and refectory (Fig. 5.16). However, test excavations in the refectory found that these benches (stone pads C23a–e) overlay large boulders which overlay the layer of burning (C27) and therefore were most likely constructed after the burning of the abbey in the early thirteenth century. On the plans (Fig.

5.16), the remains of a north–south running wall are depicted, and this was recorded in the test trench excavated. As it was only partially revealed it is not possible to give a date for this wall. From the mid sixteenth century the monastery buildings were used as a barracks known as Boyle Castle and up until the late eighteenth century were used by the Connaught Rangers. In the eighteenth century a drawing by Beranger, dated to 1779, shows one of the buildings roofed with tiles. It is possible that the refectory was roofed with tiles also. A later cobbling overlies the stone bases and would appear to have formed a rough surface. It slopes down from the side walls forming a drain along the centre of the refectory. The cobbling may have been a later phase as four of the stone pads had a channel cut into them to form drainage along the centre of the refectory.

The next phase of activity in the refectory is indicated by the remains of a post-medieval tile kiln base. The kiln was found directly inside the doorway of the refectory and was built over the cobbling and the stone pads. Based on the kiln design, the fabric manufactured in the kiln, and the artefacts recorded, it can be dated to the seventeenth century. This places the kiln in use at the time when the abbey was a barracks (Kalkreuter 2001, 24). It was defined by a layer of burning (measuring 2m in diameter and 0.22m in depth) and contained fragments of pottery, kiln furniture, tile and burnt clay. Excavations revealed that this was the basal remains of a cylindrical kiln. This type of kiln has a long date range from the Roman period right through to the nineteenth century (Dawson and Kent 2008). All that survived of the kiln structure was part of the basal levels of its western wall and a spread of burnt clay, measuring 2m in diameter. Wren (this volume) has interpreted the rows of brick as a shelter and/or windbreak, to control the airflow during the firing process. An example of a similar windbreak was recorded at a medieval kiln in Nuneaton in Warwickshire (Mayes and Scott 1984, 37). The findings from the specialist report identified this material as the remains of a temporary roof replaced with each firing. Based on the dimensions, design and the form of fabric produced at the Boyle Abbey kiln, a seventeenth-century date is indicated, similar to those in use in the seventeenth century at Barnstaple in Devon (Dawson and Kent 2008, 215). The Barnstaple kiln is similar in size, and was also an open cylinder kiln, topped with a temporary roof of clay and waster for each firing. Both kilns were fired by a pair of twin flues, and in Boyle they were orientated to the prevailing south-westerly winds. The combustion chamber at Barnstaple had central piers to support the ware chamber, and the stone base at Boyle appeared to have been utilised for the same purpose.

Wren identified three different fabrics in the tile and brick found during the 2004 excavations at Boyle Abbey: Boyle Abbey Tile 1 (BAT1), Boyle Abbey Tile 2 (BAT2) and North Devon ware, which included peg tiles, pantiles, floor tiles, roof tiles and bricks. An estimated 95% of the tiles are of BAT1 which would have been fired in the on-site kiln and from comparative evidence dates from the early seventeenth to the early eighteenth century. This coincides with the period when the abbey was in use as an army barracks and the manufacture of tiles on site was usual, especially in large construction projects like Boyle Abbey (Eames and Fanning 1988, 12). Comparative studies of peg tiles in the west and north-west for the seventeenth century were recorded at fortified structures such as Clogh Oughter Castle, Co. Cavan, dating from the first half of the century (Wren 2013, 374). The fabric (BAT1) was fired to a buff or brick orange, with swirls of both colours visible in the cross section found mainly in the pantiles. The ridge tile fragments included one with a low cockscomb cresting. The second fabric identified (BAT2) dated from the eighteenth century and may have been made at Boyle Abbey or somewhere in the vicinity of Boyle.

An examination of the pottery assemblage from this area by Meenan (see above) indicates dating from the second half of the seventeenth century until the nineteenth century. In the area of the kiln and in the layers overlying the remains of the kiln, Meenan distinguishes two groups in the assemblage; the first group comprises domestic pottery which was used when the site was occupied by the barracks and the second group comprises a corpus of saggars, probably manufactured in the kiln on the site. According to Meenan, the Sandy ware (saggers) would have been used in the kiln to protect smaller vessels; however, no glaze was evident. Meenan identified comparative examples from an excavated kiln in Bideford, North Devon, dating to the later part of the seventeenth century. The finds from the kiln waste had similar heavy profiles with approximately the same diameters and splayed sagger bases also recorded. The pottery report also found parallels from a kiln at Castle Hill, Great Torrington, North Devon. Three saggers with splayed bases were also recorded, dating from the early eighteenth century. Some vessels also made in the same fabric as the saggers were a flowerpot (92), the remains of a milk pan (81) and three shallow bowls (95, 164, 224). Ceramics from this context also included pottery dating from the seventeenth and eighteenth centuries consisting of Frechen, Sandy ware, glazed red earthenware and black glazed ware (158–63, 169–71).

A concentration of early eighteenth-century glass wine bottles was also recorded from the refectory. Examination of the post-medieval glass indicates two types of wine bottle, the first a typical early eighteenth-century, short-necked onion bottle and the second, a group of early to mid eighteenth-century French wine bottles described as 'wrythen'.

The glass report states that these have not previously been recorded in an Irish context. Hanrahan's (1978, 56) view was that 'throughout the seventeenth century and for at least a decade or two in to the 18th century, the common glass wine vessel in France remained the wanded bottle'. Miscellaneous metal objects recorded from the area of the kiln, and the layer directly above it (C19) include nails, horse equipment, locks and keys and structural items. Two iron bars identified by Scully (see above) may have formed part of a grille within the kiln. Two metal finds (690, 692) recorded in C19 were identified as forming part of a musket, similar to one found in Clogh Oughter, dating from the seventeenth century (Manning 2013).

Excavations along the exterior of the north wall revealed burials at a depth of 1.10m–1.20m and *c.* 0.40m above the natural ground. These were overlain by a black clay layer (C9) containing frequent inclusions of animal bone, glass, metal nails and post-medieval pottery and overlay a deposit of large stones (C8). A number of architectural fragments were recorded from this layer which may be associated with the construction of buttresses in the nineteenth century. This was sealed by rough cobbling (C4) which lay below the sod and topsoil.

Archaeological Excavations being undertaken in the North Aisle
Photograph by Fionnbarr Moore.

Chapter 6

Excavations Within the North Aisle

Annette Quinn

SPECIALIST CONTRIBUTIONS BY
M. Carroll, L. Lynch, S. Lyons, M. McCarthy, C. McCutcheon, F. Moore, J. Moran, R. Ó Floinn, J. O'Sullivan, D. Swift and J. Wren

Introduction

The archaeological excavations within the north aisle at Boyle Abbey were undertaken between 2006 and 2012 under Ministerial Consent No CO25 and National Museum finds registration number E2399 as part of the OPW conservation works. The main seasons of excavation along the north aisle were conducted in 2006, 2008, 2010 and 2012. The excavations focused on the north aisle, along the line of the sub-surface remains of the north wall and just outside same (Fig. 6.1) The dismantling of the north arcading and subsequent excavation of the pier bases provided a unique opportunity to examine the 'make-up' of the foundations especially given the poor structural condition of the north arcade which gave rise to the 'North Wall Project'. The north aisle arcade and six piers were dismantled by the conservation team prior to the excavations taking place. The base mouldings of each pier were left *in situ*, however, so that the archaeological team could record them in full. Once drawn and photographed, the cut stone was retrieved by the conservation team and set aside for re-use in the rebuilding phase. Six pier bases were recorded, and the numbering system utilised by the OPW was also adopted for the excavation project (Fig. 6.2).

Pier foundations

A clay surface (F369 and F383) measuring 9.3m in length east–west, 2.24m in width north–south and 0.08m in thickness was located at the east end of the north aisle in the vicinity of Piers 3, 5 and 7. The clay was a highly compacted mottled blue grey material which was cut by the pier foundation pits (F376, F386 and F385). It is likely that this clay was introduced during or as part of the construction phase of the north aisle, perhaps as a working surface from which to build the pier foundations. A similar surface (F383) further to the east was also cut by foundation pit (F389) associated with Pier 3.

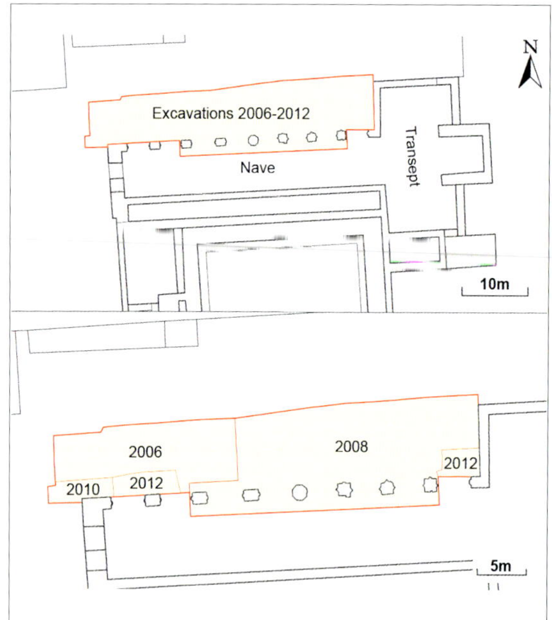

Fig. 6.1. The areas excavated between 2006 and 2012.

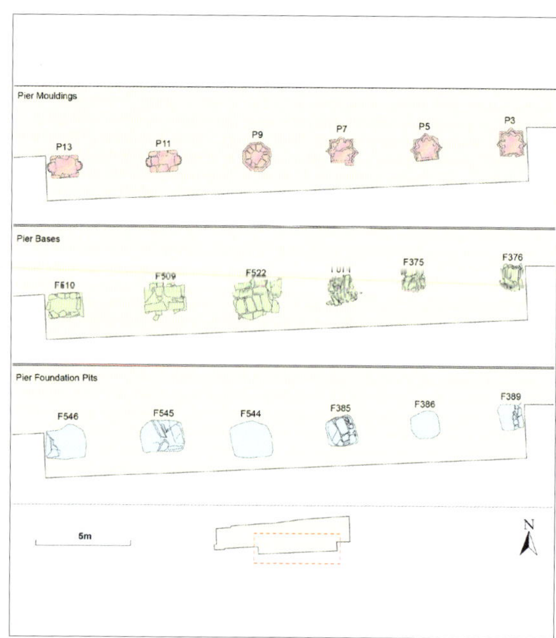

Fig. 6.2. Pier mouldings, bases and foundation pits.

The earliest recorded building phase in the body of the nave and the north aisle was the construction of the north arcade piers. In general, the foundation methods adopted for the building of these piers was similar. The pier foundations were constructed by first digging the circular/sub-circular foundation pits. The pits were then filled with large stones which formed the base/raft for the piers. No dating material was recovered from the foundation pits as their fills consisted entirely of stone and standing water indicating a high water table in this area.

Pier 3 (Fig. 6.2, Pls 6.1–4) (F298) is the easternmost pier base moulding dismantled along the aisle and measured 1.45m–1.60m in length north–south, 1.60m–1.40m in width east–west and 0.13m in depth. The foundation pit cut a silty sand layer (F383) of loose compaction with few stone inclusions, and it was not excavated as it formed the arbitrary level at which the excavation ceased. F383 abutted F369 (clay surface) which also remained unexcavated. The centre of the pier base consisted of a rubble core of irregularly shaped stones set in a matrix of orange mortar/sandy material. The pit (F389) for the foundation stones was sub-rectangular in plan, 1.55m in length north–south, 0.84m in width east–west and 0.65m in depth. The base moulding for Pier 3 (F298) directly overlay the foundation stones (F376). The foundation consisted of large irregularly shaped flat stones set within a compact brown/orange clay which formed a solid base for the pier. The pier base is square in plan with stone flanges at the north, west and east sides. Many of the cut stones were shattered and cracked possibly as a result of the pressure exerted on some as a result of the failing foundation beneath.

Pier 5 (Fig. 6.2, Pls 6.5–8) (F297) is located to the west of Pier 3. The pit for the foundation (F386) was sub-circular in plan with vertical sides and a flat base. The rising water table obscured the base of this foundation pit which measured 1.56m in length east–west, 1.34m in width north–south and 0.42m in depth. The rubble core consisted of numerous smaller stones and overlay irregularly shaped uncut slabs which sat on a bed of moderately compacted mortar-rich material. The foundation stones overlay the foundation cut (F386) and measured 1.50m east–west, 1.28m north–south and 0.42m in thickness. The foundation stones (F375) consisted of tightly placed, flat, slab-like stones surrounded by small packing stones. The clay surface (F369) surrounded the foundation stones in this location. The cut stones overlay the foundation stones (F375) and measured 1.4m–2m in length north–south, 1.70m–2.4m in width east–west and 0.13m in thickness. The base moulding was star shaped in plan with stone flanges at the centre of the north, east and west sides. It was composed of large sandstone slabs the majority of which were cracked into several pieces.

Pl. 6.1. Pier 3 foundation pit (F389) looking north.

Pl. 6.2. Pier 3 fill of foundation cut F389 looking south.

Pl. 6.3. Pier 3 base F376.

Pl. 6.4. Pier 3 moulding (F298) looking west.

The foundation pit (F385) for Pier 7 (Fig. 6.2, Pls 6.9–12) was sub-rectangular in plan with vertical sides and a base of flat stones (F392). The pit measured 1.60m in length east–west, 1.57m in width and 0.31m–0.34m in depth. The layer of flat stones at the base of the pit remained *in situ* and was set into a blue grey compacted clay material. The rubble core comprised one large stone surrounded by numerous smaller rubble stones. Overlying this was a rough layer of foundation slabs mixed with moderately compacted mortar-rich material. It consisted of large sandstone slabs the majority of which were shattered and measured 1.4m–2m in length north–south, 1.70m–2.4m in width east–west and 0.13m in thickness. Cut stones (F296) overlay the foundation slabs (F374) which consisted of medium to large stones measuring 1.56m east–west, 1.54m north–south and 0.42m in thickness, star shaped in plan with stone flanges at the centre of the north, east and west sides.

Pier 9 is located further to the west of Pier 7 (Fig. 6.2, Pls 6.13–16). The pit for the foundation base (F544) was sub-circular in plan, with vertical sides and a relatively flat base, partially obscured by the water table. The full extent of the south side of the cut was not excavated due to the limit of excavation in this area. The pit cut was found to be south of centre from the position of the upstanding pier and measured 2.5m in length east–west, 1.6m in width north–south and 0.5m in depth. The foundation pit cut layer F441 which occurred at the level where a floor would be expected (at same level as F111 to the west and F293 to the east) and in which the earliest phase of burials was interred. Slabs were set on edge and wedged together within the foundation pit (F544). The water table had risen to above these stones during the excavation. The foundation consisted of 12 large flat flagstones (F522) bonded with small stones and loosely compacted mortar. Many of the stones within this foundation layer were shattered. The flagstone foundation measured 2.4m in length east–west, 2m in width north–south and 0.70m in thickness. The foundations on the west side were abutted by a later wall (F424). The pier was octagonal in plan.

Pl. 6.5. Pier 5 foundation pit (F386) looking south.

Pl. 6.6. Pier 5 fill of foundation cut F386 looking west.

Pl. 6.7. Pier 5 base (F375).

Pl. 6.8. Pier 5 moulding (F297).

Pier 11 (Fig. 6.2, Pls 6.17–19) is situated west of Pier 9. The foundation pit (F545) was sub-rectangular in plan with vertical sides. The pit had a flat base formed of angular flagstones which remained *in situ* (unexcavated). It measured 2.14m in length east–west, 2m in width north–south and 0.7m in depth. The flagstone foundation (F509) consisted of a base of six flat undressed flagstones bonded with light yellow/beige mortar and small stones in the centre. It measured 2.10m in length east–west, 1.16m in width north–south and 0.66m in thickness. This was overlaid by the basal course of cut pier stones. The pier is rectangular in plan with engaged pier mouldings on the east and west faces.

The foundation pit (F546) of Pier 13 (Fig. 6.2, Pls 6.20–22) was rectangular in plan and measured 1.83m in length east–west, 1.65m in width north–south and 0.48m–0.56m in depth. A fragment of a rotary quern stone (E2399:510:208) was recovered from the foundations (F510) of this pier. Two pieces of the same quern stone (E2399:439:183 and E2399:439:217) were recovered from a layer (F439) which abutted the pier and overlay the primary phase of burials excavated in this location. The foundation (F510) consisted of small–medium stones bonded with a yellow/beige sandy mortar and a central rubble core. As with other pier foundations, the foundation stones were shattered. The basal layer of the pier measured 1.89m in length east–west, 1.30m in width north–south and 0.18m in thickness. It was rectangular in plan with engaged pier mouldings on the east and west faces.

A possible wall foundation (F511) was exposed at the foundation level of Piers 11 and 13 and consisted of a rough arrangement of irregular uncut stones extending from the eastern edge of Pier 11 (F509) to Pier 13 (F510). This feature overlay layer F441 and measured 2.70m in length east–west, 0.84m in width north–south and 0.20m in thickness. Although the feature occurred at the level of the foundations of both piers, it is not certain whether it related to the piers or their construction or perhaps

Pl. 6.9. Pier 7 foundation pit (F385) with blue clay F369 surrounding pit.

Pl. 6.10. Pier 7 fill of foundation pit F385.

Pl. 6.11. Pier 7 base (F374) looking north.

Pl. 6.12. Pier 7 moulding (F296) looking north.

a foundation for a later division in the aisle.

Pier 15 is located at the western end of the north aisle arcade and although it was not dismantled by the OPW, was assigned feature number F704 for reference purposes.

Construction postholes

A number of postholes were uncovered to the north and south of the north aisle wall (F19/F211) and were largely confined to the eastern and central portions of the excavation area (Fig. 6.3).

The postholes (F19/F211) included the following cut numbers (fill numbers in brackets); F277 (F276), F319 (F318), F340 (F339), F342 (F341), F347 (F346), F349 (F348) (Pls 6.23–25), F352 (F351) and F360 (F359). The dimensions of the postholes varied from 0.19m × 0.17m to 0.79m × 0.6m. The depths varied from 0.29m to 0.72m. Many contained packing stones and one example (F277) was square in plan and stone lined (Pl. 6.23). Finds from the posthole fills were few and comprised two iron nails (E2399:341:2631 and E2399:351:2634). Environmental material was lacking from the samples taken from the postholes with only nutshell and small mammal bones recovered from fill F277. No other environmental material was identified. This may suggest a clean building site at the time the north wall was constructed. The postholes were only exposed towards the eastern end of the excavation area and were situated between 0.5m and 1m north of the north wall in a roughly linear fashion. It is likely that the postholes are related to the construction of the north wall, perhaps representing a temporary scaffold-type structure.

The postholes south of the north wall (F19/F211) include F316 (F315), F354 (F353), F373 (F372), F418 (F417) and F539 (F538). They were exposed at varying levels, however, unlike the postholes to the north (F19/F211). One posthole (F316) was cut into layer F284 which underlay a modern layer

Pl. 6.13. Pier 9 foundation pit (F544).

Pl. 6.14. Pier 9 base (F522) looking north.

Pl. 6.15. Pier 9 moulding from above.

Pl. 6.16. Pier 9 moulding looking north.

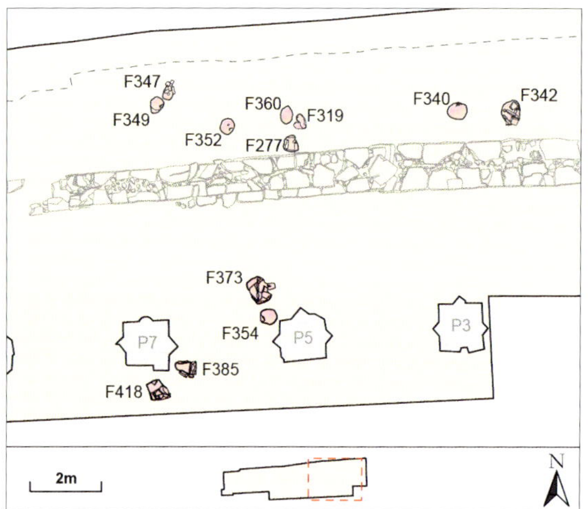

Fig. 6.3. Construction postholes at east end of north aisle.

(F221). Layer F284 was located in the nave of the church along the eastern side of the excavation area and 13 ferrous nails (E2399:284:2575–2587) were recovered from this material. No finds were recovered from the fill of the posthole.

Two postholes (F354 and F373) cut burial horizon F343 located along the eastern and central part of the excavation. Both postholes contained large packing stones within their fills, suggesting the requirement to keep the timber posts in place. They measured an average of 0.6m × 0.4m. The burial horizon (F343) produced one sherd of medieval window glass and an iron nail (E2399:343:2632 and E2399:343:2633). Given that the postholes occurred at the same level as a number of burials, it is not possible to say with certainty that they relate to the original construction of the north wall or indeed the piers but may be associated with repairs made to masonry walls during the use of the church.

Posthole F418 (F417) was located in the eastern side of the excavation area within the nave. The posthole was square in plan, stone lined and had a flat base, measuring 0.6m × 0.56m and 0.54m in depth.

One posthole (F539) was exposed roughly centrally in the excavation area within the north aisle. This posthole cut burial horizon F441, the earliest burial horizon in this part of the excavation. The latter layer produced medieval finds including the arms of a scale balance (E2399:441:202) and some medieval window glass. The posthole appears to have been isolated and may represent a temporary support structure.

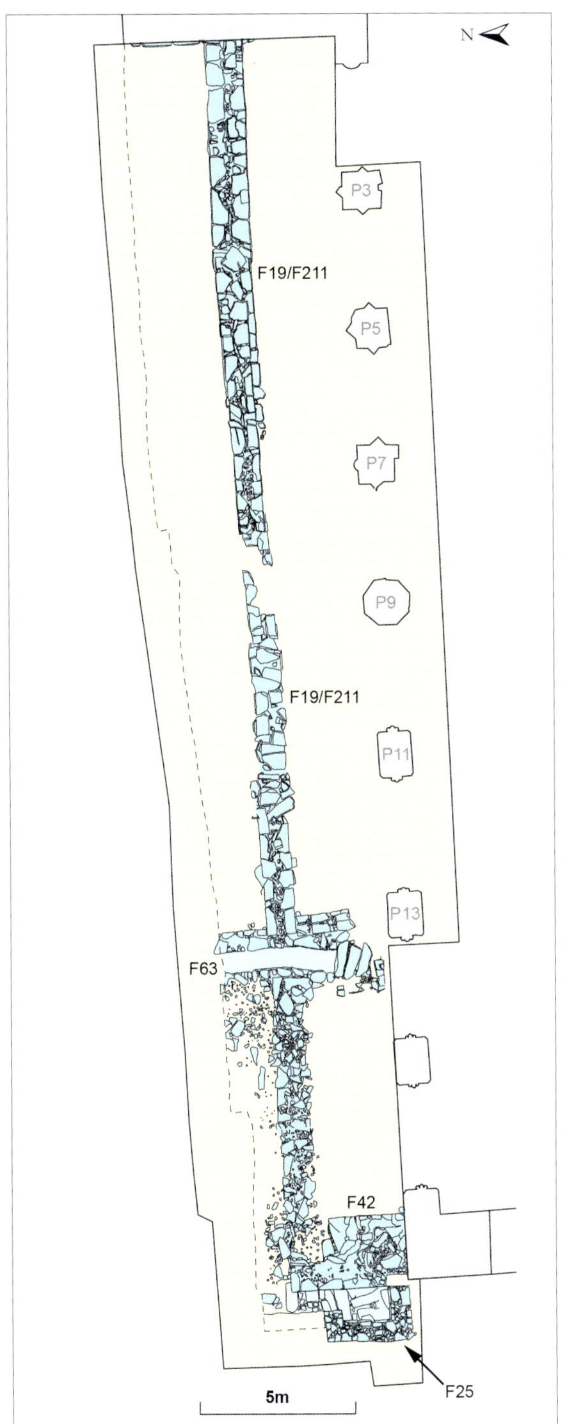

Fig. 6.4. The north wall (F19/F211) and west wall (F42).

Pl. 6.17. Pier 11 foundation pit (F545).

Pl. 6.18. Pier 11 base (F509) looking north.

Pl. 6.19. Pier 11 base moulding.

Monastic masonry remains

The medieval masonry structures exposed during the course of the excavations included the west wall (F42), the north wall of the church (F19/F211) and two exterior annexes, one (F25) abutting the western side of the west wall and the second (F312) abutting the north side of the north wall and the west side of the north transept (Figs 6.4–6).

The west wall

Foundations of the west wall (F42) in the angle of the north wall and north transept were fully exposed (Figs 6.4, 6.5, Pls 6.26, 6.27). The wall was revealed after the removal of topsoil and post-medieval layers as well as later walls (F4) and cobbles (F3). It survived to its greatest height of 1.24m in the south. Further to the north it survived to a

Pl. 6.20. Pier 13 foundation pit (F546) looking north.

Pl. 6.21. Pier 13 base (F510) looking north.

Pl. 6.22. Pier 13 moulding.

Pl. 6.23. Posthole (F277) adjacent to north wall looking east.

height of 0.9m (approximately four courses). The north-west corner of the wall survived well but the masonry was robbed out elsewhere. The west wall (F42) measured 3.97m in length north-south and 2.37m in width. It was comprised of some cut and dressed sandstone blocks of up to 2m in length which were bonded with a fine beige/orange sandy mortar type material.

A large spread of flat flagstones (F148) was exposed at the base of the west wall (F42) (Pls 6.28, 6.29) which may represent a raft type feature which supported the west wall foundations. The flagstone surface was preserved *in situ* and not excavated. It was visible for a length of 3.40m north-south and a width of 1m east-west.

The north wall

The conservation works also involved rebuilding the north wall of the church. No above ground trace of the north wall (F19/F211) was evident prior to excavation and one of the aims of the archaeological project was to uncover the buried wall (Fig. 6.4). The entire length of the north wall (F19/F211) was uncovered. It survived in varying degrees of preservation throughout this area but was generally found to be at, or close to, foundation level. Up to four courses were recorded towards the centre of the excavation area (Pls 6.30, 6.31) while only a mere foundation was apparent at the west end (F42) (Pl. 6.32). It measured 1.2m–1.4m in width at the east end of the excavation area for a distance of *c.* 12.8m west of the north transept wall. It then became much narrower as it extended towards the west, measuring 0.9m–1m in width. It was constructed of large limestone blocks (average of 0.8m × 0.3m × 0.25m in size) bonded with both an orange sandy gritty mortar and a compact grey clay towards the centre of the wall. A random rubble core of smaller irregularly shaped stones was also evident. At the west end of the site the north wall survived to just one course height (0.25m maximum height) with flat foundation stones evident underneath. No foundation trench was evident along either the north or south sides of the wall base. A stone drain (F63) was built into the north wall (F19/F211) towards the west end of the site and appears to be contemporary with the

Pl. 6.24. Posthole F347 (right) and F349 (left).

Pl. 6.25. Postholes F342 (foreground) and F340 (background) looking west.

Pl. 6.26. Post-medieval wall (F4) overlying remains of F42 (west wall, arrow).

Pl. 6.27. West wall (F42) looking south-west.

Pl. 6.28. Flagstone foundation (F148) under west wall (F42) and forming base of annex (F25) looking south.

Pl. 6.29. Flagstone foundation (F148) indicated by arrow (west side of north aisle).

Pl. 6.30. North wall (F19/F211) looking east towards north transept.

Pl. 6.31. Pier 11 (right) and 13 (left) foundation pits in foreground. North wall (F19/ F211) in background and post-medieval drain F407/ F290 to right of photo.

Pl. 6.33. Annex (F25) to west of west wall (F42) built around drain F59.

Pl. 6.32. North wall (F19/F211), drain (F63) and wall (F132). Remains of west wall (F42) in background.

Pl. 6.34. Drain (F59) capstones within annex (F25) (mid-excavation). West wall (F42) to right, looking north.

construction of the wall (Pl. 6.31). The north wall was also cut by a later drain (F407 see below) which removed its courses to foundation level.

Robber trench

It is not certain whether the north wall collapsed or was intentionally deconstructed. The presence of post-medieval walls and cobbling on site would suggest that the upstanding north wall was no longer extant by at least the mid eighteenth century or earlier. Sherds of pottery from the robber trench (F41, see below) with a date range of seventeenth–eighteenth century were recovered from the fill providing a date before which the north wall was no longer upstanding. The lower courses of the wall appear to have been intentionally deconstructed sometime in the post-medieval period therefore, probably during the later military occupation. There is direct evidence for the lower courses having been robbed out and the trench backfilled after the masonry had been removed. The width of the robbing out trench was almost exactly along the same alignment as the north wall. This would suggest that the location of the wall was known and that some masonry remained above ground to varying degrees at this time. The deposits to the north and south of the wall that had built up by this time were cut by the robbing out trench.

North wall annexes

Two small 'annexes' were uncovered during the excavations, one (F25) at the western end of the excavation area abutting the outside (west side) of the west wall (F42) and a second smaller annex (F312) in the angle of the northern side of the north wall (F19/F211) and the western wall of the north transept.

Western annex

This structure (F25) was fully uncovered (Fig. 6.5, Pl. 6.33). It abutted the exterior of the west wall (F42) of the church with a contemporary drain (F59) incorporated into its basal courses (Pls 6.34, 6.35). The annex was constructed on top of the flat flagstones (F148) that formed the foundations for the adjacent west wall (F42). This flagstone surface/'raft type' foundation also formed the base of the drain (F59). The drain was integral to the northern wall of the annex (F25) indicating their contemporaneity. The annex measured 2.9m north–south by 1.8m east–west and stood to a height of 1.2m from the top of the surviving wall to the base (internally). The building is roughly L-shaped in plan with a return on the north side to form the 'opening' or exit point for the drain (F59). The main walls were constructed of regular limestone blocks with a central rubble core of smaller irregular stones. The opening at the north measured 0.6m in width through which the drain (F59) extended.

The interior of the annex contained a number of fills which overlay the drain (F59). The basal fill (F609) consisted of a loosely compacted black silty material containing unburnt animal bone and measured approximately 0.3m in thickness. This was overlain by a deposit (F33) which was similar in consistency (a black loosely compacted silty sand with inclusions of yellow clay) although it contained a few inclusions of small stones and frequent amounts of burnt bone and charcoal. This layer resembles a deposit of discarded hearth material from a domestic context. It contained mixed finds including a twelfth- or thirteenth-century bone comb (E2399:33:11) and a bullet casing (E2399:33:603). Fill F32 overlay fill F33 and consisted of a loosely compacted mid-brown silty sand with frequent inclusions of stones and mortar. It also contained moderate inclusions of shell, burnt bone, charcoal, human teeth and animal bone fragments. It measured 1.68m north–south, 0.7m–0.8m east–west, and 0.10m–0.25m in thickness. The uppermost fill (F26) consisted of a loosely compacted mid-brown silty sand with inclusions of approximately 50% medium-sized angular stones, frequent inclusions of animal and disarticulated human remains including five disarticulated crania (Pl. 6.36). It measured 1.86m north–south, 0.35m–0.4m east–west and 0.32m–0.36m in thickness. Three metal pins (one copper alloy) (E2399:26:9, 10 and 14), a miscellaneous iron object (E2399:26:535) and a stone roof slate (E2399:26:3412) were recovered from F26. This fill was cut by a wall foundation (F605 and F4) which is described below.

The material recovered from the fills of the annex is mixed in date and its deposition was probably after the structure went into disuse. The archaeobotanical material in the samples recovered from this structure accord with the interpretation of the fills being redeposited from elsewhere in the abbey with the presence of oat and wheat. Of note also was more than 500 blackberry/bramble deposits from fill F33. Their deposition with items such as small mammal bones, weeds and cereal chaff further supports the interpretation of the layer as a domestic dump. The presence of disarticulated human skulls and long bones within the fill is direct evidence that the medieval layers within the abbey, in particular the burial horizons, had undergone significant disturbance.

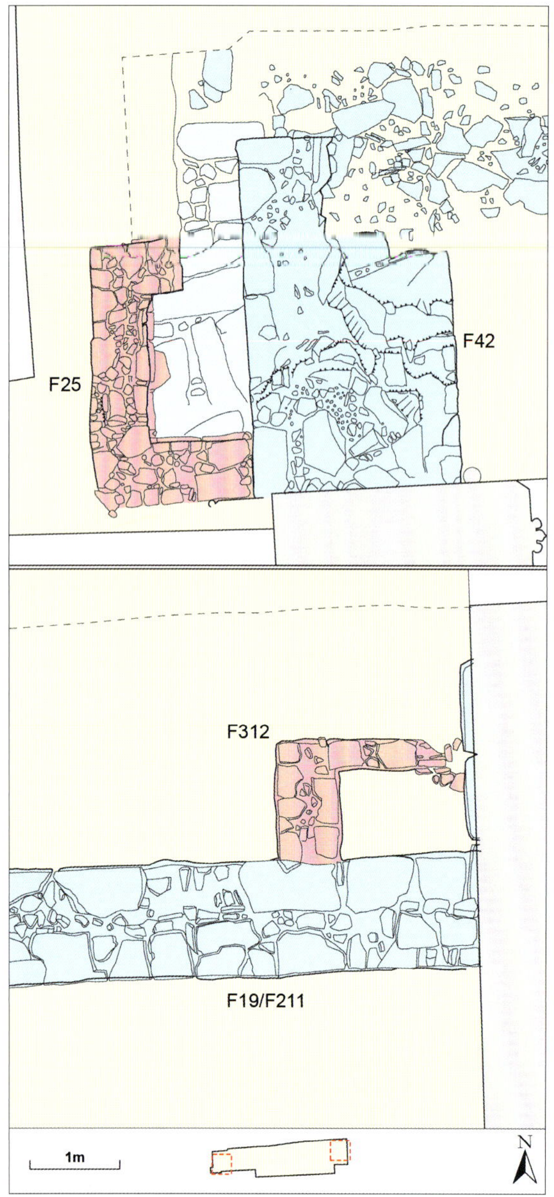

Fig. 6.5. Western annex (F25) above and eastern annex (F312) below.

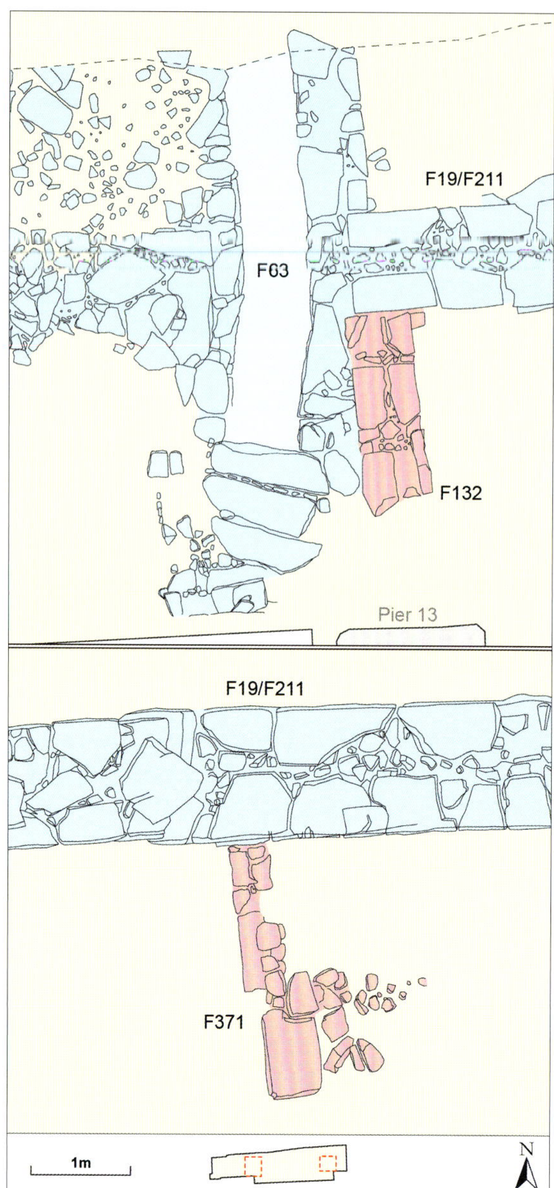

Fig. 6.6. Wall (F132) at west end of aisle and wall (F371) at east end of aisle.

The drain (F59) incorporated into the annex was comprised of two stone side walls which were capped with large flagstones (Pls 6.34, 6.35). It extended from the base of the south wall of the annex through the opening in the north wall. The drain measured 4.1m north-south and projected beyond the north church wall. It measured 0.3m in width internally and 0.48m in height (maximum). The capstones and side walls were bonded with a highly compact grey/yellow clay (F54) which sealed the drain. A similar highly compact yellow/grey clay was also placed between the side stones and the west wall (F42), presumably to ensure that the side stones remained in place.

The drain was filled with a compact grey silty clay (F58/F613). A decorated bone knife handle (E2399:58:3070) was retrieved from the fill but no other datable finds were recovered. The knife handle came from a scale tang knife, possibly late medieval in date but certainly no earlier than the fourteenth century given the proliferation of scale tang handles after this time. No modern or post-medieval finds were present within the excavation portion of drain fill. One piece of architectural stone was noted, built into the base of the southern wall of F25 and forming the side wall of the drain. There was a dearth of archaeobotanical material from fill F613 and some general indeterminate cereal grains from F58.

Easternmost annex

This small structure (F312) was built in the angle abutting the north wall (F211/F19) and the west wall of the north transept (Fig. 6.5, Pl. 6.37). It was clear that the northern courses of the annex had been cut by a later ditch (F222). It was defined by a roughly coursed wall with a central rubble core comprising smaller stones and clay which survived to one course and to 0.34m in height. It enclosed an area measuring 1.26m north–south and 1.88m east–west, 0.7m in width (0.36m on north side where it was cut away). The upper courses of this structure were overlain by a large post-medieval layer (F212). Two deposits (F313 and F317) were excavated from within the structure and consisted of loosely compacted material containing some animal bone and disarticulated human bone. No dateable finds were recovered from these fills and it is not possible to establish the exact date of the structure. The structure, however, post-dates two burials (B308 and B266) which have been dated to the thirteenth–fourteenth century implying a *terminus post quem* of *c.* fourteenth century for the annex.

Pl. 6.35. South wall of F25 showing drain (F59) integral to structure after removal of capstones and side stones (fully uncovered).

Pl. 6.36. Disarticulated crania and long bones within upper fill (F26) of F25.

Wall

This wall (F371) abutted the south side of the north wall F211 (Fig. 6.6, Pl. 6.38). It was located at the eastern end of the excavation area and extended in a north–south direction across the north aisle. It consisted of a roughly coursed foundation, loosely bonded with clay and mortar and measured 2.64m north–south, 0.75m in width, and 0.15m in height. This wall was disturbed by burial activity on its east and west sides and cut by burials B291 (F381/F382) and B288 (F367/F368)). The wall was overlain by the Phase 2 burial horizon (F343) and cut into the earliest burial horizon (F384). The only material recovered from F343 was an iron nail and a fragment of medieval window glass (E2399:343:2633 and E2399:343:2632). B288 and B291 are located in a burial horizon associated with a nearby grave (B290) which produced two silver medieval coins (E2399:378:98 and E2399:378:99). One of the coins (378:98) is illegible but the second (378:99) is an Edward III penny dating from the mid fourteenth century. This

Pl. 6.37. Annex F312 located outside north wall abutting north transept. Cut by Ditch F222 to north.

Pl. 6.38. Wall (F371) abutting south face of north wall.

Pl. 6.39. Wall F132/F440 indicated by arrow. Medieval drain F63 in centre.

provides a probable mid fourteenth-century date or earlier for this wall division in the north aisle.

Wall

This wall (F132/F440) was uncovered immediately east of the drain (F63) (Fig. 6.6, Pl. 6.39). It abutted the southern face of the north wall (F19/F211) and would have extended across the north aisle in a north–south direction. It is similar (in dimensions and form) to wall F371 and measured 2.02m north–south, 0.65m east–west, 0.39m in height and consisted of at least two courses. It was constructed using large stones forming an east and west face with a central rubble core. A large block of cut stone was re-used within this structure.

Monastic drain

A stone drain (F63) was uncovered extending north–south under the north wall from the west wall (Fig. 6.6, Pl. 6.39). The capstones of the drain were removed, and associated fills were excavated while the structure was left *in situ*, along with the north wall. The drain was well constructed, in particular on the south side of the north wall (F19/F211) where capstones remained *in situ*. North of the north wall (F19/F211) the drain became more irregular with no evidence for capstones surviving outside the church. It measured 5.5m in length and 0.6m in width (internally). The covered portion of the drain on the south side of the north wall (F19/F211) measured 2.9m in length north–south and 1.3m wide. It was filled with F78, F76/F103, F104 and F107. This drain was also uncovered in the excavations undertaken within the cloister (see Chapter 4) and can be viewed under a modern grate in the cloister today. The basal fill of the drain (F107) consisted of a yellow-brown silty sand of moderate to loose compaction. Inclusions of animal and human bone were concentrated at the northern uncapped section of the drain, similar to that described in the cloister above (see Chapter 4). It measured 3m in length north–south, 0.64m in width east–west and was excavated to 0.1m in depth. Some of this fill remained *in situ* due to the level of the water table at the time of excavation. Two ferrous nails were recovered from the fill (E2399:107:700 and E2399:107:701). This basal layer was covered by a dark grey, humic, silty clay of moderate compaction with inclusions of disarticulated human and animal bone (F104). It measured 3m in length north–south, 0.64m in width east–west and 0.25m in thickness. No finds were recovered from this material, although the archaeobotanical material retrieved from fill F104 included oat, barley, bread wheat, pea, weeds and nutshell. Over this was a grey silty clay of moderate compaction (F76/F103) with frequent inclusions of mortar and disarticulated human and animal remains, especially concentrated north of the stone-capped section of the drain. It measured 3m in length north–south, 0.64m in width east–west and 0.24m in thickness. No finds were recovered from fill F76/F103. The uppermost fill (F78) within the drain consisted of a mixed deposit of orange-brown clayey silt of moderate compaction with infrequent mortar inclusions. One sherd of pottery (E2399:78:678) was uncovered from the fill (Weser wavy band) which dates to the late sixteenth/early seventeenth century. The fill was concentrated mainly within the northern portion of the drain, outside the north wall and measured 1.6m in length east–west, 1m in width and 0.3m in thickness. The presence of a sherd of pottery within the upper fill could suggest that the find is intrusive due to the unsealed nature of the drain, or indeed that the drain was still functioning until the 1500s, or even the 1600s, when the north wall (F19) was perhaps still upstanding. In addition, three peg tiles (BAT2) were recovered from the fill and are thought to date to the eighteenth century (see Wren below). In this regard it is more likely that the fill is not secure.

Monastic floor

The remains of possible floor surfaces were noted along the north aisle in areas where burial distribution was less dense. Floor surfaces in all cases were earthen with no evidence of a tiled or stone floor. One highly compacted floor surface (F293) was noted in the eastern section of the excavation area and consisted of an almost metalled and highly compacted surface comprising 70% tiny stones and pebbles and 30% sand and clay mix of yellow/grey colour (Pl. 6.40). This floor surface was confined to within the aisle. It measured 5m east–west and extended 1.45m as far as the north wall. This layer remained *in situ* and formed the base of the excavation in this area. A number of burials cut this floor level and are discussed below.

Layer F434 also represents possible evidence for a floor surface and consisted of a highly compacted yellow/blue clay with occasional inclusions of small stones. Numerous burials were cut into this level and it was confined to the north aisle and located centrally within the excavation area. It occurred at the same level as layer F293, as described above, and measured 2.8m north–south by 2.3m east–west.

Pl. 6.40. Highly compacted floor (F293) looking east along north aisle, pier bases 5 and 7 on right.

Patchy remains of a highly compacted mortar-rich surface (F482) were encountered north of Pier 11 within the central aisle. This directly overlay layer F441, the level at which the excavation terminated. This mortar-rich surface was cut by grave cuts (F477, F479, B345 and B346). The mortar surface (F482) measured 2.3m east–west and 1.3m in width north–south.

Another highly compacted surface (F914) was noted at the eastern end of the aisle adjacent to the north transept wall (at 50.288–50.388 OD). This consisted of a beige/blue sandy clay and was cut by pits (F911 and F916) and a grave cut (F913). It was similar in consistency to the blue clay surrounding pier bases (F369). This area of highly compacted material measured 4.3m east–west and 2.9m north–south. Again, of note was the lack of burials in this location, perhaps leaving more evidence of the clay floor intact.

The burials

INTRODUCTION

The excavation focused on the entire north aisle, a strip 24m by 3.75m outside the north wall (F19/F211), and a strip 24m by 1.50m within the nave just south of the arcade wall. This provided an insight into the burial practices that took place within Boyle Abbey and the differences in grave types inside and outside the church. No indications of any graves were noted prior to excavation. Burials were encountered at 0.3m–0.4m below the current ground level (Table 6.1). The excavation revealed that burials had taken place within the

Table 6.1 Extract from Report on the Osteological remains at Boyle Abbey (Dr Linda G. Lynch)

Age	Females	Males	Sex undetermined
	n (% of females aged)	n (% of males aged)	
Young Adult (18–25 years)	8 (14.3)	8 (13.1)	–
Young Middle Adult (26–34 years)	11 (19.6)	14 (23)	–
Old Middle Adult (35–44 years)	17 (30.4)	27 (44.3)	–
Middle Adult (25–44 years)	3 (5.4)	3 (4.9)	–
Old Adult (45+ years)	17 (30.3)	9 (14.8)	–
Adults (age undetermined)	21	19	4
Total	21	19	4

aisle, outside the north wall of the church, and within the nave to the south of the piers. Four burials were selected for radiocarbon dating on the basis of spatial distribution and sex.

Evident throughout all contexts – medieval, post-medieval and modern – was the large quantity of disarticulated human bones recovered. This demonstrates the significant level of disturbance of medieval and post-medieval burials that took place within the abbey precinct.

Two hundred and twenty-two (222) burials were uncovered in the excavations and varied from full articulated skeletons to partial articulated skeletons (Fig. 6.7). Evidence for both sexes was uncovered, and a number of juveniles, infants and adolescents were recorded as well as one in utero foetus in a later burial thought to be sixteenth or seventeenth century in date (Fig. 6.8). Associated grave goods were very few, making it difficult to date any of the burials with precision. Furthermore, the burial matrices produced very few datable artefacts. The phasing of the burials as presented below is reliant on artefacts, where recovered, and AMS dating. A full analysis of the osteoarchaeological material was undertaken by Dr Linda Lynch (see Human Remains section below).

Patterns have emerged from the analysis of burial distribution, one of which was the notable lack of formal grave cuts outside the north wall and the somewhat haphazard placing of the remains when buried. The treatment of infants and juveniles is also interesting, with many buried apparently intentionally close to or abutting the south face of the north wall perhaps to afford them protection from disturbance from other grave digging.

The skeletal sample comprised 72.5% adults and 27% juveniles. It was possible to determine the age-at-death of 117 adults, and the results are presented in the Human Remains section below. Just 13.7% of adults were young adults (18–25 years) at the time of death, and 22.2% were aged 45 years and older. The majority of individuals (64.1%) were aged between 26 and 44 years at the time of death.

A number of limitations were encountered with regard to the excavation and recording of the burials. The excavation areas were excavated out of sequence; the west end was excavated first, followed by the east end and lastly the area in the centre. Furthermore, Health and Safety concerns meant that exposing full skeletons within the western half of the site (which was deepest) was difficult. Some skeletal remains extended under the base of the excavation baulks which were up to 2m deep meaning that they had to remain *in situ* until the baulks were safe for excavation in 2012. This resulted in a six-year gap between the excavation at the western end and its associated southern baulks. Weathering and erosion of the unexcavated baulks was noted when excavation recommenced in 2012. Furthermore, weather conditions experienced in 2006 and 2008 meant that the lowermost (earliest) phases of skeletons were

Fig. 6.7. All burials north and south of wall (F19/F211).

Female adult
Male adult
Indeterminate adult / adolescent
Female adolescent
Male adolescent
Juvenile / Infant
Isolated Skull
Remains without skull

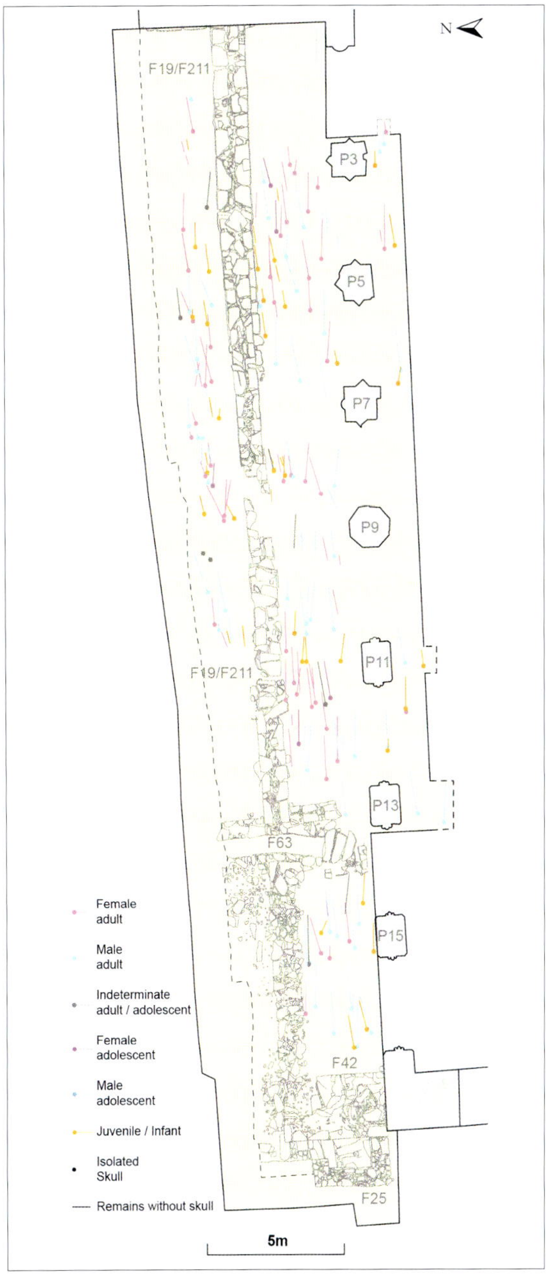

Fig. 6.8. All burials north and south of wall (F19/F211) according to sex and age.

under water due to the rising water table (despite the use of pumps on site).

The preservation of the human bone varied substantially from poor to well preserved and largely depended on the level at which the burials occurred and also the context in which they were located. For example, the burials outside the north wall were interred in a loose sandy material which was not ideal for the preservation of bone. Water influx was also an issue over much of the site where some of the burials excavated from the lowest horizons were below the water table. Disturbance of the upper burials horizons was also evident from later post-medieval features such as the buttress foundations, later walls, the ditch and post-medieval drains.

The burials will be discussed in chronological order within two locations: burials outside the north wall and those within the north aisle and nave.

BURIALS OUTSIDE THE NORTH WALL

Sixty-four burials were excavated outside the north wall and were concentrated in the eastern

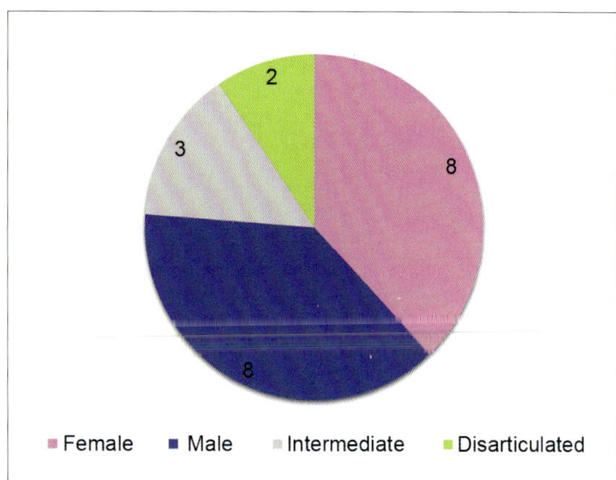

Fig. 6.9. Twelfth–early thirteenth-century burials outside north wall of church.

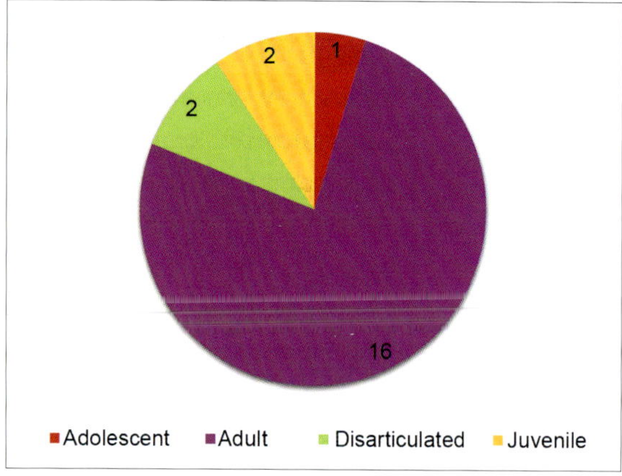

Fig. 6.10. Number of excavated skeletons according to sex.

and central sections of the excavation area. Two main burial matrices were recorded (F314/F325 and F232/F240) the former being the earliest (Fig. 6.9). Many burials were highly disturbed by both the intense burial activity in this area and by the later ditch (F222) and drain (F407/F290). The earliest phase of burial was also evident under the limit of excavation (F314). A burial (B289) was apparent in the south side of the ditch edge/cut (F222). The cranium was recovered, but the remainder of the burial was left *in situ* as there was no further requirement for excavation in this location. A second early burial (unexcavated) (B308) was partially exposed (upper portion of cranium) under annex F312 and under material F314. This burial indicates a much earlier phase of burial on the site. It is interesting to note that B289 pre-dates the possible construction postholes which were cut into the burial horizon (F314). The postholes are associated with the construction of the north wall and therefore this provides evidence for burials on the north side of the church prior to the construction of the aisle itself.

In general, grave cuts were not discernible outside the north aisle wall and the placing of the burials was far from neat, perhaps suggesting that the wrapping of bodies interred outside the church did not occur.

- Twelfth-early thirteenth-century (Fig. 6.9). Radiocarbon dating of a sample of bone (B274) from the early burial horizon (F314/F325) places it in the period cal. AD 1116–1218 (Sigma 2). This context, into which 21 burials were interred, was a yellow/brown gravel material of loose compaction. Artefactual evidence from this context included only four objects comprising a miscellaneous iron object and three nails (E2399:314:2610, E2399:314:93, E2399:314:2611 and E2399:314:2612). At the same level another layer (F325), cut by ditch F222, also contained burials. Table 6.2 details the burials which were exposed and cut into burial horizon F314/ F325. Only four burials had discernible grave cuts with the remainder undefined and haphazard. Only one grave fill produced artefactual material, which consisted of a ferrous nail (E2399:461:2927).

The placement of the burials north of the church was haphazard. One such example is burial B265 which the specialist notes retained the appearance of an unshrouded body being laid rather carelessly in the grave, with both arms falling loosely to the right. The practice, whilst unusual, is not exceptional. Specialist analysis of burial B274, also from the earliest phase of burial outside the north wall (male 45+ years), revealed that it exhibited rather unusual peri-mortem sharp-force injuries to the anterior of the sacrum: four oblique slashing-like wounds were apparent to the front of the bone. The four injuries were all orientated in the same direction and suggest a repeated action. In the living body, however, this bone is buried deep behind the abdomen and even a single, very considerable, sword-swipe would find it difficult to cut all the way through to the back. To have this repeated would be virtually impossible. These injuries may be sustained through evisceration or disembowelling. Such a punishment did form part of the medieval execution of being hung, drawn, and quartered. If this is a case of disembowelling, that method of killing would not have prohibited burial in consecrated ground. Radiocarbon dating of a sample of bone from B274 places this burial in the period AD 1116–1218 (95% probability) pre-dating the completion of the aisle. It can be surmised, however, that perhaps the north wall had been built by the time this individual was interred as he appears to have been intentionally placed outside the church.

Burial B318, thought to be a female aged 13–15 years, displayed evidence of massive erosive destruction of the bones of the lower thoracic, lumbar, and sacral vertebrae where the entire vertebrae appear to have been almost completely eroded. The destruction appears to have been caused by a serious infection, but it is difficult to ascertain precisely what that infection may be. Another young adolescent aged approximately 14–16 years old (B328) displayed joint disease as well as evidence of systemic infection. Evidence of diffuse idiopathic skeletal hyperostosis was found on burial B335 (a male aged 40–45 years).

The earliest burial phase excavated outside the north wall represents males, females, juveniles and adolescents. Figure 6.10 and Table 6.2 demonstrate that the numbers of males to females in this particular burial horizon is equal while Figure 6.11 demonstrates that adults dominated the burials in this particular phase of burial outside the north wall.

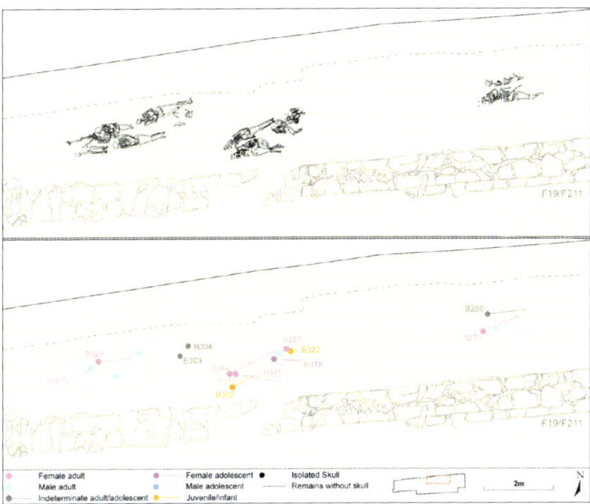

Fig. 6.11. Number of excavated skeletons according to age profile.

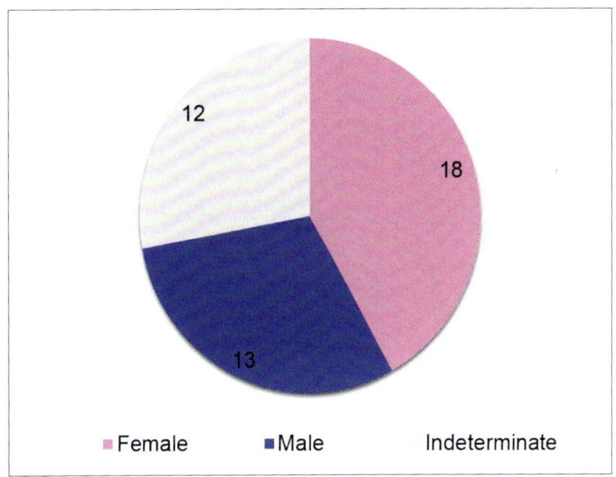

Fig. 6.12. Thirteenth–fourteenth-century burials outside north wall of church.

- Thirteenth-/fourteenth-century

This context was exposed directly under a stone surface (F227) that served to cover the 43 burials excavated outside the north wall (Fig. 6.12, Table 6.3). The burial matrix (F232/F240 and F491) was cut at the north end by the ditch (F222) resulting in numerous burials being disturbed and leaving only partial remains in places. Of particular note within this fill (F232) was the large number (43) of medieval window glass shards (E2399:232:2988–3047, E2399:232:37, E2399:232:74a and E2399:232:24) and 44 iron nails (E2399:232:2298–2340, E2399:232:72 and E2399:232:83). A piece of window lead (E2399:232:79) was also recovered. The context (F240) produced two miscellaneous iron objects (E2399:240:2514 and E2399:240:2515) and a fourteenth-century horseshoe (E2399 :240:187) as well as 35 shards of mid to late thirteenth-century medieval window glass (E2399:240:75, E2399:240:78, E2399:240:84, E2399:240:175, E2399:240:2986, E2399:240:2987, E2399:240:3027-50 and E2399:240:3053a). One hundred and twenty-eight iron nails were recovered (E2399:240:36, E2399:240:85, E2399:240:2386–2502, and E2399:240:2504-2512) and two fragments of window lead (E2399:240:2375 and E2399:240:2376).

No pathologies, traumas or conditions usual to such populations were noted by the specialist, perhaps with the exception of burial B230, a possible female aged 14–17 years who displayed extensive pathological skeletal lesions likely resulting from tuberculosis.

This burial phase excavated outside the

Table 6.2: Burial horizon (21 individuals) (F314/F325, earliest) outside north wall (F19/F211)

Burial Number	Sex	Age	Grave Fill	Grave Cut	Horizon
B265	Male	Adult	Not discernible	Not discernible	F314
B273	Female	Adult	Not discernible	Not discernible	F325 and F314
B274	Male	Adult	F328	F329	F325
B280	Indeterminate	Adult	Not discernible	Not discernible	F325
B302	Indeterminate	Juvenile	Not discernible	Not discernible	F314
B303	Disarticulated	Disarticulated	Not discernible	Not discernible	F314
B304	Disarticulated	Disarticulated	Not discernible	Not discernible	F314
B310	Female	Adult	Not discernible	Not discernible	F314
B315	Female	Adult	Not discernible	Not discernible	F314
B318	Female	Adolescent	Not discernible	Not discernible	F314
B319	Female	Adult	Not discernible	Not discernible	F314
B320	Male	Adult	Not discernible	Not discernible	F314
B322	Indeterminate	Juvenile	Not discernible	Not discernible	F314
B323	Female	Adult	Not discernible	Not discernible	F314
B324	Female	Adult	Not discernible	Not discernible	F314
B327	Male	Adult	Not discernible	Not discernible	F314
B328	Male	Adult	F451	F452	F314
B331	Male	Adult	Not discernible	Not discernible	F314
B333	Male	Adult	Not discernible	Not discernible	F314
B335	Male	Adult	F461	F462	F314
B342	Female	Adult	F489	F490	F314

north wall contained males, females, juveniles, adolescents and infants. Figure 6.13 and Table 6.3 demonstrate that the numbers of males to females in this burial horizon is relatively balanced, with 18 females and 12 males. Figure 6.14 demonstrates that adults again dominated the burials outside the north wall while infants and adolescents are poorly represented with only one of each recovered. A higher number of juveniles (9) was recovered, however.

BURIALS WITHIN THE NORTH AISLE AND NAVE

Burial practice within the aisle and the area of the nave surrounding the pier bases was in stark contrast to the burial practice adopted outside the north wall. Burial cuts and fills were evident for the most part with a much neater placement of the remains within their respective graves in the church. All burials were unmarked apart from B283, B235, B232 and B231, which were interred

Table 6.3 Burial horizon F232/F240 (43 individuals)

Burial Number	Sex	Age	Grave Fill	Grave Cut	Horizon
B203	Female	Adult	Not discernible	Not discernible	F232/F240
B204	Female	Adult	Not discernible	Not discernible	F232/F240
B205	Male	Adult	Not discernible	Not discernible	F232/F240
B206	Female	Adult	F242	F242	F232/F240
6B208	Female	Adult	F243	F244	F232/F240
B210	Female	Adult	F245	F246	F232/F240
B216	Indeterminate	Juvenile	Not discernible	Not discernible	F232/F240
B217	Female	Adult	Not discernible	Not discernible	F232/F240
B218	Male	Adult	Not discernible	Not discernible	F232/F240
B220	Male	Adult	Not discernible	Not discernible	F232/F240
B221	Female	Adult	Not discernible	Not discernible	F232/F240
B222	Female	Adult	Not discernible	Not discernible	F232/F240
B223	Male	Adult	Not discernible	Not discernible	F232/F240
B226	Male	Adult	Not discernible	Not discernible	F232/F240
B227	Indeterminate	Adolescent	Not discernible	Not discernible	F232/F240
B230	Female	Adult	Not discernible	Not discernible	F232/F240
B242	Female	Adult	Not discernible	Not discernible	F232/F240
B243	Indeterminate	Juvenile	Not discernible	Not discernible	F232/F240
B250	Indeterminate	Infant	Not discernible	Not discernible	F232/F240
B251	Male	Adult	Not discernible	Not discernible	F232/F240
B252	Female	Adult	Not discernible	Not discernible	F232/F240
B253	Male	Adult	Not discernible	Not discernible	F232/F240
B254	Indeterminate	Juvenile	Not discernible	Not discernible	F232/F240
B255	Indeterminate	Juvenile	Not discernible	Not discernible	F232/F240
B256	Female	Adult	Not discernible	Not discernible	F232/F240
B259	Indeterminate	Juvenile	Not discernible	Not discernible	F232/F240
B260	Indeterminate	Juvenile	Not discernible	Not discernible	F232/F240
B261	Female	Adult	Not discernible	Not discernible	F232/F240
B262	Male	Adult	Not discernible	Not discernible	F232/F240
B263	Male	Adult	Not discernible	Not discernible	F232/F240

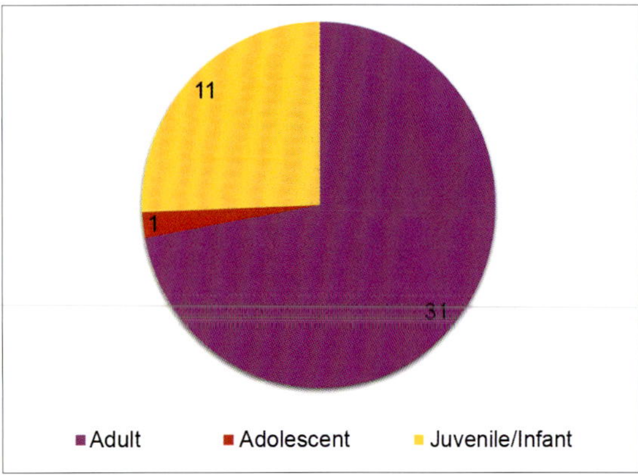

Fig. 6.13. Thirteenth–fourteenth-century burials according to age profile in burial horizon (F232/F240).

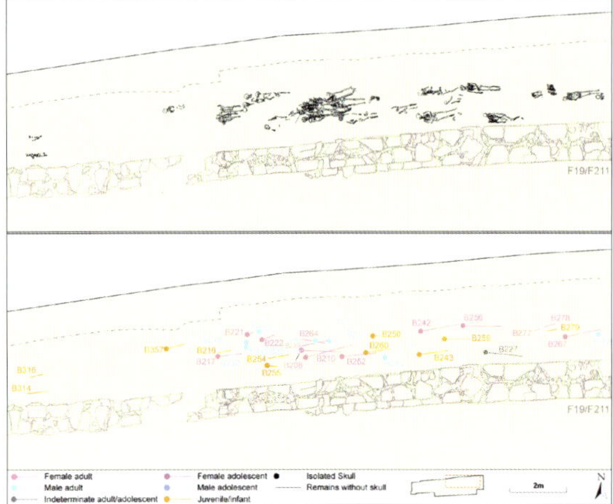

Fig. 6.14. Burial numbers according to age profile in burial horizon (F232/F240).

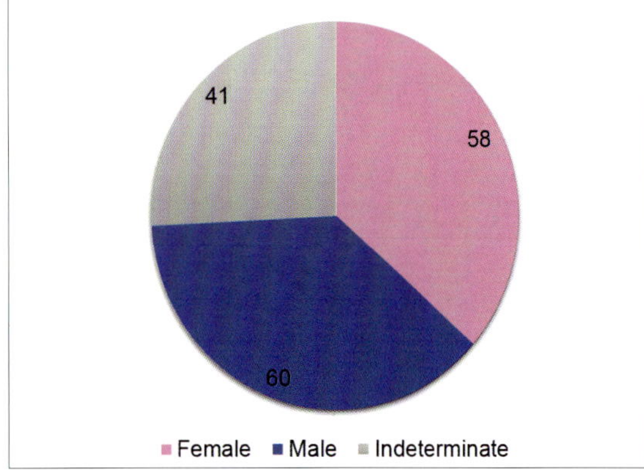

Fig. 6.15. Burial numbers according to sex within the north aisle.

under a medieval grave slab within the nave just south of the north arcade. One individual (B374) was buried under an uninscribed grave slab (E2399:534:215) immediately to the south of Pier 11 within the nave. No further grave slabs were recorded within the north aisle. An interesting statistic within the aisle was the almost equal proportion of males to females. This statistic was also noted by Linda Lynch (see Human Remains section below) in the analysis of the entire assemblage of human remains. The number of males to females is shown on Figure 6.15. This is an interesting comparison to the burials excavated at Tintern Abbey, Co. Wexford, where Ó Donnabháin (2010, 108) notes that females and males appear to have been buried in equal numbers in the transept and ambulatory, and that this was in contrast to those excavated in the presbytery, where males dominated over females. Infants and juveniles were also well represented with very few adolescents being buried (Fig. 6.16).

- Early fourteenth-century burials

  Eighty-six burials can be attributed to the earliest phase of burials within the north aisle and the portion of the nave excavated (Figs 6.17, 6.18 and Table 6.4). These burials are tabulated according to the burial phase in which they were placed. Dateable material was sparse, with a silver coin of mid fourteenth-century date being the only readily dateable artefact from the entire horizon (see below).

  At the western end of the north aisle (Fig. 6.15) the burials were highly disturbed by activity associated with the demolition of the west wall (F42) and the north wall (F19). A number of burials survived at the lower levels (F146, F125, F100 and F111). Two burials (B15 and B18) were interred in layer F146. A copper alloy stick pin (E2399:146:90) was retrieved from this layer and is likely to be medieval in date, although it is unclassified.

  Further to the east, burials B8, B9, B10, B11 and B14 were interred in layer F111. Burial B9 (F113 fill) contained four medieval window glass fragments (E2399:113:77a, E2399:113:77b, E2399:113:77c and E2399:113:77d) and three iron nails (E2399:113:715–717). Burial B10 also contained iron nails (E2399:115:107, E2399:115:108 and E2399:115:110). Burial B14 had been severely truncated by burials B9 and B10 above. This burial activity (F111) produced a number of finds including architectural stone (E2399:111:79), a mid to late thirteenth-century window glass fragment (E2399:111:74) and three iron nails (E2399:111:712, E2399:111:713 and E2399:111:714). The window glass fragment bears a trefoil motif and a suggested 4-quarry pattern (see Moran below). In terms of unusual anomalies, burial B9, a male 20–25 years old, had its right arm intentionally and completely bent at an angle underneath his supine body.

Adjacent to the west wall (F42), the earliest burials were interred in a compact yellow mottled sandy gravel silt (F100). A rowel spur (E2399:98:71) with a likely date of the late thirteenth to early fourteenth century was recovered from the layer. Burial B17 (F142 fill) contained a bead (E2399:142:89) and two shards of medieval window glass (E2399:142:104 and E2399:142:860). No unusual anomalies were apparent on B16 and B17. In the south-western corner of the north aisle, the earliest burials recovered included B711–B718 and were interred in a buff-pink sand, loosely compacted in places (F733). Nine artefacts comprising four nails (E2399:733:778–781), three miscellaneous iron objects (E2399:733:782–784), a possible pumice stone (E2399:733:47) and a fragment of window lead (E2399:733:48) were recovered from this deposit. Artefactual evidence from the grave fills includes a shard of medieval window glass (E2399:743:49) from burial B714 and window lead (E2399:745:725 and E2399:745:785). Osteological anomalies include an individual (B712) aged 17–20 years who had suffered multiple violent injuries at the time of death including an attempted decapitation. The specialist notes that the individual appears to have suffered a particularly violent death, possibly during a battle.

An isolated deposit (F734) which occurred at the same level as burial activity (F733) consisted of a loosely compacted black charcoal and ash deposit underlying F716. It produced 13 artefacts comprising a mid fourteenth-century silver coin (E2399:734:24), five window glass shards (E2399:734:33, 36 and 40–42), an iron object (E2399:734:39), a medieval copper alloy needle (E2399:734:30), three iron nails (E2399:734:44-46), an iron object (E2399:734:43) and a sherd of Saintonge green-glazed pottery (late thirteenth to early fourteenth century in date) (E2399:734:37). The layer (F734) was cut by burial B715 (F747 and F748). This earliest phase of burials (B711–B718) was sealed by another burial deposit (F716) into which many other burials were cut. A silver coin (734:24) identified as an Edward III half groat, possibly third (1344–51) or fourth (1351–77) coinage provides a fourteenth-century date which is likely for this burial activity.

The earliest burials from the central portion

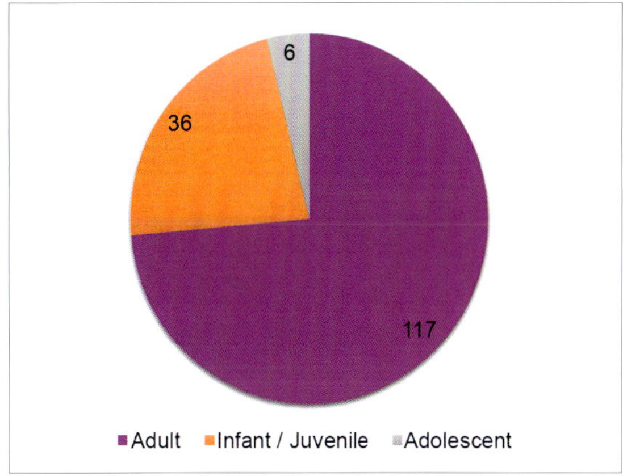

Fig. 6.16. Burial numbers according to age within the north aisle.

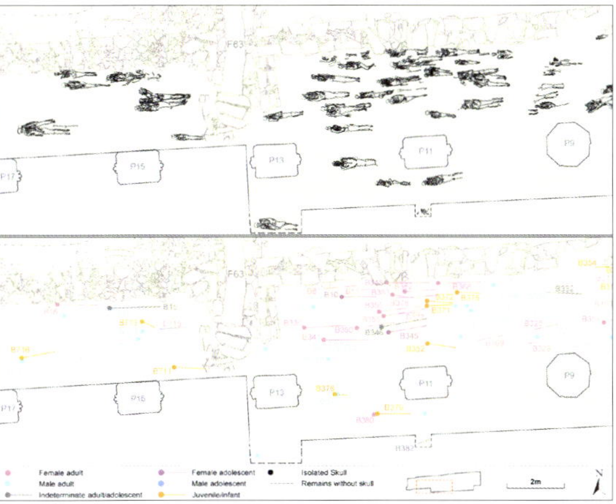

Fig. 6.17. Early fourteenth-century burials within north aisle (west side).

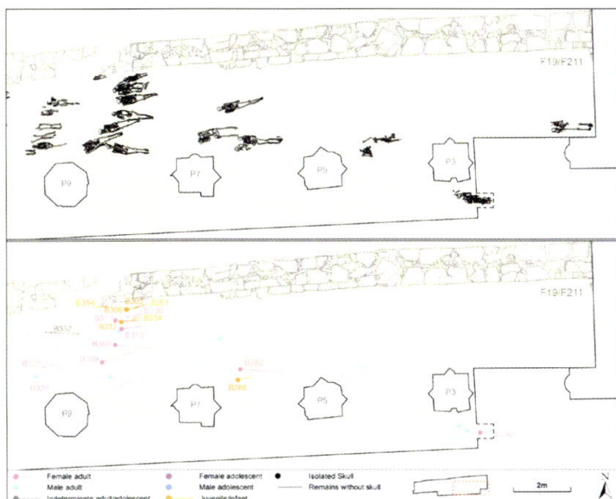

Fig. 6.18. Early fourteenth-century burials within north aisle (east side).

of the aisle were cut into a number of contexts (F441, F384, F369, F444, F434, F293) and separated and cut by post-medieval drains and buttresses. Burials were interred in a yellow-brown deposit underlying layers F438 and F439 north of Piers 13 and 11. An estimated 36 burials (Table 6.4) were interred in an area. Finds include architectural stone (E2399:441:216), two medieval window glass fragments (E2399:441:209 and E2399:441:3057), miscellaneous iron (E2399:441:2921), two iron nails (E2399:441:2922 and E2399:441:2923) and a fragment of a fine copper alloy scale balance (E2399:441:202). Grave finds were few (apart from nails) although an iron object (E2399:480:2931) and a bone pin (E2399:480:190) were recovered from burial B347. A bone pin (E2399:542:221) was also recovered from burial B376. A miscellaneous item (E2399:469:189) was recovered from the fill of burial B341 (adult female).

Burials B371 and B372, aged 5–7 years, were initially thought to be a double burial (possibly twins). Upon excavation, however, it was clear that one burial cut the other and that B371 was later than B372. The specialist suggests a familial relationship, however, given their similar age-at-death and the position of the burials. No other significant anomalies or observations were noted.

Further to the east, another layer (F384) occurring at the same level as F441 was also cut by the earliest burials. It consisted of a highly compacted orange-brown silty clay. It was cut by burials B295, B297 and B298. The burials in this location were poorly preserved and incomplete although one burial (B297) is particularly distinct due to its prone position. B297 (male 20–25 years) was 'buried in a prone position with the head to the east, his right humerus had been bent behind his neck' (see Human Remains section below). There were no skeletal indicators suggesting why he would have been buried in such a way. Lynch (below) notes that 'a prone burial is anathema to the entire central Christian concept of resurrection' and that the placement of the body face down is a technique by the living of controlling the dead and their soul and represents what is known as a deviant burial (Tsaliki 2008).

Further to the east in the vicinity of Piers 3 (F389), 5 (F375) and 7 (F374), a highly compacted blue clay (F369) was cut by the primary phase of burials (B293, B294, B296 and B299). Finds from the grave fill (F387) include a copper alloy mount (E2399:387:112), possibly used on a leather or wooden object, which is likely to be medieval in date. Further finds included three ferrous nails (E2399:387:113, E2399:387:2656 and E2399:387:2657).

Four (B275, B276, B282 and B286) additional burials were cut into layer F293 further to the north towards the north wall (F211/F19). This layer also represents one of the earliest burials matrices and consisted of a highly compacted metalled surface, possibly the remains of a floor surface. The fill (F326) of burial B275 contained a possible copper alloy mount (E2399:326:90).

Burial matrix F444 was cut by the post-medieval drain (F407) and buttress cut (F435) and was separated from the other horizons by these late features. Burials B321, B325, B326, B329, B332, B337 and B338 were interred in it. They were severely truncated by the drain (F290/F407) on the west side and the buttress cut (F435, adjacent to Pier 9) on the east side.

Burial activity (F434) to the east of the post-medieval drain (F407) was interred in a yellow-blue clay of moderate compaction. Twelve burials were cut into this layer (B309, B311, B312, B313, B334, B336, B339, B351, B354, B359, B360 and B364). Finds from the layer itself included three shards of medieval window glass (E2399:434:204, E2399:434:3056 and E2399:434:3058), while three of the 12 grave fills produced finds. A silver coin (E2399:430:176) was recovered from the lower right thorax of the adult male (B309). The coin is an Edward III silver halfpenny which is incomplete and highly abraded. It is possibly second coinage, dating from 1335–43, and suggests the burial dates from the mid fourteenth century. This is the only dateable find directly recovered from the grave fills at this level. The coin (E2399:734:24) recovered from burial activity F734 at the same level is also of mid fourteenth-century date.

A compact surface (F914) was located in the far south-east corner of the north aisle, adjacent to the north transept. This is considered to be

Table 6.4 Primary burials within the north aisle (and nave)

Burial Number	Sex	Age	Grave Fill	Grave Cut	Horizon
B8	Female	Adult	None discernible	None discernible	F111
B9	Male	Adult	F113	F114	F111
B10	Female	Adolescent	F115	F116	F111
B11	Female	Adult	None discernible	None discernible	F111
B14	Male	Adult	None discernible	None discernible	F111
B15	Indeterminate	Adult	F130	F131	F146
B16	Female	Adult	F140	F141	F100
B17	Male	Adult	F142	F143	F100
B18	Male	Adult	F144	F145	F146
B275	Male	Adult	F326	F327	F293
B276	Male	Adult	F330	F331	F293
B282	Female	Adult	F337	F338	F293
B286	Indeterminate	Juvenile	F362	F363	F293
B293	Male	Adult	F387	F388	F369
294	Male	Adult	F387	F388	F369
B295	Male	Adult	F390	F391	F384
B296	Female	Adult	F387	F388	F369
B297	Male	Adult	None discernible	None discernible	F384
B298	Male	Adult	None discernible	None discernible	F384
B299	Indeterminate	Juvenile	None discernible	None discernible	F369
B305	Indeterminate	Juvenile	F463	F464	F434
B306	Indeterminate	Juvenile	F552	F553	F434
B309	Male	Adult	F430	F431	F434
B311	Female	Adult	F459	F460	F434
B312	Indeterminate	Juvenile	F432	F433	F434
B313	Female	Adult	F554	F555	F434
B317	Male	Adult	F443	None discernible	F441
B321	Male	Adult	F445	F446	F444
B325	Female	Adult	F447	F448	F444
B326	Male	Adult	F449	F450	F444

Table 6.4 Primary burials within the north aisle (and nave) *continued*

Burial Number	Sex	Age	Grave Fill	Grave Cut	Horizon
B329	Female	Adult	F453	F454	F444
B330	Female	Adult	F455	F456	F441
B332	Indeterminate	Adolescent	F457	F458	F444
B334	Indeterminate	Infant	F556	F557	F434
B336	Female	Adult	F558	F559	F434
B337	Male	Adult	None discernible	None discernible	F444
B338	Male	Adult	None discernible	None discernible	F444
B339	Male	Adult	F471	F472	F434
B340	Male	Adult	F465	F466	F441
B341	Female	Adult	F469	F470	F441
B344	Male	Adult	F473	F474	F441
B345	Female	Adolescent	F477	F478	F441
B346	Male	Adult	F478	F479	F441
B347	Male	Adult	F480	F481	F441
B348	Female	Adult	F483	F484	F441
B349	Male	Adult	F485	F486	F441
B350	Female	Adult	F487	F488	F441
B351	Indeterminate	Juvenile	F492	F493	F434
B352	Indeterminate	Juvenile	F494	F495	F441
B354	Indeterminate	Infant	F496	F497	F434
B355	Female	Adult	F498	F499	F441
B356	Female	Adult	F500	F501	F441
B358	Male	Adult	F502	F503	F441
B359	Female	Adult	F504	F505	F434
B360	Female	Adult	F506	F507	F434
B362	Female	Adult	F514	F515	F441
B363	Female	Adult	F516	F517	F441
B364	Male	Adult	F512	F513	F434
B365	Male	Adult	F520	F521	F441
B366	Male	Adult	F528	F529	F441

Table 6.4 Primary burials within the north aisle (and nave) *continued*

Burial Number	Sex	Age	Grave Fill	Grave Cut	Horizon
B367	Male	Adult	F524	F525	F441
B368	Female	Adult	F526	F527	F441
B369	Female	Adult	F520	F521	F441
B370	Male	Adult	F527	None discernible	F441
B371	Indeterminate	Juvenile	F532	F533	F441
B372	Indeterminate	Juvenile	F532	F533	F441
B373	Male	Adult	F535	F536	F441 Nave
B374	Male	Adult	F534	F537	F441 Nave
B375	Indeterminate	Juvenile	F540	F541	F441
B376	Indeterminate	Infant	F542	F543	F441 Nave
B377	Female	Adult	F531	None discernible	F441
B378	Female	Adult	F528	F529	F441
B379	Indeterminate	Juvenile	F549	F550	F441 Nave
B380	Female	Adult	F549	F550	F441 Nave
B381	Male	Adult	F560	F561	F441 Nave
B382	Indeterminate	Adult	F2003	F2003	F441 Nave
B383	Indeterminate	Juvenile	None discernible	None discernible	F441
B711	Indeterminate	Juvenile	F737	F738	F733
B712	Male	Adult	F739	F740	F733
B713	Indeterminate	Juvenile	F741	F742	F733
B714	Male	Adult	F743	F744	F733
B715	Female	Adult	F747	F748	F733
B716	Indeterminate	Juvenile	F745	F746	F733
B717	Male	Adult	F749	F750	F733
B718	Male	Adult	None discernible	None discernible	F733
B901	Male	Adult	None discernible	None discernible	F914

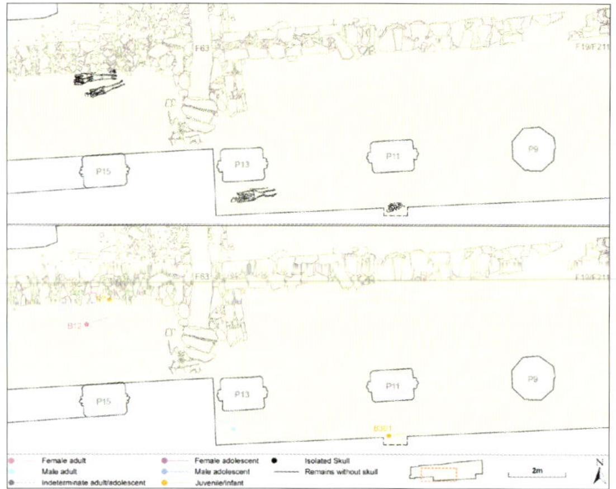
Fig. 6.19. Mid fourteenth-century burials at west side of aisle/nave.

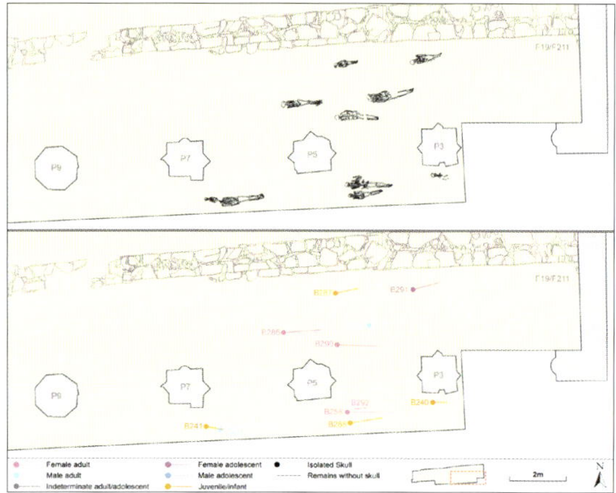
Fig. 6.20. Mid fourteenth-century burials at east side of aisle/nave.

Pl. 6.41. Grave slab E2399:273:25 (*in situ*).

similar to, if not the same layer as possible floor level (F293) discussed above. It was a highly compacted beige-blue sandy clay. One burial (B901) was cut into this material and rested on the foundation stones of the north transept.

- Mid fourteenth-century burials

A total of 16 burials were associated with this activity (Figs 6.19, 6.20 and Table 6.5).

At the western side of the aisle, in the vicinity of the medieval drain (F63), burials B7, B12 and B13 were interred in a highly compacted yellow/orange redeposited clay (F121) which sealed the lowermost burial horizon (F146) in this location. The only find was a nail (E2399:121:722).

Further to the east, towards the centre of the aisle and extending into the nave, eight burials were interred in F284 forming the latest burials in the nave. The burial matrix (F284) was a mid-grey-brown clayey sand with a yellow hue, of moderate compaction. It produced 13 iron nails (E2399:284:2575–87). The juvenile burial (B241, aged 1.5–2 years) displayed endocranial lesions indicating a possible haemorrhage from a trauma or an inflammatory condition such as meningitis. Another individual (male aged 35–39 years) displayed severe hypoplastic defects on his teeth owing to childhood diseases and dietary deficiencies. He also showed evidence of rickets indicating dietary deficiencies or lack of light (vitamin D deficiency).

Further to the north a similar layer (F343) extended into the north aisle as far as the north wall (F211/F19). The material consisted of a brown clay-rich layer of moderate compaction. The only finds retrieved from the horizon were a fragment of medieval window glass (E2399:343:2632) and a ferrous nail (E2399:343:2633). This context was cut by five burials (B285, B287, B288, B290, B291). Only one of the five grave fills (F378, B290) produced finds, consisting of two silver coins (E2399:378:98 and E2399:378:99) resting on the left pelvis of the individual, an adult female aged 45 years or over. Coin E2399:378:99 has been identified as an Edward III silver penny, possibly a third or florin coinage dating to between 1344 and 1351. The second coin (E2399:378:98) is assumed to be similar in date range but the obverse/reverse are illegible.

- Late fourteenth-/early fifteenth century burials

The eastern section of the aisle contained far more burial activity than the central or western portion of the aisle and this was evident by the numerous layers and contexts within which burials were placed (Fig. 6.21). Layer F269 was cut by a further 19 burials, some of which were incomplete and poorly preserved with grave cuts and fills not always apparent or discernible (Fig. 6.21, Table 6.6). Finds

Table 6.5: Phase 2 burials (16 individuals)

Burial Number	Sex	Age	Grave Fill	Grave Cut	Horizon
B7	Indeterminate	Infant	None discernible	None discernible	Under F69 stones
B12	Female	Adult	F117	F118	F121 (under F69 stones)
B13	Male	Adult	F119	F120	F121 and F100
B240	Indeterminate	Juvenile	F301	F302	F284 Nave
B241	Indeterminate	Juvenile	F299	F300	F284 Nave
B257	Male	Adult	F306	F307	F284 Nave
B258	Male	Adult	F304	F305	F284 Nave
B268	Indeterminate	Juvenile	F335	F336	F284 Nave
B285	Female	Adult	F357	F358	F343
B287	Indeterminate	Juvenile	F365	F366	F343
B288	Male	Adult	F367	F368	F343
B290	Female	Adult	F378	F379	F343
B291	Female	Adolescent	F381	F382	F343
B292	Female	Adult	F335	F336	F284 Nave
B301	Male	Adult	F425	F426	F284 Nave
B361	Indeterminate	Juvenile	F524	F525	F284 Nave

retrieved from the material included a fourteenth-century key (E2399:269:94) and four nails (E2399:269:2564–8). The analysis of the human remains suggests that one burial (B228, a female aged 35–45) from this layer displayed evidence of spinal fusion (possibly ankylosing spondylitis). An infant (B247, 3–9 months) displayed evidence of either scurvy or rickets, more likely the former which is a vitamin C deficiency. These burials were all sealed by context F233 into which later burials were cut.

- Marked burials in the nave

A small portion of the nave was required to be excavated to the south of the north arcade. This was to facilitate the pile foundations that were being excavated in the footprint of the pier foundations and the requirement for a sufficient 'working area' around same. The ground level within the nave, prior to excavation, was much lower than that of the north aisle. Post-medieval material (F221) directly overlay the burials in this area. After the removal of F221, an *in situ* grave slab (E2399:273:25) was uncovered within the nave just south of the north arcading (Pl. 6.41). Its removal revealed a single grave cut (F274) containing four burials as described below. Radiocarbon dating of the primary burial (B283) has indicated a date of between cal. AD 1392 and 1443. The cut of the grave (F274) when fully excavated was sub-rectangular in plan with sharp vertical sides and a flat base. It measured 1.66m east–west, 0.60m–0.65m north–south and 0.40m in depth.

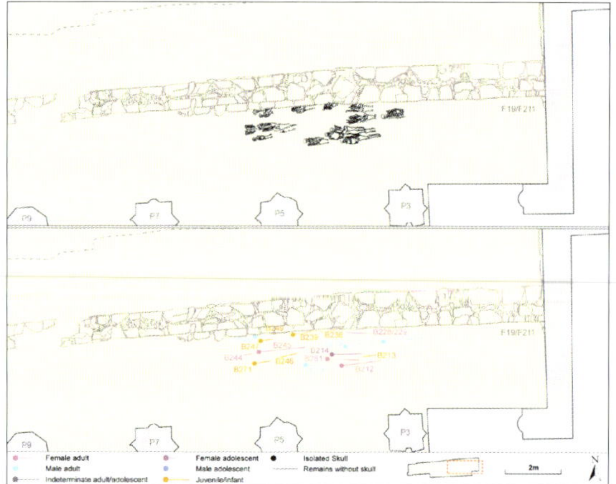

Fig. 6.21. Late fourteenth-century to early fifteenth-century burials (F269) at east side of aisle.

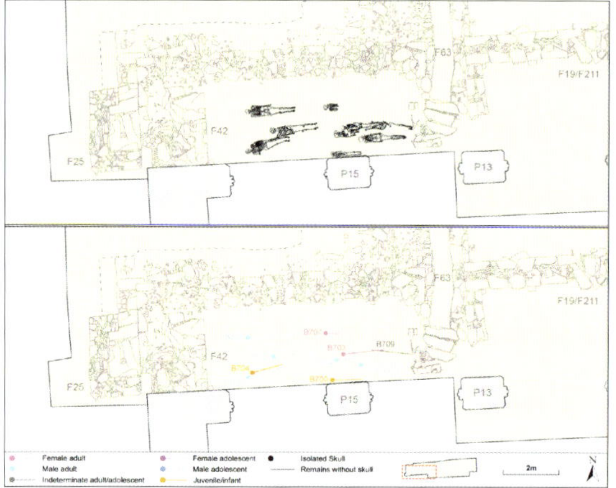

Fig. 6.22. Late fifteenth–mid sixteenth-century burials within the aisle at the west side.

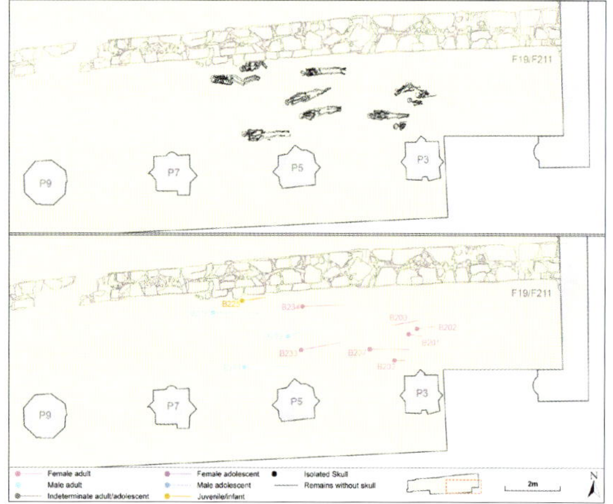

Fig. 6.23. Late fifteenth–mid sixteenth-century burials within the aisle at the east side.

The south side of the cut extended under the limit of excavation. It was filled with a brown-grey sandy silt (F273) of loose compaction with frequent disarticulated human bone inclusions. A number of iron nails (E2399:273:54, 57, 62–64 and 2574) were recovered from the fill. Although the grave was used for burial on four occasions, the fills were not distinguishable from each other. Four burials were recovered from the cut (B283, B235, B232 and B231).

The earliest burial (B283) was truncated by the burial above it (B235) and consisted of an adult male (only the left humerus and scapula survived). This was the primary burial within the grave cut. The second burial interred in this grave (B235) consisted of a female adult aged 25–30 and again was incomplete due to truncation by the overlying burial (B232). The remains were orientated exactly east–west with the arms extended by the pelvis. The second last burial interred in this grave cut (B232) was that of a male aged 25–35 years. The specialist notes a number of peri-mortem sharp-force weapon traumas to the cervical vertebrae, one of which is likely to have caused death. The last burial under the grave slab (B231) was that of a young–middle adult male aged 30–34 years (Pl. 6.42). The burial was complete with the arms extended by his side. Re-use of the grave cut to inter four individuals may suggest a familial relationship.

One individual (B374) was buried under an uninscribed grave slab (E2399:534:215), immediately to the south of Pier 11 within the nave (Pls 6.43, 6.44). This was the only burial in this grave. The skeleton was that of a young–middle adult male, aged 25–35 years. The individual had suffered a fracture to the right distal humerus (elbow) and displayed evidence of spina bifida occulta (see Human Remains section below). The individual is placed within the primary phase of burials in this location.

- Late fifteenth-/mid sixteenth-century burials

Layer F716 was located at the west side of the aisle and formed the latest material into which a further 11 burials were interred in that location. Twenty-two burials were uncovered at this level (Fig. 6.22, Table 6.7). Both the artefactual evidence and radiocarbon dating from burials B207 and B703 with a date range of cal. AD 1477–1642 and cal. AD 1458–1635 (Sigma 2) respectively, indicate a late fifteenth-/mid seventeenth-century date for the burials. The burials may belong to the last phases of monastic activity at Boyle

Table 6.6: Phase 3 burials (19 individuals) (east side of north aisle only)

Burial Number	Sex	Age	Grave Fill	Grave Cut	Horizon
B212	Female	Adult	F250	F251	F269
B213	Indeterminate	Juvenile	F551	F254	F269
B214	Female	Adolescent	F252	F253	F269
B219	Male	Adult	F261	F262	F269
B224	Male	Adult	F278	F279	F269
B228	Female	Adult	F265	F266	F269
B229	Female	Adult	None discernible	None discernible	F269
B236	Indeterminate	Juvenile	None discernible	None discernible	F269
B237	Female	Adult	None discernible	None discernible	F269
B239	Indeterminate	Juvenile	None discernible	None discernible	F269
B244	Female	Adult	None discernible	None discernible	F269
B245	Female	Adult	F308	F309	F269
B246	Indeterminate	Juvenile	F308	F309	F269
B247	Indeterminate	Infant	F310	F311	F269
B248	Male	Adult	F310	F310	F269
B249	Indeterminate	Juvenile	F310	F311	F269
B271	Indeterminate	Juvenile	F320	F321	F269
B281	Female	Adult	F344	F345	F269
B284	Male	Adult	F355	F356	F269

terminating with the dissolution in 1541.

At the east end of the north aisle, the burial matrix (F233) consisted of a dark brown material. It was cut by a post-medieval wall (F206, cut F260). The material produced 24 finds, most of which were iron nails (E2399:233:2343–52, E2399:233:2977–85). Two iron knives, medieval in date, were also recovered (E2399:233:20 scale tang and E2399:233:26 whittle tang). Eleven burials were interred into this matrix (F233), with seven of them identified as female (Fig. 6.23, Table 6.7). Finds were few, with only one iron nail and an unidentified item recovered from grave fill F285 (B234).

One of the 22 burials (B200), a female aged 30–34 years, was laid in a very distinct position, laying mostly on her right side. The arms were to the front of the torso with the left forearm over the right, and the left femur over the right. Her haphazard position in the grave is suggestive of a very hurried affair. Another male (B238, 35–39 years) had suffered at least three sharp-edged weapon injuries to the cranium: at the top left of the skull, the upper margin of the right eye, and the base of the left eye. In addition, he appears to have been struck on the side of the head, around the right ear, resulting in breaks to the back of the arch of the cheek bone and to the jaw. In addition, four left rib fragments (number of ribs affected unidentified) exhibited

Table 6.7 Phase 4 burials (22 individuals) within north aisle

Burial Number	Sex	Age	Grave Fill	Grave Cut	Horizon
B200	Female	Adult	None discernible	None discernible	F233
B201	Female	Adult	None discernible	None discernible	F233
B202	Female	Adult	F271	F272	F233
B207	Female	Adult	None discernible	None discernible	F233
B209	Female	Adult	None discernible	None discernible	F233
B211	Male	Adult	F249	F248	F255
B215	Male	Adult	F256	F256	F255
B225	Indeterminate	Juvenile	F267	F268	F255
B233	Female	Adult	F282	F283	F233
B234	Female	Adult	F285	F286	F233
B238	Male	Adult	F294	F295	F233
B700	Indeterminate	Juvenile	F712	F713	F716
B701	Male	Adult	F714	F715	F716
B702	Male	Adult	F717	F718	F716
B703	Female	Adult	F719	F720	F716
B704	Indeterminate	Juvenile	F721	F722	F716
B705	Male	Adult	F723	F724	F716
B706	Male	Adult	F725	F726	F716
B707	Female	Adult	F727	F728	F716
B708	Female	Adult	F731	F732	F716
B709	Indeterminate	Adult	None discernible	None discernible	F716
B710	Male	Adult	F735	F736	F716

sharp-force injuries indicative of horizontal slashes across the torso.

Burial matrix F716 at the west end of the north aisle overlay an earlier layer of burials and was cut by several grave cuts (F713, F715, F718, F720, F722, F724, F726, F728, F732 and F736) for burials B700–B710. Artefactual material recovered from this layer consists of 12 iron nails (E2399:711:751–61 and E2399:711:18), two architectural stones (E2399:711:22–3), two possible pot boilers (E2399:711:722–3), a miscellaneous iron object (E2399:711762) and a copper alloy mount (E2399:711:17) which may have been attached to a leather or wooden object.

- Sixteenth/seventeenth-century to nine teenth-century burials

Three sixteenth- to seventeenth-century burials (B3, B4 and B20 foetus) were also encountered after the removal of the later post-medieval walls

Pl. 6.42. Latest individual (B231) interred under grave slab E2399:273:25.

Pl. 6.43. Burial (B374) after removal of uninscribed grave slab E2399:534:215.

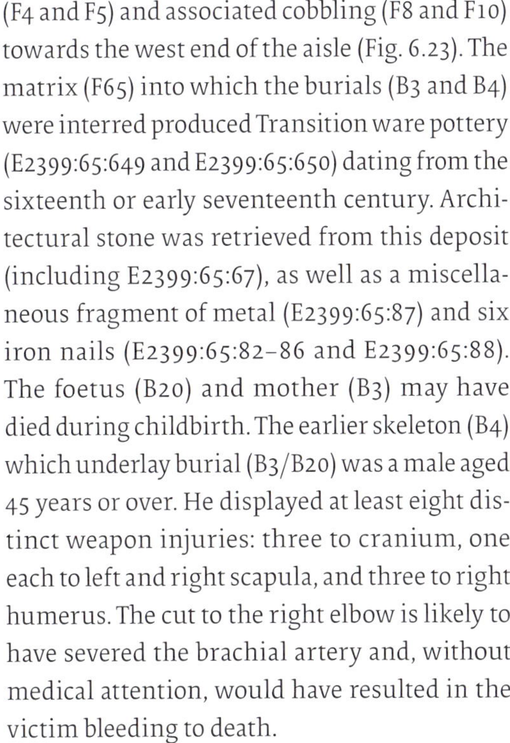

(F4 and F5) and associated cobbling (F8 and F10) towards the west end of the aisle (Fig. 6.23). The matrix (F65) into which the burials (B3 and B4) were interred produced Transition ware pottery (E2399:65:649 and E2399:65:650) dating from the sixteenth or early seventeenth century. Architectural stone was retrieved from this deposit (including E2399:65:67), as well as a miscellaneous fragment of metal (E2399:65:87) and six iron nails (E2399:65:82–86 and E2399:65:88). The foetus (B20) and mother (B3) may have died during childbirth. The earlier skeleton (B4) which underlay burial (B3/B20) was a male aged 45 years or over. He displayed at least eight distinct weapon injuries: three to cranium, one each to left and right scapula, and three to right humerus. The cut to the right elbow is likely to have severed the brachial artery and, without medical attention, would have resulted in the victim bleeding to death.

Burial B600 was uncovered immediately under the cobbles (F3) just to the east of the west wall (F42). It is likely to be the latest burial on the site, perhaps nineteenth century or later, evident from the level at which it was buried (under the topsoil and modern overburden). The burial was orientated east–west with the head unusually to the east. The skeleton was partial with the cranium missing and represents an individual aged 4–6 years. The individual had active lesions suggestive of systemic infection (L. Lynch pers. comm.).

SEALING OF BURIALS

In several places throughout the excavation, the presence of stone at the interface between the post-medieval layers and the top of the burials was notable (Pls 6.45–47). This occurred both inside the church within the north aisle and outside the church (F19/F211). The stone layers did not represent uniform cobble-like surfaces but rather a rough, uneven placement of stones over the burial. It is likely that these stone surfaces were deposited over the burials in the post-medieval period. Pottery (E2399:223:2135) from the layer directly underneath one such stony surface (F216) included a Grey Slip coated handle from a pot dating from the eighteenth

Pl. 6.44. Grave slab (E2399:534:215) south of Pier 11 looking north.

Pl. 6.45. Stone surfaces (F66 and F69) sealing underlying burials. North wall F19/F211 in centre.

Pl. 6.46. Stone surface (F216) sealing underlying burials.

century at least. Use of the church during the military occupation (from 1592 onwards) could have resulted in many medieval and early post-medieval deposits being removed or disturbed. It is possible that a layer of stone was placed over the burial ground during the post-medieval period.

The easternmost stone deposit (F216) consisted of an irregular layer of stones set within a matrix of dark brown silty sand with occasional inclusions of mortar and yellow clay (Pl. 6.46). It is probable that this surface was laid down when the north wall was still upstanding as all such stony layers respect the line of the wall on the north and south sides. This stone surface (F216) overlay deposit F223 which produced finds dating from the eighteenth century or later. The layer (F906) also consisted of a rough stone surface under layer F905 and was comprised of medium sized stones laid flat to form a rough surface. It overlay a distinct black-beige deposit (F908). One iron nail (E2399:906:817) was recovered from this deposit.

Another similar layer (F231) was located further west, within the aisle (F211/F19). This rough surface (F231) was delimited on the east side by the possible early buttress/wall (F220/F280). The deposit of stones consisted of an irregularly laid rough surface composed of *c.* 80% small to medium sized stones. It was truncated on the south. The ground level within the nave was significantly reduced by the Commissioners of Public Works in the nineteenth century. The material (F238 and F239) recorded under this stony surface produced a shard of eighteenth-century bottle glass (E2399:238:2353) and this accords well with the deposition date suggested for the aforementioned layer (F216).

In the western portion of the excavation area a similar stone deposit was encountered to the west (F69) and east (F66) of the medieval drain (F63) and to the south of the north wall (F19/F211) within the north aisle (Pl. 6.45). The roughly laid surface (F69) comprised a number of large flat stones and a broken and discarded grave slab (E2399:69:73). This deposit overlay burial B12 (F117/F118). The underlying deposit (F711) covered numerous burials. Artefactual material recovered from this layer consists of 11 iron nails (E2399:711:751–61), two architectural stones (E2399:711:22–23), two possible pot boilers (E2399:711:722–3), two miscellaneous iron objects (E2399:711:18 and 762) and a copper alloy riveted mount of unknown date (E2399:711:17).

Outside the north wall a stone surface/plinth (F230) was uncovered which consisted of a flat flagged surface of large sandstone slabs set in a mid-brown sandy clay. It measured 3.1m in length east–west, 1.6m in width north–south and 0.10m–0.20m in thickness. It was overlain by a roughly laid stone surface (F227) with inclusions of a complete quern stone (E2399:227:15) (Pl. 6.47). The stone surface (F227) overlay the latest burial activity outside the north wall (F240/F232). The finds recovered include a piece of architectural stone (E2399:227:14), five ferrous nails

(E2399:227:2203–27) and the rotary quern stone (E2399:227:15). The presence of discarded architectural stone and a quern stone again suggests a later, post-medieval date for the deposition of the stones on top of the burials.

Eighteenth-century buttresses

Evidence for two early buttress foundations abutting Piers 7 and 9 was uncovered during the excavations (Fig. 6.24).

BUTTRESS ABUTTING PIER 7

This structure (F220) was constructed of large stones with a rubble core and was built on a flat foundation of large flagstones (F280) (Fig. 6.24, Pls 6.48, 6.49). The buttress measured 3.25m in length north–south, 0.89m in width east–west and survived to 0.30m in height. The structure is unlikely to date to the monastic period since the base mouldings of the pier would have been obscured by the buttress. It was, however, constructed when the north wall was upstanding to some extent as it terminates exactly at its foundation. This buttress could represent an early attempt to support Pier 7 (F296) and could date to anytime between the post-dissolution period of the mid to late 1500s to the early 1700s. It is likely to represent one of the three buttresses shown on Beranger's sketch of 1779 (Fig. 1.8).

BUTTRESS ABUTTING PIER 9

Another buttress-type foundation (F411) and associated cut (F435) was exposed at the level of the base moulding of Pier 9 (F522) (Fig. 6.24, Pls 6.50–2). It abutted the north side of the pier base and was exposed immediately after the removal of the latest buttress base (F393). This may also represent one of the three buttresses depicted on Beranger's sketch of 1779 (Fig. 1.8). The structure was poorly preserved and was cut by a nineteenth-century drain (F290/F407) on the north side where it would have abutted the north wall.

THE ROBBING OUT OF THE NORTH WALL

The north wall is likely to have been extant when the

Pl. 6.47. Stone surface (F227) outside north wall (F19/ F211).

Pl. 6.48. Buttress (F220) and flagstone foundation (F280).

Pl. 6.49. Foundation flagstones F280 after removal of buttress (F220) looking north.

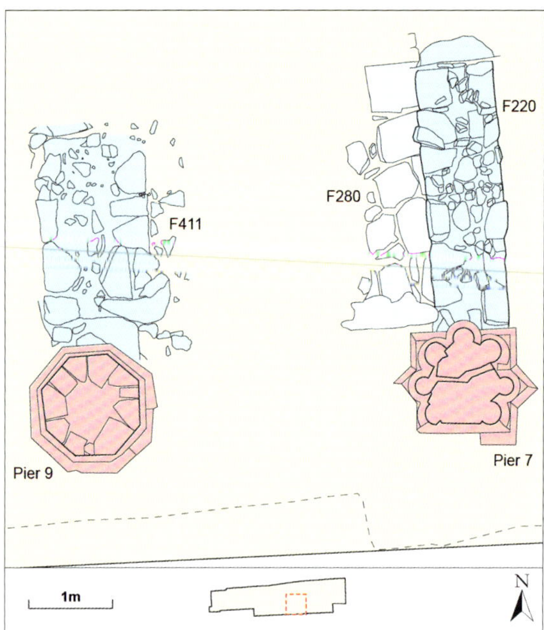

Fig. 6.24. Eighteenth-century buttresses.

early buttress (F220) abutting Pier 7 was constructed in the eighteenth century, since the buttress was neatly built against the north wall foundations. A backfilled trench (F41/F219) along the line of the sub-surface north wall was exposed almost along the full length of excavation area but not as evident where the north wall survived some three to four courses high towards the east of the site (Fig. 6.25, Pls 6.53, 6.54). It measured 29.4m in length (east–west), an average of 1m in width (north–south) and varied in depth from 0.2m to 0.8m.

The basal fills (F35/F18) consisted of a mortar-rich deposit of silty sand directly overlying the basal courses of the north wall. An inscribed medieval candlestick or chalice base (E2399:18:6) was retrieved from the base of this layer. The object is incomplete and was folded over in antiquity when deposited (see Ó Floinn below). Finds included four nails and a shard of post-medieval window glass (E2399:35:604–8). Fill F17 was excavated from the western half of the robbing out trench. A dark grey to black fine clay silt fill (F46) contained significant quantities of disarticulated human remains. The uppermost layer (F47) consisted of a grey to mid black clayey silt and included lime and sandy mortar. Fills F40, F39 and F38 were located within the cut (F41) immediately adjacent to the west wall (F42). The basal fill (F40) consisted of a mid-brown sandy silt with occasional inclusions of mortar flecks and disarticulated animal and human bone. It overlay F39 and finds, including two clay pipes consisting of a heel fragment (E2399:40:760) and an undecorated stem (E2399:40:761), were recovered. Fill F39 consisted of a grey silty clay with inclusions of mortar flecks, occasional animal and human bone. A small architectural stone fragment (E2399:39:49) was recovered. The uppermost fill (F38) consisted of a mottled grey-brown sandy silt with inclusions of mortar flecks and disarticulated animal and human bone. It was exposed under deposit F36 which overlay the fills cut of the robbing out trench (F41) and contained two iron nails (E2399:38:613–14).

Fill F215 consisted of a mixed brown sandy silt with inclusions of a pink/orange mortar and occasional inclusions of stone, animal bone and infrequent charcoal flecks. This fill was cut by a later drain (F407) and a pit (F413) in the centre of the excavation area. Numerous finds (22) were recovered from the fill and included black glazed ware (seventeenth to nineteenth century in date), an eighteenth-century bottle glass shard (E2399:215:1899), creamware (eighteenth century in date), four miscellaneous ferrous objects, nine ferrous nails, two post-medieval window glass fragments, a slate roof tile and a sherd of tin-glazed earthenware (seventeenth or eighteenth century in date).

Numerous finds were recovered from the fills of this trench including clay pipes, post-medieval window glass (potentially dating to anytime between the time the military took over the abbey in 1592 and the late 1800s) while pottery dating from the eighteenth century provides a date for the feature. It is likely that the remainder of the north wall was robbed out at roughly the same time as the early buttresses were constructed. It may be possible that the masonry from the north wall was utilised for the buttresses; however, this cannot be stated with certainty.

Pits

Two pits (F911, F916) were uncovered at the east end of the north aisle (Fig. 6.25) immediately west of the north transept door which provides access to the aisle. Given their position within the aisle, it is likely that the pits are post-dissolution (late

Pl. 6.50. Pier 9 early buttress (F411) (after removal of later buttress F393).

Pl. 6.51. Cut (F435) for earlier buttress F411 looking south towards Pier 9.

Pl. 6.52. Early buttress (F411) exposed after removal of later buttress (F393).

medieval) at the earliest but more likely to be post-medieval in date. Pit F911 measured 1.3m east–west, 1.15m north–south and 0.05m–0.1m in thickness. The cut consisted of a large oval/sub-rectangular pit with a sharp break of slope at the top at the west and south-west. The base was stony with rounded edges. It measured 2.6m north–south, 1.7m east–west and 0.9m in depth. It was filled with a deposit (F909) comprising *c.* 60% oyster shell within a brown silty sand matrix.

Pl. 6.53. Robbing out trench (F219, post-excavation) along central and eastern end of north aisle.

Pl. 6.54. Section of robbing out trench (F41/F219) in western side of north aisle.

Pl. 6.55. Ditch (F222) with cobbles (F207) subsided into cut.

Pl. 6.56. West-facing section of ditch at east end of north aisle.

This deposit underlay fill F910. Two iron objects comprising a U-shaped staple (E2399:909:820) and a miscellaneous item (E2399:909:821) were recovered. The upper fill (F910) consisted of a brown compact stony fill with inclusions of medium sized stones, animal bone fragments, occasional mortar associated with a dump of stones and lenses of pink sand. It measured 1.3m north–south, 1.3m east–west and 0.9m in thickness. A residual decorated bone knife handle

Pl. 6.57. Linear ditch (F222) post-excavation looking east.

(E2399:910:50) and a Type C whittle tang knife of thirteenth- or fourteenth-century date (910:832), a possible sixteenth- or seventeenth-century iron horseshoe (E2399:910:38), seven iron nails, and three miscellaneous iron objects were recovered. Pit F916 was sub-circular/oval in plan and measured 0.72m east–west, 0.61m north–south and 0.43m in thickness. It was filled with a mixed deposit (F915), comprising beige and black lenses mixed with a mid-dark brown sandy silt and was of moderate compaction. It contained burnt and unburnt animal bones and stones. It cut the possible medieval floor (F914).

Nineteenth-century ditch

The southern edge of an east–west orientated linear ditch (F222) was uncovered along the north side of the excavation area in the eastern and central portions of the site (Fig. 6.25, Pls 6.55–7). The ditch was uncovered after the removal of the nineteenth-century cobbles (F207/F209). Its full width was not uncovered and only a small portion of its southern side was excavated. It had gradual sloping sides and extended under the north baulk. It measured 24.3m east–west, 2m north–south (as exposed) and 0.49m in depth. The cobbles, where they overlay the ditch fills, had subsided substantially and slumped into the ditch suggesting a short time span between the backfilling of the ditch and the laying down of the cobbled surface (Pl. 6.55). The ditch cut numerous burials outside the north wall (F232/F240) and also cut the northern extent of the small annex (F312) at east end of excavation.

The basal fill (F229) consisted of a dark brown to black humic silty sand of moderate compaction with inclusions of animal and disarticulated human bone. A residual copper alloy pin (E2399:229:157), numerous iron nails, eighteenth-century bottle glass, architectural stones, a clay pipe stem, a sherd of stoneware and window glass were recovered. It underlay fill F213, cobbles F207/F209 and layer F212. Seventy-seven finds were recovered, 60 of which were nails, thought to be from disturbed coffins. A date range of nineteenth to twentieth century has been provided for the sherd of stoneware (E2399:229:88). Although some earlier finds were recovered, this sherd provides a *terminus post quem* for the feature. Upper fills F213, F408, F225, F224 and F226 contained further evidence of building collapse and seventeenth-century to nineteenth-century pottery.

Ditch

A linear ditch (F604) was partially exposed west of annex F25 extending in a north–south direction (Fig. 6.25, Pl. 6.58). Only the eastern edge was excavated. The ditch had gradually sloping sides. The base was not exposed due to the limit of excavation. Although not stratigraphically linked, this ditch is likely to be contemporary with ditch F222 as discussed above. The excavated section measured 1.64m north–south, 0.49m–0.88m east–west and 0.95m in depth and was exposed under cobbles (F3). The basal fill (F603) comprised a grey moderately compact sandy silt with inclusions of oyster shell, mortar, charcoal flecks, human bone, burnt and unburnt animal bone. Three iron nails (E2399:603:3433–4 and 3454), two miscellaneous iron objects (E2399:603:3435–6), four post-medieval

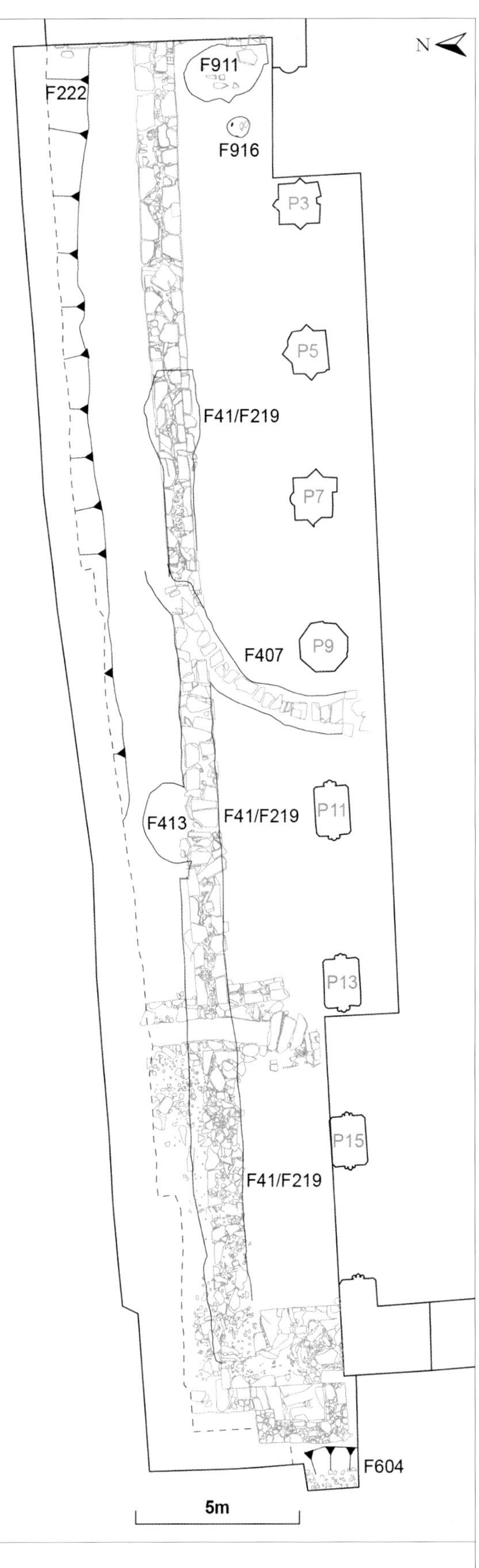

Fig. 6.25. Post-medieval features indicated in blue: robber trench (F41/F219), pits (F916 and F911), ditches (F222 and F604), drain (F407/F290) where it cuts north wall (F19/F211).

Pl. 6.58. Ditch (F604) to right looking south.

Pl. 6.59. Post-medieval drain (F407) looking north.

window glass shards (E2399:603:3429–32) and a medieval bone handle (E2399:603:3072) were recovered. This material produced very little archaeobotanical evidence with only four cereal grains retrieved from the sample. The uppermost fill (F602) underlay the cobbles (F3) and consisted of a mid brown stony material. It produced a large quantity of oat and may represent discarded domestic refuse.

Nineteenth-century drain

A stone drain (F290/F407) extended from between Piers 9 and 11 as far as the northern edge of the excavation (Fig. 6.25, Pl. 6.59). It curved sharply from the north arcading through the north wall (F19/F211) in a north-easterly direction and cut the ditch (F222) and its associated fills. Numerous burials in the north aisle were also cut by this drain in addition to the eighteenth-century buttress (F411). It measured 12m in length and 0.7m in width at the base. The fills (F289 and F406) sealing the drain consisted of a mid to dark grey silty material with inclusions of a nineteenth-century bottle glass shard (E2399:289:2591), iron nails (E2399:289:2592–4, E2399:406:2775–83), a post-medieval window glass fragment (E2399:289:2590), and five post-medieval peg tiles (E2399:406:2770–4).

The drain post-dates the nineteenth-century ditch (F222), therefore placing it in the nineteenth century or later. The presence of this nineteenth-century drain under the buttress foundation (F393) at Pier 9 is direct evidence that the buttress is a later rebuild and is not that shown on Beranger's sketch (Fig.1.8) discussed above.

Blocking of the north arcade

It would appear that during the military occupation of the abbey, the arches along the north arcade were blocked to almost half their height. These blocking walls (F234, F235 and F236, F424, F409 and F703) were dismantled by the OPW to below ground level and therefore were not visible above ground prior to the excavation (apart from F703 at the western end of the excavation which was deconstructed entirely by the archaeological team) (Pls 6.60–3). The quantity of post-medieval material (nineteenth century) that had accumulated against the northern face of the north arcading (in the vicinity of F703) suggests the likely date of the blocking. Interestingly, the arches appear to have been fully blocked up on Beranger's sketch of 1779 (Fig.1.8), itself based on an earlier drawing, but only partially blocked on Westropp's illustration of 1880–91. It is, therefore, possible that the walls dismantled by the OPW during their conservation works were a later construction which replaced earlier walls. Archaeological evidence also supports this theory in that one of the walls (F424) was built on top of a nineteenth-century drain (F290/F407). Furthermore, concrete was evident at the base of some of the walls (F234, F235 and F236). Evidence of an earlier wall (F259) was uncovered under wall F236 between Piers 7 and 9 (Pl. 6.60).

Nineteenth-century cobbles and associated walls

A cobbled surface with integrated gullies and associated walls (F4, F5, F396, F210 and F397) was exposed across the entire north aisle (Fig. 6.26, Pls 6.64–7). The cobbles are one of the latest events on

Pl. 6.60. Pier 7 base moulding and wall (F259) to south and wall (F236) to the north.

Pl. 6.62. Wall (F703) constructed between piers at west end of aisle/nave F703.

Pl. 6.61. Wall (F409) in between piers 11 and 13.

Pl. 6.63. Wall (F703) looking east.

the site being exposed in some areas just under the topsoil. The material retrieved from underneath the cobbles dates from the nineteenth century, thus providing a *terminus post quem* for the surface. Finds from underneath the cobbled surfaces within the central part of the aisle included sherds of eighteenth/nineteenth-century pearlware (E2399:212:1712–14) and transfer-printed ware (E2399:212:1716, E2399:212:1717). Further to the east, adjacent to the blocked north transept door, the material under the cobbles produced finds including two clay pipe stems (E2399:903:715 and 716), three seventeenth- to nineteenth-century pottery sherds (E2399:903:138–40) and a nineteenth-century light green glass bottle shard (E2399:903:625). The earliest evidence of cobbling (F13) was recorded at the western end of the aisle (Pl. 6.64) where a clearly defined cobbled path was exposed. The cobbles were well constructed utilising all available resources such as discarded architectural stone from engaged piers (E2399:13:17–29). One layer (F48), which underlay the cobbles in the western part of the aisle, produced an impressive sixteenth-century sword (E2399:48:80) (see Swift below).

The cobbling had subsided in places perhaps due to their placement above cut features such as ditches (F222 and F604) (Pl. 6.66). The entire cobbled surface extended over an area of 41.45m

Pl. 6.64. Cobbles (F13).

Pl. 6.65. Cobbles (F8/F10) and walls (F4 and F5) at western end of north aisle looking east.

Pl. 6.66. Cobbles (F902) in south-east corner of aisle against transept wall.

Pl. 6.68. Buttress foundation (F393, Pier 9).

Pl. 6.67. Wall (F397) looking north (note test trench excavated by Fiona Rooney to right of wall).

in length east–west, 8m in width north–south at the eastern end and only 4m in width north–south at the western end of the north aisle.

Buttresses

Five buttresses (F203, F202, F201, F383 and F394) were upstanding and abutting the north arcade prior to the commencement of excavation associated with the North Wall Project in 2006 (Figs 6.26, 6.27, Pls 6.68–71). The buttresses were integral to the survival of the arcade. The five buttresses and a connecting wall (F206) were dismantled prior to the commencement of the main season of excavation in 2008. There is direct stratigraphic evidence that the five buttresses are nineteenth century in date and may have been significantly altered in the early 1900s. Finds from the buttresses included architectural stone, eighteenth-century bottles, red earthenware tiles, seventeenth- to nineteenth-century black glazed ware, and eighteenth-century creamware. Twenty-two artefacts

Pl. 6.69. Buttress foundation (F393, Pier 9), north wall to right and cobbles F207 either side of buttress.

Pl. 6.70. Buttress (F203, Pier 3) at east end of north aisle.

Pl. 6.71. Buttress (F201, Pier 7) looking south.

were recovered from the base of the buttress (F201) including eighteenth-century creamware, eighteenth-century bottles, clay pipes, seventeenth- to nineteenth-century glazed red earthenware, North Devon gravel tempered ware (seventeenth

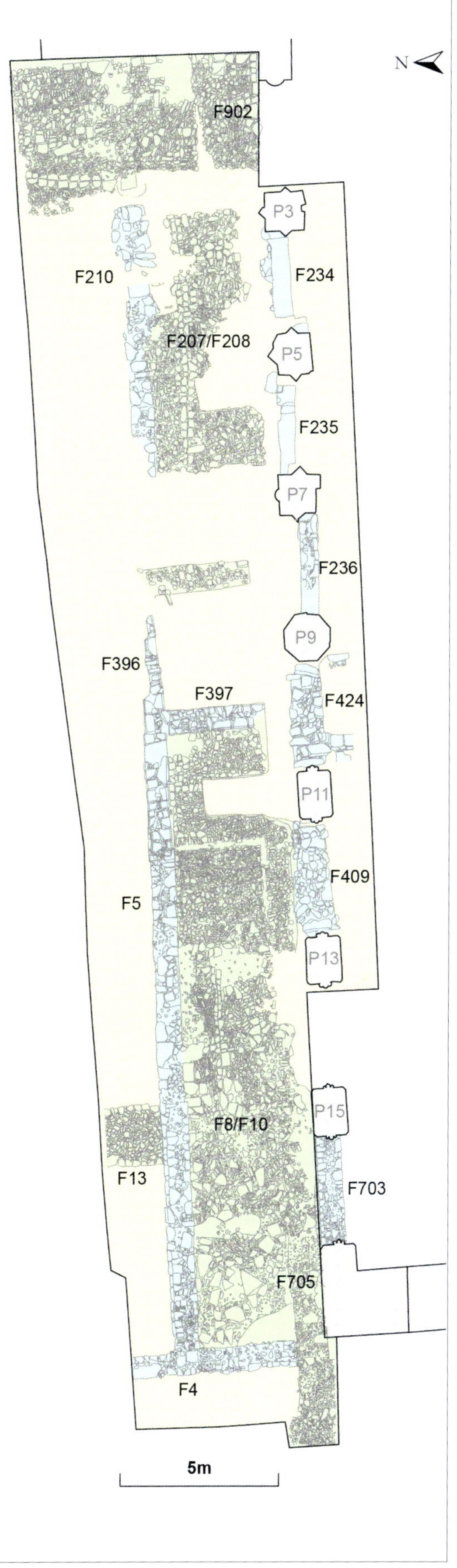

Fig. 6.26. Nineteenth-century cobbles and associated walls and blocking of the north arcade.

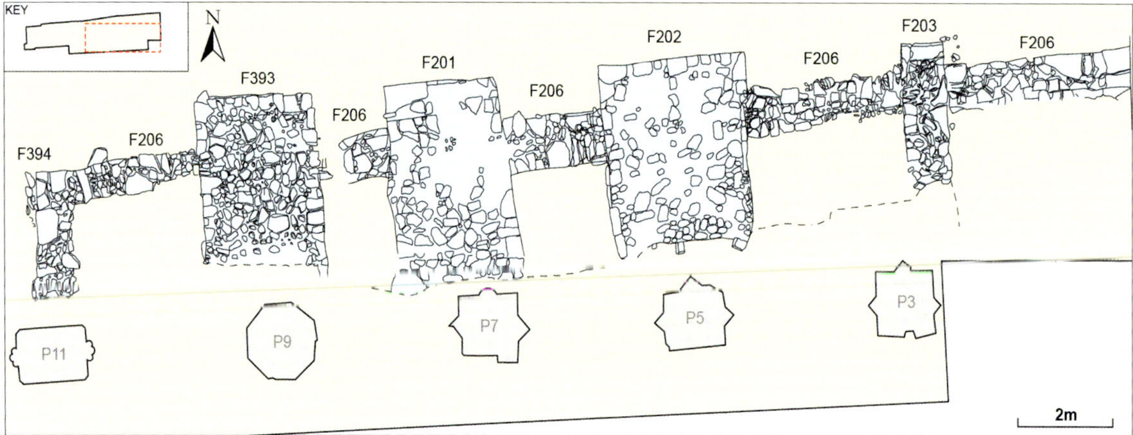

Fig. 6.27. Post-medieval buttresses.

century in date), three sherds of eighteenth- to nineteenth-century pearlware, and nineteenth- to twentieth-century stoneware.

Modern deposits

A post-medieval/modern deposit (F205/F7/F9) extended across the site from east to west and consisted of a dark brown silty clay containing modern, post-medieval and medieval finds, disarticulated animal and human bone. It is direct evidence of the disturbed nature of the site, containing 1,096 finds varying from post-medieval pottery, architectural stone, post-medieval window glass, ferrous nails, buttons (E2399:205:45 and E2399:205:48), a Victorian penny (possibly 1861) (E2399:205:30), two coins of unknown date (E2399:205:5 and 8), a possible Victoria halfpenny (E2300:205:3) and a rare St Patrick's issue farthing dated 1673 (E2399:7:1).

The Finds

Miriam Carroll

This section presents the results of the analysis of various artefacts recovered during the excavation. The National Museum finds registration number for this project is E2399. For the purposes of analysis, artefacts of varying types were grouped into a number of categories such as stone artefacts, metal artefacts, or glass, and are presented below accordingly. This impressive range of finds offers important and occasionally surprising insights into the monastic centuries at Boyle. Fragments of window glass, for example, add to what is known of the Cistercian approach to decoration within their churches. There again, albeit incomplete, the base of an inscribed medieval chalice or candlestick in gilded silver is a rare and important discovery of a liturgical object, taking us to the heart of religious life within the abbey. In contrast, we are presented with a range of knives, coins, stick pins and weaponry, including an impressive example of a late medieval sword, all of which adds to our appreciation of such sites and their interface with the secular world.

INTRODUCTION

Over 1,830 metal and non-metal objects were recovered from the excavations of the north aisle at Boyle Abbey. Of these, over 1,362 are nails or nail shafts. In addition, approximately 290 items were undiagnostic due to their fragmented or corroded nature and are consequently catalogued as miscellaneous. The remaining objects vary in their nature and function, from items of personal dress such as pins to objects of domestic use such as keys and scale balances. Items found in direct association with burials were few but where they occurred largely comprised coins, all of which are medieval in date. While a large number of finds may be attributed to the medieval period, they were frequently found in post-medieval contexts which indicates the significant disturbance that took place within the church over the centuries since its dissolution. Items pertaining to the structure and glazing of the church are also present in the assemblage in the form of window lead and items of what may be termed 'structural ironwork', such as nails, tacks and staples. Significant finds of a chalice/candlestick base and an iron sword hint at the opposing aspects of activity. The candlestick base is a reminder of the once rich corpus of such objects that would have been used within the church (see Ó Floinn below), the sword, a sharp reminder of the demise of the abbey after its dissolution and subsequent military occupation (see Swift below). A large number of items also date to the post-dissolution period of the abbey's history right up to the modern period, a testament to the how the abbey continued as a focal point within the community long after it went out of use.

The items are discussed below according to type and function and each section is followed by a catalogue.

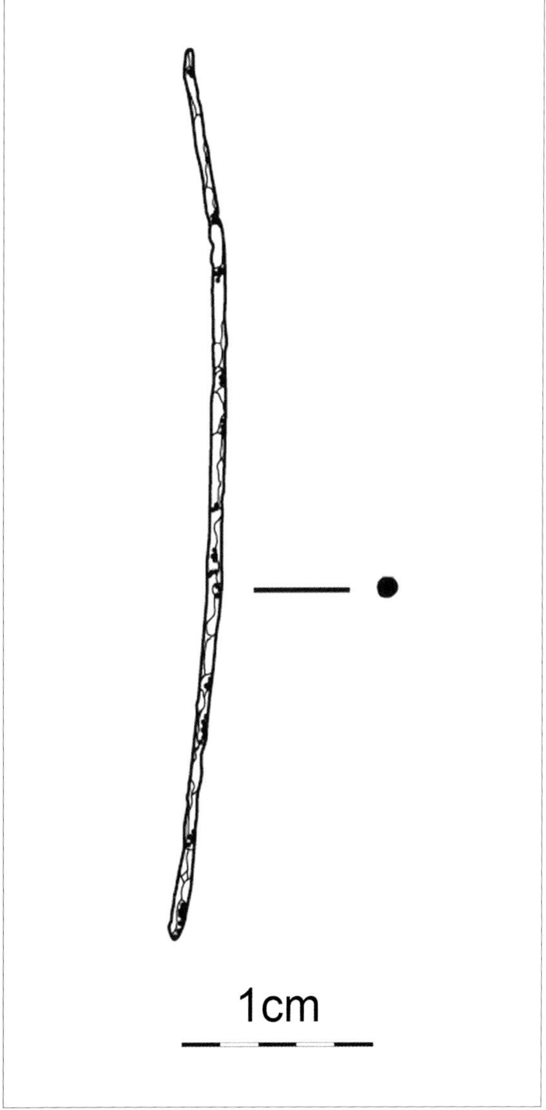

Fig. 6.28. Needle E2399:734:30. (Illustration: S. Nylund)

PINS/NEEDLES (FIG. 6.28)

Pins and/or needles are frequently classified as such if the diagnostic elements of the objects such as the eye or head are missing. In such instances a loose classification must be applied. The majority of the possible pins/needles from Boyle are of iron, with one copper alloy example. These artefacts may have been items of personal dress or indeed pins for fastening shrouds, but alternatively may be needles now lacking the distinctive eye.

CATALOGUE

Pin/needle. E2399:36:737. Fe. L. 80.9mm, Th. (shaft) 5mm, Wt. 4.2g. Possible iron needle/pin, head not extant. Shaft tapers to a narrow point. Corroded.

Pin/needle. E2399:1/2:3161. Fe. L. 35.6mm, W. 6mm, Th. 7.1mm, Wt. 3.1g. Incomplete. Pin/needle shank with head/eye extant (D. 4.3mm). Shaft folded back onto itself. Rectangular to sub-square in section. Highly corroded.

Pin/needle. E2399:26:10. Fe. L. 49.8mm, W. 3.4mm, Th. 3.2mm, Wt. 1.4g. Incomplete. Possible pin/needle shank, head not extant. Shank, rectangular/square in cross section, tapers to a fine point. Fragmented into three pieces. Conserved.

Possible pin/needle. E2399:26:9. Fe. L. 60.6mm, W. (head?) 8.3mm, Th. (shank) 3.9mm, Wt. 4.7g. Incomplete. Possible pin or unfinished needle. Shank rectangular in cross section tapers to a point. Flat rectangular sectioned 'head' at opposing end. Conserved.

Pin/needle. (illustrated, Fig. 6.28. E2399: 734:30. Cu alloy. L. 44.56mm, D. 0.76mm, Wt. 0.1g. Incomplete. Very fine shank of needle/pin. Head not extant. Shank circular in cross section. Bent and slightly flatted at one end, possibly location of head/eye. Conserved.

Needle fragment. E2399:901:25. Fe. L. 22mm, D. 1.3mm, Wt. 0.1g. Incomplete. Needle shank with small portion of eye visible at one end. Shank circular in cross section, tapers towards point (not extant). Conserved.

Pin/needle. E2399:901:26. Fe. L. 21.8mm, D. 1.5mm, Wt. 0.2g. Incomplete. Pin/needle shank. Circular in cross section. Tapers slightly towards one end. Conserved (Fig. 6.28).

PERSONAL DRESS ITEMS

- Buckles

Eight buckles or buckle frames were recovered from a variety of contexts. Iron buckles range from crude rectangular examples to those which are 'elegantly shaped'. The buckles are simple examples of iron rectangular and D-shaped frames which would have been easy for the smith to produce. E2399:205:114 has an extant pin and sheet roller. The roller is made of a separate sheet of metal which is formed into a cylinder around the outside frame of the buckle. It would have facilitated easier and tighter fastening than a rigid integral edge but may also have been related to the fashions of the time. Small buckles such as those from Boyle may have been used on girdles, shoes or saddle bags. E2399:205:114 and 121 may be medieval in date but were recovered from a post-medieval context. Similarly, E2399:230:2284 is medieval in appearance and was recovered from manual cleaning of a stone flagged surface outside the north wall F19/F211. Trapezoidal buckles such as E2399:205:1451 are known from later thirteenth- to fifteenth-century contexts in Britain but are likely to have continued in use into the post-medieval period. This example from Boyle was recovered from a post-medieval context (F205); however, its origins in the later medieval period cannot be ruled out. Its larger size may suggest use with a strap for horse equipment. A double-oval framed buckle (E2399:212:1795) was found in a post-medieval deposit (F212) in the abbey. This buckle form is known in Britain and Ireland in the later medieval period, with similar examples from mid fourteenth- to early fifteenth-century contexts in London. The form continued in use into the early eighteenth century after which it went out of use but appears to have been most prevalent from the fifteenth to the seventeenth century.

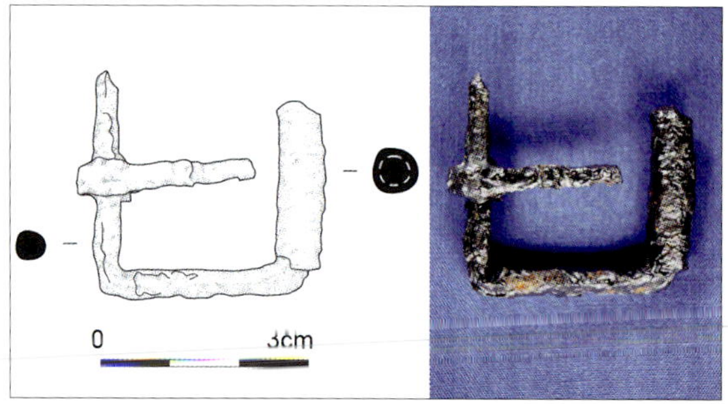

Pl. 6.72. Buckle E2399:205:114.

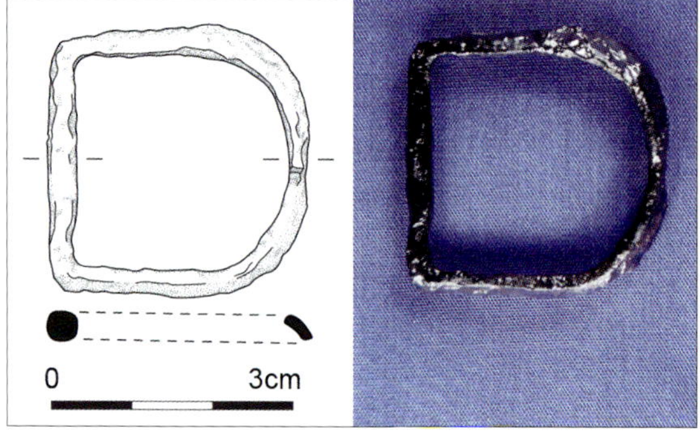

Pl. 6.73. Buckle E2399:401:137.

CATALOGUE

Buckle. E2399:205:121. Fe. L. 39.4mm, W. 25.9mm, Th. 4.6mm, Wt. 7.2g. Rectangular buckle, rectangular in section with rectangular sectioned pin extant. Possible shoe or girdle buckle. Conserved but corroded.

Buckle. (illustrated, Pl. 6.72). E2399:205:114. Fe. L. 33.6mm, W. 26.8mm, Th. 3.1mm, Wt. 6.8g. Incomplete. Portion of single looped rectangular buckle frame with rectangular sectioned pin extant. Sheet roller also present. Conserved but corroded.

Buckle. (illustrated, Pl. 6.73). E2399:401:137. Fe. L. 32.3mm, W. 33mm, Th. 4.7mm, Wt. 5.4g. Incomplete. D-shaped buckle frame, rectangular in cross section. Bar is thinner than the frame which is angled inwards slightly. Possibly post-medieval in date. Conserved.

Buckle frame. E2399:205:1451. Fe. L. 50.77mm, W. 48mm, Th. 6.5mm, Wt. 20.9g. Incomplete. Trapezoidal buckle frame, rectangular in cross section. Pin not extant. Corroded.

Buckle frame. E2399:204:520. Fe. L. 50.5mm, W. 32.6mm, Th. 4.1mm, Wt. 16.4g. Incomplete. Rectangular buckle frame, possibly D-shaped or rectangular in cross section. Pin not extant. Frame is damaged and bent. Corroded.

Buckle frame. E2399:205:1664. Fe. L. 30mm, W. 32.3mm, Th. 4.8mm, Wt. 6.5g. Incomplete. Small rectangular buckle frame, rectangular in cross section. Pin not extant, frame incomplete. Corroded.

Buckle frame. E2399:230:2284. Fe. L. 28.7mm, W. 34mm, Th. 5.7mm, Wt. 4.5g. Incomplete. Small D-shaped buckle frame, rectangular in cross section. Pin not extant and frame is incomplete. Corroded.

Buckle frame. E2399:212:1795. Fe. L. 67.1mm, W. 48mm, Th. 4.6mm, Wt. 39.g. Incomplete. Double-oval frame, one loop being smaller than the other. Frame rectangular in cross section. Pin not extant. Corroded.

- Stick pins

Three stick pins were recovered (E2399:91:63, E2399:146:90 and E2399:439:186). Two of the three are unclassified. The third pin is club-headed and pins such as these are known from eleventh- to thirteenth-century contexts elsewhere in Ireland. Club-headed pins have been recovered from contexts dating to the late eleventh to thirteenth century in Dublin and Waterford and thirteenth-century contexts in Cork (Carroll and Quinn 2003, 271). The club-headed pin came from a medieval layer within the church and may be thirteenth to fourteenth century in date.

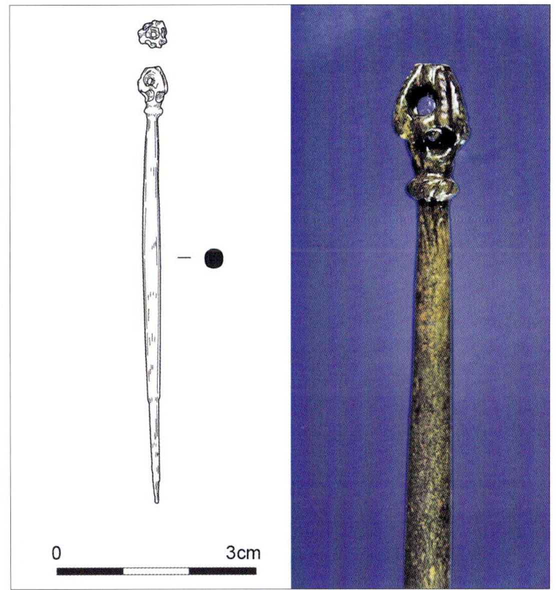

Pl. 6.74. Stick pin E2399.91.63.

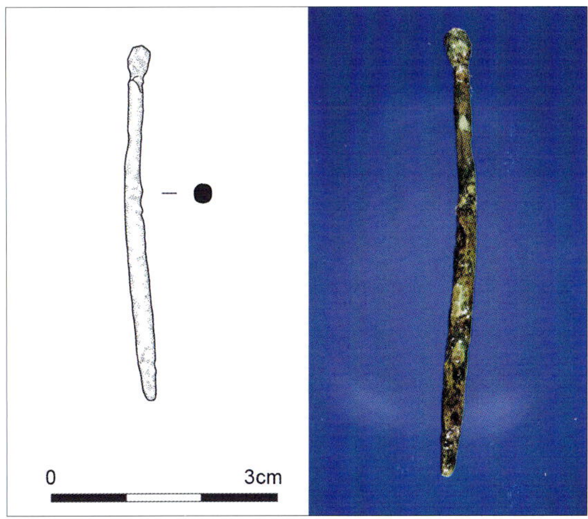

Pl. 6.75. Stick pin E2399:146:90.

CATALOGUE

Stick pin (illustrated, Pl. 6.74). E2399:91:63. Cu alloy. L. 63.7mm, W. (head) 4.4mm, D. (shank) 2.4mm, Wt. 1.5g. Complete. Unclassified. Expanded shank. Upper and mid-portion of shank circular in cross section, lower portion rectangular in section and tapers to fine point. Elaborate head with circular perforation at top and three perforations through centre. This gives the impression that head is formed by three ribbed narrow panels which meet at the top. Well-defined collar beneath head. Possible trace of rilling on neck. Conserved. Similar pins from a twelfth-century context at 40–48 South Main Street, Cork and a thirteenth-century context at Washington Street, Cork.

Stick pin (illustrated, Pl. 6.75). E2399:146:90. Cu alloy. L. 45.4mm, W. (head) 2.3mm, D. (shank) 2.5mm, Wt. 1g. Incomplete. Unclassified. Possible expanded shank circular in cross section. Shank waisted beneath head, trace of possible collar also. Shank tapers at opposing end but point not extant. Conserved.

Stick pin (illustrated, Pl. 6.76). E2399:439:186. Fe. L. 75.6mm, W. (head) 5.4mm, D. (shank) 2.7mm, Wt. 2.5g. Complete. Club-headed. Upper and mid portion of shank circular in cross section, lower potion rectangular in section and tapers to a point. Undecorated. Conserved.

- Possible pin fragment

CATALOGUE

Possible pin fragment. E2399:423:181. Fe. L. 37.7mm, W. (head?) 8.9mm, D. (shank) 3.7mm, Wt. 4.1g. Incomplete. Fragment of iron object with circular sectioned shank. Sub-circular possible head with rectangular sectioned projection on top of same. Possible collar beneath head on shank. Conserved.

- Dress hook/clasp

One dress hook or clasp (E2399:87:59) was recovered. It is an iron example with a short, but deep hook, at the end of tapering decorative openwork at the top of which is a small loop (now broken) – presumably to facilitate attachment to an item of dress or associated accessory. These items are thought to have been used in pairs on the ends of short chains or straps and had the function of joining decorative accessories together or onto a garment. Several relatively

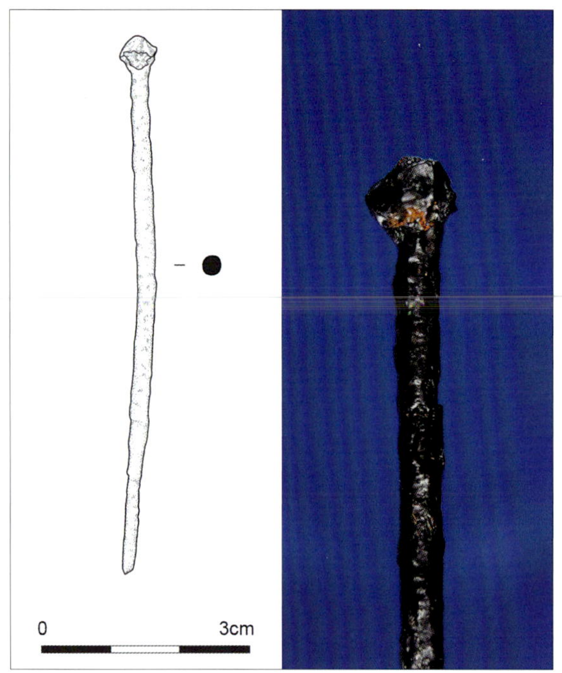

Pl. 6.76. Stick pin E2399:439:186.

similar examples are known from late fifteenth- to sixteenth-century contexts in London but are mainly of copper alloy or lead.

CATALOGUE

Dress hook/clasp (illustrated, Pl. 6.77). E2399:87:59. Fe. L. 50.8mm, W. 19.9mm, Th. 3.7mm, Wt. 4.8g. Complete. Flat openwork piece comprising two open circles at the widest part of the object below which is a triangle where object tapers towards the hooked end. Small loop on top now broken. Hook is rectangular in cross section. Conserved.

- Lace chapes

Lace chapes, as their name would suggest, functioned by protecting the ends of laces and facilitated threading them through eyelets in a garment. Lace chapes are known from both medieval and post-medieval contexts in Britain. They were almost always made of copper alloy sheeting bent into a tube. The seam of the tube may be edge-to-edge or overlapping with both construction methods apparent on the examples from Boyle. The tapered end of E2399:213:77 may be finished by neatly bending inwards

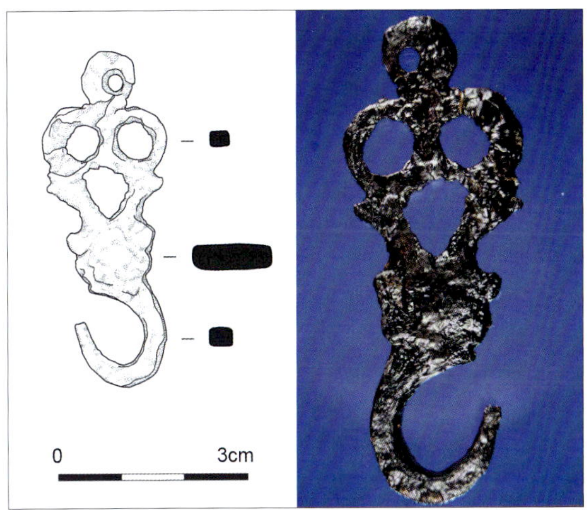

Pl. 6.77. Dress hook/clasp E2399.87.59.

and is somewhat longer than those recovered from medieval and later medieval contexts in London. The second Boyle chape E2399:26:14 is quite small and finely made, although it is unclear if the tapering end is broken.

CATALOGUE

Lace chape. E2399:213:77. Cu alloy. L. 60mm, W. 3.9mm, Th. 3.7mm, Wt. 1.6g. Complete. Sub-circular/oval in cross section. Tapers towards one end, unfinished. Comprised of folded sheet metal with overlapping seam. Bent slightly along its length. Possible remnants of organic material at wider end. Conserved.

Lace chape. E2399:26:14. Cu alloy. L. 18.6mm, W. 1.9mm, Th. 1.8mm, Wt. 0.2g. Complete. Sub-circular/oval in cross section. Tapers to one end. Comprised of folded sheet metal with edge-to-edge seam.

- Buttons

Post-medieval buttons are frequently decorated or impressed with lettering or other designs, particularly if the object was for use on a uniform. The term 'backmark' refers to the inscriptions, often in legend form, or trademarks on the backs of buttons. They are usually formed as embossed or impressed lettering at the time of the button's manufacture. Backmarks soetimes identify the manufacturer or may refer to the quality assurance of the button itself Examples of so-called quality assurance backmarks include 'warranted' and 'triple gilt' which were utilised on both military and civilian uniform buttons. Military buttons often have insignias on the outer face of the button providing information on regiments and rank. The buttons from Boyle are post-medieval in date and several possibly of the nineteenth century.

CATALOGUE

Military button. E2399:0:1. Cu alloy. D. 18.9mm, Th. 9.1mm, Wt. 4.1g. Complete. Spun two-piece button with set-back shell and inset back, fitted with a swan neck footed shank (now flattened) and mounted emblem of the 64th (2nd Staffordshire) Regiment of Foot – an infantry regiment of the British Army active between 1756 and 1881.

Button. E2399:7:3059. Cu alloy. D. 15.6mm, Th. 0.9mm, Wt. 1.4g. Incomplete. Slightly concave button back with stamped repeated foliate design. Shank not extant. Possibly nineteenth century in date.

Button. E2399:205:45. Cu alloy. D. 20.2mm, Th. 1mm, Wt. 3.1g. Incomplete. Flat button back with stamped backmark of WARRANTED in legend form beneath which is foliate design. Base of shank extant. Possibly nineteenth century in date.

Button. E2399:205:48. White metal. D. 19.9mm, Th. 1mm, Wt. 3.2g. Incomplete. Flat, plain button back with base of shank extant. Post-medieval in appearance.

Button. E2399:205:107. White metal. D. 19.9mm, Th. 0.8mm, Wt. 2.5g. Incomplete. Flat plain button back with central boss for eye, latter not extant.

Button. E2399:205:46. White metal and Fe. D. 16.9mm, Th. 3.4mm, Wt. 1.4g. Incomplete. Flat button back

Pl. 6.78. Button E2399:2:113.

with recessed oval for eye. Remnants of corroded iron button front extant.

Button. E2399:2:312. Cu alloy. D. 16mm, Th. 6mm, Wt. 1.8g. Incomplete. Flat button with WICKLOW in legend above crowned GR. Flattened looped eye on back.

Button (illustrated, Pl. 6.78). E2399:2:113. Cu alloy. D. 20.89mm, Th. 1.4mm, Wt. 4.4g. Incomplete. Flat button back with embossed backmark reading TREBLE GILT and the letter B within a diamond. Surrounded by foliate design.

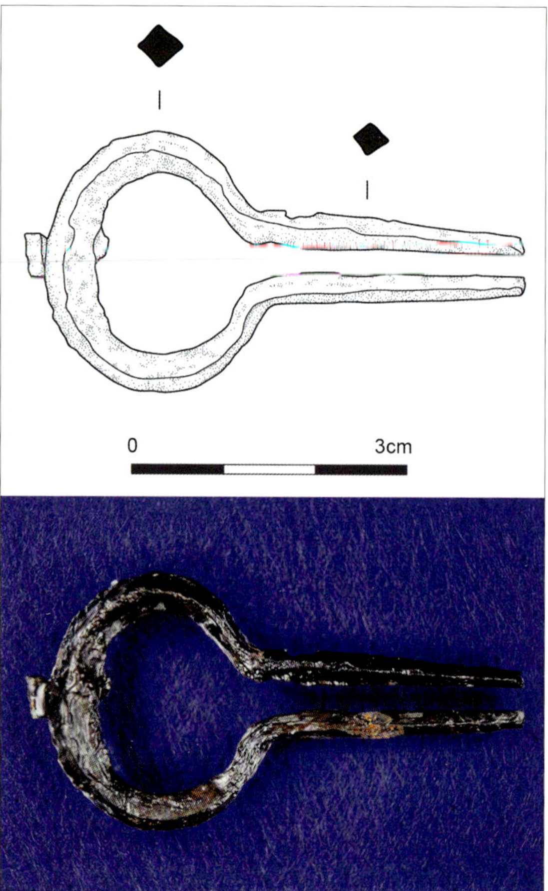

Pl. 6.79. Jew's harp E2399:439:196.

MUSICAL INSTRUMENTS

- Jew's harp

One fine example of a Jew's harp (E2399:439:196) was recovered. Although incomplete, it displays the classic shape and diamond-shaped cross section as seen on these musical instruments. Evidence is also present for the tongue, although it does not survive. This Jew's harp is also known as a trump and is an ancient folk instrument which has a wide geographical distribution. Its origins are believed to be in south-east Asia; however, it had been introduced to Europe by the eleventh century. The European Jew's harp is usually made of iron and comprises a frame made from a single piece of metal which has been formed into a rounded or looped 'head' which narrows into two parallel arms, tapering to a blunt tip. The tongue, which rarely survives in archaeological contexts, comprised a separate component which was hammered into a groove or rabbet at the top of the head. The projection of the tongue above the head is extant in the Boyle example; however, nothing more of the tongue survives. The instrument was played by holding it in one hand and lightly supporting the frame with the teeth. The metal tongue was plucked by fingers of the other hand while the mouth cavity acted as a resonator for the sound emitted by the plucking. Jew's harps have been recovered from Bective Abbey, Co. Meath, Kells Priory, Co. Kilkenny and the excavations in Cork City, from both medieval and post-medieval contexts. According to Scully (2007, 375) the Jew's harp was in large-scale commercial and social use from the late sixteenth to the late nineteenth century. The Boyle example was recovered from a layer (F439) which overlay the primary phase of burials in the aisle and is likely to be medieval in date.

CATALOGUE

Jew's harp (illustrated, Pl. 6.79). E2399:439:196. Fe. L. 55mm, W. (head)

27.6mm, Th. 4.8mm, Wt. 6.1g. Incomplete. Small Jew's harp with rounded head leading to parallel arms. Both head and arms display classic diamond-shaped cross section. Tongue is not extant apart from short projection above the head where it was hammered into a recess or groove. Conserved.

COINS

- Medieval coinage

Seven coins that may be attributed to the medieval period were recovered. Of these, five are attributed to Edward III (1327–77) and one to Elizabeth I (1558–1603).

There are numerous classes of Edward I–II coins numbered Classes 1–15c. Class 15d is attributed to Edward III as it has a Lombardic rather than a Roman N. While the legend on the obverse of coin E2399:27:7 is largely illegible, the Lombardic n is utilised on the reverse and may place this coin within the Edward III reign.

A possible Edward III halfpenny (second coinage dating from 1335–43) was recovered from the fill of grave cut F431 associated with B309 and is highly worn. This coinage consisted purely of halfpennies and farthings, which were issued at 83.3% fineness (the amount of silver each coin contained, the sterling standard of pervious coins was 92.5%). These coins are identifiable by a star which is mainly located at the end of the obverse and reverse legends; however, this was not identifiable in E2399:430:176 due to wear. An Edward III penny (E2399:378:99) was found with a second silver coin (E2399:378:98) in the fill of grave cut F379 associated with B209. The latter is illegible due to wear; however, it may belong to Edward III given its association with E2399:378:99. The penny has a possible cross patée mint mark which would provide a date of 1344–51. The outer legend on E2399:27:7 is illegible while the inner legend refers to London as the place of minting. It is possible that this coin belongs to the fourth coinage of Edward III (1351–77). A second halfgroat

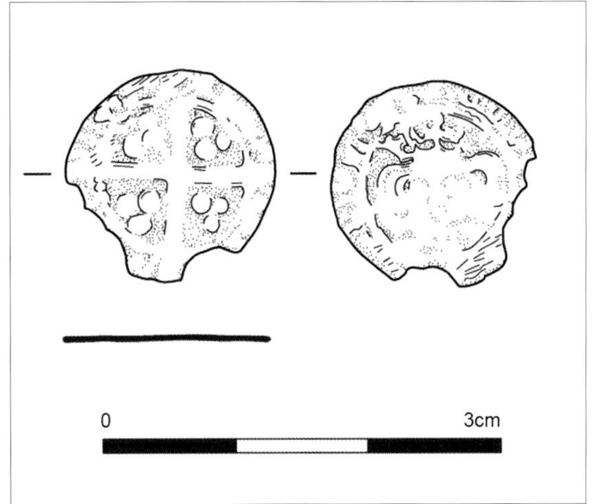

Fig. 6.29. Coin E2399:430:176. (Illustration: S. Nylund)

E2399:734:24 was recovered from a deposit (F734) located towards the west end of the church with a third example E2399:439:201 found further to the east, both of which were minted in London.

E2399:21:55 Elizabeth I silver sixpence is a fine example of a third issue coin. The mint mark is of a pheon and was used on coins dating to between 1561 and 1565. Coinage from Elizabeth I's reign is interesting because of the large number of different denominations issued, partially to alleviate a shortage of small change. Due to the large number of denominations issued, the sixpence, threepence, three halfpence and three farthings were marked with the rose behind the queen's head to distinguish them from the shilling, groat, half groat and penny. The introduction of a screw press in 1561 by Eloye Mestrelle, a French moneyer, produced coins of 'exceedingly fine workmanship'. The coins became known as 'mill money' as the machinery was partly powered by a horse-drawn mill. The coin itself (E2399:21:55) was recovered from a layer located towards the west end of the site which was cut by the robbing out trench for the north aisle wall.

CATALOGUE

Halfpenny. E2399:430:176 (Fig. 6.29). Ag. D. 15.1mm, Th. 0.4mm, Wt. 0.4g. Incomplete. Long cross coinage of Edward III. Obverse highly worn, however,

Pl. 6.80. Penny E2399:378:99.

Pl. 6.81. Halfgroat E2399:439:201.

trifoliate crown is visible. Only EDW of legend partially visible. Reverse legend not legible. Long cross and pellets visible. Possibly second coinage dating from 1335–43.

Penny (illustrated, Pl. 6.80). E2399:378:99. Ag. D. 18.2mm, Th. 0.39mm, Wt. 0.9g. Complete but worn at edge. Edward III penny. Possibly third or florin coinage. Bust with bushy hair facing. Obverse legend reads: EDWR ANGL DNS HYB (Reversed Roman 'N'). Possible cross patée mint mark which would provide date of 1344–51. Reverse: LON DON CIVI TAS (Lombardic 'n').

Halfgroat (Fig. 6.30). E2399:734:24. Ag. D. 20.4mm, Th. 0.7mm, Wt. 1.6g. Complete but heavily worn around edge. Edward III, possibly third (1344–51) or fourth (1351–77) coinage. Obverse legend worn and largely illegible. EDW visible. Bust with bifoliate crown and bushy hair. Trefoils on cusps of tressure. Outer reverse legend incomplete and illegible. Inner legend reads: CIVITAS LONDON (Lombardic 'n').

Halfgroat (illustrated, Pl. 6.81). E2399:439:201. Ag. D. 19.3mm, Th. 0.45mm, Wt. 0.8g. Complete but worn at edge. Possibly Edward III halfgroat. Crowned bust facing within tressure on obverse. Legend illegible. Long cross with triangle in centre on reverse. Outer legend illegible. Inner legend reads LONDON CIVITAS, (Lombardic n).

Halfgroat (illustrated, Pl. 6.82). E2399:27:7. Ag. D. 19.5mm, Th. 0.72mm, Wt. 1.3g. Incomplete but worn around edge. Possibly Edward III halfgroat, mint mark not visible. Partially legible obverse shows crowned bust facing within tressure. Legend partially legible – WARD – (illustrated). Reverse outer legend illegible. Inner legend reads LON.

Silver coin (illustrated, Pl. 6.83). E2399:378:98. Ag. D. 17.9mm, Th. 0.51mm, Wt. 0.8g. Complete but highly worn. Obverse legend and bust illegible. Long cross dividing pellets visible on reverse. Legend illegible.

Silver sixpence (illustrated, Pl. 6.84). E2399:21:55. Ag. D. 25.8mm, Th. 0.65mm, Wt. 2.6g. Complete. Elizabeth I sixpence dated 1561. Third issue with pheon mint mark in obverse legend. Crowned bust facing left on obverse with rose to right. Legend, partially legible, reads ELIZABETH DG ANG FR ET HIB REGINA. Obverse legend reads POSVI DEV

ADIVTOREM MEV. Square-topped shield on long cross fourchée dividing the legend, date above.

- Seventeenth-century coinage

Three coins dating to the seventeenth century were recovered from the north aisle excavations. Two are halfcrowns, of different date, which came from post-medieval/modern contexts. The earlier coin, E2399:377:96, is a silver Commonwealth halfcrown which dates to between 1649 and 1657 as it displays a sun mint mark. This type of late hammered coinage was minted in England after a period of civil war which culminated in the execution of King Charles I in London in 1649. The coins from this period bear no portrait of a king or queen as there was none. Instead, there is a simple puritan design and a legend in English rather than Latin as this was thought to be too popery. The reverse depicts conjoined shields of England and Ireland, with a date and the legend 'GOD WITH VS'. During the Commonwealth no distinctive Irish coinage was struck and it was anticipated that the coinage needs of the Irish were to be met with the new English Commonwealth gold and silver coins with their conjoined English and Irish shields, such as the halfcrown E2399:377:96. Despite the threat of confiscation of coins and minting equipment, corporations and individual merchants continued to issue tokens throughout the 1660s and 1670s. Among these was St Patrick's Money, a series of private tokens including a halfpenny and a farthing issued in 1673. E2399:7:1 is an example of a St Patrick's issue farthing. The obverse of the coin features a king playing a harp with a crown above and the legend reads FLOREAT REX, meaning 'May the king flourish'. The reverse features St Patrick holding a double long cross in his left hand, while with his right hand he is driving away snakes. To the bottom right of St Patrick is a cathedral or church building. The reverse legend reads QVIESCAT PLEBS, meaning 'May the people be at peace'.

The coin (E2399:901:20) is dated 1689 and is James II 'gun money'. Gun money was minted in Ireland by James II from June 1689 to October 1690 during the conflict with William III that followed the Glorious Revolution of 1688 (William and Mary). The name stems from the idea that the money was minted from melted down guns. However, many other brass

Pl. 6.82. Halfgroat E239: 27:7.

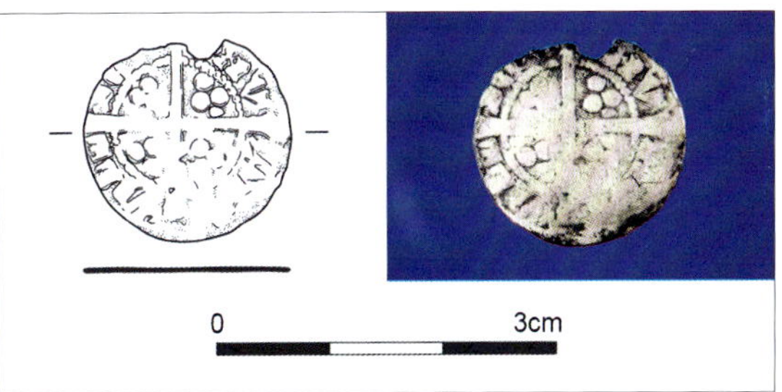

Pl. 6.83. Silver coin E2399:378:98.

Fig. 6.30. Halfgroat E2399:734:24.

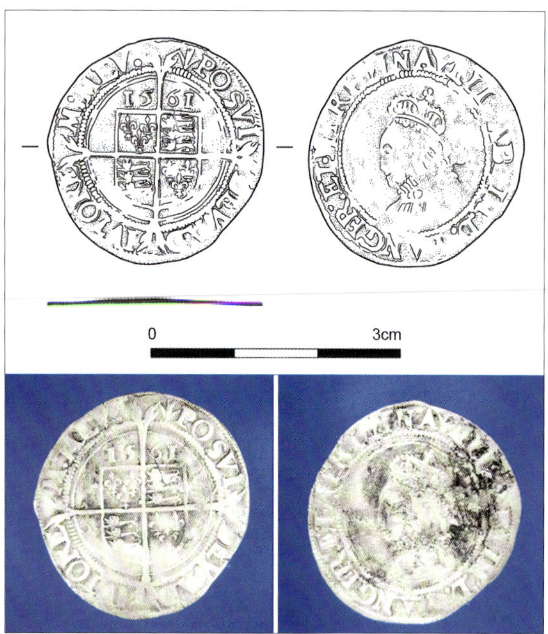

Pl. 6.84. Silver sixpence dated 1561 E2399:21:55.

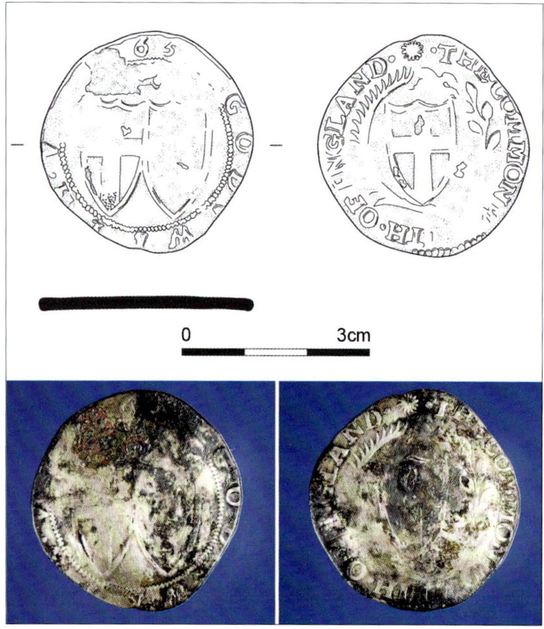

Pl. 6.85. Halfcrown E2399:377:96.

objects, such as church bells, were also used. There were two issues. The first large issue consisted of sixpences, shillings and halfcrowns (2/6d). The second, small issue consisted of shillings, halfcrowns and crowns (5 shillings). Some of the second issue were overstruck on large issue pieces, with shillings struck over sixpences, halfcrowns on shillings and crowns on halfcrowns. The most notable feature of the coins is the date because the month of striking was also included.

These coins were all recovered from post-medieval/modern context in the abbey and while they are clearly residual in same, they testify to seventeenth-century activity at the abbey, evidence for which was largely lacking in the *in situ* archaeological remains in the north aisle.

CATALOGUE

Halfcrown (illustrated, Pl. 6.85). E2399:377:96. Ag. D. 33.7mm, Th. 1.8mm, Wt. 13.4g. Complete but worn around edge. Commonwealth silver halfcrown, sun mint mark on obverse legend dates to 1649–57. Legend reads THE COMMONWEALTH OF ENGLAND. English shield in centre. Reverse legend only partially visible due to wear. Only numbers 65 of the date are legible. Conjoined Irish and English shields in centre.

Farthing (illustrated, Pl. 6.86). E2399:7:1. Cu alloy. D. 23.9mm, Th. 1.4mm, Wt. 5.4g. Complete. St Patrick's issue, *c.* 1673. Obverse depicts king playing a harp with a crown above. Legend reads FLOREAT REX. Reverse depicts St Patrick holding a double long cross with a church or cathedral to his right. Legend reads QVIESCAT PLEBS. Brass plug visible on obverse near crown.

Halfcrown (illustrated, Fig. 6.31). E2399:901:20. Cu alloy. D. 32.6mm, Th. 2.3mm, Wt. 12.9g. Complete. James II 'Gun money' 1689. Obverse displays bust facing left. Legend reads: IACOBVS ffi II ffi DEI ffi GRATIA. Crown over crossed sceptres on reverse. The figures above crown denotes coin value (halfcrown). Letter 'M' beneath crown indicates month when struck, possibly March.

- Nineteenth–twentieth-century coinage

Ten coins dating to the nineteenth to twentieth centuries were recovered from the excavations with two additional coins of unknown date due to wear. The majority of the coins are twentieth-century Irish coinage with some twentieth-century British coins also present.

Pl. 6.86. Farthing E2399:7:1.

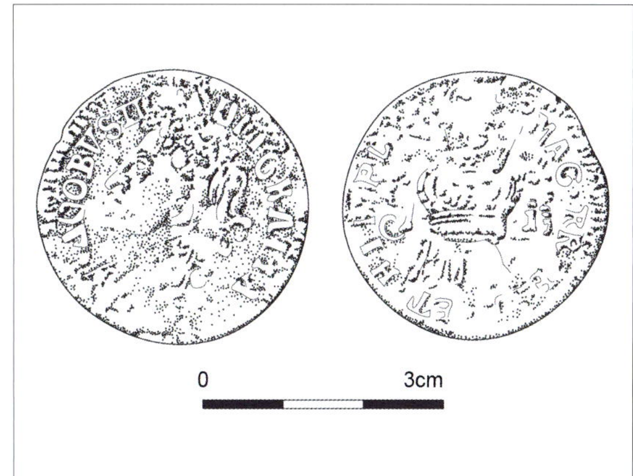

Fig. 6.31. Halfcrown E2399:901:20.

CATALOGUE

One penny. E2399:205:30. Cu alloy. D. 30.6mm, Th. 1.4mm, Wt. 8.7g. Complete. Victoria penny, 'Bun Head' issue, 1860–95. Obverse features laureate bust facing left. Legend reads VICTORIA DG BRITT REG F D. Reverse depicts seated Britannia with shield and trident with date of 186- below. Possibly 1861.

Coin. E2399:205:5. Cu alloy. D. 26.86mm, Th. 1.6mm, Wt. 7g. Complete. Obverse and reverse both illegible. Date unknown.

Coin. E2399:205:8. Cu alloy. D. 27.6mm, Th. 1.5mm, Wt. 6.9g. Complete. Obverse and reverse both illegible. Date unknown.

Halfpenny? E2399:205:3. Cu alloy. D. 21.3mm, Th. 1.9mm, Wt. 3.9g. Complete. Faint trace of bust facing left on obverse, legend illegible. Seated Britannia with shield faintly visible on reverse. Legend illegible. Possible Victoria halfpenny?

Pingin. E2399:1:178. Cu alloy. D. 30.4mm, Th. 1.7mm, Wt. 9g. Complete. Obverse depicts harp and Eire in legend with date of 1942. Reverse depicts hen and clutch of chicks facing left. The value of the coin, '1d', above hen with 'PINGIN' in exergue.

Two pence. E2399:1:179. Cu alloy. D. 25.8mm, Th. 1.6mm, Wt. 6.8g. Complete. Obverse depicts harp and Eire in legend with date of 1971. Reverse depicts stylised rendering of a bird with large beak with '2p' above.

One pence. E2399:1:180. Cu alloy. D. 20.1mm, Th. 1.4mm, Wt. 3.4g. Complete. Obverse depicts harp and Eire in legend with date of 1980. Reverse depicts peacock-like bird with elaborate tail feathers and '1P' to the right.

Halfpenny. E2399:1:181. Cu alloy. D. 16.9mm, Th. 0.9mm, Wt. 1.7g. Complete. Obverse depicts crowned bust facing right. Legend reads ELIZABETH II DG REG FD 1971. Reverse shows crown and legend reads NEW PENNY. denomination below crown.

Two pence. E2399:2:261. Cu alloy. D. 25.8mm, Th. 1.6mm, Wt. 6.8g. Complete. Obverse depicts harp and Eire in legend with date of 1985. Reverse depicts stylised rendering of a bird with large beak with '2p' above.

One pence. E2399:2:262. Cu alloy. D. 20.1mm, Th. 1.4mm, Wt. 3.4g. Complete. Obverse depicts harp and Eire in legend with date of 1980. Reverse depicts peacock-like bird with elaborate tail feathers and '1P' to the right.

One pence. E2399:2:263. Cu alloy. D. 20.1mm, Th. 1.4mm, Wt. 3.4g. Complete. Obverse depicts harp and Eire in legend with date of 1980. Reverse depicts peacock-like bird with elaborate tail feathers and '1P' to the right.

One penny. E2399:2:264. Cu alloy. D. 20.1mm, Th. 1.5mm, Wt. 3.4g. Complete. Obverse depicts crowned bust facing right. Legend reads ELIZABETH II DG REG FD 1974. Reverse shows crowned portcullis with denomination '1' beneath. Legend reads NEW PENNY.

WEAPONRY AND MILITARIA

- Projectile heads

  Larger projectile heads such as E2399:78:679 cannot be considered as arrowheads as they are likely to have been too heavy to be fired effectively from a bow. The large socket diameters of such projectile heads would indicate that they were mounted on larger shafts than conventional arrowheads. It is possible that at least some of these larger projectile objects may be crossbow quarrel heads or the heads of missiles fired from larger machines, such as a ballista. The projectile from Boyle was recovered from the upper fill of drain (F63) and is similar to large projectile heads from mid to late twelfth-century contexts in Waterford City and Kells Priory, Co. Kilkenny.

CATALOGUE

Projectile head (illustrated, Fig. 6.32). E2399:78:679. Fe. L. 144.8mm, W. (blade) 9.6mm, Th. 8.2mm, Dth. (socket) 27mm, Wt. 38.2g. Incomplete. Large, socketed bodkin-bladed projectile head. Blade, rectangular in section tapers to slightly bent point. Socket damaged but likely to be originally circular.

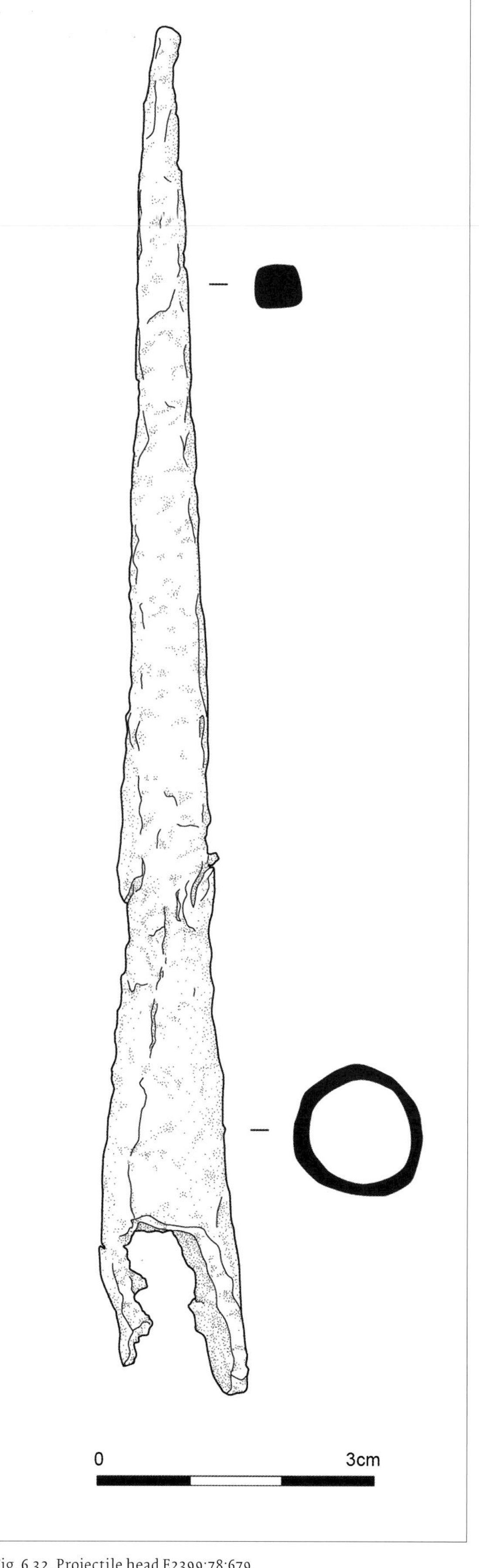

Fig. 6.32. Projectile head E2399:78:679.

- Lead shot

  Four lead shots were recovered from the excavations and are a reminder of the occupation of Boyle by the military from the late sixteenth century until the nineteenth century. The shots were all recovered from later deposits within the excavation area which produced a range of artefactual material of varying dates. In this regard, it is not possible to assign a precise date to the shot other than to ascribe them to the fairly broad time period during which guns for use with lead shot were utilised.

Gunlocks were an easily broken and readily replaceable component of a firearm whose function it was to enable the firing of the bullet or shot through the ignition of the gunpowder. Numerous types of gunlock were in use in the sixteenth to nineteenth centuries and it is by these names such as Matchlock and Flintlock that the firearms became known. Matchlock guns were used throughout the seventeenth century, and it was the standard infantry arm of the British Army until 1690. The diameter of lead shot may sometimes be indicative of the type of weapon used, although the attempted standardisation of shot size in England during the seventeenth century was not entirely successful.

CATALOGUE

Lead shot. E2399:221:2082. Pb. D. 15.4mm, Wt. 20.9g. Complete. Sub-circular with casting flash visible.

Lead shot. E2399:610:3069. Pb. D. 12.7mm, Wt. 10.7g. Complete. Small shot with possible impact mark.

Lead shot. E2399:204:1. Pb. D. 16.7mm, Wt. 29g. Complete. Circular shot, no apparent marks.

Lead shot. E2399:7:4. Pb. D. 17.7mm, Wt. 33.1g. Complete. Circular shot, no apparent marks.

- Sword
  David Swift

Description

Part of an iron sword blade (E2399:48:80, illustrated, Pls 6.87–9) was found along the north aisle. The artefact was recovered from a layer which overlay the cut of the robbing out trench for the north aisle wall, towards the western end of the site. It is a double-edged blade with a hexagonal cross section towards one end and a broad-fuller cross section as it extends towards the now folded end. A fuller is a rounded or bevelled longitudinal groove or slot along the flat side of a blade that is made using a blacksmithing tool called a spring swage or, like the groove, a fuller. A fuller is often used to lighten the blade. The fullered blade is decorated with two parallel incised lines inside which are regularly spaced motifs. No remains of any element of the hilt furniture are extant. The tang has barely survived with only a small projection of 4mm length still apparent. The sword blade had been cleanly broken in antiquity some 358mm down the length of the blade from the collar of the tang.

The top of the blade nearest the tang has been folded over and in the cleft of the fold are the remains of unidentified organic material (S. Kelly pers. comm.). The edges of this folded section are considerably thicker than the lower part of the blade indicating the presence of a *ricasso* which extends 80mm in length while being 4.44mm in thickness. A *ricasso* is an unsharpened length of blade just above the guard or handle of the sword, The centre of the folded over area is cracked. On one side of the sword some 49mm from the top of the blade is what appears to be a maker's mark. The exact detail of the mark is not clear – although it could be interpreted as a simple capital 'I'. The punched stamp measures 7mm long by 1.5mm wide. Also apparent running the length of the *ricasso* are four parallel decorative incised lines, of which the central two run longer down the length of the blade marking the edges of the fuller. The shorter pair of incised lines running close to each edge run for only the length of the *ricasso* itself. The longest discernible length of these lines is 184.1mm. The transition of the *ricasso* to the blade proper is further emphasised by two crescent shaped 'sickle' motifs. These sickle motifs are decorated with a van dyke edge on the convex side facing upwards towards the position of the hilt. The sickles act to join the outer incised lines of the *ricasso* to the longer

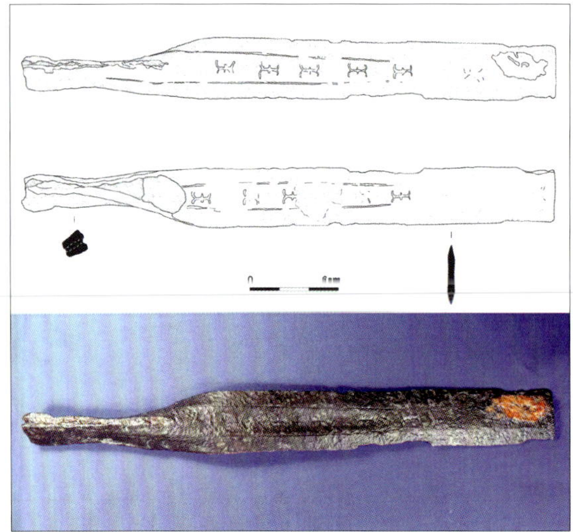

Pl. 6.87. Iron sword E2399:48:80.

inner lines where the former terminate at the blade end of the *ricasso*.

Demarked by the two central incised lines which continue past the *ricasso*, a single shallow fuller runs some 160mm down the centre of the blade on both sides. The fullers on both sides of the blade are decorated with a series of five recessed motifs adorning the blade. Each motif measures some 12mm long and they are spaced out evenly down each side of the blade, albeit with one side stretching the motifs over a somewhat longer length than the other. In form all ten motifs are very similar to each other. They could be interpreted as resembling a majuscule letter 'I' but they could also alternatively be observed as being abstract. There are no discernible remains of inlaid metal in any of the recesses. The fuller appears to start where the *ricasso* terminates at what would have been the hilt end of the sword where it is 18mm wide and gently peters out just before it reaches the fifth of the five decorative motifs on each side of the blade at 13mm in width.

The remaining extant length of the blade is an elongated hexagon in section. Over the course of the blade its profile subtly tapers from 39mm at its widest measurable point near where the hilt furniture would have been, to 34.6mm at the diamond section end where the blade is broken clear. The distal taper of the blade is more or less flat and actually rises very slightly from 4.44mm at the *ricasso* to just over 4.52mm at the extant blade end.

Discussion

The presence of a *ricasso* likely places the blade chronologically into the late medieval period in Ireland. In Europe, blades with *ricassos* could possibly date, in some relatively rare cases, to as early as the late fourteenth century (Oakeshott 1964, pl. 6.39). However, more recently a date of *c.* 1400 has been deemed somewhat safer with the type seemingly becoming more widespread over the course of the fifteenth century and into the sixteenth century (Oakeshott 1991, 198–9). Such blades are well attested to in the Irish archaeological record in the form of the Halpin Type 2 and Type 3 categories (Halpin 1986). Type 2 swords are generally dated over a wide period from the late fourteenth to the early sixteenth centuries and are generally seen as having properties of Scottish influence in various quantities (Willis 1996, 14). Type 2 swords are often interpreted as being the forerunners of the full-sized two-handed claymore which appeared in its fully developed form from as early as the late fifteenth century and which certainly began to flourish in numbers by the early sixteenth century (Wallace 1970, 10). The strongest evidence for Type 3 swords lies in the first half of the sixteenth century (Halpin 1986, 209). Oakeshott considered the Type 3 sword ring pommel hilts to be 'unmistakeably Irish' as supported by contemporary pictorial evidence, for example, by Dürer and De Heere (Oakeshott 1980,144).

Blades with *ricassos* and with incised parallel lines running down the blade are a feature of several Type 2 swords (Willis 1996, pl. 2; Halpin 1986, figs 18 and 20) and Type 3 swords (Halpin 1986, figs 26, 28 and 30). However, none of the swords in these categories bear the same decorative motifs on the fuller as the Boyle sword and many of these swords moreover do not feature a fully developed fuller at all while other swords in their categories do.

Where *ricassos* are present on Type 2 and Type 3 swords, some also feature sickle-shaped incised lines marking the end of the *ricasso*. However, none of these swords appears to feature the very distinctive van dyke edge which is seen on the Boyle sword.

One sword which is of special interest in our quest to find a parallel is a claymore which was until relatively recent times kept at Clontarf Castle in Dublin. The sword was originally part of the estate of the O'Briens, Marquesses of Thomond, and was housed at Rostellan Castle, Co. Cork, from at least 1813, though its earlier history is not known. Unfortunately, the sword was sold to a private collection in the mid 1970s. The Rostellan Castle claymore was recorded as a well-preserved classic of its type with a fuller on the blade extending for 200mm, a high collar, long langets, and quatrefoil terminals to the characteristically downward sloped quillons of the cross-guard (Halpin 1986, 228). Generally speaking, claymores are dated to between *c.* 1495 and the very early seventeenth century. However, the pommel is of 'wheel' form which would generally indicate an early to mid sixteenth-century date.

The blade was recorded as being 996.7mm in length and tapered in profile from 44.5mm at the hilt to just 38.1mm (4 inches) from the blade tip which was rounded. Also recorded on the blade were no less than five armourer's marks including the 'running wolf' of Solingen. This is no surprise as most claymore swords appear to have had their blades produced and imported from Germany (Cannan 2009, 30). Hayes-McCoy recorded that the sword blade had 'two incised lines extending upwards for 10 1/2 inches [266.7mm] from the base on either side' and 'a punched mark resembling the letter I. These occur in and about the shallow central groove [fuller] noticeable towards the base of the blade' (Hayes-McCoy 1977, 38). There are some obvious similarities with the Boyle blade regarding these latter features. Neither Halpin nor Hayes-McCoy mentions a *ricasso* on this blade but an illustration by the latter does appear to show the presence of one with the suggestion of an outer incised line nearer at least one edge of the *ricasso* also included, in addition to the two central incised lines mentioned above. The illustration also appears to demonstrate that the two long incised lines bound the fuller in much the same manner as the Boyle sword. A further piece of information, which the same illustration appears to yield, is that most of

Pl. 6.88. Iron sword E2399:48:80.

Pl. 6.89. Iron sword E2399:48:80.

the blade below the *ricasso* – very similarly to the Boyle sword – is in an elongated hexagonal section (Hayes-McCoy 1977, 44). This hexagonal section blade is a feature also seen on other claymores of sixteenth-century date held in public repositories in Britain, as at the Royal Armouries in Leeds.

At a maximum blade width of 39mm, the Boyle sword is clearly of a somewhat smaller scale than the 45mm breadth of the two-handed claymore from Rostellan Castle and may not even represent the remains of a hand-and-a-half sword – not to mention a full two-handed weapon. The similarities in finish may suggest the possibility of a date for the blade of *c.* 1495–1570; however, in the absence of important typological features such as the blade length, pommel, grip length, cross-guard and other elements of the now missing hilt furniture it is not possible to ascertain a more concise date and a range of 1400–1600 will have to suffice.

- Bullet casing/cartridges

Worldwide, there are over 800 military headstamps in existence plus some 400 or more commercial headstamps that have existed at various times. The headstamp on E2399:377:106 is illegible apart from the letter R, while a single central U comprises the headstamp on the smaller casing E2399:33:603. The latter is an intrusive find from the fill of structure F25.

CATALOGUE

Bullet casing/cartridge. E2399:33:603. Cu alloy. L. 15.3mm, D. 6.6mm, Wt. 0.6g. Incomplete. Small brass casing with headstamp of letter U. Post-medieval/modern in appearance.

Bullet casing. E2399:377:106. Cu alloy. L. 56.2mm. D. 13.2mm. Post-medieval/modern bullet casing. Only the letter R visible in headstamp.

HORSE EQUIPMENT

- Spurs

The earliest rowel spurs appeared during the thirteenth century, generally following the form of the prick spurs they were soon to replace. Most spurs had rowels by the second quarter of the fourteenth century. They are likely to have been wet and this may have been one reason for the combination of iron with copper alloy as is the case in the spur from Boyle (E2399:98:71). The Boyle rowel is also relatively small, with eight points, which would suggest a late thirteenth- to early fourteenth-century date, as large rowels had become fashionable by the mid fourteenth century. This date is supported by the shortneck, as by the early fifteenth century longer necks were more prevalent following the trend for lengthening and pointing items such as the toes of shoes and boots.

CATALOGUE

Rowel spur (illustrated, Pl. 6.90). E2399:98:71. Fe and Cu alloy. L. 60.8mm, D. (rowel) 28.8mm, Wt. 13.9g. Incomplete. Fragment of iron spur with extant copper alloy rowel held in place by iron rivet. Short neck. 8-pointed rowel.

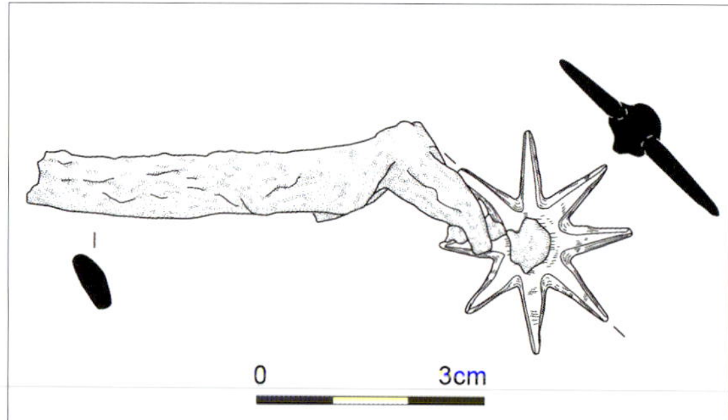

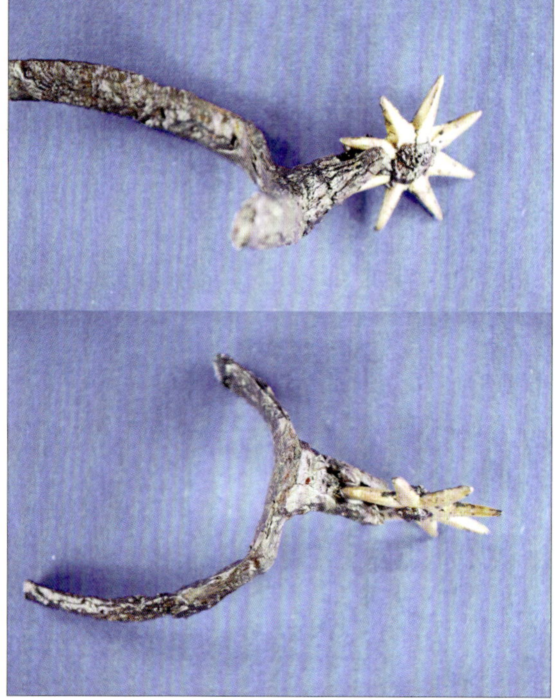

Pl. 6.90. Rowel spur E2399:98:71.

- Horseshoes and horseshoe fragments

While horseshoes have a long history of use from the medieval period to the present, several indicators exist which may be indicative of date. Calkins are one such feature but continued in use from medieval times through to the post-medieval period. Calkins consist of projections formed by turning down the heels of the horseshoe whose function was apparently to provide a better foothold on soft ground. Calkins are a feature of medieval horseshoes; however, they continued in use albeit less frequently in the post-medieval period. Horseshoe E2399:240:187 is one such shoe which has calkins but does not display the later post-medieval innovations of a toe clip and fullering groove and therefore may be fourteenth to fifteenth century in date. The majority of the remainder of the horseshoes and horseshoe fragments from Boyle Abbey came from post-medieval/modern contexts and survived in varying levels of preservation.

CATALOGUE

Horseshoe fragment. E2399:2:260. Fe. L. 134mm, W. 19mm, Th. 12mm, Wt. 117.5g Incomplete. Branch and heel of horseshoe, gently curved. No calkin visible. Two possible nails present. Highly corroded.

Horseshoe. E2399:209:1658. Fe. L. 112mm, W. of web 28mm, Th. 10mm, W. 118.6mm, Wt. 207.4g Complete. Broad arc: each heel is gently tapered and curved inwards. One heel is slightly damaged. One rough rectangular nail hole visible near centre. No calkins. One possible nail also *in situ* but unable to determine due to high level of corrosion.

Horseshoe fragment. E2399:11:454. Fe. L. 116.2mm, W. 35.3mm, Th. 6.8mm, Wt. 144g. Lower portion of branch of horseshoe, gently curved with a rectangular sized perforation near centre. One single nail extant with both shaft and head protruding from either side.

Horseshoe. E2399:7:400. Fe. L. 116.3mm, W. of web 20.1mm, Th. 11mm, W. 114.8mm, Wt. 241.6g Complete. Broad arc: each end is gently tapered and curved inwards. Four nails protrude (rough rectangular head and shaft). No calkins. Toe clip is visible at edge of centre of broad arc, which would suggest a post-medieval date.

Horseshoe fragment. E2399:205:1424. Fe. L. 118.1mm, W. 23.7mm, Th. 9.9mm, Wt. 127.5g Incomplete. Lower portion of branch of horseshoe, gently curved. No calkin visible. Possible nail rivet present but unable to determine due to high levels of corrosion.

Horseshoe. E2399:423:2809. Fe. L. 116mm, W. of web 40mm (max.), Th. 10.8mm, W. 107.8mm, Wt. 270.6g. Incomplete. Broad arc with each end gently tapered. Calkin visible at one heel while the other heel is broken off. No further detail apparent due to high levels of corrosion.

Horseshoe fragment. E2399:395:125. Fe. L. 128.3mm, W. 24.5mm, Th. 5.6mm, Wt. 130.4g. Incomplete. Lower portion of branch of horseshoe, gently curved. No calkin visible. Three rough rectangular headed nails visible, two of which are clenched at tip. One rectangular nail hole also visible. No further detail apparent due to high levels of corrosion.

Horseshoe fragment. E2399:3:343. Fe. L. 29mm, W. 24.5mm, Th. 7.4mm, Wt. 52.2g. Incomplete. Possible portion of branch of horseshoe, gently curved. No calkin visible. Highly corroded.

Horseshoe fragment. E2399:30:560. Fe. L. 117mm, W. 25.95mm, Th. 6.3mm, Wt. 105.4g. Incomplete. Lower portion of branch of horseshoe, gently curved. Three rectangular nail holes visible, one of which has a rough rectangular headed nail with clenched tip protruding. Two smaller nails also apparent. No calkin visible. Possible toe clip is visible at edge, which would suggest a post-medieval date. Highly corroded.

Horseshoe fragment. E2399:3:343. Fe. L. 77.3mm, W. 25.8mm, Th. 7.7mm, Wt. 56.9g. Incomplete. Possible portion of branch of horseshoe, gently curved. Possible nail visible but unable to confirm due to high level of corrosion. One end damaged. No calkin visible.

Horseshoe fragment. E2399:395:130. Fe. L. 117mm, W. 32.9mm, Th. 8mm, Wt. 149.1g. Lower portion of branch of horseshoe, gently curved with two rectangular perforations near centre. Possible nail at one end. Corroded.

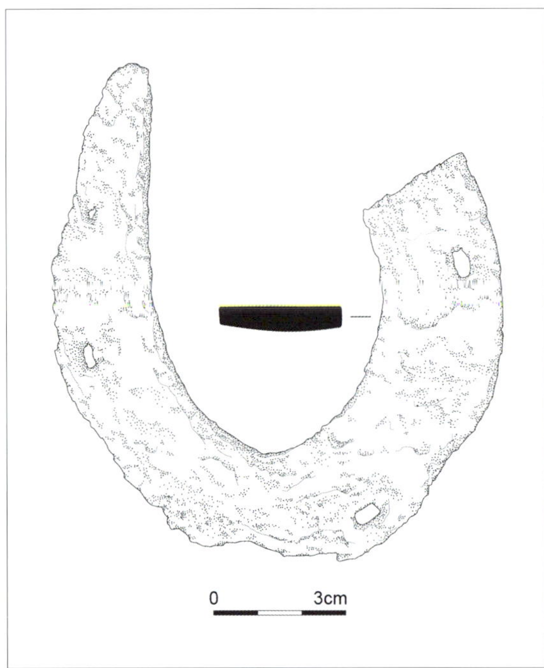

Fig. 6.33. Horseshoe E2399:910:38.

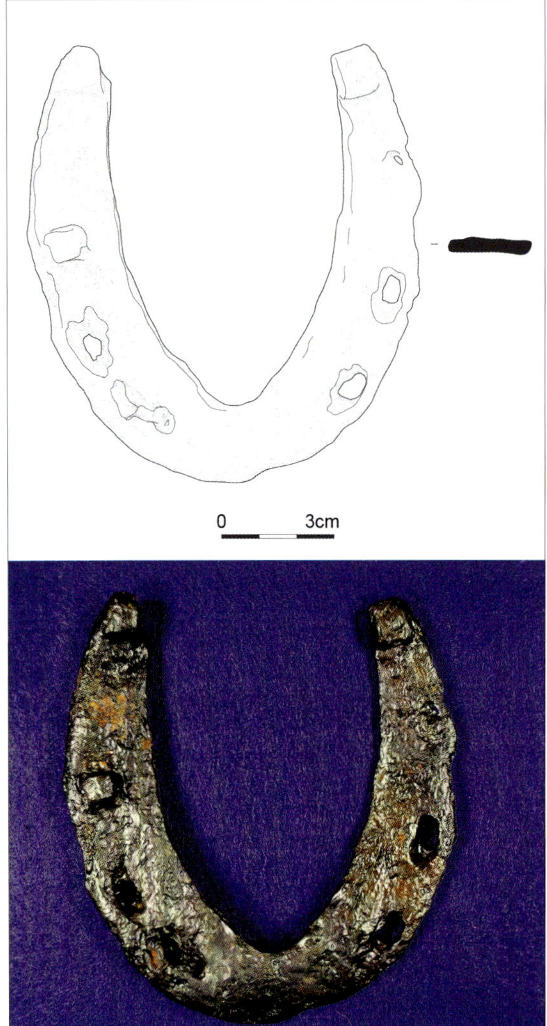

Pl. 6.91. Horseshoe E2399:240:187.

Horseshoe. E2399:205:1421. Fe. L. 114mm, W. of web 26.6mm, Th. 6.5mm, W. 113.6mm, Wt. 190.5g. Complete. Broad arc: each end is gently tapered and curved inwards. One nail protrudes (rough rectangular head). No calkins. Two rough rectangular nail holes visible on either branch. Corroded.

Horseshoe. E2399:209:1659. Fe. L. 115.6mm, W. of web 28.8mm, Th. 9.24mm, W. 107mm, Wt. 270g. Complete. Broad arc: one heel is gently tapered and curved inwards. Opposite heel slightly damaged. Three rough rectangular headed nails visible, all of which are clenched at tip. No calkins. Corroded.

Horseshoe fragment. E2399:205:1422. Fe. L. 120.1mm, W. 29mm, Th. 7.4mm, Wt. 124.5g. Incomplete. Lower portion of branch of horseshoe, including heel, which is tapered gently and curved slightly inwards. Rectangular in section. Two nails extant with both shaft and head visible, including clenched tips, which protrude from the surface on both sides. Corroded.

Horseshoe fragment. E2399:2:259. Fe. L. 152.5mm, W. 24.6mm, Th. 11.6mm, Wt. 273.5g. Incomplete. Lower portion of branch of horseshoe, including heel with visible calkin. One round head nail and shaft visible. Possible toe clip visible at one edge, which would suggest a post-medieval date.

Horseshoe fragment. E2399:204:519. Fe. L. 116.5mm, W. 29.4mm, Th. 8.4mm, Wt. 74.8g Incomplete. Lower branch and heel of horseshoe, gently curved. No calkin visible. One rectangular nail hole visible at centre of branch. Highly corroded.

Horseshoe fragment? E2399:205:1426. Fe. L. 56.9mm, W. 25.9mm, Th. 9.6mm, Wt. 55.6g. Incomplete. Possible portion of heel of horseshoe, gently curved. One end damaged. No calkin visible. Corroded.

Horseshoe fragment. E2399:205:1427. Fe. L. 107.8mm, W. 23mm, Th. 7.3mm, Wt. 57.8g.

Incomplete. Branch and heel of horseshoe, slightly bent. No calkin visible. Two nails with a possible third present. Highly corroded.

Horseshoe fragment. E2399:0:833. Fe. L. 90.6mm, W. 24.6mm, Th. 4.2mm, Wt. 38.8g. Incomplete. Lower portion of branch of horseshoe, including heel, which is tapered gently and curved slightly inwards. Rectangular in section. One nail head possibly extant at broken end. Two rough rectangular nail holes visible along length. Corroded.

Horseshoe. E2399:30:559. Fe. L. 106.3mm, W. of web 24mm, Th. 6mm, W. 114.8mm, Wt. 201.5g. Complete. Broad arc: each end is gently tapered and curved inwards. Three rough rectangular nail holes visible along edge of one branch. No calkins. Corroded.

Horseshoe (illustrated, Fig. 6.33). E2399:910:38. Fe. L. 109.6mm, W. of web 29.3mm, Th. 5.7mm, Wt. 92.9g. Incomplete. Highly corroded prior to conservation. Remains of four rectangular nail holes visible. Tapers towards surviving heel. No fullering, toe clip or calkins. Possibly sixteenth–seventeenth century in date.

Horseshoe (illustrated, Pl. 6.91). E2399:240:187. Fe. L. 119.7mm, W. of web 27.3mm, Th. 5.5mm, Wt. 108.5g. Complete. Six rectangular nail holes apparent close to edge of shoe with two extant nails. Medieval in appearance, possibly fourteenth–fifteenth century in date. Conserved.

DOMESTIC OBJECTS

- Scale and balance

One balance arm (E2399:441:202) from an equal-armed balance and a possible fragment of a folding arm balance (E2399:223:12) were recovered from the excavations. Balances or scales were used throughout the medieval period for measuring coins, precious metals or spices. The equal-armed balance is comprised of two folding arms or a rigid arm, a balancing fork and a central pin or pointer. A scale pan would have hung by chains from the end of the arm. The balancing fork and the pointer are usually attached by means of a spindle which passes through the lower ends of the fork and through a hole at the base of the pointer (Biddle 1990, 917). When the balance is in equilibrium, that is when the material in either scale pan is of equal weight, the pointer stands vertically between the fork (*ibid.*). A folding arm balance and balance forks and pointers were recovered from eleventh–thirteenth-century contexts in Waterford City (Scully 1997, 466–7). The Boyle example (E2399:441:202) differs from the Waterford balance in that the arm is rigid rather than folding. Rigid arm balances are known from medieval contexts in London.

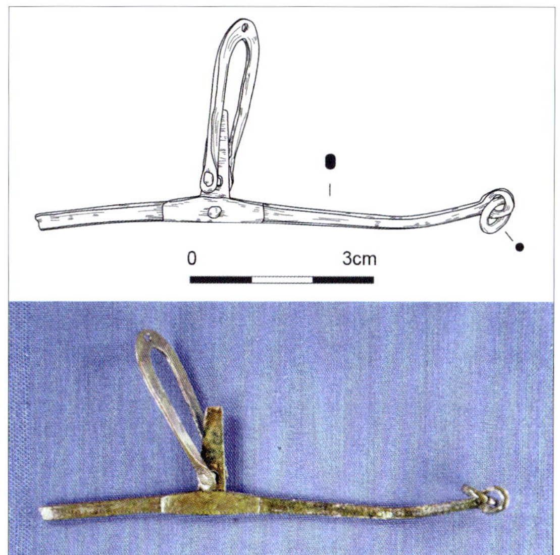

Pl. 6.92. Balance arm of scale E2399:441:202.

A fragment of a folding balance arm (E2399:223:12) came from context F223. It is incomplete but similar to other examples of folding arm balances in the archaeological record in Britain.

CATALOGUE

Balance arm (illustrated, Pl. 6.92). E2399:441:202. Cu alloy. L. 78.8mm, W. 3.8mm, Th. 1.6mm, Wt. 4.1g. Incomplete. Portion of rigid balance arm. Tapers to extant end where small ring is present in perforated terminal. Opposing end not extant. Pointer set in thicker central portion of arm, three rivets apparent here also. Thin rectangular sectioned loop/fork to facilitate hanging the arm attached by rivet through perforation at base of pointer. Upper portion of fork also perforated. Conserved.

Possible folding arm balance fragment (illustrated, Pl. 6.93). E2399:223:12. Cu alloy. L. 61.55m, W. 6.2mm, Th. 4.8mm, Wt. 6.7g. Incomplete. Fragment of copper alloy object with sub-circular sectioned shank. Rectangular 'collar' at one end from which short length of broken shank continues. Larger 'collar' at opposing end beyond which the item becomes flat with a rectangular section. Broken at either end. Possible fragment of folding arm balance. Conserved.

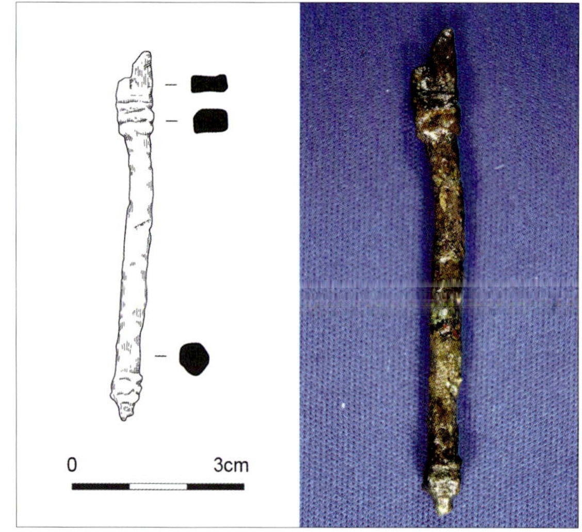

Pl. 6.93. Possible folding arm balance E2399:223:12.

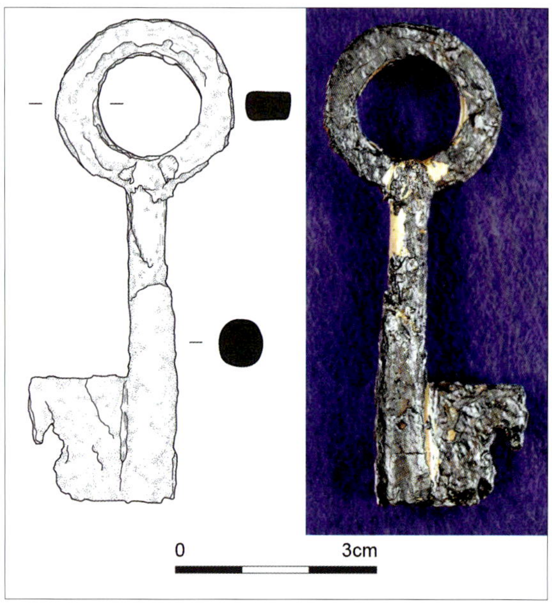

Pl. 6.94. Key E2399:212:1787.

- Keys/Padlocks

Rotary keys are those which were utilised in mounted locks on doors, caskets or chests. Such keys could technically be inserted into the lock from either side, for example on a door. Rotary keys typically comprise three distinct elements: the bow, shank and bit. The form and method of construction of these elements provide clues to the function and date of such keys. Keys with hollow shank ends, as E2399:269:94 demonstrates, may have had a corresponding pin set in the lock to help align them for the bolt. Small crude keys with circular bows and very simple bits were a long-lasting form from the late twelfth century to the late fourteenth century. While the bow on this example is likely to have been oval rather than circular, its simple form may suggest a relatively early date, possibly thirteenth to fourteenth century. Keys with oval-shaped bows have been recovered from thirteenth- to fourteenth-century contexts in London. In the absence of any other distinguishing features which would place keys E2399:269:94 and E2399:615:3071 in the post-medieval period it is possible that both are medieval in date. The small key with a circular bow (E2399:212:1787) from Boyle was recovered from a layer producing seventeenth- to nineteenth-century material but is likely to be a medieval artefact as it falls into Egan's category of small keys with circular bows and simple bits, as outlined above. Interestingly, both this key and E2399:223:68 are made of both iron and copper alloy, the folded shank of both having a copper alloy element, perhaps a lining.

Key E2399:223:68 is a well-preserved example of a hollow-shank key with a kidney-shaped bow. It was recovered from a deposit which produced both medieval and post-medieval finds but is likely to be medieval in date itself. A key with a kidney-shaped bow was recovered from a fourteenth-century context in London and Scully (2007, 364) notes that keys with kidney-shaped bows were more common in the fifteenth century. Another key with a kidney-shaped bow (E2399:200:105) came from the topsoil overlying the site. It is small and may have been used for a mounted lock on a chest or casket. Its form would suggest a later medieval or early post-medieval date.

Little evidence for barrel padlocks or their keys was recovered from Boyle Abbey. One possible barrel padlock key was found in a medieval deposit (F441). While the bit of the key is missing, its distinctive crook bow and finial allow its classification as a possible key. Barrel padlocks worked on the basis of the expansion of barbs on a spine within the padlock casing. The lock could not then be released until the barbs were compressed by a key. Barrel padlocks were used for securing a variety of items depending on their size but typically were used on chests, caskets, doors, shutters and gates. Barrel padlock keys are classified according to the form of the bit, the relationship of the bit to the shank and the form of the bow. The bit from the Boyle key is not extant therefore it cannot be classified in this regard. The bow, which was a means of suspension, is the distinctive crook type which is common on barrel padlock keys in Britain and Ireland in the medieval period. In Waterford City, barrel padlock keys all display the crook bow and were recovered from twelfth- and thirteenth-century contexts. Elsewhere in Ireland, Type 4 keys have been recovered from thirteenth- to fourteenth-century contexts in Cork, Trim Castle, Co. Meath, and Derrynaflan, Co. Tipperary. A twelfth- to thirteenth-century date for the Boyle key may be suggested therefore but cannot be stated with certainty due to the missing piece which would allow a full classification.

The keyhole plates and possible padlock fragment were all recovered from late contexts and are post-medieval in appearance.

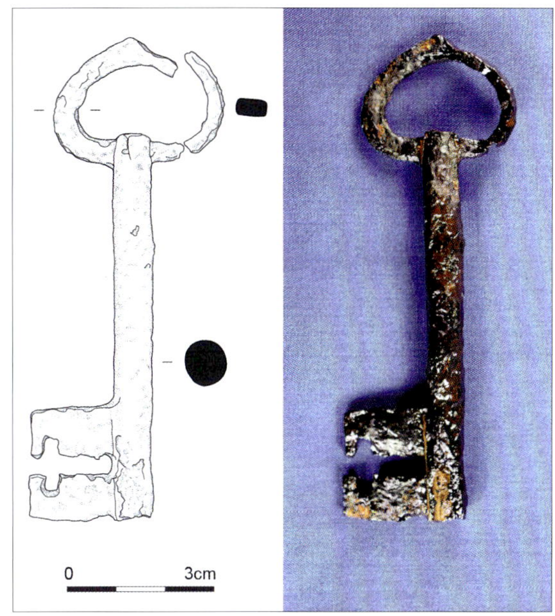

Pl. 6.95. Key E2399:223:68.

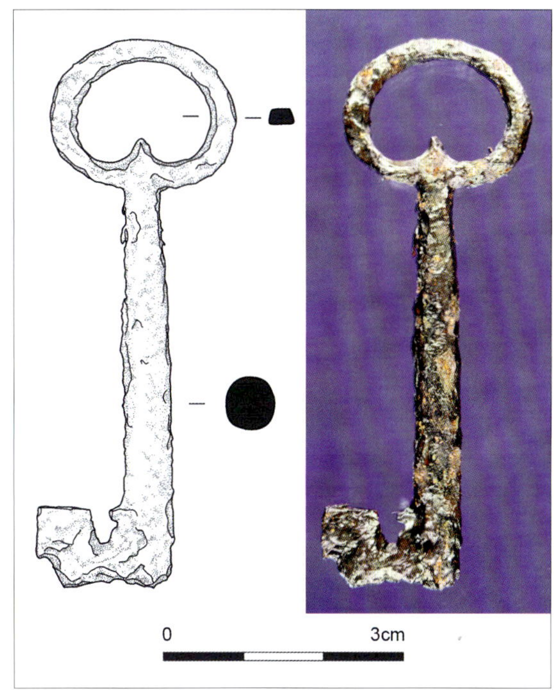

Pl. 6.96. Key E2399:200:105.

CATALOGUE

Key (illustrated, Pl. 6.94). E2399:212:1787. Fe and Cu alloy. L. 70mm, W. (bow) 26.5mm, (shank) 8.4mm, Th. (shank) 7.6mm, Wt. 11.7g. Incomplete. Rotary key with hollow shank, sub-circular in cross section. Circular bow. Possibly solid bit, incomplete. Iron key, however, core of shank may have copper alloy component as copper corrosion is apparent. Possible chest or casket key. Conserved.

Key (illustrated, Pl. 6.95). E2399:223:68. Fe and Cu alloy. L. 93.8mm, W. (bow) 34mm,

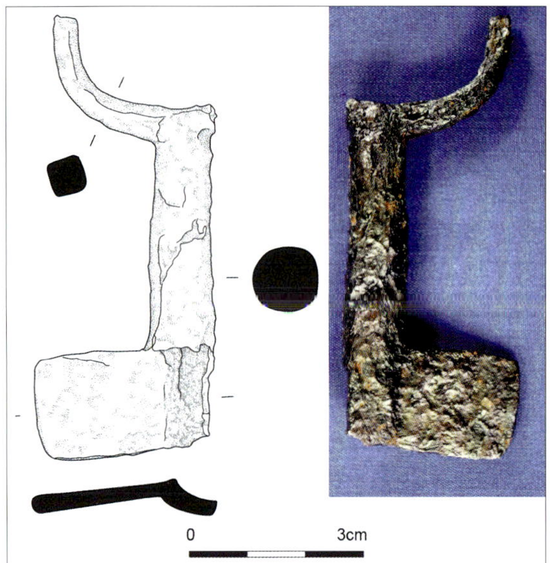

Pl. 6.97. Key E2399:269:94.

(shank) 8.8mm, Th. (shank) 7.8mm, Wt. 17.8g. Complete. Rotary key with hollow shank, circular in cross section. Kidney-shaped bow. Symmetrical clefts form the bit. Iron key, however, core of shank may have copper alloy component as copper corrosion is apparent along the fold/join of the shank. Conserved.

Key (illustrated, Pl. 6.96). E2399:200:105. Fe. L. 65mm, W. (bow) 23mm, (shank) 5.7mm, Th. (shank) 5mm, Wt. 10.1g. Incomplete. Rotary key with solid shank?, oval in cross section. Kidney-shaped bow. Bit incomplete. Conserved.

Key (illustrated, Pl. 6.97). E2399:269:94. Fe. L. 73.7mm, W. (bit) 17.2mm, Th. (shank) 8.2mm, Wt. 26g. Incomplete. Rotary key with rectangular sectioned shank, hollow close to bit. Solid rectangular bit. Bow, incomplete, possibly originally oval. Conserved.

Possible barrel padlock key. E2399:441:2921. Fe. L. 83.7mm, W. 4.6mm, Th. 3.1mm, Wt. 4.7g. Incomplete. Shank of possible barrel padlock key with distinctive crooked bow with finial. Bit not extant. Corroded.

Key. E2399:221:184. L. 54mm, W. 42.5mm, Th. 18.7mm Wt. 39.2g. Incomplete. Closed bow with two loops measuring 8.9mm and 4.5mm respectively at one end. The other end is narrower and has been broken off.

Key. E2399:615:3071. Fe. L. 70.5mm, W. (bow) 34.5mm, (shank) 8.6mm, Th. (shank) 5mm, Wt. 26.9g. Incomplete. Rotary key with rectangular sectioned shank and oval/rectangular sectioned bow. Key is damaged and twisted along shank therefore detail of bit is somewhat obscured.

Keyhole. E2399:204:522. Fe. L.61.9mm, W. 48.2mm, Th. 3.9mm, Wt. 21.4g. Incomplete with central 'keyhole' perforation (L. 10.5mm, W. 5.8mm).

Keyhole plate. E2399:218:1975. Fe. L. 49mm, W. 35mm, Th. 1.9mm, Wt. 6.9g. Incomplete with central 'keyhole' perforation. Possible perforation on one side, not fully extant, for attachment. Edges are bevelled.

Possible keyhole plate. E2399:1:176. Fe. L. 47.9mm, W. 30.6mm, Th. 3.9mm, Wt. 13.7g. Incomplete with central rectangular perforation (L. 12.3mm, W. 4.7mm).

Possible padlock fragment. E2399:218:1976. Fe. L. 36.9mm, W. 31.3mm, Th. 17mm, Wt. 21.9g. Incomplete. Fragment of possible padlock with remnants of keyhole apparent and inner moving parts. Post-medieval in appearance. Highly corroded.

- Possible shears

CATALOGUE

Shears? E2399:2:832. Fe. L. 46.1mm, W. 7.1mm, Th. 3.8mm, Wt. 4.2g. Incomplete. Incomplete bow and arm of shears. Bow and arm rectangular in section. Corroded.

Shears? E2399:205:111. Fe. L. 113.1mm, W. 7.4mm, Th. 5.5mm, Wt. 20.1g. Incomplete. Incomplete bow and arm of shears. Bow and arm rectangular in section. Corroded.

- Miscellaneous domestic objects

CATALOGUE

Hinge. E2399:209:166. Fe. L. 165mm, W. 50mm, Th. 9.7mm, Wt. 240.9g. Possible hinge with perforation (D. 5.34mm) at one end. Broken at both ends. Corroded with stone encrusted at one end.

Hinge. E2399:1:177. Fe. L. 145mm, W. 23.5mm, Th. 7.3mm, Wt. 84.8g. Thin strip of iron, with one end folded back onto itself to form loop (D. 11.4mm) at one end. Rectangular in section. The other end tapered gently to a blunt, slightly rounded end. Fragmented and highly corroded.

Hinge. E2399:221:2052. Fe. L. 98.6mm, W. 67.8mm, Th. 6.5mm, Wt. 346.5g. Incomplete? Possible hinge plate/pivot with perforation (D. 13.7mm) at one end. Other end is higher in section (13mm). Slightly bent and encrusted with stones. Highly corroded.

Handle. E2399:398:134. Fe. L. (complete) 95.2mm, L. ('C' shaped loop) 62mm, Th. (max.) 28.2mm, Wt. 501.2g. Incomplete. Bar circular in section, bent into 'C' shaped loop. Centre of loop thickest in section. Both ends bent into right angle from terminus of loop, rectangular in section. Small secondary iron attachment, rectangular in section, visible at one end.

Handle. E2399:398:163. Fe. L. (complete) 185mm, L. ('C' shaped loop) 141.2mm, Th. (max.) 15.1mm, Wt. 87.9g. Incomplete. Bar circular in section, bent into 'C' shaped loop. Centre of loop thickest in section. One end damaged. Other end bent into right angle from terminus of loop, rectangular in section.

Handle. E2399:1:175, Cu Alloy. L. (link) 20mm, L. ('L' shaped loop) 52mm, W. 32mm, Th. (max.) 9.4mm, Wt. 20g. Incomplete. Bar circular in section, bent into curved 'L' shaped loop. One end damaged. Other end bent into right angle from terminus of loop, rectangular in section.

Handle. E2399:221:2048. Fe. L. (complete) 121.8mm, L. ('C' shaped loop) 104mm, Th. (max.) 17mm, Wt. 103g. Incomplete. Bar circular in section, bent into 'C' shaped loop. Centre of loop thickest in section. One end damaged. Other end bent into right angle from terminus of loop, circular in section.

Hinge. E2399:212:1792. Fe. L. 104mm, W. 63.7mm, Th. 13.9mm, Wt. 355.8g. Incomplete? Possible hinge plate, rectangular in section, with perforation (D. 13.3mm) at one end. Other end is higher in section (10mm). Slightly curved. Highly corroded.

Possible scissors/Pruning tool. E2399:204:521. Fe. L. (handle) 56.2mm, L. (complete) 146mm, W. (blade) 11mm, W. (max.) 25.5mm, Th. (handle) 8.6mm, Wt. 99.6g. Incomplete. Possible scissors/pruning tool with visible rivet below the branch of the handle, which is incomplete. Possible blade, rectangular in section, partially extant at opposite end with accretions at terminus. Corroded.

Hinge. E2399:2:300. Fe. L. 64.1mm, W. 51.3mm, Th. 8.3mm, Wt. 64.9g. Incomplete. Thin rectangular iron fragment, slightly curved, with side hinge visible. Rectangular in section. Highly corroded and fragmented.

Prongs? E2399:206:1623. Fe. L. 168.3mm, W. 8.3mm, Th. 6.6mm, Wt. 82.3g. Rod, circular in section and slightly curved. One end tapers to a blunt point (damaged). Opposing end possibly splayed into two branches (L. 52mm) but unable to determine due to high level of corrosion.

T-Hinge? E2399:205:1431. Fe. L. 85.2mm, W. (head) 80.2mm, W. (arm) 33.1mm, Th. 9.9mm, Wt. 99.6g. Incomplete. Thin 'T' shaped iron object, with rod, circular in section, visible on one side. Two circular perforations visible, one in centre of head (D. 4.3mm) and the other on one side of arm (D. 4.2mm), for attachment. One end of arm damaged. Corroded.

Ring. E2399:45:54. Fe. D. 14.9mm, Th. 1.4mm, Wt. 0.5g. Complete. Small, thin ring, thicker and corroded where ends overlap. Possibly a link for fine chain or smaller domestic object.

Looped mount for handle. E2399:377:2655. Pb? L. 65.9mm, W. 56mm, Th. 1.9mm, Wt. 45g. Complete. Bell-shaped object with circular perforation at narrower end which seems purposely bent. Opposing wider end has two circular rivets and remnants of vessel to which the mount was attached on interior. Post-medieval/modern in appearance.

- Knives/Scabbards

Nine knives or knife fragments were recovered from the excavation. They vary from the earlier whittle tang knives, with the later scale tang knives also represented, including modern examples. Whittle tang knives display a tapered tang at the end of the blade which facilitated its insertion into a handle. Conversely, scale tang knives have broad, flat tangs which were attached to the handle using rivets. A classification of whittle tang knives was devised by Goodall (1990) and is based on the blade form. Five knife types were identified, A–E, of which three are represented here.

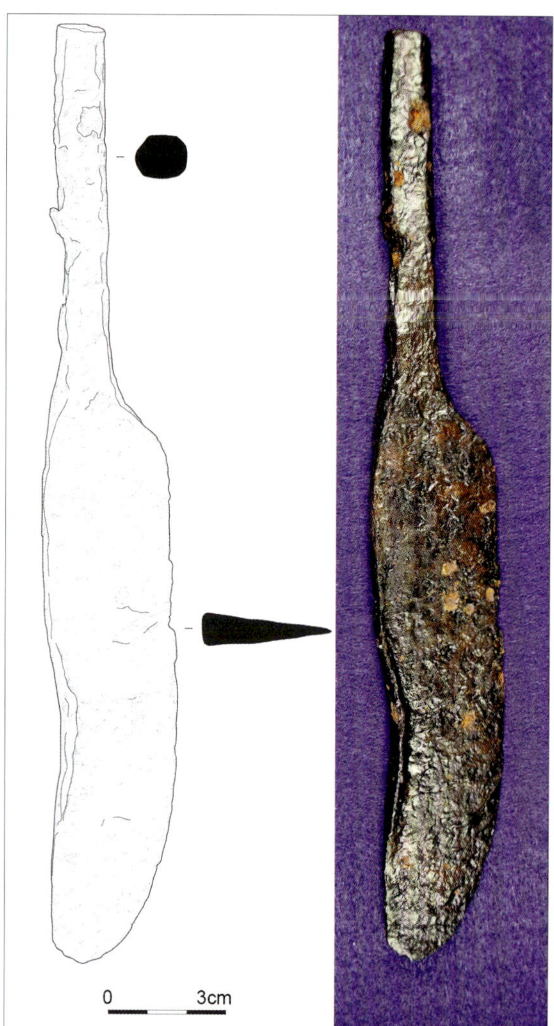

Pl. 6.98. Knife E2399:212:49.

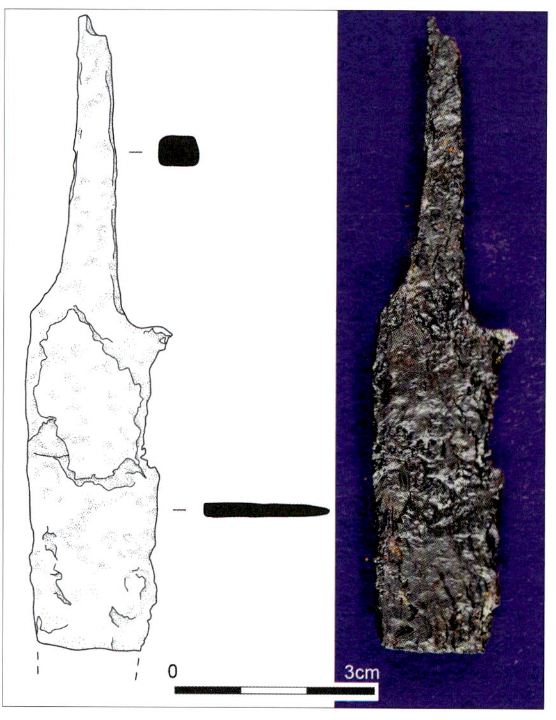

Pl. 6.99. Knife E2399:212:178.

Type B Knives

Type B knives are classified by a flat blade back which angles down to the tip and may have a straight or curved cutting edge. Type B knives occur in Winchester from the ninth to the fourteenth century.

Type C Knives

Type C knives are classified by their parallel blade and back which both taper to the tip (Goodall 1990, 844). In Winchester this knife type occurs in relatively large numbers in contexts dating from the tenth–thirteenth centuries (*ibid.*, 835). The type also occurs, albeit in smaller numbers, in eighth- to ninth-century contexts and also in fourteenth- to sixteenth-century contexts (*ibid.*).

Type D Knives

In this type the blade and the back both taper from the junction with the tang to the tip (*ibid.*, 847). Type D knives occur from the tenth century onwards in Winchester, although they appear to occur in larger numbers in the thirteenth and fourteenth centuries (*ibid.*, 835).

Type E Knives

Type E knives are defined by a curved back but may have variously shaped cutting edges (*ibid.*, 850). Type E knives from Winchester occurred in contexts dating from the tenth to the sixteenth century, although the largest numbers were recovered from twelfth- and thirteenth-century contexts (*ibid.*, 835).

As outlined above, scale tang knives differ from whittle tang knives in the form of the tang. In the former it is flat and perforated to facilitate the attachment of the handle plates by rivets. While scale tang knives and whittle tang knives were in use together during the medieval period, the scale tang variety is thought to be later, emerging in the late thirteenth or fourteenth century. For example, of the late fourteenth-century knives from the excavations in London, one-third comprised scale tangs with two-thirds being whittle tanged. In the early to mid fifteenth-century assemblage of knives, however, two-thirds were made up of scale tang knives illustrating their dominance in the later medieval period.

Knives with bolsters are thought to be a later development, with the bolster generally only appearing from the sixteenth century onwards. The bolster comprises a thickened, shaped portion of the knife between the blade and the tang. One knife with a bolster (E2399:221:178) came from Boyle. Similar bolster knives were recovered from the excavations at Kells Priory (Scully 2007, 368) and have been attributed to the post-medieval period. One bolster knife from the excavations at

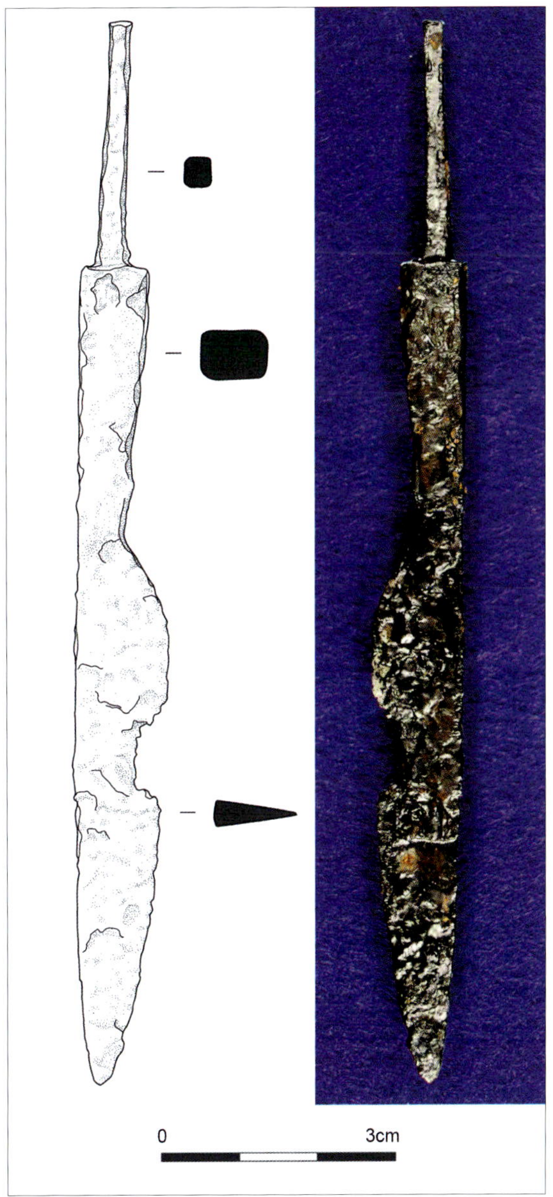

Pl. 6.100. Knife E2399:221:178.

Southampton was also dated to the sixteenth–seventeenth century. In the absence of any bolster knives positively identified as medieval in date it is reasonable to suggest that the finely made example from Boyle is also post-medieval in date, perhaps dating to the sixteenth or seventeenth century. Another example of a later knife is E2399:212:49 which is post-medieval in appearance given the large size of the blade and tang.

The somewhat unusual find of a possible socketed knife (E2399:439:193) from Boyle demonstrates the use of alternative methods of securing the blade to a handle in the medieval period. In this instance it would appear that

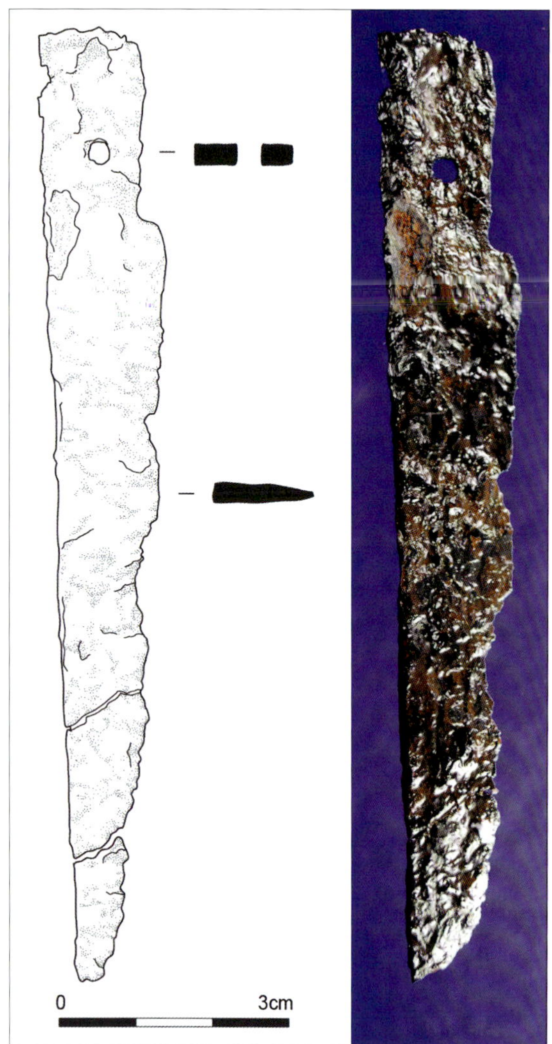

Pl. 6.101. Knife E2399:233:20.

the blade was socketed to the handle, although evidence for a rivet to secure the same was not extant. A socketed knife was recovered from a thirteenth-century context during the excavation of a moated site at Rigsdale, Co. Cork (Sweetman 1981, 203, fig. 7:15) and is suggested to be a pruning knife. The Boyle example was recovered from F439, a layer which overlay the primary phase of burials in the aisle.

CATALOGUE

Knife (illustrated, Pl. 6.98). E2399:212:49. Fe. L. 232.3mm, W. (blade) 33mm, Th. (tang) 10.7mm, Wt. 197.7g. Complete. Large knife with long, sub-rectangular sectioned tang. Large triangular sectioned blade with cutting edge which curves up to the tip. Blade back has been flattened by hammering. Post-medieval in appearance. Conserved.

Knife (illustrated, Pl. 6.99). E2399:212:1788. Fe. L. 92.5mm, W. (blade) 19.5mm, Th. (tang) 4mm, Wt. 19g. Incomplete. Type C possibly. Parallel blade and back, tip not extant therefore type not certain. Rectangular sectioned whittle tang. Conserved.

Knife (illustrated, Pl. 6.100). E2399:221:178. Fe. L. 130.3mm, W. (blade) 11.7mm, Th. (tang) 2.8mm, Wt. 12.9g. Incomplete. Straight back, blade angles gradually to the tip. Rectangular sectioned bolster between blade and whittle tang, also rectangular in cross section. Complete apart from small fragment of blade edge. Conserved.

Knife (illustrated, Pl. 6.101). E2399:233:20. Fe. L. 95.6mm, W. 15.2mm, Th. 3mm, Wt. 8.5g. Incomplete. Scale tang knife. Straight back, blade tapers towards rounded tip. Scale tang incomplete, one circular perforation extant. Conserved.

Knife (illustrated, Pl. 6.102). E2399:233:26. Fe. L. 115.8mm, W. (blade) 11.2mm, Th. (tang) 4.6mm, Wt. 15.7g. Incomplete. Type C? Parallel blade and back taper towards broken tip. Short whittle tang, rectangular in cross section. Highly corroded.

Socketed blade/knife (illustrated, Pl. 6.103). E2399:439:193. Fe. L. 111mm, W. (blade) 13.5mm, (socket) 15.1mm, Th. (blade) 3.6mm, Wt. 14.1g. Incomplete. Triangular sectioned blade tapers to a blunt tip, bent into U shape. At opposing end blade widens out into incomplete socket. Conserved. Similar object from a moated site at Rigsdale, Co. Cork (Sweetman 1981, 203, fig. 7:15), suggested by author to be a pruning knife.

Knife (illustrated, Fig. 6.34). E2399:908:819. Fe. L. 107.5mm, W. (blade) 14.2mm, Th. (blade) 4.8mm, (tang) 3.9mm, Wt. 11.7g. Complete. Type B. Straight blade back angles down to tip. Straight cutting edge.

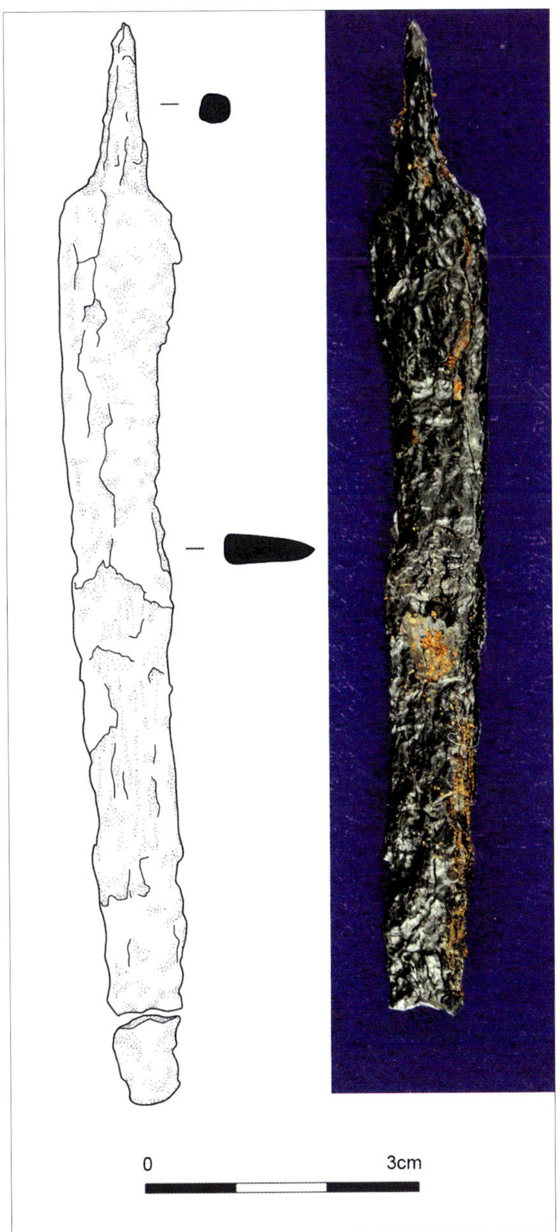

Pl. 6.102. Knife E2399:233:26.

Whittle tang, rectangular in cross section. Conserved.

Knife (illustrated, Fig. 6.35). E2399:910:832. Fe. L. 143mm, W. (blade) 17.1mm, Th. (blade) 3.6mm, (tang) 4.4mm, Wt. 29g. Complete. Type C? Parallel blade and back, taper to the tip. Blade curves down to pointed choil. Long whittle tang, rectangular in cross section, bent. Conserved.

Possible knife. E2399:32:600. Fe. L. 92.9mm, W .22.4mm, Th. 12.6mm, Wt. 28.6g. Incomplete. Type A? Iron knife. Possible short stump

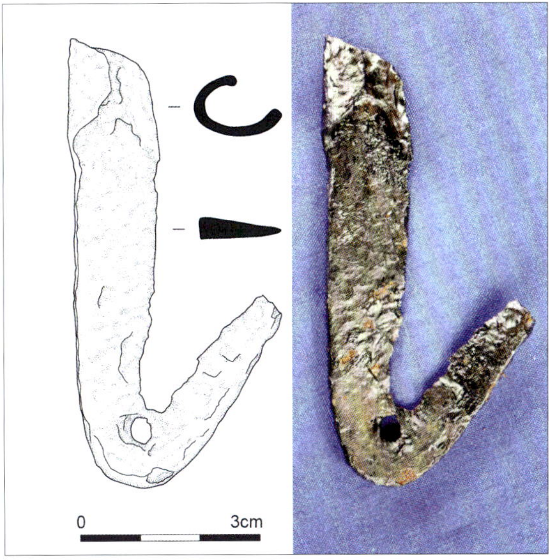

Pl. 6.103. Socketed knife E2399:439:193

of whittle tang extant. Blade triangular in section. Highly corroded and fragmented.

LEAD SEAL

Lead seals were attached to textiles from the late fourteenth to the early nineteenth century in England as part of a system of industrial regulation and taxation. Cloth seals were typically two-disc seals joined by a connecting strip. These were intended to be folded around each side of a textile and stamped closed, in a manner similar to that in which coins were stamped. The marking of newly woven cloths with seals of lead was part of the textile industry's quality control system in medieval and later times throughout Europe and thousands of different stamps have been recorded from excavated examples (Egan 1992). At its most complicated this involved checking that the cloth was of good quality and that it conformed with the statutory length, breadth and weight. A mark or seal was put on each satisfactory cloth. Without this alnage (the official supervision of the shape and quality of manufactured woollen cloth) seal the textile could not legally be sold. The cumbersome alnage system ended in 1724, but seals continued to be used as labels on cloths into the nineteenth century (*ibid.*). Regulation was at its most complex in the seventeenth century, when a single cloth might have half a dozen different seals applied to it, including that for alnage. Although the seal from

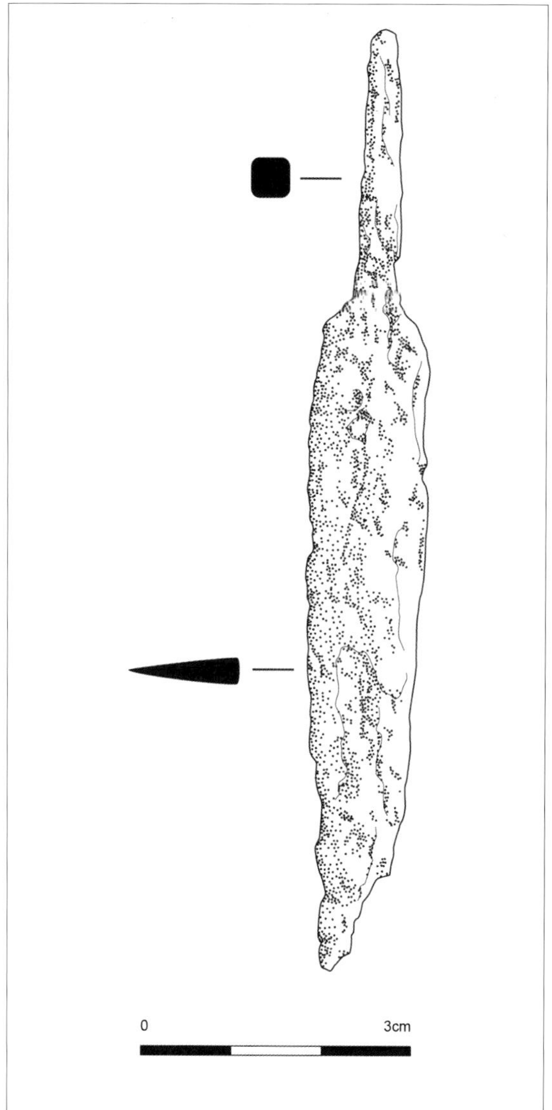

Fig. 6.34. Knife E2399:908:819.

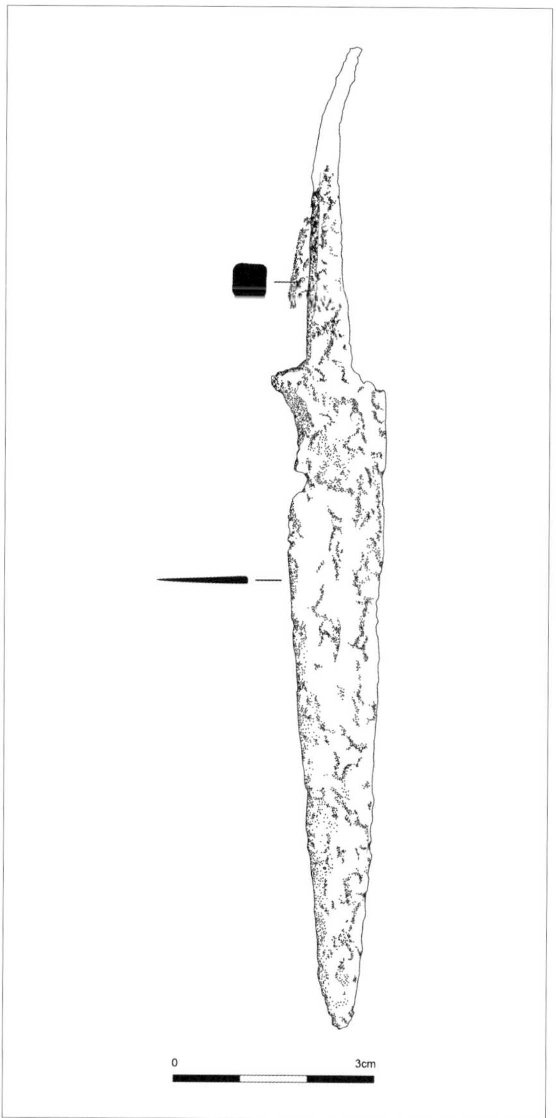

Fig. 6.35. Knife E2399:910:832.

Boyle was recovered from a post-medieval/modern deposit, its precise date is unclear. The depiction of the lion and the lettering on the back may suggest an eighteenth- or nineteenth-century date, but this is merely a tentative suggestion.

CATALOGUE

Lead seal (illustrated, Pl. 6.104). E2399:205:101. Pb. D. 18.6mm, Th. 4.8mm, Wt. 10.9 Complete? Seal depicting animal, possible lion statant (four paws on the ground) on one side. Opposing side has lettering of which only H---OR are legible.

FITTINGS AND MOUNTS

- Window lead

Windows that were glazed utilised glass which was cut into small diamonds, rectangles and squares known as 'quarries' (Noël Hume 1969, 233). The quarries were then mounted in grooved strips of lead anchored to iron frames which in turn were nailed to wooden casements (*ibid.*). According to Moran (see below), medieval window glass has not survived *in situ* in any Irish window frames, despite historical sources and archaeological evidence that confirms its widespread use in ecclesiastical buildings by the thirteenth century. One complete quarry and a number of quarry fragments were

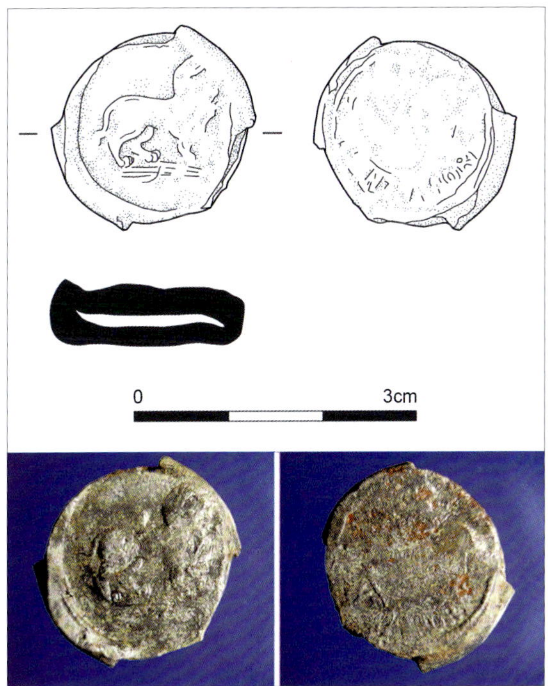

Pl. 6.104. Lead seal E2399:205:101.

recovered from the excavations at Boyle and provide direct evidence for the glazing of the abbey windows and the type of decoration used. The quarries would have been leaded together to form the overall pattern in the window and the lead fragments listed below would have fulfilled this function. A number of fragments of H-sectioned lead strips were recovered from various contexts with three pieces from F240 located outside the north aisle wall. One fragment (E2399:733:48) also came from a medieval deposit inside the aisle towards the centre of the church with two fragments (E2399:36:734 and 735) from a later deposit (F36). One piece came from the fill of a grave cut associated with burial B716 and attests to the continued repair of the windows through the lifetime of the church, at least prior to its dissolution.

CATALOGUE

Window lead. E2399:745:785. Pb. L. 42.7mm, W. 7.9mm, Th. 3.9mm, Wt. 5.6g. Incomplete. H-shaped in section. One end cut, opposing end damaged.

Window lead. E2399:733:48. Pb. L. 38.7mm, W. 7.9mm, Th. 4.7mm, Wt. 6.4g. Incomplete. H- shaped in section at one end. Opposing end is crushed. Slightly bent.

Window lead. E2399:240:2376. Pb. L. 50.9mm, W. 7.6mm, Th. 4.4mm, Wt. 7g. Incomplete. H-shaped in cross section. Broken at either end.

Possible window lead. E2399:240:2375. Pb. L. 35.8mm, W. 4.2mm, Th. 2.7mm, Wt. 3g. Incomplete. Twisted strip of lead with possible H-shaped cross section.

Window lead. E2399:240:2374. Pb. L. 18.3mm, W. 8.9mm, Th. 3.3mm, Wt. 2.5g. Incomplete. Small fragment of window lead. H-shaped cross section apparent but now misshapen.

Window lead. E2399:36:734. Pb. L. 42mm, W. 6.7mm, Th. 3.5mm, Wt. 2.2g. Incomplete. Fragment of window lead with-shaped cross section, now misshapen and twisted.

Window lead. E2399:36:735. Pb. L. 50.3mm, W. 5.6mm, Th. 3.6mm, Wt. 2.7g. Incomplete. Window lead fragment with H-shaped cross section, now misshapen. Impressed lines apparent on one surface, possibly from manufacturing process?

- Miscellaneous lead

CATALOGUE

Miscellaneous. E2399:1:174. Pb. L. 50.8mm, W. 7.9mm, Th. 6.3mm, Wt. 20.8g. Fragment of lead object, now T-shaped. Lacks distinctive H-shaped cross section. Unclear if part of window came.

Miscellaneous. E2399:125:728. Pb. L. 29.2mm, W. 1.7mm, Th. 1.3mm, Wt. 0.3g. Incomplete. Thin strip of lead, broken at either end. Possibly rectangular in cross section. Precise function unknown.

Miscellaneous. E2399:240:79. Pb. L. 62.6mm,

W. 7.6mm, Th. 3.9mm, Wt. 13.5g. Incomplete. Lead bar, rectangular in cross section. Tapers slightly towards one end. Function unknown.

Miscellaneous. E2399:125:729. Pb. L. 27.7mm, W. 3.6mm, Th. 3mm, Wt. 1.6g. Incomplete. Thin lead bar, rectangular in cross section, tapers to one end. Function unknown.

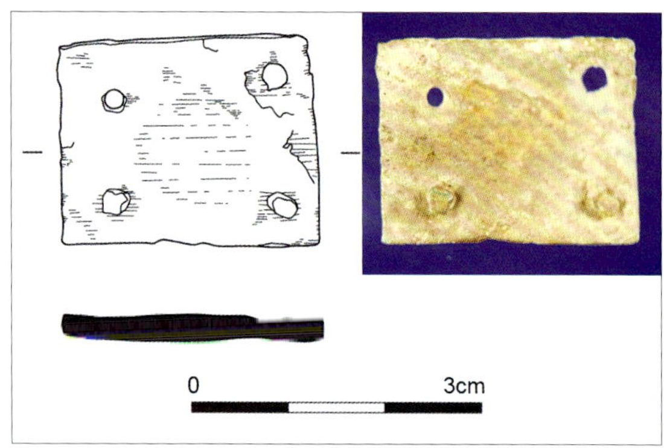

Pl. 6.105. Mount E2399:387:112.

- Mounts

CATALOGUE

Mount (illustrated, Pl. 6.105). E2399:387:112. Cu alloy. L. 26.4mm, W. 20.9mm, Th. 0.6mm, Wt. 2.6g. Incomplete. Thin, sub-rectangular mount with four circular rivet holes located towards each corner. Three rivets extant. Undecorated. Recovered from the grave fill associated with burials B293, B294 and B296. May have been utilised on leather or wooden objects. Precise function unknown.

Mount. E2399:711:17. Cu alloy. L. 122mm, W. 63.4mm, Th. 0.9mm, Wt. 46.5g. Incomplete. Flat copper alloy sheet in two fragments. Roughly rectangular in shape, slightly wider at one end. Edges broken and uneven. Three copper alloy rivets attached close to outer edges in addition to one detached rivet. Presence of rivets suggest that this item was originally mounted. Precise function unknown. Conserved.

Strap. E2399:709:750. Fe. L. 52mm, W. 23.9mm, Th. 1.6mm, Wt. 4.8g. Incomplete. Flat strap, rectangular in cross section with single sub-circular perforation (D. 3mm). Possible rivet on underside. Splayed at one end (broken). Opposing end also broken but not splayed. Conserved. Possible buckle plate.

Strap-type mount. E2399:205:123. Fe. L. 86.5mm, W. 20.4mm, Th. 1.7mm, Wt. 13.4g. Incomplete. Thin strap, rectangular in section. Shaped at one end which is perforated with remnants of rivet extant. Opposing end broken with second rivet extant. Conserved. Such mounts may have been used on wooden objects such as caskets, chests or boxes.

Mount. E2399:205:1442. Fe. L. (long arm) 68.3mm, L. (short arm) 57.2mm, W. 29mm (max.), Th. 3.3mm, Wt. 15.6g. Complete? Thin, L-shaped, strip of iron with perforation (D. 4.8mm) in centre. Rectangular in cross section. Both ends taper to a rounded point. Possible case/casket mount?

- Post-medieval/modern fittings and mounts

Several fragments of at least one coffin plate were recovered from the excavations, in proximity to the King family tomb, known as the King Monument. The plate is very fragmentary but appears to be made of lead with a copper alloy gilt on the upper, decorative surface. The decoration is an embossed foliate design within a curvilinear frame, also embossed along the edge of the plate. A winged figure, possibly a cherub, is visible on one fragment of the large group E2399:427:2837–52 and also on E2399:427:170. Coffin plates, as the name suggests, were metal plates, usually of lead, copper, pewter or brass that, were attached to the coffin lid as a decorative adornment. The plates sometimes provided details pertaining to the deceased such as the name and date of death. No lettering, however, could be discerned on the plate from Boyle. It also has small tack or nail holes at what appear to be the corners of the plate which would have facilitated attachment to the coffin lid.

Coffin plates date to at least the seventeenth

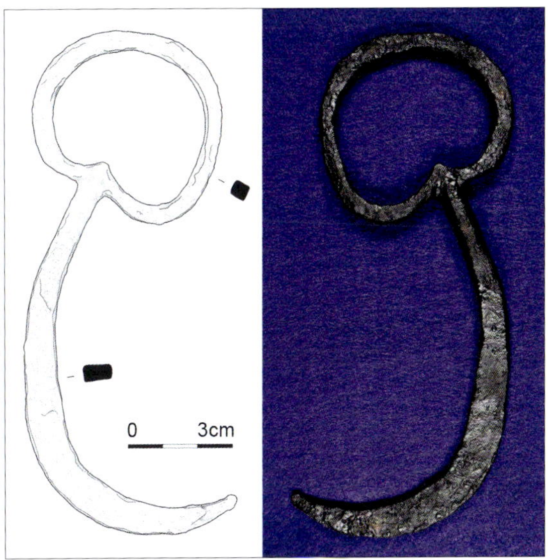

Pl. 6.106. Possible bale hook.

century and at that time were reserved for people of wealth. The use of coffin plates proliferated by the early to mid nineteenth century when they were widely available in cheap materials. By this time the cost of the plates had decreased so much that almost every family could afford to have one put on the coffin of their loved ones, while headstones were still unaffordable. As coffin plates began increasing in popularity, the practice of removing the plates from the coffin before burial became the trend, and they were often removed by the loved ones to be kept as mementos of the deceased. This practice peaked in the late nineteenth century.

The precise date of the plate is unclear as the material from which it was recovered was largely unexcavated. Given its proximity to the King Monument and the design of the plate an eighteenth- to nineteenth-century date is likely.

CATALOGUE

Fitting. E2399:11:455. Cu alloy. L. 64.2mm, D. (max.) 32.9mm, Wt. 55.4g. Cast hollow knob or fitting for pull chain. Post-medieval/ modern in appearance.

Coffin plate. E2399:427:2837–2852. Pb and Cu alloy. Numerous fragments of coffin plate with embossed foliate design. Appears to have copper alloy gilt. Largest piece dimensions: L. 60.8mm, W. 53mm, Th. 1.6mm. Total weight 29.3g. Incomplete. Possibly associated with the nearby King Monument.

Coffin plate fragment. E2399:427:170. Pb and Cu alloy. L. 62.8mm, W.45mm, Th. 1.7mm, Wt. 4.5g. Incomplete. Fragment of lead coffin plate with copper alloy gilt. Embossed design with winged figure, possibly a cherub. Possibly part of E2399:427:2837–2852 above.

Decorated mount. E2399:398:3456. Cu alloy L. 92.6mm, W. 87.4mm, Th. 3.6mm, Wt. 15.5g. Incomplete. Circular with central perforation (D. 9.2mm). Opposing circular perforations for attachment. Floral design in relief formed around central perforation.

TOOLS

- Mounts Bale Hook

  Bale hooks or cargo hooks were utilised to assist in lifting heavy loads by extending the reach and grip of the workman. As the name implies, they were frequently used to lift bales of wool, hay or other heavy items such as sacks or wooden boxes. While they often have a wooden handle set perpendicular to the hook, fully metal examples are also known. These implements would appear to be a post-medieval development in the agricultural industry when the practice of making hay into bales became more prevalent.

CATALOGUE

Possible bale hook (illustrated, Pl. 6.106). E2399:237:19. Fe. L. 136.5mm, W. (hook) 10.7mm, (handle) 56.3mm, Th. (hook) 3.2mm, (handle) 4.5mm, Wt. 55.7g. Complete. Rectangular sectioned hook with kidney-shaped handle. Hook curves and tapers to the tip. Conserved.

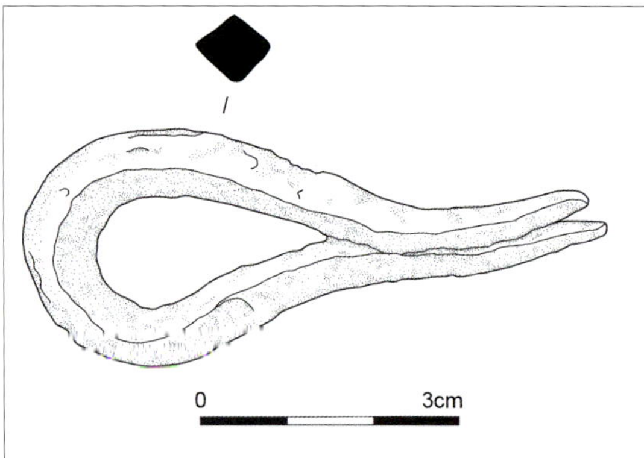

Pl. 6.107. Link E2399:14:5.

- Woodworking tools

CATALOGUE

Awl/punch? E2399:221:2051. Fe. L. 230.5mm, W. 13mm, Th. 11.3mm, Wt. 111g. Iron bar, circular in section, which tapers to a blunt point. Other end sub-rectangular in section. Highly corroded.

Punch? E2399:221:2054. Fe. L. 157.3mm, W. 11.6mm, Th. 11.9mm, Wt. 142.6g Complete? Iron bar bent into 'L' shape. Circular in section. One end rounded headed. Opposing end tapers gently to a flat, splayed terminal. Highly corroded and fragmented.

Awl/punch? E2399:209:1662. Fe. L. 189mm, W. 12.3mm, Th. 11.6mm, Wt. 78.3g. Iron bar, rectangular in section, which tapers to a point (damaged). Opposing end also damaged. Highly corroded.

Gouge. E2399:200:281. Fe. L. 124.8mm, W. 11.6mm, Th. 7.6mm, Wt. 62.5g. Iron bar, circular in section. One end damaged. Opposing end flattened and curved inwards to form gouge shape. Corroded.

- Structural ironwork

Hooks

A large iron hook, E2399:538:213, with a looped head and a spirally twisted shank was recovered. A very similar object was recovered from the excavations at Coppergate, York (Ottaway 1992, 653) and was interpreted as likely forming part of suspension gear. Such items are likely to have been utilised for hanging or suspending domestic items such as cooking pots, cauldrons, food or clothing.

CATALOGUE

Hook. E2399:538:213. Fe. L. 157mm, W. 11.7mm, Th. 6.1mm, Wt. 66g. Incomplete? Large iron hook with spirally twisted shank, rectangular in cross section. Looped head, open, slightly tapers. Conserved.

Links

One possible chain link (E2399:14:5) came from a post-medieval context. It is diamond or lozenge-shaped in cross section and is looped to form a 'head', the tapering arms then pinched together. A similar object with the same lozenge-shaped cross section came from the excavations at Coppergate, York (Ottaway 1992, 647, fig. 273.3509).

CATALOGUE

Link (illustrated, Pl. 6.107). E2399:14:5. Fe. L. 67.9mm, W. 27.7mm, Th. 7.7mm, Wt. 22.4g. Complete. Diamond-sectioned bar, looped to from 'head' with tapering arms. Conserved.

Pl. 6.109. Chalice.

made to obliterate the inscription. Somehow this fragment was lost or discarded and was incorporated into the backfill of the robbed out north wall (Ó Floinn 2013, 368).

WINDOW GLASS

Jo Moran

INTRODUCTION

An assemblage of 227 shards of window glass was recovered from the 2006–12 excavations. Of these 114 are medieval, 110 are post-medieval and three are modern. Although the medieval glass has survived in very poor condition, some fragments have been dated mid to late thirteenth century based on surviving painted patterns. The excavations covered the footprint of the north aisle at Boyle Abbey and extended slightly beyond the north wall.

MEDIEVAL GLASS

Medieval window glass has not survived *in situ* in Irish window frames, but historical sources and archaeological evidence confirm its widespread use in ecclesiastical buildings by the thirteenth century. Boyle Abbey is a Cistercian foundation and regulations were laid down by the reformed order of Cistercian monks as to what was permitted and not permitted in window glazing. It spoke out against the use of 'luxurious materials and figurative imagery in monastic art and architecture' which led to the prohibitions in the statutes of *c.* 1151 against coloured or figurative glass windows (Zakin 1979, 4). As a result, a simple ornamental type of window glass was developed known as Cistercian grisaille glass. The prohibitions may not have always been easy to enforce as the General Chapter held in 1182 asked for coloured and painted glass to be removed within two years. The prohibitions on coloured and painted glass were repeated in 1202, *c.* 1220, 1237, and 1257 (Marks 1986, 212–13). A nave window at La Bénisson-Dieu (*c.* 1200) includes small quarries of red pot-metal as part of the interlace pattern but no late twelfth-century glass has been found in England and Wales (*ibid.*, 213) and Marks believes that it 'is unlikely that coloured or figural glazing played much of a part before the last quarter of the century'.

The term *'grisaille'* is a French word meaning painting in tones of grey. It is used to describe windows composed of white glass which when leaded together give an overall impression of grey. There are two types of Cistercian grisaille glass; the earlier is plain white glass (with a green tint) leaded together into geometric patterns, sometimes called 'blankglazing', and the second is white glass painted with vegetal and floral designs and leaded into geometric patterns. There is no evidence for 'blankglazing' in Ireland to date but painted grisaille glass dated to the early to mid thirteenth century has been recovered from excavations at the Cistercian abbeys of Duiske, Graiguenamanagh, Co. Kilkenny (Bradley and Manning 1981, 419), Tintern, Co. Wexford (Lynch 2010, 144–5), and Bective, Co. Meath (Moran 2016, 90–2). A single shard was recovered from recent excavations at the Cistercian abbey at Dunbrody, Co. Wexford. Medieval window glass has also been recovered from excavations at Mellifont Abbey, Co. Louth (de Paor 1969, 157) but this appears to be later. A significant assemblage was recovered from excavations at Holycross, Co. Tipperary (C. Manning pers. comm.). Glass is listed among the assets of the Cistercian monastery at Inishlounaght, Co. Tipperary, at the time of the dissolution (White 1943, 227).

There were two methods of manufacturing medieval window glass. Cylinder or 'muff' glass was made by blowing a bubble of glass, elongating

Fig. 6.37. Quarry glass E2399:111:74.

Pl. 6.110. Quarry glass E2399:111:74.

it into a cylinder, cutting off the ends, then cutting along its length and flattening it into a sheet while still hot. This type of glass has elongated bubbles or 'seeds' and the cut edges often developed fire-rounded thickened edges. Two fragments (E2399:734:41–2) have a muff or fire-rounded edge, extremely thick (*c.* 5.8mm), and for this reason they may have been discarded during glazing. Evidence suggests that cylinder or muff glass was the most common method of manufacture for medieval 'potash' glass. Crown glass was created by transferring molten glass from the blowpipe to a pontil iron which was spun round rapidly to create a circular sheet by centrifugal force. These sheets have a characteristic bullseye in the centre and curved lines preserved within the glass. The glass was thinner towards the edge of the sheet. Cylinder glass was popular until the late seventeenth century, when crown glass was introduced to Ireland. Crown glass was then dominant up to the middle of the nineteenth century.

There is no evidence, archaeological or documentary, that glass was manufactured in Ireland before the late sixteenth century. There are references to medieval glassworkers in Dublin from the thirteenth century onwards, but it is unclear if the glassworker (vitrarius and verreour) is a glassmaker or a glazier who painted onto the glass and fused the paint to the glass in a furnace (Westropp 1920, 20).

Many of the medieval glass fragments from Boyle Abbey have 'grozed' or nibbled edges, formed by trimming the glass with a 'grozing' iron. The glass was first cut with a hot iron and then trimmed into shape by grozing, a method described by Theophilis in his treatise *De diversis artibus*, written between *c.* 1110 and 1140 (Dodwell 1986, 48–9).

THE GLASS

One complete quarry (Fig. 6.37, Pl. 6.110) and nine fragments with a painted pattern were identified in the assemblage. Many more of the fragments are likely to have had patterns but the glass has devitrified to such an extent that the painting is no longer visible. A single border quarry of white glass was also recovered

Quarry E2399:111:74 (Pl. 6.110, Fig. 6.37) was recovered from the earliest burial horizon at the west end of the north aisle. The glass was found in association with nails and architectural fragments. The quarry is opaque potash glass with a buff/cream patchy enamel-like patina on the surface. It is white glass with a blue tint but it is not a 'pot-metal' (coloured using a metallic oxide added in the pot). It is roughly square (51mm × 51mm × 3.6mm) and is painted with a foliate spray with trefoil terminals. The trefoils are boldly outlined in red/brown paint against a clear ground. The central trefoil is larger than the other two and has its head in the apex of the quarry. It has round lobes and the trefoils on either side fit neatly under its side lobes. The side trefoils have a round central lobe and slightly pointed lobes on either side.

The quarry might have been part of a four quarry pattern, as the spray is set diagonally and springs from a quarter of a central motif (Fig. 6.37). The four quarry pieces would have been set diagonally and surrounded by borders, to form part of a repeating pattern. Arrangements of this type can be seen in early thirteenth-century, non-Cistercian windows at Lincoln Cathedral, Salisbury Cathedral, Westminster Abbey (Marks 1993, 131) and S. Remi, Reims (Day 1897, 120). The suggested Boyle quarry pattern is unusual in having the central motif shared between the four quarries of the spray; elsewhere the central motif is a separate medallion of coloured glass (as at Lincoln (Fig. 6.38), Salisbury and Westminster cathedrals; Marks 1993, 131–2). The late thirteenth century reconstructed grisaille panel from Kells Priory, Co. Kilkenny, would also have had a separate central medallion (Moran 2007, 266).

The Boyle pattern is set against a clear ground while similar quarry patterns at Lincoln and Salisbury cathedrals are set against a cross-hatched ground (Fig. 6.38). Cross-hatching was used as a background to stylised patterns in the early thirteenth century but was dropped in the second half of the century (from *c.* 1260). However, as the cross-hatching disappeared the foliate patterns became more fluid, and no longer confined by the lead. The later thirteenth-century patterns are more naturalistic, as in architectural sculpture.

The Boyle Abbey quarry, with its stiff-leaf trefoil motif, is more typical of the period when cross-hatching was popular (*c.* 1220–60). It is very similar to the motif on a quarry from Lincoln Cathedral now in the V&A, London (Fig. 6.39), but without the cross-hatched background and painted borders.

Fig. 6.38. Medieval glass.

Fig. 6.39. Medieval glass from Lincoln Cathedral.

Alternatively, the Boyle quarry might have been leaded into a lattice to fill the background between panels, similar to a panel from Lincoln (Fig. 6.40).

Foliate sprays with trefoil terminals form the basis of many thirteenth-century floor tile

Fig. 6.40. Medieval glass from Lincoln Cathedral.

designs (Eames and Fanning 1988, 24). The 4-tile trefoil spray (T157) recovered from excavations at Graiguenamanagh Abbey Co. Kilkenny, is similar to the Boyle quarry and is dated to the mid to late thirteenth century (*ibid*., 27, 112). The use of the same or similar patterns on tiles and glass is well known (Zakin 1979, 2); however, Boyle Abbey did not have a tiled floor and floor tiles have not been found at other abbeys west of the Shannon (Stalley 1987, 214).

Fragments E2399:221:2030, E2399:77:61, E2399:232:3004, E2399:240:2986, E2399:221:2031, E2399:21:56 and E2399:232:2991 are very small and have the remains of a pattern painted on one side (Fig. 6.41). Although it is not possible to identify any of the grisaille patterns with certainty, they are painted against a clear ground and do not have cross-hatching. They are potentially contemporary with quarry E2399:111:74. Fragment E2399:232:37 is part of an open beaded border. A row of open circles of equal size are painted against a clear ground. Borders of this type were common from the mid twelfth to the thirteenth century, framing grisaille and figurative panels.

Fragment E2399:439:191 is an almost complete border pane of white glass with a blue-green tint. Borders of white glass form part of many grisaille patterns and framed figurative panels. They were also commonly placed between the central panel and painted border of a grisaille window for aesthetic effect. They were also used to create a border between the stonework and glass, probably because they could easily be replaced, if broken when the window was removed from its frame for repair or re-leading, and for aesthetic effect. The top edge of fragment E2399:439:191 is chamfered, probably to fit a corner.

The remaining fragments are potash glass but they have devitrified to a point where they are totally opaque and crumbling. Most have a soft orange/brown powdery crust and no longer retain their original shape or any painted patterns and it is not possible to say if they are white or coloured glass.

POST-MEDIEVAL GLASS

In the late sixteenth century, glass making went through considerable changes. Glass became thinner (1mm–3mm thick), harder and less prone to corrosion. The glass is greenish, containing less potash but higher concentrations of lime, and is referred to as a high-lime, low-alkali glass (HLLA) (Paynter 2011, 27). Glass of this type was manufactured in England following the arrival of Continental glassmakers in the late sixteenth century. One of these glassmakers, Jean Carré, obtained monopoly rights to glass production in England and Ireland in 1567 (*ibid*.). Early glasshouses have been identified in counties Cork, Derry, Laois, Offaly, Waterford and Wicklow (Farrelly 2010, 37). A glasshouse at Salterstown, Co. Derry, was making window glass between 1614 and 1618, and a glasshouse at Shinrone, Co. Offaly, was producing pale green HLLA window glass in the seventeenth century (Farrelly *et al.* 2005, 9). However, most of the window glass used in Ireland in the seventeenth century may still have been imported.

Crown glass does not appear to have been made in Ireland until the eighteenth century Imported crown glass for windows was introduced to Ireland by the end of the seventeenth century and remained in demand to the middle of the nineteenth century.

The excavations at Boyle Abbey recovered 113 fragments of post-medieval window glass, all 'white' glass, with a tint, in shades ranging from

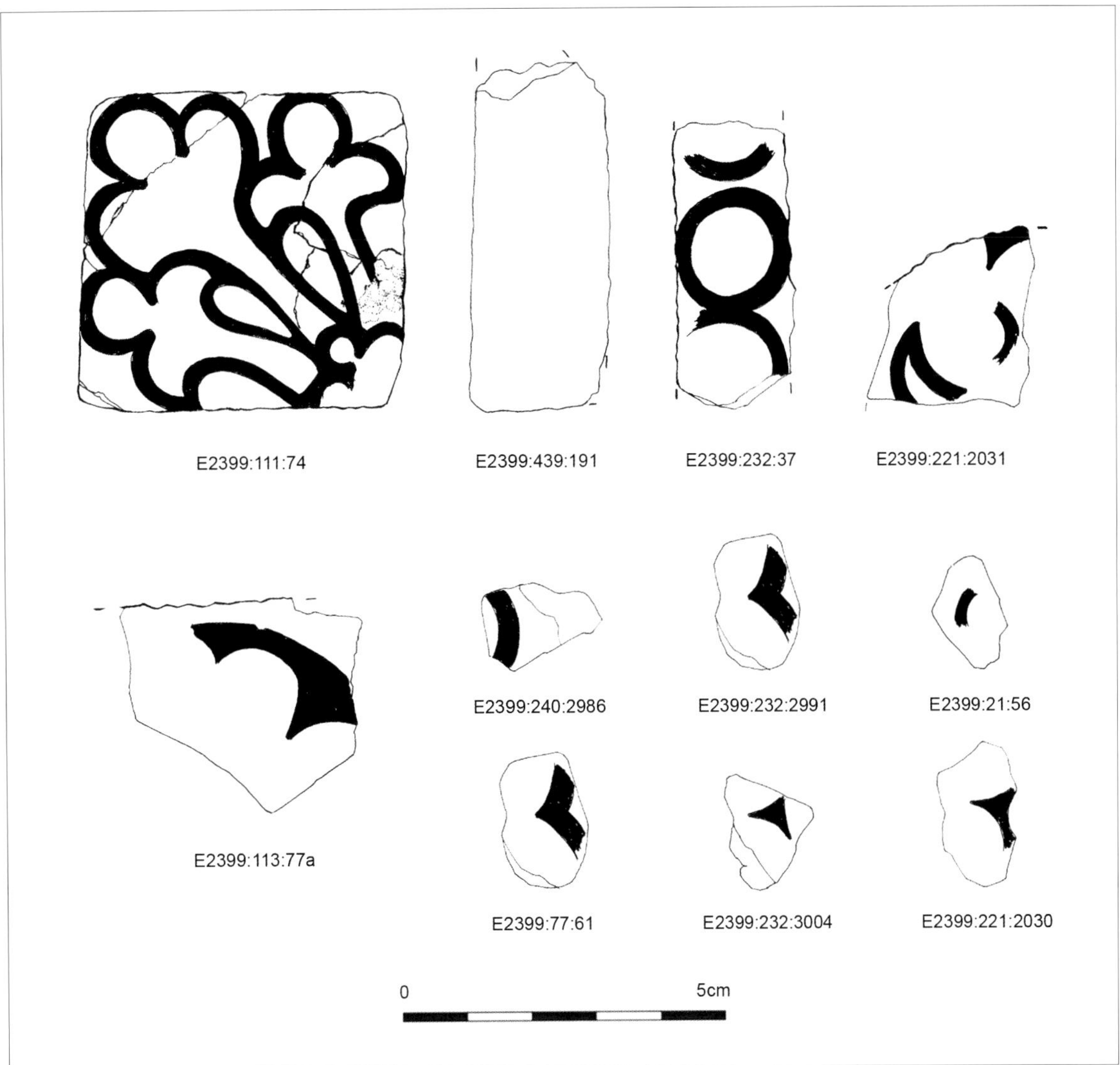

Fig. 6.41. Painted medieval glass E2399:232:2991.

dark green and olive green to pale yellow and blue-green. The fragments are thinner than medieval glass (1.5mm to 3mm thick) and more uniform, and some have retained their translucency. Some fragments have a slight iridescence on the surface, and some have a metallic patina. None have a painted pattern. The cut edges are generally diamond-cut but a few are grozed.

CYLINDER GLASS

Archaeological evidence suggests that cylinder glass (or broad glass) was the most common type of glass in Ireland in the seventeenth century – made in Ireland and also imported. It was still in common use in Ireland until the late eighteenth century. Fragment E2399:7:386 (Pl. 6.111) is an edge fragment of cylinder glass, probably discarded because of the thickness of the 'muff' edge.

The likely earliest post-medieval fragments are thin (1.5mm–3mm thick) white glass with a strong green tint (7%). The glass still retains some of its translucency but has some brown surface corrosion. These fragments have been classified as late medieval (late sixteenth century) because some have grozed edges; E2399:603:3429–30 and E2399:212:1724–25. Fragment E2399:706:161 has a grey/green patina and one grozed edge. It is argued that grozing should not be used as a date indicator because it was employed into the eighteenth century to trim quarry corners during reglazing (McGlade and Roche 2016, 118).

The majority of the fragments (72%) are thin white glass (1.5mm–2.5mm thick) with a pale, yellow-green tint, semi-translucent due to yellow-brown surface corrosion and iridescence.

Pl. 6.111. Cylinder glass fragment E2399:7:386.

Pl. 6.112. Crown glass fragment E2399;7: 385.

Many of the fragments have diamond-cut edges. Fragments E2399:207:1640, E2399:403:151 and E2399:405:2757 have two diamond-cut edges and appear to be the apexes of diamond-shaped quarries. Diamonds were used to cut glass from the late sixteenth century onwards (Brown and O' Connor 1991, 65). All the glass fragments from this context are 'white' glass with a pale yellow tint. Some have diamond-cut edges, and some have elongated bubbles known as 'seeds' suggestive of the cylinder or muff method of manufacture. Both cylinder and crown glass limited the size of the pane that could be cut and because of this the glass was cut into diamond quarries which were then leaded together into a lattice. Diamond quarry windows are likely to have glazed the abbey when it was in use as a barracks from 1592. Quarries of this type were recovered from post-dissolution contexts at Blackfriars Abbey, Waterford and are thought to have been used to repair or reglaze windows in the vicinity of the sacristy/chapel.

Two fragments of thin white glass (1.5mm) with a yellow-green and a mid-green tint are translucent and do not have any surface corrosion (E2399:7:3169-3170, E2399:201:305).

CROWN GLASS

Twenty-six fragments of crown glass were recovered (*c.* 19%). The glass is white glass with a blue-green tint, translucent apart from a slight milky iridescence on a few fragments. One of these fragments is part of a bullseye or 'bullion' (E2399:7:385 in three pieces, Pl. 6.112), 18.35mm thick close to the centre of the bullseye narrowing to 3mm. Curved lines are preserved in the glass close to the bullseye. The second bullseye (E2399:221:2024, Pl. 6.113) is also clear glass with a blue/green tint, 12.19mm thick at the centre of the bullseye narrowing to 3mm but with some iridescence on the surface. The pontil scar is visible on one side, where the pontil rod was attached.

The bullseye was often discarded as waste as it would have been considered too thick and uneven to be used in a window. The recovery of the bullseyes suggests that the crowns of glass were brought to the abbey by the glazier and cut into quarries on site for glazing or reglazing some time from the late seventeenth century onwards. Some of the crown glass fragments might be offcuts from curved-shaped quarries (Pl. 6.114).

Three fragments of modern clear white glass

without a tint were recovered, and one thick fragment of reinforced glass (E2399:218:1943-1944, E2399:205:1314, E2399:205:1315).

DISCUSSION

The medieval window glass fragments were recovered from medieval contexts and grave fills, in the area of the north arcade and aisle, and are unlikely to be original to the windows close by, which were built between 1185 and 1220 (Stalley 1987, 243).

The medieval glass fragments are grisaille glass with painted stylised patterns against a clear ground. No coloured window glass (pot-metal) and no figural fragments were identified, although only scientific analysis could tell if any of the devitrified glass was coloured.

The best-preserved medieval fragment is an almost complete square quarry painted with a trefoil spray (E2399:111:74). The trefoil is essentially an Early English rather than a Romanesque motif, stylised or 'stiff-leaf' and does not have a cross-hatched ground. Four similar quarries might have formed a group, but without a central, coloured glass medallion. However, the quarry is small and might have formed part of a border or background. The absence of cross-hatching, combined with the formal design, suggest a date for design and manufacture in the mid to late thirteenth century.

The lack of cross-hatching on the other quarry fragments suggests they may be contemporary.

Unfortunately, there is very little comparative material from Cistercian sites in Ireland. Seven fragments of painted grisaille glass were recovered from a fourteenth-century layer at Tintern Abbey, Co. Wexford, and two border quarries of plain glass were recovered from a thirteenth-century drain fill (Lynch 2010, 144–6). The grisaille fragments from Tintern have painted ornamental patterns set against cross-hatched grounds, and similar glass at Lincoln and Salisbury cathedrals has been dated to the early-mid thirteenth century (*c.* 1220–60).

Only seven fragments of painted window glass were recovered from Mellifont Abbey (de Paor 1969, 157). The illustrated fragments are too small to classify but they do not appear to have come from a thirteenth-century grisaille window; they are more likely to be contemporary with the remodelling of the south transept in the fourteenth century. Five fragments of grisaille glass with the remains of a painted pattern were recovered from excavations at Bective Abbey (Moran 2016, 90–1). Unfortunately, the fragments are in too poor a condition to identify the patterns. One small fragment of opaque potash window glass (E3686:001:071) was recovered from excavations at Dunbrody Abbey, Co. Wexford. The piece is likely to be medieval grisaille glass, with part of a painted pattern visible on one side but is too small to say more.

Analysis of glass from a number of Cistercian sites in England and Wales by Richard Marks indicates that by the second half of the thirteenth century the Cistercians were using stylised foliage

Pl. 6.113. Glass fragment E2399:221:2024.

Pl. 6.114. Glass fragment E2399:218:193-4.

against cross-hatched grounds in their grisaille, and the decoration is indistinguishable from windows in non-Cistercian indigenous houses (Marks 1986, 215–16).

Roger Stalley's analysis of Irish Cistercian architecture and sculpture suggests that between 1142 and 1200 'Irish Cistercians made serious efforts to obey the spirit of the rule in artistic matters' but by the 1200s the Cistercian attitude in sculptural decoration was changing, and there was a move away from austerity (Stalley 1979, 182).

Although very little window glass was recovered from the Boyle Abbey excavations, the stylised or stiff-leaf trefoil on the Boyle Abbey quarry suggests a similarity with the other Cistercian sites in Ireland.

CATALOGUE OF ILLUSTRATED FRAGMENTS (FIG. 6.41)

E2399:21:56. Opaque potash glass with black/brown surface weathering, shadow of a painted pattern on one side, 4mm thick.

E2399:77:61. Opaque potash glass with black/brown surface weathering, remains of painted pattern on one side, pitted on the outside surface, 4mm thick.

E2399:111:74. Square quarry of grisaille potash glass, painted with a trefoil spray against a clear ground. Opaque with cream/brown surface weathering, complete but fractured, four grozed edges, 51mm × 51mm × 4mm. Found in north aisle/nave, phase 1 burial horizon.

E2399:113:77a. Opaque potash glass, black/brown surface weathering, remains of painted pattern on one side, one grozed edge, 4mm thick. Found in grave fill, earliest burial horizon.

E2399:221:2030. Opaque potash glass, remains of painted pattern on one side, 4mm thick. Found in post-medieval overburden in the nave.

E2399:221:2031. Opaque potash glass, black/brown surface weathering, traces of a curvilinear pattern, pitting on outside surface, one grazed edge, 32mm × 26mm × 4mm. Found in post-medieval overburden in the nave.

E2399:232:37. Border quarry of potash glass, black/brown surface weathering, painted with a beaded motif, 44mm × 21mm × 4mm. Found in latest burial horizon, outside north wall.

E2399:232:2991. Opaque potash glass with black/brown surface weathering, remains of a painted curvilinear pattern on one surface, 21mm × 16mm × 4mm. Found in post-medieval overburden in the nave.

E2399:232:3004. Opaque potash glass devitrified black/brown, remains of a painted pattern on one side, 4mm thick. Found in post-medieval overburden in the nave.

E2399:240:2986. Opaque potash glass, black/brown surface weathering, remains of a painted pattern on one side, 17mm × 7mm × 4mm. Found in latest burial horizon outside the north wall.

E2399:439:191. Border quarry of opaque potash glass, one chamfered corner, 58mm × 22mm × 4.5mm. Found in the centre of the nave overlying the latest burial horizon.

ARTEFACTS OF SKELETAL MATERIAL

Miriam Carroll

INTRODUCTION

A total of 13 bone artefacts were recovered from the excavations. While the overall number of objects of skeletal material from the sizeable excavation area is small, they nonetheless attest to a range of activities on the site from the medieval period through to the nineteenth and twentieth centuries. Several of the artefacts are items of personal dress or were for personal use, while others are utilitarian in nature. Many of the items were recovered from secondary or post-medieval contexts although they themselves may be earlier in date. The objects are catalogued below according to type and are discussed accordingly.

HANDLES

Seven bone handles or handle fragments (E2399:910:50, E2399:603:3072, E2399:204:349, E2399:1/2:3115, E2399:9:437, E2399:58:3070 and E2399:205:1052) were recovered from the excavations and comprise the largest number of bone objects in the assemblage. Two main types of bone handle are common within the archaeological record in Britain and Ireland and are classified according to their method of attachment, namely whittle tang handles and scale tang handles. Whittle tang handles are fixed by pushing the pointed end of the tang into the handle which has a central narrow hollowed-out portion. Conversely scale tang handles were composite objects attached to the tang by iron or copper alloy rivets. In general, whittle tang handles are regarded as the earlier form and are largely associated with whittle tang knives.

One potentially late medieval whittle tang handle (E2399:910:50) came from this site. According to Cowgill *et al.* (2000, 25) most whittle tang handles were cylindrical with a wide diameter to prevent the handle from splitting when the knife was flexed. Such handles recovered from London were rarely decorated while decoration was more common on the later scale tang handles (*ibid.*, 25–6). The form and decoration of the handle from Boyle (E2399:910:50) would suggest a medieval date, possibly thirteenth–fourteenth century. While decorated knife handles have been recovered from excavations in Ireland, they are predominantly scale tang handles as per the evidence from excavations in Britain. In this regard the handle from Boyle is a fine and seemingly rare example of a decorated whittle tang handle. Its recovery from a possible late medieval/post-medieval pit just outside the north transept door would seem to suggest that it is a residual find.

Two scale tang handles (E2399:58:3070 and E2399:205:1052) form part of the assemblage. Scale tang handles are known from medieval contexts in Britain and Ireland with many examples from contexts dating from the fourteenth century onwards in London (Cowgill *et al.* 2000, 26). According to Cowgill (*ibid.*) the construction of scale tang handles required many more components than whittle tang handles and led to a greater used of decorative metals. This may be seen in a small way on the Boyle example (E2399:58:3070) where a tiny copper alloy rivet has been utilised in the dot of the dot-and-circle motif. The rise in popularity of scale tang handles may be attributed to the greater possibilities in terms of decoration and the ability to produce an arguably more elegant handle than the early whittle tang examples (*ibid.*). Larger scale-handles were recovered from the excavations at Kells Priory, Co. Kilkenny, one of which was identified as being late medieval in date (Hurley 2007, 419). On the basis of its decoration, the smaller example from Boyle may be medieval in date but it is unlikely to be earlier than the fourteenth century given the proliferation of scale tang handles after

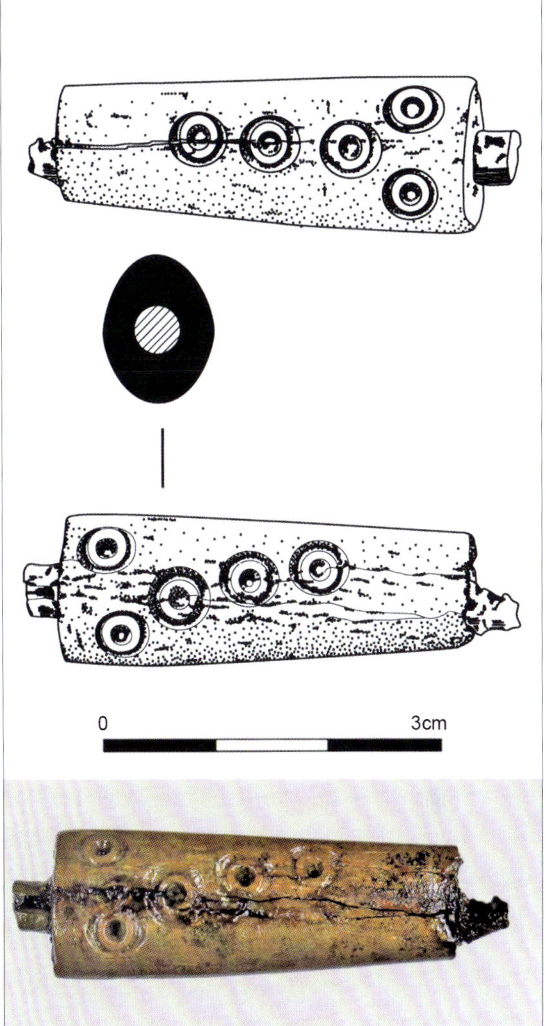

Pl. 6.115. Bone handle E2399: 910:50.

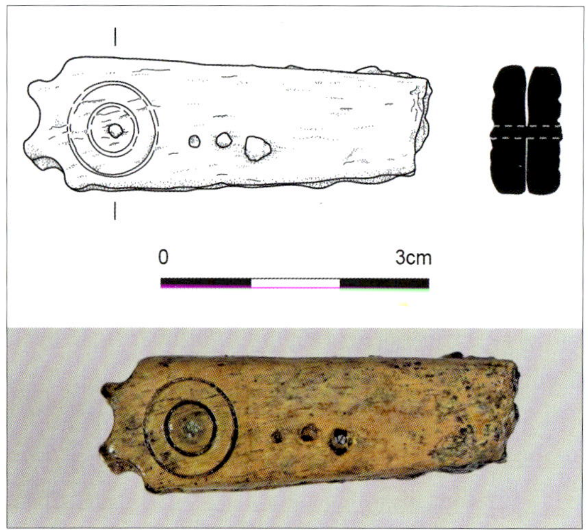

Pl. 6.116. Bone handle E2399: 58:3070.

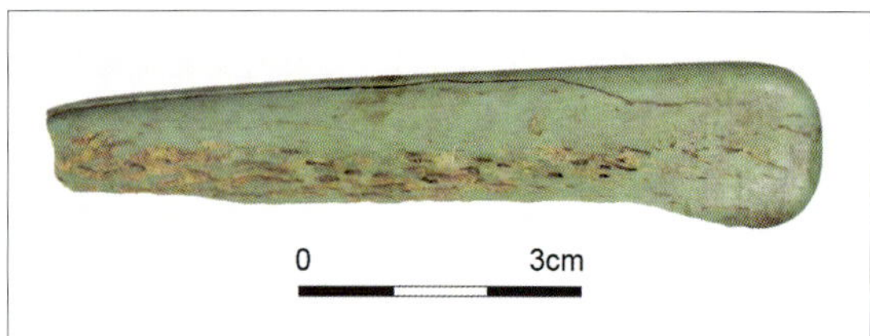

Pl. 6.117. Bone handle E2399:204:349.

Pl. 6.118. Bone handle E2399:205:1052.

this time. In this regard, a late medieval date is suggested for the handle which was recovered from a drain fill (F58).

The scale tang handle E2399:205:1052 is undecorated and fairly crudely made. The bone is also abraded and may have been exposed to the elements for some time in antiquity. The proliferation of scale tang handles from the fourteenth century onwards is well documented and supported by examples from numerous excavations in Britain and Ireland. This handle was recovered from a post-medieval context (F205) and while it may have originated from an earlier context it can only be broadly ascribed to a possible date rage of the late fourteenth to the seventeenth century.

Two additional whittle tang handles (E2399:1/2:3115 and E2399:204:349) are likely to represent a post-medieval renaissance of this handle type. Such bone and antler handles, used for table knives, are known from eighteenth and nineteenth century contexts and the rectangular form of the former example from Boyle would suggest a post-medieval date for same. A stained example (E2399:204:349), while incomplete, represents another post-medieval example of such handles and is likely to be nineteenth century in date, when it became popular to stain cutlery handles a characteristic green. A fragment of a whittle tang handle (E2399:9:437) was also recovered from a post-medieval context at the abbey; however, the date of the object itself is uncertain given its incomplete state.

CATALOGUE

Handle (illustrated, Pl 6.115). E2399:910:50. L. 35.5mm, W. 11.65mm, Th. 9.3mm, Wt. 7g. Complete. Bone handle, oval in cross section, tapers towards one end. Decorated on both surfaces with five dot-and-circle motifs. The motifs are arranged regularly on one surface with two at the widest end of the handle and three in a linear arrangement along the length. On the opposing side a similar arrangement has been attempted; however, the linear motifs are diagonal. Iron tang (whittle?) extant within centre of hollowed out handle. Small cu alloy penannular ring attached to tang at wider end of handle may suggest that this was part of a composite object and that further parts of the handle would have originally been attached to this wider end. Conserved.

Handle fragment. E2399:603:3072. L. 43.4mm, W. 10.1mm, Th. 4.5mm, Wt. 2.1g. Incomplete. Fragment of possibly rectangular sectioned whittle tang handle with faceted corners. Hollowed centre for holding tang apparent. Polished outer surface. Possibly post-medieval in date.

Handle (illustrated, Pl. 6.116). E2399:58:3070. L. 45.6mm, W. 14.4mm, Th. 8.9mm, Wt. 7.8g.

Incomplete. Composite handle comprising two rectangular sectioned bone plates joined together with small iron rivet. Tapers slightly towards one end where remnants of iron object, possibly a scale tang, are extant. Each plate is decorated with a dot-and-double-circle motif, in the centre of which is a tiny copper alloy rivet. The decoration is located at the splayed end of the handle on the upper surface of each plate. The end of both plates is also scalloped to form decorative handle end. Conserved.

Handle (illustrated, Pl. 6.117). E2399:204:349. L. 79.3mm, W. 16.6mm, Th. 8.4mm, Wt. 8.7g. Incomplete. Fragment of knife/fork handle, hollowed in centre to hold tang. D-shaped in cross section. Stained green. Nineteenth century in date.

Handle. E2399:1/2:3115. L. 77.1mm, W. 15.7mm, Th. 7.5mm, Wt. 9.5g. Incomplete. Rectangular sectioned bone handle, tapers slightly towards one end (broken). Sub-circular-oval hollow apparent at narrow end, presumably to hold tang of object. Extends into handle for length of 42.6mm. Post-medieval in appearance.

Handle fragment. E2399:9:437. L. 44.5mm, W. 16mm, Th. 6.9mm, Wt. 4.5g. Incomplete. Portion of whittle tang bone handle. Tapers towards one end where remains of hollow for tang are visible. Handle appears to have been split, possibly during use. Outer surface is decorated with shallow linear grooves extending along length of handle.

Handle (illustrated, Pl. 6.118). E2399:205:1052. L. 71.1mm, W. 17.4mm, Th. 13.4mm, Wt. 25.1g. Complete. Composite handle comprising two D-shaped sectioned bone plates joined together with two iron rivets. Tapers towards one end where remnants of iron object (possible knife) and associated scale tang are extant. Corroded metal at wider end of handle may represent an end cap. Undecorated.

PINS

Two bone pins (E2399:480:190 and E2399:542:221) were recovered from the excavations and are likely to represent items of personal dress. The former is a simple undecorated example which came from the grave fill of burial B347. Similar pins have been recovered from ninth–eleventh-century contexts in Coppergate, York (MacGregor *et al.* 1999, 1950) and are classified therein as Group 1 pins. Such pins are simple in form in which the naturally expanded and flattened distal end of the bone forms the head, while the shaft of the bone has been cut through to form a pointed shank. Not to be confused with weaving tools known as 'pin-beaters' which take a somewhat similar form, the example from Boyle is likely to have been used as an item of personal dress, possibly to secure a cloak or other item of clothing. In this regard, its recovery from the grave fill of burial B347 is noteworthy and it may be a shroud pin.

A second simple, undecorated pin (E2399:542:221), although much different in form, was recovered from the grave fill of B376. Bone pins are known from varying medieval contexts in Ireland and Britain and form another type of dress accessory to their metal counterparts, albeit utilising a different material. This example from Boyle Abbey (E2399:542:221) was recovered from a grave fill (F542) associated with burial B376 and arguably may have been an item of personal adornment for this individual or perhaps a pin for securing a shroud. Bone pins recovered from other sites in Ireland and Britain typically display a form comparable to metal pins of the time, comprising a circular sectioned shank tapering to a point with a round or sometimes flat head at the opposing end. The Boyle pin clearly differs from the usual pin form being flat with a barely differentiated head. In this regard it is unlikely to have been a hair pin and may have been utilised to secure a cloak or other item of clothing.

CATALOGUE

Pin (illustrated, Pl. 6.119). E2399:480:190. L. 109.9mm, W. (head) 13.8mm, Th. 3.8mm, Wt. 2.9g. Complete. Bone pin with sub-rectangular-oval sectioned shank,

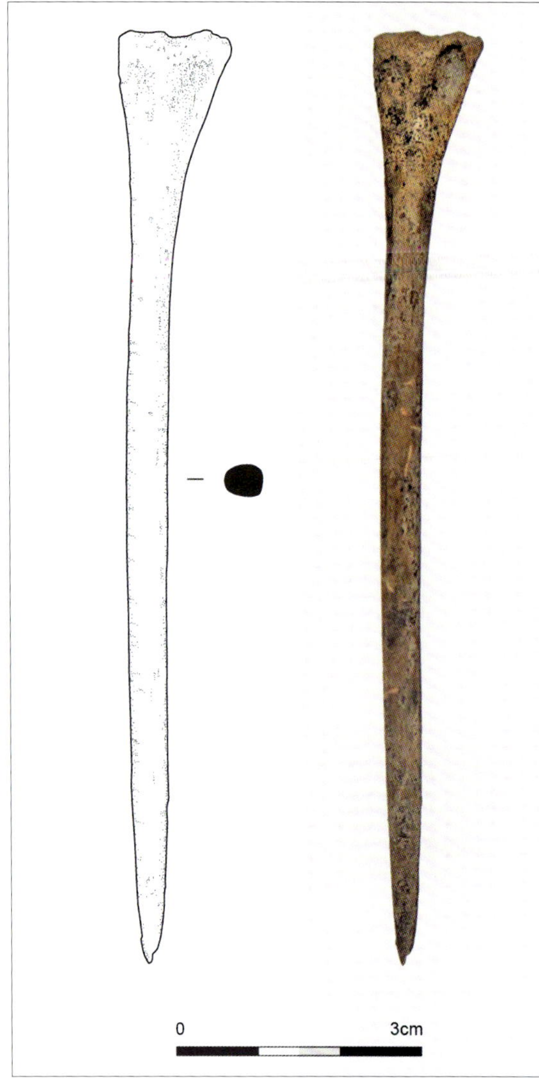

Pl. 6.119. Pin E2399:480:190.

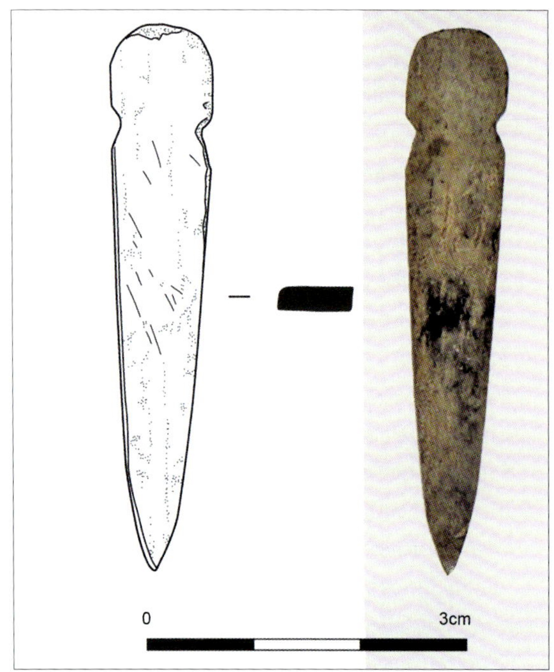

Pl. 6.120. Pin E2399:542:221.

tapers to a point. Crude rectangular sectioned head at opposing end. Undecorated.

Pin (illustrated, Pl. 6.120). E2399:542:221. L. 49.2mm, W. (head) 9.3mm, Th. 2.1mm, Wt. 1.4g. Complete. Flat bone pin, rectangular in cross section. Tapers to a point. Opposing wide end has been waisted to form a slightly rounded head, also rectangular in section. Undecorated.

DISCS

Bone discs have been recovered from medieval and post-medieval contexts in Britain and Ireland with examples from early twelfth-century contexts in Cork. The precise function of such perforated discs is unclear, and some may be waste from bone working or button making. The disc from Boyle (E2399:221:2005) was recovered from a post-medieval context which produced finds ranging in date from the seventeenth to nineteenth century. The bone disc, although incomplete, is well made and polished and therefore is unlikely to be waste. Its recovery from a post-medieval context equally does not necessarily infer a post-medieval date, although similar examples from post-medieval contexts in Galway City are of note.

CATALOGUE

Disc (illustrated, Pl. 6.121). E2399:221:2005. D. 28mm, D. (perforation) 6.9mm, Th. 2.3mm, Wt. 1.8g. Incomplete. Polished circular bone disc with central circular perforation. Portion of one side not extant.

COMBS

One almost complete bone comb (E2399:33:11) and a comb fragment (E2399:0:02) were recovered. The larger more complete comb (E2399:33:11) has been classified according to the typology of Irish combs devised by Dunlevy (1988a, 341–422). It broadly fits into her Class F combs which comprise single-sided composite combs with an arched

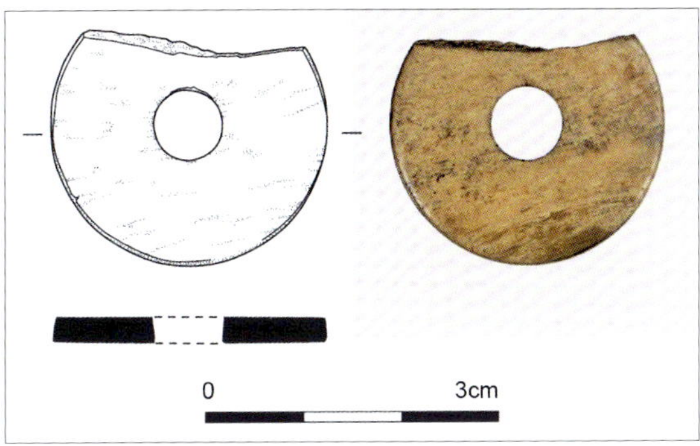

Pl. 6.121. Disc E2399:221:2005.

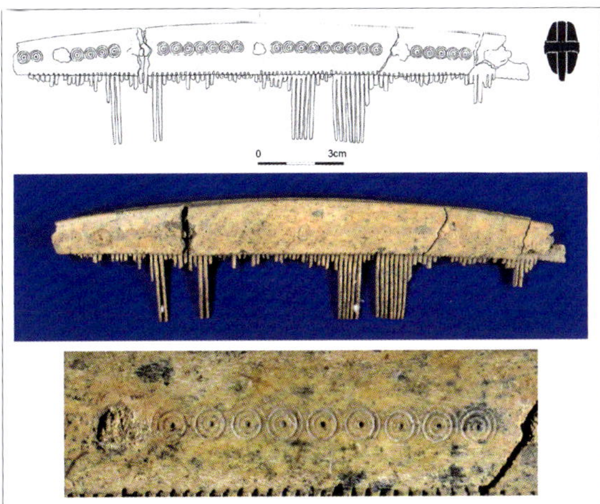

Pl. 6.122. Comb E2399:33:11.

spine (*ibid.*, 362), within which there are three major sub-classes F1, F2 and F3. The Boyle comb may fit within the F2 sub-class as it has the polished, D-shaped side plates associated with same (*ibid.*, 364), although its dot-and-double-circle decoration is also seen in sub-class F1. Despite such variations, the form of the Boyle comb is consistent with Class F; similar examples, albeit undecorated, were recovered from eleventh- and early twelfth-century contexts in Waterford City (Hurley 1997, 654–61) and from a late twelfth- to early thirteenth-century context in South Main Street, Cork City. A Class F comb also decorated with dot-and-double-circle motif was recovered from a late twelfth–thirteenth-century context at Christ Church, Cork (Hurley 1997, 243–5). According to Dunlevy (1988a, 367) Class F combs appear to have a ninth–twelfth-century date range in Ireland, 'corresponding to a period from shortly after the initial settlement of the Vikings to roughly when the Norman-style combs were generally adopted'. More recent evidence from archaeological excavations, however, imply variations to the form and a continued use into the late twelfth and thirteenth centuries in Cork, Waterford and elsewhere. In this regard the Boyle Abbey example, despite its recovery from a secondary context, is likely to date to the twelfth to thirteenth century.

eleventh- and early twelfth-century contexts in Waterford City (Hurley 1997, 654–61) and from a late twelfth- to early thirteenth-century context in South Main Street, Cork City. A Class F comb also decorated with dot-and-double-circle motif was recovered from a late twelfth–thirteenth-century context at Christ Church, Cork (Hurley 1997, 243–5). According to Dunlevy (1988a, 367) Class F combs appear to have a ninth–twelfth-century date range in Ireland, 'corresponding to a period from shortly after the initial settlement of the Vikings to roughly when the Norman-style combs were generally adopted'. More recent evidence from archaeological excavations, however, imply variations to the form and a continued use into the late twelfth and thirteenth centuries in Cork, Waterford and elsewhere. In this regard the Boyle Abbey example, despite its recovery from a secondary context, is likely to date to the twelfth to thirteenth century.

CATALOGUE

Comb (illustrated, Pl. 6.122). E2399:33:11. L. 181mm, Wth. 41.6mm, Th. 14mm. Incomplete. Class F. Single-sided composite comb with slightly arched back. Side plates D-shaped in cross section attached to composite teeth plates with small iron rivets (extant). Decorated with finely executed dot-and-double-circle motif on both sides. Saw marks apparent on base of side plates from cutting of teeth, many of which are no longer extant. The side plates taper downwards at either end (not extant). Fragmented.

Comb fragment (illustrated, Pl. 6.123). E2399:0:02. L. 16.2mm, Wth. 31.6mm, Th. 2mm. Incomplete. Fragment of double-sided comb with one wide end tooth extant. Fine teeth. Undecorated. Unknown class.

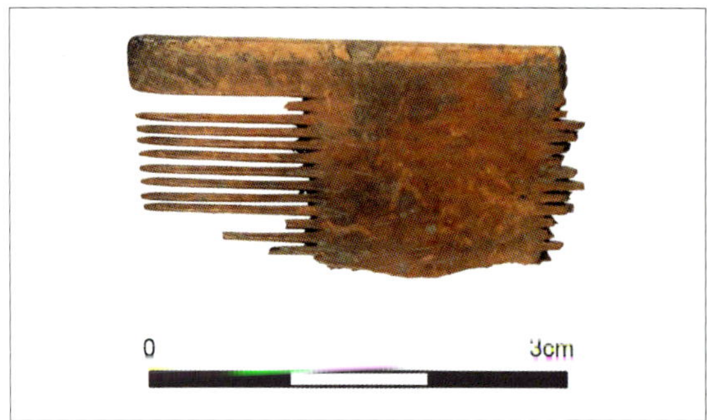

Pl. 6.123. Comb fragment E2399:0:02.

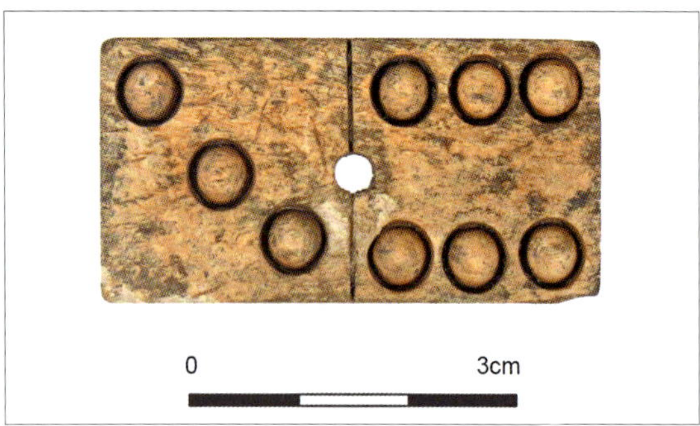

Pl. 6.124. Domino piece E2399:2:313.

GAMING PIECES

A bone domino is the only item of skeletal material (E2399:2:313) from the abbey finds assemblage which may be attributed to leisure activities, and it is from a post-medieval context. Indeed, the item is post-medieval in appearance and is likely to be mid to late nineteenth century in date given the central perforation. By the mid nineteenth century, European dominoes were still commonly manufactured from slim narrow pieces of bone, but now with an ebony wood back which was glued and then fixed to the bone with a brass pin (known as a spinner) through the centre of the tile. This development was probably due to a lack of suitable thick pieces of animal bone, requiring the ebony layer to strengthen the tile, which made it possible to stand dominoes on their edges. The perforation on the domino from Boyle is likely to have facilitated attachment of the aforementioned back to the domino and hence attributes the piece to the mid to late nineteenth century.

CATALOGUE

Domino piece (illustrated, Pl. 6.124). E2399:2:313. L. 45mm, W. 23mm, Th. 4.7mm, Wt. 6.4g. Complete. Bone domino piece with central perforation. Shallow linear groove separates three and six shallow drilled circles. Perforation may have facilitated the attachment of a wood back (not extant).

CLAY PIPES

Clare McCutcheon

INTRODUCTION

A total of 159 pieces of clay pipe were recovered during the 2006–12 seasons of excavation. Following identification and some reassembly this was reduced to 156, of which 124 are undecorated stem fragments. The narrowest of the stems measured just 2.36mm by 3.65mm in diameter but the majority were much wider with one as wide as 7.89mm by 8.10mm. The longest stem fragment surviving measured 83.77mm in length. The pipes have been divided into roughly seventeenth-, eighteenth- and nineteenth-century date with a closer date listed where a positive identification can be made.

SEVENTEENTH-CENTURY CLAY PIPES

CATALOGUE

E2399:212:1708 (illustrated, Pl. 6.125): stamped incuse with lozenges and rouletting as 221:2002 (below); without initials cannot be identified as Evans pipes. Two similar stems have been found at Boyle Abbey (E283).

E2399:221:2002 (illustrated, Pl. 6.125): stamped incuse LE between lozenges with rouletting above and below, the mark of Lluellin Evans of Bristol, dating 1661–88. Three similar stems have already been recovered at Boyle Abbey (E283).

E2399:27:536 (illustrated, Pl. 6.126): small bulbous spurred bowl, in yellow clay, uneven milled line around the rim. Used. 1610–40.

E2399:221:2000 (illustrated, Pl. 6.127): well-finished bowl, with fine milling, a stamped cartouche on the rear, with a crowned L contained within a circle of beading. The Arms of Gouda are stamped either side of the spur confirming this as a Dutch pipe dating 1750–1800 (Norton 2007, 449).

E2399:2:795 (illustrated, Pl. 6. 128): bulbous complete bowl with milling around flared rim and flat oval heel. Late seventeenth century.

E2399:2:196 (illustrated, Pl. 6.128): complete undecorated bulbous bowl. Late seventh century.

E2399:2:199: bowl fragment, flat heel. Late seventeenth century.

E2399:40:760: fragment of flat heel. Late seventeenth century.

E2399:205:689: bulbous bowl fragment. Late seventeenth century.

E2399:205:690: bowl fragment, spur. Late seventeenth century.

E2399:205:692: spur. Late seventeenth century.

E2399:229:2211: bowl fragment, flat heel. Late seventeenth century.

E2399:905:717: spur. Late seventeenth century.

Pl. 6.125. Clay pipe E2399:212:1708.

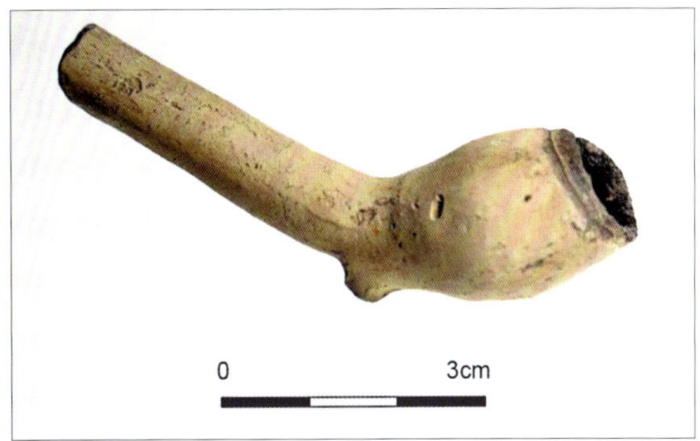

Pl. 6.126. Clay pipe E2399:27:536.

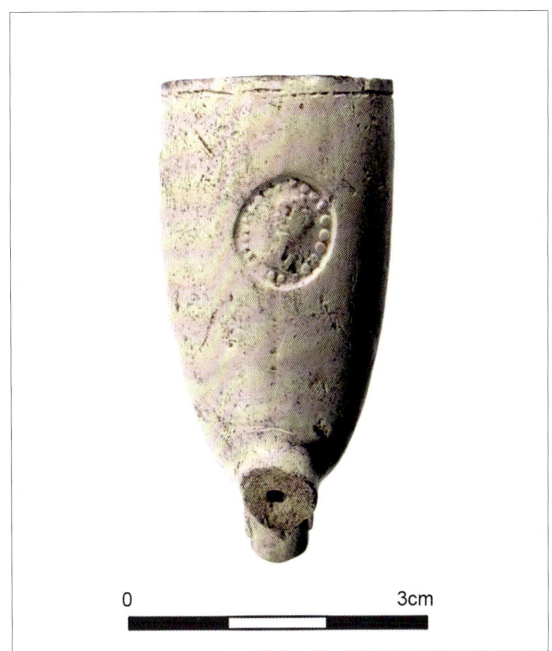

Pl. 6.127. Clay pipe E2399:221:2000.

EIGHTEENTH-CENTURY CLAY PIPES

CATALOGUE

E2399:2:198: bowl fragment.

E2399:16:494: stem fragment, red clay, well finished. Dutch. (cf. 221:2002).

E2399:15:493: bowl fragment.

E2399:30:557: stem fragment, red clay (cf. 212:1705).

E2399:204:344: bowl fragment, milling. Dutch.

E2399:204:346: bowl fragment, thin, milling.

Pl. 6.128. Clay pipe E2399:2:196.

Pl. 6.129. Clay pipe bowl E2399:2:197.

E2399:212:1705: red-firing clay, bowl fragment with flat heel.
E2399:221:2003: stem fragment, red clay, well finished. Dutch? (cf. 16:494).

NINETEENTH-CENTURY CLAY PIPES

CATALOGUE

E2399:0:720: decorated stem with indistinct relief decoration on incuse spiral band.
E2399:1:143: complete bowl, undecorated.

E2399:2:197 (illustrated, Pl. 6.129): bowl fragment, rouletted and stamped with the number 43 within a circle. This was possibly made at Knockcroghery. A similar item has previously been recovered at Boyle Abbey (E283). It is most likely that the number refers to the Year of Repeal 1843 rather than a series of addresses and may have been a Repeal type local to the Galway Roscommon area (McCutcheon below).

E2399:204:345: bowl, fragment.

E2399:204:343: bowl fragment, undecorated.

E2399:205:691: bowl fragment, milling round rim, right edge of incuse stamp.

E2399:221:1998: semi-complete bowl, hatching around rim, unmarked spur.

E2399:221:1999: complete bowl, rouletting around rim and indistinct stamp incuse on the rear of the bowl.

MOUTHPIECES

CATALOGUE

E2399:7:383: end of pipe stem, made originally as mouthpiece, worn.

GLASS BEAD

Joanne O'Sullivan

INTRODUCTION

A single glass bead was recovered from the fill of a burial (B17) located adjacent to the west wall (F42) of the north aisle.

DESCRIPTION OF THE GLASS BEAD

Bead (Pl. 6.130) E2399:142:89 is of semi-translucent, cloudy, whitish-grey glass. Of roughly globular shape, it measures 13.5mm in diameter, 12.5mm in height, with its perforation having a diameter of 1.3mm.

Manufactured using wound glass, it displays some variation in wispy greyish colour on the

Pl. 6.130. Bead E2399:142:89.

body of the bead, some pock marks and discolouration around one perforated end, indicating that the bead was exposed to weathering at some point in the past. Furthermore, half of the bead's surface displays decidedly more wear than its opposite half, suggesting that the bead was partially submerged for a time while weathering took place. This may have happened prior to its inclusion in the fill of burial B17.

DISCUSSION

This single glass bead was recovered from the fill of burial B17, the only burial to have contained such an artefact. The evidence for partial weathering visible on the bead suggests an earlier accidental surface loss. The further recovery of shards of window glass (E2399:142:104 and E2399:142:860) from the same context supports this assertion. Given the nature of the site as a place of worship and religious pilgrimage, this bead may well represent the accidental loss of a bead from a set of early rosary beads, or paternoster. Several examples of paternoster have been found in Ireland (see O'Sullivan 2014, 362), both of amber and of glass. In terms of origins, it is likely that this bead was an imported item, as there is no archaeological evidence for the manufacturing of wound glass beads in medieval Ireland thus far.

CONCLUSIONS

This singular glass bead is not immediately diagnostic, given its lack of identifiable decoration, but its location within the north aisle, combined with the other associated artefacts from the same context, indicates that it was an accidental loss of a paternoster bead that was later moved and included within the fill of burial B17.

THE POTTERY

Clare McCutcheon

INTRODUCTION

A total of 972 sherds of pottery were presented for study. Following identification and some reassembly this was reduced to 946 sherds of which two are medieval in date. Two contexts (205 and 212) were linked by pottery reassembly of a piece of unglazed red earthenware.

METHODOLOGY

The pottery was sorted visually, and the identification of the sherds has been entered on a database as per the requirements of the National Museum of Ireland. The detailed information is presented in Table 6.8. This shows the number of sherds in each fabric type, the minimum number of vessels (MNV) present and the minimum vessels represented by the sherds (MVR). The form of the vessels represented is also shown with the known date range of the material.

MISCELLANEOUS FRENCH POTTERY

This is a general term that is applied to all other white wares, clearly French rather than English in origin, that are found on Irish sites and are not as yet identifiable to a specific source. Continuing research points to the mid-west of France as the most probable location, and as possible provenances for particular types are located these groups will be isolated out of the general miscellaneous French grouping. The single body sherd (E2399:77:60, Pl. 6.131) in this assemblage falls into this vague description, that is, whiteware that is not Saintonge.

Pl. 6.131. French medieval pot sherd E2399:77:60.

Pl. 6.132. Martincamp-type pot sherd E2399:205:560.

SAINTONGE WARES

The term Saintonge has been used as something of a catch-all term in Irish ceramic studies. It is becoming increasingly apparent, however, that a number of production centres in the wider Bordeaux area shared similar clay and forms, thus making it difficult to distinguish on the basis of chemical analysis. It may be that certain vessels will be recognised by their individual decorative motifs as coming from a particular area.

- Saintonge mottled green glazed
  This is the mainstay of the Saintonge wares – tall standard jugs with minimal decoration, flat splayed bases, strap handles and applied spouts. It points up the use of pottery in the period as confined almost totally to jugs and thereby the clear association with the French wine trade (Chapelot 1983; Deroeux *et al.* 1994). As with the majority of the French wares, the clay is off-white, micaceous and containing quartz and haematite. The application of a lead glaze containing copper filings leads to the mottled effect that constitutes the primary decoration. Vertically applied thumbed strips, usually only three, or else lightly incised horizontal lines are the only other decoration. The single body sherd (734:37, Pl. 6.131) from Boyle was decorated with these lines.

MARTINCAMP-TYPE

This ware is attributed to Martincamp, located between Dieppe and Beauvais in Northern France, although 'to date, no great numbers of flasks has ever been found in Martincamp or identified as wasters of Martincamp' (Ickowicz 1993, 58). A single detached body sherd (E2399: 205:560) from a flask was found at Boyle Abbey (Pl. 6.132).

WESER WAVY BAND

This German whiteware was made at a number of centres between the Weser and Leine rivers (Hurst *et al.* 1986, 250). It was exported widely to the Low Countries and also to eastern England (*ibid.*, 251) but has been found occasionally in Ireland, particularly in Cork at the North Gate (McCutcheon, C. 1997, fig. 31.1) and at James Fort, Kinsale (McCutcheon, C. 2002, 37, fig. 13.3). A further sherd of possible Weser slipware with the typical hammer-head rim was recovered at King John's Castle, Limerick (Whyte 2016, 358). A single detached body sherd (78:678, Pl. 6.132) from a plate was found at Boyle Abbey.

FRECHEN

Grey stonewares with a mottled brown surface were made in the towns of Cologne and Frechen from the sixteenth century (Hurst *et al.* 1986, 208). Potters originally from Frechen moved to Cologne in about 1500 and were moved out in the mid sixteenth century as a consequence of the pollution from the kilns (*ibid.*). At least four jugs are represented in the Boyle assemblage, one with the remains of a coat of arms in relief, similar to, but not the same as, the widely found Arms of Amsterdam.

Table 6.8 Pottery identification, Boyle Abbey, Co. Roscommon (E2399)

Fabric	Sherds	MNV	MVR	Form	Date
Miscellaneous French	1	–	1	Jug	L12th-E13th
Saintonge green glazed	1	–	1	Jug	13th-M14th
Total medieval	2	–	2		
Martincamp	1	–	1	Flask	L16th-17th
Weser wavy band	1	–	1	Plate	L16th-E17th
Frechen	28	1	>4	Jugs	17th
Seville coarseware	3	–	1	Olive jar	17th
Total late medieval continental	33	1	7		
Transition-type ware	12	–	1	Jug	16th-E17th
North Devon gravel tempered	6	–	1	Pancheon	17th
North Devon gravel free	6	–	3	Bowls, pancheon	17th
Porcelain	6	–	3	Saucer, tea bowls?	18th
Tin-glazed earthenware	26	–	3	Chamberpot, tea bowls?	17th-18th
Mottled ware	3	–	1	Tankard	18th
Black glazed ware	66	–	10	4 pancheons, 2 bowls, 4 jars	L17th-19th
Glazed red earthenware	149	1	>9	Handled bowl, 4 bowls, 2 jars, 2 pancheons	L17th-19th
Glazed white earthenware	4	–	2	Plate, yellow cup	18th-19th
Unglazed red earthenware	26	–	4	Bowl, flowerpots	18th-19th
GRE: slip decorated	1	–	1	Jug?	18th-19th
GRE: slip coated	4	–	1	Bowl	18th-19th
Creamware	218	–	13	2 chamberpots, 9 plates, 2 conserve jars, gaming counter	18th
Painted creamware	1	–	1	Bowl	18th
White salt glazed stoneware	5	–	2	2 jars, gaming counter	18th
Pearlware	187	1	15	Cup, plates	19th

Table 6.8 Pottery identification, Boyle Abbey, Co. Roscommon (E2399) *continued*

Fabric	Sherds	MNV	MVR	Form	Date
Transfer-printed ware	124	1	28	20 plates, 2 cups, 3 bowls, jug, brown cup, brown plate	19th
Shell-edged ware	21	–	6	Plates	18th
Painted pearlware	6	–	5	Cups, 3 saucers	19th
Mochaware	8	–	1	Cup	19th
Brown glazed earthenware	1	–	1	Teapot	19th-20th
Stoneware	31	–	13	Inkwell, 9 preserve jars, 2 bottles, whiskey jar	19th-20th
Unidentified	2	–	1	Plate?	19th?
Total post medieval/modern	983	2	125		

SEVILLE COARSEWARE

Olive jars were produced in the Seville area from the Roman period through to the nineteenth century (Jennings 1981, 77) and were widely distributed to Northern Europe and America in the seventeenth century (Hurst *et al.* 1986, 66). The fabric is coarse, pink-buff in colour with a light, coloured exterior, resulting from 'the reaction of salt and calcium carbonate during firing' (Gerrard *et al.* 1995, 281). The jars were sometimes green glazed on the interior but the sherds from Boyle were unglazed.

TRANSITION WARE

The least well-known group of pottery at the moment is the so-called Transition-type ware. These vessels, principally jugs, retain many of the features of medieval pottery such as external glazing and sometimes a thumbed or slightly splayed base. The shape of the jug, however, more closely resembles the glazed red earthenwares of the seventeenth to nineteenth centuries. In addition, the handles are often in a twisted solid rod shape, very unlike the typical strap handle found on the majority of jugs in the Anglo-Norman period. This tendency to strap handles in Ireland is based on the south-west French and south-west English wares so prevalent in the medieval jugs. In northern France and London, however, the solid rod handle is most typical.

Jugs of this anomalous type are rarely found. The earliest one published in Ireland is from Ferns Castle, Co. Wexford (Sweetman 1979, 233–4, fig. 8.1). It is also the best stratified to date as the 80+ sherds were recovered from the south section of the fosse 'over the charcoal and black occupation layers but under the post-medieval pottery' (*ibid.*). One is known from Kells Priory, Co. Kilkenny (McCutcheon 2007); others from Kilcolman and Glanworth castles (McCutcheon 2005; 2009) both in County Cork. Further indications have been noted in Carrickfergus, Co. Antrim (A. Gahan pers. comm.). A dozen sherds were recovered at Boyle Abbey representing a jug (Pl. 6.133).

NORTH DEVON WARES

The production of these wares was centred on the towns of Bideford and Barnstaple in North Devon with a large-scale export trade in the seventeenth century to Ireland in particular. Considerable quantities were exported to Ireland to service the provisions trade to the North American colonies, in particular to the West Indies (Nash 1985). The pottery trade developed in Cork from 1620 with peaks in the early 1680s and in 1699 (Grant 1983, 109). The same basic fabric and glazes are used but the addition of gravel temper and slip and sgraffito patterns enhances a wide variety of vessels.

- North Devon gravel free
  This is the basic fabric, clean pink and grey firing clay, with a clear lead glaze that appears green/brown on firing. Vessels are generally jugs, bowls, chamber pots, lids etc. The six sherds from Boyle represent a pancheon, the staple basin of the seventeenth-century kitchen.

- North Devon gravel tempered
  The basic fabric is strengthened with a fine water-rolled quartz gravel to assist in opening out the thicker bodies to allow for complete and consistent drying. Larger vessels for the kitchen and dairy were made in this fabric, but the lead glaze reacts in the same way as the North Devon gravel free wares. These tripod pots were made in imitation of metal pots but with a rod handle projecting at *c.* 45° from the rim, probably to assist in steadying the pot on the fire. The six sherds from Boyle represent two bowls and a smaller pancheon, possibly a large serving dish rather than the working basin in the reinforced gravel tempered ware.

PORCELAIN

Porcelain is distinguished by its translucence and hardness in addition to the fine oriental scenes. The earliest porcelain originated in China, imported at the latter part of the Ming Dynasty (1368–1644) with shiploads arriving in the seventeenth and eighteenth centuries (Hurst *et al.* 1986, 9). Porcelain was later developed in Western Europe, both in England and France. The six sherds from Boyle appear to be the later eighteenth-century forms but the sherds are small suggesting saucers and tea bowls.

TIN-GLAZED EARTHENWARE

Tin-glazed earthenware was brought into Europe from the Near East, beginning in Italy in the twelfth century and reaching the Netherlands in the late fifteenth century. Dutch delftware producers are known to have set up production in Norwich and London in the late sixteenth century (Draper 1984, 25). Many of the Dutch patterns were carried over into English tin-glazed earthenware and it is often difficult to distinguish between English, Dutch and the occasional Irish-made piece.

This ware was used for table vessels but also for decorative wall, stove and furniture tiles and is widely recovered on Irish excavations. The 26 sherds recovered at Boyle consist of 21 undecorated all-white sherds, most likely representing a chamber pot, and a further five sherds decorated in blue and white, representing some small bowls, possibly tea bowls.

Pl. 6.133. Transition-type pottery (E2399:139:92, 98,101,111).

MOTTLED/TREACLE WARE

The fabric of these Staffordshire wares varied from fine buff to orange/red with the vessels covered in a rich dark brown slip (*ibid.*). Tankards are the most typical vessel form recovered in excavations in Ireland and the three body sherds from Boyle (204:341, 342; 205:678) represent such a vessel.

BLACK GLAZED WARE

Black glazed wares are most commonly found in Dublin and the east coast, originating from Lancashire and north Wales – the so-called Buckley wares. Both black glazed and glazed red earthenwares (see below) are the successors of the North Devon gravel tempered wares, large vessels used for the dairy, kitchen and toilet. Some tableware such as cups and jugs are also made, but equally, roof tiles are also made in these wares.

DEVON SGRAFFITO WARES

Black glazing results from the addition of iron to lead glaze on the red earthenware fabrics. The fabric is often highly fired to a near stoneware purple, although other varieties have a white marbled appearance. The fabric of the black glazed wares made in Ireland appears to be a less highly fired red earthenware (Meenan 1997, 349). Just 12 sherds were in near stoneware and seven in marbled ware from Boyle, suggesting that the majority of the black glazed sherds (46) were produced locally, possibly as local as the glazed red earthenware (see below).

GLAZED RED EARTHENWARE

Glazed red earthenware was the more commonly used dairy and kitchen ware in the area, as distinct from the black glazed wares. The fabric is generally sandy earthenware, usually oxidised buff to light orange through to brown. The clear lead glaze takes its colour from the fabric with variations due to firing conditions (Jennings 1981, 157). These are also known as brownwares and were made widely in England and Ireland in the later seventeenth and eighteenth centuries (Dunlevy 1988b, 24–5). A typical kiln was excavated at Tuam, Co. Galway, with milk pans and dishes comprising a majority of the vessels (Carey and Meenan 2004). 'Coarse pottery is made near Dromahaire and Leitrim, in quantities merely sufficient to supply the domestic demand' (Lewis 1837, II, 255) and 'in the vicinity of Roscommon are several small potteries' (*ibid.*, 523) and either of these may have supplied the needs of Boyle Abbey. A detailed description of glazed red earthenware survives for the mid nineteenth century in the town of Roscommon and many other production sites would have been similar:

> Amongst the articles manufactured in the immediate vicinity of Roscommon, may also be mentioned coarse pottery ware, consisting of pans, jugs, etc. These were mostly of a reddish, brown colour, or of brown mixed with yellow, in rude patterns, or merely mottled, and considerable quantities were brought into the markets. The clay of which these articles are made is not found on the spot, but, brought in carts from the neighbourhood of the Shannon ... (Weld 1832, 403).

The large quantity of sherds from Boyle (149) represents the typical sturdy functional vessels of the kitchen with some bowls suitable for serving at the kitchen table. The handled bowl may have been a porringer, a small bowl with a small handle that could be grasped while eating the hot porridge. There are also two large storage jars and the ever-present pancheon.

A further decoration on the glazed earthenware dishes was by the addition of white slip or thin clay under the clear lead glaze. This resulted in yellow decorations on the rich brown background. In other cases, the vessel was completely coated with a slip giving a pale to bright yellow colour with no further decoration. These match perfectly with Weld's description above of reddish-brown or brown and yellow in rude patterns.

Just one body sherd from Boyle was decorated with slip trailing (205:673) while four sherds (205:683, 684; 221:1994; 223:2135) were coated with slip – the handle, two rims and a body representing a bowl. A final sherd of earthenware is in white firing clay (901:115) with a greenish/yellow glaze, representing a plate.

CREAMWARE

In *c.* 1760, Josiah Wedgwood developed cream-coloured earthenware with a transparent lead glaze to compete with the large quantities of porcelain imported from China. In fact, it was so successful that it went on to become a substitute for tin-glazed earthenware and also affected porcelain production on the Continent, being known variously as faïence anglaise or terraglia.

These wares are very elegant with restrained decoration around the rim and with a clean cream centre on the plate and two conserve jars for marmalade or jams. Two chamber pots are represented by strong flat rims, comfortable to sit on. The gaming counter, made by rubbing the edge of a broken sherd to a rounded finish, is not classified as a vessel but rather as a modified sherd or artefact.

WHITE SALT GLAZED STONEWARE

This ware dates from the first to the last quarter of the eighteenth century (Jennings 1981, 222). The wares were made in moulds and by slip casting as well as being wheel-thrown. The fabric is that of the later creamware, but the stonewares were fired to a higher temperature. Moulding allowed for some complex patterns along the rims. The sherds at Boyle represent two jars, possibly used for preserves on the dining room table as part of the finewares.

PEARLWARE

Wedgwood's development of creamware was further refined as pearlware, with a harder-fired clay and a blue rather than a green tinge in the collected glaze. This formed the basis for many decorative forms of the later eighteenth and nineteenth centuries such as shell-edged, mochaware and transfer-printed wares. The sherds break up to small sizes and there is such a huge variety of patterns that it is very difficult to make divisions beyond the general willow pattern, floral etc.

SHELL-EDGED WARE

This is a term used for the decorative motif of a moulded border on some plates. The technique was first used on creamware but was principally associated with pearlware and was popular at Wedgwood and other Staffordshire potteries *c.* 1779–1830. Blue and green brush strokes were used to highlight the grooved modelling on the edge of the plate. The same decoration occasionally appears on the bodies of hollow wares such as jugs and teapots. Twenty-one sherds found at Boyle represent six plates, four of which were decorated with blue edging and two with the less common green.

MOCHA/BANDED WARE

This is a decorative technique on pearlware including bands and swirls of colour.

BROWN GLAZED EARTHENWARE

This is a general term used to describe the thickly glazed, late nineteenth- to early twentieth-century items such as teapots, accompanying jugs, and other such items. The single rim sherd (1:159) from Boyle represents a traditional teapot.

STONEWARE

The term is used here to cover all English stonewares, made of a clay and fusible stone, which can be fired to partial vitrification, not then requiring a glaze to make it impervious to liquids. The sherds from Boyle are from the typical later nineteenth-century bottles and jars used to contain liquids and pastes that could stain, such as ink and cleaning substances. None of the Boyle sherds had transfer-printed labels so they may have had printed paper labels instead. Smaller jars were used for preserves such as marmalade and jams while larger jars were used for salted vegetables, in the days before freezing. Two stoneware balls were recovered (F205:1053 and 1614). While the surface is not totally spherical, the largest diameter on the first (1053) is 22.75mm while the second (1614) has a diameter of 21.12mm. The purpose of these balls is unclear as, although they may have been used for games, there is little wear on the surface.

TWENTIETH CENTURY

Three sherds appear to be a modern cup, in a white clay with a bright yellow coloured glaze. A small handle (2:823), and two detached body sherds (205:1040, 1041), the latter decorated with stamped circles, may date to anytime from the mid 1930s to the 1960s.

DISCUSSION

The pottery assemblage from the 2006–12 excavations at Boyle Abbey is typical of the later post-medieval sites around Ireland. A small number of seventeenth-century vessels survive, all very sturdy and long-lived. Four German stoneware jugs are represented, and these might have had pewter or silver lids mounted on them when in use. Some sherds from the ubiquitous North Devon wares were also found, representing pancheons and bowls. These pancheons are the sturdy, hard-working basins of the seventeenth century, used for mixing, baking, washing clothes, dishes and possibly even the baby.

A large proportion of the ceramics date to the mid eighteenth century, with black glazed and glazed red earthenwares replacing the North Devon wares in the kitchen and the dairy. The dining table would have shone with the elegant cream-coloured plates of the fashionable new 'Queens ware', with restrained decorative beading or stamped pattern around the rim. As the guests play cards by candlelight with gaming counters produced from a broken plate or two, we can imagine a discreetly placed cream-coloured chamber pot, replacing the old, chipped tin-glazed earthenware one.

In the nineteenth century, the creamwares are replaced in the dining room by the busy blue and white decorations of transfer-printed ware plates. Engravings depicting scenes of earlier paintings, series of old romantic ruins or grand stately homes provide a talking point at the table. In the kitchen, the cook enjoys a well-earned cup of tea from her favourite brown teapot in her mochaware cup. Stoneware jars stand on the pantry shelves containing various preserves, pickles and salted vegetables. In the storeroom are more stoneware jars with cleaning material or ink, ready to refill the small inkwell placed upstairs in the library or study. Finally, the whiskey jar is locked away for safe keeping, to be decanted in small measures at special occasions.

Pl. 6.134. Eighteenth-century bottles.

Pl. 6.135. Late eighteenth-century Mallet-type bottle base (E2399:901:314).

BOTTLE GLASS

Clare McCutcheon

INTRODUCTION

A total of 1,218 pieces of bottle glass were presented for study, recovered from six seasons of excavation on the site. These pieces represent at least 58 bottles for wine, mineral water, gin, medicine and soda. In addition, two glass vessels and a dozen glass marbles were recovered.

EIGHTEENTH-CENTURY BOTTLES

The majority of the shards represent wine bottles. Some 895 shards represent early to mid eighteenth-century onion and mallet-shaped bottles. The first is the typical early eighteenth- century short-necked onion bottle with string ring at the top of the neck and a low kick up (Pl. 6.134). There are 17 complete rims with a further 14 partial rims surviving. The slightly later mallet-type bottles are represented more clearly by bases with the distinctive straighter sides (Pls 6.135, 6.136).

The second group of early to mid eighteenth-century bottles are oval, long necked and without string rims and are covered in wicker in the manner of modern Chianti bottles (Hanrahan 1978, 56). They are known as French wanded bottles, and were the most common bottle in France, but also found in colonial Virginia (Noël Hume 1969, 71). From this assemblage, 17 shards represent 12 bottles, recognised most clearly by the rim. Detached bodies are less easily recognised, and no bases were noted in this assemblage. Some 67 of these bottles were recovered during the 2004 excavations in the area of the former refectory (McCutcheon below).

A possible medicinal bottle (Pl. 6.137) is represented by a number of reassembled shards (205:1370–72). This is a light green, thin-walled bottle, oval with a narrow neck and a pontil mark on the base and bubbling throughout. A second medicine phial is represented by a base (11:446) and a thin body (398:2711) in pale green.

Eight shards of degraded glass (205:1374–7; 224:2195; 901:598–601; unstratified:629 and 694) represent a case gin bottle, also known as a taper

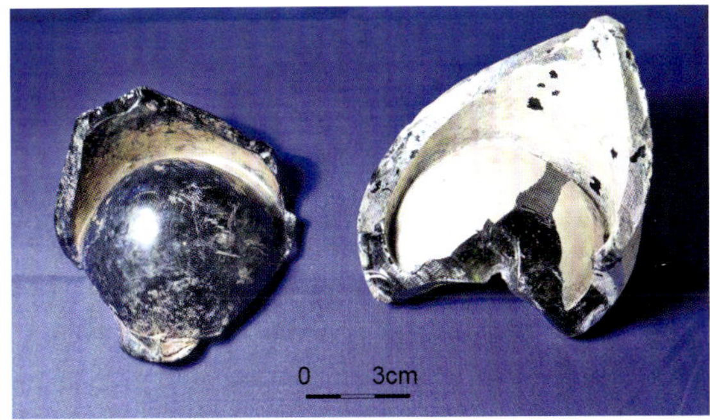

Pl. 6.136. Eighteenth-century bottle.

Pl. 6.137. Possible eighteenth-century medicinal bottle.

gin, square in section with a wider shoulder than base (Woods 2010).

NINETEENTH-CENTURY BOTTLES

A small group of 27 sherds are similar to the earlier blown glass but in a light green glass rather than the typical dark green of the wine bottles. They may represent some pharmaceutical bottles but diagnostic features such as rims were not recovered.

In the early nineteenth century, blown glass bottles were replaced by moulded bottles, primarily produced in Bristol by the Ricketts company. Some 78 shards represent five of these bottles, three circular and two oval. The centre under the base was variously marked with a nipple along with a letter or other mark.

A further innovation in the later nineteenth century was the development of the Hamilton Codd bottle, and a base and body (2:3087–3088) in an aqua green were recovered on this site. Hamilton had produced a pointed end bottle which lay on its side and kept the fizz in the mineral water, with Codd further developing the fastener in the later nineteenth century (Blakeman 2002, 34).

Another late nineteenth-century dark green bottle is represented by a base (212:1775), with the words SAXLEHNE[RS]/HUNYA[DI]/JANOS clearly embossed. This was a late nineteenth- early twentieth-century mineral water from Hungary, developed by Andreas Saxlehner and named for a fourteenth- or fifteenth-century Hungarian national hero, Hunyadi Janos, and very commonly found in the USA (Society for Historical Archaeology 2021).

Sixty-eight shards in blue, representing at least two bottles, may also have been medicinal such as the ever-popular Milk of Magnesia. One of the rims would have been stoppered with a cork and the second with an external screw top.

In the later nineteenth and early twentieth century, a variety of bottles were made in Ireland in the Irish Glass Bottling Co. based at Ringsend, Dublin. These were represented in Boyle by 48 shards of brown glass, a possible medicine bottle.

TWENTIETH-CENTURY BOTTLES

Eleven shards in a bright green metal represent a possible soda bottle. Fifty-nine shards are a variety of clear glass bottles, one fragment showing an inlaid mark on a red background, indicating possibly a mid-century date, post-paper labels and pre-plastic labels.

VESSEL GLASS

Two items of vessel glass were recovered. The first is the thick base (205:1305) of a possible firing glass so called as 'when a toast was drunk the members would strike the table simultaneously with their glass, the noise being said to resemble the firing of a musket' (Bickerton 1984, 22). The base (Dia. 56.60mm) from Boyle Abbey carries a solid fluted knop (Dia. 29.05mm) and the jagged edges of the bowl above. The glass is clear in section with an opaque-white surface.

The second vessel is also a fluted knop (205:1304), also in clear glass but this knop appears to be hollow. The knop (Dia. 25.20mm) is contained between two flat circles of glass (Dia. 24.50mm) with jagged edges below (base?) and above (bowl?). This may be a pressed glass sweetmeat dish.

MARBLES

A total of 12 glass marbles were recovered, ten of them from one feature (F2:314-323). Of these, four have central yellow centres (314–317), one is white (318), one is bright red (319) and one is a red-brown (320). A further yellow marble (F221:2008) and one decorated with a combination of blue, white and green (F205:1306) complete the nine modern glass marbles. The final three marbles were also recovered from F2 but are coloured with a white surface streak. One is blue (321), the second is green (322) and the third is a dark red (323).

Pl. 6.138. Quern stone E2399:231:18.

THE STONE

Miriam Carroll

INTRODUCTION

A total of 112 stone artefacts were recovered from the excavations, in addition to the architectural stone and grave slab fragments. A significant number of the objects came from post-medieval contexts, with 70 comprising stone/slate roof tiles. Medieval finds are represented in the form of the quern stone and quern stone fragments, although many were again retrieved from post-medieval contexts. Overall, the stone assemblage is small but is still representative of a variety of activities including food processing and preparation (querns and potboilers), the making of textiles (possible loom weight) and the later roofing of buildings, perhaps associated with the military occupation of the site. The objects are classified below according to type with each discussion followed by a catalogue.

QUERN STONES

Fourteen quern stone fragments were recovered, three of which are fragments from the same quern. Quern stones are also known as disk or rotary querns and were comprised of two flat disk-shaped stones used for grinding cereals (O'Sullivan and Downey 2006, 24). These fit into Type C of Caulfield's quern classification (Caulfield 1977, 104–38) which have a short handle set upright into a perforation in the upper stone, midway between the central perforation and the edge of the stone and are well represented in medieval contexts in Ireland (O'Sullivan and Downey 2006, 24). Rotary quern stones are a common find in medieval contexts in Ireland and numerous examples are known from Cork, Waterford and beyond.

One complete upper rotary quern stone, one incomplete and nine fragments were found in the area excavated north of the nave. All have been catalogued and some selected for illustration here. The incomplete example (E2399:439:183, 439:217 and 510:208) is in three pieces and retains the handle hole and most of the central perforation, the latter outlined by a raised band. The undersides of the stones are fire damaged. Of interest regarding this quern stone is its recovery from two different contexts within the church. Another quern fragment (E2399:227:15) formed part of a stone surface immediately outside the north wall of the church which may have served to seal the underlying burials. Conversely, however, it may be argued that as quern stones were broken, they were simply discarded haphazardly. It should also be noted that the majority of the quern stone fragments from Boyle were recovered from post-medieval contexts and therefore were not in their primary place of deposition in many cases.

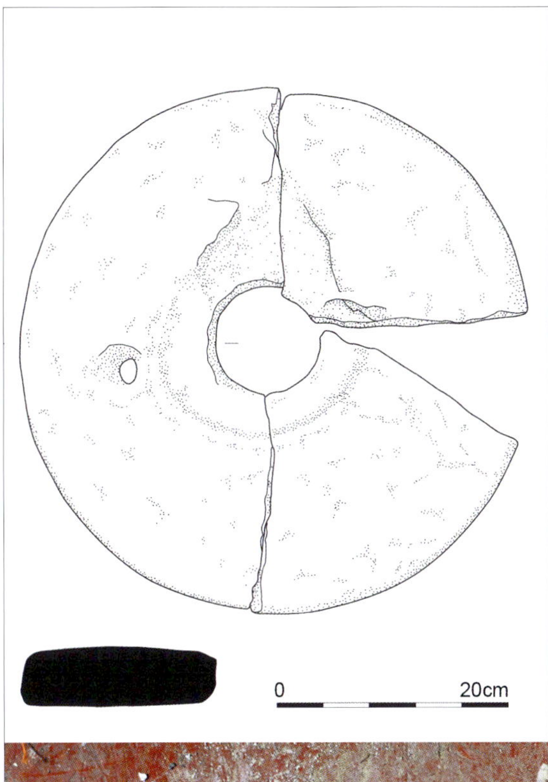

Pl. 6.139. Quern stone E2399:439:183.

All but one of the fragments retain traces of the central perforation and three have handle holes. The handle hole in E2399:324:91 has a second incomplete perforation beside it hollowed out from the base of the stone. Clearly the perforation was hollowed out from the top and base of the stone and intended to meet in the centre.

There is one possible example of a lower rotary quern stone. It is quite crude and may only have been a rough out (E2399:247:27).

CATALOGUE

Quern stone. E2399:73:664. L. 139.1mm, W. 107.8mm, Th. 28.3mm. Incomplete. Triangular fragment of rotary quern stone (upper) with chamfered edge. Lower surface flat from use. No evidence for handle hole.

Quern stone. E2399:36:732. L. 132.5mm, W. 121.4mm, Th. 40.9mm. Incomplete. Sub-triangular fragment of rotary quern stone. Lower surface flat from use. No evidence for handle hole.

Quern stone (illustrated, Pl. 6.138). E2399:231:18. L. 146.2mm, W. 133.9mm, Th. 77.1mm. Incomplete. Triangular fragment of upper rotary quern. Portion of circular perforation extant for handle.

Quern stone (illustrated, Pl. 6.139). E2399:439:183, E2399:439:217 and E2399:510:208. D. 435mm, W. 435mm, Th. 50.4mm. Incomplete. Three fragments of one upper quern stone. One segment missing. Central perforation defined by a raised band, diameter 90.9mm. Handle hole extant on upper surface, 24.5mm in diameter. Underside of stones fire damaged.

Quern stone (illustrated, Fig. 6.42). E2399:227:15. D. 490mm, Th. 61.8mm. Incomplete. Broken upper quern stone. Decorated with cruciform shape. Central circular perforation (91mm diameter). Portion of perforation for handle (37.9mm diameter).

Quern stone. E2399:247:27. Incomplete. D. 500mm, Th. 128.4mm. Part of unfinished lower quern stone, possibly a rough out. No central perforation.

Quern stone. E2399:30:45. Incomplete. L. 279mm, W. 188.4mm, Th. 54.6mm. Triangular shaped fragment of quern stone. Partial remains of central perforation. Trace of pecked groove around perforation.

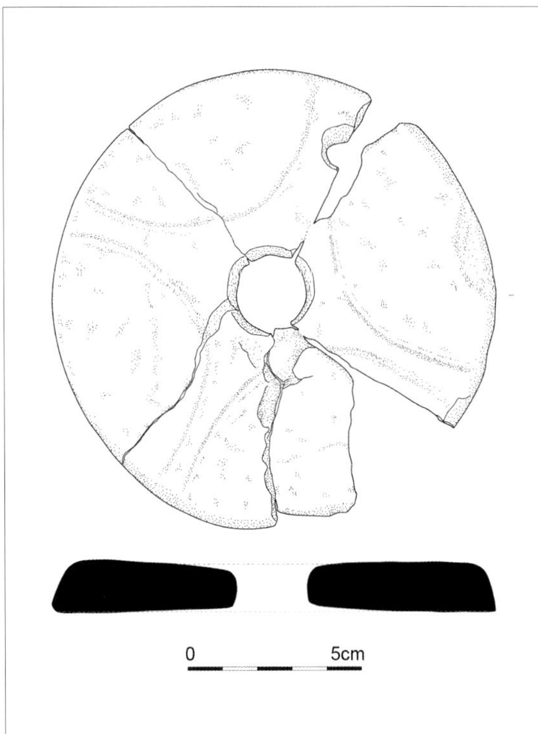

Fig. 6.42. Quern stone E2399:227:15.

Quern stone. E2399:324:91. Incomplete. L. 260.3mm, W. 216.4mm, Th. 92.5mm. Handle hole D. 34.8mm. Sub-rectangular fragment of upper quern stone with partial central perforation and handle hole extant. Damaged on upper surface. Beginnings of second handle hole on under-surface of quern forming a figure-of-eight shape with finished handle hole. Quern stone. E2399:393:128. Incomplete. L. 167.8mm, W. 120.9mm, Th. 50.2mm. Sub-triangular fragment of rotary quern stone, flat and smoothened on one surface.

Quern stone. E2399:213:156. Incomplete. L. 291.6mm, W. 224mm, Th. 88.9mm. Sub-triangular fragment of rotary quern stone, flat and smoothened on one surface.

Quern stone. E2399:401:136. L. 132.5mm, W. 121.4mm, Th. 40.9mm. Incomplete. Sub-triangular fragment of upper rotary quern stone with trace of central perforation. L. 178mm, W. 199.6mm, Th. 57.2mm.

Quern stone. E2399: unstratified. Complete. D. 245mm, Th. 84.3mm, Central perforation D. 102.7mm, Handle hole D. 40.4mm. A complete upper quern stone with concave under side.

WHETSTONES AND SHARPENING STONES

Whetstones or hone stones may be defined as pieces of abrasive rock used to sharpen metal objects (O'Connor 1991, 45). Whetstones and sharpening stones have a long period of use which spans from the Iron Age through to the post-medieval period. Throughout this time however, there is a notable lack of typological development which would assist in assigning particular forms of whetstone to specific date ranges. Whetstones and hone stones can take a variety of forms and shapes. While they may be typically regarded as block-like in shape with two broad surfaces and two narrow sides this may vary depending on the raw material used. For example, water-rolled pebbles and stones are used as whetstones and frequently retain their characteristically rounded form (*ibid.*, 48).

The majority of whetstones and hones display very smooth surfaces and some wear from their use. So-called 'pin grooves' can also be evident but are not apparent on the Boyle examples. Such marks are believed to be the result of bringing objects such as pins and awls to a point and possibly working the ends of knives (*ibid.*, 57). One complete hone stone (E2399:216:66) and a hone stone fragment (E2399:705:724) were recovered from the north aisle excavations. As outlined above, neither display any so-called pin grooves but are smooth from repeated use.

CATALOGUE

Hone stone. E2399:216:66. L. 106.2mm, W. 36.9mm, Th. 16.7mm. Complete. Rectangular stone with two broad surfaces and narrow sides. Two surfaces smooth from use.

Possible hone stone fragment. E2399:705:724. L. 42mm, W. 40mm, Th. 33.2mm. Fragment of stone, 'D' shaped in cross section. One very smooth surface.

PESTLE, MORTARS AND RUBBER STONES

Mortars may be classified as hand-operated tools which were used in conjunction with a pestle to pound or grind food. They have also been associated with the preparation of drugs and dyes (Ottaway and Rogers 2002, 2803). Mortars are generally considered to be a thirteenth-century introduction and began to replace rotary querns in urban areas as a method of hand milling by the fifteenth century. Their durability was such that they were frequently re-used in later walls. While it is thought that wooden beetles/pestles were used in conjunction with stone mortars, such items would have rapidly become worn and are likely to have had a limited period of use (Hurley 1997, 216). Stone and copper alloy pestles were more durable substances and examples of copper alloy pestles are known.

Rubber stones generally consist of rounded stones with one or more flat and/or smooth surfaces and would have fitted comfortably in the hand. They may have been used in conjunction with a larger stone (usually with a hollow in its surface) for grinding grain or other substances. One possible rubber stone was recovered from the excavations at Boyle Abbey. It came from a post-medieval context and may not be in its primary context.

CATALOGUE

Possible rubber stone. E2399:212:1786. L. 81mm, W. 64mm, Th. 34.7mm. Complete. Round stone with smooth surfaces, possibly from use.

ROOF SLATES/TILES

Roof slates appear to have been used throughout the medieval and post-medieval period in Ireland. This extended period of use is demonstrated in the Cork City excavations where slate was recovered from medieval and post-medieval contexts. There is no distinct typological development of roof tiles from the medieval to the post-medieval period (Carroll and Quinn 2003, 313). Frequently, these objects become fractured and broken once they were discarded after use.

Seventy roof tiles and roof tile fragments came from the excavations at Boyle Abbey. They would appear to represent discarded and/or collapsed roofing material and would have been attached via the circular/sub-circular perforations apparent in some examples. As outlined above, these objects frequently become fragmented and there are many examples which, although they do not have an extant perforation, are regarded as possible roof tile fragments given their similarity in form and material to other perforated examples. Different types of stone were utilised for the Boyle roof tiles, with both slate and sandstone examples represented in the assemblage. For example, a number of stone tiles and tile fragments were recovered from material overlying the robbed out west wall (E2399:606:3437–3443) and are made of thin pieces of sandstone. Conversely, slate examples came from other contexts and serve to demonstrate the use of different types of roofing material in the abbey precinct during its occupation. Many of the tiles came from post-medieval contexts and, while typologically do not display any distinctively late features, many are likely to be post-medieval in date.

CATALOGUE

Roof tile fragment. E2399:37:610. L. 167.35mm, W. 97.4mm, Th. 16.57mm. Incomplete. Fragment of stone roof tile with circular perforation (D. 8.70mm). Narrows towards one end which is broken.

Roof tile fragment. E2399:215:159. L. 79.76mm, W. 82.54mm, Th. 8.48mm. Incomplete. Fragment of stone roof tile with circular perforation (D. 9.30mm).

Possible roof tile fragment. E2399:221:1992. L. 79.18mm, W. 50.51mm, Th. 8.12mm. Incomplete. Small fragment of stone roof tile with no perforation extant. Possible roof tile.

Possible roof tile fragment. E2399:26:3412. L. 47.72mm, W. 36.96mm, Th. 7.92mm. Incomplete. Small fragment of possible roof tile, perforation not extant.

Slate fragment. E2399:2:773. L. 85.70mm, W. 57.30mm, Th. 8.72mm. Incomplete. Small slate fragment, no diagnostic features. Possible roof slate fragment.

Slate fragment. E2399:2:774. L. 117.10mm, W. 79.75mm, Th. 7.30mm. Incomplete. Sub-rectangular slate fragment, no diagnostic features. Possible roof slate fragment.

Slate fragment. E2399:218:1931. L. 137.10mm, W. 48.57mm, Th. 4.35mm. Incomplete. Sub-rectangular slate fragment, no diagnostic features. Possible roof slate fragment.

Slate fragment. E2399:218:1932. L. 88.73mm, W. 79.94mm, Th. 6.66mm. Incomplete. Small slate fragment with portion of circular perforation extant. Possible roof slate fragment.

Slate fragment. E2399:1:115. L. 180.05mm, W. 87.49mm, Th. 7.17mm Incomplete. Slate fragment, no diagnostic features. Possible roof slate fragment.

Slate fragment. E2399:1:116. L. 197.14mm, W. 120.89mm, Th. 6.40mm. Incomplete. Sub-rectangular slate fragment, no diagnostic features. Possible roof slate fragment.

Slate fragment. E2399:1:117. L. 44.91mm, W. 41.30mm, Th. 3.93mm. Incomplete. Small slate fragment, no diagnostic features. Possible roof slate fragment?

Slate fragment. E2399:206:537. L. 65.24mm, W. 57.74mm, Th. 7.20mm. Incomplete. Small slate fragment, no diagnostic features. Possible roof slate fragment?

Slate fragment. E2399:206:534. L. 105.45mm, W. 52.31mm, Th. 4.29mm. Incomplete. Small slate fragment, no diagnostic features. Possible roof slate fragment?

Possible stone roof tile fragment. E2399:206:533. L. 90.37mm, W. 43.10mm, Th. 4.29mm. Fragment of flat stone object, possible roof tile.

Slate fragment. E2399:206:536. L. 71.52mm, W. 41.17mm, Th. 3.87mm. Incomplete. Small slate fragment, no diagnostic features. Possible roof slate fragment?

Slate fragment. E2399:206:535. L. 88.53mm, W. 71.77mm, Th. 6.54mm. Incomplete. Small slate fragment, no diagnostic features. Possible roof slate fragment?

Slate fragment. E2399:206:538. L. 110.46mm, W. 89.39mm, Th. 7.90mm. Incomplete. Small slate fragment, no diagnostic features. Possible roof slate fragment?

Slate fragment. E2399:206:540. L. 106.58mm, W. 83mm, Th. 4.64mm. Incomplete. Small slate fragment, no diagnostic features. Possible roof slate fragment?

Slate fragment. E2399:206:539. L. 175.60mm, W. 65.45mm, Th. 13.61mm. Incomplete. Small slate fragment, no diagnostic features. Possible roof slate fragment?

Possible stone roof tile fragment. E2399:30:550. L. 122.47mm, W. 79.22mm, Th. 12.11mm. Fragment of flat stone object, possible roof tile?

Slate fragment. E2399:204:324. L. 104.45mm, W. 47.76mm, Th. 8.58mm. Incomplete. Small slate fragment, no diagnostic features. Possible roof slate fragment.

Slate fragment. E2399:204:323. L. 85.76mm, W. 72.76mm, Th. 9.48mm. Incomplete. Small slate fragment, no diagnostic features. Possible roof slate fragment.

Slate fragment. E2399:221:1982. L. 53.26mm, W. 25.57mm, Th. 2.65mm. Incomplete. Small slate fragment, no diagnostic features. Possible roof slate fragment?

Slate fragment. E2399:221:1983. L. 84.75mm,

W. 52.41mm, Th. 4.64mm. Incomplete. Small slate fragment, no diagnostic features. Possible roof slate fragment?

Roof slate fragment. E2399:221:1984. L. 105.21mm, W. 82.88mm, Th. 7.71mm. Incomplete. Sub-rectangular slate fragment with circular perforation (D. 4.40mm). Trace of ferrous staining around perforation.

Possible stone roof tile fragment E2399: 207:1635. L. 119.10mm, W. 117.90mm, Th. 9.34mm. Fragment of flat stone object, possible roof tile.

Possible stone roof tile fragment. E2399:36:731. L. 219.72mm, W. 163.20mm, Th. 15.91mm. Large fragment of possible roof tile. Perforation not extant.

Possible stone roof tile fragment. E2399:37:754. L. 197.34mm, W. 130.54mm, Th. 12.74mm. Incomplete. Large fragment of stone roof tile with portion of circular perforation extant.

Stone roof tile fragment. E2399:37:755. L. 93.55mm, W. 75.9mm, Th. 10.1mm. Incomplete. Fragment of stone roof tile with circular perforation (D. 8.39mm).

Possible stone roof tile fragment. E2399:37:756. L. 106mm, W. 71mm, Th. 7.1mm. Incomplete. Fragment of flat stone object, possible roof tile?

Possible stone roof tile fragment. E2399:608:3449. L. 195.3mm, W. 111.5mm, Th. 13.1mm. Sub-rectangular fragment of possible roof tile.

Possible stone roof tile fragment. E2399:608:3448. L. 198.3mm, W. 90.8mm, Th. 13.9mm. Irregular fragment of possible roof tile.

Possible stone roof tile fragment. E2399:608:3445. L. 131.5mm, W. 125.2m, Th. 8.9mm. Sub-rectangular fragment of possible roof tile. Perforation not extant.

Possible stone roof tile fragment. E2399:608:3447. L. 77.3mm, W. 75.8m, Th. 4.41mm. Sub-rectangular fragment of possible roof tile. Perforation not extant.

Possible stone roof tile fragment E2399:608:3450. L .130.8mm, W. 122.8mm, Th. 10.4mm. Irregular fragment of possible roof tile.

Possible stone roof tile fragment. E2399:608:3451. L. 213.4mm, W. 115.8mm, Th. 13.2mm. Irregular fragment of possible roof tile.

Possible stone roof tile fragment. E2399:608:3452. L. 164.1mm, W. 141.7mm, Th. 14mm. Irregular fragment of flat stone object, no perforation, possible roof tile?

Possible stone roof tile fragment. E2399:608:3446. L. 150mm, W. 135mm, Th. 12mm. Fragment of possible roof tile.

Possible stone roof tile fragment. E2399:606:3443. L. 200.8mm, W. 131.9mm, Th. 14.1mm. Sub-rectangular flat stone object, no perforation. Possible roof tile.

Possible stone roof tile fragment. E2399:606:3441. L. 111.1mm, W. 76mm, Th. 5.5mm. Irregular fragment of flat stone object, no perforation. Possible roof tile.

Possible stone roof tile fragment. E2399:606:3439. L. 96.6mm, W. 62.9mm, Th. 6.9mm. Sub-rectangular fragment of flat stone object, no perforation, possible roof tile.

Possible stone roof tile fragment. E2399:606:3438. L. 81.7mm, W. 52.1mm, Th. 9mm. Irregular fragment of flat stone object with portion of circular perforation. extant. Possible roof tile?

Possible stone roof tile fragment.

E2399:606:3440. L. 100.8mm, W. 74.5mm, Th. 8.7mm. Irregular fragment of flat stone object with no perforation. Possible roof tile.

Possible stone roof tile fragment. E2399:606:3437. L. 85.1mm, W. 83.2mm, Th. 8.1mm. Irregular fragment of flat stone object with no perforation. Possible roof tile?

Possible stone roof tile fragment. E2399:606:3442. L. 111.9mm, W. 109mm, Th. 7mm. Irregular fragment of flat stone object with incomplete circular perforation (D. 8mm in visible extant). Possible roof tile.

Possible stone roof tile fragment. E2399:15:496. L. 39mm, W. 30.6mm, Th. 3.8mm. Small sub-rectangular fragment of flat stone object with no perforation. Possible roof tile?

Stone roof tile fragment. E2399:15:495. L. 102.4mm, W. 77.5mm, Th. 10mm. Sub-rectangular fragment with portion of perforation extant. Possible roof tile fragment.

Stone roof tile fragment. E2399:15:498. L. 123.1mm, W. 77.4mm, Th. 8.6mm. Triangular fragment of stone roof tile with portion of circular perforation extant.

Stone roof tile fragment. E2399:15:497. L. 150.6mm, W. 146.8mm, Th. 10.5mm. Sub-rectangular fragment of stone tile with circular perforation extant (D. 7mm).

Slate fragment. E2399:2:187. L. 79.6mm, W. 70.8mm, Th. 7.5mm. Incomplete. Small slate fragment with portion of perforation extant. Possible roof slate fragment.

Slate fragment. E2399:2:184. L. 114.8mm, W. 72.7mm, Th. 8.3mm. Incomplete. Irregular slate fragment, no diagnostic features. Possible roof slate fragment.

Slate fragment. E2399:2:183. L. 120.4mm, W. 69mm, Th. 8.4mm. Incomplete. Small slate fragment, no diagnostic features. Possible roof slate fragment.

Possible roof tile fragment. E2399:705:699. L. 87.1mm, W. 71.8mm, Th. 7.4mm. Incomplete. Small fragment of stone tile, perforation not extant. One edge chamfered, opposing edges broken.

Stone tile fragment. E2399:705:700. L. 67.9mm, W. 32.9mm, Th. 10.6mm. Incomplete. Small L-shaped fragment of stone tile with portion of perforation extant.

Stone tile fragment. E2399:705:701. L. 112.5mm, W. 68.9mm, Th. 13.7mm. Incomplete. Sub-rectangular stone tile fragment, with portion of perforation extant.

Stone tile fragment. E2399:705:698. L. 85.4mm, W. 76.9mm, Th. 15.5mm. Incomplete. Sub-rectangular fragment of stone tile. Perforation not extant.

Stone tile fragment. E2399:705:703. L. 64.9mm, W. 50.5mm, Th. 7.6mm. Incomplete. Sub-rectangular stone tile fragment with one cut edge. Perforation not extant.

Stone tile fragment. E2399:705:702. L. 75.3mm, W. 45.3mm, Th. 6.3mm. Incomplete. Stone tile fragment, triangular. Perforation not extant.

Stone tile fragment. E2399:700:697. L. 92.3mm, W. 88.7mm, Th. 11.5mm. Incomplete. Sub-rectangular stone tile fragment, perforation not extant.

Stone tile fragment. E2399:705:706. L. 72.5mm, W. 42.4mm, Th. 8.1mm. Incomplete. Stone tile fragment, with portion of circular perforation extant.

Stone tile fragment. E2399:705:705. L. 187.6mm, W. 140.9mm, Th. 11.8mm. Incomplete. Sub-rectangular stone tile fragment with mortar adhering to both surfaces.

Stone tile fragment. E2399:705:704. L. 68.1mm,

W. 41.3mm, Th. 7.6mm. Incomplete. Rectangular stone tile fragment with one chamfered edge. Perforation not extant. Possible roof tile.

Stone tile fragment. E2399:205:533. L. 85.9mm, W. 43mm, Th. 6.9mm. Incomplete. Small rectangular fragment of possible stone roof tile.

Slate fragment. E2399:205:534. L. 101.9mm, W. 52.7mm, Th. 3.9mm. Incomplete. Irregular fragment of slate, possibly from roof slate.

Slate fragment. E2399:205:535. L. 86.6mm, W. 71.3mm, Th. 6.7mm. Incomplete. Sub-rectangular slate fragment, possible from roof slate.

Slate fragment. E2399:205:536. L. 70mm, W. 35.6mm, Th. 3.8mm. Incomplete. Small fragment of roof slate with V-shaped notch at one edge.

Slate fragment. E2399:205:537. L. 78.6mm, W. 59.5mm, Th. 7.7mm. Incomplete. Sub-rectangular slate fragment, possibly from roof slate.

Slate fragment. E2399:205:538. L. 104.2mm, W. 91.5mm, Th. 7.1mm. Incomplete. Sub-rectangular slate fragment with one curving edge. Possibly roof slate fragment.

Roof slate fragment. E2399:205:539. L. 158mm, W.65.5mm, Th. 13.7mm. Incomplete. Rectangular roof slate fragment with trace of circular perforation (incomplete).

Roof slate fragment. E2399:205:540. L. 104.8mm, W. 80mm, Th. 4.3mm. Incomplete. Roof slate fragment with portion of circular perforation extant.

WEIGHTS

One possible loom weight or net sinker (E2399:1:142) was recovered from the excavations. As with many of the finds in the Boyle assemblage, this item was recovered from a post-medieval/modern context and is likely to be residual therein.

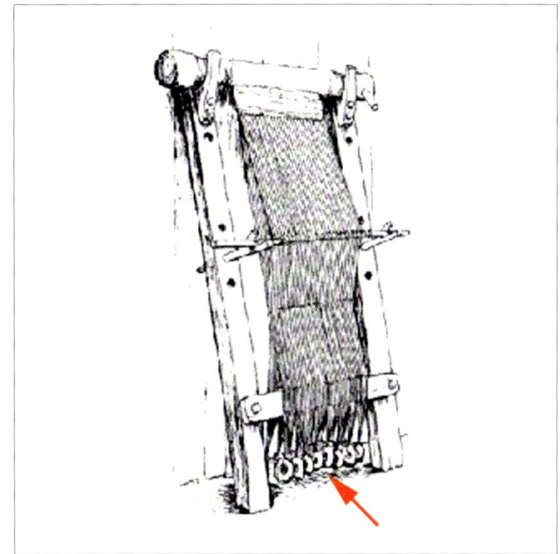

Fig. 6.43. Sketch of a vertical loom.

After the thread was spun as part of the weaving process, it was woven into cloth using a large vertical loom; the warp threads were weighted with heavy stone or clay loom weights as shown in Figure 6.43.

CATALOGUE

Possible net sinker/loom weight fragment. E2399:1:142. L. 59.9mm, W. 23mm, Th. 23.9mm. Incomplete. With evidence for central perforation, not fully extant. Unclear if the perforation was originally straight sided.

STONE DISCS

The discs recovered vary in size and form but generally consist of flat circular discs with roughly worked or chipped edges. Similar items have been recovered from medieval contexts in Waterford City and post-medieval contexts in Cork (Carroll and Quinn 2003, 310).

Seven slate/stone discs were recovered from the excavations, from a variety of contexts. Some examples came from post-medieval/modern contexts, while others were recovered from somewhat earlier deposits, such as E2399:69:654. The precise function of these items is unknown, although it has been suggested that they may have been utilised as lids, or perhaps as counters.

CATALOGUE

Possible slate disc. E2399:2:186. L. 49.7mm, W. 47.5mm, Th. 5.8mm. Incomplete. Sub-circular slate disc with one flat, smooth surface and one side straight edged.

Slate disc. E2399:2:185. L. 55mm, W. 49.7mm, Th. 7.6mm. Incomplete. Sub-circular slate disc with one flat, smooth surface.

Disc. E2399:229:2205. L. 90.4mm, W. 89.9mm, Th. 13.9mm. Incomplete. Roughly shaped stone disc, D-shaped in cross section. Edges rounded but damaged.

Disc. E2399:30:558. L. 59.6mm, W. 55.5mm, Th. 31.2mm. Complete. Roughly shaped stone disc. Edges rounded but rough.

Disc. E2399:69:654. L. 57.7mm, W. 55.3mm, Th. 9.5mm. Complete. Roughly shaped sub-circular stone disc. Edges rounded but rough.

Disc. E2399:45:624. D. 14mm, Th. 14.4mm. Complete. Roughly shaped circular stone disc. Edges rounded but rough.

Disc. E2399:43:617. L. 58.3mm, W. 54.9mm, Th. 12.2mm. Complete. Roughly shaped sub-circular stone disc. Edges rounded but rough.

HAMMERSTONES AND POTBOILERS

Two possible hammerstones (E2399:32:44 and 0:726) were recovered from the excavations. The former has an irregular depression on one surface which may be as a result of its repeated use. Hammerstones may have been used for a variety of purposes including food preparation.

Potboilers are stones which prevented the build-up of calcareous deposits on vessels such as cauldrons by being placed in the vessel as the water was boiled. Four possible potboilers form part of the Boyle Abbey stone assemblage and all display signs of being affected by heat. Examples of hammerstones and potboilers have been recovered from the Waterford City excavations (McCutcheon 1997, 405–06) and several from the Cork City excavations (Carroll and Quinn 2003, 317–8).

CATALOGUE

Possible hammerstone. E2399:32:44. L. 123.1mm, W. 108.2mm, Th. 81.4mm. Complete. Sub-circular stone with small irregular depression on one surface, possibly from use.

Possible hammerstone. E2399:0:726. L. 79mm, W. 70.9mm, Th. 36.7m. Incomplete. Quartz. Sub-circular stone with one rounded surface. Depression at centre (D. 30mm), possibly from use.

Possible potboiler. E2399:30:47. L. 64.4mm, W. 64.2mm, Th. 39.2mm. Complete. Round stone with one slightly smooth, flat surface.

Possible potboiler. E2399:229:2209. L. 66.3mm, W. 56mm, Th. 36.7m. Complete. Heat- shattered, rounded upper surface with opposing surface broken.

Possible potboiler. E2399:711:723. L. 66mm, W. 51.8mm, Th. 27.6mm. Oval stone with one rounded surface. Opposing side not extant. Heat affected on rounded side.

Possible potboiler. E2399:711:722. L.68.8mm, W. 66.7mm, Th. 40.1mm. Sub-circular heat-affected stone.

QUARTZ CRYSTAL AND PEBBLES

The intentional deposition of quartz stones and pebbles in Christian burials in Ireland is well documented. In a thirteenth-century cemetery in Ballyshannon, Co. Donegal, quartz was deliberately interred with the body and was frequently placed in the individual's hand (Ó Donnchadha 2007). Much earlier examples are also known where the seemingly pre-Christian custom of burying quartz pebbles within the grave continued well into the seventh century and sometimes as late as the ninth century (Bhreathnach 2009, 1). Excavations at Dunmisk Fort, Co. Tyrone, uncovered over 400 graves mainly in the south-east quadrant of the enclosure. Most of the burials, which are believed to be early medieval in date, were extended in simple graves orientated roughly east–west. Several of the graves were covered with quartz pebbles (Edwards 2002, 130).

Four pieces of unworked quartz were found at Boyle Abbey in burial horizons F240/F232 and F233. While not found in direct association with a burial, the occurrence of these quartz pieces within the cemetery may be indicative of intentional deposition particularly given the well-documented association with burial in Ireland. The quartz items themselves are in a natural form and do not appear to have been worked. Some of the pebbles are smooth but may be water rolled.

CATALOGUE

Quartz pebble. E2399:232/240:80. L. 38.8mm, W. 32.7mm, Th. 17.6mm. Complete. Rounded quartz pebble stone with one smooth flat surface.

Quartzite stone. E2399:240:2374. L. 51.8mm, W. 41.2mm, Th. 24mm. Complete. Round stone with smooth surfaces, possibly from use, but also possibly water rolled.

Quartz pebble. E2399:232/240:82. L. 42.5mm, W. 29.3mm, Th. 18.9mm. Complete. Round quartz pebble with smooth surfaces. Water-rolled?

Quartz. E2399:233:17. L. 30.4mm, W. 20.1mm, Th. 9.5mm. Incomplete. Irregular fragment of flat piece of quartz. Incomplete. Rectangular fragment of flat stone object, possible plaque fragment.

Possible plaque fragment. E2399:2:189. L. 63.2mm, W. 59.5mm, Th. 18mm. Incomplete. Irregular fragment of flat quartzite object, possible plaque fragment.

Pumice stone? E2399:733:47. L. 56.7mm, W. 53.1mm, Th. 40.4mm. Sub-circular/oval stone. Extremely porous surface.

Pebble. E2399:745:725. L. 34mm, W. 28.9mm, Th. 24.9mm. Oval, possibly water-rolled pebble. Found in association with B716.

GRAVE SLABS

INTRODUCTION

Prior to the excavation there were no visible remains of any marked graves, either within the nave floor or north aisle. Ten grave slabs were recovered from the excavations along the north aisle, two of which marked *in situ* burials (E2399:273:25 and E2399:534:215). The remainder were recovered from later contexts and were in a fragmentary condition. Some were recovered from stone surfaces laid to seal burials and others from nineteenth-century cobbled surfaces and so were in a secondary position.

IN SITU MEDIEVAL GRAVE SLABS

- Inscribed grave slab
  Fionnbarr Moore

An *in situ* grave slab (E2399:273:25) was uncovered beneath a layer of post-medieval material (F221) just south of the north aisle arcade. It is a rectangular, well-cut, limestone slab bearing a Latin cross (damaged at its base) with embossed roundels at the terminals and crossing point and an inscription in Irish on its wide face, with both cross and inscription running along its full length (Pl. 6.44). The slab covered a single grave cut (F274), orientated east–west, which contained four burials, with radiocarbon dating of the primary burial within the grave (B283) indicating a date of between cal. AD 1392 and 1443. This burial was truncated by the burial above it (B235); it comprised the partial remains of an adult male, presumably the remains of the person commemorated in the inscription, namely

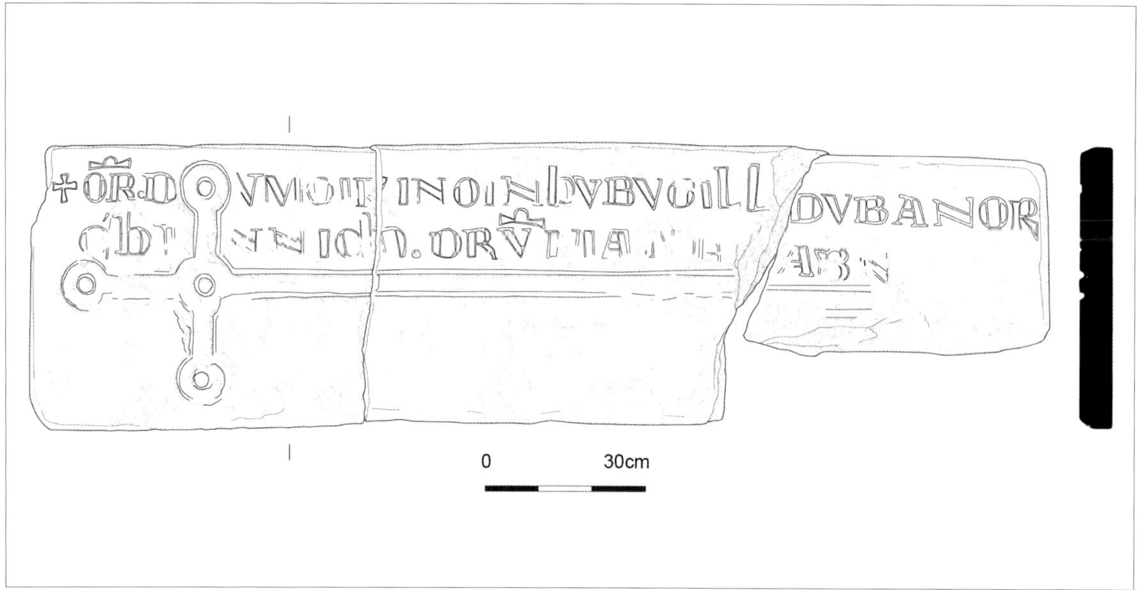

Fig. 6.44. Inscribed grave slab E2399:273:25.

Moirenn. The subsequent burials within the same grave cut consisted of a female adult, aged 25–30 years (B235), a male aged 25–35 (B232) who appears to have had a violent end and a young-middle adult male, aged 30–34 years (B231). As suggested by the archaeological excavators, the re-use of the grave cut to inter four individuals may suggest a familial relationship (see this chapter, Burials within the north aisle and nave).

The grave slab measures 1.88m in length by 0.52m in width and is 9.5cm in thickness. The lower part of the slab was broken off in antiquity and one half of that end, containing the word DUBANOR and the letters ABN, was also recovered in the excavation. The most likely reading of the inscription is:

OR DO [U]MOIRIN DINBU BUOILL ORCHINNICH DRUMIARILL followed by ABN

which can be translated as 'A prayer for poor [U]Moirenn of Boyle who was Airchinnech of Druimiarla' where *dinbu* is derived from *dindba* meaning poor, an early borrowing into Irish from the Latin word *indigini* (DIL). The use of the letter V for U in the inscription is a result of the practice in medieval Latin and in later Gothic scripts where V and U were interchangeable. The *airchinnech* (spelt Orchinnich) was the chief steward in a monastery, an important position in which the monk in question would have overseen the running of the monastic estates and property.

The cross, while simple in design, is finely executed and would appear to have been carved after the inscription as the letter at the start of the name [U]Moirin is partly cut by it and the O of DO is in fact the roundel at the terminal of the left arm of the cross. The inscription, more lightly executed than the cross, is preceded by a small Greek cross and there is a reduced angel-like figure over the word OR (a prayer) at te start of the inscription. The cross is carved deeply, giving the impression it is in relief while it is in fact flush with the face of the stone. The arms and shaft are gently rounded while the embossed roundels at the terminals and crossing point give it the appearance of a studded metal processional cross, which may well be the inspiration for it, being in a region and in the same county that produced the eighth-century Tully Lough processional cross (Kelly 2003, 9–10). There is a similar cross on a sandstone grave slab from Cloonburren in south Roscommon (RMP RO056-011001-) with 'circular terminals, circles at the crux and fleur-de-lis in the angles' (M. Moore pers. comm.).

The person bearing the name [U]Moirenn has not yet been identified in the sources, nor the place name Drumiaril (Drumiarla) (C. Devane pers. comm.).

CATALOGUE

Inscribed grave slab (illustrated, Fig. 6.44, Pl. 6.42). E2399:273:25. L. 1.88m, W. 52cm, Th. 9.5cm.

UNINSCRIBED GRAVE SLAB

Annette Quinn

This grave slab was uncovered to the south of Pier 11 within the nave. One individual (B374) was buried in this grave, a young-middle adult male, aged 25 to 35 years. The individual had suffered a fracture to the right distal humerus (elbow) and displayed evidence of spina bifida occulta (see Lynch below). The slab was trapezoidal in shape with no decoration or inscriptions.

CATALOGUE

Grave slab. E2399:534:215. Complete. L. 1.69m, W. 54cm, Th. 7cm. Simple trapezoidal shaped uninscribed grave slab marking burial B374.

OTHER GRAVE SLAB FRAGMENTS

Annette Quinn and Miriam Carroll

All of the following grave slabs were retrieved in a largely fragmentary condition from post-medieval contexts.

CATALOGUE

Inscribed grave slab (Fig. 6.45). E2399:69:73. Incomplete. L. 51.5cm, W. 32.5cm, Th. 6.2cm. Incomplete rectangular slab. Part of shaft and base of cross in relief. Broken and re-used as stone surface covering burials in north aisle.

Cross-inscribed grave slab (Fig. 6.46). E2399:15:75. Complete. L. 50cm, W. 23cm, Th. 13.4cm. Small rectangular block with simple incised Latin cross on one surface.

Fig. 6.45. Inscribed grave slab E2399:69:73.

Grave slab. E2399:221:117. Quartzite grave slab fragment, comprising two pieces, one measuring L. 116.4m, W. 40.6mm, Th. 19.9 and the other L. 72.4mm, W. 62.1mm, Th. 20.6mm. The latter is triangular, with flat surfaces on both sides and slightly rough flat edges. The other fragment is irregular shaped, with slightly rough flat edges and flat surfaces on both sides, with the letters 'a' and a possible 'u' inscribed on one side. There is very slight evidence of the 'a' on one edge of the other fragment.

Grave slab. E2399:2:188. L. 31.2mmm, W. 30.8mm, Th. 14mm. Incomplete. Sub-square fragment of flat stone object, possible slab fragment.

Grave slab. E2399:2:189. Incomplete. L. 63.2mm, W. 59.5mm, Th. 18mm. Incomplete. Irregular fragment of flat quartzite object, possible slab fragment.

Grave slab. E2399:416:174. Incomplete. L. 46cm, W. 41cm, Th. 12.2cm. Fragment of

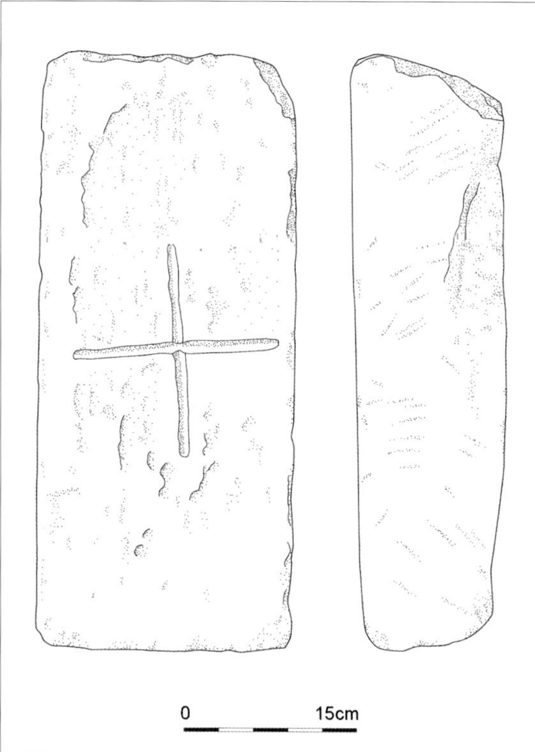

Fig. 6.46. Cross-inscribed grave slab E2399:15:75.

slab with shaft of cross in relief formed by two parallel lines.

Grave slab. E2399:212:76. Incomplete. L. 294mm, W. 179mm, Th. 99mm. Fragment of an inscribed and decorated grave slab. Part of a cross in relief with outline circle and possible foliate decoration extant.

Grave slab. E2399:212:9. Incomplete. L 310.4mm, W. 173.7mm, Th. 94mm. Small fragment of grave slab with trace of possible foliate decoration inside a border in relief.

ARCHITECTURAL STONE

Annette Quinn

INTRODUCTION

Most of the architectural stone retrieved from the excavation along the north aisle came from post-medieval contexts including deposits, walls, buttress bases and demolition layers. Most of this material is of sandstone and appears to date from the thirteenth century (Dornan 2009).

Some of the architectural stone, as one would expect, came from windows, doors and arches. The majority of pieces came from engaged columns or clustered piers (see Chapter 3). Others, although roughly shaped and/or bearing toolmarks, have no distinguishing features to identify their original location or purpose. Many engaged column fragments were re-used in a nineteenth-century cobbled surface across the north aisle (F13). The pieces were found adjacent to where they would have originated at the west side of the nave. The architectural stone is catalogued and is in permanent storage on site in Boyle Abbey. A representative sample of the architectural stone was chosen for illustration and discussion.

COLUMNS/PIERS

A number of fragments of columns/piers were recovered from the excavation from various contexts, mainly post-medieval stone surfaces or from redeposited demolition layers. Fragments from the engaged pilasters in the nave were retrieved as well as column imposts and miscellaneous fragments.

ENGAGED PILASTERS FROM COLUMNS/PIERS IN NAVE

Twelve pieces of loose architectural stone likely to have originated from engaged columns in the abbey were recovered from various contexts. Some fragments (E2399:13:18–23, E2399:13:25–27, 29 and 37) are likely to have originated from the west corner of the nave and were retrieved from a nineteenth-century cobbled surface (F13; Pl. 6.140) along the north aisle. They are likely to be thirteenth century in date.

CATALOGUE

Column fragment. E2399:13:18. D. 15cm, H. 15cm. Section of column with triple fillets from engaged pilasters in the west corners of the nave.

Column fragment. E2399:13:19. D. 15cm, H. 14cm. Section of column with triple fillets from engaged pilasters in the west corners of the nave.

Pl. 6.140. Architectural fragment E2399:13:18.

Column fragment. E2399:13:20. Incomplete. D. 15cm, H. 11cm. Section of column with triple fillets from engaged pilasters in the west corners of the nave.

Column fragment. E2399:13:21. D. 15cm, H. 13cm. Section of column with triple fillets from engaged pilasters in the west corners of the nave.

Column fragment. E2399:13:22. Incomplete. D. 15cm, H. 10cm. Section of column with triple fillets from engaged pilasters in the west corners of the nave.

Column fragment. E2399:13:23. D. 15cm, H. 14cm. Section of column with triple fillets from engaged pilasters in the west corners of the nave.

Column fragment. E2399:13:25. D. 15cm, H. 13cm. Section of column with triple fillets from engaged pilasters in the west corners of the nave.

Column fragment. E2399:13:26. D. 15cm, H. 13cm. Section of column with triple fillets from engaged pilasters in the west corners of the nave.

Column fragment. E2399:13:27. D. 15cm, H. 13cm. Section of column with triple fillets from engaged pilasters in the west corners of the nave.

Column fragment. E2399:13:29. D. 16cm, H. 19cm. Section of column with triple fillets from engaged pilasters in the west corners of the nave.

Column fragment. E2399:13:37. Complete. D. 15cm, H. 15cm. Section of column with triple fillets from engaged pilasters in the west corners of the nave.

Column fragment. E2399:394:131. Incomplete. D. 15cm, H. 10cm. Section of column with triple fillets from engaged pilasters in the west corners of the nave.

Column fragment. E2399:108:704. L. 82.1mm, W. 48.8mm, Th. 40.5mm. Incomplete. Fragment of column with one fillet apparent. Rectangular in cross section.

Column fragment (Fig. 6.50). E2399:212:13. Incomplete. L. 43cm, W. 18cm, H. 15cm. Damaged on all sides, moulded at either end. Possibly part of a column.

COLUMN IMPOSTS

One fragment of a column impost was recovered from a nineteenth-century wall associated with a cobbled surface. An impost or impost block is the projecting block resting on top of a column above a capital or embedded in a wall serving as the base for the springer or lowest voussoir of an arch.

CATALOGUE

Column impost. E2399:396:138. L. 29cm, W. 41.5cm. Impost decorated with pellets. Three extant pellets on both sides.

VOUSSOIRS

A fragment of a voussoir (E2399:213:152) was recovered from the fill of a post-medieval ditch (F222). The context (F213) consisted of a mortar-rich fill

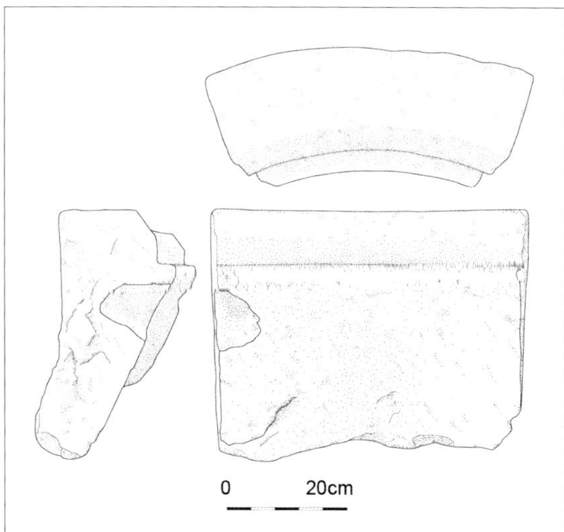

Fig. 6.47. Voussoir E2399:213:152.

and is likely to be a dumped demolition layer. The origin of the piece is likely to be from the north–south arcading.

CATALOGUE

Voussoir (illustrated, Fig. 6.47). E2399:213:152. L. 260mm, W. 200mm, Th. 80mm. Incomplete fragment. Broken voussoir which is chamfered and recessed with centring hollow.

HOOD AND KEEL MOULDINGS

Three fragments from hood mouldings were recovered from the excavations, one of which was chosen for illustration. The fragment (E2399:229:60) was recovered from the fill of a post-medieval ditch (F222). The fill contained items of both medieval and post-medieval date and, similar to other fills of the ditch, is likely to be a dumped demolition layer. The additional pieces were also recovered from post-medieval contexts.

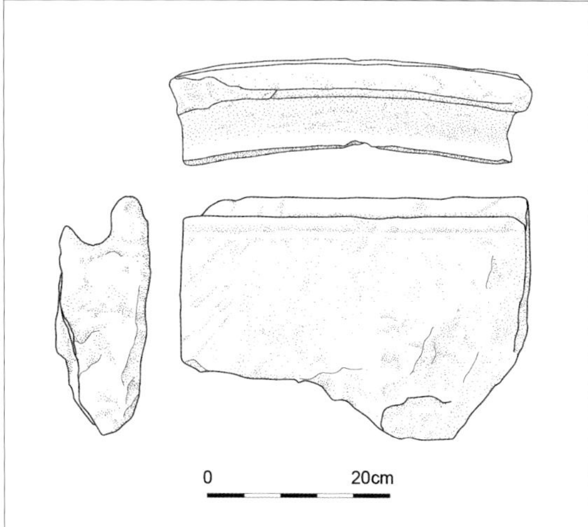

Fig. 6.48. Hood moulding E2399:229:60.

CATALOGUE

Hood moulding (Fig. 6.48). E2399:229:60. L. 360mm, W. 230mm, Th. 100mm. Incomplete fragment. Section of a hood moulding with keel mouldings separated by a hollow chamfer.

Keel moulding. E2399:32:43. Incomplete. L. 25cm, W. 10cm, Th. 10cm. Small fragment of keel moulding. Fragmented and broken.

Keel moulding. E2399:209:11. Incomplete. L. 27.3cm, W. 26.3cm, Th. 109.89cm. Section of hood moulding with keel moulding separated by a hollow chamfer.

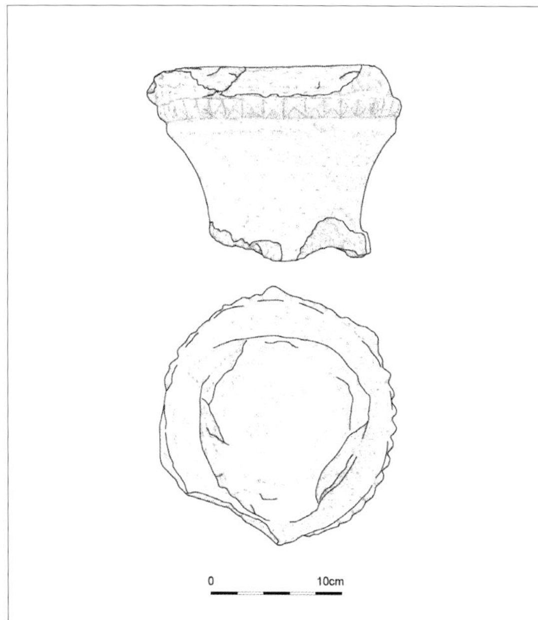

Fig. 6.49. Pier capital E2399:247:179.

PIER CAPITALS

A broken capital was recovered from a layer (F247) which occurred at the interface between the medieval burials and the post-medieval activity. The

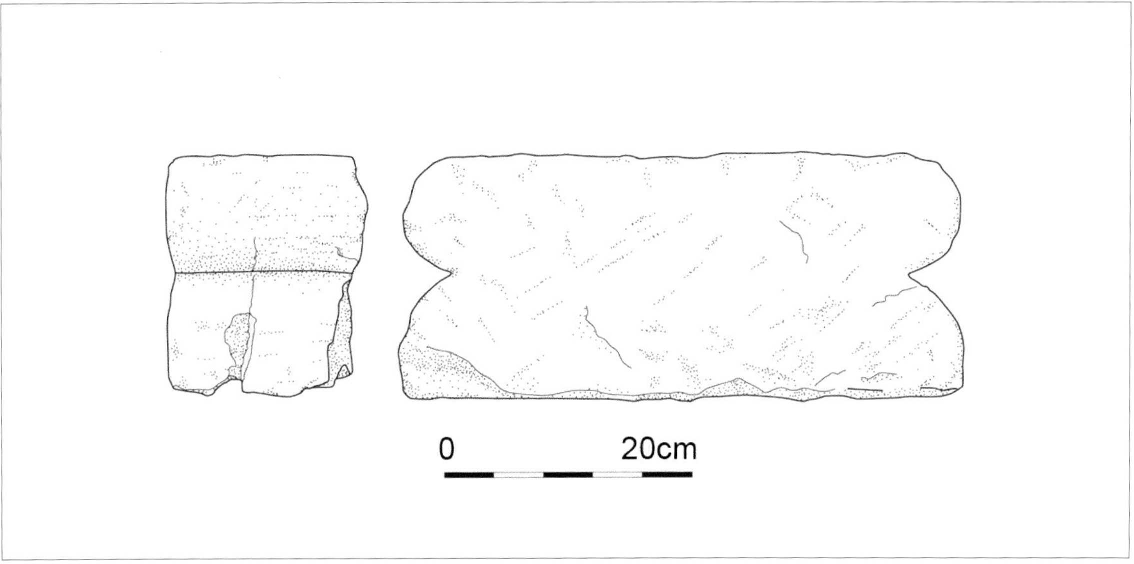

Fig. 6.50. Column fragment E2399:212:13. (Illustration: S. Nylund)

layer also included nails and other architectural fragments and building stone and is likely to be a dumped layer from demolition. The capital, of Romanesque style, may have originated from the early windows in the east gable and fits with some fragments of beaded chevron included in the 2004 Carved Stone Inventory (Dornan 2009).

CATALOGUE

Capital (Fig. 6.49). E2399:247:179. D. 180mm, Incomplete and damaged. Small capital with nail head ornament.

MISCELLANEOUS

The following items are catalogued as miscellaneous due to their fragmentary condition.

CATALOGUE

Miscellaneous. E2399:108:703. L. 81.1mm, W. 55.2mm, Th. 51.6mm. Incomplete. Possible column fragment with curving dressed edge.

Miscellaneous. E2399:1:119. L. 67.6mm, W. 39.5mm, Th. 25.2mm. Incomplete. Sub-rectangular fragment with two flat surfaces, one smooth. Parallel grooves on upper narrow surface. Original function unknown.

Miscellaneous. E2399:44:621. L. 108.5mm, W. 70.1mm, Th. 70.2mm. Incomplete. Fragment of stone, possibly originally rectangular in cross section.

Miscellaneous. E2399:147:730. L. 87.9mm, W. 58.4mm, Th. 26.4mm. Incomplete. Slightly curving architectural stone fragment with filleted edge, D-shaped in cross section. Incised linear groove beneath. Diagonal dress marks apparent.

Miscellaneous. E2399:108:702. L. 99.5mm, W. 97.7mm, Th. 48.1mm. Incomplete. Circular column fragment with rough edges apart from one small section which is flat with diagonal dress marks.

Miscellaneous. E2399:125:727. Incomplete. L. 85.7mm, W. 63mm, Th. 29.5mm. Rectangular fragment of architectural stone with pellet decoration along edge; three pellets (D. 20.6mm) with a fourth damaged at the end (D. 15.4mm).

Miscellaneous. E2399:9:425. L. 90.3mm, W. 77.5mm, Th. 24.9mm. Incomplete. Sub-rectangular fragment with rounded edge, D-shaped in profile. Linear groove beneath.

CLAY BUILDING MATERIALS

Joanna Wren

INTRODUCTION

This assemblage consisted of 446 sherds of post-medieval clay building material, including peg tiles, pantiles, floor tiles and roof tiles. The largest single grouping was the peg tiles, which formed 35% of the collection.

METHODOLOGY

Four different fabrics were identified. Two of these were used in the manufacture of a number of different forms of tile and were probably locally made. They were numbered Boyle Abbey Tile one and two (BAT1, BAT2). The first fabric (BAT1) was used in the manufacture of peg tiles, ridge tiles and pantiles and the vast majority of the assemblage (71%) was comprised of roof tiles in this fabric. The second fabric (BAT2) was used to make peg tiles and bricks (11%). The rest of the assemblage consisted of floor tiles made in gravel tempered fabric imported from North Devon and roof tiles and pantiles made in red earthenwares.

The tiles were grouped according to these fabrics and then subdivided on the basis of form. They were weighed as the most accurate way of assessing quantity. The total numbers and weights of each form of tile were recorded according to context. All percentages used in the text are based on weight. The report is divided for discussion on the basis of the fabric groupings and ordered chronologically. Dating is based on a combination of typology, contextual information and comparative material from other sites.

BAT1 FABRIC (PEG TILES, PANTILE AND RIDGE TILE)

Some 316 sherds came from tiles made in this hard, coarse fabric, which fired to buff or brick orange, with swirls of both colours visible in cross section. It contained sparse angular inclusions of red or buff matter, and voids where material had burnt out during firing. Sherds made in BAT1 fabric were widespread throughout the site and they included examples of at least three different forms of tiling. Only 70% of the sherds were complete enough to classify and the majority of these (57%) were identified as peg tiles, with smaller amounts used for making pantiles (25%) and ridge tiles (3%).

These tiles all date to the post-medieval period when the abbey was in use as an army barracks. The excavations uncovered the remains of structures along the original north aisle, possibly part of a military stables. An estimated 18% of the sherds in BAT1 fabric were found in layers associated with the construction of these buildings, with the majority (61%) found amongst rubble and occupation debris connected with their demolition. Thirty per cent came from unstratified or modern levels and one sherd (E2399:441:2920) was found amongst intrusive material in a medieval burial horizon (F441).

- Peg tiles

  Amongst the sherds in this fabric, 109 were identified as coming from peg tiles. These were clay imitations of the flatter forms of roofing, like slates or wooden shingles, which functioned better on the steep roofs used in the wet Irish climate. They consisted of flat rectangular slabs of clay with peg holes and/or clay nibs along their upper edges. They were attached to the roof in horizontal rows, using pegs or clay nibs and each row overlapped the one below it. The exposed lower sections were usually protected with a glaze.

  No nibs survived on the Boyle Abbey tiles and they would have been attached using pegs or nails. The remains of holes were found on 35 of them including 24 sherds with round holes and 11 sherds with square holes. The tiles with round holes were found in the same contexts as the square ones and their use was probably arbitrary, determined by an individual tile-maker's preference. None of the sherds showed evidence for glaze.

  An estimated 18% of the peg tiles were found in deposits associated with the construction of the buildings on the north aisle, some of which also contained pottery dating to the late seventeenth and eighteenth centuries (C. McCutcheon pers. comm.). Another 61% of the sherds were found amongst later deposits of rubble (F7, F401, F701 etc.) and occupation debris (F205) associated with their demolition. These layers produced a mix of pottery, ranging in date from the late eighteenth century to the late nineteenth/early twentieth century (C. McCutcheon pers. comm.). The final 21% of these tiles came from unstratified or modern levels.

- Pantiles
  Another 40 sherds, made in BAT1 fabric, came from pantiles. These tiles were a post-medieval development of earlier curved roof tiles and they were used on the body of the roof. The pantiles in BAT1 fabric have a slightly different deposition pattern to the peg tiles in the same fabric in that none of them occur in the earlier construction levels. Instead, 36% of these tiles came from the later demolition deposits and 64% of them were from unstratified or modern levels.

- Ridge tile
  The remains of one ridge tile (E2399:393:2658), made in BAT1 fabric, were recovered from a later buttress (F393). The ridge tile had a flattened U shape in cross section, and it was plain without any sign of cresting, decoration or glaze.

BAT2 FABRIC (PEG TILES AND BRICK)

Fifty-one sherds were made in this coarse dark red fabric, which contained frequent inclusions of quartzite and unidentified cream matter all *c.* 1mm in size. The vast majority of them (95%) were from peg tiles, but there were also two sherds from bricks.

- Peg tiles
  None of the peg tiles had nibs but the remains of round peg holes survived on 11 sherds and they would probably have been attached to the laths on the roof with wooden pegs. Once again none of the sherds showed evidence for glaze. Seven of the peg tiles (14%) came from layers associated with the construction of the outbuildings along the north aisle, but the vast majority of them (75%) were found amongst rubble associated with their demolition.

- Bricks
  Both bricks were thick and were probably handmade, factors which combine to suggest a date in the eighteenth century for their manufacture (Lynch and Roundtree 2009, 15). One sherd came from demolition rubble and the other was from the topsoil.

NORTH DEVON GRAVEL TEMPERED WARE (FLOOR TILES)

Four sherds came from plain floor tiles made in a gravel tempered fabric imported from North Devon. Gravel tempered floor tiles are rare in Ireland, but they do occur. In particular, tiles in this fabric decorated with relief motifs with dates ranging from the late sixteenth to the eighteenth century have been found in Dublin, Waterford, Carrickfergus (Eames and Fanning 1988, 50) and Cork. The floor tiles at Boyle Abbey came from topsoil.

RED EARTHENWARES (PANTILES, ROOF TILES)

This category is a generic term used to cover different forms of post-medieval building material made in red earthenware fabrics. A total of 74 sherds of roof tile in these fabrics were recovered from the site. Only 41 of them were complete enough to identify as pantiles.

- Pantiles
  The pantile sherds were made in a very distinctive sandy brick red fabric. Pantiles made in similar fabrics are common throughout Ireland and are usually found in contexts dating to the seventeenth and eighteenth centuries. As discussed above, pantiles are used on the body of the roof as a post-medieval development of earlier curved roof tiles. Forty-one per cent of these tiles were from the demolition rubble and occupation debris above the cobbles in the north aisle. The other 59% were from unstratified and modern levels.

DISCUSSION

The most significant aspect of this assemblage is the fact that it consists mostly of tiles made in one fabric (BAT1). Similar tiles were found during excavations in 2004 along the north wall of the nave and at the site of the abbey's refectory where the remains of a post-medieval pottery kiln were

Pl. 6.141. Peg tile E2399:395:2681.

Pl. 6.142. Peg tile E2399:207:1636.

uncovered (see Rooney above). A number of tile sherds were recovered from within the kiln debris and the assemblage also included kiln wasters in BAT1 fabric. It is quite possible therefore, that the BAT1 tiles were either made at this kiln or another similar one within the abbey grounds. Tilemakers often manufactured on site (Eames and Fanning 1988, 12) particularly when they were involved in more elaborate building programmes, such as that at the Boyle army barracks.

The majority of the more diagnostic BAT1 sherds came from peg tiles. Eight per cent of these were found in deposits associated with the construction of the outbuildings along the north aisle. It is possible that these tiles were used on one of these outbuildings and that these small quantities of tile are accidental debris from roof construction. Indeed, it is quite likely that the uncrested ridge tile (E2399:393:2658) found re-used in one of the buttresses came from the same roof.

The other 62% of the peg tiles, found in the later demolition layers, were probably deposited when the roof collapsed or was dismantled. The demolition levels appeared to have been subject to some modern disturbance as they contained pottery with a wide date range, from the late eighteenth to the early twentieth century (C. McCutcheon pers. comm.). The construction levels, however, were more intact, and the ceramic evidence here indicates a date in the late seventeenth or eighteenth century for the construction of the outbuildings.

Comparative evidence indicates a seventeenth-century date for the peg tiles. The fashion was for peg tiled roofing in the west and northwest during the seventeenth century. For the most part these tiles have been found at fortified structures in lakeland regions. At Clogh Oughter Castle, Co. Cavan. in particular, the remains of a collapsed roof of peg tiles were uncovered in secure contexts, which dated them to the first half of the seventeenth century (Wren 2013, 374). Similar tiles were found in an early seventeenth-century context at Portumna Castle, Co. Galway, (C. Manning pers. comm.) and amongst seventeenth-century material at Limerick Castle (Wren 2015, 472).

As well as debris from these outbuildings it seems likely that the rubble deposits included building debris dumped from other parts of the site. The pantiles in BAT1 fabric, for example, do not occur in the construction levels in this area and may have originated on a roof in another area. Likewise, the gravel tempered floor tiles could have come from another building, presumably one with a more domestic function where a tiled floor was appropriate.

As discussed above, an eighteenth-century date is likely for the second fabric (BAT2) based on the kind of bricks it was used to make. The fact that both bricks and roof tiles were made in this fabric could suggest that it too was locally made, if not at the abbey somewhere in the wider vicinity of Boyle. These bricks and tiles may also have originated on the outbuildings in the north aisle. Pictorial evidence, however, suggests that these buildings were demolished by the late eighteenth century at the latest and these smaller amounts of tile, in BAT2 fabric, may also have been dumped from another part of the site. Finally, the pantiles made in the sandy red earthenwares are common throughout Ireland, usually in contexts dating to the seventeenth and eighteenth centuries.

CATALOGUE

E2399:395:2681 (Pl. 6.141). Peg tile made in BAT1 fabric with round holes.

E2399: 207:1636 (Pl. 6.142). Peg tile made in BAT1 fabric with two square holes.

E2399:393:2658 (Pl. 6.143). Uncrested ridge tile made in BAT1 fabric.

E2399:15:489 (Pl. 6.144). Peg tile made in BAT2 fabric with round peg hole.

Pl. 6.143. Uncrested ridge tile E2399:393:2658.

FAUNAL REMAINS
Margaret McCarthy

The recovered animal bones represent occupational debris spanning almost nine centuries of the use of Boyle Abbey from the middle of the twelfth century to the twentieth century (Table 6.9 and Table 6.10). Faunal material was found in many features across the site and was divided into two broad chronological groups, based on pottery and coin finds. The smallest samples came from features associated with the Cistercian abbey and the community of monks who resided there from AD 1161 to 1569. Following the dissolution of the monastery, the buildings were used as a garrison during the Elizabethan settlement of County Roscommon. The abbey continued to be used as a military barracks until the end of the nineteenth century (1892) and the largest samples of animal bones have been dated to this latest phase of occupation.

The distribution of bones across the site was uneven, and while some fragments were recovered from features including pits, ditches and drains, the vast majority of the assemblage derived from extensive build-up layers that accumulated across the site over nine centuries of occupation. The excavated graves within the abbey also contained animal bones, all of which are considered to be either residual or intrusive.

The total assemblage comprises 14,150 fragments of bone representing a mixture of primary butchery waste and meal remains of both the Cistercian community and the military personnel who occupied the abbey during the eighteenth and nineteenth centuries. Many of the medieval layers were truncated during the military occupation of the abbey when the buildings were modified for accommodation and the stabling of horses, and this activity would have resulted in a certain amount of reworking and contamination of bone. From the upper layers, much of the post-medieval animal bone came from contexts which had been disturbed or which could not be closely dated. The continuous occupation of the site over nine centuries has meant that much of the animal bone came from layers of uncertain origin and it was not possible to chart changes in diet and animal exploitation from the medieval period to the post-medieval period as accurately as had been hoped.

Pl. 6.144. Peg tile E2399:15:489.

The assemblage consists almost exclusively of the remains of domestic animals such as cattle, sheep, goat, pig, horse, dog, cat and domestic poultry. The analysis demonstrates continuity in food consumption from the twelfth century to the twentieth century, with cattle and sheep being the primary sources of meat, both in terms of raw counts of the total number of identified fragments (NISP) and from estimates of the minimum number of individuals (MNI) present. The total medieval sample (3,371 fragments) is small considering that the remains span five centuries of occupation and it might be inferred from this that the monks practised an organised system of waste disposal in designated areas of the abbey, outside the excavated areas. Cattle bones significantly outnumbered those of sheep, and pigs were the least well represented of the main livestock species. If the sample is typical of the husbandry methods employed by the Cistercian monks, the indications are that the fattening of cattle solely for meat production was not commonly practised. The small sample size and the fragmented nature of the bones prevented a determination of the ratio of males to females, but it is assumed that both cows and steers were kept, cows as dairy animals and oxen for ploughing and other forms of heavy traction. Body part representation indicates that beef and mutton derived from complete carcasses, from animals bred in the abbey lands and driven on the hoof to the kitchen area to be slaughtered and dismembered for cooking. The very low frequency of pig bones might suggest that the monks were engaged in intensive arable farming and while sheep and cattle would have been important suppliers of manure for fertilizing the fields, pigs would have posed a threat to crops as they are difficult to manage in an open environment (Harris 1997, 152).

In the seventeenth century, Boyle Abbey changed from becoming a place of mixed farming during the Cistercian phase of habitation to one of meat consumption during its military occupation. Notwithstanding the mixed nature of the samples, there is evidence that systems of animal management changed between the medieval and post-medieval periods and the higher frequency of cattle and sheep that were slaughtered when they had just reached adulthood suggests a concentration on meat production by farmers supplying meat to the garrison. The metrical sample was too small to determine the sex of the individuals as this may have confirmed a higher incidence of bulls and steers, animals bred solely for the provisioning of meat. There is no doubt that the military personnel were fed principally with beef and mutton and, from the representation of skeletal elements, it is clear that animals continued to be driven on the hoof into the barracks as there are many concentrations of cattle and sheep bones, dumped after large-scale primary carcass processing. The somewhat limited metrical data showed a change in cattle size from the medieval period to the later phases of occupation indicating that improved breeds of cattle became common in the region during the post-medieval period, at a time when significant advances were being made in livestock breeding across Europe.

Where specific identification was possible, sheep bones outnumbered those of goat, and for both periods goats were represented almost entirely by their horncores. Just two post-cranial bones were positively identified suggesting that goat meat was not consumed to any great extent in either period of occupation of the abbey. The monks probably kept a few goats for milk, to be slaughtered and eaten when they were no longer required for this purpose. For the medieval period, age estimation indicates that sheep were not bred primarily for food and while the animals would eventually have been eaten, the bones have to be seen as indicating a resource that is broader than

Table 6.10 The variation of principal stock animal fragments against feature types in the post medieval period

	Horse	Cattle	Sheep	Pig	TNF*
Cobble surfaces	0.5%	74%	25%	0.5%	214
Drains	6%	76%	12%	6%	17
Walls	1%	78%	18%	3%	74
Buttress remains	5%	68%	26%	1%	86
Layers/Deposits	2%	70%	24%	4%	3041
Trench/Ditch fills	0.4%	74%	18%	7.6%	494
Pits	–	83%	6%	11%	18

TNF* Total number of fragments

food. Sheep husbandry seems to have been aimed at the production of wool, this product being the mainstay of the medieval economy, and Cistercian communities across Europe were actively involved in the trade. In contrast to the medieval assemblage, the age ranges for sheep from the post-medieval layers indicate a higher proportion of individuals that were slaughtered primarily for meat, animals bred specifically to supply the garrison. Although the sample of measurable bones is limited, there is a suggestion that sheep increased in size during the post-medieval period, indicating that an improved breed was introduced into the Boyle region at this time. A population rise during the seventeenth century generated an increased demand for meat which would have encouraged producers to breed animals with a larger body mass.

Pork was not consumed to any great extent during either period of occupation and the small recovered samples suggest that there was no great tradition of pig farming in the region. Pig bones were considerably less common than at Bective Abbey (Beglane 2016) and Tintern Abbey (McCormick 2010), providing 7% of the total identifiable sample from the medieval deposits and just 4.7% from the post-medieval period. This notably low proportion of pigs may be due to a number of factors, such as the location of Boyle in an area better suited to cattle and sheep herding, or it may reflect an increase in the amount of arable land at the expense of woodland which would have deprived pigs of their natural habitat. The presence of bones of young pigs from both periods echoes the pattern observed at many medieval urban and monastic sites and indicates that a certain number of pigs were reared within the abbey for breeding and rubbish recycling.

Horses were kept during both periods of occupation although their remains were more abundant in the post-medieval layers reflecting the military occupation of the abbey at this stage. The bones from the medieval layers are all from adult individuals that would have given many years of service as riding and pack animals. Most are complete but were not found in articulation which may be partly due to the reworking of specimens originally discarded as complete skeletons. The medieval Church prohibited the eating of horseflesh and there are no butchery marks on the bones to suggest that this rule was not observed by the monks at Boyle Abbey. Dogs and cats were the most popular non-meat animals kept and the presence of both rats and mice provides ample reason for the keeping of these animals to control the vermin population. Some dogs were of a medium or large type and may have performed guarding and hunting duties while the smaller terrier-sized individuals from the post-medieval period would have made useful ratters in a barracks where horses were kept and stabled.

Both the medieval and post-medieval occupants of Boyle Abbey seem to have relied almost exclusively on domestic livestock for meat provisioning and there is very little evidence for the

Table 6.9 The variation of principal stock animal fragments against feature types in the medieval period

	Horse	Cattle	Sheep	Pig	TNF*
Deposits/Layers	6%	68%	20%	6%	1080
Masonry remains	–	47%	40%	13%	15
Drains	1%	59%	24%	16%	91
Flagstone surfaces	–	–	100%	–	3
Pits/Postholes	–	88%	9%	3%	154
Graves	1%	48%	37%	14%	73
Buttress F411	–	100%	–	–	3

TNF* Total number of fragments

exploitation of the local wild environment. The few butchered post-cranial deer bones indicate that these game animals were occasionally hunted and their carcasses brought back to the abbey for dismemberment. A few sawn antler offcuts show that bone-working for the production of artefacts was practised on a small scale by the monks; the antler present is entirely from red deer (*Cervus elaphus*) and there is no evidence for fallow deer (*Dama dama*) which would have been present in Ireland at this stage. Wild boar was not established among the medieval remains, and apart from a few finds scattered unevenly across the deposits, wild species of birds are also very rare, despite what must have been a plentiful locally available resource of native wildfowl including winter migrants along the riverbank and nearby lakes. Nor is there much evidence for the consumption of rabbits, also surprising as the keeping of rabbits in warrens was commonly practised during the medieval period.

Domestic fowl dominate the medieval avian assemblage, and the presence of young chicken bones indicates that hens were kept by the monks for the provision of eggs and meat. Goose bones were also identified, and these large birds not only supplemented the meat diet but would also have been useful producers of eggs, down and feathers. The few duck bones may represent domestic duck, but it is also possible that the bones are from the wild strain of the species, mallard (*Anas platyrhynchos*). Less common are edible wild bird taxa, which include single finds of two duck species, teal (*Anas crecca*) and tufted duck (*Aythya fuligula*), both of which could have been captured from rivers and lakes in the vicinity of the abbey. A single bone of woodpigeon (*Columba palumbus*) was recovered. The domestic form of rock doves (*Columba livia*) was bred in captivity by religious orders during the medieval period and it is presumed that this was also the case at Boyle Abbey. Non-edible wild bird species include jackdaw (*Corvus monedula*), common sandpiper (*Tringa hypoleucos*) and starling (*Sturnus vulgaris*), commensal birds living locally in trees and hedges and frequenting the monastery for a regular supply of waste foodstuffs.

Fish also formed part of the diet, but the limited assemblage cannot truly reflect the original amount and range of species that was consumed. It might have been expected that the medieval deposits would have produced larger quantities of fish bone given the strict fasting rules that were imposed by the Church during this period. The small sample suggests that either many bones were lost by natural decay or that fish waste was discarded in unexcavated areas of the site. Two members of the gadid family were identified: cod (*Gadus morhua*) and whiting (*Merlangius merlangus*), both regarded as important commercial food fishes during the medieval period. Element distribution suggests that marine fish reached the abbey with the heads still attached as skull bones and vertebrae are equally well represented. Salmon (*Salmo salar*) and eels (*Anguilla anguilla*) would have been locally available, and the documentary sources refer to the monks of Boyle having plentiful eels for capture. Sprat (*Sprattus sprattus*) and scad (*Trachurus trachurus*) bones represent very small fish which may have originated from the stomach contents of the larger marine fish found at the site.

The faunal assemblage from Boyle Abbey, when viewed in its wider chronological context, can be considered a useful addition to a limited number of pre-existing monastic assemblages and the analysis has provided additional data to further our understanding of animal exploitation in the medieval and post-medieval periods in Ireland. For comparative purposes, the information from the Cistercian abbeys of Bective (Beglane 2016) and Tintern (McCormick 2010) is drawn on as well as from other rural and urban medieval sites. The formation processes in operation at all sites seem to be very similar, namely small-scale domestic butchery of whole animals with maximum exploitation of available animal products. The monks' diet relied on a somewhat narrow economic base focused almost exclusively upon domestic livestock with very little input from either wild mammals or wild species of birds. The recovery of bones of newborn lambs and piglets implies some husbandry within the precinct of the abbeys, representing animals brought in during lambing and farrowing seasons.

At all sites, the animals present suggest that the monks practised a mixed farming economy focusing on dairying and wool production and producing their own meat. As far as can be determined, the subsistence economies show some variation between the sites in terms of livestock husbandry and economy. When the relative proportions of the three main domestic animals are compared, it is clear that cattle and sheep were more frequent at Boyle than at Bective Abbey (Beglane 2016) and Tintern (McCormick 2010). The monks living in Bective Abbey seem to have focused on sheep farming and the age-slaughter patterns clearly show that the community was actively involved in the local economic system through the supply of wool into the urban market for export to Europe and perhaps beyond. Although the proportion of sheep bones is high at Bective Abbey, the dietary importance of sheep as meat providers would always have been secondary to the larger cattle.

The monks at Boyle, on the other hand, seem to have specialised more in cattle husbandry and the kill-off pattern suggests that dairying was an important and even a prominent function of the cattle herd. The impression that stock rearing appears to have been more common at Boyle Abbey than at Bective Abbey is an indicator that the monastery in Roscommon was more peripheral in terms of intensity of trading with a large urban market, such as would have been available for the community at Bective Abbey, being geographically closer to Dublin. When the age profiles of sheep are compared, it appears that a greater proportion of older females were held back for breeding purposes by the monks in Boyle. The low proportion of goat bones and the tertiary role of pigs are broadly similar with other sites, although it would appear that pork was more commonly consumed by the monks at Bective Abbey and Tintern Abbey than it was at Boyle Abbey. Ageing data for the pigs at Boyle are also typical for pigs with most animals slaughtered before adulthood and just a few being kept as breeding stock. The range of fish from Boyle Abbey is similar to that recorded from Bective Abbey (Hamilton-Dyer 2016), where the bones mostly represented marine species with a lesser reliance on riverine species such as eels and salmon. At all sites, there is little to suggest that the monks enjoyed a high-status elite diet through a wide range of fish, wild birds and wild fauna for example. The monks seem to have been virtually reliant on their own produce and only occasionally varied their diet with locally procured wild fauna and wild birds. At all sites, one would have expected the sea to have been a more important source of food given that these are monastic assemblages dated to a period when the Church imposed very strict regulations on fasting (Murray and McCormick 2005).

The animal bone samples from Boyle Abbey, whilst of uncertain origin in terms of depositional history, are not without interest and have provided some insight into a range of domestic activities for both periods of occupation. The data on taxa frequency and ageing add to the evidence for diet and animal husbandry practices in a medieval religious institution and trace some differences from this period to dissolution and the subsequent use of the abbey as a military barracks. The

Table 6.11 List of samples analysed

Feature	Cut number	Fill number	Sample number	Processed sample weight
Medieval				
Stone annex structure	F25	F26	601	1.1g.
Stone annex structure	F25	F609	603	7.2g
Stone annex structure	F25	F33	2	8.6g
Grave cut	F533	F532	5	5.6g
Grave cut	F274	F273	5	0.4g
Grave cut	F250	F251	2	5.8g
Grave cut	F472	F471	16	0.5g
Grave cut	F460	F461	15	0.7g
Grave cut	F421	F420	13	0.4g
Posthole	F277	F276	6	3.4g
Posthole	F342	F341	11	0.2g
Posthole	F340	F339	10	0.7g
Ditch	F222	F229	3	6.2g
Ditch	F604	F603	600	0.4g
Ditch	F604	F602	35	10.4g
Ditch	F604	-	58	6.6g
Drain at base of F25	F59	F613	605	2.1g
Drain at base of F25	F59	F58	4	0.4g
Drain at North Wall F19/F211	F63	F104	8	12.2g
Charcoal-rich layer	–	F90	6	8.3g
Charcoal-rich layer	–	F90	6	0.1g

Cistercian community flourished in Boyle from the beginning of the twelfth century until the abbey was dissolved in AD 1569. It is well documented that the Cistercians were progressive arable and pastoral farmers and the community in Boyle was undoubtedly self-sufficient in all areas of food provisioning. Good provisioning would seem to have continued during the military occupation and documentary sources record that the monks stayed on at the abbey and may have continued to farm and supply meat to the occupants of the garrison. Meat must also have been supplied by outside producers, most probably from farming communities in the rural hinterland of the town. When all the evidence from the Boyle Abbey assemblage is considered, it suggests that a significant transition occurred between the medieval and the post-medieval period with the abbey becoming a consumer site, rather than a producer site after AD 1692 due to the arrival of an armed force in need of direct meat provisioning.

Table 6.11 List of samples analysed *continued*

Feature	Cut number	Fill number	Sample number	Processed sample weight
Late Medieval to Post-Medieval				
Deposit	–	F68	3	12.9g
Deposit	–	F429	14	6.1g
Deposit	–	F34	1	7.5g
Deposit	–	F84	5	3.4g
Deposit	–	F139	11	5.7g
Deposit	–	F709	1	4.3g
Deposit	–	F908	3	1.8g
Post-Medieval				
Post-medieval pit	F911	F910	2	3.4g
Post-medieval pit	F916	F915	4	2.8g

ARCHAEOBOTANICAL REMAINS: ENVIRONMENTAL EVIDENCE

Susan Lyons

SOIL SAMPLING STRATEGY AND SCOPE OF WORKS

A total of 26 processed samples were selected from the excavation to recover archaeological remains and ecofacts that would help with interpreting activities at the site and provide suitable environmental material for radiocarbon dating. This report presents the results of the archaeobotanical (plant macrofossil) analysis from all phases of archaeological excavation (Table 6.11).

ARCHAEOBOTANICAL RESULTS

The plant macro-remains identified from Boyle Abbey were preserved by carbonisation. The results of the plant assemblage and other ecofacts identified are presented in Table 6.12.

CARBONISED CEREALS, FIELD CROPS AND WILD TAXA

- Cereal grains
  Carbonised cereal grains were recorded from the majority of the samples, but most notably from the medieval stone annex F25 (F609), medieval ditches F222 and medieval drains F604, F59 and F63, and late medieval to post-medieval waste deposits F34, F68, F84, F139 and F429.

  Predominantly the charred grain was in a poor state of preservation, displaying signs of abrasion and erosion. These appear in the table as Cerealia and accounted for 53% of the charred grain recorded (Fig. 6.51). Cereal grains can become eroded and abraded as a result of charring at high temperatures, if the grain was damp when burnt or if this material had degraded due to redeposition and/or exposure.

- Oat (Avena sp.)
  was the dominant identified species recorded from the Boyle Abbey excavations making up 24% of the plant assemblage. Most of the grain was free of the palea/lemma (hulls), which are required in identifying between oat types. However, based on the size of the oat grain (*caryopsis*) and the absence of the large 'suckermouth'-type lemma bases it seems likely that the common oat type (*A. sativa*) is the prominent species present in the assemblage. Barley (*Hordeum sp.*),

Table 6.12 Composition of archaeobotanical remains from Boyle Abbey, Co. Roscommon

	Medieval									Medieval / Late Medieval				
	Stone annex structure			Drain			Postholes North Wall			Burial: Ph 1			Burial: Ph 3	Burial: N aisle
	F25	F25	F25	F59	F59	F63	F277	F342	F340	F460	F472	F533	F250	F274
	F26	F609	F33	F613	F58	F104	F276	F341	F339	F461	F471	F532	F251	F273
	601	603	2	605	4	8	6	11	10	15	16	5	2	5
	1.1g	7.2g	8.6g	2.1g	0.4g	12.2g	3.4g	0.2g	0.7g	0.7g	0.5g	5.6g	5.8g	0.4g
Latin name														
CEREALS: CARBONISED														
Hordeum vulgare	–	–	–	–	2	–	–	–	–	–	–	–	–	–
Hordeum spp.	–	3	–	–	–	2	–	–	–	–	–	–	–	–
Avena sativa	–	–	–	–	1	–	–	–	–	–	–	–	–	–
Avena spp.	14	15	–	–	–	36	–	–	–	–	–	41	42	–
Triticum aestivum/ compactum	–	–	–	–	–	2	–	–	–	–	–	–	–	–
Triticum spp.	1	–	–	–	–	–	–	–	–	–	–	1	8	–
Secale cereale	–	–	–	–	–	–	1	–	–	–	–	–	–	–
Cerealia	6	277	11	101	5	–	3	–	–	–	–	9	36	–
Culm nodes	–	–	–	–	–	4	–	–	–	–	–	–	–	–
Total cereal counts	21	295	11	101	8	44	4	–	–	–	–	51	86	–
LEGUMES/FLAX														
Pisum sativum	–	–	–	–	1	–	–	–	–	–	–	–	–	–
cf Pisum sp.	–	–	–	–	–	–	–	–	–	–	–	–	–	–
Vicia hirusta	–	–	–	–	–	–	–	–	–	–	–	–	–	–
Vicia spp.	–	–	–	–	–	–	–	–	–	–	–	–	–	–
Vicia/Lathyrus spp.	–	–	–	–	2	1	–	–	–	–	–	–	–	–
Linum usitatissimum	–	–	–	–	–	–	–	–	–	–	–	–	–	–
Total legume counts	–	–	–	–	3	1	–	–	–	–	–	–	–	–

Table 6.12 Composition of archaeobotanical remains from Boyle Abbey, Co. Roscommon *continued*

	Medieval / Late Medieval							Post Medieval		19th century				No date			Total
	Deposit							Pit		Linear ditch				Burial: other	Charcoal-rich layer		
	–	–	–	–	–	–	–	F916	F911	F604	F604	F604	F222	F421	–	–	
	F709	F68	F429	F34	F84	F139	F908	F915	F910	F603	F602	–	F229	F420	F90	F90	
	1	3	14	1	5	11	3	4	2	600	35	58	3	13	6	6	
	4.3g	12.9g	6.1g	7.5g	3.4g	5.7g	1.8g	2.8g	3.4g	0.4g	10.4g	6.6g	6.2g	0.4g	8.3g	0.1g	
Latin name																	
CEREALS: CARBONISED																	
Hordeum vulgare	–	85	12	–	5	53	3	–	–	–	–	–	–	–	–	–	157
Hordeum spp.	7	–	–	–	22	–	–	5	6	1	4	–	3	–	5	–	34
Avena sativa	–	–	23	–	14	–	2	–	–	–	–	–	–	–	–	–	38
Avena spp.	5	141	12	26	43	–	–	5	11	–	55	11	2	–	18	4	375
Triticum aestivum/ compactum	–	25	2	–	21	2	–	–	–	–	–	1	–	–	8	–	52
Triticum spp.	5	8	–	–	17	–	–	3	2	–	–	–	1	–	–	2	40
Secale cereale	–	1	–	–	–	2	–	–	–	–	–	–	–	–	–	–	4
Cerealia	42	119	22	67	207	72	14	11	30	3	10	18	15	–	34	1	977
Culm nodes	–	6	2	–	2	–	–	–	–	–	5	–	–	–	–	–	14
Total cereal counts	59	385	73	93	331	129	19	24	49	4	74	30	21	–	65	7	1984
LEGUMES/FLAX																	
Pisum sativum	–	8	–	–	–	–	–	–	–	–	–	–	1	–	–	–	8
cf Pisum sp.	–	–	–	–	–	–	–	–	–	–	–	–	–	–	–	–	
Vicia hirusta	–	–	–	–	1	–	–	–	–	–	–	–	–	–	–	–	1
Vicia spp.	–	28	–	–	–	–	–	–	–	–	–	–	–	–	–	–	28
Vicia/Lathyrus spp.	–	3	–	–	2	–	–	2	–	–	1	1	–	–	–	–	6
Linum usitatissimum	–	2	–	–	–	–	–	–	–	–	–	–	–	–	–	–	2
Total legume counts	–	41	–	–	3	–	–	–	–	–	1	1	1	–	–	–	53

Table 6.12 Composition of archaeobotanical remains from Boyle Abbey, Co. Roscommon *continued*

	Medieval									Medieval / Late Medieval				
	Stone annex structure			Drain			Postholes North Wall			Burial: Ph 1			Burial: Ph 3	Burial: N aisle
	F25	F25	F25	F59	F59	F63	F277	F342	F340	F460	F472	F533	F250	F274
	F26	F609	F33	F613	F58	F104	F276	F341	F339	F461	F471	F532	F251	F273
	601	603	2	605	4	8	6	11	10	15	16	5	2	5
	1.1g	7.2g	8.6g	2.1g	0.4g	12.2g	3.4g	0.2g	0.7g	0.7g	0.5g	5.6g	5.8g	0.4g
Latin name														
WILD TAXA: CARBONISED														
Ranunculus sp.	–	–	–	–	–	–	–	–	–	–	–	–	–	–
Chenopodium sp.	–	–	–	–	1	1	–	–	–	–	–	–	–	–
Fallopia colvolvulus (L.) Á Löve	–	–	–	–	–	–	–	–	–	–	–	–	–	–
Polygonum sp.	–	–	–	–	–	–	–	–	–	–	–	–	1	–
Rumex cf acetosella L.	–	–	–	–	–	–	–	–	–	–	–	–	–	–
Rumex sp.	–	–	–	–	1	–	–	–	–	–	–	–	–	–
Aethusa cynapium L.	–	–	–	–	–	–	–	–	–	–	–	–	–	–
Spergula arvensis L.	6	–	–	–	–	–	–	–	–	–	–	3	–	–
Prunus spinosa L.	–	–	–	–	–	3	–	–	–	–	–	–	–	–
Galium cf aparine L.	–	–	–	–	–	1	–	–	–	–	–	–	–	–
Lapsana communis L.	–	–	–	–	–	–	–	–	–	–	–	–	1	–
Lamium sp.	–	–	–	–	–	–	–	–	–	–	–	–	–	–
Raphanus raphanistrum L.	–	1	–	–	–	1	–	–	–	–	–	–	–	–
Carex sp.	–	–	–	–	–	–	–	–	–	–	–	–	–	–
Seed indet.	–	–	–	–	6	–	–	–	–	–	–	–	–	–
Total seed/fruit counts	6	1	–	–	8	6	–	–	–	–	–	3	2	–

Table 6.12 Composition of archaeobotanical remains from Boyle Abbey, Co. Roscommon *continued*

	Medieval									Medieval / Late Medieval				
	Stone annex structure			Drain			Postholes North Wall			Burial: Ph 1			Burial: Ph 3	Burial: N aisle
	F25	F25	F25	F59	F59	F63	F277	F342	F340	F460	F472	F533	F250	F274
	F26	F609	F33	F613	F58	F104	F276	F341	F339	F461	F471	F532	F251	F273
	601	603	2	605	4	8	6	11	10	15	16	5	2	5
	1.1g	7.2g	8.6g	2.1g	0.4g	12.2g	3.4g	0.2g	0.7g	0.7g	0.5g	5.6g	5.8g	0.4g
WILD TAXA: UNCARBONISED														
Prunus spinosa L.	–	–	–	–	–	1	–	–	–	–	–	–	–	–
Carex spp.	–	–	–	–	–	9	–	–	–	–	–	–	–	–
Total wild taxa seed counts	–	–	–	–	–	10	–	–	–	–	–	–	–	–
OTHER PLANT REMAINS: CARBONISED														
Charcoal	–	1.2 g	–	–	0.2 g	0.3 g	0.3 g	0.2 g	0.2 g	–	0.2 g	1.5 g	0.8 g	0.2 g
Nutshell	–	-	–	–	0.1 g	0.1 g	0.1 g	–	–	–	–	–	0.2 g	0.1 g
OTHER ECOFACTS: UNCARBONISED														
Nutshell	–	–	–	–	–	1 g	–	–	–	–	–	–	–	–
Mammal bone	0.1 g	0.2 g	–	–	–	–	0.1 g	–	–	++	–	0.1 g	–	–
Mollusca	–	–	–	–	–	–	–	–	–	–	–	–	–	–
Insect remains	–	–	–	–	–	+	–	–	–	–	–	–	–	–

Table 6.12 Composition of archaeobotanical remains from Boyle Abbey, Co. Roscommon *continued*

	Late Medieval/Post Medieval							Post Medieval		19th century			
	Deposit					Layer		Pit		Ditch			Linear Ditch
	–	–	–	–	–	–	–	F916	F911	F604	F604	F604	F222
	F709	F68	F429	F34	F84	F139	F908	F915	F910	F603	F602	–	F229
	1	3	14	1	5	11	3	4	2	600	35	58	3
	4.3g	12.9g	6.1g	7.5g	3.4g	5.7g	1.8g	2.8g	3.4g	0.4g	10.4g	6.6g	6.2g
Latin name													
WILD TAXA: CARBONISED													
Ranunculus sp.	–	1	–	–	–	–	–	–	–	–	–	–	–
Chenopodium sp.	–	2	–	–	–	–	–	–	–	–	–	–	–
Fallopia colvolvulus (L.) Á Löve	–	–	–	–	–	–	–	–	–	–	–	–	–
Polygonum sp.	–	1	–	–	3	–	–	–	–	–	–	–	–
Rumex cf acetosella L.	–	–	–	–	1	–	–	–	–	–	–	–	–
Rumex sp.	–	3	–	–	–	–	–	–	–	–	–	–	–
Aethusa cynapium L.	–	–	–	–	1	–	–	–	–	–	–	–	–
Spergula arvensis L.	–	30	–	–	–	–	–	–	–	–	–	–	–
Prunus spinosa L.	–	–	–	–	–	–	–	–	–	–	–	–	–
Galium cf aparine L.	–	3	–	–	–	–	–	–	–	–	–	–	–
Lapsana communis L.	–	–	–	–	–	–	–	–	–	–	–	–	–
Lamium sp.	–	1	–	–	–	–	–	–	–	–	–	–	–
Raphanus raphanistrum L.	–	8	–	–	–	–	–	–	–	–	–	–	–
Carex sp.	–	8	–	–	–	–	–	–	–	–	–	–	–
Seed indet.	–	–	–	–	–	–	–	–	–	–	–	–	–
Total seed/fruit counts	–	57	–	–	5	–	–	–	–	–	–	–	–

Table 6.12 Composition of archaeobotanical remains from Boyle Abbey, Co. Roscommon *continued*

	Late Medieval/Post Medieval							Post Medieval		19th century			
	Deposit					Layer		Pit		Ditch			Linear Ditch
	–	–	–	–	–	–	–	F916	F911	F604	F604	F604	F222
	F709	F68	F429	F34	F84	F139	F908	F915	F910	F603	F602	–	F229
	1	3	14	1	5	11	3	4	2	600	35	58	3
	4.3g	12.9g	6.1g	7.5g	3.4g	5.7g	1.8g	2.8g	3.4g	0.4g	10.4g	6.6g	6.2g
WILD TAXA: UNCARBONISED													
Prunus spinosa L.	–	–	–	–	–	–	–	–	–	–	–	–	–
Carex spp.	–	–	–	–	–	–	–	–	–	–	–	–	–
Total wild taxa seed counts	–	–	–	–	–	–	–	–	–	–	–	–	–
OTHER PLANT REMAINS: CARBONISED													
Charcoal	3.6g	0.1g	0.6g	–	0.7g	–	5.6g	3g	7.2g	–	6.6g	0.7g	–
Nutshell	0.1g	0.5g	–	–	2g	0.3g	0.2g	0.3g	0.1g	–	–	–	0.1g
OTHER ECOFACTS: UNCARBONISED													
Nutshell	–	–	–	–	–	–	–	–	–	–	–	–	0.1g
Mammal bone	0.7g	0.5g	–	–	–	0.2g	–	0.4g	–	0.1g	–	0.2g	–
Mollusca	–	–	0.7g	–	–	–	–	–	–	–	–	–	–
Insect remains	–	–	–	–	–	–	–	–	–	–	–	–	–

Table 6.12 Composition of archaeobotanical remains from Boyle Abbey, Co. Roscommon *continued*

	No Date			
	Burial: other	Charcoal-rich layer		Total
	F421	–	–	
	F420	F90	F90	
	13	6	6	
	0.4g	8.3g	0.1g	
Latin name				
WILD TAXA: CARBONISED				
Ranunculus sp.	–	–	–	1
Chenopodium sp.	–	–	–	4
Fallopia colvolvulus (L.) Á Löve	–	–	–	–
Polygonum sp.	–	1	–	5
Rumex cf acetosella L.	–	–	–	1
Rumex sp.	–	–	–	4
Aethusa cynapium L.	–	–	–	1
Spergula arvensis L.	–	–	–	39
Prunus spinosa L.	–	–	–	3
Galium cf aparine L.	–	–	–	4
Lapsana communis L.	–	–	–	1
Lamium sp.	–	–	–	1
Raphanus raphanistrum L.	–	–	–	10
Carex sp.	–	–	–	8
Seed indet.	–	–	–	6
Total seed/fruit counts	–	–	–	88
WILD TAXA: UNCARBONISED				
Prunus spinosa L.	–	–	–	1
Carex spp.	–	–	–	9
Total wild taxa seed counts	–	–	–	10
OTHER PLANT REMAINS: CARBONISED				
Charcoal	–	–	–	33.3g
Nutshell	–	–	–	4.2g
OTHER ECOFACTS: UNCARBONIZED				
Nutshell	–	–	–	1.1g
Mammal bone	0.1g	0.1g	–	2.8g
Mollusca	–	–	–	0.7g
Insect remains	–	–	–	–

predominantly hulled barley (*H. vulgare*) made up 10% of the identified plant remains, while wheat (*Triticum sp.*), identified as the bread/club variety (*T. aestivo-compactum*), accounted for 5%. Less than 1% of the grain was identified as rye (*Secale cereale*) (Pl. 6.145).

- Cereal chaff
  Cereal chaff in the form of culm nodes was recovered from medieval drain F63 and medieval ditch F604 and deposits F68, F84 and F429 (Pl. 6.146). Chaff is classified as the remains of cultivated cereals left behind after threshing and crop processing. Cereal chaff by its very nature is light and papery so fragments and separates quite easily as a result of threshing and can disintegrate during the carbonisation process. It is difficult to quantify chaff fragments as the exact intact elements are unknown and represent a multitude of cereal remains fragments.

- Legumes/Flax
  The pulse crop/legume assemblage made up 3% of the overall plant remains recorded from Boyle Abbey. While most of the material identified was made up of indeterminate vetch/pea (*Vicia/Lathyrus spp.*) seeds, evidence for field pea (*Pisum sativum*) was also present (Pl. 6.147). These legumes are made up of a variety of species and can be difficult to differentiate if the hilum is absent. Since vetch seeds are much smaller than pea or bean seeds, this feature is easily burnt away during the carbonisation process. This material was recorded in low incidences from ditches F222 and F604, drains F59 and F63 and deposit F84. The highest frequency of legume seeds was recovered from deposit F68. Flax (*Linum usitatissimum*) made up just less than 1% of the plant assemblage. The plant survives in seed form and was identified from deposit F68.

- Wild taxa
  A notable number of weed seeds (5%) was recorded in relatively low frequencies from drains F63 and F59 and deposit F84. The highest incidence of seeds was recovered from deposit F68. Species common to cultivated ground and areas of disturbance were identified – goosefoot (*Chenopodium sp.*), knotgrass (*Polygonum sp.*), black bindweed (*Fallopia convolvulus*) dock (*Rumex sp.*), sheep's sorrel (*Rumex acetosella*), corn spurrey (*Spergula arvensis*), fool's parsley (*Aethusa cynapium*), cleavers (*Galium aparine*), charlock/wild radish (*Raphanus raphanistrum*) and nipplewort (*Lapsana communis*). Woodland species indicators, such as blackthorn (Prunus spinosa), were also present along with

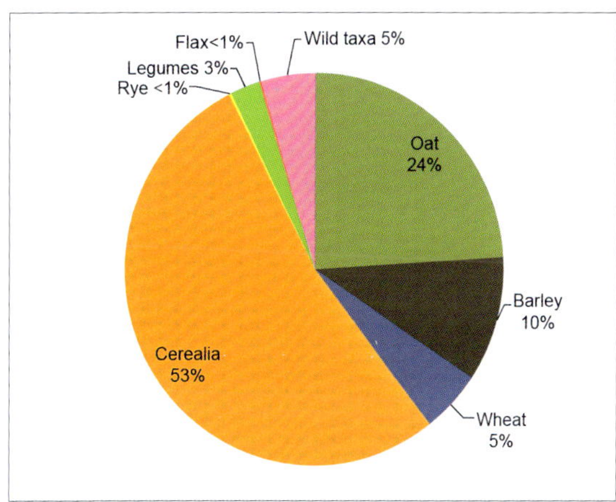

Fig. 6.51. Percentage of carbonised plant remains from Boyle Abbey.

Pl. 6.145. Carbonised cereal grains recovered from Boyle Abbey. (Photo: S. Lyons)

Pl. 6.146. Carbonised cereal chaff (culm nodes). (Photo: S. Lyons)

Pl. 6.147. Carbonised field pea (*Pisum sativum*) seeds. (Photo: S. Lyons)

buttercup (*Ranunculus sp.*), reflecting more open meadows/grassland and sedges (*Carex sp.*) indicative of a range of habitats, such as heaths, wet meadows and marshy areas.

- Nutshell
  Fragments of carbonised nutshell, identified as hazelnut shell were recorded in relatively low concentrations (<1 gram) from posthole F277, ditch F222, drains F63 and F59, pits F911 and F915 and deposits F68, F84, F139, F709 and F908.

OTHER ENVIRONMENTAL REMAINS

- Uncarbonised nutshell remains
  Fragments of uncharred hazelnut shell were identified from drain F63 and ditch F222.

- Insect remains
  Indeterminate insect remains were noted from drain F63 and ditch F222. It is difficult to ascertain if this material is archaeological or modern.

- Mollusca
  A low incidence of terrestrial shells was noted from deposit F429. It was not within the scope of this analysis to identify this material.

- Small mammal bone
  Unburnt bone from what was gleaned to be small mammal species was removed from stone annex F25, posthole F277, ditch F604, charcoal-rich layer F90 and deposits F68, F139, F709 and F908.

DISCUSSION

The samples analysed from the archaeological excavations at Boyle Abbey represent features and deposits associated primarily with occupational activities dating from the medieval period through to the post-medieval period. The archaeobotanical remains identified reflect domestic waste (cereals, legumes and flax) and gathered foodstuffs as well as flora from the various habitats that were growing in and around the site. A variety of plant species recorded also has a history of anthropogenic use and may have been growing in a more controlled environment, such as in gardens or orchards at the site. These plant remains provide information about the local arable economy, crop processing techniques and the diet of the people who resided there as well as offering an insight into what the local environment may have looked like.

MEDIEVAL ARABLE AGRICULTURE AND SITE ECONOMY

Cistercian monasteries required a good supply of arable lands to produce two staples of the monastic diet: bread and ale (Lynch 2010, 78). Several grades of bread were produced by the Cistercians; the highest quality, made of wheaten flour, was consumed by the abbot and his guests, a brown variety was eaten as a staple of the monks themselves, while a coarser variety made of oatmeal, rye or barley flour was given to the lay brothers and labourers (*ibid.*). Ale production preferably required malting barley, although oat and wheat were also used as an admixture (*ibid.*, 83). It is difficult to ascertain, however, if cereals were being dried for brewing activities at Boyle Abbey since there were no obvious signs of grain sprouting from the assemblage. Sprouting grain can be indicative of germination, which were recorded in ones and twos, are most likely residual and so their exact context, nature and chronology are difficult to ascertain. Oat and barley, which were recorded in lesser quantities from the site, are both crops which can grow well in the humid, wet Irish climate and will tolerate poorer soils. This allows them to thrive in areas less suited to the cultivation of other crops, such as wheat. They produce dark, coarse bread and are often combined with wheat and rye to form a maslin mix. Both crops were also used as animal fodder during the medieval period; however, their suitability in brewing beer and ale increased their crop status during this period (Kelly 1998). Based on the graded breads consumed by the Cistercian order, this preponderance of oat and barley from Boyle Abbey could represent the daily staple bread consumed by the monks, lay brothers and labourers at the abbey. This could therefore be evidence of a working site, where active agriculture and grange maintenance was being carried out.

The low wheat values recorded is interesting in the context of the site as wheat represents potentially high-status occupation and was the prominent crop recorded from the Cistercian occupation at Bective Abbey. During the early historic period, wheat was seen as a luxury crop associated with supreme kings and bishops (Kelly 1998) and continued to be a crop favoured by the Anglo-Norman population in the later medieval period. Wheat cultivation was very labour intensive and not as economically viable as oat or barley (McClatchie 2003, 398), which could account for its absence from the site at Boyle. The cultivation of wheat sees an increase in the twelfth and thirteenth centuries, with the arrival of the Anglo-Normans (Monk 1986, 34). Wheat flour was of superior quality and was used to produce luxury bread, which was lighter than the coarser darker breads of oat and barley. Monastic/penitential bread was a common staple as the Benedictine rule of the Cistercians and Augustinian orders required coarse flat bread to be consumed. This was made from an inferior flour of barley, oats and pulses baked on ashes or made into dried biscuits. Only the finest wheat flour was permitted on Sundays and in the making of the wafer-thin sacramental host, which could also explain why wheat was under-represented at Boyle Abbey.

Values for rye are low from the majority of

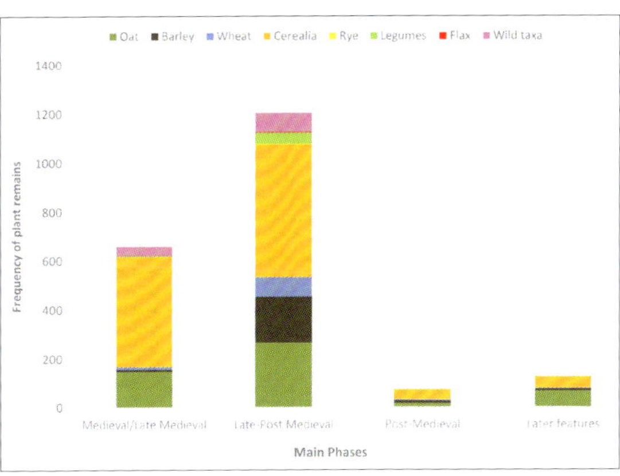

Fig. 6.52. Distribution of plant macrofossil remains from main phases of excavation at Boyle Abbey.

a process used in malting and brewing practices (Van der Veen 1989, 304).

Wheat was a commonly cultivated crop of the Cistercian congregation as a whole. Evidence from thirteenth-century account records for the monastery at Bonnefont in southern France, for example, mentions that wheat was widely cultivated along with rye (Berman 1986, 76). The thirteenth- and fourteenth-century account rolls for Beaulieu Abbey, Hampshire in England also details wheat, oat and barley as among its favourable crops (Hockey 1975, 26). In Ireland, lists of grain supplies were documented in the dissolution extents of the sixteenth century, giving valuable information about the type of grain each abbey was producing (Lynch 2010, 92). Oats and wheat were popular crop types recorded from Irish Cistercian houses at Baltinglass, Co. Wicklow, Duiske, Co. Kilkenny and St Mary's, Dublin. Wheat and oats take priority over barley at Kells Priory in the thirteenth century and there is an early reference to using peas at the site, suggesting a shift to using a system of crop rotation perhaps (*ibid*.). This emphasis on wheat and oat from Kells is also reflected from the archaeobotanical evidence from thirteenth-century occupation at Bective Abbey (Lyons 2016).

In contrast, oats followed by barley were the main crops recorded from all phases recorded at Boyle Abbey, with values for barley, oat and wheat rising in frequency during the later post-medieval phase of the site (Fig. 6.52). Rye grains were recorded in very low numbers and found in medieval, late medieval and post-medieval layers at the site. While this is evidence that rye was being dried and therefore cultivated at the site, the grains,

Irish medieval sites (McCormick *et al.* 2011), so not unusual in the context of Boyle Abbey. Rye cultivation is absent from many of the thirteenth- and fourteenth-century manorial records and any documentary evidence relates only to smaller holdings. During the fifteenth century rye, along with other grains, was being extensively cultivated as part of an export trade to England, Scotland and Wales. While rye would have been consumed in mixed grain-based produce, such as bread, it has been surmised that it was reserved for thatching. This would therefore help explain its absence in the archaeological record within food processing debris. Its presence at Boyle Abbey could also represent a low level of contamination within a different crop, where it may have been growing as a weed. Other explanations for its occurrence on site could be that it was growing on marginal areas, where it would be out competed by other cereals (particularly on saline or acidic soils).

Ecological factors must also have proved significant in crop cultivation from different areas of the country. Wheat favours dry conditions and mineral-rich soils and may have been rarely grown in damper climates. Interestingly, wheat dominates on medieval sites in mixed crop assemblages in eastern rather than western areas (McCormick *et al.* 2011), which could explain its absence from the Boyle Abbey crop assemblage. In contrast, barley and oat are more versatile crops and can be cultivated on most soils. This, together with the fact that barley and oat were used as both human and animal food, undoubtedly accounts for their higher frequency from many sites, as revealed by a national study of archaeobotanical remains conducted through the Early Medieval Archaeology Project (McCormick *et al.* 2011, 50). Interestingly, a similar composition of cereal grains was recorded from medieval, late medieval and post-medieval deposits at Tulsk Fort, Co. Roscommon, located approximately 30km south of Boyle Abbey. Oat and barley also dominated this assemblage, while wheat was under-represented, perhaps indicating that environmental rather than cultural factors may have played a part in arable agricultural practices in this region. It must also be recognised, however, that wheat and rye were more often sown in the winter, while barley and oat were sown in the spring (Lynch 2010, 75). This may also account for the low incidence of wheat and rye in the assemblage, indicating that seasonal crop harvests were being used or stored on site.

LATER MEDIEVAL/POST-MEDIEVAL

Oats remain relatively higher during the post-medieval phases and later, while barley and wheat decline, relative to the number of samples analysed. The high value for oat is not unusual in this context as archaeobotanical evidence is revealing that it was the most commonly grown crop type during the late medieval and post-medieval period, particularly outside the environs of the eastern Pale regions. The pulse crop/legume assemblage recorded at the site is largely from the late medieval to post-medieval phase, albeit low, and indicates that these species were likely to have been part of the local arable economy. Their emergence in later medieval Ireland coincided with the arrival of the Anglo-Normans, probably as part of their crop rotation agriculture (Monk 1986, 34). These plants have the ability to increase soil quality, through nitrogen-fixing, which improves crop yields, suppresses weed growth and prevents soil erosion. They are documented as being used primarily for animal fodder and as a foodstuff in times of famine or a bad harvest in later medieval Ireland. A recent archaeological project on pulse crops in medieval and post-medieval Ireland has revealed that these cultivated plants are largely absent in western areas (Lyons and McClatchie 2012). To date, the only known evidence for bean/pea has been recorded from late medieval deposits at Mackney, Co. Galway (*ibid.*). These plant remains are more often associated with enclosed sites or those of high status (*ibid.*), most likely growing in gardens or as mixed crops with other cereal crops. As well as cultivated legumes (field pea) 'wild' legumes are found at many medieval sites in Ireland, particularly vetches (Vicia spp.). While there is no documentary evidence for the cultivation of vetches during this period, there are extensive historical sources for their cultivation in medieval England, principally as fodder and also as famine food (Campbell 2000, 228–30). It has been argued that by the fourteenth century, the scale and distribution of vetch cultivation on some English demesnes signal their status as a significant field crop (Campbell 1988, 196). This also corresponds with the earliest accounts of vetches being used on a large scale to feed draught animals. Similar mixed pea and vetch assemblages have also been recorded from later medieval deposits at Carrickmines Castle, Co. Dublin and at Bective, Co. Meath (Lyons 2016, 179–99). Wheat occurs frequently on Irish archaeological sites where legumes are also present, which is interesting because wheat is a rather demanding crop that requires good quality nitrogenous soils (Lyons and McClatchie 2012). The higher frequency of wheat and legumes from the late medieval to post-medieval phase at Boyle could therefore signal that such a technique was being implemented into the arable system at the site.

The presence of flax in seed form from Boyle Abbey was very low and found only in a late medieval deposit (F68). The presence of flax from medieval and later sites adds to the diversity of crops cultivated in Ireland during this time. The cultivation of flax, obtained from the stalks by retting, would have enabled the production of linen, provided animal fodder from the leaves and oil from the crushed seeds, which had uses in cooking and lighting. Linseed was eaten with grains and pulses in breads and stews as archaeological evidence from Viking Birka can attest. Evidence for flax, together with other food plant remains, was recorded from eleventh-century cess deposits at Fishamble Street, Dublin, a thirteenth-century cesspit from John Dillon Street, Dublin, Waterford and South Main Street, Cork. While it was also identified from other thirteenth- and fourteenth-century sites in Dublin, Cork and Wexford (Bourke 1995, 35), its status as a foodstuff during this period still remains elusive, primarily because documentary evidence for flax cultivation in the medieval period is rare. Later medieval sources from England suggest that it grew as a garden crop, indicating small-scale cultivation on individual holdings and in gardens. Flax would have grown well and produced higher yields on smaller plots, where nutrient-rich loamy soils from organic debris were common.

DISTRIBUTION OF ARCHAEOBOTANICAL REMAINS

While charred plant macrofossil remains were identified from a range of contexts and features at Boyle Abbey (Fig. 6.53), it has been established,

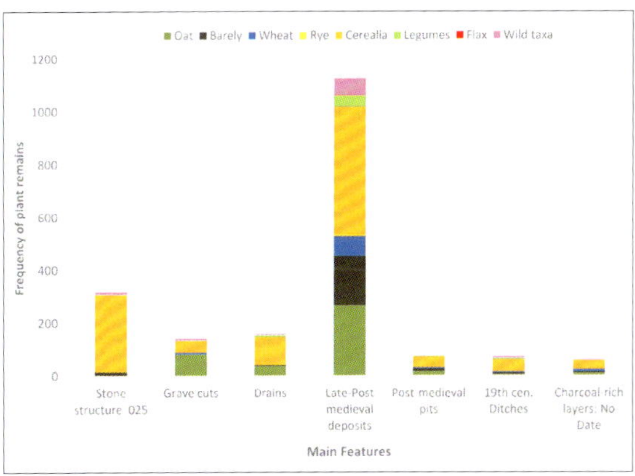

Fig. 6.53. Distribution of plant macrofossil remains from main features at Boyle Abbey.

based on the high number of abraded cereal grains, that these remains were dumped or redeposited residues from numerous kilning events that occurred over the lifetime of occupation at the site. While no corn-drying kiln was identified from this phase of excavation, the presence of a keyhole kiln (F12) recorded from excavations at the abbey between 1982 and 1984 (see Ann Lynch above) is evidence that crop drying was being practised at the site. This feature is provisionally dated to the sixteenth century; however, since no soil samples were taken from the kiln, there are no comparative archaeobotanical data to help with this discussion. These indeterminate grains would have experienced prolonged erosion if they were constantly reworked across the site over time, most probably in clays that were used as levelling or infilling deposits as the abbey expanded and contracted over time. While a notable frequency of cereal grains was recorded from the stone annex F25 (F26, F33 and F609), the remains were poorly preserved and suggests they were redeposited from another source. Similarly, contemporary drains F59 (F613) and F63 (F104) and burials F250 (F251) and F533 (F532) are also likely to contain reworked cereal debris from a number of unknown sources. The highest frequency of plant remains (>1000 individual grains and seeds) was undoubtedly recovered from a number of late medieval to post-medieval deposits (F34, F68, F84, F139, F429, F708 and F908). Oat, wheat, barley, rye, legumes, flax and wild taxon were all well represented here and this implies that there may have been a shift in arable agricultural practices at the site during this late medieval to post-medieval phase of occupation. This high volume of grain, coupled with the only corn-drying kiln excavated dating to this phase (Lynch 2012), strongly suggests an increase in crop processing, in the form of grain drying at the site. Perhaps this activity was now being carried out directly by the occupants at Boyle, particularly as this is the phase that had the best evidence for cereal chaff and cereal processing waste. The decline in the volume of cereal remains from post-medieval and later periods probably reflects the absence of any primary arable activities, such as crop processing and drying, at Boyle during the time after the dissolution of the abbey in the sixteenth century and its later modification into a military garrison (Stalley 1987).

SUMMARY

The archaeobotanical analysis from Boyle Abbey has revealed evidence for arable farming during the medieval to the post-medieval period. Whether the crops were being dried or stored directly at the site or not was difficult to establish from this suite of evidence as no primary features associated with a corn-drying kiln or granary were identified. A kiln recorded during the 1982–4 excavations by Ann Lynch (see Chapter 4), however, does provide archaeological evidence that crop drying was being undertaken at the site certainly during the sixteenth century. Instead, the distribution of remains from this analysis has revealed that food and crop processing debris was being dumped and redeposited across the site as domestic rubbish. This would account for the high incidence of poorly preserved grains from the samples and the presence of other occupational debris ecofacts, such as nutshell, weed seeds, cereal chaff, animal bone, molluscs and other small finds. Continuous occupation at Boyle Abbey from the late medieval through to the post-medieval period would inevitably have caused deposits and clays to be reworked and redistributed through levelling and infilling deposits, which would cause grain abrasion.

The archaeobotanical assemblage comprised a mix of cereal crops (oat, barley, wheat and rye), cultivated plants (field pea, legumes and flax), wild taxa and fruit and nut remains. The majority of these remains were confined to the late medieval to post-medieval phase of occupation, strongly suggesting that occupants engaged with more arable crop processing during this time. This material provides a snapshot of the range of cultivated and possibly gathered food plants consumed at Boyle Abbey during the late medieval to post-medieval period. While cereal-based foodstuffs were commonly recorded in literary sources, the fruits and nuts identified give some insight into other natural resources exploited to supplement the monastic self-sufficient lifestyle and suggests that they maintained and managed gardens and orchards. Oat and barley dominated the cereal component, while wheat and rye were relatively under-represented. It has been surmised that both environmental and cultural factors may have played a part in this composition. Oat and barley were more versatile and grew in poor soils, which would be consistent with arable growing in the west of Ireland. The daily bread of Cistercian monks, lay brothers and labourers was also made of oatmeal, legumes and barley, while wheat was reserved for high quality bread making in producing the communal host and for visiting dignitaries. The decline in cereal remains is apparent from the post-medieval period and later, most probably as a result of the abbey being dissolved and its re-occupation as a military garrison in the sixteenth and seventeenth centuries.

HUMAN REMAINS: SUMMARY OF OSTEOARCHAEOLOGICAL FINDINGS FROM EXCAVATIONS 2006–12, BOYLE ABBEY

Dr Linda G. Lynch

INTRODUCTION

The skeletal remains of 222 individuals, including an apparent in utero infant, were recovered during the 2006–12 archaeological investigations at Boyle Abbey. This represents a relatively good sample size in terms of osteoarchaeological analysis. The level of preservation of the skeletal remains varied across the site; however, overall, more than half of individuals were classed as 'poor' or 'very poor' in terms of preservation. This, along with a range of other inherent biases, obviously complicates the interpretation of the extant skeletal evidence. Nevertheless, the osteoarchaeological analysis has greatly added to knowledge of the period. This section represents an executive summary of the main findings of that analysis and is not intended as a detailed osteological report (see Lynch 2017).

The assemblage of burials, almost exclusively medieval in date, represents a particular cohort, or group of cohorts, which may be outside the 'norm' of some contemporary cemeteries. Firstly, at least some of the individuals buried here would have been monks and lay brothers attached directly to the abbey itself. Secondly, who was permitted burial within the confines of the abbey would have been controlled and may have tended towards the wealthier individuals in society who, it may be surmised, had better and more consistent access to adequate nutrition, and who may have been less exposed to disease and physical stress than poorer individuals in a community. Crucially, however, there are also a number of individuals whose skeletal remains indicate undoubted significant physically debilitating disease: these burials may be linked more to the role of the monastery as an infirmary. Therefore, perhaps there are also individuals of 'low' status buried here. Interestingly, there are also some indicators of deviant burials at Boyle Abbey.

OSTEOARCHAEOLOGICAL ANALYSIS

Juveniles were, perhaps not surprisingly, relatively uncommon within the sampled burials, representing just over a quarter of individuals (27.5%, 61/222). More particularly, infants (<1 year) accounted for just over one in ten juveniles, and this included just two neonates. Infant mortality would have been high in the past, prior to the advancement of modern medicine, and infants would normally have formed the largest group in a mortality curve. Infants, however, are quite often under-represented in excavated Irish historic cemeteries, for a wide variety of reasons, with one of the most probable being that infants were typically buried elsewhere, not in a cemetery such as Boyle but in a variant of the classic post-medieval cillín.

Almost three out of four individuals excavated were adults (17+ years), representing a total of 72.5% (161/222) of the total. Interesting, given the monastic nature of the site, the sexes were equally represented, with 49% (77/157) female and 51% (80/157) male. This contrasts with evidence from other comparable sites in Ireland where there is typically a prevalence of male burials. In terms of ages-at-death, most individuals were aged between 25 and 45 at the time of death: there was a clear lack of younger and older individuals. However, a nuanced bias could be traced within the latter group as to who the older adults were. Almost one-third of females (30.3%, 17/77) were aged over 45 years at the time of death, compared with just 14.8% (9/80) of males. Given the higher risk to the lives of women through pregnancy and childbirth at the time, this is somewhat unexpected, and suggests a bias towards, perhaps, a matriarchal group.

Pl. 6.148. B340 (male 35–39 years), severe calculus on mandibular teeth. (Photo: L. Lynch)

In terms of dental diseases and conditions, there were some expected results, as well as some evidence of subtle differences. Overall, the dentitions, and the evidence of diet, were as would be expected in an Irish medieval population. Calculus (calcified plaque, reflective of both diet and oral hygiene) deposits were very common (94.2% of teeth and 99.1% of individuals), and the deposits were often significant (Pl. 6.148). There was no variation between females and males. Carious lesions (dental decay) were identified in 5.7% of teeth and 39.6% of adult individuals, with females more typically affected, and the prevalence rates are broadly typical of an Irish population prior to the adoption of refined carbohydrates and sugars. Ante-mortem tooth loss, which may be linked with both calculus and caries, was significantly more prevalent in females and was of greater severity. This may have somewhat masked the true prevalence of caries. Higher prevalence rates of caries in females is a common finding in many archaeological populations, typically due to physiological variations, but cultural and social issues may also be important. However, it may also suggest that diet, perhaps unsurprisingly, varied by gender. It may be argued that, with the surely monastic nature of some of the

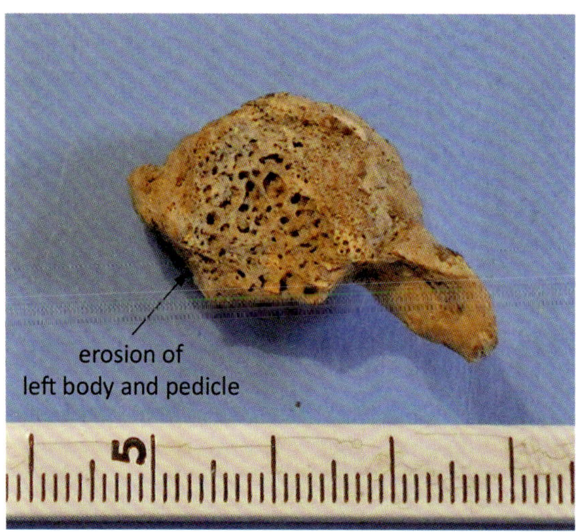

Pl. 6.149. B318 (possible female 13–15 years), superior view of unidentified thoracic body, anterior to top, note smooth trabecular exposure and complete erosion of left pedicle, bacterial or fungal infectious disease. (Photo: L. Lynch)

burials, at least some men would have had access to a wider, more varied, and perhaps richer diet. This is not borne out in the dental evidence (or indeed in the skeletal evidence, see below). Dental abscesses, indicative of infection which may have been fatal, were present in 28% of all adults, while periodontal disease (gum disease) was very common (77.6%). In terms of general health, the medieval adults buried in Boyle Abbey were shorter (average 156.5cm for females, n 50, and 167.9cm for males, n 62) than many of the contemporary averages. While there are many factors that could account for this, it may be linked to poor nutrition in childhood. A number of juvenile remains suggested that they too were skeletally small for their age-at-death. However, rather than clear indicators of stresses in childhood, the shortened statures may be evidence of adaptation and survival.

Other evidence of childhood stresses, such as dental enamel hypoplastic defects, were somewhat more illustrative. These defects were found in just over one-fifth of adults (21.6%, 24/111), which is not particularly high, and there was little difference between females and males. However, the analysis indicates that males endured stresses earlier in childhood than females, suggesting gender-based differences in childrearing. For example, perhaps male children were weaned earlier than female children. Interestingly, males also exhibited higher prevalences of dental crowding, rotation, and/or developmental deformities in the teeth. It is possible that childhood stresses account for some of the relatively diminutive statures in the Boyle Abbey adults but, while there are indications of differences in childhood stress between the sexes, in timing if not in prevalence, there is no indication of considerable and widespread general stress as manifested by enamel hypoplastic defects.

The other classic indicators of physiological stress are in specific porous lesions, porotic hyperostosis and cribra orbitalia, which manifest in the cranium. Almost a quarter (24.3%) of all observable adults had evidence of the former condition, while nearly a fifth (18.7%) of observable adults had the latter condition. When compared with contemporary examples, the prevalence rates were within the norm for the time. There were higher prevalence rates of porotic hyperostosis in adult males than in females, although cribra orbitalia was marginally lower in males. Overall, the bias may be linked both to the dental evidence of variation in stress in childhood between the sexes and the higher numbers of older females. These metabolic conditions were more common in younger adults and in the older juvenile (7–12 years) group, hinting at illnesses that may have contributed to the demise of cohorts of that particular age. A possible case of vitamin D deficiency (rickets) was also identified in an adult male, while an infant and an adolescent appeared to suffer a vitamin C deficiency (scurvy). Overall, the evidence of these particular metabolic conditions suggested this group were not under significant physiological stress.

Non-specific infection, primarily in the form of periosteal lesions, may also be a good indicator of general health. It was identified in 7.5% (12/161) of adults and 14.8% (9/61) of juveniles. The prevalence rate in the adults was broadly expected, given the context of the site in question. Males were more typically affected than females, a trend common in many archaeological populations. The higher prevalence in the juveniles was particularly biased toward younger individuals, including infants, suggesting infections were common in that group: infection is a serious issue with regards to weaning in societies with poor hygiene practices and no access to modern medicine. Interestingly, the lesions were lacking in the older juveniles, despite the fact they exhibited higher prevalence of metabolic disease: this suggests a subtle change in overall cause of death in juveniles within different age groups. In the adolescent group, evidence of serious infections in the form of tuberculosis, and possible other bacterial or fungal infection, was recorded (Pls 6.149, 6.150).

In terms of other pathological lesions, degenerative joint disease (DJD) was very common (76.4%) and had similar prevalence rates in females and males, despite the prevalence of older females. More detailed examinations revealed that DJD was actually more severe in adult males, suggesting significant physical activity and again highlighting variation in life experience by gender, although both females and males may have had a similar exposure to labour in youth. There may be some links with the Cistercian dedication to manual labour, but the evidence is also reflective of the time period in general. There was also some evidence that suggested that females who engaged in significant physical labour at a young age were at a higher risk of mortality.

Evidence of trauma was identified in 17.4% of adults and, while there was little difference in overall prevalence rates between females and males, males aged between 25 and 45 years of age were more likely to suffer traumatic injuries. Many of the traumas comprised classic bone fractures, the majority of which had healed, or were healing, at the time of death. Most probably occurred as a result of accidents and/or repeated stresses, and patterns indicate gender-based variation. This latter bias was most demonstrably evident in the skeletal evidence of violent trauma. Peri-mortem sharp-force injuries were identified in 5% of adults, with the overwhelming majority being male. A female adult had suffered a single weapon injury, while seven males had sharp-force traumas, with most exhibiting multiple injuries (Pl. 6.151). The injuries are indicative of violent death and/or assaults on the dead. Swords may have been the primary weapon in most instances. However, axes and knives were probably also used and there was evidence of a penetrating injury from a square-profiled point, possibly an arrowhead or a spike from a poleaxe. Decapitations or attempted decapitations were identified, as well as one example of possible evisceration or disembowelling.

It is apparent that a number of individuals buried at Boyle Abbey had serious physical problems,

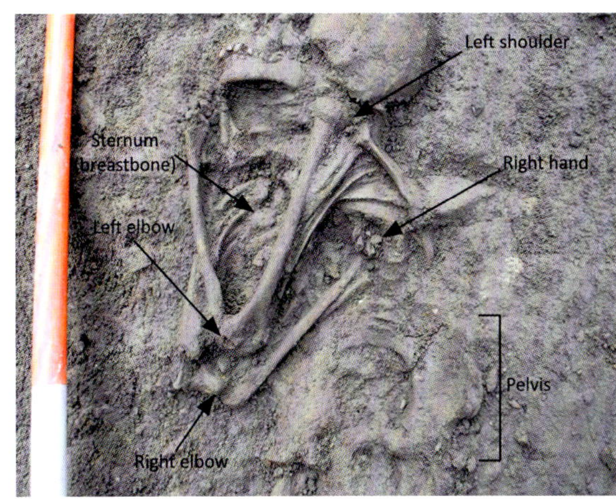

Pl. 6.150. B318 (possible female 13–15 years), *in situ*, detail. (Photo: A. Quinn)

Pl. 6.151. B712 (male 17–20 years), C1 and base of cranium, right black arrow indicates first weapon injury, left black arrow indicates second injury, botched decapitation. (Photo: L. Lynch)

which would potentially have had negative consequences in terms of quality of life. The monastic foundation at Boyle was obliged, by its very nature, to care for the poor, old, sick, and dying, and there may be evidence of the burial of victims of some of the more extreme debilitating conditions. Spinal fusion was observed in a number of female and male adults: three females may have suffered from ankylosing spondylitis, one male had spinal fusion related to degeneration, while a female and a male had fusion possibly associated with a fracture. Spinal fusion can result in other physiological problems, particularly if there is associated kyphosis and/or scoliosis (bending of the spine). Some of these may have required care as provided by the abbey. Interestingly, three males exhibited lesions which were indicative of diffuse idiopathic skeletal hyperostosis. This disease is noteworthy as, in historical contexts, it is often associated specifically with males within monastic foundations, who would have had a high

Pl. 6.152. B313 (female 40–44 years), right ilium with lytic erosions, possible metastatic carcinoma. (Photo: L. Lynch)

Pl. 6.153. B313 (female 40–44 years), superior margin of sixth right rib, with ovoid lytic erosions and destruction of trabecular bone, possible metastatic carcinoma. (Photo: L. Lynch)

calorific intake. However, the prevalence at Boyle was not particularly high. Interestingly though, all three men were aged over 40, had extensive evidence of DJD, and two were buried in very similar positions, all suggesting that they may have had something in common, that is, they may have been monks. Other individuals who may have been cared for within the abbey include those with diseases such as the possible erosive arthropathies (joint diseases), which could have had serious impacts on the life of a person at a time when physical labour was so essential. In addition, one old female had a fracture to the lower end of the right tibia (shin) bone. Suffering a presumed associated possible infection, she died probably less than a month later. Another elderly female died within weeks of a pelvic fracture, possibly as a result of complications.

The skeleton of an adolescent female (Pls 6.149, 6.150) exhibited the clearest evidence of just how traumatic life could be without modern medical care. This juvenile had suffered severe destruction of the lower spine, which had essentially dissolved, and resulted in complete collapse of the torso. Although having some traits of tuberculosis, the lesions do not conform to the classic signs. The disease may be another bacterial infection, or it may relate to a fungal infection. The impact on the life of this individual could have been nothing less that catastrophic, with spinal collapse, torso compression, and apparent paralysis. Despite this, the girl clearly survived a considerable time, which allowed the skeletal lesions to manifest to such a degree. Another adolescent female also exhibited evidence of debilitating tuberculosis. A female adult exhibited lesions suggestive of metastatic carcinoma (Pls 6.152, 6.153), which, when she was alive, would have had a profound impact on her lifestyle.

Finally, there are a number of noteworthy points to be made on the modes of burial. The majority were traditional Christian individual supine extended burials, orientated with the head to the west. But there were variations. One young juvenile was buried with the head to the east, a position traditionally associated with clerics but certainly not exclusively so. In this case, this juvenile with active lesions of a systemic infection, appears to represent a possible clandestine burial within the abbey in the post-medieval period. Two double burials were recorded. One was a female with an infant aged 6–12 months lying on her right arm. These individuals may or may not have been related. A full-term infant was also found in the abdominal area of another female. The infant's head was orientated toward the pelvic cavity of the female suggesting their deaths occurred during childbirth: the infant was larger than average in size.

A number of unusual positionings of bodies during burial were also noted. The aforementioned female with the infant on her arm, was buried slightly on her left side with her left leg tightly flexed. The reason is unknown. The skeleton of another female suggested that she had been rather carelessly cast into the grave. Her skeleton exhibited some unusual pathological lesions, suggestive both of possible violence and a repeated occupational activity. Perhaps she simply had no relatives to oversee her burial, but she was still deemed worthy of interment here. A male adult was similarly,

Table 6.13 Results of C14 dating

Beta	Technique	Submitter Number	Calendar Calibration (95.4% Probability)
478908	E2399:B283 Left Humerus	520 +/- 30 BP	95.4% probability (84.9%) 1392–1443 cal AD (558–507 cal BP). (10.5%) 1324–1345 cal AD (626–605 cal BP)
478907	E2399:B207 Left Fibula Fragment	330 +/- 30 BP	95.4% probability (95.4%) 1477–1642 cal AD (473–308 cal BP)
478906	E2399:B274 Left Femur Fragment	890 +/- 30 BP	95.4% probability (59.5%) 1116–1218 cal AD (834–732 cal BP). (35.9%) 1040–1108 cal AD (910–842 cal BP)
478905	E2399:B703 Left Fibula Fragment	350 +/- 30 BP	95.4% probability (54.1%) 1538–1635 cal AD (412–315 cal BP). (41.3%) 1458–1530 cal AD (492–420 cal BP)

though nowhere near as dramatically, carelessly placed in the grave. More unusual were two other burials, both of adult males. One appeared to be buried with his right arm flexed at a right angle behind his back. While it should not be taken as a sign the hand was deliberately tied, it does hint at a possible aberration. The other male was more clearly a deviant burial. This young male was buried in a prone position with the head to the east and his right arm bent behind his neck. There were no real skeletal indicators which marked him as 'different', although he did have a defect in the left kneecap which resulted in osteoarthritis, despite his young age. A prone burial is anathema to the entire central Christian concept of resurrection, particularly at a time when there would have been a strong belief in corporeal resurrection. The position indicates fear of the dead (necrophobia) and a need to control them after death, both physically and spiritually. Yet the individual was still buried within the hallowed grounds of Boyle Abbey.

C14 DATING OF BURIALS

Four burials were selected for radiocarbon dating where artefactual evidence was lacking and also in order to achieve a balance both in terms of spatial distribution (east/west and inside/outside church) and sex (female/male). Table 6.13 presents the burials submitted for C14 dating. The higher probability technique has been used and is presented in the table; however, the lesser probability of 68% can also be used depending on further evidence, for example, artefactual, from a site. The Beta Analytic reports are also presented for reference (Table 6.13 and Figs 6.54–7).

CONCLUSIONS

The osteoarchaeological analysis of this large sample of skeletal remains has revealed important data on the lives and deaths of those associated with medieval, and later, Boyle Abbey. This pertains to the monks, who presumably are represented in the assemblage but, of course, cannot be definitively identified, and also to all the other people – men, women, and children – who were allowed to be buried here.

In terms of health, age and sex were factors which had an influence on the nature, severity, and impact of the stress, as was the physical work undertaken, and the diseases endured, and this appears to have been the case from infanthood. Of those who were buried here, men, in general, appear to have endured earlier stress and women lived longer. The older women were quite distinct and may indeed represent an elite and privileged group. In terms of physiological stresses, it was

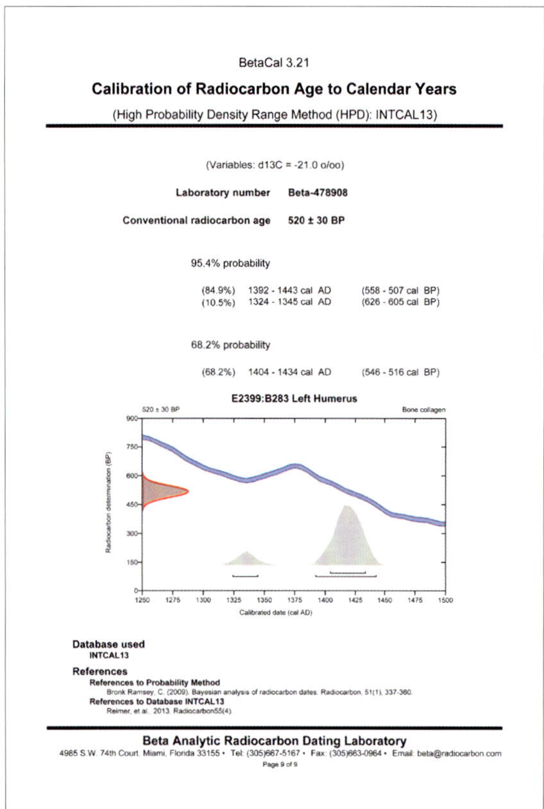

BetaCal 3.21

Calibration of Radiocarbon Age to Calendar Years

(High Probability Density Range Method (HPD): INTCAL13)

(Variables: d13C = -21.0 o/oo)

Laboratory number **Beta-478908**

Conventional radiocarbon age **520 ± 30 BP**

95.4% probability

(84.9%)	1392 - 1443 cal AD	(558 - 507 cal BP)
(10.5%)	1324 - 1345 cal AD	(626 - 605 cal BP)

68.2% probability

(68.2%)	1404 - 1434 cal AD	(546 - 516 cal BP)

Database used
INTCAL13

References
References to Probability Method
Bronk Ramsey, C. (2009). Bayesian analysis of radiocarbon dates. Radiocarbon, 51(1), 337-360.
References to Database INTCAL13
Reimer, et.al., 2013. Radiocarbon55(4).

Beta Analytic Radiocarbon Dating Laboratory
4985 S.W. 74th Court, Miami, Florida 33155 • Tel: (305)667-5167 • Fax: (305)663-0964 • Email: beta@radiocarbon.com
Page 9 of 9

Fig. 6.54. C14 report for B283.

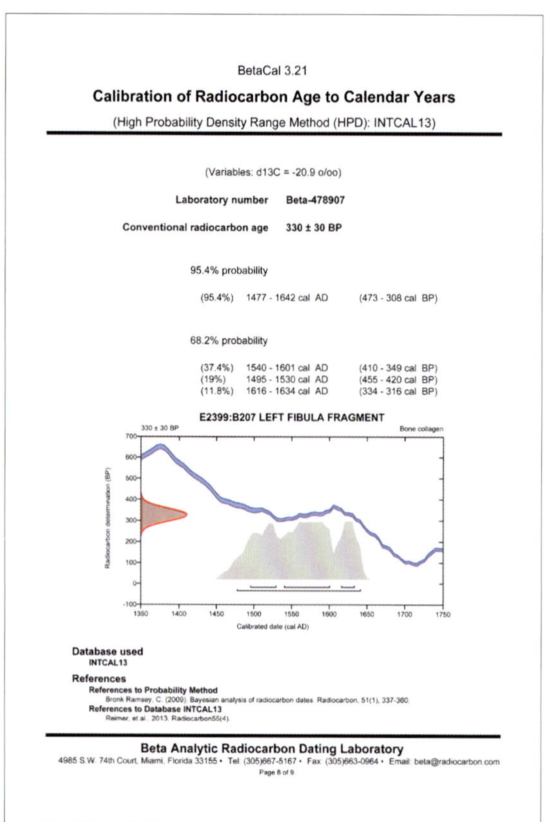

BetaCal 3.21

Calibration of Radiocarbon Age to Calendar Years

(High Probability Density Range Method (HPD): INTCAL13)

(Variables: d13C = -20.9 o/oo)

Laboratory number **Beta-478907**

Conventional radiocarbon age **330 ± 30 BP**

95.4% probability

(95.4%)	1477 - 1642 cal AD	(473 - 308 cal BP)

68.2% probability

(37.4%)	1540 - 1601 cal AD	(410 - 349 cal BP)
(19%)	1495 - 1530 cal AD	(455 - 420 cal BP)
(11.8%)	1616 - 1634 cal AD	(334 - 316 cal BP)

Database used
INTCAL13

References
References to Probability Method
Bronk Ramsey, C. (2009). Bayesian analysis of radiocarbon dates. Radiocarbon, 51(1), 337-360.
References to Database INTCAL13
Reimer, et.al., 2013. Radiocarbon55(4).

Beta Analytic Radiocarbon Dating Laboratory
4985 S.W. 74th Court, Miami, Florida 33155 • Tel: (305)667-5167 • Fax: (305)663-0964 • Email: beta@radiocarbon.com
Page 8 of 9

Fig. 6.55. C14 date for B207.

clear that early exposure may have contributed to an early demise for some individuals. On the whole, however, the indicators of stress are not abnormally high, and are somewhat reflective both of the date and nature of the cemetery.

While it is probable that this sample is biased in nature, as burial here would often have been for the privileged, there are also indications that a number of individuals had suffered from severe, and undoubtedly, debilitating diseases and this may be a reflection of the role of the monastery as an infirmary for the poor and ill. Therefore, perhaps there are indeed individuals of 'low' status buried here also.

Interestingly, there are some indicators of deviant burials at Boyle Abbey, most vividly in the form of a prone burial. It may represent some clandestine use of this prestigious site.

GENERAL DISCUSSION

Annette Quinn

The excavations undertaken in Boyle Abbey between 2006 and 2012 focused on the entire north aisle, outside the hitherto buried remains of the north wall, and also a portion of the nave centred on the north arcade. The excavation provided an opportunity to examine the building foundations in this location as well as the burials both inside and outside the church. Evidence of later activity was also recorded on the site, spanning some 200 years through to the eighteenth century, during which time Boyle was under military occupation (Stalley 1987; Kalkreuter 2001). The Commissioner of Public Works subsequently took over the abbey in the late nineteenth century. The material culture from medieval contexts was scarce with few finds from grave fills. What was abundantly clear, however, was the level of disturbance that had taken place within the abbey as a whole, evident from the numerous medieval finds, disarticulated human bone, as well as copious amounts of animal bone, in later contexts up to the twentieth century. Much of the material culture retrieved from the excavations was recovered from secondary contexts, which was not unusual given the post-dissolution activity on the site. The north side of the abbey appears to have been used as a dumping ground in later years, evident

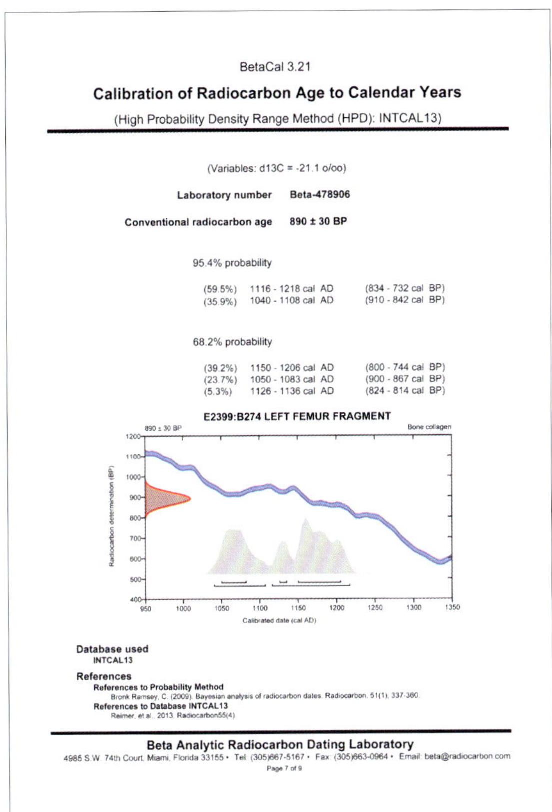

BetaCal 3.21

Calibration of Radiocarbon Age to Calendar Years

(High Probability Density Range Method (HPD): INTCAL13)

(Variables: d13C = -21.1 o/oo)

Laboratory number **Beta-478906**

Conventional radiocarbon age **890 ± 30 BP**

95.4% probability

(59.5%) 1116 - 1218 cal AD (834 - 732 cal BP)
(35.9%) 1040 - 1108 cal AD (910 - 842 cal BP)

68.2% probability

(39.2%) 1150 - 1206 cal AD (800 - 744 cal BP)
(23.7%) 1050 - 1083 cal AD (900 - 867 cal BP)
(5.3%) 1126 - 1136 cal AD (824 - 814 cal BP)

E2399:B274 LEFT FEMUR FRAGMENT

Database used
INTCAL13

References
References to Probability Method
Bronk Ramsey, C. (2009). Bayesian analysis of radiocarbon dates. Radiocarbon, 51(1), 337-360.
References to Database INTCAL13
Reimer, et.al., 2013, Radiocarbon55(4)

Beta Analytic Radiocarbon Dating Laboratory
4985 S.W. 74th Court, Miami, Florida 33155 • Tel: (305)667-5167 • Fax: (305)663-0964 • Email: beta@radiocarbon.com
Page 7 of 9

Fig. 6.56. C14 report for B274.

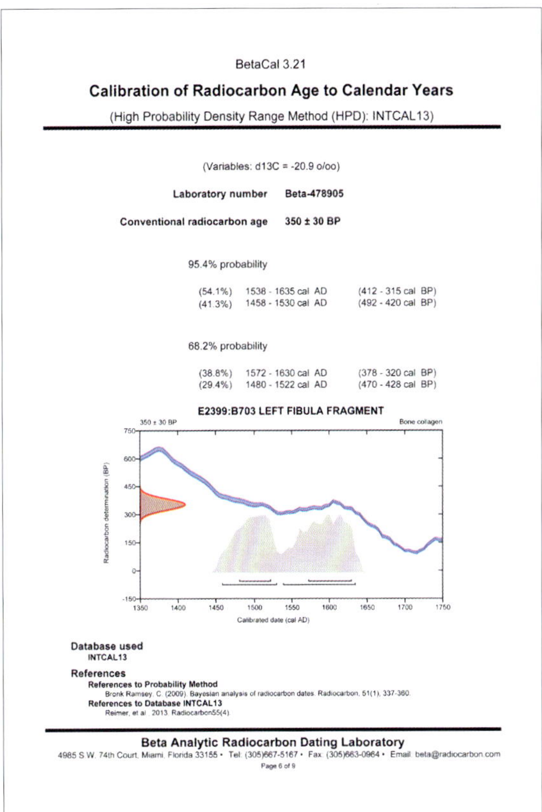

BetaCal 3.21

Calibration of Radiocarbon Age to Calendar Years

(High Probability Density Range Method (HPD): INTCAL13)

(Variables: d13C = -20.9 o/oo)

Laboratory number **Beta-478905**

Conventional radiocarbon age **350 ± 30 BP**

95.4% probability

(54.1%) 1538 - 1635 cal AD (412 - 315 cal BP)
(41.3%) 1458 - 1530 cal AD (492 - 420 cal BP)

68.2% probability

(38.8%) 1572 - 1630 cal AD (378 - 320 cal BP)
(29.4%) 1480 - 1522 cal AD (470 - 428 cal BP)

E2399:B703 LEFT FIBULA FRAGMENT

Database used
INTCAL13

References
References to Probability Method
Bronk Ramsey, C. (2009). Bayesian analysis of radiocarbon dates. Radiocarbon, 51(1), 337-360.
References to Database INTCAL13
Reimer, et.al., 2013, Radiocarbon55(4)

Beta Analytic Radiocarbon Dating Laboratory
4985 S.W. 74th Court, Miami, Florida 33155 • Tel: (305)667-5167 • Fax: (305)663-0964 • Email: beta@radiocarbon.com
Page 6 of 9

Fig. 6.57. C14 report for B703.

from the twentieth-century material in the upper contexts under the topsoil.

THE MONASTIC FOUNDATIONS AND ASSOCIATED STRUCTURES

The monastic foundations consisted of the pier bases, the sub-surface north wall and the west wall. Associated medieval drains as well as a number of postholes were also uncovered. Some other building additions, which are also potentially medieval, are discussed below. Boyle belonged to the Clairvaux filiation of Cistercian abbeys, via its mother house at Mellifont, but it is also set apart by its lengthy building campaign and stylistic architectural variations. The building campaign(s) lasted from approximately AD 1170 until 1220. In terms of a date for the construction of the pier bases, it is widely accepted that the first four along the eastern part of the north arcading were built between 1170 and 1200 (Kalkreuter 2001, 51; see Stalley above) and due to the intervening years of sieges on Boyle Abbey that the remainder of the nave's north arcade would have been completed sometime between 1202 and 1220.

THE PIERS

The excavation revealed that the entire north arcade had been built utilising the same type of foundations despite the architectural variation evident in the piers themselves. The foundations were simple and consisted of stone-filled pits with an upper layer of flat flags, sometimes proud of the cuts. The latter flagstone surfaces formed the footings for the base mouldings themselves. No dating evidence in the form of charcoal or artefactual evidence was recovered from the foundations which may have provided a more accurate construction date. The stones within both the foundation pits and under the base mouldings were shattered and somewhat loosely placed. All of the excavated examples were subject to a fluctuating water table which may have resulted in the constant washing away of any bonding material that was originally used, thus undermining the structural integrity of the piers. The easternmost foundations showed more signs of subsidence than their western counterparts, with the underlying foundation stones being completely shattered and crumbled. It can be concluded, therefore, that the leaning wall at Boyle was undoubtedly the result of the poor foundations which lay beneath the piers, perhaps a consequence of the constant change in water levels. The soft ground may have resulted in the uneven settling of the north arcade foundations and the subsequent leaning of the wall. In 1471 Boyle was flooded at Beltaine (May Day) (see Chapter 2).

THE NORTH WALL

The north wall of the abbey was not visible above ground prior to the excavation. In part, the aim of the project was to locate this wall, in turn allowing for its conservation and partial reconstruction. The full length of the north wall was uncovered. It survived to varying degrees, with the best-preserved elements found towards the centre of the aisle, and with only fragmentary remains towards the west. Evidence for a trench along the alignment of the north wall was recorded during the excavations. Sherds of pottery from its fill (dating from the seventeenth and eighteenth centuries) were recovered providing a date after which the north wall was no longer extant above ground. Beranger's sketch of 1779 (Fig. 1.8) shows the northern side of the abbey with three buttresses but does not depict the north wall. Both the excavated and pictorial evidence would suggest that the wall is likely to have been demolished at some time during the 1700s, prior to 1779. There is also evidence that the north wall may have been built in two phases, the earlier phase apparent as a wider foundation at the east end of the aisle. In the later phase of building, the wall is narrower and was built on top of the wider wall foundations. A slight change in orientation was also noted at foundation level, a variation that may not have been apparent in the upstanding wall. It is possible that these construction phases coincided with the building of the two phases of piers along the north arcade, beginning with the eastern piers and ending with those to the west. It is interesting to note that the variation in the north wall foundation occurs opposite the third 'clustered pier' (Pier 7), the style of which, according to Stalley, may have been abandoned due to its complicated and expensive form (Stalley 1987, 90).

When the earlier buttress (F220, Pier 7) was being built, perhaps at the beginning of the eighteenth century or even earlier, the north wall, or at least its foundations, was extant. This is evident as the buttress (F220) was neatly built against the north wall foundations. It may be suggested, therefore, that the wall was still upstanding at that time.

A number of postholes were uncovered along the outside of the north wall with additional, although fewer, examples within the north aisle. They were uncovered at the base of the excavation area after removing the primary phase of burials in this location. On the outside of the church the postholes were aligned roughly parallel to the north wall and it can be surmised that they were used during the construction of the latter or indeed as part of repairs to same. The postholes comprised small pits, some of which were packed with large angular stones.

The recovery of 114 shards of medieval window glass has revealed evidence for the window types used in the north wall. The stylised or stiff-leaf trefoil patterned glass found in Boyle Abbey, whilst more in keeping with Anglo-Norman religious houses. This differs from other thirteenth-century grisaille glass recovered from Irish, English and Welsh sites due to the absence of cross-hatching and a coloured medallion. The Boyle trefoil spray may pre-date other thirteenth-century Cistercian grisaille found to date (*c.* 1220 onwards) and may be contemporary with the completion of the nave and west end of the church between 1202 and 1220. Their recovery from medieval burial horizons and some grave fills is not too surprising since one would expect glass windows to break and require repair especially given the constant attacks on the abbey in the thirteenth century and after. The windows in the north aisle are likely to have been lancet windows.

THE WEST WALL

Traces of the west wall also survived, particularly on its west side where up to six courses were extant (up to 1.24m in height). The eastern face of the wall was poorly preserved with only a mere foundation surviving at the base of the excavation area. The building methods utilised for this wall were interesting in that it was constructed on top of a flat flagstone surface (similar to a modern raft type foundation). No evidence of a wall foundation trench was recorded.

THE MONASTIC DRAINS

The drains that were excavated remind us of the constant need to drain water away from the abbey, a problem that would appear to have been realised when the church was being constructed. The drain (F63) excavated in the north aisle was also uncovered in the excavations in the cloister. This drain can be seen today in the northern cloister walk under a modern metal cover/grill. The drain excavated in the northern cloister walk in 1984 was likely to have been constructed as an integral part of the abbey. This concurs with the results of the later excavations in the aisle as the same drain was built into the base of the north wall. The drain was flowing in a northerly direction, however, away from the abbey.

The drain was built of upright side stones with capstones forming the cover and it extended through the base of the north wall foundations where it exited the church. The drain was undoubtedly constructed in the medieval period and the material recovered from the fills suggests its continued use into the post-medieval period. The occupation of Boyle Abbey by the military in 1592 saw the continued use of some of the then functioning medieval features such as drains. It is not unusual, therefore, that sixteenth- or early seventeenth-century pottery and clay building material dating to the 1700s were found within its fills. A second box drain (F59) was uncovered within a small annex (F25) built against the north-west corner of the church abutting the west wall (F42). It is likely that this drain is also medieval as the structure built around it is medieval in date, albeit later than the church. A medieval decorated bone knife handle was retrieved from the fill of this drain (E2399:58:3070).

MONASTIC FLOOR

There is evidence for a number of highly compacted clay surfaces within the north aisle, particularly where burials were in low occurrence. Therefore, the original medieval floors consisted of highly compacted clay with inclusions of gravel-like material and pebbles. There is no surviving evidence of medieval floor tiles, or indeed any form of paved floor surface, from either the monastic church or the cloister buildings at Boyle.

THE CEMETERY POPULATION IN BOYLE ABBEY

- Demographics
  In terms of the demographic profile of the excavated human remains in the north aisle and outside the north wall, adults accounted for almost three-quarters of the individuals, with juveniles making up just over a quarter of the sample. Infants appear to be under-represented although it may be the case that certain areas within the abbey were favoured for infant burial. It is suggested by Lynch (Human Remains section above) that infants may have been buried elsewhere. Of those infants and juveniles excavated, it was noted that they were interred close to or abutting the north aisle wall interior, perhaps intentionally. This pattern was not the case outside the north wall, where less care was taken in the placement of the dead. It is suggested by the excavator that the placing of the infant and juvenile remains almost against the wall foundations may have afforded the individuals more protection from disturbance from other grave digging. Larger samples would be required to confirm this, however.

- Sex
  An interesting overall statistic was the ratio of females to males of the excavated sample (49% female to 51% male). In an Irish context, the Boyle Abbey cemetery population appears to be quite unique in terms of comparable numbers of female and male adults. The Annals of Boyle contains numerous references to the funerals of privileged secular figures, and this is an indication of the close contact kept between the lay population and the monks, perhaps reflected in the almost equal distribution of male to female burials within the north aisle. For instance, Devane (see Chapter 2) notes in her history of the site that 'women were also buried in Boyle Abbey in the medieval period', and that in 1253, when the daughter

of the earl of Ulster and wife of Milo Costello died, she was interred in Boyle. The earliest burials outside the church (AD 1116–1218) demonstrate that there did not appear to be any preference of male over female burials in this early phase of monastic activity with equal numbers of each sex.

- Health
In terms of the health of the individuals, degenerative joint disease was the most common pathological lesion in the skeletons, being apparent in just over three-quarters (76.4%) of all adults. Overall, the indicators of stress were not abnormally high, and are somewhat reflective of both the date and nature of the cemetery. While it is probable that this sample is biased in nature, as burial here would often have been for the privileged, there are also indications that a number of individuals had suffered from severe and undoubtedly debilitating diseases and this may reflect the role of the monastery as an infirmary for the poor and ill (see Human Remains section above).

- Trauma and violence
Evidence of trauma is also an important factor to consider in the assessment of populations. It can reveal information on hazards which may have been common in populations, as well as evidence of violence. According to Lynch (above), a total of 17.4% of all adults exhibited some evidence of trauma, which included fractures, sharp-force and piercing injuries, some healed, others not. The nature of the trauma, the specialist notes, comprised classic bone fractures probably as a result of occupational activities, most of which were either healed or healing at the time of death.

In addition to the occupational traumas of the monastic population the skeletal assemblage displayed evidence of actual violence with peri-mortem sharp-force trauma identified in 5% of adults. Victims of such violence may have been denied burial in consecrated ground on the basis that they died without the Last Rites and/or that they may have been strangers to, or indeed enemies of, the community that actually buried them. Some such individuals may have been disposed of clandestinely, while other victims of violence were clearly allowed normal burial. In Boyle Abbey, a single female adult had suffered at least one sharp-force trauma injury, while seven males had suffered violent and brutal deaths. Injuries were as a result of weapons including swords, axes, knives, and also at least one penetrating weapon, with a square-profiled point, such as an arrowhead or a spike in a poleaxe.

The youngest victim of violence was a male (B712) aged just 17–20 years. He appears to have suffered a particularly violent death, possibly during a battle. There is mention of repeated pilgrims dying on their way to Boyle Abbey as, according to Kalkreuter (2001, 24), 'since 1231 the monastery had become a focal point of local pilgrimage and that the monastery may have held relics of some sort'. Devane (see Chapter 2) also notes that there are numerous references to Boyle as a place of pilgrimage throughout the Middle Ages and fatalities among the pilgrims at times show how hazardous a journey it was. Injuries on B274 (male 45+ years) suggest he may have been eviscerated or disembowelled, a practice that would not 'normally' allow the individual to be buried within consecrated ground. A sample of this bone was dated to cal. AD 1116–1218 for the individual. A similar individual buried at Hulton Abbey in England indicated he had been convicted of high treason and had suffered the ultimate punishment of being hung, drawn, and quartered, yet was still buried in an abbey.

A number of individuals buried at Boyle Abbey had serious physical problems, which would potentially have had negative consequences in terms of quality of life. One individual (B318, 13–15 years, possible female) stands out as it demonstrates how difficult life could be without modern medicine. The juvenile had suffered 'severe destruction of the lower spine, which had essentially dissolved, and resulted in complete collapse of the torso' (Lynch, Human Remains section above) and had some traits of tuberculosis. It is possible that the individual was paralysed, at least from the waist down, as a result of the dissolving of the bones of the spine and the subsequent spinal collapse.

- Unusual burial positions in Boyle Abbey
  The majority of individuals were buried in the traditional Christian manner, supine and extended, with the head to the west. A number of exceptions were, however, noted during the excavation. A post-medieval individual (juvenile, B600, 4–6 years) was buried just under the topsoil in the area of the north aisle with the head to the east, but in a supine position. According to Lynch, the individual had active lesions suggestive of systemic infection and it is likely to have been a clandestine burial.

  One adult female (B336) had the remains of an older infant (B334, 6–12 months) lying on her right arm. One male (B9), located at the western side of the aisle, was buried with his right arm bent behind and across his back. Even more unusual in the context of Boyle Abbey was a male (20–25 years old, B297), who was buried in a prone position with his head to the east. His right arm had been bent behind his neck.

CISTERCIAN DIET

The overall number of medieval contexts within the excavation area were few and consisted mainly of grave cuts and fills as well as the structures such as the medieval drains and masonry remains discussed above. The greatest amount of material culture and environmental material was retrieved from secondary and tertiary contexts. The high numbers of medieval finds in post-medieval contexts demonstrates the level of disturbance that took place within the abbey. While the finds and environmental material shed some light on what items were used in the monastery as well as the diet of both the monks and the later military, their retrieval in later contexts is less secure. The vast majority of faunal material and archaeobotanical remains recovered from the medieval levels were not within their primary contexts. The north aisle was a place of burial and not directly associated with domestic activity where one would expect to recover such material. Consequently, the majority of the faunal remains were recovered from post-dissolution and post-medieval contexts as one would expect. Comparative analysis with other sites where the faunal and archaeobotanical material was retrieved from secure, primary domestic contexts providing direct evidence of the monastic diet, for example at Bective Abbey, is problematic.

Animal bones were not found in great abundance in the medieval layers within the church. Small amounts of bone were recovered from surface deposits, mainly burial horizons, grave fills, construction posts, masonry remains, drains and a stone annex building (F25) associated with one of the drains. The medieval faunal sample is reflective of the organised nature of the monks who had designated areas for the disposal of domestic refuse within the abbey precinct. Cattle was by far the favoured meat of the Cistercians accounting for 67% of the identifiable total. Sheep accounted for 20% of the medieval sample and an ageing analysis established from the state of fusion of the long bones indicated that most sheep were killed between two and five years of age which suggests a mixed economy aimed at the production of wool, woolfells and meat.

The recovery of faunal remains from the drains (F63 and F59) and annex (F25) is such that, while the structures themselves are medieval, the fills may not be solely medieval in date. This is particularly the case for the drain fills, which may have functioned up to and beyond the military period. The recovery of rat, mouse and pigmy bones suggests that other items may also have been carried into the drains.

The ages of the animals from these contexts suggest that the monks engaged in a mixed farming economy with older cattle and sheep being kept not just for their meat but also for their secondary products. Both would have provided milk; oxen were probably used for ploughing and sheep would certainly have been kept for wool, the mainstay of the Cistercian economy. It is also interesting to note that the Cistercians in Boyle engaged in a more arable economy evident by the low numbers of pig bones.

The range of fish from Boyle is similar to that recorded from Bective Abbey (Hamilton-Dyer 2016, 170–8), where the bones mostly represented marine species with a lesser reliance on riverine species such as eels and salmon. There is little to suggest that the monks enjoyed a high-status elite diet with a wide range of fish, wild birds and wild fauna. The monks seem to have been virtually reliant on their own produce and only occasionally varied their diet with locally procured wild fauna and wild birds. One would have expected the sea to have been a more important source of food given that these are monastic assemblages dated to a period when the Church imposed very strict regulations on fasting (Murray and McCormick 2005).

The archaeobotanical remains identified reflect domestic waste (cereals, legumes and flax) and gathered foodstuffs, as well as flora from the various habitats that were growing in and around the site. The low wheat values recorded at Boyle Abbey is interesting as wheat represents potentially high-status occupation and appears to be the most common crop recorded from Cistercian sites such as Bective Abbey, Co. Meath. Wheat cultivation, however, was very labour intensive and not as economically viable as oat or barley. There are historical references to the theft of barley from the monks at Boyle and as Devane (see Devane above) notes 'one such concession was a rent of 25 bushels of barley due annually from three cantreds in Connacht as a gift from Ua Conochobair. The justiciary Maurice Fitzgerald was mandated in 1233 to find out if his predecessor, Richard de Burgo, had divested the monks of their rights, and, if this was the case the monks should be paid the rent owed to them ... the inferred inquiry into the theft of the monks' barley did not deter Richard from plundering Boyle Abbey in 1235'.

Ecological factors must also have proved significant in crop cultivation in different areas of the country. According to Lyons (see above) wheat favours dry conditions and mineral-rich soils and may have been rarely grown in damper climates. Interestingly, wheat dominates on medieval sites in mixed crop assemblages in eastern rather than western areas (McCormick *et al.* 2011), which could explain its absence from the Boyle Abbey crop assemblage. It can be concluded therefore that environmental rather than cultural factors may have played a part in the type of arable agricultural practices in both Boyle and the western region. The distribution of plant remains from Boyle Abbey has revealed that food and crop processing debris was being dumped into open features and redeposited across the site as domestic rubbish. This accords with other environmental evidence such as the faunal remains. The bread of Cistercian monks, lay brothers and labourers was also made of oatmeal, legumes and barley, while wheat was reserved for high quality bread making in producing the communion host and for visiting dignitaries. The decline in cereal remains is apparent from the post-medieval period and later, most probably as a result of the abbey being dissolved and its re-occupation as a military garrison in the sixteenth and seventeenth centuries.

MATERIAL CULTURE OF THE CISTERCIANS

The few medieval pottery sherds, only two from the excavations, is perhaps not surprising as the north aisle served as a place of burial. Similarly, only one possible sherd of medieval pottery was recovered from the excavations in the cloister (see Ann Lynch above). The lack of medieval pottery within post-medieval contexts, however, is a little unusual as numerous medieval finds such as knives, stick pins and coins were retrieved from these contexts. The excavations in the cloister also highlighted that the artefactual evidence related mainly to the post-medieval period and similar to the north aisle, all objects were found in redeposited contexts. As the excavator noted, the lack of artefacts relating to the monastic period is disappointing but not surprising given the limited area excavated and the extent of post-dissolution destruction of the cloister area. There is no doubt that artefacts dating to the monastic period existed at Boyle Abbey and this is evident by the numerous metal artefacts found in disturbed contexts. Although the artefacts are not within their original context, they do provide direct evidence of the types of items being used by the Boyle community in the monastic period.

POST-MEDIEVAL ACTIVITY IN BOYLE ABBEY

The later activity at Boyle Abbey was intense with the introduction of drains, ditches, cobbling, walls and buttresses. A large quantity of nineteenth-century material was retrieved from under the cobbled surface, and this was consistent across the entire north aisle. It is highly likely that within this part of the monastery, barracks activity was confined to the north side of the abbey church with the blocking of the north arcade, the construction of three buttresses (as shown on Beranger's sketch of 1779, Fig 1.8) and the dismantling of the remainder of the north wall. The structural integrity and buttressing of the north arcade must have been a priority during the military use of the north side of the abbey rather than its use as outbuildings. The eighteenth century witnessed the demolition of the north wall masonry which at this stage may already have been largely collapsed. In the nineteenth century there was a lot of activity including the cutting of a ditch on the north and west sides of the abbey, construction of a drain, laying down of cobbled surfaces across the site soon after the ditch was backfilled and the addition of two buttresses as well as the taking down or significant rebuilding of the three earlier buttresses.

The nature and quantity of material recovered from the ditch (F222) indicate that it was utilised for dumping refuse. Bottles, broken clay pipes, large quantities of animal bone and numerous disarticulated human bones were recovered from the fills of the ditch. The quantity of disarticulated human bone and ferrous nails is also indicative of the fact that numerous burials were disturbed during the cutting and backfilling of this ditch feature. Some of the material recovered is likely to be earlier in date and finds such as the copper alloy pin are thought to be residual. Given that the ditch cut through numerous burials, the presence of earlier material within the fills is not unusual.

The large quantity of clay building material dating from the seventeenth and eighteenth centuries is another reminder of the later use of the abbey as an army barracks. The dumping of large quantities of discarded tile may be indicative of the destruction of a barrack building somewhere in the abbey precinct. The clay building material is likely to be linked directly to the kiln excavated by Rooney (see above).

MILITARY DIET

The faunal material from the post-medieval contexts includes animal bones from the period 1592 until the 1800s and beyond. Again, given the large amount of disturbance along the north aisle in the form of buttresses and drains and activity into the twentieth century, this is not surprising. It is highly likely that the north aisle area was taken up by three buttresses during the early 1700s or before. The post-medieval animal bone sample consisted of 8,914 mammalian fragments, 4,014 of which were identifiable to species. The majority of these came from general occupation layers and spreads distributed across the excavated area and dated to the nineteenth century. Of the assemblage, cattle dominated the diet and interestingly evidence that larger cattle were present in the post-medieval deposits was noted by the specialist (McCarthy see above). Improved breeds of cattle had become more common in Boyle during the post-medieval period. There would seem to have been some change in the ages of animals eaten by the military personnel, representing a change in animal husbandry practices during the seventeenth and eighteenth centuries, focusing in particular on the supply of animals for meat provisioning. The more frequent use of saws, compared to the earlier phase, indicated a development in butchery technology during the eighteenth and nineteenth centuries. Horses were in higher numbers than the preceding period which tallies with the later use of the site as a barracks. Most of the horse bones recovered belonged to mature animals and from the scarcity of cut marks it is clear that horses were not important as meat producers (M. McCarthy pers. comm.). In general, the abbey had changed from becoming a place of meat production in the Cistercian period to one of meat consumption in the later period and it is likely that the military acquired their beef from outside producers. The archaeobotanical material was represented by barley, oat and wheat in very low numbers and indeterminate carbonised cereals. Blackberry/bramble was also recovered. Fruit remains could be telling signs of once cess deposits, which were dumped into open features such as ditches and drains. It is also possible that they represent discarded waste debris from other domestic/industrial activities, such as cooking, food preparation, fruit-processing or dyeing.

CONCLUSIONS

Excavations along the north aisle of Boyle Abbey, conducted as part of the overall conservation project, provided a unique opportunity to gain information on the site as a monastic foundation, burial ground and military barracks. Deconstruction of the north arcade, in advance of its conservation, allowed for the excavation of the late twelfth- to early thirteenth-century pier foundations. Excavations also located the buried north wall of the church and uncovered medieval burials associated with it. This has provided a rare opportunity to analyse a medieval monastic community, and has revealed significant data on diet, pathologies, and disease.

A number of objects recovered are hugely noteworthy. Retrieval of the chalice or candlestick base from the site is of great significance. It provides direct evidence for the liturgical objects utilised at the abbey during the medieval period and its enigmatic script is alluring. Similarly, uncovering of the inscribed medieval grave slab provides valuable insight into the types of grave markers used at Boyle, albeit in seemingly limited numbers. Medieval artefacts from primary contexts were few; however, fourteenth-century silver coins recovered with some burials adds to the information regarding the date of the latter but also how the coins retained their value to the individual even after death. The later occupation of the site also left behind important artefacts including the iron sword, serving as a reminder of its sometimes violent history.

Boyle Abbey is a special site given its continuous occupation from medieval times into the nineteenth century. The military occupation and later guardianship by the Commissioners of Public Works provided a continuity of use that is rarely seen at such monastic sites. The fate of the abbey's buildings was dependent on its military occupiers and this resulted in its partial destruction.

A carved face discovered on a corbel in Pier 1.

Chapter 7

Conservation and Restoration of the North Arcade Wall

Mary-Liz McCarthy, Kevin Clancy and Denis Walsh

Introduction

Conservation is the process of caring for structures and places and of managing change to them in such a way as to retain their character and special interest. It is the aim of good conservation practice to preserve the authentic fabric which contributes to the special interest of the structure. The works to Boyle Abbey were carried out in line with this best conservation practice and in accordance with the recommendations of the principal international charters. These include the Venice Charter of 1964 and the Burra Charter of 1979–2013.

Before formulating proposals for works to an historical monument, it is essential to achieve a thorough understanding of its development, its cultural significance, and its current condition. Investigations are carried out in order to identify causes of current issues and involve a thorough review of any recorded historic documents on the site. It is also important that all works are specified by experts with a knowledge of and experience in working on historic sites and structures.

At Boyle Abbey, the first step was to compile a detailed conservation report on the abbey. This looked at the historic development of the site and included high-level survey and investigations into its current condition. This was carried out by a multi-disciplinary team who had specific skill sets necessary for work on such a sensitive structure.

The recommendations detailed in the report took into account best practice guidelines, including the conservation principles of minimal intervention and reversibility. Rather than take down the entire north aisle arcade, it was decided to take down the minimal amount possible. Recognising that this would result in the conserved aisle arcade being not entirely plumb, the decision had the benefit of allowing us to tell a fuller story of the structural issues within the feature. Where possible, historic fabric such as damaged stone was repaired rather than replaced. Lost sections of carved stone were not necessarily replaced, except for one face of

Fig. 7.1 Thomas James Westropp's drawing of Boyle Abbey (1880–91).

Pier 3 where new cut stone was provided. This was dressed differently to allow the intervention to be discernible on closer inspection.

Before the programme of works, although it was fully appreciated that the large buttresses and insert walls between the piers of the north arcade formed part of the story of the building, there could be no doubt that they were also highly disruptive visually. In the event, the decision was taken to remove them completely. The removal of the insert walls raised an issue in relation to security. Thus, the ensuing decision to replicate the general form of the north aisle structure was made not only to address issues of security, but also to allow for an area of display within the abbey. The scar from the roof of the medieval north aisle could be clearly seen and the foundations of its outer (north) wall were found during excavation, thus providing crucial evidence as to its plan. To avoid conjectural restoration, it was agreed that the lost aisle would be recreated in modern material, distinct from, but sympathetic to, the historic fabric of the building. The new aisle structure is also completely reversible, having 'light-touch' connections to the north arcade.

Background to problems with the north arcade

Reports of the Commissioners of Public Works record carrying out works to the structure in 1894 and again in 1904–5 (Carrig Conservation 2005, 5). By the time the abbey came under their guardianship, five buttresses had allegedly been in place for 70 to 80 years (Commissioners of Public Works 1896, 80; Commissioners of Public Works 1905, 15). A notable incline in the north arcade is recorded in the 1904 report (*ibid.*). The north aisle arcade is approximately 37m long, up to 10.5m high and generally 1.1m thick. There are three clustered piers at the east end, a fourth central pier of octagonal plan, then three much more substantial, rectangular piers towards the western end. There are eight arches, with the detailing in the later four westerly examples varying slightly from the four to the east (Pl. 7.1).

It is thought that the first (eastern) section of the north arcade had started to settle before the remainder of the arcade was constructed in the early decades of the thirteenth century, and this may have had an impact on the form of pier used for the

Pl. 7.1. Detail showing differences in arch styles.

remainder of the arcade; these are of a more robust form. This might also be attributed to changes in stylistic trends. Trial pits excavated as part of the initial works in 2004 showed the footings of the piers to have a degree of corbelling, broadening onto wider base stones. In 2004, these were approximately 650mm below the internal ground level but originally they were probably 400mm below internal ground level. This manner of footing was not unusual for buildings of this type. However, the ground beneath the piers was found to be quite poor for a depth of approximately 1m to 1.5m. Founding structures onto poor ground invariably results in uneven settlement of the structure.

While there may have been some settlement of the structure from its earliest existence, any inclination of the arcade was probably not too apparent. The most dramatic movement of the arcade is likely to have occurred following the removal of the north aisle. The date of this is unknown, but it is likely to have occurred between the mid 1500s and the mid 1600s, possibly while the abbey was in use as a barracks (see Chapter 6). The bays of the arcade itself were also likely to have been infilled at this time for security reasons. Similarly, the date of construction of the buttresses is unknown. They were certainly in place well before 1779 based on the drawing of the east and north sides of the abbey by Gabriel Beranger dating to this year (Fig. 1.8). Three substantial buttresses are shown against the north aisle wall with the degree of vegetation over the wall and buttresses indicating that they had been constructed against the roofless abbey a number of years prior to Beranger's visit. The individual bays of the north arcade are not apparent on this drawing, indicating that they were completely infilled; as noted above, this probably occurred during the military occupation of the site. The most likely instigators for the building of the buttresses are the King family in the late 1600s or early 1700s (Carrig Conservation 2005, 23).

Features which are likely to be the buttresses appear to be indicated on the 1838 Ordnance Survey map and may represent all five buttresses. They are certainly indicated on a later edition dating to *c.* 1890. The next illustration of the abbey dates from between 1880 and 1891 and was drawn by Thomas James Westropp in his Sketches of Ireland (Fig.

7.1) (Westropp 1880–91 i, 256). This illustration shows three buttresses against the north arcade. Given that the Commissioners of Public Works report from 1904–5 indicates that all five buttresses were in place for *c*. 80 years by that time, however, two of the buttresses may have been omitted by the illustrator. By this stage, the three bays at the western end of the north arcade have been partially opened to about the tops of the piers.

The first firm documentary evidence of works is found in the annual report of 1904, though this in turn makes reference to previous works carried out in 1894, including the removal of ivy and repair of walls where masonry had become dislodged. The report describes the buttresses as being 'almost useless, having been built with stones of small stone size, and the great portion, especially near the top, packed with clay, scarcely any mortar having been used except on the outer faces' (Commissioners of Public Works 1905, 15). During the 1904–5 phase of works, the tops of the walls throughout were cleaned down and concreted: 'The loose masonry of the four buttresses at northern wall of nave was taken down and rebuilt with concrete, and they were carried up several feet higher in order to support the top of the nave wall'. The north arcade was recorded as being two feet six inches (0.76m) out of plumb at this time (*ibid*.). The Commissioners' report from year end 1940 documents further work on the abbey, including the removal of ivy and extensive pointing and weathering, carried out to stabilise the condition of the fabric (Commissioners of Public Works 1939–40). In 1975, cracks on the buttresses were monitored to check for further movement but the concrete laid over the crack has not moved and led to further cracking. A series of drawings of the abbey was prepared by the OPW in the late 1970s which show the inclination of the arcade as it was at that point (Fig. 7.2).

Initial survey and recommendations

Carrig Conservation, in association with Lisa Edden Consulting Structural Engineer, was appointed in April 2004 to provide 'building forensic services' at Boyle Abbey. The brief was to assess and make recommendations for the structural stability and the consolidation of the north arcade at the abbey. The objective was to assess the current stability of the arcade, the effect and possibility of removing the massive buttresses, and possible alternative methods of providing stability to the arcade as a whole. A detailed condition survey and structural appraisal of the interior and exterior of the north arcade were carried out to gain an understanding of the degradation of its fabric. The report was completed in February 2005 (Carrig Conservation 2005) (Fig. 7.3, A, B).

Desktop research was carried out in order to gain a better understanding of the construction history of the abbey, and to establish the significance of the construction process that had triggered the structural problems with the north arcade. This research was used to understand site investigations carried out throughout 2004. A nomenclature was developed for the arcade, with numbers assigned to the bays travelling from the east end of the wall westwards. The piers were referred to by the numbers of the bays they stood between, with Pier 3/4, for example, standing between the third and fourth bays. The piers were renumbered when developing a numbering system to dismantle the wall. A visual inspection of the wall was carried out from a scaffold erected at Bay 4. In addition to this visual inspection, three trial pits were excavated, and two boreholes were drilled to investigate the subsoil conditions.

The geological map of the area shows Boyle Abbey situated very close to the junction of the Palaeozoic Lower Carboniferous devonian Shales and Sandstones with the Lower Carboniferous Limestone (Fig.1.4). The borehole investigations carried out on the site showed fill overlying very soft clay/silt over dense clayey gravel and probable top of weathered rock at between 3m and 3.4m below the external ground level. Limestone or sandstone fragments were retrieved in the lower levels of the boreholes to 3.5m and 4m below ground level. The water level rose to 2.3m below ground level, to the top of and slightly above the level of the good bearing strata. It should be noted that the external ground level at the time of the investigations was approximately 1m above that internally (Carrig Conservation 2005, Appendix 5).

The composition of the pier foundations has been described above. This type of construction

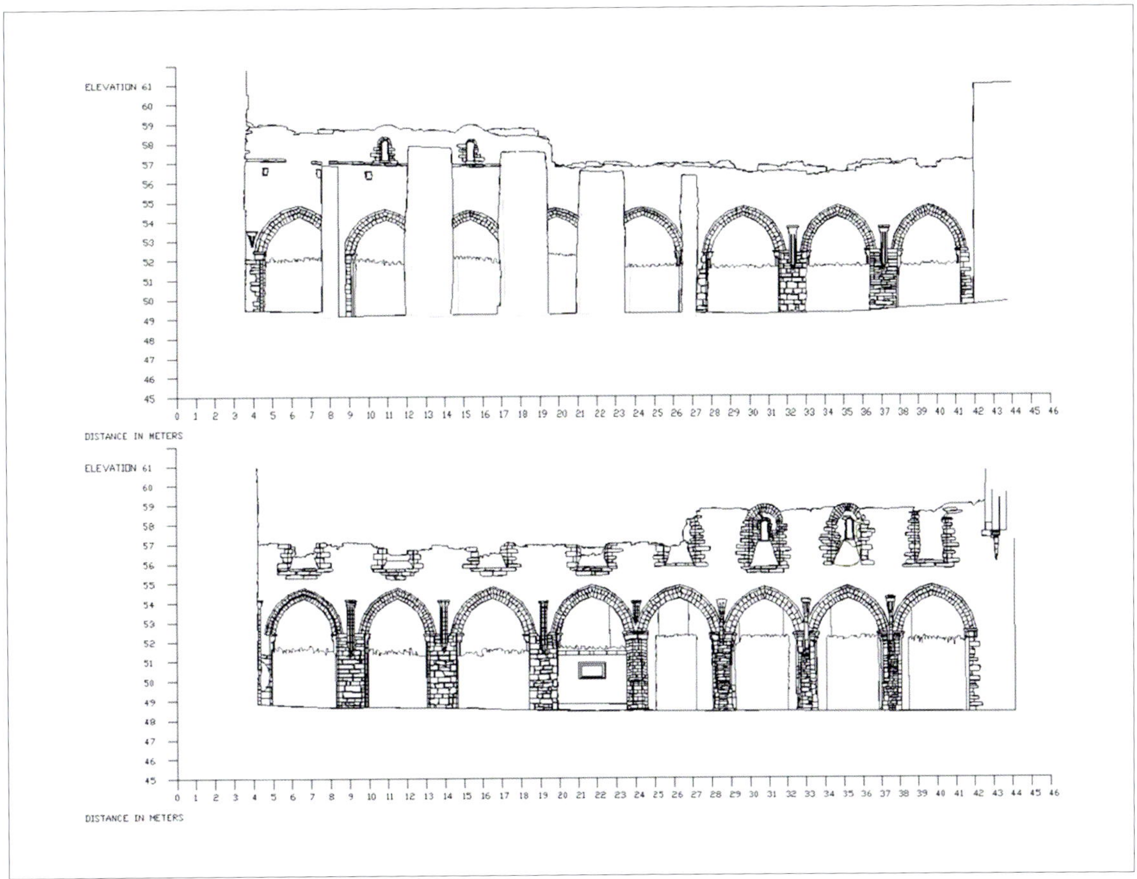

Fig. 7.2. OPW drawings of Boyle Abbey, late 1970s.

Fig. 7.3. (A, B) Condition drawings (after Carrig 2005).

Pl. 7.2. North elevation of nave.

Pl. 7.3. View of top of wall showing lean.

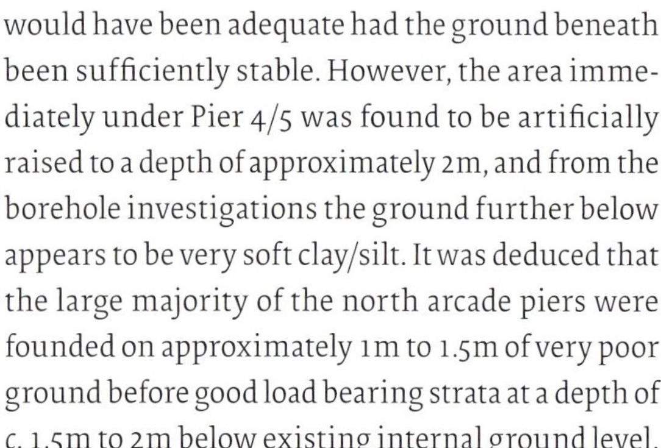

would have been adequate had the ground beneath been sufficiently stable. However, the area immediately under Pier 4/5 was found to be artificially raised to a depth of approximately 2m, and from the borehole investigations the ground further below appears to be very soft clay/silt. It was deduced that the large majority of the north arcade piers were founded on approximately 1m to 1.5m of very poor ground before good load bearing strata at a depth of *c.* 1.5m to 2m below existing internal ground level.

There were five substantial masonry buttresses to the first five piers, with those to Piers 2/3, 3/4 and 4/5 being so massive that much of the bay openings had been obscured (Pl. 7.2). The buttresses were founded approximately 500mm to 750mm above the foundation level of the pier footings, indicating that the external ground level had been significantly raised with building debris, graves, and other material. The shallow foundations of the buttresses places their construction in the eighteenth century.

The visual survey of the arcade identified a significant lean outwards at the top, which was at its greatest near the centre of the wall, namely at Bays 3, 4, and 5 (Pl. 7.3). The degree of lean was less, but not insignificant, to either side of these three bays, but as the arcade reached the presbytery to the east and the west wall at the opposite end, the inclination was at zero. Thus, the presbytery and the west wall provided substantial buttressing to the arcade. The inclination was measured at 1.5m over a height of 10.5m at Pier 3/4 and 1.3m over a height of 8.6m at Pier 4/5 (Pl. 7.4). The inclination was not planar, rather there was a double curvature in the shape of the wall. The movement appeared to have stabilised in recent decades but given the poor ground onto which the foundations of both the arcade and its foundations were founded, the recommencement of the movement was thought to be a significant risk. A cement mortar plaque placed across a crack to the east side of the buttress at Pier 3/4 with a date of '20-10-75' showed no evidence of cracking and therefore any movement.

A condition survey of the stonework was carried out concurrently with the structural investigations and found little sign of cracking in the wall. However, there was evidence of many repairs, insertions of stone, and other treatment, all of which implied previous failures to the stonework. It was found that there had been considerable removal of stone to the north side of many of the piers, which had been replaced by buttress stonework. There had also been much replacement of cluster stones with plain masonry and cement to the south faces of Piers 1/2, 2/3 and 3/4. The loss of some stone had left remaining sections of the cut stone under threat.

Pl. 7.4. View of Piers 3–4 showing curvature of the wall.

The effects of the outward movement on the inside of the north wall could be seen in the twisting and compression of stones. In some cases, the bases of the piers had been compressed into the ground. The degree of the tilt meant that the structural integrity of almost two-thirds of the elevation had been undermined with the building material suffering greatly as a result. Fractures to stones, which were the result of mechanical stresses, had occurred. Piers 3/4 and 4/5 had a heavy tilt, resulting in fractured stone to their bases, undermining their structural integrity. It was noted that the fractures present in the stone would only further deteriorate due to freeze-thaw action, which would further undermine the structural integrity of the building, allowing more fractures to occur.

The movement in the arcade had resulted in joints in the stone opening up with moisture ingress accelerating the dissolution of mortar, including washing away the bedding mortar. Along the parapet the bedding mortar was found to have deteriorated to a high degree with gravity being the only factor holding some of the stonework in place. Open joints were also noted in the voussoirs of the arcade arches, with only the structure of the arch in question continuing to hold the voussoirs in place. In all, the arcade had been a ruin and roofless for a number of centuries. It had suffered the ill-effects of bombardment from the elements on all sides over this time. The weathering stones at the top of the wall were for the most part missing, with the result that water had been allowed to percolate down into the masonry. Furthermore, the inclination of the arcade allowed for a different mechanism of erosion than would have been the case had the structure remained vertical. For much of its length, the arcade had been reduced to the sill-level of clerestory windows (Fig. 7.2), but two clerestory windows survived intact. These were at the point in the wall with the greatest curvature and the stone to the openings had been affected by the movement in the arcade.

A number of remedial options were explored during the site investigations, including rebuilding on new foundations, underpinning the existing piers and carrying out some rebuilding, installing

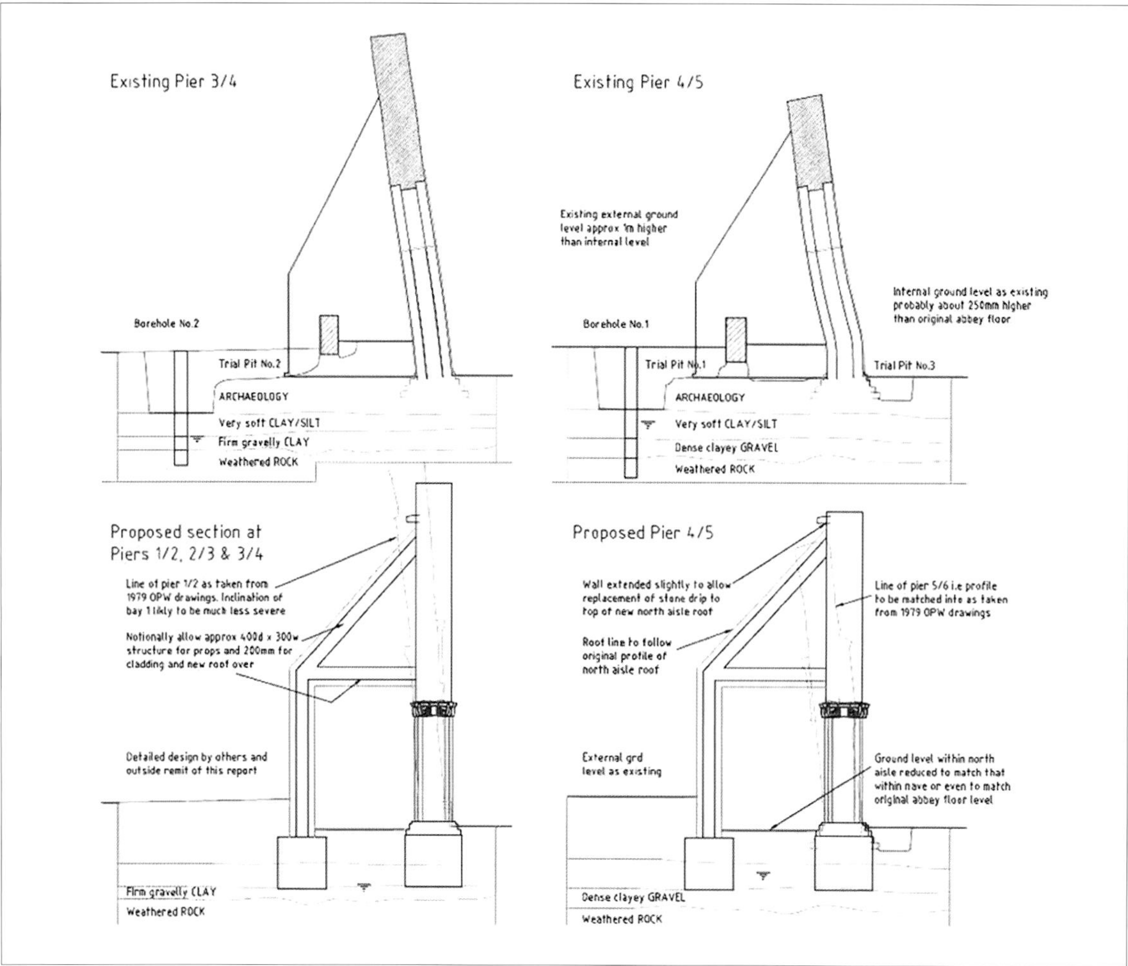

Fig. 7.4. Section drawings of north arcade. (OPW)

modern flying buttresses, reinforcing the existing wall with stainless-steel rods, restraining the arcade with rods through the nave into the grounds of the abbey, and constructing a new north aisle complete with roof to prop and strut the north arcade.

The following facts and requirements were considered carefully in arriving at the agreed solution:

- Removal of the five buttresses and replacement with something that obscures less of the arcade was highly desired.
- Removal of the in-fills between piers was also highly desired, but building security should not be compromised.
- The amount of badly deformed and missing stones from the first four piers meant that these piers required extensive intervention
- The deformation of the arcade was so extensive that removal of the buttresses would not be possible without serious disruption to the fabric.
- Any works within the ground would affect archaeology. The preference was to leave archaeology in place. The second preference was to have the opportunity to fully examine and record the archaeology.

The key recommendation of the report which discussed these options (Carrig Conservation 2005) was that a section of the arcade from the centre of Bay 1 to the centre of Bay 5 should be rebuilt. Initially, whilst recognising that the deformation of the wall was dramatic, a complete rebuild was not viewed as either essential or good conservation practice. On further consideration, however, such was the inclination and fragility of the wall between the two identified bays, including the condition of the piers, that it was accepted that stabilisation of this section of the arcade would be virtually impossible, with its rebuilding essential to its future survival.

The rebuilt section of the arcade was to be set

on new mass concrete pad foundations into the clayey gravel or rock. Any attempts to de-water to allow construction of new foundations was to be made with extreme caution to prevent further settlement of the existing structure. It was recommended that a new north aisle be constructed to provide substantial buttressing for the arcade itself. The north aisle should be constructed on concrete trench foundations into the clayey gravel or rock. Any reinforcement was to be stainless steel at a minimum for longevity. These new works were to have a lifespan substantially longer than 50 years. The new aisle structure was to be the new line of building security, allowing the removal of the infill walls between the arches (Fig. 7.4).

The retained sections of the arcade were to be carefully repointed and grouted with lime mortar/grout and damaged stones were to be replaced; this would strengthen these sections of the structure. The rebuilding of this section would also allow for the removal of the bulky and visually obtrusive buttresses. However, if the arcade beyond this section was to be retained, the reordering would have to be carried out with careful detailing and a very thorough examination of the sequence of construction. Whether the rebuilt section of arcade was to be constructed plumb (or with some deformation to meld with the retained sections), all of this work would need a helping hand to maintain its long-term stability.

The Boyle Abbey condition report, with its recommendations for remedial works, was submitted to the National Monuments section of the then Department of the Environment, Heritage, and Local Government (DEHLG) so that Ministerial Consent could be obtained to carry out the work, as the site is a National Monument. Consent was sought for a phased conservation programme that included archaeological excavation, repair of stonework *in situ*, and dismantling and rebuilding of five of the arcade bays. Ministerial Consent for the works was issued in January 2006.

In 2008, an addendum to the Consent (Carrig Conservation 2008) was requested after further investigation identified that rebuilding the dismantled section of the arcade would result in a significant difference between it and the existing structure. Though the lean of the arcade was at its most significant at Bays 3, 4 and 5, there was still a notable lean at Bay 6. The difference would be a total of 500mm at the top at the junction of the two sections, with this difference reducing downwards. However, there would also be a difference of *c*. 200mm at the springing point of the arch from the pier, resulting in an overhang of the arch over the side of the pier.

An architectural model was produced of the western end of the arcade to illustrate the problems with the plan as it currently stood. This architectural model clearly showed the difference between the sections of the arcade and also the problem of the rebuilt arch overhanging the pier. The necessity of rebuilding the arcade plumb would mean that there could be no scope for attempting to diminish the overhang.

From a structural point of view, the condition of the pier between Bays 6 and 7 was examined. It was agreed that this pier might not be solid enough to support the weight of the rebuilt arcade and therefore was in need of some intervention. This pier was also coming under significant stress due to the lean of the wall. Following these discussions, the decision was reached whereby the dismantling of a further pier, that between Bays 6 and 7, together with half of the subsequent arch would be necessary. Thus, a total of six piers along the arcade were dismantled rather than the initial five proposed. The removal of this extra pier and section of arcade allowed for a reduction in the variation between the walls to a measurement which could easily be eradicated during the rebuilding phase.

Methodologies

Once the decision had been taken to dismantle and rebuild the north arcade, a methodology needed to be put in place that was safe, effective and would allow the work to be carried out according to best conservation practice. Through an extended process of discussion with all of the design team members, and particularly with the OPW's skilled team of masons, a methodology was set out, which it was felt was both rigorous enough and flexible enough to allow the project to proceed successfully. Throughout the project, work was very much based on the collaborative relationship between the OPW's Dromahair District Works Team and

Fig. 7.5. Survey of south elevation of nave in 2006. (OPW)

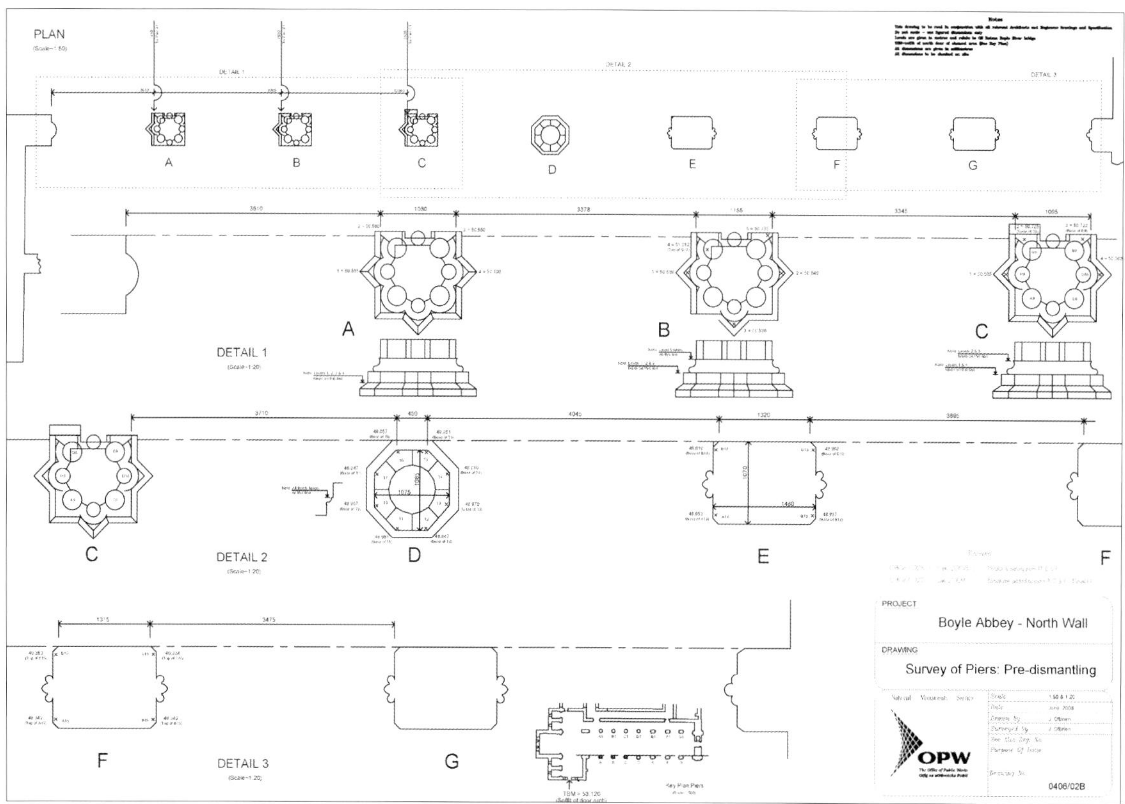

Fig. 7.6. Drawing of base of piers *c.* 2006. (OPW)

the design team. Assistance on mortar analysis and stone cutting was provided by the Athenry and Portumna OPW Districts.

There were essentially four main components to the project plan or methodology devised:

- Recording – creating a record of the wall in its current state
- Numbering – devising a numbering system and numbering the stones *in situ*
- Dismantling – according to a pre-agreed methodology
- Storage – in a pre-established storage area.

Recording

Survey and recording of the wall in advance of dismantling relied on a combination of photogrammetric survey, rectified photographic survey, 3-D laser scan survey and many record photographs taken by the OPW, DEHLG and other project members. The keeping of a photographic record continued throughout the project, documenting all phases through to completion.

A rectified photographic survey of the north arcade was carried out by the OPW before the project commenced and this informed decision-making. A photogrammetric survey of the wall had been carried out in the late 1970s and this was scanned to allow for the development of a preliminary numbering system by the OPW. This survey allowed for each stone to be identified and given a unique number. In 2006, a laser scan survey, which was a requirement of Ministerial Consent, was carried out which provided a detailed record of the wall prior to dismantling including plans, elevations and sections (Fig. 7.5). The OPW carried out an accurate plan survey of the wall in 2006 to establish the exact location of piers before the dismantling stage of the project commenced. OPW carried out a further detailed survey and levelling of both bottom courses, pier stones and foundation stones to assist with rebuilding the piers before their removal by archaeologists (Fig. 7.6). This survey was extremely important as the measurements recorded at this stage would be the only means of ensuring the piers would be reconstructed in their original location due to

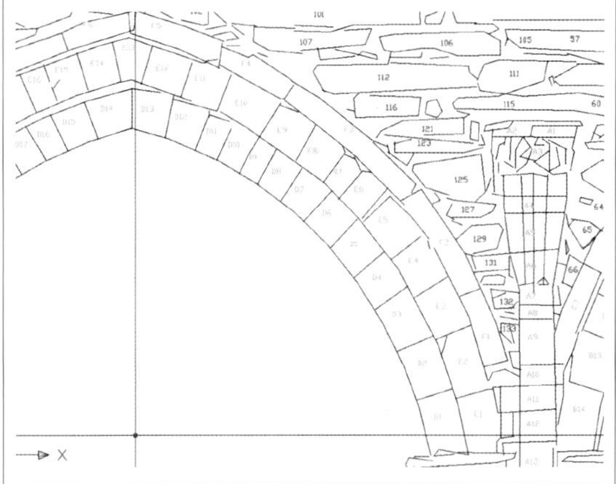

Fig. 7.7. The stones were numbered in advance of being dismantled.

the archaeological investigations and foundation works as part of the rebuild phase.

Numbering

A numbering system (Carrig Conservation no date) was devised in consultation with the design team and with the project masons. In many ways this was the biggest task, especially in terms of the detailed revisions and the amount of thought needed to devise a system that would be clearly legible, easily identifiable, last the duration of the project, and conform to the masons' traditional working practices. It was also a system that needed to have a series of built-in checks and controls, in the unlikely event that one element of the plan was to go awry.

The agreed final system considered the arcade in its five principal elements – Rubble Stone, Piers, Windows, Arches, and Corbels. Each element was treated differently within the system. This system was seen as being accurate enough, without being overly complex, to allow an efficient and flexible working model. All visible stones in the rubble wall were numbered individually with stones not currently visible numbered by the dismantling team as the buttresses came down and the numbers marked on printed drawings. A grid was placed over the elevation and the stones were numbered according to the courses within each section. Only stones that fell within the grid lines were numbered within the grid (Fig. 7.7). The rubble stone was numbered in a linear fashion and the walls numbered from east to west (Pl. 7.5).

Cut stone was not numbered according to the

Pl. 7.5. Detail of numbered stone prior to dismantling.

individual grids, as it was felt it would be better to keep each element together as a unit. Each window was given a letter – WA, WB, WC – and each stone within the window given a number – WA1, WA2, and so on. Individual courses of each arch were lettered A, B, C/ D, E, F/G, H, I/J, K, L, and so on and the individual voussoirs within each course were numbered from east to west and inner to outer course. Essentially, the inner course of the most easterly arch was numbered A1, A2, A3, etc. with the inner course of the arch at Bay 5 numbered P1, P2, P3. The arches were numbered on their faces prior to dismantling, with the numbers transferred to the skyward surfaces as each stone was removed from the wall. Each corbel was given a letter – A, B, C – and each stone within each corbel was numbered (Pl. 7.6). The system for numbering the piers was devised at a later point in the dismantling project, namely when these were due to be taken down. As there are different styles of piers in the building, separate numbering systems for the different styles needed to be devised. Each pier was assigned a letter – A, B, C, and so on – (this differed from the numbering system used in the first phase of the project) with the stones in each pier receiving a unique number based on an approach which took cognisance of their unique design.

In addition to the numbering system outlined above, different paint colours were used for inner and outer walls and for adjacent bays for ease of identification. A waterproof, removable paint was used for numbering the stone. The numbering system was trialled on a purpose-built mock-up at the OPW's Dromahair Depot. This trial also included the identification of a suitable paint. Once numbering was complete, all numbers were thoroughly recorded on both drawings and photographs and numbered drawings continued to be updated throughout the project.

Storage

As part of the development of a numbering system, a storage system (Carrig Conservation no date) was also devised. This identified a designated storage position relevant to the type of stone and its location within the wall. The rubble stone walls were rebuilt in reverse on the ground within the nave in sections only up to a safe height. Once the safe height was reached, a new layer was started (Pl. 7.7). The inner and outer faces of the wall were laid

Pl. 7.6. Detail of corbel with numbers applied.

Pl. 7.7. The stones were stored in the nave

parallel to one another and each stone was laid in place directly as it came down from the wall. All stone was carefully isolated from the ground and weatherproofed and secured when not in use. The cut stone was laid out on the scaffold at a level corresponding to its position in the wall (Pl. 7.8). The bays of the scaffold were numbered, and a record made of which stones were contained in each bay. The stone was protected from the scaffold planks by a protective membrane and layer of hemp cloth, with the stone also covered with hemp and tarpaulin to make it weatherproof and secure (Pl. 7.9). The corbels were stored as set pieces, with each one in an individual crate or box. These were then placed within a secure lock-up on site. The capitals were also stored within the secure lock-up. The piers were rebuilt in reverse within the nave, directly to the south of a pier's original location. As with the walls, the stone from the pier was to be isolated from the ground and protected from the elements. Once stone was in its storage location, a photographic record of this was to be made.

Dismantling methodology

Once the numbering and storage systems had been put in place, a strict methodology for dismantling was developed. Hand tools were used to loosen masonry; electrical tools were only acceptable in areas where modern cement mortar had been used, as in the buttresses for example, and were to be operated in a highly controlled manner. Stone was moved to the designated storage location in a manner that would ensure no damage was caused. During dismantling, any features or changes were clearly noted on the drawings, including any changes in the numbering system. Photographs were taken of any features found during dismantling. This included the presence of carved stone within the core fill material. Measurements were taken at 50mm–100mm intervals across the width of the wall and recorded to ensure the wall was rebuilt at as close to its original depth as possible.

Mortar sampling

It was determined that 15–20 samples of mortar would be required to carry out analysis and identify the correct mortar for rebuilding the north arcade. Each sample was given a reference number and its location marked on the drawings. Samples included core, bedding and pointing mortars and the samples were evenly dispersed across the entire span of the wall. They were taken at regular intervals during dismantling. These samples were submitted for laboratory analysis to identify the correct repair mortars to be used during rebuilding. Both core bedding and pointing mortar samples were taken. A mortar mock-up session was held on site to trial the replacement mortars and to ensure that they could be effectively used in the rebuilding of the wall.

Sourcing of replacement stone

It was necessary to source replacement sandstone to substitute for material that could not be re-used as a result of damage from movement of the wall. To this end, petrographic analysis was carried out on a sample of stone from the arcade to identify the origin of the stone and also ascertain potential

Pl. 7.8. The cut stone was loaded on to a scaffold

sources of replacement stone. Following detailed research and testing, it was found that the sandstone used for the cut-stone elements of the abbey was derived from the Boyle Sandstone Formation. However, it was not possible to obtain any new quarried stone from the original source, so a suitable replacement source had to be located. Through research in the locality around Boyle, and following petrographic analysis, blocks of sandstone were identified which proved a match for the medieval arcade and were therefore seen as suitable replacement stone. As part of the dismantling procedure, any stones that were noted to be damaged beyond re-use were recorded on drawings and replacement stone provided during rebuild.

Dismantling phase

Following the actual recording and numbering of the arcade, a dismantling methodology was developed and agreed with input from the OPW National Monuments Team, OPW Dromahair District Works Team and the design team. Briefly, this involved the deconstruction of the arcade and its temporary drystone reconstruction in the presbytery area of the abbey.

Having established the original line of the arcade, cut lines between the section of wall to be dismantled and reconstructed and the elements which were to be retained at either end were agreed. The positions of the cuts would allow a smooth transition between the reconstructed wall and the original elements retained in place. The process of dismantling the arcade safely required that the massive supporting buttresses would be progressively dismantled from the top down and a little at a time.

This approach also facilitated the recording and numbering of the newly revealed, carved cut and random masonry stones in line with the relevant methodologies, followed by dismantlement and storage as previously described. This temporary drystone wall was built 'upside down' to safe manual handling heights, so that the reconstruction process would be safe, easy and foolproof in the context of replacing stones in their exact original position.

Carved and cut stones were managed differently. The carved stones were laid out on custom-designed scaffolding decks, in close proximity to their position in the original arcade. Similarly, the cut stones of the Gothic arches were laid loose flat upon the adjacent deck, in a mirror image of their original position. This storage and location strategy allowed for safe, easy and exact replacement of carved and cut stones.

Pl. 7.9. Cut stone on the scaffold was protected

During the dismantling phase of the works, a carved face was discovered on a corbel to Pier A. It was located on the upper surface, towards the back of the stone and therefore completely hidden once the stone had been placed into the arcade. The face was oval in outline with a broad forehead and a nose in slight relief. This head appears to have been a mason's mark and was never to be seen. It was recorded and then placed back into the wall during the rebuilding phase (Pl. 7.8).

To enable the OPW masonry works team to accomplish these complex and exacting activities safely, the design team provided the design, drawings and details for false and other temporary works, bespoke scaffolding and work decks. Traditional centring was erected to each of the severely out of plumb arches during the dismantling phase to prevent the arches collapsing and protect the cut stones. As the arches were significantly out of plumb, the centring was built to fit as required for each arch. The false works, temporary works, scaffolding and decks were also used for the reconstruction stage of the project.

Arguably, the most important aspect of the dismantling phase was the necessity for temporary works to the sections of the arcade that were to be retained in position. As well as the installation of timber centring to support arches, temporary structures were designed and installed to support the original walls and arches that were being retained. A combination of bespoke timber temporary buttresses and structural steel temporary flying buttresses was used to ensure the lateral stability of the retained sections. All of the temporary works were designed to be supported on ground level to respect the underlying archaeology and permit safe archaeological excavation. In addition to safe storage of large quantities of carved and cut stones, the bespoke scaffolding system was modified to accommodate lifting hoists and runway beams installed for the safe handling and placement of such stones as exceeded the safe manual handling Health and Safety Regulations.

The scaffolding installation was further enhanced and modified to support a temporary roof over the reconstruction stage of the works, which was a vital intervention, primarily for quality but also for programming reasons. Scaffolding is a temporary structure, which provides a safe means of working at height. To achieve this, scaffolding must comply with technical standards and be designed to take account of the loadings. SGB Cuplok is a proprietary scaffolding system and was used to form the scaffolding throughout the project. As a modular system it was ideally suited for use at Boyle Abbey. The main purposes of the scaffolding at Boyle were to provide a safe means of access to the works and a safe working platform for the dismantling and reconstruction of the arcade. In addition, there were many secondary requirements that the scaffolding had to satisfy. In particular:

- The scaffolding provided several means for the safe handling of materials, in particular the large masonry stones.
- Some of the stonework that was taken down from the north wall was stored on the scaffolding.
- The scaffolding allowed for the movement of materials, both vertically and horizontally.
- The scaffolding provided protection against the elements for OPW employees and the complete project team and for the reconstruction works.

There were two areas where scaffolding was erected. The first was an internal scaffold, which was erected inside the abbey itself; this extended the full width and length of the abbey and remained in place for the full duration of the works. The second area was outside of the north wall; this external scaffolding was erected along the line of the north arcade and was dismantled several times at various stages in the reconstruction works.

There were three main phases of the scaffolding at Boyle Abbey:

1. The first phase involved the dismantling of the north wall. An internal scaffold was erected to provide access internally and for the movement and storage of materials. The external scaffold was erected to provide access to the outside face of the wall and was complicated by the leaning nature of the north wall.
2. The main purpose of the scaffolding during the second phase was to provide storage of the stone, while the foundations to the north arcade were reconstructed. To provide access to the work, the external scaffolding was dismantled, leaving the internal scaffolding in place to store the stone.
3. The internal scaffolding was adapted for the third phase and external scaffolding was erected to allow access to reconstruct the north arcade. In addition, a Haki roof was erected over the arcade and the scaffolding enclosed using protective sheeting. These served to provide an improved working environment and to protect the works during inclement weather.

Because the works involved the handling of large quantities of heavy stone masonry, there were a number of additional safety features incorporated into the scaffolding. These included:

- A materials lift was installed in the middle of the internal scaffold. This served the main lifts of the scaffold and allowed for the vertical movement of stone to and from the main storage area.
- An external hoist was installed on the external scaffold, which provided a means of delivering lime mortar, tools and materials to the north wall.
- A runway rail system was installed above the top lift of the scaffolding. This supported the hoist, which was used to lift individual stones back into the arcade. The rail system

Pl. 7.10. View of new timber and stone side aisle structure

allowed the hoist to be slid in both horizontal directions, along and across the arcade. This minimised manual handling and allowed stones to be lifted by the hoist and easily set into position in the arcade.

Assure Health and Safety Consultants (Niall O'Donovan) coordinated the design of the scaffolding and advised on amendments during the construction stage on site. Upon completion of dismantlement to original ground level, including foundation stones, and following rigorous archaeological excavations, new piled foundations and pile caps were installed. The phasing of the dismantlement of the arcade and the installation of the temporary structures required close collaboration between all the disciplines involved in the project, with the archaeological imperatives to the forefront at all times.

Reconstruction phase

NEW FOUNDATION FOR NORTH AISLE WALL

Geophysical site investigation established the fundamental underlying reason for the failure of the original foundations of the north arcade. It was constructed on a soft, silty layer of soil. The decision to do this seems to have been quite risky, even for the time, and may have been influenced by issues related to the high water table and the difficulty of construction in that context. Moreover, the builders were faced with the potential of having to dig out approximately two metres of poor material before reaching a good bearing stratum. After due consideration of the same issues, it was decided to construct new reinforced concrete pad foundations, each supported by four small diameter piles. The pile type was selected on the basis of the following criteria:

- Adequate load capacity
- Ease of access for installation
- Ease of installation
- Minimum size of piling rig
- Minimum size of pile
- Minimum vibration impact during installation.

As part of the reconstruction, very careful consideration was given to the presentation of the bases of the piers by the OPW National Monuments, Works Team and the design team. To achieve this end, the original floor level of the nave of the abbey church was established with reasonable certainty. So that the cut base stones of the piers could be presented consistent with their original place and congregational viewpoint, the pile caps were cast at a level that would accommodate a new foundation stone upon which the original piers were reconstructed. Thereafter, the reconstruction of the arcade simply involved the reversal of the dismantling, storage, and recording numbering methodologies, with the addition of fresh mortar bedding. As the arcade was reconstructed to be plumb, piers were first reconstructed to corbel level (referring to numbered stones for each pier) and the timber centring used in the dismantling phase was adjusted for the new arch position.

PIER RECONSTRUCTION

The decision to reinforce the reconstructed piers was made for the following reasons:

- The original core filling had a very high clay content, which affected load bearing capacity.
- The load bearing capacity of the piers was compromised by the extent of structural deterioration of the stone fabric that had occurred over time.
- In order to re-use as much original stone as possible, much of which was fractured, the core of the piers would need to have enhanced load bearing capacity.
- In the context of a full restoration of Boyle Abbey being undertaken at some future time, the reconstructed piers would be an enabling factor in such a project.
- Duplex stainless-steel bars were selected for the pier reinforcement on the basis of: (a) Greater corrosion resistance than 'ordinary' austenitic stainless steel (b) Higher strength than 'ordinary' austenitic stainless steel.

For all of these reasons a limecrete core and duplex stainless-steel reinforcement was incorporated in the reconstruction process. This also enabled a modern side aisle 'lean-to' structure to be added, and the additional wind and gravity loads which it imposed to be safely supported and resisted by the reconstructed arcade.

NEW SIDE AISLE STRUCTURE

Taking into account best conservation practice, the presentation of the north arcade, and the visual opening up and revelation of the internal spaces of Boyle Abbey, good site visitor management and security, and possibilities for permanent and occasional exhibitions and events, it was decided that a modern glass envelope supported by a glulam timber and stainless-steel frame would be the most appropriate design solution (Pl. 7.10).

The new form was intended to acknowledge and echo the original medieval north aisle structure, whilst at the same time allowing for the expression of twenty-first-century materials. In addition, the new structure was designed to be completely reversible, with minimum connection to the conserved arcade. The new foundation for the north aisle structure is in the form of a reinforced concrete sill beam supported on piles. The sill beam and piles were installed through the centre of the remnants of the original external aisle wall, with the 'rebuilt' wall constructed around the piles. A clear distinction was made between new and old in the form of a layer of bituminous sheet membrane. The reasoning for this is essentially the same as that for the new foundations of the arcade.

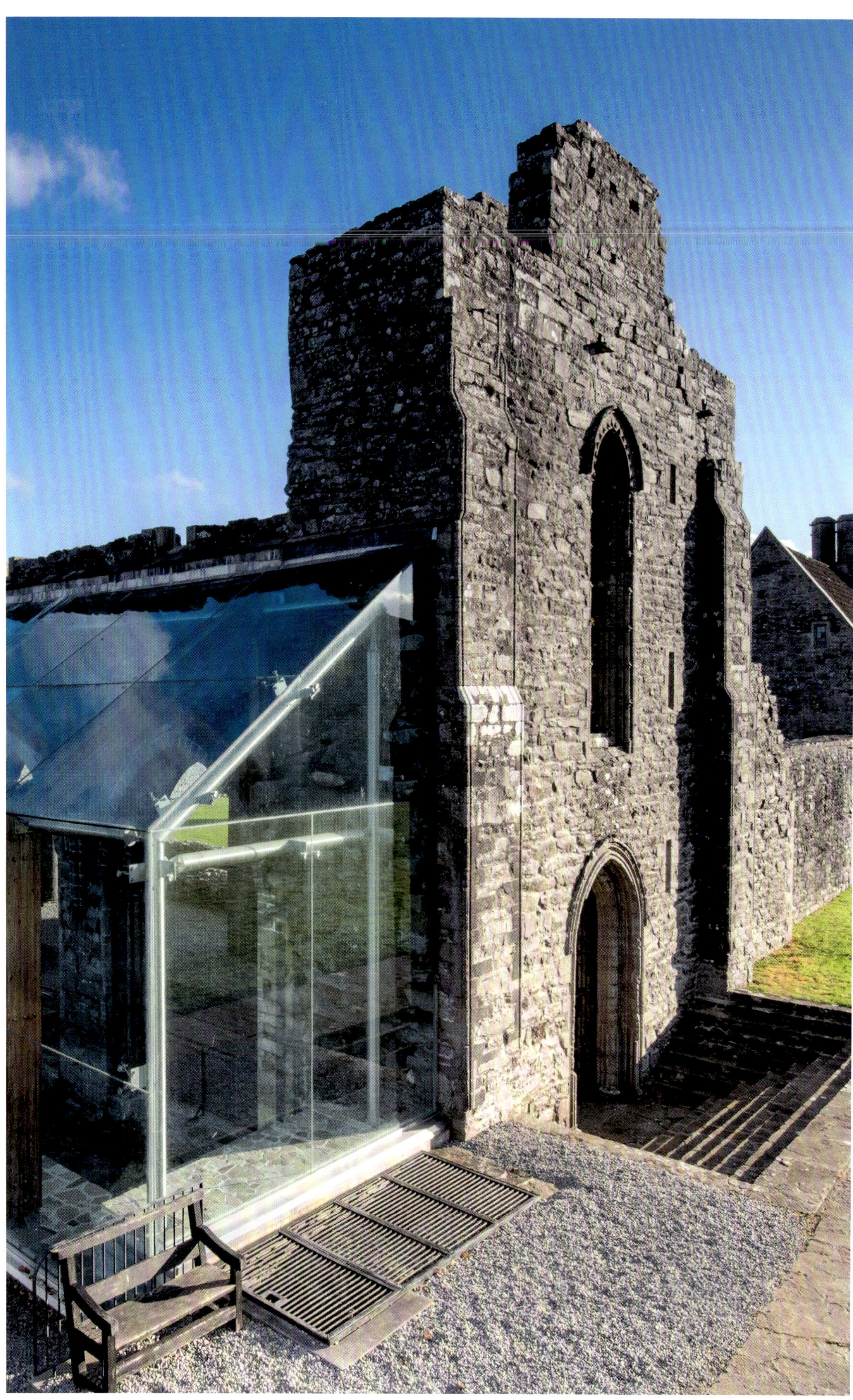

Post conservation view of Boyle Abbey.

Chapter 8

Discussion and Conclusions

Geraldine Stout

Today, at Boyle Abbey the north aisle arcade stands proud with its rich carving shimmering in the newly built glass surround. It is a testimony to the care and consideration given by a specialist team to the preservation of this masterpiece of architecture for another generation. Two major phases of conservation have ensured the better presentation of the abbey ruins at Boyle and their safety for the foreseeable future. The opportunities afforded for excavation by the conservation programmes have produced a considerable body of new material which has thrown light on many aspects of the long history of the site. A comprehensive history of the site and study of its architecture have provided a broader context within which to review this new material.

Foundation

In 1148 a group of 12 Cistercian monks and their abbot set out from Mellifont Abbey, Co. Louth, with the aim of establishing the first Cistercian house in Connacht, but there were a number of false starts before they finally settled at Boyle, Co. Roscommon in AD 1161. This is not unusual in the history of Cistercian sites. In spite of the care and preparation which went into the foundation of Cistercian abbeys, as many as one-third of all communities across Europe found it necessary to transfer to a new location, often within a decade or so of the initial settlement. For instance, of the 75 abbeys in England and Wales, at least 30 changed their site at least once (Robinson 2006, 47). This may have resulted from adverse physical conditions or friction with the locals. The buildings at these temporary sites were probably of wood. The most common sequence of events was that the patron accepted responsibility for providing the initial buildings in advance of the founding colony's arrival (*ibid.*, 51). In England, at least three sites have produced substantial timber constructions namely Bordesley (Worcestershire), Fountains (North Yorkshire) and Sawley (Lancashire). Five timber buildings have been excavated at Sawley covering the period 1150–90. Two of these were fed with piped water supplies (Coppack *et al.* 2002, 30–45, 101–5). At Valle Crucis in Wales, structural timbers were re-used as part of the footings beneath the south range suggesting the earlier presence of temporary lodgings elsewhere at the site (Robinson 2006, 52).

Building phases and architectural styles

A study of the architecture of Boyle Abbey has highlighted the incremental nature of medieval monastery building and the role of the Cistercians in bringing international design to the peripheries of Europe. In this volume, Stalley traces the sequence of building at Boyle Abbey identifying three distinct medieval phases (see Chapter 3); the first major phase of building (1170 to 1201) included the presbytery, transepts, the first four cylindrical piers on the south side of the nave, a guest house, infirmary, house for the novices and the cloistral buildings. This initial building phase at Boyle naturally reflects a degree of affiliation with the architecture of St Bernard's Clairvaux derived from their mother house at Mellifont with carved detailed clearly embedded in Hiberno-Romanesque tradition. The pointed barrel vault over the presbytery, the pointed choir arch and stone vaulted entrances to the transept chapels compare well with other abbeys and demonstrate clear influence from France via Mellifont, in particular from the region of Burgundy. The abbey church reflects the so-called 'Bernardine plan' which occurred throughout the Clairvaux affiliation and was almost universally employed at Cistercian abbeys across Europe. The genesis of the plan itself has been traced back to the new church built at Clairvaux *c.* 1135–45 (Fig. 8.1). Boyle is similar in scale to Baltinglass, Co. Wicklow, and Jerpoint, Co. Kilkenny, and the Welsh abbeys of Margam and Whitland in plan (Robinson 2006, 74.)

After 1201 the second phase of building work (1201–15) resumed on the nave of the church including the first four bays of the north arcade and the upper walls with clerestory. Changes in pier design, from cylindrical to clustered form, represent Boyle's unique version of what had become fashionable in England during the second half of the twelfth century, confirming that a new team of masons had arrived at the monastery. Stalley (see above) highlights the care and attention to detail demonstrated in the second phase of piers in the north arcade which were specifically designed with wooden choir stalls in mind.

The foundation methods adopted were similar, although the easternmost arches showed more signs of subsidence with the foundation stones being heavily shattered. Pier foundations were constructed by first digging the sub-circular foundation pits which were then filled with large stones that formed the base/raft for the piers. The entire north arcade had been built using the same type of foundation methods despite the architectural variation evident in the piers themselves. The north aisle wall may have been built in two chronological phases, the earlier phase apparent as a wider foundation at the east end of the aisle. During the 1980s excavations, the south wall of the nave was exposed to foundation level sitting on a footing that projects from the base of the wall and indicated a single-phase construction in the earlier (twelfth-century) phase (see Chapter 3). In this phase the wall was narrower and built on top of the wider wall foundations, using a temporary scaffold-type structure reflected in the presence of postholes. The foundations of the west gable wall were constructed directly on top of a flat raft of large flagstones. The stone annexes were built during this phase and the north wall of the church, which was built on flat foundation stones. A stone drain was built into the north wall and continued through the nave to the cloister. Floor surfaces in all cases were clay with no evidence of a tiled or stone floor

The third phase of building (1215–20) involved the last four bays of the nave and the west façade. The architecture of this phase is closely related to practices in the west of England in the years around 1200, the so-called west country 'school' of masons that operated in the area around the Bristol Channel and influenced masons working on Christ Church cathedral in Dublin. The architecture of the third campaign at Boyle had repercussions throughout Connacht where it influenced church architecture. Formal consecration of the church took place in 1220 when the entire church was completed and roofed. It has been suggested that the change in

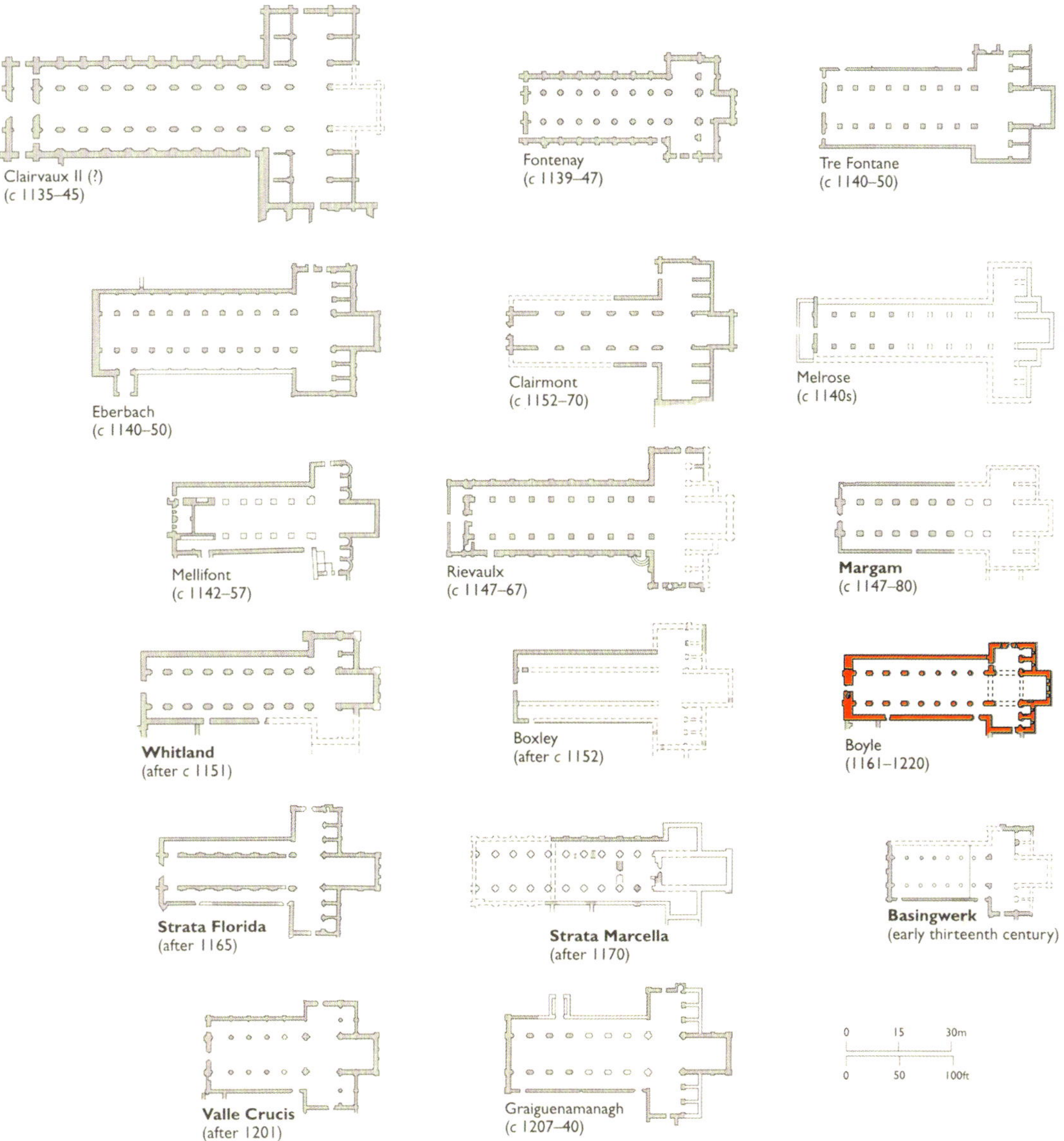

Fig. 8.1. Cistercian abbey churches with 'Bernardine plan' (after Robinson 2006).

pier from clustered to a simple octagon in the north arcade in this phase of building may have marked the location of the screen separating the monks' choir from that of the lay brothers. It is also intriguing that the capital carvings decorated with figures or animals in a typically Romanesque manner are all to be found in the area of the church occupied by the lay brothers, rather than the choir monks.

Boyle Abbey cloistral buildings conform to the general layout of Cistercian abbeys with a series of buildings serving both domestic and religious purposes surrounding a rectangular cloister garth. The introduction of the square or rectangular cloister was one of the most revolutionary aspects of Cistercian architecture (Stalley 1987, 51). Evidence uncovered during the 1980s excavations at Boyle threw much light on the form and layout of the medieval cloister (see Ann Lynch above). An original doorway leading from the nave onto the west cloister walk was revealed which provided access for the lay brothers in the west range. The west walk had a trampled clay surface, but excavations of the cloister garth revealed a flagged surface. A substantial drain running across and under the south nave wall continues beneath the cloister walk and highlights the concern for water management on a site that was constantly prone to flooding. Lynch has postulated that a second smaller box drain

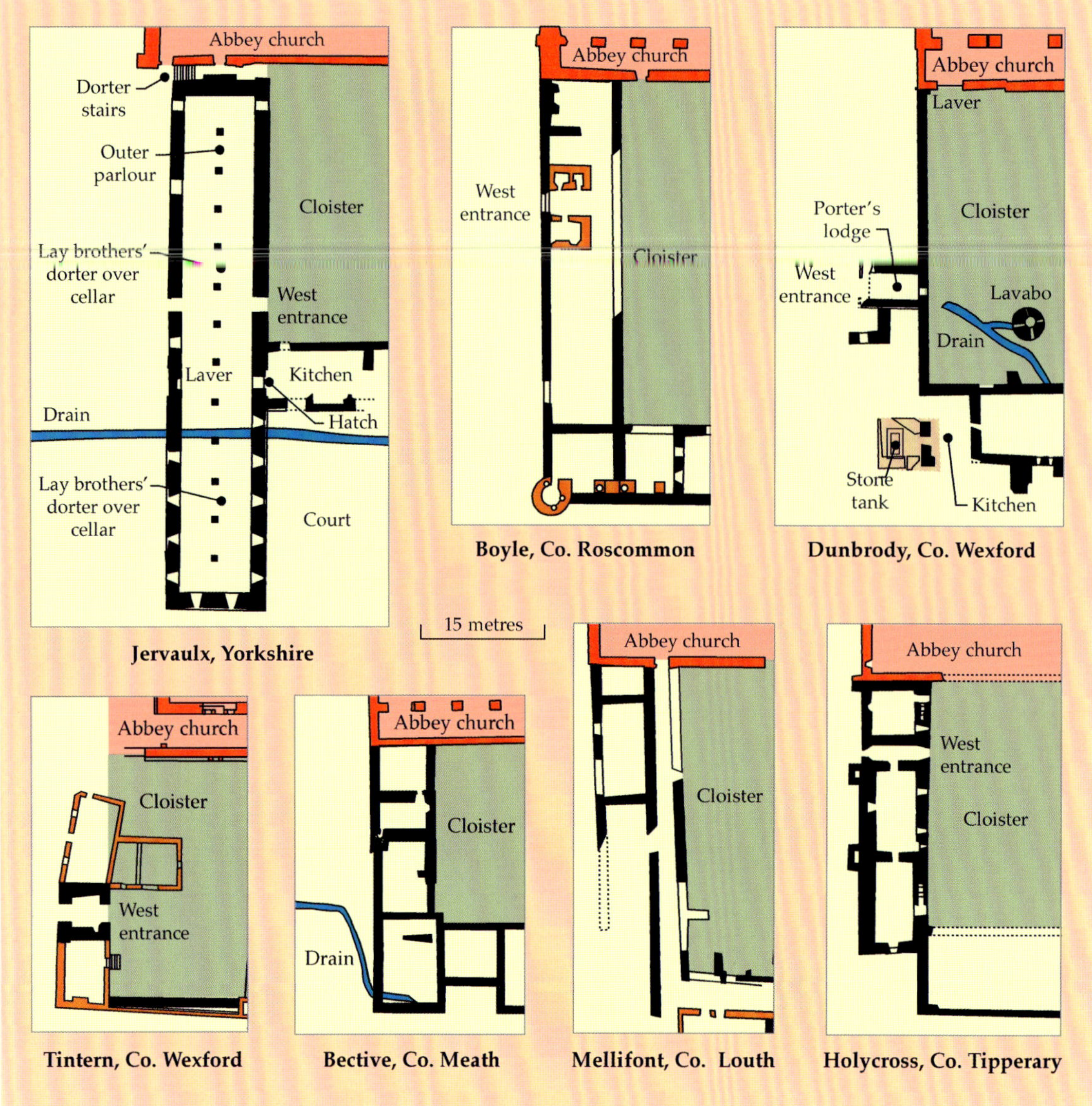

Fig. 8.2. Comparative plans of west ranges in Irish Cistercian abbeys (after Stout and Stout 2016).

uncovered in the west walk, running under the cloister arcade wall, could have served a lavabo sited within the cloister garth, similar to that revealed during excavations at the Cistercian abbey at Dunbrody, Co. Wexford (Stout 2016). The latter used lengths of lead pipe which were similar to lead pipes that formed part of the water supply mechanism found at Mellifont Abbey (de Paor 1969). Unfortunately, post-medieval modifications at Boyle Abbey resulted in the removal of much of the east range but the spectacular nature of the surviving chapter house and parlour doorways shows how impressive the original buildings would have been.

Clearly, drainage was the serious issue at Boyle Abbey and resulted in major structural problems over the centuries. The abbey's location on the bank of a river that is prone to flooding put it in a precarious position. Its geographic location in the west of Ireland, which has a higher than average annual rainfall, exacerbated the situation. The leaning arcade at Boyle was undoubtedly a result of the poor foundations that lay beneath the piers, a consequence of the constant change in water levels. Flooding was a natural hazard for monasteries sited by rivers, as most Cistercian abbeys were. Outside Ireland at Waverly Abbey in Surrey, one of the very first monasteries founded in Britain (1201, 1203) major storms resulted in flooding of their conventual buildings. At Meaux in Yorkshire, by the Humber estuary, a great flood drowned many of its men and animal stock in 1235. Also, Stanlaw abbey, by the Mersey estuary in Cheshire, was flooded in

1287, and monks had to retreat to Whalley abbey (Williams 1998, 146).

Given their preference for a riverside location, the Cistercians were renowned for their expert drainage systems (Stalley 1987, 169–70). The builders at Boyle did endeavour to manage water on their site with a substantial drain built into the north wall of the abbey church and continued through the nave to the cloister. At other Irish Cistercian sites impressive drains have been identified, for example, Jerpoint Abbey, Co. Kilkenny and Grey Abbey, Co. Down where a stone-lined sewer passes under the *rere dorter* (latrine), the floor of the refectory and kitchens and runs into the river and lough. A substantial stone-lined drain was excavated at the south end of the dormitory range at Tintern Abbey, Co. Wexford (Lynch 2010, 88–92.) At Bective Abbey, Co. Meath, a well-built stone-paved drain was uncovered below the southern end of the lay brothers' range and ran under the west wall continuing outside it (Stout and Stout 2016, 30–1).

Ann Lynch (see above) has argued that the inner wall of the west range was built against the nave wall and on top of the north–south drain, indicating that what is traditionally the lay brothers' accommodation was constructed late in the building campaign, possibly in the second quarter of the thirteenth century or even later. Boyle is one of nine Cistercian abbeys in Ireland with evidence for a west range and one of at least six that incorporate a western entrance into the abbey (Stout 2016, 58) (Fig. 8.2). Entrance to the abbey avoided the east range, the business side of the abbey, and the north which was dominated by the church. The location of entrances in the west may also highlight the lack of priority given to the lay brothers' range. After the church, the tallest and most imposing room in a Cistercian abbey was the refectory (Stalley 1987, 169–70). It was stipulated in their statutes that the refectory was one of the structures that had to be in place before a founding colony could be sent out to a new location. The refectory at Boyle runs parallel to the south cloister walk, a standard Bernardine scheme, derived ultimately from the plan of St Gall. This plan is found on four other Irish abbeys, Abbeyknockmoy, Co. Galway, Monasteranenagh, Co. Limerick, Hore, Co. Tipperary, and Dunbrody, Co. Wexford. It is a feature of the primary stone layouts of Cistercian abbeys in England and Wales. In Waverly in Surrey, a similar stone-built refectory was laid out in the 1130s and others have been identified from the mid twelfth century at Fountains, Furness, Kirkstall and Rievaulx in the north of England (Robinson 2006, 202).

Excavations at Boyle Abbey also threw light on medieval materials and methods of construction. Flat flagstones were exposed at the base of walls forming what may have represented a raft or plinth for the wall (Chapter 6). Similar construction techniques were revealed in recent excavations at an Augustinian abbey at Ballintubber, Co. Mayo (Archaeology and Heritage Consultancy Ltd 2019, 21).

The majority of the medieval iron finds were used in the timberwork of the church, furniture and other items such as chests. Structural ironwork includes nails, tacks, rivets, staples and brackets. There are also wood working tools such as wedges, gouges, punches and an awl. These finds highlight the quantities of timber used in these great stone buildings. From the late twelfth century, a change in building practices put pressure on reserves of mature timber. Large timbers were used in the construction of large-scale stone buildings for scaffolding and centring (Carpenter and Moss 2015, 85). The excavation at Boyle Abbey revealed construction postholes which may be the remains of a temporary working scaffold (Chapter 6). The best surviving examples of medieval structural timbers are preserved in the roofs of medieval stone buildings such as St Patrick's cathedral and Christ Church cathedral, Dublin. Timber was usually worked while still green shortly after felling. Erection on site of prefabricated structures was facilitated by a system of markings seen at Christ Church (*ibid.*, 86). Many religious houses cultivated their own mature woodlands for use in maintenance and rebuilding such as Mellifont (White 1943, 122). Recent excavations at Ballintubber Abbey produced structural ironwork including nails (Archaeology and Heritage Consultancy Ltd 2019). It was roofed and shingled with oak.

Items pertaining to the glazing of the church are present in the Boyle assemblage in the form of window glass and window lead. Boyle Abbey is a Cistercian foundation and regulations were laid down by the reformed order of Cistercian monks as to what was permitted and not permitted in window glazing within the abbey. (For the twelfth-century statutes, see Waddell 2002). As a result, a simple ornamental type of window glass was developed known as Cistercian grisaille glass. One complete quarry and a number of quarry fragments were recovered from the excavations at Boyle and provide direct evidence for the glazing of the abbey windows and the type of decoration used. The Boyle Abbey quarry, with its stiff-leaf trefoil motif, and painted grisaille glass dated to the early to mid thirteenth century and is similar to medieval glass recovered from excavations at the Cistercian abbeys of Duiske, Graiguenamanagh, Co. Kilkenny (Bradley and Manning, 1981, 419), Tintern, Co. Wexford (Lynch 2010, 144–5), and Bective, Co. Meath (Stout 2016, 90–2). A single sherd was recovered from excavations at the Cistercian abbey at Dunbrody, Co. Wexford. Medieval window glass has not survived *in situ* in Irish window frames, but historical sources and archaeological evidence confirm its widespread use in ecclesiastical buildings by the thirteenth century. Although the medieval glass has survived in very poor condition, some fragments have been dated to the mid to late thirteenth century based on surviving painted patterns.

Burial, memorial and patronage

The excavations at Boyle between 2006 and 2012 focused on the north aisle, an area outside the north wall and a narrow portion of the nave, immediately south of the north arcade (see Quinn above). This has provided a wealth of information on burial within Boyle Abbey and highlighted differences in burial practices inside and outside the church. Burial was taking place at Boyle Abbey from as early as the twelfth century right through to the sixteenth/seventeenth century with evidence for burials on the north side of the church prior to the construction of the aisle itself. The primary burial phase produced a radiocarbon date with a broad range (AD 1116–1218) encompassing the pre-foundation date of AD 1161. However, it is more probable that the earliest burial phase occurred when the monastic community had been established on the site. This phase of burials outside the north wall represents males, females, juveniles and adolescents. The earliest burials outside the church demonstrate that there did not appear to be any preference of male over female burials in this early phase of monastic activity with equal numbers of each sex. Grave cuts were not discernible here and the placing of the burials was far from neat, suggesting that wrapping of bodies interred outside the church did not occur. It was a common practice in medieval cemeteries for burials to occur in relatively shallow and irregularly placed graves without permanent markers. Being buried within the holy space was of utmost importance whereas visual commemoration was of secondary consideration (Pearson 1999, 47).

Burial practice within the aisle and the small portion of the nave surrounding the pier bases was in stark contrast to the burial practice adopted outside the north wall. There was greater care taken with the grave and interment. Burial cuts and fills were evident for the most part with a much neater placement of the remains within their respective graves in the church. A significant statistic within the aisle was the almost equal proportion of males to females. This is an interesting comparison with burials excavated in Tintern Abbey where Ó Donnabháin (2010, 102–25) notes that females and males appear to have been buried in equal numbers in the transept and ambulatory and that this was in contrast to those excavated in the church presbytery where males dominated. Evidence for both sexes was uncovered, and a number of juveniles, infants and adolescents were recorded as well as one in utero foetus in a later burial thought to be sixteenth to seventeenth century in date. The treatment of infants and juveniles is also interesting, with many buried intentionally close to or abutting the north aisle wall interior perhaps affording them protection from disturbance from other grave digging.

Ten grave slabs were recovered from the excavations along the north aisle, two of which marked *in situ* burials. Items found in direct association with burials were few and largely comprised coins, all of which are medieval in date. An *in situ* grave slab (E2399:273:25) was uncovered within the nave just south of the north arcading. Radiocarbon dating of the primary burial (B283) from the grave has indicated a date of between cal. AD 1392 and 1443. The re-use of the grave to inter four individuals may suggest a familial relationship.

The earliest burial phase at Boyle represents all members of Boyle society – males, females, juveniles and adolescents. Clearly this tells us that the abbey served as a community graveyard from its foundation. It was a commonly held belief in medieval times that interment within the bounds of the holy space of the monastery could dramatically increase one's chances of salvation. However, the early regulations of the order from the late 1140s forbade burials within the bounds of monasteries with the exception of a very few selected individuals (Hall 2005, 364). There is a significant body of legislative material on the burial of laity and other patrons in Cistercian abbeys and cemeteries (*ibid.*, 363–418). Cistercian legislation was initially strict about burial of lay people in their abbeys, in line with the perceived practice of St Benedict expanded in the *Exordium Parvum*, written before 1147, which says '… And because neither in the Rule nor in the Life of St Benedict did they read that this same teacher… had given anyone burial there, except his sister, they accordingly renounced all these things…' (*ibid.*, 364). In 1190 in a series of statutes prepared for codification, it was decreed that if a man died wishing to become a monk, before being professed as a novice, he was to be buried as a familiar. This encouraged the early acceptance of death-bed professions. In 1202, guests, servants, family members and their wives, founders and travellers who died on their journey might all be buried in the cemetery. By 1217 the General Chapter announced that the burial of seculars in Cistercian cemeteries was allowed if they had chosen this and if they had a licence of their priest. The wives of family members, however, were the only women permitted burial in Cistercian cemeteries. The first reliably dated statute concerning church burial is not until 1180 – only kings, queens and bishops might be buried inside the church and abbots in the chapter house. This highlights the status of the Boyle church burials. According to Cistercian custom, abbots were buried in the chapter house, a practice known to have been followed in Ireland during the twelfth and thirteenth centuries. This was probably the original location of the abbot's slab from Boyle (which remains the only monument with a specifically Cistercian character) (Stalley 1987; 2010). Excavations at the altar of Mellifont uncovered the remains of an ecclesiastic holding a silver chalice, who was almost certainly a bishop (de Paor 1969, 126).

A useful comparison to burial practices at Boyle Abbey is Melrose Abbey, located in the frontier region of medieval Scotland. It had links with the lay society on both sides of the English-Scottish border and one of the most important Cistercian houses in Scotland. *The Chronicle of Melrose* records significant interments at Melrose Abbey, including those of lay people. The chronicle mentions 23 burials of people and only one of these was a cleric, namely William, bishop of Glasgow (1233–58) buried near the high altar, and five of them were female. The five women buried at Melrose came from the top strata of Melrose benefactors (Jamroziak 2005, 326).

The remains of older women at Boyle also appear to be a quite distinct group and may represent an elite and privileged class. The Annals of Boyle contains numerous references to the funerals of lords and ladies, and this is an indication of the close contact kept between the lay population and the monks, perhaps reflected in the almost equal distribution of male to female burials within the north aisle. Devane (see Chapter 2) also mentions women buried in Boyle Abbey in the medieval period, and that in 1253, when the daughter of the earl of Ulster and wife of Milo Costello, died, she was interred in the Abbey of Boyle.

Burial and memorial of patrons was an important aspect of monastic life in the medieval period. Benefactors desired to be associated with a particular religious house in death. In addition to spiritual benefits, it was an expression of their position in society. The burials of donors cemented the relationship between them and the monastery endowed by them and ensured their perpetual presence within the monastic space and within the minds of the community (Jamroziak 2005, 331). The patrons and benefactors also provided a level of protection for the abbey. At Melrose the abbey was caught up in Anglo-Scottish warfare but was protected by either English or Scottish kings with various degrees of success. At the foundation of a religious house, a lord could persuade his tenants to donate a sum of money to their lord's new foundation in exchange for a promise of interment in its cemetery (Westerhof 2005, 33). During the 1180s, abbot Leonard of St Mary's Abbey, Dublin, angered local clergy by proclaiming the spiritual advantages that would accrue if one chose to die in the Cistercian habit and be buried in a Cistercian graveyard (Gwynn 1949, 110–25). Certainly, this attracted many of Boyle Abbey's benefactors, who retired to die in their local Cistercian abbey. Cistercian communities were particularly keen to acquire the bodies of their founders and benefactors and Boyle became a necropolis for the McDermots of Moylurg. Endowment and burial were closely entwined (Stalley 1987, 205ff). Founders were allowed burial in the second half of the twelfth century (*ibid.*, 35) and they are usually found in front of the high altar. Towards the end of the twelfth century the burial of bishops and other ecclesiastics became common practice in some Cistercian churches (Gajewski 2005, 58). At Clairvaux, St Malachy and St Bernard were amongst the first bishops to be buried in the altar of the church, in 1148 and 1153 respectively.

In England, at Bordesley Abbey (Worcestershire), the pattern of burial in the monastic church revealed by excavation suggests that it increasingly accepted lay burials from the late thirteenth century (Wright *et al.* 2005, 357). The excavation of a large proportion of the abbey church and the external eastern cemetery has provided two sizeable burial populations for detailed analysis and comparison. The mixed age and sex group from the abbey church comprises lay benefactors and their families, while the group from the cemetery is mostly male and adult, and arguably largely monastic. Here, like Boyle, there was also an absence of grave markers.

In terms of the health of the Boyle Abbey community, degenerative joint disease was the most common pathological lesion in the skeletons being apparent in just over three-quarters of all adults. Overall, the indicators of stress were not abnormally high, and are somewhat reflective of both the date and nature of the cemetery. While it is probable that this sample is biased, as burial here would often have been for the privileged, there are also indications that a number of individuals had suffered from severe, and undoubtedly, debilitating diseases and conditions such as tuberculosis, spina bifida and meningitis. This may reflect the role of the monastery as an infirmary for the poor and infirm. There was also evidence for severe injuries; one individual had been disembowelled, another suffered a sharp-force trauma to the back, and a male had suffered multiple injuries with at least three sharp-edged weapon injuries to the head, broken cheek bone and jaw, and broken ribs.

Diet and food economy of Boyle

The Cistercians were amongst the strictest orders following the rule of St Benedict, which deemed that only the sick in the infirmary could consume meat, with the monks and lay visitors being limited to fish, dairy products, fowl and vegetables. The rule stated that everybody should abstain from the meat of four-footed animals except the weak and the sick (Ervynck 1997). The original rule allowed for a choice of one or two cooked dishes (*pulmentaria*) with a flavouring of eggs in addition to cheese or fish, plus a dish of fruit or vegetables and a pound of bread (Harvey 1993). In 1335 Pope Benedict XII allowed that meat could be served to Cistercian monks on Sundays, Mondays, Tuesdays and Thursdays except during fasts such as Lent and Advent. This had to be eaten in a separate dining room (Beglane 2016, 126–69).

The diet at Boyle Abbey was closely linked to the economy of the abbey and the evidence suggests a reliance on animals reared on monastery lands. The Cistercians in Boyle practised animal husbandry so there would have been considerable quantities of meat available. Even for newly founded monasteries, adherence to the rule was often more of an ideal than an actuality, and when a range of sites across Europe were examined it was clear that the level of faunal remains was often too high to be accounted for by the consumption of meat by guests or the sick (Ervynck 1997; 2004).

The faunal assemblage from Boyle Abbey is small. Nevertheless, it provides an insight into the diet and farming practices of the monastic community. Beef was by far the favoured meat with mutton and pork also present. Sheep accounted for 20% of the medieval sample and an ageing analysis established from the state of fusion of the long bones indicates that most sheep were killed between two and five years of age. This suggests a mixed economy aimed at the production of wool, woolfells and meat. The presence of sheep fits with the known connection between the Cistercian order and sheep rearing so that sheep are noted at a number of monastic sites (McCormick 1991). The skeletal elements present also indicate that live animals were slaughtered in the immediate environs of the abbey, presumably as meat was required. The ages of the animal stock from the medieval period also indicate that older cattle and sheep were being kept not just for their meat but also for their secondary products.

The range of fish from Boyle Abbey is similar to that recorded from Bective Abbey (Hamilton-Dyer 2016, 170–8), where the bones mostly represented marine species with a lesser reliance on riverine species such as eels and salmon. This is surprising, given the proximity of the abbey to a river.

Farming practices

When the results from Boyle Abbey are compared with the faunal evidence from another Cistercian monastery at Bective, Co. Meath, it highlights the regional diversity in animal husbandry practised. Whereas at Boyle cattle is dominant with sheep less so, the assemblage at Bective was dominated by sheep/goat with cattle and pig less prominent (Beglane 2016, 126–69). From a comparative point of view, the dominance of cattle was also clear in the animal bone assemblage from another west of Ireland Augustinian abbey at Ballintubber, Co. Mayo indicating a regional bias. At the latter site, cattle, sheep/goats, pig as well as dog, cat and horse were identified. Cattle were the most important species at this site, followed by sheep/goat and pigs (Coogan 2019, 88). Archaeobotanical remains identified from the Ballintubber site reflect domestic waste (cereals, legumes and flax) and gathered foodstuffs as well as flora from the various habitats that were growing in and around the site. Interestingly, wheat dominates on medieval sites in mixed crop assemblages in eastern rather than western areas which could explain its absence from the Boyle Abbey crop assemblage (McCormick *et al.* 2011).

Material cultures

Many of the objects found on the excavations are lost items of personal dress such as bone pins and stick pins including a club-headed example which is known from eleventh- to thirteenth-century contexts elsewhere in Ireland. These also include a dress hook or clasp and lace chapes recovered from the excavations. The discovery of a silver chalice or candlestick base is a reminder of the once rich corpus of such altar pieces used in the church. It is one of a small number of altar vessels recovered from Irish Cistercian sites such as Dunbrody and Mellifont, which show evidence for re-use or reworking before they were buried. Ó Floinn (2013, 362–73) has suggested that this probably occurred at the time of the dissolution of the monasteries. Evidence for craft-working includes that of bone used to make handles for knives, bone pins, combs and gaming pieces.

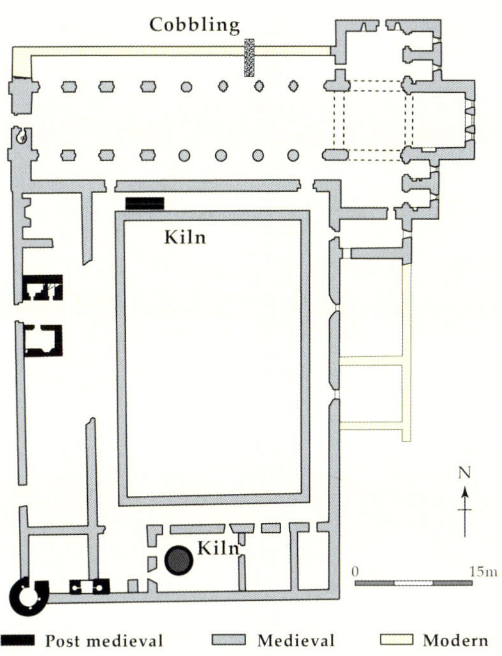

Fig. 8.3. Plan of post-medieval remodelling at Boyle Abbey.

Evidence for serious injuries was identified (see above) on some of the human remains and weapons used in warfare were recovered from the excavation. These include large projectile heads similar to examples from mid to late twelfth-century contexts in Waterford City and Kells, Co. Meath, which may have been used with a crossbow, and an impressive late medieval sword with a decorated, double-edged blade (see Chapter 6), a sharp reminder of the more turbulent times in the abbey.

Commercial activity is reflected in the discovery of a balance arm from a scale and a possible fragment of a folding arm balance. Balances or scales were used throughout the medieval period for measuring coins, precious metals or spices. Of further interest are the seven medieval coins found at the site, mainly attributed to Edward III (1327–77). Lead seals found at the abbey were similar to those attached to textiles from the late fourteenth to the early nineteenth century in England as part of a system of industrial regulation and taxation. Cloth seals were typically two-disc seals joined by a connecting strip.

There is a great scarcity of medieval pottery. Just two sherds of French pottery were recovered from the excavations and only one possible sherd of medieval pottery was recovered from the cloister.

Post-medieval remodelling

Evidence uncovered during the 1980s and 2004 excavations threw much light on the post-medieval remodelling at Boyle Abbey; in its aftermath there was wide-scale demolition (Fig. 8.3). The monastery was extensively modified following its dissolution between the late sixteenth century and the end of the eighteenth century when the abbey was occupied by an English garrison and transformed into a barracks. One of the most evocative finds of the 1980s excavation surely is the fragment of a silk vestment with sun-bleached adult hair attached, found amongst the flagstones in the cloister garth and probably lost during the time of the dissolution. At Boyle the original monastic entrance in the west was maintained and the gatehouse modified. The prestigious east range was badly damaged and the monastic kitchen at the west end of the south range was re-used with a large fireplace inserted. A circular tower was added at the south-west angle and the wall of the west range was rebuilt to form part of the defences of the barracks. Within the new cloister-turned-courtyard, the cloister arcades were cleared away and the entire cloister area cobbled and re-used for industrial purposes. A corn-drying kiln was constructed on the site with a paved, open-ended structure, probably used for storage and as a hearth.

Excavations uncovered the remains of outbuildings along the original north aisle of the abbey church, possibly part of a military stables where ceramic roof tiles and pottery dating from the late seventeenth and eighteenth centuries were found. It is possible that a rough placement of stones was put over the burial ground during this period. Arches along the north arcade were blocked to almost half-way up their height during the military occupation. A later cobbled surface with integrated gullies and associated walls was also exposed across the entire north aisle and dated to the nineteenth century.

Archaeological excavations carried out in 2004 in the area of the refectory revealed that this was also cobbled and used for industrial activity (see Chapter 4). A kiln was erected in the seventeenth century, which made pantiles, peg tiles and ridge tiles for re-roofing of the cloistral buildings. This was an open cylinder kiln similar in design to those in use in the seventeenth century at Barnstaple in Devon. It would have been topped with a temporary roof of clay and was fired by a pair of twin flues, orientated to the prevailing south-westerly winds. A Jacobean-style house with stone chimney and ovens was constructed in the western end of the south range at some stage in the late sixteenth to seventeenth century.

Boyle Abbey was one of many religious houses in Ireland that were converted to alternative uses in the period after the Acts of Suppression. Many leading Crown favourites took advantage of their position to transform cloistral buildings into residential mansions. In England as many as half of the dissolved houses were put to new uses (Aston 1973, 231–55). What marks Boyle as different is its post-medieval use as a barracks. This is exceptional when compared with many other abbey conversions in the country. Some comparison can be made with the post-medieval use of the Franciscan friary at Carrickfergus, Co. Antrim. In 1566, as part of the Elizabethan consolidation of English influence on the eastern seaboard of Ulster, it was entrenched as the fortified 'Queen's Storehouse' (Hamlin and Brannon 2003, 252–66). Also, in 1604 Sir Thomas Phillips, an English soldier, gained custody of the Dominican friary at Coleraine, Co. Londonderry, and built a fortification of its perimeter (*ibid.*, 260). In Wales, during the Civil War of the 1640s, the Fowler family defended Cwymhir for the Royalist cause by fortifying the Cwymhir Abbey (Robinson 1998, 95).

Many of the abbeys in Ireland like Boyle continued to be players in the political struggles of

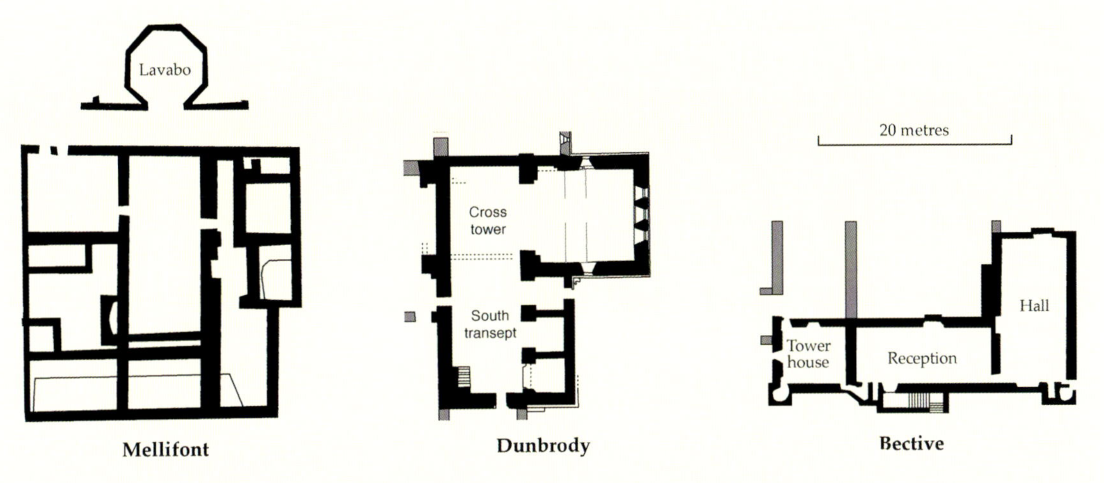

Fig. 8.4. Comparative plans of post-medieval abbey remodelling in Ireland.

the post-medieval period. These monasteries share similar approaches to their remodelling including the removal of the cloister walks at Dunbrody and Mellifont, instantly creating a courtyard (Fig 8.4). The Moore family, originally from Kent in the south of England, became the owners of three dissolved Cistercian estates in Ireland: Mellifont Abbey, Monasterevin, Co. Kildare, and St Mary's Abbey, Dublin (Stout *et al.* 2016, 191–226). Mellifont, like Boyle, played a significant role in the political events of that period. It was situated, like Boyle, in a strategic position which separated the territories occupied by the English from those held by the Irish. A lease of the site, its abbey and lands was made to Edward Moore by Queen Elizabeth in 1566 for 21 years. From Mellifont Sir Edward Moore vigorously defended the Crown position between unconquered Ulster and the Pale and regularly provided the Crown with intelligence regarding the O'Neill dynasty in the north. His son Garret Moore was later granted a troop of 25 horses. In the early seventeenth century the cloister area, including the site of the west range and part of the south and east ranges, became the cobbled forecourt to the Moore House built out of the ruins of the abbey church. The east end of the south range was used for storage. The west range was adapted for use as stables while the cloister garth was converted into a courtyard.

Tintern Abbey, Co. Wexford, witnessed its post-dissolution conversion into a domestic residence by the Colclough family from 1562 (Lynch 2010). Bective Abbey, Co. Meath, also underwent a major conversion to a fortified Tudor mansion (Stout 2016, 66ff). The mansion was designed around the south range, the cloister and the earlier south-west tower that acted as a pivot for the two domestic wings. The abbey church was largely demolished except for the south-west transept. The Cistercian abbey at Dunbrody, Co. Wexford, was also converted into a Tudor residence in the sixteenth century (Stout 2016, 97–123). Edward Etchingham erected a fine manor within the abbey buildings and the cloister served as its bawn.

Post-medieval military diet

In the post-dissolution period at Boyle Abbey there are noticeable changes in provisions with larger cattle being processed owing to the development of butchery techniques and the use of saws. This is typical of sites from this period such as Bective Abbey (Beglane 2016, 160). Improved breeds of cattle became more common in Boyle during this time. There were changes in the age of slaughter of animals eaten by the military personnel during this later period. A corn-drying kiln within the walls of Boyle Castle indicates that grain would have supplemented their diet.

Post-medieval material culture

Post-medieval finds from the excavations reflect the military use of the abbey as a barracks. Gunflints from muskets and pistols and lead shot, probably manufactured on site, were recovered. Also found were remnants of Matlock guns used throughout the seventeenth century as it was the standard infantry arm of the British Army until 1690. Lost or discarded buckles and buttons from uniforms survived including one with the mounted emblem of the 64th (2nd Staffordshire) Regiment of Foot, an infantry regiment of the British Army active between 1756 and 1881.

The military occupation of the abbey continued into the eighteenth century and domestic finds from this period were recorded in the excavations in the refectory, cloister area and north aisle. The pottery comprises tableware dating from the middle of the seventeenth century until the nineteenth century. These were largely foreign exports of middling class transported into the north-west of the country. Their dining tables shone with elegant, decorated cream plates. They also used local glazed red earthenware more commonly found in the dairy and kitchen. These include pans, jugs, storage jars and bowls. The occupants smoked from clay pipes and drank French wine. Wine bottles were recovered from the refectory and part of this assemblage consisted of a form of French wine bottle with no string ring and described as a 'wrythen'. This is the first record of this bottle type recovered in Irish excavations. In France they were used throughout the seventeenth century through to the first two decades of the eighteenth century. A large number of items recovered date right up to the modern period, a testament to how the abbey continued as a focal point within the community long after it went out of use by a monastic community.

Abbreviations

AB	Freeman, A.M. (ed.) 1924 –7 'The annals in Cotton MS Titus A. XXV', *Revue Celtique* 41 (1924), 301–30; 42 (1925), 283–305; 43 (1926), 358–84; 44 (1927), 336–61.
AConn	Freeman, A.M. (ed.) 1944 *Annála Connacht: the annals of Connacht.* Dublin.
AClon	Murphy, D. (ed.) 1896 *Annals of Clonmacnoise.* Dublin.
AFM	O'Donovan, J. 1848–51 *Annala Rioghachta Eireann: annals of the kingdom of Ireland by the Four Masters*, 7 vols. Dublin.
ACL	Hennessy, W.M. 1871 *Annals of Loch Cé, a Chronicle of Irish affairs from A.D. 1014 to A.D.* 1590, 2 vols. London.
ASH	Colgan, J. 1645 *Acta sanctorum veteris et majoris Scotiae seu Hiberniae.* Louvain, reprinted 1947. Dublin.
AT	Stokes, W. (ed.) 1895–97 'The annals of Tigernach', *Revue Celtique* 16 (1895), 374–419, 17 (1896), 6–33, 119–265, 337–420, 18 (1897) 9–59, 150–97, 267–303.
AU	Hennessy, W.M. and Mac Carthy, B. (eds) 1887–1901 *Annála Uladh: annals of Ulster*, 4 vols. Dublin.

BCC	Ó Domhnaill, M. (comp.) 1532 Kelleher, A.O. and Schoepperle, G. (eds) *Betha Colaim Chille*, Repr. 1994. Dublin.
Cal. Car. MSS.	Brewer, J.S. and Bullen, W. (eds) 1867–73. *Calendar of the Carew manuscripts, preserved in the archepiscopal library at Lambeth*, 5 vols. London.
Cal. Pap. Reg.	Twemlow, J.A. (ed.) 1921 *Calendar of Papal Registers relating to Great Britain and Ireland, xi, 1455–64*. London.
CCPH	Her Majesty's Stationery Office 1883–1976 *Calendar of the Cecil papers in Hatfield House*, 24 vols. London.
CDI	Sweetman, H.S. (ed.) 1875–86 *Calendar of documents relating to Ireland*, 5 vols. London.
CR	Kavanagh, S. (ed.) 1932–49 *Commentarius Rinuccinianus*, 6 vols. Dublin.
CSP	Public Record Office 1856–72 *Calendar of state papers, domestic series, of the reigns of Edward VI, Mary, Elizabeth and James*, 12 vols. London.
CSPI	Public Record Office 1860–1912 *Calendar of state papers relating to Ireland*, 23 vols. London.
DIL	Royal Irish Academy 1852–1976 *Dictionary of the Irish Language*. Dublin.
Fiant	Nicholls, K.W. (ed.) 1994 *Irish Fiants of the Tudor sovereigns during the reigns of Henry VIII, Edward VI, Philip and Mary, and Elizabeth I*, 4 vols. Dublin.
GC	Brewer, J.S., Dimock, J.F. and Warner, G.F. (eds) 1861–91 *Giraldi Cambrensis opera*, 8 vols. London.
HD	Ware, J. no date *Annales Dominicani de Roscoman*. Unpublished manuscript.
INSTAR	Irish National Strategic Archaeological Research Programme.
JGAHS	Journal of Galway Archaeological and Historical Society
Met. Dinn.	Gwynn, E. (ed.) 1903–35 *The Metrical Dindshenchas*, 5 vols. Dublin; repr. 1991.
SG	O'Grady, S.H. (ed.) *Silva Gadelica, a collection of tales in Irish*, 2 vols. London.
SCGOC	Canivez, J.M. 1933–5 *Statuta capitulorum generalium ordinis Cisterciensis*, 4 vols. Louvain.
TT	Colgan, J. 1647 *Trias Thaumaturga*. Louvain, repr. 1997, Dublin.

Bibliography

- Allan, J., Cramp, C. and Horner, B. (2007). The post-medieval pottery at Castle Hill, Great Torrington, North Devon. *Proceedings Devon Archaeological Society* 65, 135–81.

- Allan, J., Horner, B. and Langman, G. (2005). *Proceedings Devon Archaeological Society* 63, 167–203.

- AlQahtani, S.J., Liversidge, H.M. and Hector, M.P. (2010). Brief communication, The London atlas of tooth development and eruption. *American Journal of Physical Anthropology* 142, no. 3, 481–90. Available online at atlas.dentistry.qmul.ac.uk/.

- Archaeological Consultancy Ltd. (2004). Archaeological pre-development testing at Boyle Abbey. Unpublished report. Dublin.

- Archaeology and Heritage Consultancy Ltd. (2019). Final report on the archaeological excavations at Ballintubber Abbey, Co. Mayo, (Ministerial Consent C702). Unpublished report for the National Monuments Service.

- Archdall, M. (1786). *Monasticon hibernicum: or, a history of the abbeys, priories, and other religious houses in Ireland* Dublin.

- *Archivium Hibernicum*. (1949). XV.

- Aston, M. (1973). English ruins and English history: the dissolution and the sense of the past. *Journal of the Warburg and Courtauld Institutes* 36, 231–55.

- Aubert, M. (1947). *L'Architecture Cistercienne en France*. Vanoest, Paris.

- Australia ICOMOS. (2013). The Burra Charter. [Online] Available at australia.icomos.org/wp-content/uploads/The-Burra-Charter-2013-Adopted-31.10.2013.pdf (Accessed 01/10/2021).

- Barnard, T.C. (2000). *Cromwellian Ireland: English government and reform in Ireland 1649–60*. Oxford.

- Barnes, E. (1994). *Developmental defects of the axial skeleton in paleopathology*. Niwot, CO.

- Beglane, F. (2016). The faunal remains from Bective Abbey. In G. Stout and M. Stout, *The Bective Abbey project, Co. Meath: excavations 2009–12*, 126–69. Dublin.
- Beirne, F.M. (ed.). (2000). *The diocese of Elphin: people, places and pilgrimage*. Blackrock.
- Berman, C.H. (1986). Medieval agriculture, the southern French countryside, and the early Cistercians: a study of forty-three monasteries. *Transactions of the American Philosophical Society* 76, no. 5, 1–179.
- Bhreathnach, E. (2009). Mapping death: boundaries, territories and people in Ireland from 1st to 8th centuries AD. Unpublished summary report. INSTAR ref no. 16700.
- Bickerton, L.M. (1984). *English drinking glasses 1675–1825*. Princes Risborough, Buckinghamshire.
- Biddle, M. (1990). Dress and hair pins. In M. Biddle *Object and economy in medieval Winchester* ii, 552–60. Oxford.
- Biddle, B. and Barclay, K. (1990). Sewing pins and wire. In M. Biddle *Object and economy in medieval Winchester* ii, 560–71. Oxford.
- Bieler, L. (ed.). (1979). *The Patrician texts in the Book of Armagh*. Dublin.
- Blakeman, A. (2002). *Bottles and pot lids: a collector's guide*. London.
- Blom, D.E., Buikstra, J.E., Keng, L., Tomczak, P.D., Shoreman, E., Stevens-Tuttle, D. (2005). Anemia and childhood mortality: latitudinal patterning along the coast of pre-Columbian Peru. *American Journal of Physical Anthropology* June 127(2), 152–69.
- Boessneck, J. (1969). Osteological differences between sheep (*Ovis aries Linné*) and goats (*Capra hircus Linné*). In D.R. Brothwell and E. Higgs (eds), *Science in archaeology, a survey of progress and research*, 331–9. London.
- Bourke, E. (1995). Life in the sunny south-east: housing and domestic economy in Viking and medieval Wexford. *Archaeology Ireland* 9, no. 3, 33–6.
- Bradley, J. and Manning, C. (1981). Excavations at Duiske Abbey, Graiguenamanagh, Co. Kilkenny. *Proceedings of the Royal Irish Academy* 81C, 397–426.
- Brady, C. (ed.). (2002). *A Viceroy's vindication? Sir Henry Sidney's Memoir of Service in Ireland, 1556–1578*. Cork.
- Brakspear, H. (1931). A west country school of masons. *Archaeologia* 36, 1–18.
- Brewer, J.S. and Bullen, W. (eds). (1867–73). *Calendar of the Carew manuscripts, preserved in the archepiscopal library at Lambeth*, 5 vols. London.
- Brewer, J.S., Dimock, J.F. and Warner, G.F. (eds). (1861–91). *Giraldi Cambrensis opera*, 8 vols. London.
- Brown, S. and O'Connor, D. (1991). *Medieval craftsmen: glass-painters*. London.
- Burton, J. and Kerr, J. (2011). *The Cistercians in the Middle Ages*. Boydell Press.
- Byrne, F.J. (1973). *Irish kings and high-kings*. London.
- Byrne, J. (2004). *Byrne's dictionary of Irish local history*. Cork.

- Campbell, B. (1988). The diffusion of vetches in medieval England. *Economic History Review* 41, 193–208.
- Campbell, B. (2000). *English seigniorial agriculture, 1250–1450*, Cambridge.
- Canivez, J.M. (1933–5). *Statuta capitulorum generalium ordinis Cisterciensis*, 4 vols. Louvain.
- Cannan, F. (2009). *Scottish arms and armour.* Oxford.
- Carey, A. and Meenan, R. (2004). Excavation of a post-medieval pottery kiln, Tuam, Co. Galway. *Journal of the Galway Archaeological and Historical Society* 56, 37–45.
- Carlson, D., Armelagos, G. and Van Gerven, D. (1974). Factors influencing the etiology of cribra orbitalia in prehistoric Nubia. *Journal of Human Evolution* 3, 405–10.
- Carney, J. (ed.). (1943). *Topographical poems by Seán Mór Ó Dubhagáin and Giolla-na-Naomh Ó hUidhrín.* Dublin.
- Carpenter A. and Moss, R. (2015). Materials and methods. In A. Carpenter and R. Moss, *Art and architecture of Ireland, volume I: medieval c.400–c.1600*, 83–120. Dublin.
- Carrig Conservation. (2005). Boyle Abbey condition report. Unpublished report for the OPW. Dublin.
- Carrig Conservation. (2008). Addendum to Boyle Abbey condition report. Unpublished report for the OPW. Dublin.
- Carrig Conservation. (no date). Boyle Abbey North Wall Project method statement for numbering and dismantling system. Unpublished report for the OPW. Dublin.
- Carroll, M. and Quinn, A. (2003). Stone artefacts. In R.M. Cleary and M.F. Hurley (eds), *Excavations in Cork city 1984–2000*. Cork City Council, Cork.
- *Catholic Encyclopaedia*. (1913). VIII,163.
- Caulfield, S. (1977). The beehive quern in Ireland. *Journal of the Royal Society of Antiquaries* 107, 104–38. Champney, A. 1910 *Irish ecclesiastical architecture*. London.
- Chapelot, J. (1983) The Saintonge pottery industry in the later Middle Ages. In P. Davey and R. Hodges (eds), *Ceramics and trade*, 49–53. Sheffield.
- Chibnall, M. (ed.). (1973). *Ecclesiastical history of Orderic Vitalis, iv.* Oxford.
- Childs, J. (2007). *The Williamite Wars in Ireland*. London.
- Clark, J. (1995). *The medieval horse and its equipment; medieval finds from excavations in London*. 5.
- Clyne, M. (2005). Archaeological excavations at Holy Trinity Abbey, Lough Key, Co. Roscommon. *Proceedings of the Royal Irish Academy* 105C, 23–98.
- Coleman-Smith, R. and Pearson, T. (1988). *Excavations in the Donyatt Potteries*. Chichester, Sussex.
- Colgan, J. (1645). *Acta sanctorum veteris et majoris Scotiae seu Hiberniae*. Louvain, repr. Dublin 1947.
- Colgan, J. (1647). *Trias Thaumaturga*. Louvain, repr. Dublin 1997.

- Commissioners of Public Works. (1896). *Sixty-third annual report of the Commissioners of Public Works in Ireland, year ending 1895*. Dublin.
- Commissioners of Public Works. (1905). *Seventy-second annual report of the Commissioners of Public Works in Ireland, year ending 1904*. Dublin.
- Commissioners of Public Works. (1939–40). *108th annual report of the Commissioners of Public Works in Ireland*. Dublin.
- Conway, Fr. Colmcille. (1958). *The story of Mellifont*. Dublin.
- Coogan, A. (2019). Appendix 2: animal bone report. In Archaeology and Heritage Consultancy Ltd, Final Report on the archaeological excavations at Ballintubber Abbey, Co. Mayo, (Ministerial Consent C702). Unpublished report for the National Monuments Service, 88–99.
- Coppack, G, Hayfield, C. and Williams, R. (2002). Sawley Abbey: the architecture and archaeology of a smaller Cistercian abbey. *Journal of the British Archaeological Association* 155, 22–114.
- Cowgill, J.M., de Neergaard, M., Griffiths, N. (1987). *Knives and scabbards: Medieval finds from excavations in London*. London, Her Majesty's Stationery Office.
- CRSBI. (2020). Corpus of Romanesque sculpture in Britain and Ireland. [Online] Available at www.crsbi.ac.uk/ (Accessed 01/10/2001).
- Cunningham, B. (2010). *Calendar of State Papers, Ireland, Tudor Period 1568–1571*.
- D'Alton, J. (1845). *The history of Ireland, from the earliest period to the year 1245, when the Annals of Boyle, which are adopted and embodied as the running text authority, terminate: with a brief essay on the native annalists, and other sources for illustrating Ireland, and full statistical and historical notices of the barony of Boyle*. Dublin.
- Davis-Weyer, C. (1971). *Sources and documents, early medieval art 300–1150*. Englewood Cliffs, NJ.
- Dawson, D. and Kent, O. (2008). The development of the bottle kiln in pottery manufacture in Britain. *Post-Medieval Archaeology* 42, no. 1, 201–26.
- Day, L.F. (1897). *Windows: a book about stained and painted glass*. London.
- de Paor, L. (1969). Excavations at Mellifont Abbey, Co. Louth. *Proceedings of the Royal Irish Academy* 68C, 109–64.
- Dennehy, E. and Lynch, L. (2001). Unearthed secrets: a clandestine burial-ground. *Archaeology Ireland* 15, no. 4, 20–3.
- Department of the Environment, Heritage and Local Government. (2010). *Roofs; a guide to the repair of historic roofs*. Dublin.
- Deroeux, D., Dufournier, D. and Herteig, A.E. (1994). French medieval ceramics from the Bryggen excavations in Bergen, Norway. *Bryggen Papers Supplementary series* 5, 161–208.
- Dillon, M. (1961). The inauguration of O'Conor. In J.A. Watt, J.B. Moral and F.X. Martin (eds), *Medieval studies presented to Aubrey Gwynn, S.J.*, 186–202. Dublin.
- Dodwell, C.R. (ed. and trans.) (1986). Theophilus: the various arts (*De diversis artibus*). Oxford.

- Donkin, R.A. (1978). *The Cistercians: studies in the geography of medieval England and Wales*. Toronto.
- Doran, L. (2004). Medieval communication routes through Longford and Roscommon and their associated settlements. *Proceedings of the Royal Irish Academy* 104C, no. 3, 57–80.
- Dornan, A. (2009). Report on the inventory of carved stone at Boyle Abbey, Co. Roscommon. Unpublished OPW report. Dublin.
- Draper, J. (1984). *Post-medieval pottery 1650–1800*. Princes Risborough, Buckinghamshire.
- Dugdale, W. (1693). *Monasticon Anglicanum or the history of the ancient abbies, and other monasteries, hospitals, cathedral and collegiate churches, in England and Wales with divers French, Irish, and Scotch monasteries formerly relating to England*. London.
- Dunlevy, M. (1988a). A classification of early Irish combs. *Proceedings of the Royal Irish Academy*, 88C, 341–442.
- Dunlevy, M. (1988b). *Ceramics in Ireland*. Dublin.
- Dunne, L. and Kiely, J. (2013). Archaeological excavation report: Adare Castle. *Eachtra Journal*, 16, 89.
- Eachtra Archaeological Projects (2009). A ringfort with killeen burials at Mackney, Co. Galway (E2444). [Online] Available at eachtra.ie/index.php/journal/e2444-mackney-co-galway/ (Accessed 01/10/2021).
- Eames, E. and Fanning, T. (1988). *Irish medieval tiles*. Dublin.
- Edwards, N. (2002). *The archaeology of early medieval Ireland*. London.
- Ervynck, A. (1997). Following the rule? Fish and meat consumption on monastic communities in Flanders (Belgium). In G. De Boe and F. Verhaeghe (eds), *Environment and subsistence in medieval Europe: papers of medieval Europe, Brugge 1997 Conference*, 67–81. Brussels.
- Ervynck, A. (2004). *Orant, pugnant, laborant:* the diet of the three orders in the feudal society of medieval north-western Europe. In S.J. O'Day, W. Van Neer and A. Ervynck (eds), *Behaviour behind bones: the zooarchaeology of ritual, religion, status and identity*, 215–23.Oxford.
- Esser, K.H. (1953). Über den Kirchenbau desHl. Bernhard von Clairvaux. *Archiv für Mittelrheinische Kirchengeschichte* 5, 195–222.
- Farrelly, J., O'Brien, C. and Paynter, S. (2005). *The 17th-century glasshouse at Shinrone, Co. Offaly, Ireland*. Portsmouth.
- Farrelly, J. (2010). From sand and ash: glassmaking in early seventeenth-century Ireland. In J.M. Hearne (ed.) *Glassmaking in Ireland: from the medieval to the contemporary*. Dublin and Oregon: Irish Academic Press, 33–54.
- Fergusson, P. (1984) *Architecture of solitude: Cistercian abbeys in twelfth- century England*. Princeton, NJ.
- Flanagan, M-T. (1998a). The context and uses of the Latin charter in medieval Ireland. In P. Huw (ed.), *Literacy in medieval Celtic societies*, 113–32. Cambridge.
- Flanagan, M-T. (1998b) Strategies of lordship in pre-Norman and post-Norman Leinster. In C. Harper-Bill (ed.), *Anglo-Norman studies XX, Proceedings of the Battle Conference 1997*, 107–26. Woodbridge.

- Flanagan, M-T. (2005). Irish royal charters and the Cistercian order. In M-T. Flanagan and J.A. Green (eds), *Charters and charter scholarship in Britain and Ireland*. Basingstoke.
- Flower, R. (1927). The origin and the history of the Cottonian annals. *Revue Celtique* 44, 336–44.
- France, J. (1998). *The Cistercians in medieval art*. Stroud, Gloucestershire.
- Freeman, A.M. (ed.). (1924–7). The annals in Cotton MS Titus A. XXV. *Revue Celtique* 41 (1924), 301–30; 42 (1925), 283–305; 43 (1926), 358–84; 44 (1927), 336–61.
- Freeman, A.M. (ed.). (1936). *The Compossicion Booke of Conought*. Dublin.
- Freeman, A.M. (ed.). (1944). *Annála Connacht: the annals of Connacht*. Dublin.
- Gaffney, H. (1961). A martyr's rosary in Black Abbey. *The Kilkenny People*, Friday, 27 January.
- Gajewski, A. (2005). Burial, cult, and construction at the Abbey church of Clairvaux. In J. Hall and C. Kratzke (eds), Sepulturae Cistercienses: *Burial, memorial and patronage in medieval Cistercian monasteries*, 47–85. Cîteaux, France.
- Gerrard, C.M., Guitérrez, A., Hurst, J.G. and Vince, A.G. (1995). A guide to Spanish medieval pottery. In C.M. Gerrard, A. Guitérrez and A.G. Vince (eds), *Spanish medieval ceramics in Spain and the British Isles*, 281–95. Oxford.
- Grant, A. (1975). The animal bones and appendix B: the use of tooth wear as a guide to the age of domestic animals. In B. Cunliffe (ed.), *Excavations at Portchester Castle, i, Roman*, 378–408, 437–50. London.
- Grant, A. (1983). *North Devon pottery: the seventeenth century*. Exeter.
- Grauer, A.L. (1993). Patterns of anaemia and infection from Medieval York. *American Journal of Physical Anthropology* 91, no. 2, 203–13.
- Griesser, P.B. (ed.). (1946). *Registrum epistolarum abbatis Stephani de Lexinton. Analecta Sacri Ordinis Cisterciensis* 2, 1–118.
- Griffith, M.C. (ed.). (1991). *Calendar of Inquisitions formerly in the office of the Chief Remembrancer of the Exchequer*. Dublin.
- Gwynn, A. (1949). The origins of St Mary's Abbey, Dublin. *Journal of the Royal Society of Antiquaries of Ireland* 79, 110–25.
- Gwynn, A. and Hadcock, R.N. (1970). *Medieval religious houses, Ireland*. London.
- Gwynn, E. (ed.). (1903–35). *The Metrical Dindshenchas*, 5 vols. Dublin, repr. 1991.
- Hahn, H. (1957). *Die frühe kirchenbaukunst der Zisterzienser*. Berlin.
- Hall, J. (2005). The legislative background to lay burial. In J. Hall and C. Kratzke (eds), Sepulturae Cistercienses: *Burial, memorial and patronage in medieval Cistercian monasteries*, 363–418. Cîteaux, France.

- Halpin, A. (1986). Irish medieval swords *c.* 1170–1600. *Proceedings of the Royal Irish Academy* 86C, no. 5, 183–230.
- Hamilton-Dyer, S. (2016). Bird and fish bones from Bective Abbey. In G. Stout and M. Stout, *The Bective Abbey project, Co. Meath: excavations 2009–12*, 170–8. Dublin.
- Hamlin, A. and Brannon, N. (2003). Northern Ireland: the afterlife of monastic buildings. In D. Gaimster and R. Gilchrist (eds), *The archaeology of reformation* 1480–1580, 252–66. Belfast.
- Hanrahan, P. (1978). Bottles in the Place Royal collection. *Material Culture Review/Revue de la Culture Matérielle* 6, 52–73.
- Harbison, P. (ed.). (2000). *Drawings and notes from an eighteenth-century gentleman*. Dublin.
- Harbison, P. (2001). 'Irish artists on Irish subjects': the Cooper collection in the National Library. *Irish Arts Review* 17, 61–9.
- Harbison, P. and Shields, J. (2002). *Our Treasures of antiquities: Beranger and Bigari's antiquarian sketching tour of Connacht 1779 based on material in the National Library and the Royal Irish Academy.*
- Harris, M. (1997). The abominable pig. In C. Counihan and P. van Esterik (eds), *Food and culture: a reader*, 150–60. Abingdon-on-Thames, Oxfordshire.
- Harvey, B. (1993). *Living and dying in England, 1100–1540: the monastic experience*. Oxford.
- Hayes-McCoy, G.A. (1977). *Sixteenth century Irish swords in the National Museum of Ireland*. Dublin.
- Hengen, O.P. (1971). *Cribra Orbitalia; pathogenesis and probable etiology. Homo* 22, 57–75.
- Hennessy, W.M. (1871). *Annals of Loch Cé, a Chronicle of Irish affairs from A.D. 1014 to A.D. 1590*, 2 vols. London.
- Hennessy, W.M. and Mac Carthy, B. (eds) 1887–1901 *Annála Uladh: annals of Ulster*, 4 vols. Dublin.
- Henry, F. (1970). *Irish art in the Romanesque period. (1020–1170)*. London.
- Her Majesty's Stationery Office. (1883–1976). *Calendar of the Cecil papers in Hatfield House*, 24 vols. London.
- Herbert, M. (1988). *Iona, Kells and Derry: the history and hagiography of the monastic familia of Columba*. Oxford.
- Hillson, S. (1986). *Teeth*. Cambridge.
- Hockey, S.F. (ed.). (1975). *The Account Book of Beaulieu Abbey*. London Royal Historical Society.
- Hogan, E. (1910). *Onomasticon Goedelicum*. Dublin.
- Hogan, F. (1992). Gelasius O'Cullenan O.Cist., Martyr – Abbot of Boyle. *Hallel, A Review of Monastic Spiritualilty and Liturgy* 17, no. 2.
- Hurley, M.F. (1987). 1987 Kilferagh, Co. Kilkenny. In Cleary, M.F. Hurley and E.A. Twohig (eds), *Archaeological excavations on the Cork/Dublin gas pipeline* (1981–2), 88–100. Cork.

- Hurley, M.F. (1997). Stone artefacts. In R.M. Cleary, M.F. Hurley and E. Shee Twohig (eds), *Skiddy's Castle and Christ Church Cork: excavations 1974–7* by D.C. Twohig, 206–22. Cork.

- Hurley, M.F. and Scully, O.M.B. (eds). (1997). *Late Viking age and medieval Waterford: excavations 1986–92*. Waterford.

- Hurley, M.F. (2007). The bone artifacts. In M. Clyne, *Kells Priory, Co Kilkenny: Archaeological excavations by T. Fanning and M. Clyne*, 415–23.

- Hurst, J.G., Neal, D.S. and van Beuningen, H.J.E. (1986). *Pottery produced and traded in north-west Europe 1350–1650*. Rotterdam.

- Ickowicz, P. (1993). Martincamp ware: a problem of attribution. *Medieval Ceramics* 17, 51–60.

- ICOMOS, icomos.org/en (Accessed 01/10/2021).

- ICOMOS Ireland, icomos.ie/ (Accessed 01/10/2021).

- ICOMOS. (2005). The Venice Charter 1964 [online]. Available at icomos.org/venicecharter2004/ (Accessed 01/10/2021).

- *Irish Penny Magazine*. (1833). 201–4.

- James, B.S. (1953). *The letters of St Bernard of Claivaux*. London.

- Jamroziak, E. (2005). Making friends beyond the grave: Melrose Abbey and its lay burials in the thirteenth century. In J. Hall and C. Kratzke (eds), Sepulturae Cistercienses: *Burial, memorial and patronage in medieval Cistercian monasteries*, 323–35. Cîteaux, France.

- Jennings, S. (1981). *Eighteen centuries of pottery at Norwich*. Norwich.

- Jennings, B. (O.F.M/1949). 'Fr. Bernard Culenen is the cardinals of propoganda' in 'miscellaneous Documents II, 1625–1640' in *Archivium Hibernicum*.

- Kalkreuter, B. (2001). *Boyle Abbey and the School of the West*. Bray, Co. Wicklow.

- Kavanagh, S. (ed.). (1932–49). *Commentarius Rinuccinianus*, 6 vols. Dublin.

- Kelly E.P. (2003). The Tully Lough cross. *Archaeology Ireland* 17, no. 2, 9–10.

- Kelly, F. (1997). *Early Irish farming: a study based mainly on the law-texts of the seventh and eighth centuries AD*. Dublin.

- Kelly, F. (1998) *Early Irish farming: the evidence of the law texts*. Dublin.

- Kerrigan, M. (1985). Garrisons and barracks in the Irish Midlands, 1704-1828. In *Journal of the Old Athlone Society* 2(6), 100-08.

- Kerrigan, M. (1995). *Castles and fortifications in Ireland* 1485-1945. Cork.

- Kinder, T. (2002). *Cistercian Europe: architecture of contemplation*. Cambridge.

- Knusel, C. (2000). Bone adaption and its relationship to physical activity in the past. In M. Cox and S. Mays (eds), *Human osteology in archaeology and forensic science*, 381–402. London.

- Lane, S. (1997). Clay pipes. In R.M. Cleary, M.F. Hurley and E. Shee Twohig (eds), *Skiddy's Castle and Christ Church Cork: excavations 1974–7* by D.C. Twohig, 224–38. Cork.
- Lanigan, J. (1822) *An ecclesiastical history of Ireland*, 3.
- Leask, H.G. (1960). *Irish churches and monastic buildings, ii, Gothic architecture to AD 1400*. Dundalk.
- Lewis, S. (1837). *Topographical dictionary of Ireland...*, 2 vols. London.
- Lyons, S. and McClatchie, M. (2012). New insights into legume production in early medieval and medieval Ireland. Unpublished report for the Royal Irish Academy Research Grant 2012.
- Lyons, S. (2016). The environmental remains from Bective Abbey. In G. Stout and M. Stout *The Bective Abbey Project, Co. Meath: Excavations 2009–2012*, 179–99. Wordwell.
- Lynch, A. (2010). *Tintern Abbey, Co. Wexford: Cistercians and Cocloughs. Excavations 1982–2007*. Dublin.
- Lynch G., Roundtree, S., and Shaffrey and Associates. (2009). *Bricks: a guide to the repair of historic brickwork*. Dublin.
- Lynch, L.G. (2017). Osteoarchaeological report on human skeletal remains excavated at Boyle Abbey, Co. Roscommon. In A. Quinn, Archaeological excavations at Boyle Abbey 2006–12, consent no. C025. Unpublished report for Tobar Archaeological Services.
- McCarmick, W. (1691). *A further impartial account of the actions of the Inniskilling men*.
- McClatchie, M. (2003). The plant remains. In R.M. Cleary, M.F. Hurley (eds) *Cork City Excavations 1984–2010*. Cork City Council, 391–413.
- McCormick, F. (1991). The effects of the Anglo-Norman settlement on Ireland's wild and domesticated fauna. In P.J. Crabtree and K. Ryan (eds), *MASCA research papers in science and archaeology: supplement to volume 8*, 40–52. Philadelphia, PA.
- McCormick, F. (2010). Appendix iv: the faunal remains. In A. Lynch (ed.), *Tintern Abbey, Co. Wexford: Cistercians and Colcloghs: excavations 1982–2007*, 227–32. Dublin.
- McCormick, F., Kerr, T., McClatchie, M. and O'Sullivan, A. (2011). *The archaeology of livestock and cereal production in early medieval Ireland AD 400–1100*. EMAP Report 5.1.
- McCutcheon, C. (1997). The pottery and roof-tiles. In M.F. Hurley, *Excavations at the North Gate, Cork, 1994*, 75–101. Cork.
- McCutcheon, C. (2002). The pottery and roof tiles. In M.G. O'Donnell, Excavations at James Fort, Kinsale, 1974–98. *Journal of the Cork Historical and Archaeological Society* 107, 34–42.
- McCutcheon, C. (2005). Pottery. In Klingelhöfer, E., Collins, T., Lane, S., McCarthy, M., McCutcheon, C. McCutcheon, S., Moran, J, and Tierney, J., Edmund Spenser at Kilcolman Castle: the archaeological evidence. *Post-Medieval Archaeology* 39, no. 1, 133–54.

- McCutcheon, C. (2007). The medieval pottery. In M. Clyne, *Kells Priory, Co. Kilkenny: archaeological excavations by T. Fanning and M. Clyne*, 316–38. Dublin.

- McCutcheon, C. (2009). The medieval pottery. In C. Manning, *The history and archaeology of Glanworth Castle, Co. Cork: excavations 1982–4*, 95–8. Dublin.

- McCutcheon, S.W.J. (1997). The stone artefacts. In M.F. Hurley and O.M.B. Scully, *Late Viking age and medieval Waterford, excavations 1986–92*, 404–32. Waterford.

- MacErlean, John S.J. 1922, 'Eoin Ó Cuilleanaín, Bishopot Raphie 1525–1664' in Archivium Hibernicum, 1, 77–121. Maynooth.

- McGlade, S. and Roche, N. (2016). Flat glass (windows and mirrors). In A. Giacometti (ed.), Rathfarnham Castle 2014. Unpublished excavation report for the OPW, 108–26.

- McKenna, Fr. L. (ed.). (1939–40). *Aithdioghluim Dána*, 2 vols. Dublin.

- Mac Niocaill, G. (1959). *Na manaigh liatha in Éirinn, 1142–1600*. Dublin.

- Manning, C. (2009). *The history and archaeology of Glanworth Castle, Co. Cork: excavations 1982–4*. Dublin.

- Manning, C. (2013). *Clogh Oughter Castle, Co. Cavan: archaeology, history and architecture*. Dublin.

- Marks, R. (1986). Cistercian window glass in England and Wales. In C. Norton, and D. Park (eds), *Cistercian art and architecture in the British Isles*, 211–27. Cambridge.

- Marks, R. (1993). *Stained glass in England during the Middle Ages*. Toronto.

- Mayes P. and Scott K. (1984). *Pottery kilns at Chilvers Cotton, Nuneaton*. London.

- Meenan, R. (1997). Post-medieval pottery. In M.F. Hurley and O.M.B. Scully, *Late Viking age and medieval Waterford: excavations 1986–92*, 338–55. Waterford.

- Metcalfe, W.C. (1885). *A book of knights banneret, knights of the bath, and knights bachelor, made between the fourth year of king Henry VI and the restoration of king Charles II ... and knights made in Ireland, between the years 1566 and 1698*. London.

- Meyer, K. (ed.). (1906). *The triads of Ireland*. Dublin.

- Mitchell, C.F. (1944). *Building construction and drawing – a text book on the principles and details of modern construction*. London.

- Miwadi. (2021). About us [online]. Available at miwadi.ie/about-us (Accessed 01/10/2021).

- Moloney, C. (2009). Final report on the archaeological investigations at Dunbrody Abbey, Co. Wexford 2007. Unpublished report for the National Monuments Service.

- Monk, M.A. (1986). Evidence for macroscopic plant remains for crop husbandry in prehistoric and early historic Ireland: a review. *Journal of Irish Archaeology*, 3, 31–3.

- Monk, M.A, and Kelleher, E. (2005). An assessment of the archaeological evidence for Irish corn-drying kilns in the light of the results of archaeological experiments and archaeobotanical studies. *Journal of Irish Archaeology* 14, 77–114.

- Mooney, C. (2000). A short history of the Diocese of Elphin. In F.M. Beirne (ed.), *Diocese of Elphin: people, places and pilgrimage*, 25–57. Blackrock, Co. Dublin.

- Moore, F. (2007). Ardfert Cathedral: summary of excavation results. Dublin.

- Moore, F. (2015). The Cistercian Abbey of Boyle, Co. Roscommon. *Archaeology Ireland, Heritage Guide No.70*.

- Moorhouse, S. (1988). Documentary evidence for medieval ceramic roofing materials and its archaeological implications: some thoughts. *Medieval Ceramics* 12, 33–5.

- Moran, J. (2007). The window glass. In M. Clyne, *Kells Priory, Co. Kilkenny: archaeological excavations by T. Fanning and M. Clyne*, 261–316. Dublin.

- Moran, J. (2016). Glass from Bective Abbey. In G. Stout and M. Stout, *The Bective Abbey project, Co. Meath: excavations 2009–12*, 90–2. Dublin.

- Murphy, D. (ed.). (1896). *Annals of Clonmacnoise*. Dublin.

- Murray, E. and McCormick, F. (2005). Environmental analysis and the food supply. In J. White Marshall and C. Walsh (eds), *Ilaunloughan Island: an early medieval monastery in County Kerry*, 67–80. Dublin.

- Nash, R.C. (1985). Irish Atlantic trade in the seventeenth and eighteenth centuries. *William and Mary Quarterly* 42, no. 3, 329–56.

- Ní Ghradaigh, J. (2003). But what exactly did she give?: Derbforgaill and the Nuns' Church. In H. King (ed.), *Clonmacnoise Studies, ii*, 175–203. Dublin.

- Nicholls, K.W. (ed.). (1994). *Irish Fiants of the Tudor sovereigns during the reigns of Henry VIII, Edward VI, Philip and Mary, and Elizabeth I*, 4 vols. Dublin.

- Noël Hume, I. (1961). The glass wine bottle in colonial Virginia. *Journal of Glass Studies* 3, 90–117.

- Noël Hume, I. (1969). *A guide to artifacts of colonial America*. Repr. 1991. New York.

- Norton, C. (1986). Table of Cistercian legislation. In C. Norton and D. Park (eds), *Cistercian art and architecture in the British Isles*, 317–93. Cambridge.

- Norton, J. (2004). Clay pipes. In E. FitzPatrick, M. O'Brien and P. Walsh (eds), *Archaeological investigations in Galway city, 1987–98*, 427–47. Bray, Co. Wicklow.

- Norton, J. (2007). The clay pipes. In M. Clyne, *Kells Priory, Co. Kilkenny: archaeological excavations by T. Fanning and M. Clyne*, 445–52. Dublin.

- Norton, J. and Lane, S. (2013). Pipe dreams: a directory of clay tobacco pipe-makers in Ireland. *Archaeology Ireland* 27, 31–6.

- Oakeshott, E. (1964). *The sword in the age of chivalry*. Woodbridge, Suffolk.

- Oakeshott, E. (1980). *European arms and armour.* Woodbridge, Suffolk.
- Oakeshott, E. (1991). *Records of the medieval sword.* Woodbridge, Suffolk.
- Ó Domhnaill, M. (comp.). (1532). Kelleher, A.O. and Schoepperle, G., (eds) *Betha Colaim Chille*, Repr. 1994. Dublin.
- Ó Donnabháin, B. (2010). Burials in the abbey. In A. Lynch, *Tintern Abbey, Co. Wexford: Cistercians and Cocloughs. Excavations 1982–2007*, 102–25. Dublin.
- Ó Donnchadha, B. (2007). The oldest church in Ireland's 'oldest town'. *Archaeology Ireland* 21, no. 1, 8–10.
- Ó Floinn, R. (2013). A medieval bronze pax from Dunbrody Abbey, Co. Wexford, and the fate of ornamenta from suppressed religious houses in Ireland. In S. Duffy (ed.), *Princes, prelates and poets in medieval Ireland: essays in honour of Katharine Simms*, 362–73. Dublin.
- Ó Lochlainn, C. (1940). Roadways in Ancient Ireland. In J. Ryan (ed.), *Féil-sgríbhinn Eóin Mhic Néill: essays and studies presented to professor Eoin MacNeill on the occasion of his seventieth birthday, May 15th 1938*, 465–74, 594. Dublin.
- Ó Raithbheartaigh, T. (1932). *Genealogical tracts.* Dublin.
- Ó Riain, P. (1985). *Corpus genealogiarum sanctorum Hiberniae.* Dublin.
- Ó Riain, P. (2011). *A dictionary of Irish saints.* Dublin.
- O'Connor, L. (1991). Iron Age and early Christian whetstones. *Journal of the Royal Society of Antiquaries of Ireland* 121, 45–76.
- O'Conor, K. (2002). English settlement and change in Roscommon during the late sixteenth and seventeenth centuries. In A. Horning, R. Ó Baoill, C. Donnelly, P. Logue (eds), *The post-medieval archaeology of Ireland 1550–1850*, 189–203.
- O'Donovan, J. (1844). *The genealogies, tribes and customs of Hy Fiachrach, commonly called O'Dowda's Country. Now first published from the Book of Lecan, in the library from the Royal Irish Academy, and from the genealogical manuscripts of Duald Mac Firbis, in the library of Lord Roden; with a translation and notes, and a map of Hy-Fiachrach.* Dublin.
- O'Donovan, J. (1848–51). *Annala Rioghachta Eireann: Annals of the kingdom of Ireland by the Four Masters*, 7 vols. Dublin.
- O'Donovan, J. (1852). *The tribes of Ireland: a satire, by Aenghus O'Daly, with poetical translation by the late James Clarence Mangan, together with an historical account of the family of O'Daly; and an introduction to the history of satire in Ireland.* Dublin.
- O'Dwyer, B.W. (1970). *The conspiracy of Mellifont 1226–31.* Dublin.
- O'Dwyer, B.W. (1972). The Annals of Connacht and Loch Cé and the monasteries of Boyle and Holy Trinity. *Proceedings of the Royal Irish Academy* 72, 83–101.

- O'Dwyer, B.W. (1979). *The conspiracy of Mellifont 1216–30*. Dublin.
- O'Dwyer, B.W. (ed.). (1982). *Stephen of Lexington: letters from Ireland, 1228–9*. Kalamazoo, MI.
- O'Grady, S.H. (ed.) *Silva Gadelica, a collection of tales in Irish*, 2 vols. London.
- O'Hanlon, J. (1875). *Lives of Irish saints, iii*. Dublin.
- O'Rorke, T. (1900). *The history of Sligo: town and county*, 2 vols. Dublin.
- Ortner, D.J. (2003). *Identification of pathological conditions in human skeletal remains*. London.
- O'Sullivan, J. (2014). Glass and amber beads. In M.H. Hurley and C. Brett (eds), *Archaeological excavations at South Main Street 2003–05*, 361–62. Cork.
- O'Sullivan, M. and Downey, L. (2006). Quern stones. *Archaeology Ireland* 20, no. 2, 22–5.
- Ottaway, P. (1992). *Anglo-Scandinavian ironwork from 16–22 Coppergate*. London.
- Ottaway P. and Rogers, N. (2002). *Craft, industry and everyday life: finds from medieval York*. London.
- Paynter, S. (2011). *Archaeological evidence for glassworking: guidelines for best practice*. London.
- Pender, S. (ed.). (1939). *A Census of Ireland*. Dublin.
- Pearson, M.P. (1999). *The archaeology of death and burial*. Texas.
- Prendergast, J.P. (1875). *The Cromwellian settlement of Ireland*. Dublin.
- Pritchard, F. (1991). Pins. In G. Egan and F. Pritchard *Medieval finds from London, dress accessories c. 1150–1450*. 297–304.
- Prummel, W. and Frisch, H.J. (1986). A guide for the distinction of species, sex and body side in the bones of sheep and goat. *Journal of Archaeological Science* 13, 567–77.
- Public Record Office. (1856–72). *Calendar of state papers, domestic series, of the reigns of Edward VI, Mary, Elizabeth and James*, 12 vols. London.
- Public Record Office. (1860–1912). *Calendar of state papers relating to Ireland*, 23 vols. London.
- Robinson, D.M. (ed.). (1998). *The Cistercian abbeys of Britain*. London.
- Robinson, D.M. (2006). *The Cistercians in Wales: architecture and archaeology 1130–1540*. London.
- Robinson, D.M. (2017). The architecture of the medieval Cistercian church and cloister. In P. Beacham (ed.), *Buckfast Abbey: history, art and architecture*, 32–71, 252–55. London.
- Rogers, J. and Waldron, T. (1995). *A field guide to joint disease in archaeology*. Chichester, Sussex.
- Royal Irish Academy. (1852–1976). *Dictionary of the Irish Language*. Dublin.
- Scully, O.M.B. (1997). Metal artefacts. In M.F. Hurley and O.M.B. Scully (eds), *Late Viking age and medieval Waterford: excavations 1986–92*, 438–89. Waterford.

- Scully, O.M.B. (2007). The ferrous artefacts. In M. Clyne, *Kells Priory, Co. Kilkenny: archaeological excavations by T. Fanning and M. Clyne*. Dublin.
- Sharkey, P.A. (1927). *The heart of Ireland*. Boyle, Co. Sligo.
- Shiels, D. (2013). Military artefacts. In C. Manning *Clogh Oughter Castle, Co. Cavan, archaeology, history and architecture*. Archaeological Monograph Series: 8.
- Silver, I.A. (1971). The ageing of domestic animals. In D.R. Brothwell and E. Higgs (eds), *Science in archaeology: a survey of progress and research*. Bristol.
- Simington, R.C. (ed.). (1949). *Book of survey and distribution*, i. Dublin.
- Smith, B. 1991 The Armagh/Clogher Dispute and the 'Mellifont conspiracy': diocesan politics and monastic reform in early thirteenth century Ireland. *Seanchas Ardmhacha* 14, no. 2, 26–38.
- Smith, K.A. (2010). Spiritual warriors in citadels of faith: martial rhetoric and monastic masculinity in the long twelfth century. In J. Thibodeaux (ed.), *Negotiating clerical identities, priests, monks and masculinity in the Middle Ages*, 86–110. London.
- Society for Historical Archaeology 2021 Hunyadi Janos - Bitterquelle [online]. Available at sha.org/bottle/soda.htm#Bitterquelle (Accessed 01/10/2021).
- Stalley, R.A. (1971). *Architecture and sculpture in Ireland 1150–1350*. Dublin.
- Stalley, R.A. (1979). The medieval sculpture of Christ Church cathedral. *Archaeologia* 106, 107–22.
- Stalley, R.A. (1980). Mellifont Abbey: a study of its architectural history. *Proceedings of the Royal Irish Academy* 80C, 263–354.
- Stalley, R.A. 1981 The Romanesque sculpture of Tuam. In A. Borg and A. Martindale (eds), *The vanishing past: studies of medieval art, liturgy and metrology presented to Christopher Hohler*, 179–95. Oxford.
- Stalley, R.A. (1987). *The Cistercian monasteries of Ireland*. New Haven, CN.
- Stalley, R.A. (1994). Saint Bernard, his views on architecture and the Irish dimension. *Arte medievale, periodico internazionale di critica dell'arte medievale* 2, anno 8, n. 1, tomo secondo, 13–20.
- Stalley, R.A. (1995). Choice and consistency: the early Gothic architecture of Selby Abbey. *Architectural History* 38, 1–24.
- Stalley, R.A. (1996). Decorating the lavabo: late Romanesque sculpture from Mellifont Abbey. *Proceedings of the Royal Irish Academy* 96C, 237–64.
- Stalley, R.A. (1999). Hiberno-Romanesque and the sculpture of Killeshin. In P.G. Kane and W. Nolan (eds), *Laois history and society*. Dublin.
- Stalley, R.A. (2000). The construction of the medieval cathedral c.1030–1250. In K. Milne (ed.), *Christ Church cathedral: a history*, 53–74. Dublin.

- Stalley, R.A. (2012). The Cistercian monasteries of Ireland revisited. In P. Harbison and V. Hall (eds), *A carnival of learning: essays to honour George Cunningham and his 50 conferences on medieval Ireland in the Cistercian Abbey of Mount St Joseph's, Roscrea, 1987–2012*, 205–17. Roscrea.

- Stalley, R.A. (2012). Cathedral building in thirteenth-century Ireland. In R.A. Stalley (ed.), *Irish Gothic architecture: construction, decay and reinvention*, 15–53. Dublin.

- Stokes, W. (ed.). (1887). Vita tripartita: *the tripartite life of Patrick with other documents relating to that saint*, 2 vols. London.

- Stokes, W. (ed.). (1895–97). The annals of Tigernach. *Revieu Celtique* 16 (1895), 374–419, 17 (1896), 6–33, 119–265, 337–420, 18 (1897) 9–59, 150–97, 267–303.

- Stout, G. (2015). The Cistercian grange: a medieval farming system. In M. Murphy and M. Stout (eds), *Agriculture and settlement in Ireland*, 28–68. Dublin.

- Stout, G. (2016). The abbey of the port of St. Maria, Dunbrody, Co. Wexford: an architectural study. In I.W. Doyle and B. Browne (eds), *Medieval Wexford: essays in memory of Billy Colfer*, 97–123. Dublin.

- Stout, G. and Stout, M. (2016). *The Bective Abbey project, Co. Meath: excavations 2009–12*. Dublin.

- Stout G., Loeber, R. and O'Brien, K. (2016). Mellifont Abbey, Co. Louth: a study of its post-dissolution architecture 1540–1727. *Proceedings of the Royal Irish Academy* 116C, 191–226.

- Stuart-Macadam P. (1985). Porotic hyperostosis: representative of a childhood condition. *American Journal of Physical Anthropology* 66, 391–8.
- Sweetman, H.S. (ed.). (1875–86). *Calendar of documents relating to Ireland*, 5 vols. London.

- Sweetman, P.D. (1979). Archaeological excavations at Fern Castle, Co. Wexford. *Proceedings of the Royal Irish Academy*, 79C, 217–45.

- Sweetman, P.D. (1981). Excavations of a moated site at Rigsdale, County Cork 1977–78. *Proceedings of the Royal Irish Academy* 81C, 132–205.

- Sweetman, P.D. (1982). Some pottery and clay pipe finds from the Royal Hospital, Kilmainham, Dublin. *Dublin Historical Record* 35, no. 2, 71–4.

- Teagasc and the EPA n.d. The Irish Soil Information System [online]. Available at http://gis.teagasc.ie/soils/map.php (Accessed 01/10/2021).

- Trimble, W.C. (1919–21). *History of Enniskillen with reference to some manors in Co. Fermanagh and other local subjects*. Enniskillen.

- Tsaliki, A. (2008). Unusual burials and necrophobia: an insight into the burial archaeology of fear. In E.M. Murphy, Deviant Burials in the Archaeological Record. *Studies in Funerary Archaeology* 2, 1–16.

- Twemlow, J.A. (ed.). (1921). *Calendar of Papal Registers relating to Great Britain and Ireland, xi, 1455–64*. London.

- Twemlow, J.A. (ed.). (1921). Charred grain assemblages from Roman-period corn dryers in Britain. *Archaeological Journal* 146, 302–19.

- Verstraten, F. (2003). Both king and vassal: Feidlim Ua Conchobair of Connacht 1230–65. *JGAHS* 55, 13–37.

- Waddell, C. (ed.). (1999). Narrative and legislative texts from early Cîteaux. *Cîteaux: Commentaria cistercienses, studia et documenta*, 9, 1–524.

- Waddell, C. (2002). Twelfth-century statutes from the Cistercian General Chapter. *Citeaux: Commentaria cistercienses, studia et documenta* 12. Available online at www.citeaux.org/twelfth-century-statutes-from-the-cistercian-general-chapter-f/ (Accessed 01/10/2021).

- Wallace, J. (1970). *Scottish swords and dirks.* London.

- Walsh, P. (ed.). (1948). Beatha Aodha Ruaidh Uí *Dhomhnaill, as Leabhar Lughaidh Uí Chlérigh*. Repr. 1988. Dublin. Irish Texts Society [Cumann na Scríbheann nGaedhilge]. No. 42. Dublin.

- Ware, J. (no date). *Annales Dominicani de Roscoman.* Unpublished manuscript.

- Weld, I. (1832). Statistical survey of the county of Roscommon drawn up under the direction of the Royal Dublin Society. Dublin.

- Westerhof, D. (2005). Celebrating fragmentation: the presence of aristocratic body parts in monastic houses in twelfth and thirteenth-century England. J. Hall and C. Kratzke (eds), Sepulturae Cistercienses: *Burial, memorial and patronage in medieval Cistercian monasteries*, 27–45. Cîteaux, France.

- Westropp, M.S.D. (1920). *Irish glass: a history of glass-making in Ireland from the sixteenth century.* Dublin.

- Westropp, T.J. (1880–91). *Sketches of Ireland 1880–91*, i. Dublin.

- White, N.B. (ed.). (1943). *Extents of Irish monastic possessions, 1540–41*. Dublin

- White, H., Paynter, S. and Brown, D. (2015). *Archaeological and historic pottery production sites: guidelines for best practice.* London.

- White N.B. (ed.). (1943). *Extents of monastic possessions.* Dublin.

- Whyte, E. (2016). Later medieval and post-medieval pottery. In K. Wiggins, *A place of great consequence: archaeological excavations at King John's Castle, Limerick, 1990–8*, 354–67. Dublin.

- Williams, D.H. (1998). *The Cistercians in the early Middle Ages.* Leominster, Herefordshire.

- Willis, T. (1996). Scottish 'twa handit Swerdis'. *Park Lane Arms Fair Catalogue* 13, 12–25.

- Wincott Heckett, E. (2005). 'The apparel oft proclaims the man': late sixteenth and early seventeenth-century textiles from Bridge Street Upper, Dublin. In F. Pritchard and J.P. Wild (eds), *Northern archaeological textiles*, 108–14. Oxford.

- Wincott Heckett, E. (2009). Textiles. In F. Delaney, E2444 – Mackney, Co. Galway: ringfort with killeen burials, 480–98. Unpublished archaeological excavation report for the National Monuments Service.

- Wincott Heckett, E. (2014). Textiles. In M.F. Hurley and C. Brett (eds), *Archaeological excavations at South Main Street, 2003–5*, 220–5. Cork.

- Woods, C. (2010). Case gin bottles. [Online] Historic glasshouse. Available at antiquebottles-glass.com/case-gin-bottles/ (Accessed 01/10/2021).

- Wren, J. (2006). Medieval and post-medieval roof tiles. In C. McCutcheon, *Medieval pottery from Wood Quay, Dublin*, 177–95.

- Wren, J. (2010). Roof tiles. In A. Lynch, *Tintern Abbey, Co. Wexford: Cistercians and Colcloughs: excavations 1982–2007*, 138–44. Dublin.

- Wren J. (2013). Roof tiles. In C. Manning, *Clogh Oughter Castle, Co. Cavan: archaeology*, history and architecture, 372–5. Dublin.

- Wren J. (2015). Ceramic floor and roof tiles. In K. Wiggins, *A place of great consequence: archaeological excavations at King John's Castle, Limerick, 1990–8*. Limerick.

- Wright, S.M., Hirst, S. and Astill, G. (2005). Patronage, memorial and burial at Bordesley Abbey. In J. Hall, and C. Kratzke (eds), Sepulturae Cistercienses: *Burial, memorial and patronage in medieval Cistercian monasteries*, 353–72. Cîteaux, France.

- Zakin, H.J. (1979). *French Cistercian grisaille glass*. London.